third edition

e-marketing

judy strauss

Associate Professor of Marketing
University of Nevada, Reno

adel el-ansary

Donna L. Harper Professor of Marketing
Coggin College of Business Administration
University of North Florida

raymond frost

Professor of Management Information Systems
Ohio University

PEARSON
Prentice
Hall

P...... *......ernational*

If you purchased this book within the United States or Canada
you should be aware that it has been wrongfully imported
without the approval of the Publisher or the Author.

Senior Editor: Wendy Craven
Editor-in-Chief: Jeff Shelstad
Assistant Editor: Melissa Pellerano
Editorial Assistant: Danielle Serra
Media Project Manager: Anthony Palmiotto
Marketing Manager: Michelle O'Brien
Marketing Assistant: Amanda Fisher
Managing Editor: John Roberts
Permissions Coordinator: Suzanne Grappi
Associate Director, Manufacturing: Vincent Scelta
Production Manager: Arnold Vila
Manufacturing Buyer: Michelle Klein
Cover Design: Kiwi Design
Cover Illustration: Alexandra Maldonado/SIS, Inc.
Printer/Binder: Maple-Vail

Credits and acknowledgments borrowed from other sources and reproduced, with permission,
in this textbook appear on the appropriate page within the text.

Pearson Education LTD.
Pearson Education Australia PTY, Limited
Pearson Education Singapore, Pte. Ltd
Pearson Education North Asia Ltd
Pearson Education Canada, Ltd.
Pearson Educación de Mexico, S.A. de C.V.
Pearson Education -- Japan
Pearson Education Malaysia, Pte. Ltd
Pearson Education, Upper Saddle River, New Jersey

10 9 8 7 6 5 4 3 2
ISBN 0-13-122793-9

this book is dedicated to

cyndi and malia

tarik, waleed, eman, and noor

raymond jr. and david

Contents

14 Customer Relationship Management

The Cisco Story

End of Part 4

Practitioner Perspectives

Part V Global Perspective

15 E-Marketing in Emerging Economies

The EthioGifts Story

Preface

Marketers have been using electronic tools for many years, but the Internet and other information technologies created a flood of interesting and innovative ways to provide customer value. Short text message coupons to cell phones based on user location; consumer behavior insights based on offline and online data combination; inventory optimization through online bidding; a single-minded focus on ROI and associated performance metrics—these and more are on the cutting edge of e-marketing in 2003. New opportunities create lots of questions, however, especially in the aftermath of the dot-com crash. How can firms leverage new technologies to maximum benefit? How much commitment should marketers make to electronic marketing programs? Is our ROI on target for that Internet project? In this book, we attempt to answer these and many other questions.

E-marketing is traditional marketing using information technology but with some twists. The Internet and other technologies affect traditional marketing in three ways. First, they increase efficiency in established marketing functions. Second, the technology of e-marketing transforms many marketing strategies. Finally, it has fundamentally changed consumer behavior though a power shift from firms to mouse-holders. The marketing transformation results in new business models that add customer value, build customer relationships, or increase company profitability. The Internet also serves as an efficient marketing planning tool for both secondary and primary data collection. In addition, electronic technologies affect the 4 P's:

- Product—Internet technologies spawned a variety of innovative products for creating, delivering, and reading messages as well as services such as reverse auctions, business-to-business (B2B) market exchanges, and interactive games. What's next? Keep your eye on the wireless market!
- Pricing—The Net turned pricing strategies upside down. Bartering, bidding, dynamic pricing, and individualized pricing are now quite common online. Shopping agents create transparent pricing for identical product offerings at various online retailers.
- Distribution (Place)—E-marketers use the Net for direct distribution of digital products (e.g., news stories and live radio) and for electronic retailing. But tremendous value occurs behind the scenes: Supply chain management and channel integration create efficiencies that can either lower customer prices or add to company profits. Online retailers line the dot-com graveyard, so today's e-marketers must be very careful to stick to solid business practices.
- Promotion—The Net assists with two-way communication: one-to-one Web pages, e-mail conversation, short text messaging, and e-mail conferencing via newsgroups and mailing lists. The Net is also an advertising medium in its own right, but it has not realized the revenue promise predicted in the late 1990s, and we explain why. E-marketers also use the Net for promotions,

and sending electronic coupons and digital product samples directly to consumers.

One of the most important applications of electronic marketing involves customer relationship management. Companies are experimenting with a myriad of technologies to discover and meet the needs of these savvy and demanding customers.

The book you have in your hands is the third edition of *E-Marketing* (first edition was named *Marketing on the Internet)*. We expanded the scope from 10 to 16 chapters to build on two important areas: the strategic perspective and global issues in e-marketing. It includes new areas such as performance metrics and wireless strategies for mobile devices. This book discusses many offline electronic marketing techniques that employ information technology, such as point-of-purchase scanning devices and databases; however, it focuses on the Internet due to its widespread and increasing use for e-marketing.

Several popular books exist to shed light on the problems, opportunities, and techniques of e-marketing, and we have used them in our classes with some success. This textbook is different in these important ways.

1. We explain electronic marketing not as a list of ideas and techniques, but as part of a larger set of concepts and theories in the marketing discipline. In writing the book we discovered that most new terminology could be put into traditional frameworks for greater understanding. To this end, we present **new visual models** that show the concept relationships for each part and chapter in this edition. We strongly believe that new electronic strategies are more likely to succeed if selected using the marketing planning process, especially as the Internet continues to mature.

2. The text focuses on **cutting-edge business strategies** that generate revenue while delivering customer value. As well, we devote many pages to **performance metrics** to monitor their success.

3. We highly recommend that **marketers learn a bit about the technology** behind the Internet, something most of us are not drawn to naturally. While it is not necessary to be able to set up e-commerce servers, knowledge of the possibilities for their use will give savvy marketers an advantage in the marketplace. This book attempts to educate marketers gently in important technology issues, showing the relevance of each concept.

4. While this book describes e-marketing practices in the United States, the text also takes a **global perspective** describing market developments in both emerging and developed nations. The book includes 12 articles written by practitioners from the United States, Mexico, and Ghana. They present cutting edge practices from the field.

5. This book does not cover Web site design. This is a topic we love to teach, our students enjoy learning, and one that is included in many Internet marketing courses. Unfortunately, it is also beyond the scope of this book.

However, please check out our new companion book, *Building Effective Web Sites* (Prentice Hall, 2001).

6. The Web site that accompanies this text is an important part of the work (www.prenhall.com/strauss). Designed as an instructor's manual, it contains important information about designing and teaching an e-marketing course. Especially important is a section on Internet exercises for student application of the concepts.

7. As teachers, we present Internet marketing in a format that we believe will enhance learning. We organize chapters to parallel principles of marketing texts and provide learning tools such as chapter objectives, summaries, and exercises. We have used this format successfully since 1996 in our Internet classes, and we hope it will work well for you, too.

A MOVING TARGET

We might as well raise a flag from the start and mention that this book is a snapshot of e-marketing techniques in summer 2002. The Internet is a rapidly changing medium, enterprising entrepreneurs constantly have cool new ideas, and, thus, some things in this book will be out of date before it is off the press. This is especially true for the statistics and screen captures we used: Approximately 40% of all Web site references we provided in the second edition no longer exist! We encourage readers to explore on their own, checking out the veracity of our remarks in the light of a moving target. To assist in this process, we give reference to Web sites and reference materials throughout.

AUDIENCE

We wrote this book to assist every student of electronic marketing who wants to learn this topic one step at a time. This primarily includes graduate and undergraduate university students, but the book also will aid other individuals who want to learn more about electronic marketing. Important background includes basic marketing and computer knowledge, although we provide short explanations of terminology and concepts to be sure all readers are up to speed. Various sections of the book should appeal to those with differing levels of experience. For example, the chapter body starts at the beginning of a topic and builds, eventually integrating sophisticated concepts. "Leveraging Technology" and "Ethics and Law" chapters are quite challenging, presenting cutting-edge topics.

BOOK ORGANIZATION

This book elaborates on e-marketing planning and marketing mix topics from a strategic perspective. Part I begins with setting the context for marketing planning. Part II discusses technology, legal, and ethical environments. Part III begins the e-marketing strategy discussion in depth, and Part IV continues with marketing mix and customer relationship management strategy and implementation issues. Finally,

Part V is devoted to the global perspective; however, global issues are mentioned throughout the book. The following table displays the book's organization, and the next paragraphs provide learning objectives for each chapter.

PART I: E-MARKETING IN CONTEXT	PART II: E-MARKETING ENVIRONMENT	PART III: E-MARKETING STRATEGY
1. The Big Picture 2. Strategic E-Marketing 3. The E-Marketing Plan	4. Leveraging Technology 5. Ethical and Legal Issues	6. Marketing Knowledge 7. Consumer Behavior 8. Targeting Market Segments and Communities 9. Differentiation and Positioning
PART IV: E-MARKETING MANAGEMENT	**PART V: GLOBAL PERSPECTIVE**	
10. Product 11. Price 12. Distribution 13. The Internet for E-Marketing Communication 14. Customer Relationship Management	15. E-Marketing in Emerging Economies 16. Country Profiles from the Six Continents	

Part I: E-Marketing in Context

Chapter 1: The Big Picture
The key objective of this chapter is to develop an understanding of the background, current state, and future potential of e-marketing. You will learn how e-marketing both influences and is influenced by legal, technological, and market-related factors.

Chapter 2: Strategic E-Marketing
The main goal of this chapter is to understand strategic planning and the way companies seek to achieve their objectives through strategies involving e-business and e-marketing. You will become familiar with common e-business models implemented at different organizational levels and with the application of metrics to monitor progress toward objectives.

Chapter 3: The E-Marketing Plan

This chapter explains the importance of creating an e-marketing plan and presents the six steps in the e-marketing planning process. You will see how marketers incorporate information technology in plans for effectively and efficiently achieving e-business objectives such as increasing revenues and slashing costs.

Part II: E-Marketing Environment

Chapter 4: Leveraging Technology

The key objective of this chapter is to develop a basic understanding of the current and emerging technologies that facilitate e-marketing planning and implementation. You will explore product, pricing, distribution, and promotion technologies and learn how e-marketers are using technology for relationship marketing.

Chapter 5: Ethical and Legal Issues

In this chapter we explore the ethical and legal issues that e-businesses face in marketing online. You will learn about the current and emerging issues that have caused concern among a variety of stakeholders, including e-businesses and consumers.

Part III: E-Marketing Strategy

Chapter 6: Marketing Knowledge

Chapter 6 develops an understanding of why and how e-marketers turn marketing research into marketing knowledge. You will learn about the three categories of Internet data sources, consider the ethics of online research, look at key database analysis techniques, and explore the use of knowledge management metrics.

Chapter 7: Consumer Behavior

The primary objective of this chapter is to develop a general understanding of the online consumer population. You will learn why billions of consumers do not use the Internet and explore the context in which online consumer behavior occurs, the characteristics and resources of online consumers, and the outcomes of the online exchange process.

Chapter 8: Targeting Market Segments and Communities

In this chapter we examine the various bases for market segmentation, the classifications and characteristics of market segments and communities, and the main coverage strategies for targeting selected segments. You will also gain a better understanding of the size and growth of various important market segments and communities on the Internet.

Chapter 9: Differentiation and Positioning

Chapter 9 provides an overview of how and why e-marketers use differentiation and positioning. You will learn about the differentiation strategies used by online businesses and the bases for positioning or repositioning companies, products, and brands on the Internet.

Part IV: E-Marketing Management

Chapter 10: Product

In Chapter 10 we analyze the development of consumer and business products that capitalize on the Internet's properties and technology by delivering online benefits through attributes, branding, support services, and labeling. You will become familiar with the challenges and opportunities of e-marketing enhanced product development, Internet product classifications, and new-product trends.

Chapter 11: Price

The primary goal of this chapter is to examine how Internet technology is influencing pricing strategies. You will gain an understanding of both the buyer's and the seller's perspectives of pricing online, consider whether the Net is an efficient market, and learn about fixed pricing as well as the return to dynamic pricing.

Chapter 12: The Internet for Distribution

This chapter develops an understanding of the Internet as a distribution channel, identifies online channel members, and analyzes the functions they perform in the channel. You will learn how the Internet presents opportunities to alter channel length, restructure channel intermediaries, improve the performance of channel functions, streamline channel management, and measure channel performance.

Chapter 13: E-Marketing Communication

The primary goal of this chapter is to understand the Internet as a tool for efficiently and effectively exchanging marketing communication messages between marketers and their audiences. You will learn how each marketing communication tool can carry messages over the Internet and how marketers buy and use promotional space on the Net as a communication medium.

Chapter 14: Customer Relationship Management

The main objective of this chapter is to provide an overview of the purpose and process of building a company's relationship capital through customer relationship management (CRM). You will learn about CRM's benefits, its three facets, and the seven building blocks needed for effective and efficient e-marketing CRM.

Part V: Global Perspective

Chapter 15: E-Marketing in Emerging Economies

Chapter 15 examines the unique challenges and opportunities facing e-marketers that target or operate within countries with emerging economies. You will learn how consumer behavior and attitudes, payment methods, technological issues, and both economic and technological disparities within nations can influence e-marketing in less developed countries.

Chapter 16: Country Profiles from the Six Continents

Finally, Chapter 16 helps you to gain an understanding of the main country-by-country differences in Internet access, usage, and shopping as a foundation for segmenting and targeting specific markets. You will learn about some of the barriers to Internet adoption and e-commerce in selected countries and see how these barriers are being addressed.

End-of-Chapter Material

The end of each chapter includes both review and discussion questions to enhance learning. There are also chapter summaries and key terms.

Important End of Part Resources

Special sections at the end of each of the five parts include activities and Internet exercises to allow deeper exploration of chapter material, plus a list of savvy Web sites for further research. As well, accomplished CEOs and top-level managers working in the business of e-marketing wrote *Practitioner Perspective* pieces. These discuss issues important to those on the front line, and some take a stab at predicting the future of the Net. They are truly incredible and interesting: Don't miss them.

PEDAGOGICAL FEATURES

We included many features in *E-Marketing* to enhance learning. Based on our cumulative years of teaching experience, we've identified the best practices in university teaching and integrated items that work well for us.

Marketing concept focus: In each chapter we review several marketing concepts and then tell how the Internet is related to the concept. This technique provides a bridge from marketing principles that the student already knows and presents material in a framework for easier learning. In addition, as things change on the Net, students will understand the new ideas based on underlying concepts.

Learning objectives: Each chapter begins with a list of objectives that, after studying the chapter, students should be able to accomplish. Given our active learning preference, the objectives are behavioral in nature.

Best practices from real companies: A company success story starts each chapter. Students will find these to be exciting introductions to the material. They are all new case histories for this edition and, thus, include very current examples of firms that do it right.

Graphical frameworks in each chapter: We created unique e-marketing visual models to show how each chapter fits among other chapters in the entire part. In addition, several chapters feature models for within-chapter understanding.

Chapter summaries: Each chapter ends with a summary of its contents. While these summaries capsulate the chapter guts, they were not created so that students can read them in lieu of the chapter content.

Key terms: Also at the end of each chapter is a list of important terms in the chapter. This will assist the student in checking for understanding.

Review and discussion questions: Questions at the chapter end are aimed at both knowledge-level learning and higher levels of application, synthesis, and evaluation.

Exercises: When students become actively engaged in the material, learning is enhanced. To this end we include several activities and Internet exercises at the end of each part.

Glossary: Most people don't brag about a glossary, but we were unable to find a comprehensive glossary focusing on e-marketing, so we included one in this book. The Internet has spawned an incredible amount of new terminology, and we want to help readers understand the landscape.

INSTRUCTOR SUPPORT MATERIALS ON WEB SITE

This is the third edition of a book about a moving target. No one has quite laid out the territory the way we have in *E-Marketing*. To assist in developing courses we've designed a Web site to serve as an instructor's manual.

Web site location: www.prenhall.com/strauss

1. **Web site:** The Web site serves as instructor's manual and water cooler for sharing ideas about teaching Internet marketing classes. On the site are traditional instructor's manual items as well as class assignments, links to Internet marketing syllabi, and other materials to enhance teaching from this book. Contact your Prentice Hall representative or the authors to gain password access to protected areas.

2. **Test bank:** A test bank is available to faculty adopting this textbook. Question items focus on chapter learning objectives and other important material. They include items at all levels of learning from knowledge through application and evaluation.

3. **PowerPoint Slides:** The Web site holds files containing slides for lectures to accompany each chapter. This is to aid those wanting to present book material in class lectures.

4. **E-mail the authors:** We encourage e-mail from faculty using this textbook. Send questions, suggestions for improving the text, and ideas about teaching the class.

ACKNOWLEDGMENTS

The most pleasant task in this project is expressing our appreciation to the many individuals who helped us create this work. We are always amazed that the scope of the job requires us to request, plead, cajole, and charm a number of folks into helping us. Our gratitude is enormous.

First, we would like to thank our students over the years. We teach primarily because we love working with our students. They inspire us, teach us, and keep us on our toes.

Next we want to thank Prentice Hall, especially Jeff Shelstad and Wendy Craven, for giving us a place to showcase our ideas. John Roberts worked diligently to bring this book to press on schedule. We also appreciate the support of our institutions, the University of Nevada, Reno, Ohio University, and the University of North Florida. Next, we appreciate the fine work of Marian Wood, who carefully edited our words and provided extremely insightful suggestions. Cyndi Jakus designed the chapter introductory pages, managed the difficult task of obtaining permissions for reprinting screen shots, helped with the glossary and references, and formatted the entire book.

There are other individuals who contributed significantly to this book's content. Brian O'Connell contributed the interesting and timely "Ethical and Legal Issues" chapter, and Al Rosenbloom wrote the fascinating chapter on "E-Marketing in Emerging Economies." Many practitioners wrote essays on cutting-edge topics and you'll find their names and work at the end of each part to the book. We appreciate the fact that they took time from their busy days to contribute to student education. Finally, we thank the many individuals who wrote country profiles for Chapter 16: Their work provides an insider's view of e-marketing on the six contents.

Several others provided excellent assistance: Kasia Banasiak and Debra Robison assisted with research. Ewa Charazinska, Sean Harrington, and Katherine Klement helped with research and writing for Chapter 9. Chad Waters edited and enhanced the "Savvy Sites" section, and David Lan tested and greatly improved the end-of-part activities and Internet exercises. Jackie Parks and Judith Matthews spent long hours editing, and Tia Seitler helped organize copyright permissions.

Finally, the support and encouragement to accomplish a major piece of work come from friends and family. To them we are indebted beyond words.

ABOUT THE AUTHORS

Judy Strauss and Raymond Frost have collaborated on Web development, academic papers, practitioner seminars, and three books since 1995. They also developed a new course in 1996, "Marketing in Cyberspace." This book developed from that course and has significantly evolved along with changes in e-marketing. For this edition of *E-Marketing*, Adel I El-Ansary joined the team. He brings significant experience and expertise in e-marketing and marketing strategy, both from academic and practitioner viewpoints.

Judy Strauss is Associate Professor of Marketing at the University of Nevada, Reno and Chair of the Managerial Sciences Department. She has published academic papers in Internet marketing, advertising, and marketing education. Strauss is co-author of *Building Effective Web Sites* and the *E-Marketing Guide*. She has had many years of professional experience in marketing, serving as entrepreneur as well as marketing director of two firms. She currently teaches undergraduate and M.B.A. courses in marketing communications, Internet marketing, and marketing management. Strauss earned a doctorate in marketing at Southern Illinois University, and a finance M.B.A. and marketing B.B.A. at University of North Texas. Contact: jstrauss@unr.edu.

Adel I. El-Ansary is the Donna L. Harper Professor of Marketing at the University of North Florida. He is co-author of *Marketing Channels,* 1st through 6th editions, Prentice-Hall, 1977–2001 and contributor to the *Encyclopedia of Marketing, Encyclopedia of Economics, American Marketing Association Marketing Encyclopedia,* and the *Logistics Handbook.* His articles are published in major journals including the *Journal of Marketing, Journal of Marketing Research, Journal of Marketing Channels, Journal of Retailing, Journal of the Academy of Marketing Science, Journal of Macro Marketing, Journal of Personal Selling and Sales Management,* and *Internal Marketing Review.*

Raymond D. Frost is a Professor of Management Information Systems at Ohio University. He has published scholarly papers in the information systems and marketing fields and is an associate editor of *The Journal of Database Management*. Frost is co-author of *Building Effective Web Sites* and the *E-Marketing Guide*. Dr. Frost teaches database, electronic commerce, and information design courses. He has received Ohio University's prestigious University Professor teaching award. Dr. Frost is working on publications in data modeling and database pedagogy. He is co-author of a forthcoming book, *A Visual Introduction to Database: An E-Business Perspective*. Dr. Frost earned a doctorate in business administration and an M.S. in computer science at the University of Miami (Florida), and received his B.A. in philosophy at Swarthmore College.

1 chapter

1 the big picture

learning objectives

The key objective of this chapter is to develop an understanding of the background, current state, and future potential of e-marketing. You will learn how e-marketing both influences and is influenced by legal, technological, and market-related factors.

After reading this chapter, you will be able to:

- Explain how the Internet and information technology advances offer benefits and challenges to consumers, businesses, marketers, governments, and society.
- Distinguish between e-business and e-marketing.
- Identify some important legal and technological factors that affect e-marketing.
- Describe the composition of the Internet and the use of intranets, extranets, and the Web.
- Outline the characteristics of the three major markets for e-business.

If you have an unhappy customer on the Internet, he doesn't tell his six friends, he tells his 6,000 friends.

jeff bezos
president
Amazon.com

The Google Story

What performs 150 million searches a day, speaks 74 languages, reaches 32 countries, and is the 15th-most-visited U.S. Web site? The answer is Google.com, the privately owned, growing, and profitable dot-com firm. By some estimates, Google's 2001 revenues hovered around $70 million, while it doubled its number of employees and earned about $15 million in profit.

This success is particularly remarkable because Google entered the market in 1998, well after other search engines were firmly entrenched with loyal customers. How did Google do it? First, it got the technology right at a low cost. Co-founders Sergey Brin and Larry Page figured out how to pack eight times as much server power in the same amount of space as competitors by building their own system from commodity hardware parts. Second, they invented an innovative new search strategy: ranking search query page results based not only on keywords but also on popularity—as measured, in part, by the number of sites that link to each Web page. This meant that users' search results were packed with relevant Web sites. Finally, the founders maintained a customer focus, used simple graphics, allowed no advertising on the home page, and allowed only banner ads without graphics so search result pages download faster and are easier to read.

Google generates revenues from two B2B markets. It sells its search services to 130 Web sites such as Yahoo.com and AOL.com; it also sells keyword banners to Web advertisers. In a firm where 15% of employees hold a Ph.D., the innovation continues. The profitability is likely to continue as well, because Google pays close attention to user value, keeps costs low, and delivers eyeballs to advertisers.

I think that there's a world market for maybe five computers.

thomas watson
IBM chair
1943

The Emergence of E-Marketing

As the growth of Google.com shows, some marketing principles never change. Markets always welcome an innovative new product, even in a crowded field of competitors, as long as it provides customer value. Also, Google's success shows that customers trust good brands and that well-crafted marketing mix strategies can be effective in helping newcomers enter crowded markets. Nevertheless, organizations are scrambling to determine how they can use information technology profitably and to understand what technology means for their business strategies. Marketers want to know which of their time-tested concepts will be enhanced by the Internet, databases, wireless mobile devices, and other technologies. The rapid growth of the Internet and subsequent bursting of the dot-com bubble has marketers wondering, "What next?" This book attempts to answer these questions through careful and systematic examination of successful **e-marketing** strategies in light of proven traditional marketing practices.

What Is E-Marketing?

E-marketing is the application of a broad range of information technologies for:

- Transforming marketing strategies to create more customer value through more effective segmentation, targeting, differentiation, and positioning strategies;
- More efficiently planning and executing the conception, distribution, promotion, and pricing of goods, services, and ideas; and
- Creating exchanges that satisfy individual consumer and organizational customers' objectives.

This definition sounds a lot like the definition of traditional marketing. Another way to view it is that e-marketing is the result of information technology applied to traditional marketing. E-marketing affects traditional marketing in two ways. First, it increases efficiency in traditional marketing functions. Second, the technology of e-marketing transforms many marketing strategies. The transformation results in new business models that add customer value and/or increase company profitability (see Chapter 2).

What Is E-Business?

E-business is important, powerful, and unstoppable. But what is it, exactly? IBM coined the term *e-business*, and the Gartner Group fleshed it out to mean the continuous optimization of a firm's business activities through digital technology. **Digital technologies** are things like computers and the Internet, which allow the storage and transmission of data in digital formats (1's and 0's). In this book we use the terms *digital technology* and **information technology** interchangeably. E-business involves attracting and retaining the right customers and business partners.

It permeates business processes, such as product buying and selling. It includes digital communication, e-commerce, and online research, and it is used by every business discipline. **E-commerce** is the subset of e-business focused on transactions.

The Big Picture

Easy, inexpensive, and quick access to digital information transforms economies, governments, societies, and businesses. Digital information enhances economies through more efficient markets, more jobs, information access, communication globalization, lower barriers to foreign trade and investment, and more. However, the Internet's impact is not evenly distributed across the globe. The approximately 530 million users connected to the Internet worldwide represent just 8.5% of the global population. In fact, developed nations hold only 15% of the world's population but account for 88% of all Internet users (see www.weforum.org). One estimate puts U.S. Internet users at 182 million, representing 64% of the population (Nielsen//NetRatings). At the same time, stories abound about indigenous peoples in remote locations gaining health, legal, and other advice or selling native products using the Internet. Clearly, the Internet is having a huge impact.

A networked world creates changes that some see as undesirable. Societies change as global communities based on interests form, and worldwide information access slowly decreases cultural and language differences. Some say that the existence of a truly global village will have the effect of removing cultural differences—and that this is not good. Furthermore, easy computer networking means that work and home boundaries are blurring. Although this makes working more convenient, it may encourage more workaholism and less time with family. Yet another issue is the digital divide. This is the idea that Internet adoption occurs when folks have enough money to buy a computer, the literacy to read what is on Web pages, and the education to be motivated to do it. Internet critics are justifiably concerned that class divisions will grow, preventing the upward mobility of people on lower socioeconomic levels and even entire developing countries. Meantime, governments are working to solve some of these problems, but they have other important worries, such as how to collect taxes and tariffs when transactions occur in cyberspace in a borderless world.

In the business world, the digital environment is enhancing processes and activities across the entire organization. Disciplines work together in cross-functional teams using computer networks to share and apply knowledge for increased efficiency and profitability. Financial experts communicate shareholder information online, file required government statements, and invent new ways to value risk, return, and capital investments in dot-com firms that have high sales and few profits. Human resources personnel use the Net for electronic recruiting and training; an increasing number are managing organizational knowledge and work flow through corporate Web portals. Production and operation managers can adjust manufacturing based on the Internet's ability to give immediate sales feedback—resulting in truly just-in-time inventory and building products to order.

Strategists at top corporate levels are leveraging the Net to apply the firm's knowledge in building and maintaining a competitive edge. Digital tools allow execs easy access to data from their desktops and show results of the firm's strategies at the click of a mouse. In a 2002 survey of thousands of U.S. top executives, at least half mentioned important e-business benefits of building better-quality customer relationships, finding more business partners and other development opportunities, and building better brand visibility (Exhibit 1 - 1). This study emphasizes the importance of marketing and logistics functions, because all of these benefits (except for partner development) are typically marketing responsibilities.

Tough Times

The first generation of e-business was like a gold rush. New start-ups and well-established businesses alike created a Web presence and experimented a lot. Many companies quickly attracted huge sales and market share, but only a handful brought anything to the bottom line. In early 2000 one estimate listed 21 firms with 12-month sales growth between 100% and 500%—but all had negative profits. Notable in that list were CDNow, Lycos, DoubleClick, E*Trade, and Amazon.com. Since January 2000, however, over 500 Internet firms have shut down in the United States alone. Having gone through the boom and the bust in developed nations (the Internet is still booming in many emerging economies), we are now firmly entrenched in what Gartner Group calls the *trough of disillusionment* (Exhibit 1 - 2). According to Gartner, the disillusionment is based 30% on the technology recession and 70% on disappointment with e-business results. This is a time when marketers return to their traditional roots and rely on well-grounded strategy and sound marketing practices. During the dot-com shakeout from 2000-2002, there was much industry consolidation. Some firms, such as Levi Strauss, stopped selling online both because it was not efficient and because it created *channel conflict*. Other firms merged, with the stronger firms acquiring smaller ones, although in at least one case an e-business firm took over a traditional firm: AOL purchased Time-Warner. All of this is typical in a maturing market environment.

Benefit	% Mentioning
Better-quality customer relationships	61
More business development opportunities	50
Better brand visibility	50
Drive fat from supply chain	42
Reduce time-to-market	33
Increase customer quantity	25

Exhibit 1 - 1 The Most Important Benefits of E-Business to U.S. Executives
Source: "Key Business and Marketing. . ." (2002)

Gartner Group predicts that a *true* e-business model will emerge, and by 2008 the "e" will be dropped, making electronic business just part of the way things are done. This sounds plausible, although the timing is uncertain. Some say that "E-business has become just business. E-commerce has become just commerce. The new economy has become just the economy" (Aronica and Fingar 2001). Others say that this is far from the truth—for them, e-business will always have its own models, concepts, and practices. Time will tell.

An example of a firm that has already gone through the entire cycle is Charles Schwab, which allowed e.Schwab.com to cannibalize the larger brick-and-mortar securities firm in 1998. Dubbed "eat your own DNA" by former CEO Jack Welch of General Electric, Schwab astutely pitted the online and offline business models against each other and allowed the most profitable methods to win. The e.Schwab model resulted in lower prices, incorporation of successful e-marketing strategies, and faster-growing accounts and assets. For this brokerage firm, e-business is just business.

E-Marketing in Context

Just where does e-marketing fit into this picture? To answer that, we describe a framework for understanding e-marketing's role in the business environment.

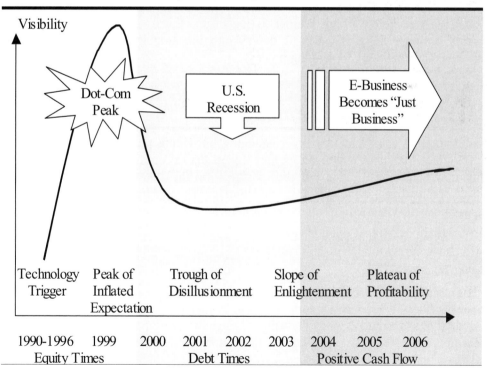

Exhibit 1 - 2 There Is Hope After the Trough of Disillusionment
Source: Adapted from Raskino and Andren of Gartner Research (2001).

Environment, Strategy, and Performance (ESP)

E-marketing flows from the organization's overall e-business strategies and selected business models. As depicted in Exhibit 1 - 3, it starts with the business environment, where legal, technological, competitive, market-related, and other environmental factors external to the firm create both opportunities and threats. Organizations perform SWOT analyses to discover what strengths and weaknesses they have to deploy against threats and opportunities. This SWOT analysis leads into e-business and e-marketing strategy. Firms select e-business strategies and e-business models, and then marketers formulate strategy and create e-marketing plans that will help the firm accomplish its overall goals. The final step is to determine the success of the strategies and plans by measuring results. **Performance metrics** are specific measures designed to evaluate the effectiveness and efficiency of the e-business and e-marketing operations. This is so important in today's e-business climate that media reports seem to be full of references to ROI (return on investment) and other measures of success for e-business strategies and tactics featured in the model.

The ESP model might just as easily depict a brick-and-mortar business process—by removing a few "e's." This underscores the idea that e-businesses are built on sound practices and proven processes but with important e-transformations and e-marketing practices, as discussed in this book.

This chapter examines the environmental factors in the ESP model, whereas Chapter 4 (technology) and Chapter 5 (legal and ethical) explore these important factors in more depth. Chapter 2 delves into the strategy area, and Chapter 3 discusses the e-marketing planning process.

E-Marketing Environment

The marketing environment is ever changing, providing plenty of opportunities to develop new products, new markets, and new media to communicate with customers, plus new channels to reach business partners. At the same time, the environment poses competitive, economic, and other threats. This section introduces three key environmental factors that affect e-marketing: legal, technological, and market-related factors.

Legal Factors

Current and pending legislation can greatly influence e-marketing strategies. Chief among these are laws concerning privacy, digital property (including copyright), expression, and fraud. Privacy is difficult to legislate, yet it is critically important to consumers who routinely yield personal information over the Internet. One hot issue involves opt-out e-mail. This occurs when users must uncheck a Web page box to avoid being put on a company's e-mail list. Some legislators want to outlaw this practice because few users read the Web page carefully enough to notice the opt-out

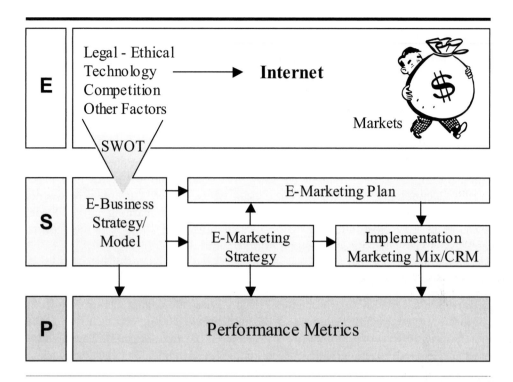

Exhibit 1 - 3 E-Marketing in Context: The ESP Model

box. Digital property problems began in the Web's early days and continue to puzzle firms and legislators alike. In a medium where content is freely distributed, it can be freely ripped off—not a good thing for the content authors. Spam, offensive content, and other forms of personal expression conflict with user rights and, thus, form an ongoing discussion among legislators. How can governments balance freedom of expression against consumer needs? Finally, new technology brings new opportunities for fraud. Although regulatory agencies are working hard to prevent fraud, enforcement is difficult in a networked world.

Technology

Technological developments are altering the composition of Internet audiences as well as the quality of material that can be delivered to them. For example, about 20% of the U.S. population enjoys high-bandwidth connections—primarily cable modems and DSL lines—that enable delivery of multimedia content. Some Web sites are beginning to create three forms of content: a high-speed multimedia form, a standard PC offering, and a handheld format for wireless devices such as cell phones. The proliferation of wireless devices creates a new set of design challenges as firms try to squeeze content onto tinier screens. Also important are technology concerns in developing countries. As communication infrastructures improve and more people use handheld devices, new geographic markets develop. Further, e-marketing is evolving through software advances. For instance, technologies that target consumers according to their online behavior are becoming increasingly sophisticated. Incorporating these technologies into Web site design can give a firm a distinct competitive advantage.

Technology lowers costs. Many firms have saved money on staff and paperwork via electronic order processing, billing, and e-mail. Conversely, technology can be a costly investment. Web page development can cost millions of dollars, and large e-commerce operations require expensive hardware and software, especially if they use extensive data gathering and distribution applications. Meanwhile, technology is emerging for improved security, new payment instruments, and low bandwidth. Over time, new technologies continue to emerge, which make current investments obsolete. Finally, putting technology to use entails a steep learning curve. Firms must, therefore, pay close attention to both technology and strategy if they are to succeed with a viable business model, on or off the Internet.

What Is the Internet?

The **Internet** is a global network of interconnected networks. This includes millions of corporate, government, organizational, and private networks. Many of the computers in these networks hold files, such as Web pages, that can be accessed by all other networked computers. Every computer, cell phone, or other networked device can send and receive data in the form of e-mail or files over the Internet. These data move over phone lines, cables, and satellites from sender to receiver. The Internet, then, consists of computers with data, users who send and receive the data files, and a technology infrastructure to move, create, and view or listen to the content. Three important types of networks form part of the Internet:

- **Intranet**—A network that runs internally in a corporation but uses Internet standards such as HTML and browsers. Thus, an intranet is like a mini-Internet but only for internal corporate consumption.

- **Extranet**—An intranet to which value chain partners have admission for strategic reasons. The access is normally only partial.

- **Web**—The portion of the Internet that supports a graphical user interface for hypertext navigation with a browser such as Netscape or Internet Explorer. The Web is what most people think about when they think of the Internet.

However, e-marketing involves much more than these technologies.

It's Bigger Than the Internet

Electronic marketing reaches far beyond the Web. First, many e-marketing technologies exist, including those used in customer relationship management, supply chain management, and electronic data interchange arrangements predating the Web. Second, non-Web Internet services such as e-mail and newsgroups are emerging as effective avenues for marketing. Some of these services are beginning to converge, such as Web-based e-mail. Third, the Internet holds more than one Web.

There is the Web that most users access from PCs. Then there are subsets of the Web with content specially formatted for the unique display properties of one of the following appliances: Web TV, personal digital assistants, cell phones, or text-only browsers. Fourth, there are offline electronic data-collection devices such as bar code scanners. Finally, there is the portion of the Web containing high-bandwidth content for users who have either cable modems or digital subscriber loop (DSL) connections.

Internet Properties and Marketing Implications

Marketers who grasp what Internet technologies can do will be better poised to capitalize on information technology. Exhibit 1 - 4 displays a list of basic properties that give Internet technology the ability to transform business practice. Compare these properties to those of the telephone. Referring to the property descriptions, the telephone is a mediating technology, has global reach, and has network externality. In contrast, the Internet has properties that create opportunities beyond those possible with the telephone, television, postal mail, or other communication media. It is these differences that excite marketers and have them wondering how to best capitalize on them.

These Internet properties not only allow for more effective and efficient marketing strategy and tactical implementation, but also they actually change the way marketing is conducted. For example, the fundamental idea of digitizing data (bits not atoms) has transformed media and software delivery methods as well as created a new transaction channel. Also, the Internet as information equalizer has shifted the balance of power from marketer to consumer.

Internet technologies have changed traditional marketing in a number of critical ways:

- **Power shift from sellers to buyers.** Both individual and business buyers are more demanding than ever because they are just one click away from a plethora of global competitors, all vying for their business. In this environment, buyer attention is the scarce commodity and customer relationship capital a valued asset.

- **Death of distance.** Geographic location is no longer a factor when collaborating with business partners, supply chain firms, or customers, or just chatting with friends. The Internet made place less important and allows many buyers and sellers to bypass traditional intermediaries.

- **Time compression.** Time is not a factor with Internet communication between firms and their stakeholders. Online stores can be open 24/7; people can communicate as their schedules permit; times zones disappear for managers collaborating with partners on other continents.

- **Knowledge management is key.** In the digital world, customer information is easy and inexpensive to gather, store, and analyze. Managers can track marketing results as they are implemented, receiving play-by-play reports. However, turning huge databases into meaningful knowledge to guide strategic decisions is a major challenge.

- **Interdisciplinary focus**. Marketers must understand technology to harness its power. They do not have to personally develop the technologies, but they need to know enough to select appropriate suppliers and direct technology professionals.
- **Intellectual capital rules.** Imagination, creativity, and entrepreneurship are more important resources than financial capital.

Property	Marketing Implications
Bits not atoms	Information, products, and communication in digital form can be stored, sent, and received nearly instantaneously. Text, audio, video, graphics, and photos can all be digitized, but digital products cannot be touched, tasted, or smelled.
Mediating technology	Peer-to-peer relationships, such as auctions and music file sharing, and business partnerships can be formed regardless of geographic location. Technology allows timely communication and data sharing, such as with businesses in a supply chain.
Global reach	Opens new markets and allows for worldwide partnerships, employee collaboration, and salesperson telecommuting.
Network externality	Businesses can reach more of their markets with automated communication, and consumers can disseminate brand attitudes worldwide in an instant.
Time moderator	There are higher expectations from consumers about communication with companies and faster work processes within companies.
Information equalizer	Firms employ mass customization of communication, and consumers have more access to product information and pricing.
Scalable capacity	Firms pay for only as much data storage or server space as needed and can store huge amounts of data.
Open standard	Companies can access each other's databases for smooth supply chain and customer relationship management. This equalizes large and small firms.
Market deconstruction	Many distribution channel functions are performed by nontraditional firms (e.g., Edmunds.com and online travel agents) and new industries emerged (e.g., ISPs).
Task automation	Self-service online lowers costs and makes automated transactions, payment, and fulfillment possible.

Exhibit 1 - 4 Internet Properties and Marketing Implications
Source: Properties adapted from Afuah and Tucci (2001).

E-Business Markets

Sergio Zyman, formerly chief marketing officer of Coca-Cola, has been quoted as saying, "Marketing is supposed to sell stuff." One way information technology helps sell stuff is by facilitating relationships before and after the transaction with prospects, customers, partners, and supply chain members. Yet all the latest technology can't help marketers sell stuff if they don't identify appropriate markets. Exhibit 1 - 5 highlights three important markets that both sell and buy to each other: businesses, consumers, and governments. Although this book focuses on the B2C market with some coverage of B2B activities, all three are briefly described next. Note that after B2C and B2B markets, the B2G and C2C markets are where most e-business activity occurs.

Business Market

The business market is huge because a higher proportion of firms are connected to the Internet than consumers, especially in developing countries. Much of the B2B online activity is transparent to consumers because it involves proprietary networks that allow information and database sharing. Consider FedEx, the package delivery firm. This company maintains huge databases of business customer shipping behavior and account information. Its customers can schedule a package pick-up using the Web site, track the package using a PC or handheld PalmPilot, and pay the shipping bill online. Sometimes the shipping order is automatically triggered when a consumer buys something online from a FedEx client; then FedEx sends e-mail

	To Business	To Consumer	To Government
Initiated by Business	Business-to-Business **(B2B)** *FreeMarkets* www.freemarkets.com	Business-to-Consumer **(B2C)** *CDNow* www.cdnow.com	Business-to-Government **(B2G)** *Western Australian Government Supply* www.ssc.wa.gov.au/
Initiated by Consumer	Consumer-to-Business (C2B) *Better Business Bureau site* www.bbb.org	Consumer-to-Consumer **(C2C)** *eBay* www.ebay.com	Consumer-to-Government (C2G) *GovWorks* www.govworks.com
Initiated by Government	Government-to-Business (G2B) *Small Business Administration site* www.sba.gov	Government-to-Consumer (G2C) *California state site* www.state.ca.us	Government-to-Government (G2G) *GovOne Solutions* www.govonesolutions.com/

Exhibit 1 - 5 E-Business Markets
Source: Wood (2001) with minor adaptation (p. 2).

notification of its delivery progress to the retailer.

Information technology created tremendous efficiencies in the B2B market, yet businesses that sell online face increasing competition due to globalization and lower market entry barriers brought about by the Internet. Because the Net contributes to market deconstruction, many firms are changing their entire supply chain structures—which often results in conflict between different marketing channels. This is especially true when manufacturers sell directly to consumers online, thus taking business from retail partners. On the other hand, many firms experience greater interdependence in their value chain due to electronic collaboration practices. Other challenges and opportunities for firms include:

- How can firms serve both offline and online customers well? For example, what if a customer purchases a product online and then tries to return it at the brick-and-mortar store? Or what if the customer buys online and telephones with a question? Firms must integrate both back-end and front-end procedures for quality customer service.

- How can firms operate in a sea of data? They need to turn data into knowledge that can then be used to profitably build the business. Information overload is a real problem, and employees have little time to solve this on a daily basis. Firms that do it right gain access to the right information at decision-making time and realize higher profits.

- New-product opportunities and ways of generating revenue abound in the digital economy. Chapter 10 describes some of these opportunities.

Finally, the Internet allows for strange bedfellows. Companies in unlikely industries find it relatively easy to forge partnerships that supply value to customers. Consider, for example, the joint venture that created MSNBC (Microsoft and the NBC television network). In this environment, firms compete not only for customers but also for partners and sometimes even form partnerships with rivals. As an example, the major airlines came together to form an airline reservations hub—thus undercutting online travel agents. As another example, the major U.S. auto manufacturers have a shared procurement hub to link to their suppliers.

Consumer Market

The Internet is a global market with opportunities existing in unimagined locations, which is why e-marketers must understand consumers in potential geographic segments. For example, with an annual average income of US$300, Vietnamese citizens who opt to spend 28% of their salary on online services do not have much purchasing power. Further, there are waiting lists for automobiles in Vietnam, so an online branding campaign might be a waste of resources. Conversely, Iceland and Denmark are two of the most wired countries in the world with over 60% Internet penetration. Also, consumers in many countries pay by the minute for local phone access. This is a tremendous deterrent to the kind of casual surfing practiced by Internet users in developed nations. In addition, the infrastructure in some countries does not support high-speed modems. Content delivered to these countries may, therefore, have to be light on bandwidth. Chapters 15 and 16 look at global Internet markets in more detail.

Apart from emerging economies, the consumer market is huge and quite active online. In one large study of 37 countries, 28% of consumers said they have shopped online or plan to shop online in the next six months, and 15% purchased offline as a direct result of online information ("The Global E-Commerce Report. . ." 2002). U.S. consumers are the biggest online shoppers, spending US$53 billion in 2001, an increase of nearly 20% from 2000 (see www.comscore.com). Here are a few of the major trends affecting the consumer market (see Chapter 7 for more in-depth analysis).

Revenge of the Consumer

Until the late 1930s, when the U.S. government stepped in to protect consumers, the slogan *caveat emptor* ("let the buyer beware") was on everyone's lips. Snake oil salesmen made impossible claims and consumers had no recourse. Things got better in the early part of the twentieth century when firms employed the product orientation, believing that the path to profits was making better products. But then the days of the sales orientation appeared along with aggressive and deceptive sales practices. Both of these marketing philosophies ignore customer needs, leading to the marketing concept: the idea that firms can satisfy customer needs and make a profit at the same time. In the late 1900s, however, consumers were not convinced. The rebellion started with television channel surfing using the remote control. Consumers did not seem to appreciate that commercials pay for broadcast TV programs.

At the start of the 21st century, consumers have control via the mouse. While this control is not yet complete, it soon will be: When television, radio, print media, entertainment, and shopping all converge seamlessly on a computer-like device, consumers will truly have information on demand. One hundred years of exposure to marketing strategies have made consumers more demanding and more sophisticated, and marketers will have to become better at delivering customer value. As noted earlier, the balance of power is shifting to consumers—one of the most fundamental changes to marketing because of the Internet. Marketers have practically lost control of brand images and must consistently underpromise and overdeliver or be found out under the bright lights of the globally networked community.

Consumer Needs

What do customers want in the information economy? Privacy is one need. Customers want marketers to keep their data confidential, and they don't want to be bothered by sales calls at home during dinner. They also want to safeguard children from Web sites they find objectionable. Consumers want marketers to ask permission before sending commercial e-mail messages. And they want e-commerce to provide convenience, self-service, speed, good customer service, personal attention, and value. Fortunately, e-marketing can meet all these needs.

E-marketing tools and processes allow firms to deliver on the marketing concept to individual consumers in ways that could rarely be achieved in the past. The Internet allows for **mass customization**, so individuals can now contact firms electronically over the Internet and receive responses tailored to their needs. Business can also customize and personalize products and communications to strengthen long-term relationships with customers. Amazon.com, for example, presents personalized Web pages to users (Exhibit 1 - 6). Also, when customers have a problem with a Dell computer, they can visit the company's Web site, type the five-character service code identifying their personal information and exact computer model, and then type in their questions. Responses immediately appear in each customer's e-mail, based on the key words in the question, along with an invitation to telephone if more information is needed. As another example, consumers create personalized Web pages and portals for sending specific data to their wireless devices—all possible through automatic application of digital information.

Government Market

The U.S. government is the world's largest buyer, purchasing over $200 billion in goods and services every year (see www.isbdcorp.org/gmag). Add to this the purchasing power of U.S. states, counties, cities, and other municipal agencies, and this makes for a huge market. The governments of other countries are also major purchasers. The state government of Western Australia, for instance, annually buys

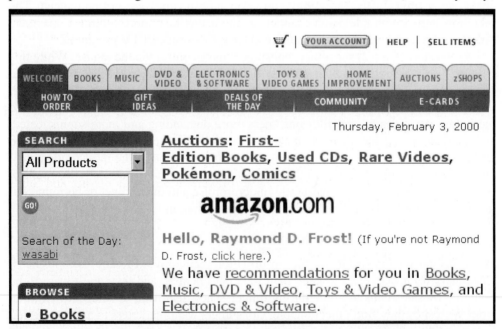

Exhibit 1 - 6 Amazon.com Uses Mass Customization to Personalize Web Pages
Source: www.amazon.com Amazon.com is a registered trademark or trademark of Amazon.com, Inc. in the United States and/or other countries. © 2000 by Amazon.com. All rights reserved.

A\$6 billion in goods and services and authorizes more than 40,000 work contracts (www.ssc.wa.gov.au/).

Businesses wishing to sell to governments face challenges unique to this market. Government agencies have many rules for suppliers to follow regarding qualifications, paperwork, and so on. Additionally, firms often must compete to be on the government list of approved suppliers, and then compete yet again for specific work contracts through a bidding process. Government agencies are generally very particular about timely delivery of quality products at reasonable prices. The good news is that small and large businesses usually have an equal chance of selling to governments and that government Web sites announce their buying needs in advance of the bidding process.

A debate has erupted in recent years about whether U.S. government agencies should accept advertising on their Web sites. Proponents suggest that advertising fees would subsidize the government costs and lower taxes; opponents worry about the ethics of mingling government and business in this way, as well as cluttering government sites with ads. The argument recently boiled down to this analogy: Is a government Web site more like a city bus or a park, with one accepting ads and the other not? This debate may be moot because even though government Web sites attract many visitors, they have difficulty competing for advertising dollars with huge commercial Web sites such as Yahoo!

What's Next?

Regardless of the current disillusionment with e-business, many solid successes exist today and exciting new growth areas will soon emerge. *Fortune* magazine has identified seven trends that will help businesses move forward into e-marketing during the next few years (Kirkpatrick 2002):

1. **Integrating IT software.** Twenty-six percent of companies will spend money to integrate all the pieces of corporate technology, such as linking front-end customer service software with back-end order fulfillment systems.

2. **Boom in Web services. Web services** will move more deeply into finding universal standards for Internet-related software. Microsoft's dot-net and Sun's Java are two competing architectures, for example.

3. **Collaboration software.** This allows employees, advisors, consultants, and other team members to work on projects while in different geographic locations. For example, "Napster for Marketers" is peer-to-peer software that one consulting firm uses to collaborate on marketing plans with ad agencies, designers, and others.

4. **Dealing with too much data.** Better customer relationship management software is helping firms reinforce customer loyalty by analyzing the mountain of data about previous behavior to suggest new products. For example, a flight attendant would be able to ask if a passenger wants coffee with sugar instead of the usual, "What do you want to drink?"

5. **Data security.** Techies are spending lots of time and money trying to protect data from hackers and viruses.

6. **Wireless is here to stay.** Technologies such as 802.11 and Bluetooth use short-range signals to link a variety of computing and handheld devices in homes, offices, and retail stores.

7. **Growth in portable computing**. Inexpensive computer storage and small machines will aid people who want to work at home, in the car or train, or virtually anywhere. Devices such as IBM's 9-ounce Metapad hold 5 gigabytes of data and will change the way people work.

The following scenarios show why marketers are excitedly preparing for the next phase of e-business growth.

> John Customer's cell phone rings as he enters the I-5 freeway on ramp on his way to work—it is a text message (Newell and Lemon 2001, p. 4):
> It is time for your 15,000 mile service. It looks like you are headed for the city. If you will take the next exit to our dealership, we will have a driver waiting to take you to your office. We will service your car and deliver it to you in the city this afternoon.
> **<u>Click Here to tell us you are coming. We will be ready.</u>**

> This from Bill Gates regarding what Microsoft envisions for the Longhorn PC operating system project (Schlender 2002):
> Why can't my computer protect me from distractions by screening phone calls and e-mails, and why can't it track me down when I'm out of the office or forward things to me automatically?

And what about *calendar commerce*? Because 60% to 70% of businesspeople have electronic calendars (using PalmPilot or Windows CE handheld devices), why not help them keep track of things automatically (Eitel-Porter 2001)? Weather.com will send a five-day local forecast to wireless devices with a link back to the site. Think of the possibilities—companies can beam a series of maintenance appointments for equipment, stock options expiration dates, or product shipping dates to a calendar; or a concert promoter can send the dates for season tickets directly into customers' electronic calendars. Similarly, OpenGrid's MobilePlanIt allows conference attendees to download conference schedules through infrared stations at the conference. We used this at Internet World and found that when we scrolled the schedule and found an event we wanted to attend it only took a stylus tap to move it to the PalmPilot calendar—very nifty.

Now innovative marketers that have some knowledge of technology have a chance to jump into e-marketing. This book will give you the basics, along with plenty of new ideas.

Read On

The book is organized into five parts and 16 chapters (see Exhibit 1 - 7). Part I, E-Marketing in Context, introduces strategic e-marketing and the e-marketing plan. Part II, E-Marketing Environment, expands on the technological and legal environments. Part III, E-Marketing Strategy, deals with e-strategy formulation, including the marketing knowledge base and customer behavior data needed for designing segmentation, targeting, differentiation, and positioning strategies. Part IV, E-Marketing Management, covers marketing mix and customer relationship management best practices. Finally, Part V, The Global Perspective, presents important developments from the six continents, with a focus on emerging economies.

Part I E-Marketing in Context

  1 The Big Picture
  2 Strategic E-Marketing
  3 The E-Marketing Plan

Part II E-Marketing Environment

  4 Leveraging Technology
  5 Ethical and Legal Issues

Part III E-Marketing Strategy

  6 Marketing Knowledge
  7 Consumer Behavior
  8 Targeting Market Segments and Communities
  9 Differentiation and Positioning Strategies

Part IV E-Marketing Management

  10 Product
  11 Price
  12 Distribution
  13 Integrated Marketing Communication
  14 Customer Relationship Management

Part V Global Perspective

  15 E-Marketing in Emerging Economies
  16 Country Profiles from the Six Continents

Exhibit 1 - 7 E-Marketing at a Glance

Summary

E-business is the continuous optimization of a firm's business activities through digital technology. E-commerce is the subset of e-business focused on transactions. E-marketing is marketing infused with technology, boosting efficiency and transforming marketing strategies to create new business models that add customer value and/or increase company profitability.

The dynamic marketing environment poses competitive, economic, and other threats even as it offers opportunities to develop new products, new markets, new media, and new channels. Three key environmental factors that affect e-marketing are legal, technological and market-related factors. Legislation covering privacy, digital property, expression, and fraud can greatly influence e-marketing strategies. Technological advances are changing Internet audiences and the quality of material they can access; improving marketing precision; affecting costs; and forcing firms to learn about new technology as they develop strategies for viable business models.

The Internet consists of computers with data, users who send and receive the data files, and a technology infrastructure to move, create, and view or listen to the content. An intranet is a network that runs internally in a corporation using Internet standards. An extranet is an intranet to which value chain partners are admitted for strategic reasons. The Web is the part of the Internet that supports a graphical user interface for hypertext navigation with a browser. The Internet's properties allow for more effective and efficient marketing strategy and tactical implementation and are changing marketing by shifting power from sellers to buyers; eliminating distance as a concern; allowing communication without regard to time zones; enabling the collection, storage, and analysis of customer information; emphasizing an interdisciplinary focus; and using intellectual capital as a more important resource than financial capital.

E-business occurs primarily in three markets—**business to business (B2B)**, **business to consumer (B2C)**, and **business to government (B2G)**, although businesses also become involved in the **consumer to consumer (C2C)** market. The majority of dollars change hands in the B2B market, with many firms connected to the Internet. Information technology is creating efficiencies while increasing competition. The consumer market is huge and active online, but the shifting balance of power means that marketers have almost lost control of brand images. The government market consists of numerous states, cities, counties, municipal agencies, and countries buying goods and services. Business must pay close attention to the rules for selling to this market. A number of trends are affecting the ability of marketers to tap new growth areas and become successful e-marketers.

Key Terms

Business to Business (B2B)

Business to Consumer (B2C)

Business to Government (B2G)

Consumer to Consumer (C2C)

Digital technologies

E-business

E-commerce

E-marketing

Extranet

Information technology

Internet

Intranet

Mass customization

Performance metrics

Web

Web services

Exercises

Review Questions

1. Define e-business and e-marketing.

2. What are performance metrics and why are they important?

3. What are some of the key legal issues that affect e-marketing?

4. How does technology both raise and lower costs for companies?

5. As a technology, how does the Internet compare with the telephone?

6. What are some of the marketing implications of Internet technologies?

7. What are the three main markets of e-business, and how do they differ?

8. In the context of e-marketing, what does "revenge of the consumer" mean?

Discussion Questions

9. As a marketer, do you agree with the U.S. executives who say "better-quality customer relationships" is one of the most important e-business benefits? Why?

10. As a consumer, are you likely to benefit when e-business becomes "just business" in the near future? Explain your answer.

11. Some economists suggest that the increase in e-commerce within the B2B market will lead to greater competition and more goods and services becoming commodities—that is, solely competing on price. How do you think this is likely to affect buyers within the B2B market? How would it affect sellers?

12. What concerns about consumer privacy are raised by the increased use of wireless computing and handheld devices outside the home or workplace?

2 strategic e-marketing

learning objectives

The main goal of this chapter is to understand strategic planning and the way companies seek to achieve their objectives through strategies involving e-business and e-marketing. You will become familiar with common e-business models implemented at different organizational levels and with the application of metrics to monitor progress toward objectives.

After reading this chapter, you will be able to:

- Explain the importance of strategic planning, strategy, e-business strategy, and e-marketing strategy.
- Distinguish between a business model and an e-business model and identify the main e-business models at the activity, business process, and enterprise levels.
- Discuss the use of metrics and the Balanced Scorecard to measure e-business and e-marketing performance.

We have the right model for the Internet age. . .[including] a partnership of trust and communication among our people, our customers, and our suppliers.

michael dell

After seven years of effort, Amazon.com finally proved that the online retailing business model can be profitable. Amazon reported its first ever net profit in the fourth quarter of 2001—$5 million, along with $59 million in operating profit. Although first-quarter 2002 results were not positive and the firm is not yet out of the woods, it is headed in the right direction. According to an analyst with Deutsche Bank, Alex Brown, Amazon has changed its business objectives: "Prior to 2001 it was all about growth at the expense of profits, and last year was about profits at the expense of growth. I think this year they will try to find a balance."

Amazon, a pure-play dot-com survivor, is quite adept at leveraging its competencies into many different e-business models. First is its core business—online retailing. Sales of books, music, and videos account for half of Amazon's sales and represent the only profitable retail division. In the past two years, Amazon has cut inventory by 25%, tightened operations, and doubled sales—a good, but tough, formula for operating profitability.

Second are Amazon's co-branding partnerships with Borders, Circuit City, Target, and Toys "R" Us (among others). These partnerships brought $225 million of the firm's $1.1 billion in revenue in the fourth quarter of 2001, with an amazing 45% gross margin (nearly twice Amazon's retail margin). Although these partnerships carry differing commitments, they typically involve Amazon's licensing of online storefront technology or earning fees for customer service and product fulfillment (delivery). Other deals, such as an Expedia partnership, give firms access to Amazon's 29 million customers in exchange for a flat fee and percentage of sales. This co-branding business model is more profitable than the retailing model because it involves the less costly automated services, e-commerce experience, or huge customer base. In fact some say that Amazon is now a hybrid company, both selling merchandise and offering technology services. Indeed, the business objective is to add two new partners a year.

Amazon also uses two other important e-business models. Amazon created the first affiliate program (called Amazon Associates), giving 600,000 Web site owners a 15% commission for referring customers who purchase at Amazon. Also, customers can auction items on the site. Amazon's future success depends on strategic planning and careful management of its existing business models.

What you measure is what you get: The performance measures you use affect the behavior of your managers and employees.

david norton and robert kaplan
harvard business school

Strategic Planning

Amazon, like every other marketer on and off the Web, uses strategic planning to get ready for a profitable and sustainable business future. **Strategic planning** is the "managerial process of developing and maintaining a viable fit between the organization's objectives, skills, and resources and its changing market opportunities" (Kotler 2003 p. 89). Two key elements of strategic planning are the preparation of a SWOT analysis and the establishment of strategic objectives.

SWOT Analysis

The **SWOT** analysis (strengths, weaknesses, opportunities, and threats) examines the company's internal strengths and weaknesses with respect to the environment and the competition and looks at external opportunities and threats. Opportunities may help to define a target market or identify new product opportunities, while threats are areas of exposure. For example, when Amazon.com seized the opportunity to sell online, it had no significant competition. Its biggest threat was a full-scale push by one of the large bookstore chains to claim the online market. The company's greatest weakness was that it had no experience selling books or even processing credit card transactions. What's more, it had no experience boxing books for shipment and originally packed them on the floor until a visiting carpenter suggested building packing tables (Spector 2000). The company's greatest strength was a smart and talented team that stayed focused and learned what it didn't know. Fortunately for Amazon, the big stores were caught napping. The delay by the bookstore chains gave Amazon the opportunity to establish its brand online. Barnes & Noble (www.bn.com) did not fight back until Amazon was on the eve of a stock offering. By then it was too late.

Bear in mind that a company's strengths and weaknesses in the online world may be somewhat different from its strengths and weaknesses in the brick-and-mortar world. Exhibit 2 - 1 displays a few of the key capabilities needed by e-business firms. Barnes & Noble has enormous strengths in the brick-and-mortar world but these do not necessarily translate into strengths in the online world. Barnes & Noble can easily find itself in the unfortunate position of channel conflict—having to explain to channel partners why customers can purchase for less online than in the store. However, Amazon has no potential channel conflict because it only sells online.

Strategic Objectives

Armed with the results of the SWOT analysis, the firm can set objectives in a number of high-level areas, such as:

- **Growth.** How much can the firm reasonably expect to grow in terms of revenues, and how fast? The answer to these questions involves a thorough understanding of the competition, product life cycles, and market factors.

Internal Capability	Examples
Customer interactions	E-commerce, customer service, distribution channels
Production and fulfillment	SCM, production scheduling, inventory management
People	Culture, skills, knowledge management, leadership, and commitment to e-business
Technology	ERP systems, legacy applications, networks, Web site, security, IT skills
Core infrastructure	Financial systems, R&D, HR

Exhibit 2 - 1 Key Internal Capabilities for E-Business
Source: Adapted from Kalakota and Robinson (1999).

- **Competitive position.** How should the firm position itself against other firms in the industry? Viable positions are industry leader (Microsoft), price leader (Priceline.com), quality leader (Mercedes), niche firm (Google.com), best customer service (Dell.com), and so forth.

- **Geographic scope.** Where should the firm serve its customers on the continuum of local to multinational?

- **Other objectives.** Companies often set objectives for the number of industries they will enter, the range of products they will offer, the core competencies they will foster, and so on.

For example, Amazon switched direction in 2001, choosing profitability instead of growth as a strategic objective. Next, companies select appropriate strategies to accomplish their strategic objectives.

Strategy

The term *strategy* has been used to describe everything from "the course we chart, the journey we imagine and, at the same time, the course we steer, and the trip we actually make (Nickols 2000 p. 6)." Although the term is used in many different contexts to mean many different things, most strategists agree that **strategy** is the means to achieve a goal. It is concerned with how the firm will achieve its **objectives**, not what its goals are. Interestingly, strategy has its roots in military action. For example, the country's objective is to win the war, its strategy is to deploy troops to a particular country, and its **tactics** are to land a particular battalion in a specific location at a specified day and time. This translates well to business strategy because the firm sets its growth and other objectives, then decides which strategies it will use to accomplish them. The tactics are detailed plans to implement the strategies.

It is important to note that objectives, strategies, and tactics can exist at many different levels in a firm. Thus far, we've been discussing high-level corporate strategic planning. Functional areas within a firm also develop goals, strategies, and tactics to support corporate-level objectives. If a firm wants to grow by 10% in the coming year, the marketing function may set supporting goals to introduce new products and increase market share. Similarly, finance, human resources, and other functional areas set goals to help achieve the firm's overall objectives.

From Strategy to Electronic Strategy

How does strategy differ from e-business strategy? **E-business strategy** is the deployment of enterprise resources to capitalize on technologies for reaching specified objectives that ultimately improve performance and create sustainable competitive advantage. Thus, when corporate-level (also called *enterprise-level*) business strategies include information technology components (Internet, digital data, databases, and so forth), they become e-business strategies. Therefore:

E-Business Strategy = Corporate Strategy + Information Technology

As one example, the Sharper Image specialty retailer might have two key strategies for reaching its growth goals: First is the corporate-level business strategy of building new retail stores in shopping malls and other locations, and second is the e-business strategy of selling products on its Web site. Using strategic planning, the Sharper Image would elect to use an e-business strategy only after careful analysis of its internal capabilities and the needs of its customers, retail competitors, and other environmental issues. Exhibit 2 - 2 depicts the way in which e-business strategy flows from the firm's environmental analysis.

In a parallel fashion, marketing strategy becomes **e-marketing strategy** when marketers use digital technology to implement the strategy:

E-Marketing Strategy = Marketing Strategy + Information Technology

Strategic e-marketing is the design of marketing strategy that capitalizes on the organization's electronic or information technology capabilities to reach specified objectives. In essence, strategic e-marketing is where technology strategy and marketing strategy wed to form the organization's e-marketing strategy. As discussed in Chapter 1, technology and its unique properties have given some new life to traditional enterprise and marketing strategies.

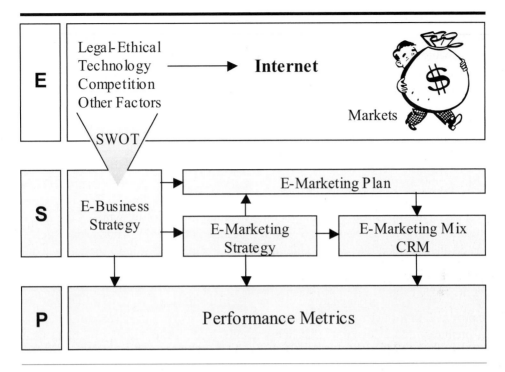

Exhibit 2 - 2 Focusing on Strategy and Performance

For example, the Sharper Image maintains a customer database available to all employees. Regardless of whether a customer buys from the store, the catalog, or the Web site, or whether contact is made by phone, in person, through e-mail, or by postal mail, employees can access the computerized database for up-to-date account activity and information when dealing with customers. This responsive service keeps customers happy and supports Sharper Image's customer relationship management e-marketing strategy—ultimately supporting the corporate growth strategy.

Most strategic plans explain the rationale for the chosen objectives and strategies. This is especially true for a single e-business project trying to win its share of corporate resources and top-management support. Kalakota and Robinson (1999) suggest four appropriate types of rationale:

1. Strategic justification shows how the strategy fits with the firm's overall mission and business objectives, and where it will take the firm if successfully accomplished.

2. Operational justification identifies and quantifies the specific process improvements that will result from the strategy. For example, if CRM (customer relationship management) software is proposed, how will that translate to increased customer retention and higher revenues?

3. Technical justification shows how the technology will fit and provide synergy with current information technology capabilities. For example, is there interoperability along the currently integrated supply chain?

4. Financial justification examines cost/benefit analysis and uses standard measures such as ROI (return on investment) and NPV (net present value).

From Business Models to E-Business Models

There is one more piece of this puzzle to explain before we get into the really interesting content of new e-business and e-marketing strategies. The term *business model* is often mentioned in print and by executives. According to one respected researcher, "A business model is the method of doing business by which a company can sustain itself—that is, generate revenue" (Rappa 2002, p. 1). Another researcher suggested that a business model contains three streams: the value proposition, the revenue stream, and the logistical stream (relating to supply chain issues) (Nickols 2000). Based on current use of the term, we suggest that a **business model** is a method by which the organization sustains itself in the long term and includes its value proposition for partners and customers as well as its revenue streams.

A business model does not exist in a vacuum. It relates to strategy in that a firm will select one or more business models as strategies to accomplish enterprise goals. For instance, if the firm's goal is to position itself as a high-tech, innovative company, it might decide to use the Internet to connect and communicate with its suppliers and customers, as does Dell Computer (see opening quote).

Presented with many opportunities, how does a firm select the best business models? The authors of *Internet Business Models and Strategies* suggest the following components as critical to appraising the fit of a business model for the company and its environment (Afuah and Tucci 2001):

- **Customer value.** Does the model create value through its product offerings that is differentiated in some way from that of competitors?

- **Scope.** Which markets does the firm serve, and are they growing? Are these markets currently served by the firm, or will they be higher risk new markets?

- **Price.** Are the firm's products priced to appeal to markets and also achieve company share and profit objectives?

- **Revenue sources.** Where is the money coming from? Is it plentiful enough to sustain growth and profit objectives over time? Many dot-com failures overlooked this element.

- **Connected activities.** What activities will the firm need to perform to create the value described in the model? Does the firm have these capabilities? For example, if 24/7 customer service is part of the value, the firm must be prepared to deliver it.

- **Implementation.** The company must have the ability to actually make it happen. This involves the firm's systems, people, culture, and so on.

- **Capabilities.** Does the firm have the resources (financial, core competencies, and so on) to make the selected models work?
- **Sustainability.** The e-business model is particularly appropriate if it will create a competitive advantage over time. This means it will be difficult to imitate and that the environment will be attractive for maintaining the model over time.

E-Business Models

Traditional business models such as retailing, selling advertising, and auctions have been around ever since the first business set up shop. What makes a business model an e-business model is the direct connection with information technology:

E-Business Model = Business Model + Information Technology

Thus, an **e-business model** is a method by which the organization sustains itself in the long term *using information technology*, which includes its value proposition for partners and customers as well as its revenue streams. For example, the Internet allows media, music, and software firms to deliver their products over the Internet, creating a new distribution model that cuts costs and increases value. E-business models that take advantage of the Internet properties described in Chapter 1 may be seen as part of a subset sometimes called **Internet business models**.

E-business models can capitalize on digital data collection and distribution techniques without using the Internet. For example, when retailers scan products and customer cards at the checkout, these data can become a rich source of knowledge for inventory management and promotional offers—e-marketing without the Internet. Similarly, when these data are available through the firm's proprietary computer network (Intranet), the firm is applying e-marketing without the Internet. Even though the Internet spawned the vast majority of e-business models, it is very important to remember that e-marketing and e-business models may operate outside the Internet. For simplicity, we use the term *e-business models* to include both Internet and offline digital models throughout the rest of our discussion.

Value and Revenue

As part of its e-business model, an organization describes the ways in which it creates value for customers and partners. Business partners might include supply chain members such as suppliers, wholesalers, and retailers, or firms with which the company joins forces to create new brands (such as the Microsoft and NBC alliance to create MSNBC). Firms deliver stakeholder value through e-business models by using digital products and processes. Whether online or offline, the value proposition involves knowing what is important to the customer or partner and delivering it better than other firms. **Value** encompasses the customer's perceptions of the product's benefits, specifically its attributes, brand name, and support services. Subtracted from benefits are the costs involved in acquiring the product, such as monetary, time, energy, and psychic. Like customers, partners evaluate value by determining whether the partnership provides more benefits than costs.

Value = Benefits – Costs

Information technology usually—but not always—increases benefits and lowers costs to stakeholders. E-marketing strategies capitalize on the Internet's properties to add many general benefits, thus increasing stakeholder value (Exhibit 2 - 3). Conversely, they can decrease value when Web sites are complex, information is hard to locate, and technical difficulties interrupt data access or shopping transactions.

As shown in Exhibit 2 - 3, e-business strategies help firms to decrease internal costs, often improving the value proposition for customers and partners. They can also increase the enterprise revenue stream, an important part of the e-business model.

E-Marketing Increases Benefits

- Online mass customization (different products and messages to different stakeholders)
- Personalization (giving stakeholders relevant information)
- 24/7 convenience
- Self-service ordering and tracking
- One-stop shopping

E-Marketing Decreases Costs

- Low-cost distribution of communication messages (e.g., e-mail)
- Low-cost distribution channel for digital products
- Lowers costs for transaction processing
- Lowers costs for knowledge acquisition (e.g., research and customer feedback)
- Creates efficiencies in supply chain (through communication and inventory optimization)
- Decreases the cost of customer service

E-Marketing Increases Revenues

- Online transaction revenues such as product, information, advertising, and subscriptions sales; or commission/fee on a transaction or referral
- Add value to products/services and increase prices (e.g., online FAQ and customer support)
- Increase customer base by reaching new markets
- Build customer relationships and, thus, increase current customer spending (share of wallet)

Exhibit 2 - 3 E-Marketing Contributes to the E-Business Model

Menu of Strategic E-Business Models

A key element in setting strategic objectives is to take stock of the company's current situation and decide the level of commitment to e-business in general and e-marketing in particular. The possible levels of commitment fall along a continuum that is appropriately represented as a pyramid since few businesses occupy the top position (Exhibit 2 - 4). As a general rule, the higher the firm travels up the pyramid, the greater its level of commitment to e-business, the more its strategies are integrated with information technology, and the greater the impact on the organization. Also, the more strategic moves are at the top, while the more tactical activities are at lower levels; as a result, higher levels carry more risk than lower levels for most firms.

Bear in mind that one firm's activity may be another's enterprise-level strategy. For example, electronic transaction order processing (e.g., selling products on a Web site) may be a small activity for a ski shop with 1% of its business from the online channel, but it is an enterprise-level activity for FedEx, the package delivery service.

It is also important to note that the lowest level of commitment—not shown on the pyramid—is no e-business involvement at all. Research shows that many small local retailers and other small businesses are at this level and should remain there because of their capabilities. For example, it is unlikely that the local independently owned dry cleaner could benefit much from e-business strategies.

In consulting with CEOs worldwide, the Gartner Group poses these questions prior to embarking on any e-business strategies:

1. Are the business models likely to change in my industry? If they are not, there is no reason to get involved. If they are, answering this question suggests a strategic direction for the firm.

2. What does the answer to question 1 mean to my company? The answers vary by size, industry, location, and more.

3. When do I need to be ready? This involves thoughtful competitive analysis.

4. How do I get there from here? This is where e-business strategy comes in.

E-Business Models at Various Levels of Commitment

Each level of the pyramid indicates a number of opportunities for the firm to provide stakeholder value and generate revenue streams using information technology. Because there is no single, comprehensive, ideal taxonomy of e-business models, we categorize the most commonly used models based on the firm's level of commitment (Exhibit 2 - 5). This scheme is not perfect either, because the level of commitment for each model varies by firm, as previously mentioned. Also, the activity-level items generally add value by shaving costs but may not generate a direct revenue stream. Nonetheless, we present this as a good menu of strategic opportunities, arranged by level of commitment to e-business, focusing primarily on models that involve e-

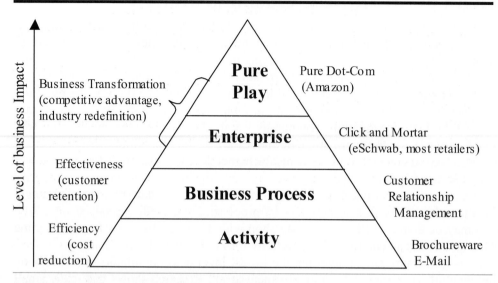

Exhibit 2 - 4 Level of Commitment to E-Business
Source: Adapted from www.mohansawhney.com.

marketing. We'll briefly describe many models here and expand upon them in later chapters.

Although we are discussing individual e-business models, many firms combine two or more e-business models. For example, Amazon.com is an both an online retailer and auctioneer. It also uses many processes and activities listed in the exhibit, such as content publishing and customer relationship management.

Activity Level E-Business Models

The lowest level of the pyramid affects individual business activities that can save the firm money if automated using information technology or the Internet. In this low-risk area, the firm realizes cost reductions through e-business efficiencies (e.g., putting order processing, competitive intelligence, or surveys online). The following is a very brief description of activity-level models:

1. **Online purchasing.** Firms can use the Web to place orders with suppliers, thus automating the activity. Normally this is not a marketing function, but when retailers such as Wal-Mart created automated order processing throughout the supply chain, it had a huge marketing impact.

2. **Order processing.** This occurs when online retailers automate Internet transactions created by customers.

3. **E-mail.** When organizations send e-mail communications to stakeholders, they save printing and mailing costs.

4. **Content publisher.** In this model, companies create valuable content or services on their Web sites, draw lots of traffic, and sell advertising. In another type of

content publishing, the firm posts information about its offerings on a Web site, thus saving printing costs: This has been dubbed **brochureware.**

5. **Business intelligence (BI).** This refers to the gathering of secondary and primary information about competitors, markets, customers, and more.

6. **Online advertising.** As an activity, the firm buys advertising on someone else's e-mail or Web site. When the firm sells advertising, it is engaging in content sponsorship, a higher-level process.

7. **Online sales promotions.** Companies use the Internet to send samples of digital products (e.g., music or software) or electronic coupons, among other tactics.

8. **Pricing strategies.** With dynamic pricing, a firm presents different prices to various groups of customers, even at the individual level. Online negotiation through auctions is one type of dynamic pricing initiated by the buyer instead of the seller. Technology allows this activity to be automated.

Business Process-Level E-Business Models

The next level of the pyramid changes business processes to increase the firm's effectiveness.

Customer relationship management (CRM) involves retaining and growing business and individual customers through strategies that ensure their satisfaction with the firm and its products. CRM seeks to keep customers for the long term and to increase the number and frequency of their transactions with the firm. In the context of e-business, CRM uses digital processes and integrates customer information collected at every customer "touch point." Customers interact with firms in person at retail stores or company offices, by mail, via telephone, or over the Internet. The

Activity Level	Business Process Level	Enterprise Level
1. Order processing	1. Customer relationship management (CRM)	1. E-commerce, direct selling, content sponsorship
2. Online purchasing	2. Knowledge management (KM)	2. Portal
3. E-mail	3. Supply chain management (SCM)	3. Broker models Online exchange, hub Online auction
4. Content publisher	4. Community building online	4. Agent models Manufacturer's agent Catalog aggregator Metamediary Shopping agent Reverse auction Buyer's cooperative Virtual mall
5. Business intelligence (BI)	5. Database marketing	
6. Online advertising	6. Enterprise resource planning (ERP)	
7. Online sales promotions	7. Mass customization	
8. Dynamic pricing strategies online		

Exhibit 2 - 5 E-Business Model Classification

results of interactions at all these touch points are integrated to build a complete picture of customer characteristics, behavior, and preferences.

Knowledge management (KM) is a combination of a firm's database contents, the technology used to create the system, and the transformation of data into useful information and knowledge. KM systems create a storehouse of reports, customer account information, product sales, and other valuable information managers can use to make decisions.

Supply chain management (SCM) involves coordination of the distribution channel to deliver products more effectively and efficiently to customers. For example, when a user orders from certain Web sites, FedEx's computers receive the instruction to pick up product from a warehouse and deliver it quickly to the customer. Similarly, when consumers buy a product at the grocery store, the bar code scanner at the checkout tells the store's computer to reduce the inventory count by one and then automatically orders more cases of the product from warehouses or suppliers if inventory in the back room is low.

With **community building**, firms build Web sites to draw groups of special-interest users. In this model, firms invite users to chat and post e-mail on their Web sites with the purpose of attracting potential customers to the site. Firms often gather e-mail lists of like-minded users from these communities for future e-mail marketing campaigns. Through community building, marketers can create social bonds that enhance customer relationships.

Affiliate programs occur when firms put a link to someone else's retail Web site and earn a commission on all purchases by referred customers. Amazon.com pioneered this e-business model. When viewed from an Amazon affiliate's perspective, it is operating as a selling agent for Amazon's products.

Database marketing involves collecting, analyzing, and disseminating electronic information about customers, prospects, and products to increase profits. This is one of the fastest-growing strategies for e-marketers. Database marketing systems can be a part of the firm's overall knowledge management system.

Enterprise resource planning (ERP) refers to a back-office system for order entry, purchasing, invoicing, and inventory control. ERP systems allow organizations to optimize business processes while lowering costs. Note that many ERP systems predate the Web. ERP does not fall under the marketing function, but it is so important that it must be included in this list.

Mass customization refers to the Internet's unique ability to customize marketing mixes electronically and automatically to the individual level. Firms use this practice when they collect information from customers and prospects, and use it to customize products and communication on an individual basis for a large number of people.

Enterprise-Level E-Business Models

At the enterprise level of the pyramid, the firm automates many business processes in a unified system—demonstrating a significant commitment to e-business. Firms relying heavily on these models (such as Dell Computer) believe that their future will depend on e-business activities.

E-commerce refers to online transactions: selling goods and services on the Internet, either in one transaction or over time with an ongoing subscription price (e.g., *Wall Street Journal Online*). Online retailers are firms that buy products and resell them online. One type of online retailer sells physical products and uses traditional transportation methods to deliver them. The other type sells digital products such as media, software, and music and delivers them via the Internet (and usually ground transportation too). Many online retailers maintain brick-and-mortar stores as well. **Direct selling** refers to a type of e-commerce in which manufacturers sell directly to consumers, eliminating intermediaries such as retailers. **Content sponsorship** online is a form of e-commerce in which companies sell advertising either on their Web sites or in their e-mail. It is called content sponsorship because this model sprang from the media, which depend on advertising sales to pay for editorial content.

A **portal** is point of entry to the Internet, such as the Yahoo! and AOL Web sites. They are portals because they provide many services in addition to search capabilities. For example, they are destinations for news, games, maps, shopping, and so forth in addition to being jump-off points for content provided by others. AOL uses its portal to communicate with members, help them find other Web sites, offer entertaining content, and conduct e-commerce—driving $33 billion in sales a year to partner merchants.

Online brokers are intermediaries that assist in the purchase negotiations without actually representing either buyers or sellers. The revenue stream in these models is commission or fee based. Examples of firms using the brokerage model are E*Trade (**online exchange**), Converge B2B exchange for electronic components, computer products and networking equipment, and eBay (**online auction**). Brokers usually create a market space for exchanges to occur, taking a piece of the action. A **B2B exchange** is a special place because it allows buyers and sellers in a specific industry to quickly connect. Online auctions occur in both B2B and B2C markets, with the online broker providing the Web site and technology in exchange for a commission on all sales.

Unlike brokers, **online agents** tend to represent either the buyer or the seller and earn a commission for their work. **Selling agents** help a seller move product. There are many of these in the B2B market. In the B2C market, affiliate programs, discussed earlier, are also an example of the selling agent model.

Manufacturer's agents represent more than one seller. In traditional marketing, they often represent manufacturing firms that sell complementary products to avoid conflicts of interest. However, in the virtual world, they generally create Web sites to help an entire industry sell product. For example, Travelocity.com, the online travel agent, is a manufacturer's agent in the travel industry. Another interesting model, the **catalog aggregator**, brings together many catalog companies to create a new searchable database of products for buyers.

A special type of agent is the **metamediary**—so called because it represents a cluster of manufacturers, online retailers, and content providers organized around a life event or major asset purchase (Sawhney 1999). Consumers facing life events such as weddings or major asset purchases such as cars require a cohesive set of cognitively related products and information. The metamediaries assemble all the content and services in one location for the customer's convenience and receive a fee from selling firms. These sites show how the Web adds value and lowers costs through market deconstruction, giving consumers everything they want at the right time and in the same place.

Purchasing agents represent buyers. In traditional marketing, they often forge long-term relationships with one or more firms; on the Internet, however, they represent any number of buyers, often anonymously. For example, **shopping agents** help individual consumers find specific products and the best prices online (e.g., www.mysimon.com). Another model, the **reverse auction**, allows individual buyers to enter the price they will pay for particular items at the purchasing agent's Web site, and sellers can agree or not. Purchasing agents often help buyers form cooperatives online for the purpose of buying in larger quantities to reduce prices. An online purchasing agent is called a **buyer cooperative** or a *buyer aggregator*. Buyers' cooperatives are quite common in offline B2C markets and in online B2B and B2C markets. Purchasing agent models are growing and evolving because they are based on the idea of increasing buyer control online.

A **virtual mall** is similar to a shopping mall in which multiple online merchants are hosted at a Web site. This as an agent model because the firm with the Web site hosting the mall usually builds the site, promotes it, and takes a fee for its services.

Pure Play

The final level of the pyramid is comprised of Internet pure plays. **Pure plays** are businesses that began on the Internet, even if they subsequently added a brick-and-mortar presence. We do not include pure plays in Exhibit 2 - 5 because they start right at the top of the pyramid rather than progressing upward as do traditional brick-and-mortar firms. For example, E*Trade is a pure play, beginning with only online trading. Interestingly, E*Trade now has several retail storefronts in major cities. Pure plays face significant challenges: They must compete as new brands and take customers away from established brick-and-mortar businesses. The successful ones have been able to do so by industry redefinition (i.e., changing the rules of the game) (Modahl 2000). One way to change the rules is to invent a new e-business model, as Yahoo! and eBay did. In fact, some observers believe that eBay has the only truly viable pure play model in existence. The key to pure play success is offering greater customer value. For example, Buy.com increases customer value by utilizing a content sponsorship model combined with direct sales. The ad inventory sold on the site helps to subsidize prices for the consumer. Most fallen angels in the dot-com crash were pure plays that lacked viable e-business models.

An Optimized System of E-Business Models

We defined e-business in Chapter 1 as the continuous optimization of a firm's business activities through digital technology. Regardless of commitment level, this means that firms usually combine traditional business and e-business models. Some firms adopt only one or two of these processes, which shows commitment at the business process level. The best examples of players at the enterprise level are click-and-mortar enterprises such as Schwab, which combined its online and offline brokerages in a unified system. Other examples include Barnes & Noble, Lands' End, and many other brick-and-mortar operations that have successfully migrated online. These businesses face unique challenges since customers view them as unified businesses and expect a high degree of coordination between online and offline operations. Thus, a customer would like to be able to access the same Schwab account whether from her home computer late at night or from her local brokerage office—and she can. The danger at the enterprise level is that the established corporate culture might squash e-commerce initiatives or slow them down with the best of intentions. To avoid these problems, many businesses have spun off their e-commerce operations as wholly owned subsidiaries or pure plays so they can compete without the weight of the parent business. While this strategy may be successful, reuniting the parent and child operations can be difficult.

A fully optimized e-business that uses the Internet to sell is the sum of multiple e-business activities and processes: e-commerce, business intelligence, customer relationship management, supply chain management, and enterprise resource planning as represented in the following equation:

$$EB = EC + BI + CRM + SCM + ERP$$

Performance Metrics

The only way to know whether a company has reached its objectives is to measure results. **Performance metrics** are specific measures designed to evaluate the effectiveness and efficiency of an organization's operations. For example, if the company wants 5% of its sales to come from the online channel, it needs to continually measure revenue from various channels to see if it is achieving the goal. Armed with this information, the company can make corrections to be sure it accomplishes the goal. For instance, Skechers USA, the trendy shoe producer, found many problems by using special software to track visitors on its Web site. As a result, it changed the site to offer faster access to product photos and require fewer clicks to view and purchase products. The result was a 70% increase in sales ($227.5 million) from the first quarter in 2000 to the same period in 2001 (Jarvis 2001).

Because strategy is the means to the end—the way of accomplishing objectives—performance metrics should be defined along with the strategy formulation so the entire organization will know what results constitute successful performance (refer to Exhibit 2 - 2 for the role of performance). Nickols (2000) put it well:

> Strategy, then, has no existence apart from the ends sought. It is a general framework that provides guidance for actions to be taken and, at the same time, is shaped by the actions taken. This means that the necessary precondition for formulating strategy is a clear and widespread understanding of the ends to be obtained. Without these ends in view, action is purely tactical and can quickly degenerate into nothing more than a flailing about. (p. 6)

When a company designates the performance metrics it will use to measure strategy effectiveness, it is doing two important things. First, it is translating its vision, strategy, or e-business model into components that have measurable outcomes that various departments can use to create action plans. Second, the performance metrics communicate to employees what results are valued by the firm. When employee evaluations are tied to the metrics, people will be motivated to make decisions that lead to the desired outcomes. Even though the metrics are usually set by top management, successful firms collect employee input throughout the process so the measurements are relevant and the organization gains consensus on their importance. Thus, the adage, "What you measure is what you get."

There are several well-known performance metrics systems. One, called Six Sigma, is the topic of Krishna Narayanan's practitioner article at the end of Part II in this book. We discuss another here—the Balanced Scorecard.

The Balanced Scorecard

For years, firms valued financial performance or market share as the most important success measures. The large firms fostered competition among their brand groups or retail outlets and measured success by the bottom line (profits). Many still do. During the mid- to late-1990's, the dot-com firms ignored financial measures and focused on growth, much to their dismay. These approaches are narrowly focused and place more weight on short-term results rather than addressing the firm's long-term sustainability.

These weaknesses paved the way for enterprise performance management systems that measure many aspects of a firm's achievements. The **Balanced Scorecard**, developed by two Harvard Business School professors in 1990, is one such system. Fifty percent of organizations worldwide have adopted the Balanced Scorecard with excellent results ("The E-Commerce Balancing Act" 2000). The scorecard approach links strategy to measurement by asking firms to consider their vision, critical success factors for accomplishing it, and subsequent performance metrics in four areas: customer, internal, innovation and learning, and financial (Exhibit 2 - 6). In the following sections we describe typical goals and metrics in each perspective. However, it is important to remember that each firm defines the specific measures for each box—the system is very flexible.

Customer Perspective		Internal Business Perspective		Innovation and Learning Perspective		Financial Perspective	
Goals	Measures	Goals	Measures	Goals	Measures	Goals	Measures

Exhibit 2 - 6 The Balanced Scorecard Has Four Perspectives

Four Perspectives

The customer perspective uses measures of the value delivered to customers. These metrics tend to fall into four areas: time, quality, performance and service, and cost. They can include measures such as time from order to delivery, customer satisfaction levels with product performance, amount of sales from new products, and industry-specific metrics such as equipment up-time percentage or number of service calls.

The internal perspective evaluates company success at meeting customer expectations through its internal processes. The items with greatest impact in this area include cycle time (how long to make the product), manufacturing quality, and employee skills and productivity. Information systems are a critical component of the internal perspective for e-business firms.

The innovation and learning perspective, sometimes called the growth perspective, is one of the Balanced Scorecard's unique contributions. Here, companies place value on continuous improvement to existing products and services as well as on innovation in new products. These activities take employees away from their daily work of selling products, asking them to pay attention to factors critical to the firm's long-term sustainability—especially important for e-business firms. Measures in this area include number of new products and the percentage of sales attributable to each; penetration of new markets; and the improvement of processes such as CRM or SCM initiatives.

If the projected outcomes result from the previous perspectives and performance metrics, the financial perspective will be on target too. Financial measures include income and expense metrics as well as return on investment, sales, and market share growth. Companies must be careful to relate measurements from the first three perspectives to the financial area whenever possible.

Each firm will select metrics for the four perspectives based on its objectives, business model, strategies, industry, and so forth. The point is to understand what the company wants to accomplish and devise performance metrics to monitor the progress and see that the goals are reached.

Scorecard Benefits

The Balanced Scorecard system helps a firm obtain timely information to update its strategy. Its four perspectives balance long-term and short-term measures and evaluate every part of the firm and how each contributes toward accomplishing selected goals. It also helps firms leverage their relationships with partners and supply chain members. The scorecard can be used by all types of organizations, both profit and not-for-profit, and in all industries, if they select appropriate metrics.

The Balanced Scorecard has many other specific benefits. First, it provides a way to go beyond financial metrics in measuring many different aspects that lead to effective and efficient performance. Second, it creates a long-term perspective for company sustainability. Third, it forces companies to decide what is important and translate those decisions into measurable outcomes that all employees can understand. Next, it is a great communication tool because employees can use the scorecard as a guide to coordinate their efforts. In addition, it supports employee evaluation in that individual performance can be tied to successful outcomes on the metrics. Also, it provides a way to measure intangible as well as tangible assets. This is especially important for firms using e-business models because knowledge, information, and innovation are critical to their success. Finally, the Balanced Scorecard is valuable because of its flexibility in allowing firms to select appropriate metrics for their goals, strategies, industry, and specific vision.

Many firms have successfully implemented the Balanced Scorecard. Hilton Hotels attributes its number-one ranking in customer satisfaction during 2000 and highest industry profits to this approach (Jackson and Baskey 2000). In another example, Wells Fargo Bank created Online Financial Services in the early Internet days to capitalize on new technologies. Its goal was to migrate current customers and draw new customers to the online channel. Using the scorecard as a roadmap to provide value to customers and to be sure internal processes and the technology could handle the anticipated volume, Wells Fargo beat its goal of 1 million customers within a short time ("The E-Commerce Balancing Act" 2000).

In the early 1990s, Apple Computer developed a Balanced Scorecard to move the focus back to innovation and away from purely financial measures and market share. Although the results and further refinements have not been reported, consider the measures Apple selected (Kaplan and Norton 1993):

- Customer perspective: Market share and customer satisfaction (as measured both internally and by J.D. Powers & Associates secondary data).
- Internal perspective: Core competencies of user-friendly interfaces, powerful software architectures, and effective distribution systems.
- Innovation and learning perspective: Employee understanding of the company strategy (as measured by a survey).

- Financial perspective: Shareholder value (based on stock prices).

Applying the Balanced Scorecard to E-Business and E-Marketing

E-business firms are swimming in data. They have databases full of customer information, Web site logs that automatically record every page users visit and how long they stay, customer service records, sales data from many different channels, and so forth. One service firm reported: "Since I've got all these things to measure, I'm paralyzed by all the opportunities." In spite of these difficulties, measurement is vital to success. When Forrester Research surveyed executives at 51 companies, 63% said measurement is extremely or very important today versus only 24% in 2000. Sixty-one percent of the executives further stated that they are focusing more on return on investment (ROI) as a measure today (Cutler 2001). This chapter presents an overview of the problem; throughout the book, we'll expand on performance metrics that seem to be working in the e-business environment.

E-business firms using the Balanced Scorecard must address a few special considerations. One is whether they should use leading or lagging indicators to measure performance. For example, the number of customers who actually bought from the Web site last month is an excellent and important lagging indicator of performance but may not predict how the e-commerce initiative is doing as well as measuring the number of site visitors this month. If a firm understands the correlation between these two numbers, it might use both. Another decision involves the level of detail. For instance, when a firm buys advertising on a Web site, it will want to measure the traffic it gets from the ad, how many people convert to a purchase, and how much they buy. Many firms also track marketing communication effectiveness over time. Finally, because e-business models evolve quickly and new opportunities arise suddenly, e-business firms often find some experimental tactics leading strategy change. This means they must review their scorecard measures often and revise strategy statements and measures in line with hot new ideas—otherwise the organization will experience inner turmoil.

Metrics for the Customer Perspective

The most important of these metrics measure customer loyalty and lifetime value. However, many other metrics can help a firm optimize customer value: for example, customer perceptions of product value, appropriateness of selected targets, and customer buying patterns. The firm must also measure value created for partners and other supply chain members because many can easily partner elsewhere if they are not satisfied. As an example, Exhibit 2 - 7 displays several possible measures for some customer goals of an e-business firm.

Customer Perspective	
Example Goals	**Possible Measures**
Build awareness of a new Web site service	Survey target awareness of service
	Number of visitors to the site
Position firm as high tech	Survey target attitudes
Increase number of software downloads from the Web site	Number from Web site log
High customer satisfaction with Web site	Survey of target at Web site
	Number of visits and activity at site
High customer satisfaction with value of online purchasing	Number of complaints (e-mail, phone)
	Number of abandoned shopping carts
	Sales of online versus offline for same products
Increase the amount or frequency of online sales from current customers	Mine the database for change in frequency of purchases over time
Build customer relationships	Number of purchases per customer over time (using cookie data)
	Customer retention percentage
Appropriate target markets	Data mining to find purchase patterns by targeting criteria
Buy-to-delivery time faster than competition	Number of days from order to delivery
	Competition delivery times
Increased coupon use from Web coupons	Number who redeem
Build communities on the site	Number of registrations to community
	Number of posts to community bulletin board
Value for Business Partners	
Increase number of affiliates in program	Number of affiliates over time
Cross-sell to partner sites	Number of visitors to partner site from our site

Exhibit 2 - 7 Customer Perspective Scorecard for E-Business Firm

Metrics for the Internal Perspective

The internal perspective is critical to a successful e-business. Many goals in this perspective affect human resources, information technology, and other areas that directly and indirectly affect marketing. Of particular note is that the entire supply chain is considered *internal* in this analysis. Obviously the manufacturing firm cannot control the employees of its online retailers. At the same time, neither business customers nor consumers differentiate among firms in a supply chain—they just want quality products on demand. Thus, recent work on the Balanced Scorecard includes measures for the entire supply chain. See Exhibit 2 - 8 for example goals and measures in the internal perspective.

Internal Perspective	
Example Goals	**Possible Measures**
Improve the quality of online service	Target market survey Number of customers who use the service Time to run the service software from Web site
Quality online technical help	Amount of time to answer customer e-mail Number of contacts to solve a problem Number of problems covered by Web site FAQ Customer follow-up survey
Quick product cycle time	Number of days to make the product
High product quality for online service	Product test statistics on specific performance measures
Web server size adequate and operational 24/7	Number of actual simultaneous Web page requests ÷ maximum possible Percentage of up-time for server Number of mirrored or backup sites
Optimized number of customer service reps responding to online help	Number of inquiries to customer service rep ratio
Superior Web site content management	Number of updates per week Web site log traffic pattern statistics
Optimized inventory levels	Average number of items in warehouse Inventory turnover Supplier speed to deliver product
Supply Chain Value to Firm	
High supplier satisfaction	Supplier profits from our firm's orders
Partner value	Number of visitors from partner site to ours and number that purchase Partner contribution to product design

Exhibit 2 - 8 Internal Perspective Scorecard for E-Business Firm

Metrics for the Innovation and Learning Perspective

The innovation and learning perspective typically falls under the human resources umbrella. Two exceptions include product innovation and continuous improvement of marketing processes, both very important for e-business firms due to rapid changes in technology. See Exhibit 2 - 9 for a few sample goals and measures affecting marketers.

Innovation and Learning Perspective	
Example Goals	**Possible Measures**
Online service innovation	Number of new service products to market in a year Number of new service features not offered by competitive offerings Percent of sales from new services
Continuous improvement in CRM system	Number of employee suggestions Number/type of improvements over time
High Internet lead to sales conversion	Revenue per sales employee from Internet leads Number of conversions from online leads
Increased value in knowledge management system	Number of accesses by employees Number of knowledge contributions by employees
Successful penetration of new markets	Percentage of the firm's sales in each new market

Exhibit 2 - 9 Innovation and Learning Scorecard for E-Business Firm

Metrics for the Financial Perspective

Marketing strategies clearly drive revenues, online and offline. They can affect profits as well, but other operational factors enter the equation when figuring company expenses. Nevertheless, marketers who manage brands have responsibility for their profits. When marketers propose new products or online services, they must forecast the potential sales over time, estimate the expenses to deliver that level of sales, and project the amount of time needed to break even (create enough revenues to cover expenses and start-up investments). In most cases, the product or internal project with the fastest break-even period or best potential for meeting the firm's return on investment hurdle will get funded.

Two of the most frequently used metrics are profits and return on investment. This section will outline basic ideas without considering taxes and other details. Net profits are revenues minus expenses (Exhibit 2 - 10). Revenues are the actual amount of dollars customers give the firm in exchange for products. Expenses include many things, most commonly the variable costs for producing the product, the selling costs (advertising, free product giveaways, and other customer acquisition costs), delivery, customer support, and other administrative costs.

Return on investment (ROI) is calculated by dividing net profit by total assets (fixed plus current). Marketers often evaluate ROI for specific e-business projects by dividing the project's profits by its investment dollars—such as the research, development, and testing funds needed to introduce the new service. As an example, a firm might invest $100,000 in software to analyze Web traffic patterns, use the results, change the Web site for better usability, and realize an additional $75,000 in

	Net Profit	**Firm-Wide Return on Investment**
Formula	Net Profit (before taxes) = Sales Revenue *minus:* 1. Cost of goods sold 2. Expenses (sales, marketing, delivery, overhead, miscellaneous)	ROI = $\dfrac{\text{Net Profit}}{\text{Total Assets}}$ Total Assets: 1. Fixed assets 2. Current assets (cash + inventory + accounts receivable)
Example	$1 million in sales *minus* ($500,000 cost of goods sold, $250,000 marketing costs and $200,000 administrative costs) = $50,000 net profit (5%)	ROI = $\dfrac{\$50,000}{\$2,000,000}$ ROI = 2.5 %

Exhibit 2 - 10 Net Profit and ROI Simple Formulas

e-commerce revenues: a 75% ROI.

The financial perspective scorecard relies heavily on sales, profit, and return figures. Exhibit 2 - 11 presents some common performance metrics used by e-marketers.

Financial Perspective	
Example Goals	**Possible Measures**
Increase market share for online products	Market share percentage (firm's sales as percentage of industry sales)
Double-digit sales growth	Dollar volume of sales from one time period to the next
Target 10% ROI within one year for each new product	ROI
Lower customer acquisition costs (CAC) in online channel	CAC (costs for advertising, etc. divided by number of customers)
Increase conversion rates at Web site	Number of orders divided by number of visitors to site
Increase individual customer profit	Average order value Profit contribution over time less CAC
Achieve at least a 10% net profit in first year of new product	Net profit as percentage of sales

Exhibit 2 - 11 Financial Perspective Scorecard for E-Business Firm

Balanced Scorecard for Raytheon's E-Business

To see the Balanced Scorecard in action, consider how Raytheon Co. applied it to the company's e-business. "It works for Raytheon; I don't see why it can't work for everyone"(p. 1). (Melymuka 2001). Following are many of the measures Raytheon established for its Web site business:

- **Customer perspective**
    - o Loyalty: percentage who return to site within a year; time between visits; duration of visit; conversion rate; percentage who give personal information; percentage of e-mail addresses collected out of all traffic.
    - o Transactions: unique visitors each month; online sales abandoned; percentage of orders correct; time to respond to a customer; percentage of orders filled on time.
- **Internal perspective**
    - o Web site: time to load a Web page; network up-time and scalability.
    - o Supply chain excellence: inventory levels; inventory turns; order confirmation time; percentage of products built to order.
    - o Complementary channels: percentage of total revenue generated online.
- **Innovation and learning perspective.** Average time from concept to start; speed to match a rival's site; speed at which the competition will match the site; time between relaunches.
- **Financial perspective.** Return on invested capital; market capitalization migration (changing value).

Although performance metrics affect the entire firm, this book focuses on e-marketing metrics. Many of the measures mentioned earlier will be described in more detail in later chapters. For example, in Chapter 13, Integrated Communication Mix, we present metrics that help firms determine the effectiveness of their marketing communication. In chapter 6, Marketing Knowledge, we discuss how firms generate the numbers they need to calculate metrics.

In the next chapter, we move to the e-marketing plan and discuss how this plan flows from corporate e-business strategies and how the marketing mix and CRM enter the picture (Exhibit 2 - 2). The e-marketing plan is a management guide and road map that paves the way to achieving performance goals.

Summary

A business or e-business needs strategic planning to develop and maintain the proper fit between the organization's objectives, skills, and resources and its ever-changing market opportunities. Two key elements of strategic planning are the preparation of a

SWOT (strengths, weaknesses, opportunities, and threats) analysis and the establishment of strategic objectives for growth, competitive position, geographic scope, and other areas.

Strategy is defined as the means to achieve a goal. E-business strategy is the deployment of enterprise resources to capitalize on technologies for reaching specified objectives that ultimately improve performance and create sustainable competitive advantage. E-marketing strategy is the use of digital technology to implement an organization's strategy. In contrast, strategic e-marketing is the design of marketing strategy that capitalizes on the organization's electronic or information technology capabilities to reach specified objectives.

A business model is a method by which the organization sustains itself in the long term and includes its value proposition for partners and customers as well as its revenue streams. An e-business model is a method by which the organization sustains itself in the long term using information technology, including its value proposition for partners and customers as well as its revenue streams. Firms deliver value by providing more benefits in relation to costs, as perceived by customers and partners. E-marketing improves the value proposition by increasing benefits, decreasing costs, and increasing revenues.

Companies can become involved in e-business at the activity level, business process level, enterprise level, or through a pure play. Commitment is lower at the activity level and rises with each level. The main e-business models at the activity level include online purchasing, order processing, e-mail, content publisher, business intelligence, online advertising, online sales promotion, and dynamic pricing strategies. The main e-business models at the business process level are customer relationship management, knowledge management, supply chain management, community building online, database marketing, enterprise resource planning, and mass customization. The main e-business models at the enterprise level are e-commerce, portal, online broker, online agent, manufacturer's agent, metamediary, purchasing agent, and virtual mall. Pure plays are businesses that began on the Internet, even if they later added a brick-and-mortar presence.

Performance metrics are specific measures designed to evaluate the effectiveness and efficiency of an organization's operations. The Balanced Scorecard links strategy to measurement by asking firms to consider their vision, critical success factors for accomplishing it, and subsequent performance metrics in four areas: customer, internal, innovation and learning, and financial. The customer perspective uses measures of the value delivered to customers. The internal perspective evaluates company success at meeting customer expectations through its internal processes. The innovation and learning perspective looks at continuous improvement to existing products and services as well as innovation in new products. The financial perspective looks at income and expense metrics as well as return on investment, sales, and market share growth. Each firm selects metrics for the four perspectives based on its objectives, business model, strategies, industry, and so forth. In this way, the firm can measure progress toward achieving its objectives.

Key Terms

Affiliate programs

B2B exchange

Balanced Scorecard

Brochureware

Business intelligence

Business model

Buyer cooperative

Catalog aggregator

Community building

Content sponsorship

Customer relationship management (CRM)

Database marketing

Direct selling

E-business model

E-business strategy

E-commerce

E-marketing strategy

Enterprise resource planning (ERP)

Internet business models

Knowledge management (KM)

Manufacturer's agents

Mass customization

Metamediary

Objectives

Online agents

Online auction

Online brokers

Online exchange

Performance metrics

Portal

Purchasing agents

Pure play

Return on investment (ROI)

Reverse auction

Selling agents

Shopping agents

Strategic e-marketing

Strategic planning

Strategy

Supply chain management (SCM)

SWOT

Tactics

Value

Virtual mall

Exercises

Review Questions

1. What is strategic planning and why do companies prepare a SWOT analysis during the strategic planning process?
2. How does e-business strategy relate to strategy on the corporate level?
3. Define e-marketing strategy and explain how it is used.
4. How does an e-business model differ from a business model?

5. What is the formula for determining value?

6. What are the four levels of commitment to e-business and what are some examples of each?

7. What is customer relationship management (CRM) and why do companies create strategies in this area?

8. How is e-commerce defined?

9. What is an Internet pure play, and what are some examples?

10. What is the Balanced Scorecard and how do companies use it in e-business?

Discussion Questions

11. Why is it important for an e-business model to create value in a way that is differentiated from the way competitors' models create value?

12. Based on the opening vignette and your examination of the Amazon.com site (or your experience as a customer), what strategic objectives do you think are appropriate for this e-business? What performance metrics would you use to measure progress toward achieving these objectives—and why?

13. The Balanced Scorecard helps e-businesses examine results from four perspectives. Would you recommend that e-businesses also look at results from a societal perspective? Explain your response.

14. Should e-businesses strive to build community with noncustomers as well as customers? Why or why not?

chapter

3 the e-marketing plan

learning objectives

The primary goal of this chapter is to explain the importance of creating an e-marketing plan and present the six steps in the e-marketing planning process. You will see how marketers incorporate information technology in plans for effectively and efficiently achieving e-business objectives such as increasing revenues and slashing costs.

After reading this chapter, you will be able to:

- Discuss the nature and importance of an e-marketing plan and outline its six steps.
- Describe the tasks that marketers complete in tiers 1 and 2 as they create e-marketing strategies.
- Show the form of an e-marketing objective and highlight the use of an objective-strategy matrix.
- List some key revenues and costs identified during the budgeting step of the e-marketing planning process.

If I had one hour to chop down a tree, I'd spend the first 30 minutes sharpening the axe.

abraham lincoln (commonly attributed)

After years of declining circulation and revenue, Playboy Enterprises CEO Christie Hefner revitalized the company in the 1990s with a plan to add multimedia content channels such as cable TV, digital media, video, and the Internet to its *Playboy* magazine format. The plan was based on a thorough understanding of the firm's assets and unique franchise and covered ways of leveraging these to meet customers' needs. Playboy's assets included a strong brand, a base of 4.5 million readers, extensive editorial and advertising sales experience, and—of course—the Playboy Bunnies. Hefner applied these strengths to new marketing distribution opportunities. A major objective was to reach new audiences that might then try *Playboy* magazine. To accomplish this, Hefner and her team designed complementary products for the different media channels rather than repeating the magazine's content online. They created Playboy TV as sexy entertainment for couples, differentiated from the one-at-a-time readers of the magazine. They also designed the Internet offerings to take full advantage of the medium's interactivity and multimedia carrying capabilities.

Playboy.com came online in 1994 as the first U.S. Web site for a nationally circulated magazine, complete with a marketing plan for generating revenues from four main sources:

- **Advertising.** Entice traditional advertisers to extend their magazine reach to new online markets.
- **E-commerce.** Sell Playboy-brand items and other products online.
- **Online gaming.** Online gambling is legal in two-thirds of all countries and is estimated to be a $3 billion global market. The Playboy version displays horse races, sends an e-mail to registered users to notify them when their horse is running, and provides betting tips from popular Playboy Bunnies.
- **Online events.** Users can join the Cyber Club for $60 a year and view behind-the-scenes content.

Not missing a chance to cross sell, the Web site includes teaser streaming video vignettes and program schedules for the Playboy TV channel, as well as subscription information for the magazine. These strategies have achieved Playboy's goal of diversifying the business. Print publishing revenues are only 45% of the business, and 100,000 users belong to the Cyber Club. Although the company is still losing money, and its online division is not yet profitable, losses are not as high as magazine industry averages. The company is betting on online gaming to draw future revenues (Hefner speech 2001; www.hoovers.com).

It's not the strongest or most intelligent that survive, but the ones most responsive to change. c h a r l e s d a r w i n

Overview of the E-Marketing Planning Process

How can information technologies assist marketers in building revenues and market share or lowering costs? How can firms identify a sustainable competitive advantage with the Internet when so little is understood about how to succeed? The answer lies in determining how to apply digital data and information technologies both effectively and efficiently. The best firms have clear visions that they translate, through the marketing process, from e-business objectives and strategies into e-marketing goals and well-executed strategies and tactics for achieving those goals. This marketing process entails three steps: marketing plan creation, plan implementation, and plan evaluation/corrective action. This chapter will examine the first of these steps: the e-marketing plan.

Creating an E-Marketing Plan

The **e-marketing plan** is a blueprint for e-marketing strategy formulation and implementation. It is a guiding, dynamic document that links the firm's e-business strategy (e-business model) with technology-driven marketing strategies and lays out details for plan implementation through marketing management. The intent of the marketing plan is to guide delivery of the desired results measured by performance metrics according to the specifications of the e-business model imbedded in the firm's e-business strategy (refer to Exhibit 3 - 1 to see where the e-marketing plan fits in the process).

The e-marketing plan serves as a road map to guide the direction of the firm, allocate resources, and make tough decisions at critical junctures (Kalakota and Robinson 1999). Many companies short-circuit this process and develop strategies ad hoc. Some of them are successful, but many more fail. The Gartner Group correctly predicted that up to 75% of all e-business projects would fail due to fundamental flaws in planning. Nonetheless, some of the best firms discover successful e-commerce tactics accidentally and then use those experiences to build a bottom up plan. Such was the case with eSchwab, the online stock trading firm, which allowed its online channel successes to change the entire brick-and-mortar firm. Whether the result of top-down or bottom-up planning, firms must plan for long-term sustainability.

This chapter is structured around a six-step traditional marketing plan. It presents a generic plan that includes a menu of tasks from which marketers can select activities relevant to their firm, industry, brands, and internal processes. It assumes that a higher-level corporate plan is already in place, outlining the firm's goals, e-business strategies, and selected enterprise-level e-business models. If this is not the case, marketers must go through the environmental scan and SWOT analyses prior to creating the plan (see Chapter 2). Two common types of e-marketing plans are the napkin plan and the venture capital plan, discussed next.

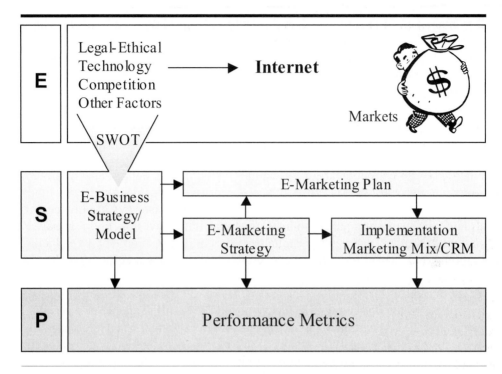

Exhibit 3 - 1 E-Marketing Plan—Strategy Formulation and Implementation

The Napkin Plan

In what one marketer calls the *napkin plan*, many dot-com entrepreneurs were known to simply jot their ideas on a napkin over lunch or cocktails and then run off to find financing. The big-company version of this is the just-do-it, activity-based, bottom-up plan. As an example, an employee has an idea about how to set up a Web site or build a database and convinces management to just do it. For example, an e-marketing student who works for a local ski shop approached the owner, asking for $500 for software and $50 a month for Web hosting to start an experimental e-commerce site. He placed a few pictures of skis on the site and included information about how to call the store to order. The site brought in several orders a week, quickly paying off the investment. These ad hoc plans sometimes work and are sometimes even necessary given a stodgy corporate culture, but they are not recommended when substantial resources are involved. This is because sound planning and thoughtful implementation are needed for long-term success in business and e-business. This principle became increasingly evident during the dot-com shakeout.

The Venture Capital E-Marketing Plan

Small to mid-sized firms and entrepreneurs with start-up ideas usually begin with a *napkin plan* and do not initially go through the entire traditional marketing planning process. One reason is that one or two leaders generally plan the whole venture, intuitively understanding the marketing environment and how their hot new idea is positioned for success. Such was the case for Jerry Yang and Dave Filo when in 1994 they started *Jerry's Guide to the World Wide Web*—later named *Yahoo!* However, as the company grew and needed capital, Jerry and Dave had to put together a comprehensive e-marketing plan. Without an emphasis on strategic planning, Yahoo! would not be a dot-com survivor.

Where does an entrepreneur go for capital? Some of it is debt financed through bank loans, though most of it is equity financed. Start-up companies tap private funds (friends and family), **angel investors**, and venture capitalists (VCs). In general, friends and family are the smallest sources of capital, angel investors invest hundreds of thousands of dollars, and venture capitalists invest millions of dollars. Even banks, corporations, and consulting firms have established **venture capital** branches to finance Internet start-ups. Some VCs are even financing companies operated out of college dorm rooms.

Regardless of the dot-com crash, plenty of money is still available to e-business entrepreneurs. The conventional wisdom is that money is scarce, when talent is really the scarce resource. Obviously, investors aren't stupid. They are looking for a well-composed business plan, and more importantly, a good team to implement it. Two quotes from a well-known venture capitalist, Arthur Rock, who helped to finance Intel, Apple, and Teledyne, say it best:

> "I invest in people, not ideas."

> "If you can find good people, if they're wrong about the product, they'll make a switch, so what good is it to understand the product that they're talking about in the first place?"

This kind of thinking relieves some of the planning pressure on entrepreneurs—but does not eliminate the need for planning to maximize organizational resources. The plan prepared by entrepreneurs for VCs should be about eight to ten pages long and contain enough data and logic to prove that (1) the e-business idea is solid and (2) the entrepreneur has some idea of how to run the business. William Sahlman (1997) of Harvard University identifies nine questions that every business plan should answer:

1. Who is the new venture's customer?
2. How does the customer make decisions about buying this product or service?
3. To what degree is the product or service a compelling purchase for the customer?
4. How will the product or service be priced?
5. How will the venture reach all the identified customer segments?
6. How much does it cost (in time and resources) to acquire a customer?

7. How much does it cost to produce and deliver the product or service?

8. How much does it cost to support a customer?

9. How easy is it to retain a customer?

Venture capitalists typically look for an exit plan—a way to get their money and profits out of the venture within a few years. These days, the golden exit plan is to go public and issue stock in an initial public offering (IPO). As soon as the stock price rises sufficiently, the VC cashes out and moves on to another investment. VCs don't even pretend that all their investments will be successful. But if even one out of 20 is an Amazon.com or eBay.com, the risk was well worth the reward. The employees of these start-ups typically work for very low wages—deferring their compensation in stock options. The buzz on the street for college graduates is to get shareholder's equity—potentially far more remunerative than a good salary with an established firm. This, of course, makes the VCs happy since their cash layout is lower and the employees have a strong incentive for the venture to succeed. A good VC will nurture the business and jump in to help when the going gets rough. However, the stock market runs hot and cold on Internet IPOs, though when they are hot they are white hot! Of particular interest to investors are projects that tap new markets with high margins. At first there was a boom in B2C investments, and then B2B investments. Some observers feel that both markets are getting saturated, although there is always opportunity for a better mousetrap. Some say it is the mobile market (wireless Internet) that is about to take off.

A Six-Step E-Marketing Plan

Six key planning elements include a situation analysis, the link from e-business to e-marketing strategy, the plan objectives, an implementation plan, the budget, and a plan for evaluating success (Exhibit 3 - 2). We cannot overemphasize the need to include feedback mechanisms to assess the plan's success and to use in making course corrections along the way. This is especially true in the fast-paced e-business environment. In fact, some marketers recommend contingency plans and "trigger points" that if reached will invoke strategy refinement.

A good way to think about the marketing plan is through the analogy of preparing for a football game. While reviewing game films, a situation analysis reveals each team's strengths and weaknesses (e.g., the home team has a good passing game, the visitors have an excellent run defense). A likely objective would then be to win the game by throwing the ball. Strategies are developed to meet this objective (e.g., use play action to draw in the coverage; throw deep). Next, tactics implement the strategies (e.g., use a play action pass on first down; run on second down to keep them honest, pass on third down). Finally there is Monday morning quarterbacking with the postgame evaluation.

Consider how Playboy Enterprises, featured in the chapter-opening example, progressed through these six steps for expanding into the Internet channel. The firm found an opportunity (Internet) and a strength (editorial material) in its SWOT analysis, identified targets for the online channel, and decided how to differentiate and position the brand for the Web (different content and multimedia delivery). It then set objectives of diversifying the business and created an implementation plan for the plan, including a description of the online product, e-commerce tactics, Cyber Club pricing, and more. As part of the planning process, they will have created a budget and continuously monitored Web site sales and traffic numbers, as well.

	Step	Tasks
1	Situation analysis	Review the firm's environmental and SWOT analyses. Review the existing marketing plan and any other information that can be obtained about the company and its brands. Review the firm's e-business objectives, strategies, and performance metrics.
2	Link e-business with e-marketing strategy	Identify revenue streams suggested by e-business models. **Tier 1** Perform marketing opportunity analysis to identify target stakeholders. Specify brand differentiation variables. Select positioning strategy. **Tier 2** Design the offer, value, distribution, communication, and market/partner relationship management strategies.
3	Objectives	Identify general goals. Select target-specific goals.
4	Implementation plan	Design e-marketing mix tactics: <ul><li>product/service offering</li><li>pricing/valuation</li><li>distribution/supply chain</li><li>integrated communication mix</li></ul> Design relationship management tactics. Design information gathering tactics. Design organizational structures for implementing the plan.
5	Budget	Forecast revenues. Evaluate costs to reach goals.
6	Evaluation plan	Identify appropriate performance metrics.

Exhibit 3 - 2 Marketing Plan Process

Step 1—Situation Analysis

Some people feel that planning for e-marketing means starting from scratch. Nothing could be further from the truth. Working with existing business, e-business, and marketing plans is an excellent place to start.

The organizational e-business plan might contain a SWOT analysis similar to the example depicted in Exhibit 3 - 3, leading to the firm adopting an e-business strategy of e-commerce. E-marketers take over from here, collecting information on how to sell on the Web, perhaps focusing on e-mail. The current marketing plan will be loaded with information of vital importance about the firm's products, the markets currently served, and so forth. The firm's pricing philosophy may dictate online pricing strategies for electronic commerce. The distribution plan will identify areas where the products are currently sold and suggest geographic gaps that might be receptive to e-commerce. Promotion plan information will give clues about how the Internet fits with the firm's current advertising, sales promotion, and other marketing communications. Also in the plan is information about the firm and brand positioning in the marketplace. Internet planners must decide how closely Web site content and promotion will follow current positioning strategies. Using this and newly collected information, the marketer moves to strategy formulation.

Step 2—Link E-Business with E-Marketing Strategy

After reviewing the marketing and e-business plans, marketers conduct strategic planning to help achieve the firm's e-business goals. An important part of the process is to define potential revenue streams. In the Playboy example, the firm selected e-commerce as one goal, planning to bring in money from selling selected products online. After reviewing the e-business goals, marketers create supporting e-marketing strategies. For clarification we present this as tier 1 and tier 2 strategies;

Opportunities	Threats
1. Hispanic markets growing and untapped in our industry.	1. Pending security law means costly software upgrades.
2. Save postage costs through e-mail marketing.	2. Competitor X is aggressively using e-commerce.
Strengths	**Weaknesses**
1. Strong customer service department.	1. Low-tech corporate culture.
2. Excellent Web site and database system.	2. Seasonal business: Peak is summer months.

E-Business Goal: Initiate e-commerce within one year.
Metric: Generate $500,000 in revenues from e-commerce during the first year.

Exhibit 3 - 3 SWOT, Objective, and Metric Example from E-Business Plan

however, in practice, the two are interrelated (Exhibit 3 - 4). In tier 1, marketers design segmentation, targeting, differentiation, and positioning strategies. In tier 2, they deal with the 4P's and relationship management by creating strategies around the offer (product), value (pricing), distribution (place), and communication (promotion). Further, marketers design customer and partner relationship strategies (CRM/PRM).

Tier 1 E-Marketing Strategic Planning

Marketers conduct a **market opportunity analysis (MOA),** including both demand and supply analyses, for *segmenting* and *targeting.* The **demand analysis** portion includes market segmentation analyses to describe and evaluate the potential profitability, sustainability, accessibility, and size of various potential segments. **Segment analysis** in the B2C market uses descriptors such as demographic characteristics, geographic location, selected psychographic characteristics (such as attitude toward technology and wireless communication device ownership), and past behavior toward the product (such as purchasing patterns online and offline). B2B descriptors include firm location, size, industry, type of need, and more. These descriptors help firms identify potentially attractive markets. Firms must also understand segment trends—are they growing or declining in absolute size and product use?

Firms use traditional segmentation analyses when they enter new markets through the online channel; however, if the firm plans to serve current markets online, it will delve more deeply into these customers' needs. Which of the firm's customers will want to use the Internet? How do the needs of customers using the firm's Web site differ from those of other customers? For example, most Internet users expect e-mail to be answered within 24 hours but will be satisfied if a postal letter is answered within weeks. In addition, firms often discover new markets as these customers find their way to the Web site. Marketers can use cookies, database analyses, and other techniques to discover how best to serve these new markets.

The purpose of a **supply analysis** is to assist in forecasting segment profitability as well as to find competitive advantages to exploit in the online market. Only by carefully analyzing competitive strengths and weaknesses can a firm find its own performance advantages. Therefore, firms should review the competition, their e-marketing initiatives, and their strengths and weaknesses prior to developing e-marketing initiatives. Firms must also try to identify future industry changes—which new firms might appear online, and which will drop away? For example, iGo's competitive advantage is a huge database of battery information. This firm knows which battery goes with every appliance and can ship it to customers within hours.

With a thorough MOA, the company can select its target market and understand its characteristics, behavior, and desires in the firm's product category. Furthermore, firms will want to understand the value proposition for each market. In our previous example (Exhibit 3 - 3), marketers might decide to target several Hispanic markets. Similarly, the apparel retailer Brooks Brothers found that Japanese visitors spent about twice on its Web site as other visitors and, therefore, built a Japanese-language version of the site (Jarvis 2001).

Another tier 1 step toward defining e-marketing strategy includes identifying brand *differentiation* variables and *positioning* strategies. Based on an understanding of both the competition and the target(s), marketers must decide how to differentiate their products from competitors' products in a way that provides benefits perceived as important by the target. In Playboy's case, management had to create brand strategies for differentiating among magazine, cable TV, and Internet products. Flowing from this is the positioning statement: the desired image for the brand relative to the competition. If this was already decided upon in the traditional marketing plan, e-marketers must decide if it will be effective online as well. If planning for a new brand or market, e-marketers must decide on branding strategies of differentiation and positioning at this point in the process.

Tier 2 E-Marketing Strategic Planning

In conjunction with tier 1 strategies, marketers design tier 2 strategies. This is an iterative process because it is difficult to know what the brand position should be without understanding the offer that comprises the brand promise (i.e., the benefits the firm promises to customers). Following are some of the tier 2 strategies covered in detail in subsequent chapters.

The Offer: Product Strategies

The organization can sell merchandise, services, or advertising on the Web site. It can adopt one of the e-business models discussed in Chapter 2, such as online

Exhibit 3 - 4 Formulating E-Marketing Strategy in Two Tiers

auctions, to generate a revenue stream. The firm can create new brands for the online market or simply sell selected current or enhanced products in that channel. Obviously, the previous analyses will reveal many options. If the firm offers current brands online, it will need to solve many different problems, such as the way colors appear differently on a computer screen than in print. The most astute firms take advantage of information technology capabilities to alter their online offerings. For example, Dell Computer allows product customization in a jiffy: Customers configure the computer they want to buy using an online form, and the database returns a page that includes current information about the computer and its price.

The Value: Pricing Strategies

A firm must decide how online product prices will compare with offline equivalents. To do this, firms consider the differing costs of sorting and delivering products to individuals through the online channel as well as competitive and market concerns. Two particularly hot online pricing trends are:

- **Dynamic pricing**—This strategy applies different price levels for different customers or situations. For example, a first-time buyer or someone who hasn't purchased for many months may receive lower prices than a heavy user, or prices may drop during low demand periods. The Internet allows firms to price items automatically and "on the fly" while users view pages, as mentioned in the Dell example.

- **Online bidding**—This presents a way to optimize inventory management. For instance, Circus Circus in Reno, Nevada, allows guests to bid for hotel rooms on slow days, instructing its reservation agents to accept various minimum bid levels depending on occupancy rates for any given day. Priceline.com, eBay.com, and many B2B exchanges operate exclusively using this strategy.

Distribution Strategies

Many firms use the Internet to distribute products or create efficiencies among supply chain members in the distribution channel. For example:

- **Direct marketing**—Many firms sell directly to customers, bypassing intermediaries in the traditional channel for some sales. In B2B markets, many firms realize tremendous cost reductions by using the Internet to facilitate sales.

- **Agent e-business models**—Firms such as eBay and E*Trade bring buyers and sellers together and earn a fee for the transaction.

Marketing Communication Strategies

The Internet spawned a multitude of new marketing communication strategies, both to draw customers to a Web site and to interact with brick-and-mortar customers. Firms use Web pages and e-mail to communicate with their target markets and business partners. Companies build brand images, create awareness of new products, and position products using the Web and e-mail. Database marketing is key to maintaining records about the needs, preferences, and behavior of individual customers so companies can send relevant and personalized information and persuasive communication at strategic times.

Relationship Management Strategies

Many e-marketing communication strategies also help build relationships with a firm's partners, supply chain members, or customers. However, some firms up the ante by using customer relationship management (CRM) or **partner relationship management (PRM)** software to integrate customer communication and purchase behavior into a comprehensive database. They then use CRM software to retain customers and increase average order values and lifetime value. Other firms build *extranets*—two or more proprietary networks linked for better communication and more efficient transactions among firms (PRM).

Step 3—Formulate Objectives

In general, an objective in an e-marketing plan takes the form:

- task (what is to be accomplished),
- measurable quantity (how much), and
- time frame (by when).

Assume that Amazon wants to increase the number of associates in its affiliate program from 600,000 to 700,000 in one year. This type of objective is hard to set, easy to evaluate, and a critical part of the e-marketing plan. The plan will often include the rationale for setting each objective—why each is desirable and achievable given the situation analysis findings, e-marketing, and e-business strategy.

Typical E-Marketing Objectives

While e-commerce transactions are an exciting dimension of an e-business presence, other objectives are also worthwhile, especially when the firm is using technology only to create internal efficiencies such as target market communication. In fact, most e-marketing plans aim to accomplish multiple objectives such as:

- increase market share.
- increase sales revenue (measured in dollars or units).
- reduce costs (such as distribution or promotion costs).
- achieve branding goals (such as increasing brand awareness).
- improve databases.
- achieve customer relationship management goals (such as increasing customer satisfaction, frequency of purchases, or customer retention rates).
- improve supply chain management (such as by enhancing member coordination, adding partners, or optimizing inventory levels).

E-Marketing Objective-Strategy Matrix

One simple way to present the firm's e-marketing strategies and accompanying goals is through an objective-strategy matrix. This is a graphical device that helps marketers better understand their implementation requirements (Exhibit 3 - 5). Each cell contains a *yes* or *no*, depending on how the marketer will link particular goals and strategies.

Step 4—Design Implementation Plan to Meet the Objectives

Now comes the part everyone enjoys: deciding how to accomplish the objectives through creative and effective tactics. This is where the marketer selects the marketing mix (4 P's), relationship management tactics, and other tactics to achieve the plan objectives and then devises detailed plans for implementation (the action plans). They also check to be sure the right marketing organization is in place for

Online Goals	Online Strategies				
	Online Advertising	Database Marketing	Direct E-Mail	Online Sales	Viral Marketing
Find affiliates	No	No	No	No	Yes
Gather customer information	No	Yes	Yes	Yes	Yes
Improve customer service	No	Yes	Yes	Yes	No
Increase brand name awareness	Yes	Yes	Yes	Yes	Yes
Sell goods or services	Yes	Yes	Yes	Yes	Yes
Enhance company image	Possibly	Yes	Yes	Yes	Yes
Engage in suggestive selling	Possibly	Yes	Yes	Yes	Yes
Generate sales leads	No	No	Yes	Yes	Yes

Exhibit 3 - 5 E-Marketing Objective-Strategy Matrix
Source: Adapted from Embellix eMarketing Suite.

implementation (i.e., staff, department structure, application service providers, and other outside firms).The right combination of tactics will help the firm meet its objectives effectively and efficiently.

E-marketers pay special attention to *information-gathering* tactics because information technologies are especially adept at automating these processes. Web site forms, feedback e-mail, and online surveys are just some of the tactics firms use to collect information about customers, prospects, and other stakeholders. Other important tactics include:

- Web site log analysis software helps firms review user behavior at the site and make changes to better meet the needs of users.

- *Business intelligence* uses the Internet for secondary research, assisting firms in understanding competitors and other market forces.

Step 5—Budgeting

A key part of any strategic plan is to identify the expected returns from an investment. These can then be matched against costs to develop a cost/benefit analysis, ROI calculation, or internal rate of return (IRR), which management uses to determine whether the effort is worthwhile. During plan implementation, marketers will closely monitor actual revenues and costs to see that results are on track for accomplishing the objectives. The following sections describe some of the revenues and costs associated with e-marketing initiatives.

Revenue Forecast

In this budget section, the firm uses an established sales forecasting method for estimating the site revenues in the short, intermediate, and long term. The firm's historical data, industry reports, and competitive actions are all inputs to this process. An important part of forecasting is to estimate the level of Web site traffic over time, because this number affects the amount of revenue a firm can expect to generate from its site. Revenue streams that produce Internet profits come mainly from Web site direct sales, advertising sales, subscription fees, affiliate referrals, sales at partner sites, commissions, and other fees. Companies usually summarize this analysis in a spreadsheet showing expected revenues over time and accompanying rationale.

Intangible Benefits

The intangible benefits of e-marketing strategies are much more difficult to establish, as are intangible benefits in the brick-and-mortar world. How much brand equity is created, for example, through an American Airlines program in which customers receive periodic e-mail messages about their frequent-flyer account balances? What is the value of increased brand awareness from a Web site? Putting a financial figure on such benefits is challenging but essential for e-marketers.

Cost Savings

Money saved through Internet efficiencies is considered soft revenue for a firm. For example, if the distribution channel linking a producer with its customers contains a wholesaler, distributor, and retailer, each intermediary will take a profit. A typical markup scheme is 10% from manufacturer to the wholesaler, 100% from wholesaler to the retailer, and 50% to the consumer. Thus, if a producer sells the product to a wholesaler for $50, the consumer ultimately pays $165. If the producer cuts out the intermediaries (disintermediation) and sells its product online directly to the consumer, it can price the product at $85 and increase revenue by $30. Whether or not this translates into profits depends on the cost of getting the product to the consumer. Other examples include the $5,000 a marketer might save in printing and postage for a direct-mail piece costing $1.00 per piece to 5,000 consumers, or the $270 million Cisco actually saved in one year on handling costs for its online computer system sales.

E-Marketing Costs

E-marketing entails many costs, including costs for employees, hardware, software, programming, and more. In addition, some traditional marketing costs may creep into the e-marketing budget—for example, the cost of offline advertising to draw traffic to the Web site. For simplicity, this section will discuss technology-related cost items only. Consider that the cost of a Web site (except the most basic) can range from $5,000 to $50 million; for pure play dot-coms, costs may be even higher. Following are just a few of the costs site developers incur:

- **Technology costs.** These include software, hardware, Internet access or hosting services, educational materials and training, and other site operation and maintenance costs.

- **Site design.** Web sites need graphic designers to create appealing page layouts, graphics, and photos.

- **Salaries.** All personnel who work on Web site development and maintenance are budget items.

- **Other site development expenses.** If not included in the technology or salary categories, any other expenses will be here—things such as registering multiple domain names and hiring consultants to write content or perform other development and design activities.

- **Marketing communication.** All advertising, public relations, and promotions activities, both online and offline, that directly relate to drawing site traffic and enticing them to return and purchase are pegged here. Other costs include search engine registration, online directory costs, e-mail list rental, prizes for contests, and more.

- **Miscellaneous.** Other typical project costs might fall here—expenses such as travel, telephone, stationery printing to add the new URL, and more.

Step 6—Evaluation Plan

Once the e-marketing plan is implemented, its success depends on continuous evaluation. This means e-marketers must have tracking systems in place before the electronic doors open. What should be measured? The answer depends on plan objectives. Review the balanced scorecard for e-business (in Chapter 2) to see how various metrics relate to specific plan goals.

In general, today's firms are quite ROI driven. As a result, e-marketers must show how their intangible goals, such as brand building or CRM, will lead to higher revenue down the road. Also, they must present accurate and timely metrics to justify their initial and ongoing e-marketing expenditures throughout the period covered by the plan.

S u m m a r y

The e-marketing plan is a guiding, dynamic document for e-marketing strategy formulation and implementation. The purpose is to help the firm achieve its desired results as measured by performance metrics according to the specifications of the e-business model within the e-business strategy. Although some dot-com entrepreneurs use a napkin plan to informally sketch out their ideas, a venture capital e-marketing plan will help show that the e-business idea is solid and the entrepreneur has an idea of how to run it.

Creating an e-marketing plan requires six steps. The first is to conduct a situation analysis by reviewing environmental and SWOT analyses, existing marketing plans and company/brand information, and e-business objectives, strategies, and performance metrics. Next, e-marketers link e-business with e-marketing strategy in 2 tiers. In tier 1, e-marketers conduct a marketing opportunity analysis to develop segmentation, targeting, differentiation, and positioning strategies. In tier two, they develop strategies for the 4 Ps and relationship management. In the third step, e-marketers formulate objectives, usually setting multiple objectives; they may use an objective-strategy matrix to guide implementation.

In the fourth step, e-marketers develop a suitable 4 P's marketing mix, select appropriate relationship management tactics, design information-gathering tactics, and select other tactics to achieve their objectives. They must also devise detailed implementation plans during this step in the process. In the next step, e-marketers prepare a revenue forecast to estimate the expected returns from the plan's investment and detail the e-marketing costs to come up with a calculation that management can use to determine whether the effort is worthwhile. In the final step of the plan, e-marketers use tracking systems to measure results and evaluate the plan's success on a continuous basis.

Key Terms

Angel investors

Demand analysis

Direct marketing

Dynamic pricing

E-marketing plan

Market opportunity analysis (MOA)

Online bidding

Partner relationship management (PRM)

Segment analysis

Situation analysis

Supply analyses

Venture capital (VC)

Exercises

Review Questions

1. What are the six steps in an e-marketing plan?

2. Why do entrepreneurs seeking funding need a venture capital e-marketing plan rather than a napkin plan?

3. What is the purpose of the marketing opportunity analysis and the segment analysis?

4. What four elements in tier 1 and five elements in tier 2 are devised for e-marketing strategy?

5. What is the purpose of an e-marketing objective-strategy matrix?

6. How do managers use budgeting within the e-marketing planning process?

7. Why do e-marketing plans need an evaluation component?

Discussion Questions

8. If you had money to invest, what would you look for in a venture capital e-marketing plan?

9. What kinds of questions should a firm ask in developing an e-marketing plan to serve customers in current markets through an online channel?

10. Why is it important for e-marketers to specify not only the task but also the measurable quantity and time frame for accomplishing an objective?

11. Why would the management of American Airlines expect its e-marketers to estimate the financial impact of intangible benefits such as building brand equity through e-mail messages to frequent flyers?

Practitioner Perspective

Networking "One-Armed Bandits:" How the Internet and customer relationship management will reshape the gaming industry

Brian Casey is the marketing director for IGT Gaming Systems. International Game Technology (IGT) is a world leader in the design, development, and manufacture of microprocessor-based gaming and lottery products and software systems in all jurisdictions where gaming and lotteries are legal. Brian also teaches Principles of Internet Marketing at the University of Nevada, Reno.
E-mail: brian.casey@igt.com

Legalized gaming continues to grow throughout the United States and the world. A phenomenon in recent years has been the proliferation of online gambling sites offering traditional table games, slot games, and sports books. Currently, most countries consider online gaming illegal, including the United States, but as revenue estimates put the industry at over $16 billion in five years, most governments and traditional gaming companies are taking a closer look at how online gaming will fit into the overall industry.

The Modern Slot Machine

Unlike the old mechanical slot machines of the past (often referred to as "one-armed bandits"), modern-day gaming machines are a complex mix of mechanical and computer equipment. Many machines still use mechanical spinning reels while others incorporate an entirely digital output through a monitor. However, both types of machines rely on a computer processor to process the game result based on a random number generator. Once a wager is made and the handle is pulled, the computer inside the machine runs the game program and the result is displayed either as symbols on a reel or cards in a poker deck. Every event from the amount wagered per game, the amount paid per game, and the result of the game is stored inside the slot machine's computer.

The Modern Casino Floor

Each gaming machine on a modern casino floor is linked together in a local area network (LAN). This makes sense since each gaming machine is essentially a computer. This LAN of gaming machines can be monitored by a network computer system designed specifically for the casino floor. Since the slot's computer captures every machine event, the gaming system's servers through the LAN can collect and accumulate these data in a central location.

Player Tracking Systems

In addition to the game specific data collected, each machine has the capability to collect information on each player (customer) through individual player cards. The casino issues these cards as a part of their customer loyalty programs. As the customer plays the machine, the system stores information such as length of play, in/loss amounts, and average wager. Based on analyses such as recency, frequency, and monetary value (RFM analysis), casinos can reward their best customers with free play, food and beverage comps, or a free night stay at the casino.

Internet and Intranet Gaming

Given the network structure of the modern casino floor, it's easy to see how the Internet and intranets could easily be used as digital distribution mechanisms for gaming devices. Gaming machines on the floor could become clients on the network with game servers distributing each game over the network. Machines on the casino floor may become "thin clients" acting as no more than a browser on a PC performing minimal application processing. Slot and poker games could then be accessed and played on the casino floor, in the hotel rooms, in the sports book, or even by the pool on a tablet PC running over an 802.11 wireless network.

Once a game server can distribute games over an intranet, distributing the same games over the Internet is the next logical step. Therefore, the casino can now extend the physical gaming experience on the casino floor to the virtual realm of the Internet.

CRM Through a System-Centric Casino Operation

By the end of 2001, there were over 1,500 online casinos. These online casinos have spent millions in advertising to acquire customers. The slot games featured on these Web sites are often generic and lack the quality of their offline counterparts on the physical casino floors. But most significantly, the online casinos lack the brand recognition the major casino properties have built over years of operation in key gaming jurisdictions throughout the world.

As the casino floor of the future advances to a more system-centric operation utilizing game servers and game download, large casino properties with well-known brand names and large customer databases are in the unique position to leverage these strengths. Since customer events and information can be captured in real-time and stored in massive databases, unique opportunities for customized marketing programs exist, and the marketing promise of mass customization can be realized by the gaming industry. For example, a future gaming entertainment experience for a casino customer may consist of the following: (1) the customer creates an account on a well-known casino's Web site and begins to play his favorite poker game online, (2) the customer plays enough to earn points toward a free weekend at the casino's property in Las Vegas, (3) upon arrival at the casino, the customer checks in at a kiosk in the lobby using his player card (smart card technology), (4) the system credits his card with $200 of free play on any of the casino's gaming devices, (5) the customer sits down in front of a gaming device consisting of a flat-panel LCD touch screen and inserts his player card, (6) credits appear on the screen and his favorite poker game appears. . .the same game he played at home.

Although it will be some time before the United States and other governments adopt legalized online gaming regulations, the promise of delivering a customized and consistent entertainment experience will drive innovation of casino floor gaming systems both by the equipment manufacturers and the casino properties.

Practitioner Perspective

Bricks and Mortar, the Internet, or Traditional Catalogs?

Daryle Scott is the president and CEO of Venus Swimwear, Inc. and WinterSilks, LLC. Venus is the world's largest cataloger of women's swimwear and WinterSilks is the world's catalog leader in silk apparel. Daryle is a frequent speaker at Stetson University and the University of North Florida. dvscott@venusswimwear.com.

Can you remember the days in the not too distant past when the Internet was going to be *the* way the world did business? It was supposed to replace brick-and-mortar retail locations and make catalogs a thing of the past. That's not quite what happened and, in fact, most *pure* Internet companies born in the stock bubble of the late 1990s went under and gave way to traditional retailers and catalogers.

As a cataloger for over 20 years, the Venus family of companies launched its various Web sites (one for each catalog title) in 1998. All sites were profitable from the very first year and since then our various Web sites account for an ever-increasing percentage of our total business. But we have found, along with most other catalogers, that the Internet is really just one more method by which our customers can choose to order. With over 20% of our sales now coming to us via the Internet we estimate that fully 90% of those are coming from customers with catalogs in their hands. The Internet is merely the method by which they have chosen to place their order.

We distribute over 60 million catalogs per year, and once a catalog lands in the home of Jane Consumer we really don't care if she elects to order via our toll-free number, the enclosed order form and envelope, or goes to our Web site to place her order. The Internet is primarily just another tool for collecting orders. Yes, there is incremental new business generated on the Web that is unrelated to our catalogs, but it is not nearly high enough to generate an acceptable ROI on the creation and maintenance of our various Web sites—thus, we see the Internet as a customer convenience tool. In one of the largest studies done to date, Land's End concluded that without a catalog there was no Internet.

Some catalogers report receiving up to 50% of their orders via the Internet, but almost all of those companies are using special "Internet only" incentives to entice customers to order via the Net instead of the more traditional toll-free number. It is less expensive to process an order via the Internet since we avoid the cost of the toll-free call and the labor cost of the order taker, but the savings is minimal. We estimate the total savings to be no more than $1.00 per order once we include all costs associated with processing an order via the Internet versus the more traditional toll-free number. While we don't have traditional "order takers" involved with taking Internet orders there is still direct labor for the personnel dedicated to "live chat" on the Internet, and we find those people essential in order to provide a quality customer service experience for our customers. Many companies that are driving larger percentages of their traffic to the Net are doing so by offering discounts that are far in excess of the cost savings on those orders.

No doubt the Internet is important and will be increasingly important as time goes on, but the real winners in the future will be the companies that master all of the various customer "touch" points. When your customers have the opportunity to purchase your products through *any* channel *they* choose—bricks and mortar, the Internet, or traditional catalogs—that's true customer service. In business today and tomorrow, customer service is still the name of the game. Companies too heavily focused on just one channel stand to lose market share to those companies that will eventually master all three. It has been proven that the total dollars a company receives from a given customer per year will increase as the firm increases the opportunities the customer has to do business with it.

Savvy Sites

American Association of Advertising Agencies www.aaaa.org	The AAAA is a national trade organization headquartered in New York and represents the advertising agency industry.
Balanced Scorecard www.balancedscorecard.com	A group of firms that uses the balanced scorecard and reports on its successful application and news. Note that www.bscol.com, the Balanced Scorecard Collaborative, Inc., also has good information on this topic.
Business 2.0 www.business2.com	A great resource for articles about e-business. It even includes discussion groups where you can chat about e-business, marketing, or B2B.
Business Marketing Association www.marketing.org	This organization is designed for business-to-business marketing professionals.
CNET www.cnet.com	CNET provides a wealth of general information about computing and the Internet.
CRN www.crn.com	This site features breaking news stories on e-business. It also provides free e-mail newsletters.
Computerworld www.computerworld.com	This online version of the print magazine features cutting-edge information on a variety of industry topics.
eMarketer www.emarketer.com	This is a great source to find the latest in *eNews* as well as providing statistics.
ESOMAR www.esomar.nl	ESOMAR is a marketing organization that brings professionals together and promotes the use of opinion and marketing research for decision making.

InfoWorld www.infoworld.com	InfoWorld provides in-depth coverage of current tech issues, trends, and new products and technologies.
Internetweek www.internetweek.com	*Internetweek* features news stories about electronic commerce from a technical perspective. It focuses on supply chain, Web development, security, and IT services.
Internet World www.internetworld.com	*Internet World* has articles on e-business and current technology trends.
MarketingPower.com www.marketingpower.com	This is the American Marketing Association's Web site. It features industry news, marketing information, business info, and best practices.
MetaCrawler www.metacrawler.com	MetaCrawler is a metasearch engine and advertises that it consistently receives top ratings.
Public Relations Society of America www.prsa.org	With 17,000 members, PRSA is the world's largest organization for public relations professionals. This site features news about public relations case studies, continuing education opportunities, and, of course, membership information.
Wilson Internet Services www.wilsonweb.com	This is an excellent site to find articles on Internet marketing gathered from a variety of publications.
ZDNet www.zdnet.com	This site provides a great amount of different information with sections devoted to tech news and business on the Internet.

Activities

1. Visit the shopping agent MySimon at www.MySimon.com. Do a search for this book (*E-Marketing*). What is the lowest price available for the book? The highest? Compare these prices with those found at brick-and-mortar sites Borders (partnered with Amazon) and Barnes and Noble. Check out used book store site www.half.com (partnered with Ebay.) Explain in terms of value why customers might buy the book at a higher price.

2. Visit www.Dell.com. Write down what you think the firm's goals are for its Web site. Then make a list recommending relevant performance metrics from each of the four perspectives.

3. Flip through a magazine, looking at the ads. Write down each mention of a Web site and in what context the mention appeared. In what percentage of the ads were Web sites mentioned?

4. Visit www.google.com and do a search for your favorite car. What banner ad appeared on the results page? Now do a search for your favorite music group. What banner ad appeared on the results page? What conclusion can you draw about targeted advertising?

5. Visit the McDonald's Web site. List each stakeholder it reaches and tell what basic content is targeted to each stakeholder.

6. Consider a local business that you know about and sketch a bare bones e-marketing plan for it.

7. Find the Web site for a firm that offers Web site building services. What steps does it recommend? What does it charge to develop a Web site?

8. Go to the Web site for your university and describe how well you think the site fulfills the marketing objectives of the university. Suggest improvements.

9. See if you can find the portion of your university's Web site that is for students and employees only (intranet). What information is contained on those pages? Should outsiders be excluded from accessing the pages? Why or why not?

Internet Exercises

Internet Exercise: The Marketing Concept

Web sites can demonstrate the marketing concept by exhibiting a company's special features to customers and prospects. Many sites target customer segments by language, gender, and age, providing slightly different content for each target. In general, Web users want to know about product benefits. However, sites that give visitors something of interest beyond product descriptions create additional value. The most attractive site advantages tend to be interactive in nature. For example, e-mail and surveys allow for customer feedback; intelligent agents can find the right shoe for the customer's needs; and retail locators tell the customer where she can buy the shoe that she needs. Complete the following chart to indicate which benefits are supported on the Web sites of three athletic shoe companies. Then decide which firm is the most customer oriented.

Benefit	Nike www.nike.com	New Balance www.newbalance.com
Retail locator		
Nonproduct information		
Multiple languages		
Multiple targets: gender		
Multiple targets: age		
Multiple targets: different sports		
Customer feedback		
Intelligent agents		
Fun to surf?		

For Discussion

1. Of the foregoing benefits, which three do you think are the most important? Why?
2. Over all which site better embodies the marketing concept? Why?
3. Suggest one or more customer benefits not listed previously that the "better" site contains.
4. Based on your analysis of Nike's site, is it interested in relationship marketing? Support your answer.

Internet Exercise: Strategic Planning for Online Marketing

Online book selling is big business. The first successful online bookseller was Amazon.com, an exclusively online retailer. The company quickly established itself as the market leader. Attracted by the profit potential, Barnes & Noble, Borders, and others have followed suit. More recently Amazon has diversified into many other lines of business: music, video, electronics, toys, and online auctions. Is this a good strategy for Amazon? To partially answer this question, conduct an analysis of the online music industry. Complete the table by first visiting www.bizrate.com and identifying two of Amazon's toughest online music store competitors in addition to CDNow. Then review the BizRate comments and visit each competitor's site to finish the table. If BizRate isn't currently rating two other music stores, do a search at Google.com and find two competitors to rate yourself.

	Amazon www.amazon.com	CDNow www.cdnow.com	Other Competitor	Other Competitor
Who rated site for BizRate?				
BizRate overall customer rating				
Products sold in addition to CDs				
Market positioning *				
Competitive advantage *				
Competitive weakness *				

*Infer from viewing site and ratings.

For Discussion

Analyze Amazon's strategy by answering the following questions.

1. How does Amazon compare to its competition in the music industry?
2. What is Amazon's mission statement? You can guess at this by reading about the company at www.amazon.com.
3. Does the music business fit with Amazon's mission? Why or why not?
4. Should Amazon be in the music business? Justify your response.
5. Is there any synergy between Amazon's many product areas? If so, what is it?
6. Years ago Sears used to advertise that "Sears has everything!" Is Amazon becoming the Sears of the Internet? If so, is this a good strategy?
7. Does Amazon pursue different product strategies in its U.K. and German operations?
8. Based on what you have learned, do you think Amazon is pursuing the correct strategy? Why or why not?

chapter

4   leveraging technology

learning objectives

The key objective of this chapter is to develop a basic understanding of the current and emerging technologies that facilitate e-marketing planning and implementation. You will explore product, pricing, distribution, and promotion technologies and learn how e-marketers are using technology for relationship marketing.

After reading this chapter, you will be able to:

- Outline some of the technologies that e-marketers are using for product-related strategies.

- Describe how consumers' use of shopping agents affects companies' pricing strategies.

- Highlight key online distribution technologies related to bandwidth and market opportunities, content filtering, and transaction security.

- Discuss how e-marketers use proxy servers, search engine technology, log files and cookies, and targeted or rotating ad banners for integrated marketing communication.

- Explain how e-marketers use technology for relationship marketing.

Elegance is how smoothly the technology slips past the user's consciousness and gets out of the user's way.

brent
lowensohn
kaiser foundation
health plan inc.

How can a company transform 25 million rows of daily Web log data into marketing knowledge? This is the challenge for AutoTrader.com, the automotive marketplace offering more than 2 million new and used vehicles with price comparisons, performance reviews, and financing and insurance resources. Over 6 million monthly visitors view more than 200 million pages, including pages where advertisers sell cars. Clearly, AutoTrader has a lot of data to analyze for e-marketing purposes.

To make sense of it all, AutoTrader created the *Management Dashboard*, a marketing tool powered by SAS statistical data analysis software. The dashboard reports on the following:

- Visitor demographics and customer behavior online—analyzed by U.S. region.
- Analytics about the advertisements served on the site Web pages.
- Key site metrics such as number of visitors and the makes and models of cars viewed.

As an example, SAS software evaluates 30 million monthly vehicle searches, categorizing them by city, state, and zip code, as well as make, model, year, and price. The regional sales force can then quickly answer inquiries about Web traffic in different localities. The firm also uses an Oracle database, extracting e-mails, leads, and other information to generate more than 100 month-to-date reports for marketing managers.

What does AutoTrader gain from all this information? First, it knows which vehicles are in demand in various regions, which helps participating car dealers and individual sellers. Second, it can fine tune the Web site based on traffic patterns. Third, and most importantly, AutoTrader can demonstrate the value of advertising on its site. Advertisers receive automatically generated reports about how many times their cars were viewed, how many visitors asked for a map to the brick-and-mortar location, and how many e-mail inquiries were received about the cars. Finally, these reports help AutoTrader bill its e-commerce partners.

In the last four years the trend was faster and bigger. Now it's about smarter.

mike volpi
cisco systems

The Marriage of Marketing and Technology

The divide between computer technology folks and marketing managers is narrowing, as seen at AutoTrader.com. Marketing managers increasingly need to understand the capabilities of new media so they can develop and implement an effective marketing plan. This chapter presents a small sampling of some technologies that facilitate e-marketing in each phase of the marketing mix: product, price, distribution, and marketing communication. A section on relationship marketing technologies concludes the chapter.

Product Technologies

E-marketers can use a wide variety of technologies to support their product strategies. Among these are technologies for building Web sites; forms, languages, and standards; multimedia capabilities; database marketing; and protection against computer viruses and denial of service attacks.

Building a Web Site

The process of building and publishing a Web page has become greatly simplified in recent years. Originally all Web pages were constructed using a language called HyperText Markup Language (**HTML**). HTML is still used today but other languages have been added to support interactive Web pages. These include HTML forms, Java, dynamic HTML, XHTML, and XML. Each of these languages creates a computer program that runs either on the Web server or the user's browser. Where the program runs makes a difference in terms of response time. Any program running on the server will have slow response times whereas programs running on the browser will have instantaneous response. HTML forms are processed on the server after the user presses the submit button—which is why users sometimes have to wait for processing. If the user has to wait too long, she may abandon the transaction. Java, dynamic HTML, and XHTML all run on the browser. One important use of these technologies is for instantaneous form verification. For example, if the user types in a credit card number that is one digit short, a helpful warning message can be instantly flashed on the screen.

HTML Forms

HTML forms are the most familiar tool of all. These consist of text boxes, check boxes, radio buttons, and drop-down lists. When completing a survey or ordering online, the customer fills out an HTML form. Creating the form is relatively easy. The hard part is processing the information that the customer enters. The processing is performed on the server by separate programs, which are mainly either Common

Gateway Interface (**CGI**) scripts or Active Server Pages (**ASP**). Both CGI and ASP are relatively difficult to master and require a professional programmer, but both perform the same functions. The CGI scripts are typically found on servers running the Unix operating system. Active server pages are typically found on servers running Microsoft Windows NT or 2000. Both of these languages can be used to write programs from scratch or to tie together off-the-shelf software modules. Our recommendation is to use off-the-shelf modules whenever possible. Why reinvent the shopping cart?

Java

Java is a general-purpose computer language developed by Sun Microsystems that can be used to develop interactive Web sites. Java comes bundled with both Netscape and Internet Explorer and, therefore, is a safe platform for which to develop content. Java is fast. Programs developed in Java run very quickly on the user's computer system. Java is also flexible. Programs may be written to support animation, streaming media, financial calculators, 3D visualization, or almost any other task. Java is safe. Programs run in a protected memory space where they cannot infect or otherwise damage the user's computer system. The major drawback is that Java is difficult to program. While a Java Development Kit (**JDK**) can simplify the process to some extent, Java is generally a language for professional programmers. The difficulty of programming in Java and problems with early versions created a clamor in the developer community for enhancements to HTML that would provide many of the interactive functions of Java without the heavy-duty programming. That call was answered by a group of technologies that collectively became known as Dynamic HTML.

Dynamic HTML (DHTML)

Dynamic HTML (DHTML) encompasses a range of enhancements to the HTML standard to make it more interactive, more capable of multimedia, and better suited to professional page layout. These enhancements include JavaScript, cascading style sheets (CSS), plug-ins, and ActiveX. These technologies are not a coordinated set but rather an ad hoc collection that is supported to a greater or lesser extent by different browsers.

JavaScript

Despite its name, JavaScript has nothing to do with Java. **JavaScript** was developed by Netscape and then became an industry standard. The name was chosen because of the cachet surrounding the Java language. The most prevalent use of JavaScript is to create the fancy buttons and rollover effects seen on so many Web sites today. Although early users of JavaScript had to program these features, many are now automatically generated by authoring tools such as Dreamweaver or are available for use from sites such as the JavaScript Source (javascript.internet.com). Another popular use of JavaScript is to check user input for errors and issue warning messages (i.e., "please fill in all required fields"). Marketers use JavaScript to detect the user's browser version and monitor size and send a version of the Web page optimized for the user's machine. JavaScript can also be used to create calculators, clocks, games, and many other applications. Part of the charm of JavaScript is that developers can't hide the JavaScript code, allowing an easy answer to the question, "How did they do that?"

ActiveX

ActiveX is a competitor to Java but works only on Windows machines. It has not achieved nearly the market share of either Java or JavaScript. ActiveX is tightly integrated with the Windows operating system. As a result, Macintosh and other non-Windows users cannot run ActiveX routines. Therefore, developers who program in ActiveX risk alienating a portion of the user base. A second consequence is that ActiveX programs can access the file system on the user's computer. For certain applications, allowing file access is useful but it also opens up the possibility of privacy abuse.

Plug-Ins

Plug-ins are most often used to play multimedia content encoded in a specific format. Each plug-in is a small program that must be downloaded and installed on the user's computer. Because users are disinclined to download and install software for fear of viruses, developers are reluctant to create content that requires a plug-in. However, some plug-ins are so prevalent that they have a large installed base of users. Developing content for these plug-ins is much safer. Content is created using the plug-in's companion development tool. Part of the attraction of plug-ins is that some of the development tools can create very glitzy content with relatively little effort. Some of the best-known plug-ins include:

- **RealPlayer**—The RealNetworks RealPlayer plays streaming audio and video on the user's computer. It is one of the most widely available plug-ins. RealPlayer can play audio and video over low-bandwidth connections—by compressing files and by playing the multimedia as it streams rather than forcing a complete download before playing. Competitors for RealPlayer include Windows Media Player and Apple QuickTime.
- **Acrobat**—Adobe Acrobat allows professional page layouts to be saved and transferred over the Internet without making them into HTML documents. Most importantly, the Acrobat developer can lock the document so that it cannot be altered, an especially useful feature for e-books, forms, legal documents, and any document requiring content security.
- **Flash**—Macromedia Flash plays animations on the user's computer. Flash content can include charts, graphics, sounds, scrolling lists, tickers, and movie clips. Flash

files are relatively small and, therefore, use little bandwidth. The secret is vector graphics—a mathematical description of each graphic. The alternative is to transfer information about each pixel of every graphic.

Cascading Style Sheets (CSS)

Cascading style sheets (**CSS**) assist with precise formatting of text and graphics on the Web page. CSS also enable relatively painless sitewide updates. The developer chooses names for each page element (e.g., bodytext, heading1, heading2, and so forth) and then describes the style or formatting that should be applied to each element. A later change to the style description automatically updates the formatting of that element wherever it appears in the site. Without style sheets, the developer would have to reformat each element individually. For example, assume that heading1 was first defined as Arial, 18 point, bold. Later, changing this heading to Verdana, 24 point, not bold would require only a single change to the style sheet. If heading1 appears on hundreds of pages, this single point of update saves a lot of time and reduces the possibility of errors.

Style sheets help satisfy a long-standing developer goal: the separation of a document's content from its presentation. The content has named styles (e.g., heading1) applied to it, but the definition of how those styles should be displayed is stored in a separate file. Style sheets have two significant advantages:

- Styles need only be updated in one place to make global changes throughout a Web site.
- Companies can more easily enforce uniform graphic standards using styles.

While all of the DHTML technologies mentioned previously can produce dynamic Web pages (pages created on the fly for individual users), they should be used with caution because some older browser versions can support them in a limited way, if at all. One solution is to create multiple versions of each page on a Web site, then send the users the page with the technology that their browser can best use. Conversely, coordinating the content of different page versions might not be worth the effort.

XHTML

XHTML, the currently endorsed HTML standard, has two major goals. The first is to bring more uniformity to the HTML language by requiring *every* tag to have a matching end tag. Currently tags such as **
, **<p>, **<li>**, and others do not have a required end tag. The second goal is to increase the separation between document content and presentation, as in the use of cascading style sheets. CSS is encouraged by deprecating certain HTML tags such as the **<font>** tag. Deprecating a tag advises but does not mandate the developer community to stop using that tag. Netscape and Internet Explorer continue to support tags long after they are deprecated. If they did not do this, millions of Web pages would suddenly become inaccessible.

XHTML can be seen as an intermediate step toward the real direction that the Web may be heading—toward XML.

XML

XML completes the separation of document content and presentation. By so doing, it opens up a significant business application—Web enabling business databases and the exchange of information from those databases. The importance of this development cannot be underestimated. It is at the core of Microsoft's .net strategy. Using XML, consumers can request online account information, product availability and information, and other data items which are sent from database to Web page instantaneously on demand. Businesses can easily exchange data with their supply chain partners, gaining a significant competitive advantage. Just-in-time inventories mean more efficiency. We are only beginning to see the impact of these developments.

However, XML has two major drawbacks. The first is lack of support for the standard by Netscape. Therefore, XML formatted pages will have a very unpredictable display on a Netscape browser. The second drawback is that XML is relatively difficult to program. As a result XML is really only accessible to professional programmers. Developers have three options. They can learn XML and become professional programmers. They can use an XML authoring tool such as Microsoft Word to automatically generate XML. The final option is to ignore the standard in the same way that many developers ignored java. Time will tell.

Multimedia

One of the hottest trends and greatest challenges for content providers is the delivery of **multimedia** content over the Web. It's a challenge because most home connections to the Web are slow (low bandwidth) and multimedia requires **high bandwidth** also known as **broadband**. There are four solutions to the problem:

1. Speed up the home Internet connection using a high-bandwidth wired or wireless connection. One reason AOL merged with Time Warner was to use the latter company's cable division to distribute high-bandwidth content via cable modems.

2. Compress the multimedia content into smaller packets of information. Almost all data can be compressed either by eliminating detail (lossy compression) or by squeezing the detail into a smaller packet (lossless compression). Lossless compression looks for patterns in the data that can be represented mathematically. For example, rather than saving each pixel on the screen separately, bounded areas of color could be saved by specifying the border and the interior color. RealNetworks has pioneered the compression of multimedia. It began with compression of audio (**RealAudio**) and moved to compression of video (**RealVideo**). The compression is so powerful that it operates over a low-

bandwidth connection, albeit with rather choppy delivery. Another popular compression technology for music is **MP3**, which can reduce CD recordings to one-tenth their original size. While MP3 utilizes lossy compression, the loss is so slight that it sounds to many like CD-quality sound. (Visit GifWizard at www.gifwizard.com for a free demo of compression of your own Web page.)

3. Stream the multimedia so that the user can play a piece of it while the rest downloads. The alternative, of course, would be to wait for the entire audio or video clip to download before listening to any of it.

4. Distribute multiple copies of the multimedia content around the Internet so that it is closer to the end users. Delays that might be caused by the Internet itself are avoided by distributing content.

Combinations of all of the preceding techniques may be employed to speed content delivery over the Internet. However, the most important is to speed up the Internet connection to the home. Currently, about 24 million households in the United States have high-speed connections—and this number is expected to grow. Already the installed base is large enough to support Web sites that cater to multimedia content.

Database Marketing

Database marketing technologies utilize relational databases to store tables of information that can be mined for information about clients and used to generate promotional campaigns. A relational database is a collection of tables that collectively contain information about a common subject. Relational databases such as Oracle and DB2 utilize a very powerful query language called SQL that can extract specific or summary information from the database.

Imagine that a firm is managing an e-mail promotion campaign and has the following tables in a database: clients, their interests, products, and client responses to the campaign.

Client

ID	Last	First	e-mail	income
001	Stutz	Joel	jstutz@miami.edu	150,000
002	Grauer	Bob	bgrauer@aol.com	200,000

Interest

Client$ID	Subject
001	tennis
001	football
001	cars
002	soccer

002	reading
002	tennis

Product

ID	Description
AAX	$10 coupon
ZZP	$20 coupon on purchase of $100 or more

Response

Client$ID	Product$ID	DateSent	DateResponded	Action
001	AAX	12/10/00	12/15/00	click-through
002	AAX	12/10/00	12/13/00	purchase
002	ZZP	1/5/01	1/6/01	purchase

Now picture this database loaded with records about thousands of clients. E-marketers would start first with the client and interest files. Information in these two files enables marketers to target by demographics (e.g., income) or psychographics (e.g., interests). The client and interest tables are linked by repeating the client id in the interest table. Note that in the interest table the field is named client$id to indicate that it matches the id field in the client table. Thus, the marketer knows that Joel Stutz, client 001, has tennis, football, and cars as interests. Let's say that the marketer is targeting only people earning over $100,000 who are also are interested in tennis. A quick scan through the data shows that both clients qualify.

However, databases with millions of records cannot be visually scanned. To quickly extract information from large databases requires a query written in Structured Query Language (**SQL**), the language used by Relational Database Management Systems (**RDBMS**). The RDBMS maintains and protects the database tables. Normally, marketers do not write SQL queries but rather have programmers provide them with a series of custom reports. Nonetheless, the queries are not that difficult to write. For example, to answer the query posed earlier (people earning over $100,000 who are also are interested in tennis) requires:

```
SELECT    *
FROM      client, interest
WHERE     client.id = interest.client$id
AND                 client.income > 100,000
AND                 interest.subject = 'tennis' ;
```

The most difficult line in the query appears in the WHERE clause. Here the computer is told to match the id fields from the two tables (client.id = interest.client$id)—exactly what we did visually.

Next the marketer targets offer AAX, which is a $10 coupon, to both clients in the segment. The response file records when the offer was sent, the response date, and the user's action (which might be nothing, click-through, aborted purchase, and so forth). The response table is linked to both the client and product tables by repeating the client id and product id in the table. This shows that Joel Stutz, client 001, received a $10 coupon, product AAX. Based on the data, the promotion generated one sale; however, it was 100% effective on click-through and 50% effective on generating a sale—very high numbers.

How does the user data get into the database? One of the best ways is by asking the user to fill out a short survey during the registration process at a Web site. This is an explicit method of data acquisition. But data could also be gathered implicitly. Say, for example, that the user exhibits a pattern of frequenting pages on a site dealing with in-line skating. Software can be programmed to conclude from this that the user has an interest in the sport and automatically add a new row to the interest table to record this information. Note that the more the customer interacts with the Web site, the more information that can be gathered and used for even more precise targeting.

Computer Viruses

Computer viruses are an e-marketer's nightmare. The biggest problem is that they reinforce consumer perceptions that the Internet is not secure. Computer viruses are intrusive pieces of computer code that secretly attach to existing software, reproducing themselves and wreaking havoc with data. Harmful viruses can spread throughout a computer network, overwriting data files with nonsense, while pranks might be as small as making the computer beep on a certain day of the month when the user strikes a particular keyboard letter. Four common types of viruses are macro viruses, worms, Trojan horses, and boot viruses. Macro viruses attach to data files and infect Microsoft Word or Excel when users open the infected data file. Worm viruses replicate rapidly, eating up memory. Trojan horses do not replicate and are usually activated at a certain date or event such as a keystroke combination. Boot viruses reside on floppy disks and destroy operating systems when users mistakenly boot the computer with a disk inserted.

Computer viruses can appear in data, e-mail, or software from any source. In 2000, the "I Love You" virus and its variants made the rounds of the world's computers and caused billions of dollars worth of damage in a matter of days. The virus was transmitted via e-mail and mostly affected users of Microsoft's Outlook e-mail program. Why? Outlook, which is tightly integrated with Windows, allows small programs called scripts to run on the user's computer in order to automate tasks. Although this means that users can customize the program to their needs, it also means that the scripts can run almost any Windows command—including the delete command. In this case, the virus writers sent a script as a file attachment that deleted files on the user's computer. The virus also looked up addresses in the

Outlook address book and sent all of the user's contacts a copy of the virus as well. The result was very rapid dissemination of a very destructive virus. Variants that followed were even more sophisticated and destructive. Knowing that users would be on the lookout for "I Love You" in the subject line, one variant randomly generated a new subject line on each transmittal. Knowing that antivirus programs would be scanning messages in search of the virus script, that same variant modified the script slightly on each transmittal so as to escape detection. The end result was a game of cat and mouse between the virus writers and the antivirus writers with the poor user victimized in the middle.

What can e-marketers do? The best place to stop a computer virus is before it reaches the end user. All e-mail messages pass through a mail server that stores the messages on a disk drive in users' mailboxes. Software can be installed on the mail server to scan all incoming messages for known viruses and destroy them if identified as containing a virus or quarantine them if suspected. In this way, the virus never reaches the end user and infection is avoided. Antiviral software can also be installed on each individual computer. One robust antiviral program is McAfee Anti-Virus (www.mcafee.com). Also popular is Symantec's Norton AntiVirus (www.symantec.com). Similar software can scan messages for spam and take equivalent actions. Both technologies are a boon for marketers because they keep the Internet clear of destructive or unwanted content, helping to focus user attention on the desired content.

Denial of Service Attacks

In 2000, denial of service (**DoS**) attacks were mounted on some of the most heavily trafficked Internet sites including Yahoo! and E*Trade. A DoS attack occurs when a hacker floods a computer system with millions of requests for information and effectively exceeds its ability to respond. The bogged down computer must then deny service to legitimate users trying to contact the Web site. The attack can shut down the site for hours until the attacking computer is identified and neutralized. DoS attacks caused e-commerce companies such as Yahoo! and E*Trade to lose millions of dollars while their sites were down and shook consumer confidence in the security of the Internet. One remedy for a DoS attack is to distribute multiple copies of a Web site around the country in the hope that all sites will not be attacked simultaneously. Infrastructure companies are also working together to develop procedures for early detection and neutralization of attacks.

Price Technologies

Shopping agents are a key technology that e-marketers need to understand when planning pricing strategies. A shopping agent helps consumers shop by eliminating the time-consuming drudgery of compiling all the information they need to complete a purchase. A shopping agent knows which stores to visit, provides accurate product and price information, helps buyers compare product features and prices, negotiates specials on their behalf, and completes the transaction with the click of a button.

The technology that shopping agents employ is called **parallel pull**. What appears to the user to be one shopping agent is actually a number of agents that simultaneously (in parallel) collect (pull) information from relevant Web sites worldwide. The entire process takes only minutes (in some cases seconds), during which time hundreds of pieces of relevant information are collected, categorized, and even sorted for the user. The process is speedy because the agents quickly translate the query into the format required by each individual merchant. The merchants benefit because the agents attract customers to their sites. And the agents benefit by selling preferred placement and advertising inventory as well as by collecting referral fees.

When it is easy for consumers to price-shop and when they perceive little product or merchant differentiation, then markets behave like commodity markets, with all prices reaching similar levels. Fortunately for marketers, most consumers are brand sensitive about their merchants. They tend to pick merchants with whom they have had a good experience or about whom they have received a good recommendation. So as they look at the price-sorted results from the shopping agent the consumer is looking for a familiar merchant name. See Chapter 11 for more about how shopping agents affect the efficiency of the Internet as a market.

For whom is the agent really working? Some agents such as PriceSCAN pride themselves on representing only the buyer's interests. They do not charge vendors a fee for listing. Other agents may charge a fee for listing and additional fees for preferred placement in the listings. This model is similar to the Yellow Pages that allows vendors to place ads early in the listings. Unlike the Yellow Pages, however, the consumer has access to pricing information and is usually able to sort the listings by price even if the initial list is ordered by preferred placement. One weakness of this model for consumers is that vendor selectivity is not prominently mentioned on the site; thus, a user believes the agent is searching all relevant sites.

Distribution Technologies

Among the technologies e-marketers use for distribution are those that increase bandwidth, allow users to filter content, and increase transaction security.

Bandwidth and Market Opportunities

Complex infrastructure systems bring a variety of utilities to the consumer's home. These include the telephone, cable TV, water, and electric power. In most cases the consumer does not know or care how the infrastructure that delivers these systems works. What interests the consumer are benefits. For example, the consumer might be interested in receiving 25 more TV channels or being able to videoconference from home. To provide these additional services would require major infrastructure improvements behind the scenes.

Bandwidth refers to the carrying capacity of an information channel—the amount of information that can squeeze through an information pipe. That pipe might be a telephone or cable TV wire. Greater bandwidth results in greater information delivery speed through that pipe. A lack of bandwidth leaves the consumers waiting for Web content to download. Bandwidth is measured in bits per second. Modems are used to pump information over a telephone line. The fastest modems operate at about 50,000 bits per second. How much information does this represent? It takes about 10 bits to form one character such as the letter *A*. So a channel carrying 50,000 bits per second (i.e., 50 Kbps or 50 kilobits per second) could carry about 5,000 characters per second. If the words in this document contained an average of five letters each, this would be 1,000 words sent from person A to person B in 1 second— quite fast.

$$\frac{50,000 \text{ bits}}{\text{second}} * \frac{1 \text{ character}}{10 \text{ bits}} = \frac{5,000 \text{ characters}}{\text{second}}$$

Text travels very efficiently over the Internet, although graphics do not. A photograph could easily require 500,000 bits. At 50,000 bits per second, the photograph would take 10 seconds to transmit

$$500,000 \text{ bits} * \frac{1 \text{ second}}{50,000 \text{ bits}} = 10 \text{ seconds}$$

Full-motion video requires 32 frames per second, each one of which requires 500,000 bits. This means that full-motion video is just not possible at telephone modem speeds.

Just how fast does transmission need to be to support various media types? What are the bandwidth requirements? Advances in compression methods change these numbers constantly, but the following table serves as a rough guide:

Media Type	Minimum Number of Bits per Second	Abbreviation
Text	25,000	25 Kbps
Graphics (pictures)	50,000	50 Kbps
Sound	100,000	100 Kbps
Video	1,000,000	1 Mbps

Bandwidth is important to e-marketers for several reasons. First, one major marketing opportunity, developing low-involvement brands, is not possible without increases in bandwidth. Branding soap, for example, requires creating an emotional feel-good experience for the consumer. This atmosphere is best created by the multimedia sight and sound experience of television. High-quality multimedia on the Web is only available for high-bandwidth users. Those users can comfortably enjoy the following services:

- Personal selling and customer service via the computer as a videoconferencing device
- Phone calls delivered over the Internet
- Delivery of music CDs over the Web
- Delivery of movies over the Web
- Real-time virtual reality

The Internet is currently in a curious stage of development. The information channels that form the Internet backbone have amazing carrying capacities and are constantly being upgraded by firms such as Cisco, Sprint, and AT&T. However, the last link along the path to the Internet, the telephone line to the consumer's home, is woefully outdated and is a bandwidth stranglehold because the line was never designed to carry anything other than voice communications. Voice communications do not require a tremendous amount of bandwidth. The latest round of 56K modems (56,000 bits per second) have just about squeezed as much information out of the phone line as is possible without major infrastructure changes—which are on the way.

Digital Subscriber Line (DSL)

Digital subscriber line (**DSL**) technology refers to a family of methods for transmitting at speeds up to 8 Mbps (8 million bits per second) over a standard phone line. DSL uses the phone line already installed in consumer homes, allowing users to simultaneously make phone calls and surf the Web because the data travel outside of the audible voice band. Users must install a DSL modem; some computer manufacturers offer these as a preinstalled item, and some phone companies supply them.

All the major phone companies have deployed or are planning to deploy the infrastructure to support DSL technology, but some technical issues remain. One of the more serious issues is that in many neighborhoods phone companies saved money by installing hardware that channels traffic from multiple homes onto a single line back to the phone company. This grouping is not compatible with DSL, which requires that each phone line from every home extend all the way back to the phone company's central office. However, industry insiders are optimistic that the technical difficulties can be overcome. And the difficulties must be quickly overcome or the phone companies will lose the high-speed data market to the cable companies, which are already widely disseminating their infrastructure.

Cable Modems

While the phone companies are sorting out the DSL issues, the cable companies have gotten a head start with cable modems. The cable companies have banded together into two consortiums. In one example, Time Warner, Time Warner/Advance-Newhouse, and MediaOne Group Inc. formed a consortium called Road Runner. These consortiums help to set standards and share development costs.

The consortiums have attracted venture capital. As an example, Compaq Computer and Microsoft each invested $212.5 million in Road Runner. Clearly the personal computer industry has a stake in selling computer upgrades to consumers who need beefed up machines to handle the additional bandwidth.

Cable modems allow transmission of Internet traffic over the cable TV wire connected to the home. The speed of transmission over a cable modem ranges between 500 Kbps and 2.5 Mbps. Cable companies do not face the same daunting infrastructure issues that the phone companies face. In fact the major problem cable companies may face is having too many subscribers! This is a problem because subscribers in a cable neighborhood share bandwidth. The more subscribers who share, the less bandwidth there will be to repartition. Therefore, if a neighborhood becomes saturated with subscribers, each subscriber will experience delays.

The big advantage that the cable companies have is early market penetration. The early adopters opted for cable modems because they were the first technology available. This early usage also gives cable modems the advantage of diffusion via word of mouth. Another advantage is that the cable companies solved their infrastructure issues early and can now focus on establishing value-added services such as:

- Video-on-demand
- CD-quality audio
- Online games available for download and purchase

Each value-added service provides a barrier to entry for the phone companies. Why purchase a service with fewer features? And because providing each service requires a learning curve, phone companies will have difficulty catching up. One way the phone companies could compete is through price. As the following table shows, the prices seem fairly comparable, despite significant regional variations in price. In some cases the companies will wave the installation fee if the user signs up for an extended period of service.

Cost Comparison

	DSL	Cable Modem
Monthly charge	$30 to $100	$35 to $55
Installation fee	$60 to $300	$80 to $175
Bandwidth	32 Kbps to 8 Mbps	500 Kbps to 2.5 Mbps

Other Broadband Options

Two smaller competitors in the broadband game are satellite and wireless. Satellite broadband is offered through DirecPC. The major limitation is limited bandwidth that does not scale well with subscriber increases. **Wireless** relies on towers to relay signals in a mode very similar to that of cell phones. The technology seems to have a very bright future. Personal data assistants (PDAs), notebook computers, and other wireless devices are best served by wireless communication. These devices are growing rapidly in popularity and are quite ubiquitous in Europe and Japan. Users want access anytime from anywhere.

Wireless access is best categorized by distance and bandwidth. Some systems are designed to work over a range of miles—effectively replacing wired access to the home. Other systems operate over a range of up to hundreds of feet—providing local connectivity within the home or office. In either scenario, the bandwidth of the system determines its suitability as a broadband connection.

With cell phone towers already in place in many areas, Web access via cell phone would seem to be a natural outgrowth. The cell phone network is very reliable and in many areas the communication is already digital. The problem is bandwidth. The cell phone network was designed to handle low-bandwidth voice communications. As a result data communication over the network is relatively slow. Third-generation **(3G) cell phone** networks should help solve the bandwidth problem, because they will transfer data up to 10 times faster than traditional cell phone networks.

Wireless local area networks (WLANs), which are receiving considerable attention, can span distances of up to hundreds of feet. Major players such as Hewlett-Packard are investing in the infrastructure to provide WLANs to hotels and airports. The major issues are ease of connectivity and the number of different devices that can be interconnected.

One of the most important standards for WLANs is called **Wi-Fi**, also known as IEEE 802.11b. Wi-Fi networks operate at 10 Mbps within a range of about 300 feet. To reach the Internet every Wi-Fi network must connect back to a wired network. Some home users use Wi-Fi to share an Internet connection among multiple computers within their homes. Connecting to the network is relatively easy. In fact, some Wi-Fi adopters allow passersby on the street to tap into their home networks—effectively providing free wireless bandwidth. Some areas have enough of these altruistic providers that commuters can maintain a free Internet connection by hopping from network to network. However, free wireless upsets the providers of high-bandwidth connections (the phone and cable companies). Their customers are effectively redistributing bandwidth that was sold to them in violation of their subscription agreements.

Wireless ISPs (WISPs) offer connectivity to Wi-Fi networks for a small daily fee. The major issue for these fee-based services is how to recover revenues when their subscribers roam to other WISP networks. iPass makes software that supports roaming and hopes to become a de facto standard.

Wi-Fi networks can be found in Starbucks cafes, hotels, airports, and college campuses. For the real road warrior, Nokia has released a wireless modem capable of connecting to both cell phone and Wi-Fi networks.

Content Filtering

One growing segment of Web users is children under the age of 18. Many families are concerned that their children will be exposed to pornography, violence, or other unwanted material online. Even children not seeking material perceived as objectionable may be exposed to it by the results of an innocent search. For example, a search for "fun for girls" using one of the top search engines resulted in 13 of the first 20 pages linking to sex sites.

There are many solutions to serve the needs of user segments that do not want exposure to this type of material. One group of solutions aims to curb exposure to offensive material through education and/or legislation. Another group of solutions aims to limit exposure by use of technology. Education- and legislation-based solutions include:

- Educate children not to pursue offensive online material.
- Ban offensive material through legislative means.
- Require/encourage providers of offensive material to put age warnings on their sites (i.e., "if you are under 18 do not enter here").
- Require/encourage providers of offensive material to run an age verification system. Such systems require users to purchase a password using a credit card. The presumption is that minors do not have access to credit cards.
- Require/encourage providers of offensive material to rate their material using industry-standard ratings similar to those used by the film industry.

Technology-based solutions include:

- Ask the Internet service provider (ISP) to filter the content coming to the user.
- Filter the content right on the user's own computer.

All of these solutions have their merits and drawbacks and have been the subject of lively debate. This section focuses only on solutions that are technologically based—using computer software to monitor and filter content.

Content can be filtered by software running on any computer along the path from the user's computer to the Internet. In the corporate world employees are typically barred from objectionable sites by software running on a corporate computer that serves as the gateway to the Internet. This computer is called a **proxy server**. All communication to and from any corporate computer to the Internet passes through the proxy server. This is a very efficient solution and even allows employers to record attempted accesses to objectionable sites—taking disciplinary action when desired.

The home user typically does not have access to a similar service because ISPs are reluctant to filter content on their site since many users want to access this type of material. Notable exceptions to this reluctance include America Online (AOL) and Prodigy Internet, which provide families with multiple passwords. The children can then be restricted to a kid's area of the service. Some countries, such as China and Vietnam, filter content at the ISP level for everyone (adults as well as children). Incidentally, censorship is at the heart of the ethics debate on this issue.

Normally, the home user installs software on her computer to filter content. A number of products can perform this task, including NetNanny, CyberSitter, Cyber Patrol, and SurfWatch. As their names indicate, these products are intended to impede children's access to the questionable sites. Many provide password overrides so other household members can have full Internet access if they wish. Most products provide free updates as the list of objectionable sites grows, and many are customizable, allowing users to add or remove items from the list.

One way the products operate is by maintaining "can go" and "can't go" lists. Under the "can't go" scenario, the products maintain a list of banned sites—tens of thousands of sites. Each time the child attempts to access a site, the software checks the site address against the list of banned sites. If there is a match, the software can take one of the following actions:

1. Make a silent record of the access for the parent to see later but do nothing else.

2. Mask out objectionable words or images from the accessed site.

3. Block any access to the banned site.

4. Shut down the browser completely.

Under the "can go" scenario, the child can visit only sites that are on an approved list and nothing else. These might include such G-rated sites as www.disney.com. The parents can always add to this list according to requests from the children. Again, the same series of actions would be available should a child try to access a site not on the "can go" list.

Vendors update the "can't go" lists periodically and allow users to download the updated lists from their Web site. Updates are a major concern—especially for the "can't go" list, since new adult sites are constantly coming online. These sites can still be blocked with the words in the site name (e.g., www.cybersextalk.com) or the words in the Web page itself (e.g., "this site contains graphic sex"). Even incoming e-mail or MS-Word documents can be scanned. In all cases the same list of foregoing action options is available.

The products can also monitor outgoing e-mail messages to ensure that children do not give away private information such as name, phone number, or address to a cyber pedophile. To accomplish this, the software is programmed to recognize the name, phone number, and address of household members and then scan for these in any outgoing message.

Many feel that these **content filtering** products do provide the level of protection that families need. Some communities also install content filtering software in public libraries. These products are an example of a unique marketing mix that is tailored to a target market based both on demographics (age) and psychographics (beliefs). However, none of these products is foolproof, because Web sites change too quickly and determined kids are very clever.

Transaction Security

A study conducted for Lycos (www.lycos.com) by CyberDialogue/findsvp (www.cyberdialogue.com) (now Fulcrum Analytics) in 1998 revealed that transaction security is the number-one concern of all users online—and a greater concern among women than it is among men. The other concerns are summarized in Exhibit 4 - 1.

Is this a legitimate concern? Are users afraid of the unknown or are their fears the result of media hype? Ironically, transactions are probably much more secure on the Internet than in the brick-and-mortar world. To understand why this is so requires exploring the technology behind transaction security.

Credit Card Number Theft

There are three places that a credit card number could potentially be stolen on the Internet. It could be stolen from a user's home or business computer; it could be stolen in transit from the user's computer to the merchant's Web site; or it could be stolen once it reaches the merchant's site. How likely is each of these scenarios?

1. **Stolen from the user's computer**: Very unlikely considering that most users do not store credit card numbers on their computers.

2. **Stolen in transit**: Almost impossible and in fact this has never been reported. Encryption algorithms (described later) make this possibility very remote.

3. **Stolen at the merchant's site**: Probably the most legitimate user concern. There are three possibilities:

   a. The merchant may be fraudulent.
   b. The merchant may be honest but have a dishonest employee.
   c. The merchant may be honest but fail to protect its database of credit card numbers from hackers.

One way e-marketers are addressing transaction security is through the use of encryption algorithms.

Issue	Extremely Concerned or Very Concerned
Security of credit card transactions	86%
Protecting privacy	75%
Censorship	72%
Hate group Web sites	47%
Depiction of violence	38%
Pornography	30%

Exhibit 4 - 1 Top Issues for Online Users

Encryption Algorithms

Encryption algorithms cannot stop dishonest merchants or employees, but they are designed to protect transaction information in transit. Try to read the following encrypted phrase:

> JCRRA JQNKFCAU

You may have guessed that the key to decrypt this message is 2. All letters have been shifted two characters to the right in the alphabet.

> A-B-C-D-E-F-G-H-I-J-K-L-M-N-O-P-Q-R-S-T-U-V-W-X-Y-Z

To decrypt we shift back two letters to the left.

> J becomes **H**
> C becomes **A**
> R becomes **P**
> R becomes **P**
> A becomes **Y**

Continuing to decrypt reveals the message "HAPPY HOLIDAYS." Encryption on the Internet works in a similar fashion except that the key is a very big number, which is almost impossible to guess, and the encryption scheme is a good deal more sophisticated than shifting along the alphabet. In fact the industry standard RSA encryption scheme (named after the inventors Rivest, Shamir, and Adleman) has never been broken outside of university laboratories, and then only with weeks of effort by high-speed computers. This means a user's information is quite secure in transit.

When two computers on the Internet communicate in secure mode, the messages are encrypted in both directions. Both Netscape and Internet Explorer have the ability to communicate with a Web site in secure mode. The user's browser encrypts her credit card number and then sends it to the merchant; the merchant in turn encrypts confidential information sent back to the user. Each side uses a key to decrypt the other's message.

But how does the user get the merchant's key? If the merchant sends the key unencrypted, it could be stolen in transit. As amazing as it may seem, this is not a problem. In fact, merchants willingly give out what is known as a **public key**. However, the encryption algorithms are so clever that while the public key can encrypt the message, the same key cannot decrypt it. Only a complementary **private key**, which the merchant does not distribute, can decrypt the message, a process involving complex polynomial calculations and very large prime numbers.

The software used to handle the encryption is part of the merchant's commerce server. A tiny lock, which appears in the browser window, indicates encrypted communication with the merchant. The design of this lock symbol may have limited the growth of electronic commerce: The consumer might be more reassured by a larger symbol, a change in screen color, or any other significant visual cue that the transaction is secure. Where browsers failed, merchants picked up the cue. Before entering secure mode, many merchants transfer the user to a page that explains the security of the transaction. See Exhibit 4 - 2.

Exhibit 4 - 3 shows that the user has chosen to enter secure mode. Note how Amazon continues to reassure the user even on the secure mode screen!

Encryption protects the transaction while it is in transit between the user's computer and the retailer. Sometimes, however, the retailer does not adequately protect the records stored on its computer. In one security breach, the online storefronts of ESPN SportsZone and NBA.com were "broken into." The hacker stole the credit card numbers and e-mail addresses of hundreds of customers. As proof, he then sent each person an e-mail message containing his or her card number.

How does this happen? Most Web servers are very secure if properly installed and maintained. But in the rush to get things done, information system professionals sometimes get sloppy. Passwords are set to easily guessed names, passwords are loosely shared, or some accounts are enabled without passwords. Hackers usually begin by obtaining access to an account with very limited access to protected computer resources. Using that account they compromise an account with a bit more access. They continue to work their way up from account to account until they have sufficient access to compromise the system.

Exhibit 4 - 2 Amazon Guarantees Safety of Online Transactions

Source: www.amazon.com. Amazon.com is a registered trademark or trademark of Amazon.com, Inc. in the United States and/or other countries. © 2000 by Amazon.com. All rights reserved.

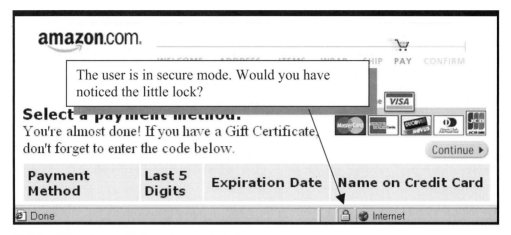

Exhibit 4 - 3 User Enters Secure Mode
Source: www.amazon.com Amazon.com is a registered trademark or trademark of Amazon.com, Inc. in the United States and/or other countries. © 2000 by Amazon.com. All rights reserved.

Merchants can protect themselves by trying to break into their own systems or hiring professionals to do so. Professionals are able to recognize flaws in the security system of the merchant's computer and suggest remedies to make it more secure. There are even computer programs such as Smurf, PingOdeath, and Satan Scan that merchants can use to attack their own sites. And, of course, there are corresponding intrusion detection systems, such as Real Secure and Entrust, which can notify the merchant of an actual attack by recognizing the digital signatures of these attack programs. These software systems experience short but sweet product life cycles: First, a new attack program comes along, then a detection program is upgraded to counteract it, then a new attack program is designed, and the cycle continues with increasing sophistication.

IMC Technologies

E-marketers use a variety of technologies for integrated marketing communication. Among these are proxy servers, search-engine listings, log files and cookies, and rotating and targeted ad banners.

Proxy Servers

Banner ads are typically sold on a basis of cost per thousand (CPM) impressions. This cost varies by site and even by page within site. Accurate counting of the number of impressions is critical to the revenue stream of a content site. Specifically, undercounting impressions robs the content provider of revenue.

Undercounting has become a significant problem as a result of a technology that copies entire Web sites and then lets users view the copies—a technology that makes the Web seem faster for users. The device that makes the copies is called a *proxy server.* Clever solutions have been developed to count the number of times that a proxy server serves out a copy. See Exhibit 4 - 4.

So how big is the problem of undercounting? According to a study by the MatchLogic Corporation, which was independently audited by Ernst & Young, undercounting averages 76% and in some cases can be as high as 674%. That represents a tremendous loss of revenue for companies selling ad inventories, but the problem is even more serious. Most of the proxy servers are in corporations, and the demographics of users in those corporations represent precisely the affluent demographics that advertisers try to reach. Thus, undercounting not only affects size counts but also biases user demographic descriptions. There are some other problems, as well:

1. The Web site records one less impression for which it can charge the advertiser.

2. The Web site records one less page view that it can report to its investors.

3. Even though the advertiser creates several ads to be shown in rotation, the ads never rotate on the page. The same ad is seen over and over again, leading to ad burnout and potential loss of effectiveness.

4. The page could grow stale over time if the content is not updated frequently.

The MatchLogic solution goes straight to the heart of the problem: how many eyeballs see an ad. When advertisers purchase impressions, they really want to reach that number of people. In fact, this solution improves on TV and other traditional

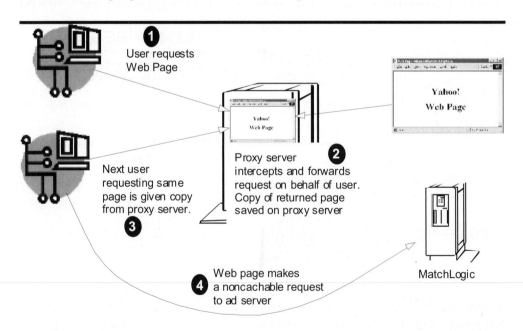

Exhibit 4 - 4 Circumventing the Proxy Server

media audience measurement because Nielsen and others only know if the TV set is tuned to a program and do not count the number of people who actually watch commercials during a show (versus how many go to the refrigerator). Screen space being small as it is, and consumer navigating behavior being focused and intense, banners receive relatively good advertising exposure on the Web. By the way, when requesting a Web page the status line at the bottom of the browser window includes comments like "contacting ad server" in between comments about contacting the requested site.

How Search Engines Work

The Web contains billions of pages. Realistically it would be impossible for the search engines to search the entire Web every time someone types in a search term. The task would take days to complete. Therefore, search engines actually do the searching up to a month in advance and store the results in a huge database. They send automatic programs called **spiders** out on the Web to go from site to site, page by page and word by word, as shown in Exhibit 4 - 5. These spiders build up a massive index or database of all the words found, where they were found, how many times they appear on each page, and so on. When users type in a search term, this is the database that is actually queried. Because it is an indexed database, the query returns the results almost instantly. The results are generally returned in order of

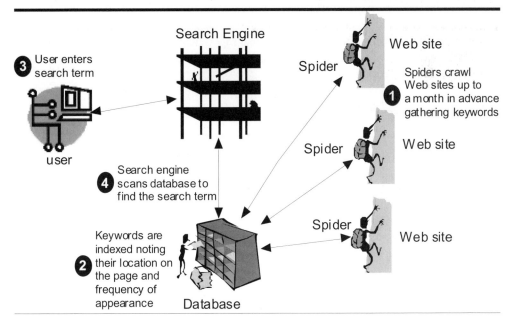

Exhibit 4 - 5 How Search Engines Work

relevance with the most relevant site appearing first. But how does the search engine define relevance?

It is the search engine's job to figure out which sites are most likely to be relevant to the search term. Here the spider aids it. The spider does more than just count words. It also looks for the location of those words on the page. For example, if the word is in the title of a page, it is given a higher relevance value than a word appearing in the body text. The spiders are also trained to avoid sites that attempt to trick them by repeating words many times in a row. One technique is to ignore repeats that are not separated by at least, say, seven other words. This guards against someone loading a page with, for example, Mazda, Mazda, and Mazda. The actual techniques used are becoming trade secrets since producing a search engine that returns truly useful results is actually a point of product differentiation and, therefore, provides a competitive advantage. Nonetheless, one Web site, SearchEngineWatch (www.searchenginewatch.com), reveals many of the secrets for each of the search engines.

One search engine maintains a competitive edge by relying on user behavior to form its rankings. Google (www.google.com) ranks sites according to how many links point to the site from other Web sites. A popular site should have more links pointing to it than one that is less popular. Internet giant Yahoo! has adopted Google as its search engine.

E-marketers would like their sites to appear high in the search engine rankings—preferably on the first page. Fortunately, specialized companies can help by carefully studying the search engines to determine their algorithms for ranking pages. The analysis provides information that can be used to redesign pages so they will rise in the rankings. Some of these companies have rather catchy names, such as Did-It, MoreVisibility, and SpiderBait.

Log Files and Cookies

Visitors on the Web, like visitors to a sandy beach, leave footprints wherever they go. The footprints are left in two places—on the computer visited and on the user's own computer. The computer visited maintains a log of all computers that visit the site and exactly which pages they see. The log is in the form of a table, which looks similar to this:

Date	Time	Visitor Address	Page Viewed
1/10/2003	10:30am	FrostR.ohiou.edu	Baking recipes
1/10/2003	10:31am	FrostR.ohiou.edu	Cookies
1/10/2003	10:32am	FrostR.ohiou.edu	Chocolate chip
1/10/2003	10:40am	FrostR.ohiou.edu	Sign off

A real **log file** records much more data. However, even in this simple example, one can tell that the computer FrostR.ohiou.edu (belonging to Frost at Ohio University) navigated quickly down to the recipe for chocolate chip cookies and then stayed there for 8 minutes before leaving the site. This type of information collected from thousands of users tells e-marketers which pages are popular, who are repeat users, the days and times that the site is most heavily used, and so forth. The analysis also forms the basis for site redesign as marketers learn which pages are most popular. Note that the log file only identifies the computer. This makes it difficult to monitor user behavior if more than one user shares the computer—as is the case in university computer labs.

The second way to track behavior on the Web is by use of cookies. **Cookies** are files stored on the user's computer. Each site a user visits may write a cookie on the computer. Suppose a user is a repeat visitor to a site that requires a password. The site could authenticate this user by looking up her password in a cookie from a previous session. It could also use the cookie to store her purchase choices in an electronic shopping basket prior to checkout. Cookies are more reliable than computer addresses because a computer's address may change every time it is restarted. See Exhibit 4 - 6.

Both log files and cookies can be helpful for customizing products and services for the user community. However, most users do not understand how extensively their behavior is being tracked. This raises a question about the ethics of gathering information about people without their knowledge and explicit consent—an ethical issue that is being hotly debated.

Rotating and Targeted Ad Banners

Using the browser's refresh or reload button on Yahoo!'s Web site usually results in a change in the banner ad displayed on the page. Yahoo! sells its inventory of banner

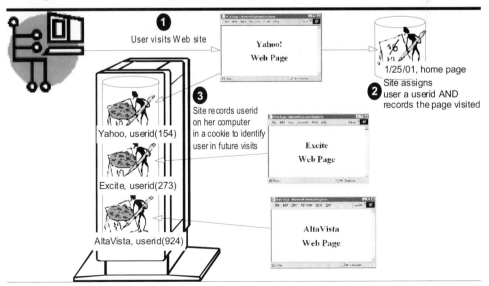

Exhibit 4 - 6 How Cookies Are Stored

slots on a rotating basis. Advertisers are guaranteed a certain number of impressions over a period of time, but other ads will be interspersed with theirs. This is not unlike the ads that rotate on a scoreboard during professional sporting events. However, sporting events have a distinct advantage—they know the characteristics of their audience and, therefore, can target ads to their needs. Magazines and newspapers have a similar feature called selective binding. Advertisers in *Time* magazine, for example, can select from among over 200 different versions to reach markets ranging from doctors, business executives, and students to very specific geographic areas. It is likely that the issue of *Time* that you receive as a student will contain different ads and even a few different articles than issues created for other markets. To achieve the same level of efficiency in the online world, the industry developed targeted ads. The ad changes or rotates based on the search words that a user types into the search engine. Targeted ads cost more per impression because advertisers are more effectively able to reach their target based on psychographics (interests of users).

Even more impressive are ad networks such as DoubleClick that can track and target users as they move from site to site. DoubleClick does this by storing a cookie on the user's computer to identify each user by number. Whenever the user visits a site in the DoubleClick network, DoubleClick reads the cookie, looks up and/or modifies the user's profile, and then targets an appropriate ad. See Exhibit 4 - 7. The process is very effective from a direct-marketing point of view and extremely successful. DoubleClick delivers billions of ads *each day*!

Is DoubleClick tracking you? Find the cookie files on your hard drive to see. Internet Explorer stores each cookie in a separate file in the Cookies directory. Netscape Navigator, by contrast, places all of the cookies in the same file called cookies.txt. Use the Windows "find files" feature to search for *cookie*. This will find cookies.txt (for Netscape) as well as the Cookies directory (for Internet Explorer). You can open cookie files in a text editor by double-clicking on them. Exhibit 4 - 8 shows the contents of a cookie file for a newly installed computer. The user has visited exactly one site, www.travelocity.com. However, since Travelocity uses DoubleClick as its ad server, a DoubleClick cookie is also written to the user's computer.

At this point the user has two cookies on her computer—one from Travelocity and one from DoubleClick. The Travelocity cookie will allow Travelocity to greet the user by name on a subsequent visit. The DoubleClick cookie will be used to track the user around the Internet. The next time that the user visits a site on the DoubleClick network, DoubleClick will be able to target an ad to that user for a travel-related service. This type of marketing is often called **closed loop marketing** because it functions as long as the user visits one of the Web sites on the loop or network.

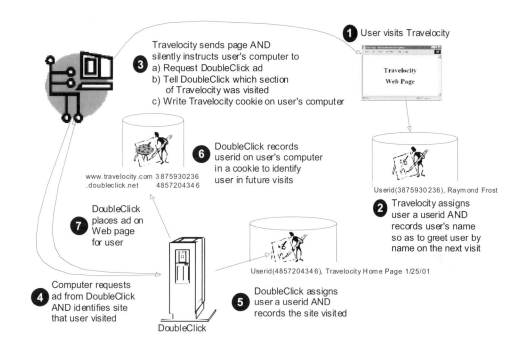

Exhibit 4 - 7 Tracking Users Site to Site

Tracking users across multiple sites raises some ethical issues concerning the user's privacy. Is it ethical to record information about the user without the user's knowledge or consent? This issue is investigated in more detail in Chapter 5. Currently, users who do not wish to be tracked have three options. First, they can disable cookies in their browser. In practice this option is not effective since many Web sites will not provide content if cookies are disabled. The second option is to delete the cookie files at the end of each session. To delete cookies in Internet Explorer choose **Tools → Internet Options → General → Delete Cookies**. Again, this is not a very practical option since most users would probably forget to do so. The third option is to purchase a product such as Intermute (www.intermute.com) that blocks all requests to the ad server. If the user's computer never contacts the ad server, the ad server cannot write a cookie—and without the cookie tracking is not possible. But how many people know this?

A technical solution has been developed that would give sites needed information to serve customers without compromising user privacy. It is called the Platform for Privacy Preferences (**P3P**). The idea behind P3P is that users specify in advance how much information they are willing to reveal to a Web site and under

```
# Netscape HTTP Cookie File
# http://www.netscape.com/newsref/std/cookie_spec.html
# This is a generated file!  Do not edit.
www.travelocity.com   FALSE    /    FALSE    3875930236   grtng  1
.doubleclick.net       TRUE     /    FALSE    4857204346   id     A
```

Exhibit 4 - 8 Netscape Cookie File (cookie.txt)

what conditions. That information is stored on each user's computer. When the user visits a participating site, the user's browser reviews the P3P policies of that site and compares them against the stored policies on the user's computer. For example, the policy might state that the site only collects data on its home page that are found in standard HTTP access logs. If this is acceptable to the browser, then it loads the page. This saves the user from having to read the privacy policy of each site— something that users very seldom do. If the site requests information that the user deems sensitive, then the user receives a warning. Similarly, the user could be warned if the site participates in closed loop marketing. Today the standard is completely voluntary. However, P3P is supported by Internet Explorer and may gain in acceptance. To review your P3P settings in Internet Explorer choose **Tools →** **Internet Options → Privacy**. Critics of P3P claim that it is not easy to use, effective, or enforceable.

Relationship Marketing Technologies

Relationship marketing online involves personalization (greeting by name) and customization (changing a site's content to match a user's preferences). Personalization is much easier to implement than customization. However, both technologies rely on database-driven Web sites.

A database-driven Web site stores all of its content in a database. When the user requests a Web page, a program extracts content from the database and creates the page in a fraction of a second. That program is normally written by an MIS (or IT) professional in a language such as ASP. Another tremendous advantage of database-driven Web sites is that they are easy to update. Change the content in the database and the Web page is automatically updated the next time it is accessed. Most database-driven Web sites have a separate administrative program to allow updates to the database. The ease of update is especially important for sites that rapidly change content such as CNN.com. The news writers enter their stories in the administrative program, which updates the database, thereby instantly publishing the changes on the Web site.

Exhibit 4 - 9 shows relationship marketing in action at Amazon. Amazon uses a database-driven Web site that incorporates personalization and customization. The process begins when the user first registers with Amazon. Amazon records information about the user in its user database file, a simplified form appearing in Exhibit 4 - 10.

Exhibit 4 - 9 Amazon Welcome Screen

Source: www.amazon.com. Amazon.com is a registered trademark or trademark of Amazon.com, Inc. in the United States and/or other countries. © 2000 by Amazon.com. All rights reserved.

Amazon then stores the user's userid in a cookie file on the *user's* computer. A simplified form of the cookie file appears in Exhibit 4 - 11.

On a return trip to the Amazon site, the user's computer sends the userid value (12345) from the cookie file to Amazon's server. Amazon's server uses that number to look up the user's record (12345, Frost, Raymond D., 8 Web Way, Athens, 45701, 4444 5555 6666 7777) in its database. The server merges the user's name with its home page, inserting the personalized greeting ("Welcome Back, Raymond D. Frost") in the appropriate spot. The process is not unlike a mail merge in a word processor except that only one document is created.

Userid	Last	First	Street	City	Zip	Credit Card #
12345	Frost	Raymond	8 Web Way	Athens	45701	4444 5555 6666 7777
76543	Strauss	Judy	10 Net Lane	Reno	89557	3333 2222 9999 8888

Exhibit 4 - 10 User Database File

.amazon.com	Userid	= 12345
my.yahoo.com	Userid = 88875	
.hotwired.com	Userid	= 55235

Exhibit 4 - 11 Simplified Cookie File

But Amazon doesn't stop there. Note the line after the greeting: "We have recommendations for you in books." Clicking on this link brings up Exhibit 4 - 12. The exhibit shows a recommendation in an area in which the author has recently ordered books—romance set in Southeast Asia. This is an example of customization.

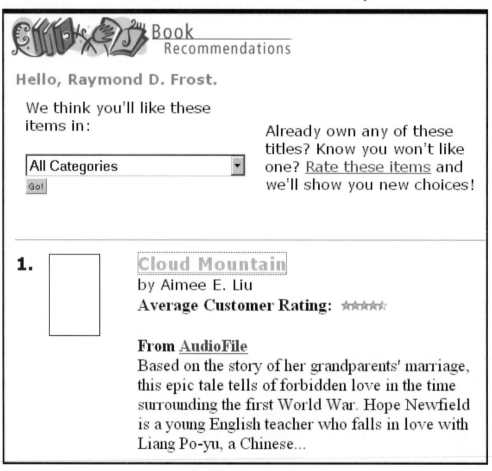

Exhibit 4 - 12 Amazon's Customized Recommendations

How did Amazon identify the author's preferences? It maintains a separate file containing all the orders for its users. A simplified form of the file looks like Exhibit 4 - 13.

Using the userid (12345), Amazon can look up the last titles ordered. The same file contains books that other users have ordered. Note how in this example two users who ordered books that the author ordered also purchased *Cloud Mountain*. Assume that there are thousands of users following the same pattern. The pattern would then be enough to place *Cloud Mountain* on the recommendation list.

To Review the Process Once Again

First Purchase

1. The user makes a purchase with Amazon.
2. Amazon stores the user's full information in its user file.
3. Amazon stores the purchase record in its orders file.
4. Amazon stores the user's userid (not the full user record) in a cookie file on the user's computer.

Subsequent Visits

1. Amazon pulls the cookie record from the user's computer to find the Userid.
2. The userid is used to look up the user's record.
3. The name is extracted from the user's record and merged with the Web page to produce a personal greeting.
4. The userid is used to look up the user's order history from the orders file.
5. Collaborative filtering software is used to find patterns among other users' orders, which can help to recommend book titles.

While Amazon wrote many of the programs used to manage CRM services, other companies prefer to buy established solutions. Some companies specializing in CRM software solutions include:

Userid	Title
12345	The Language of Threads
12345	Night of Many Dreams
76543	Cloud Mountain
76543	The Language of Threads
22233	Cloud Mountain
22233	Night of Many Dreams

Exhibit 4 - 13 Amazon Orders File

- Siebel Systems (www.siebel.com)
- E.piphany (www.epiphany.com)
- Oracle (www.oracle.com)
- PeopleSoft (www.peoplesoft.com)
- SAP (www.sap.com)
- SAS (www.sas.com)
- Net Perceptions (www.netperceptions.com)

In some cases the software vendor provides consultants to help with installation and fine tuning of the software. However, in many cases a company interested in CRM will hire a consulting firm such as Accenture to both choose the software vendor and install and tune the software.

Summary

Marketing managers increasingly need to understand the capabilities of the new media in order to develop effective marketing plans. These technologies apply to all 4 P's of marketing.

E-marketers need various technologies to support their online product strategies, including technologies for building Web sites; forms, languages, and standards; multimedia capabilities; database marketing; and protection against computer viruses and denial of service attacks. HTML is used to design Web pages. Other languages that support interactive Web pages include HTML forms, Java, dynamic HTML, XHTML, and XML. Other important technologies are ActiveX, plug-ins, and cascading style sheets. While multimedia will one day be omnipresent on the Web, now e-marketers face serious bandwidth problems in delivering multimedia. Solutions include increasing bandwidth, compressing, streaming, and distributing the content closer to the end user. Database marketing technologies use relational databases to store tables of information that marketers can mine for information about customers and use to generate promotional campaigns online.

Computer viruses are intrusive pieces of computer code that secretly attach to existing software, reproduce themselves, and wreak havoc with data. Four common types of viruses are macro viruses, worms, Trojan horses, and boot viruses. A denial of service attack occurs when a hacker floods a computer system with millions of requests for information—which exceed the system's ability to respond. The computer must deny service to legitimate users trying to contact the Web site.

E-marketers must understand how consumers use shopping agents so they can plan effective online pricing strategies. Shopping agents scan multiple Web sites simultaneously to retrieve product and pricing information and may deliver added benefits, as well. Some agents represent the buyer's interests; others charge e-marketers for listing and preferred placement.

Distribution technologies are used to increase bandwidth, filter content, and increase transaction security. Four ways to increase bandwidth are DSL, cable modems, satellite, and wireless. Cable modems are by far the most popular, but many eyes are focused on the future of wireless. Content filtering is a good example of a technological solution to the policy problem of how to screen out undesirable material for certain Internet users or, conversely, allow targeted users (such as children) to access only certain sites. Although e-commerce transactions are very secure, the public still has misgivings about online use of credit cards. To address these concerns, marketers are using encryption algorithms and reassuring users at every stage of the purchase process.

E-marketers use integrated marketing communication technologies such as proxy servers, search-engine listings, log files and cookies, and rotating and targeted ad banners. Proxy servers create the problem of unrecorded impressions. Fortunately, solutions exist to ensure accurate counting of ad impressions. Marketers need to understand how search engines work so they can devise strategies for raising the ranking of their companies on result listings. Web sites track user movement using log files and cookies. Using this knowledge to better serve the visitor and redesign the Web site is a marketing challenge. One of the most sophisticated applications of technology is for targeted and rotating ad banners using cookies. While these techniques are controversial, they are often very effective.

Relationship marketing online involves personalization (greeting users by name) and customization (changing a site's content to match a user's preferences). Cookies allow Web sites to greet customers by name and make recommendations based on past purchases. E-marketers can also offer customized recommendations to individual users based on collaborative filtering techniques.

Key Terms

3G cell phone

ActiveX

ASP

Bandwidth

Broadband

Cable modem

CGI

Closed loop marketing

Content filtering

Cookie

CSS

DoS attack

DSL

Dynamic HTML

Encryption

High bandwidth

HTML

Java

JavaScript

JDK

Log file

MP3

Multimedia

P3P

Parallel pull

Plug-in

Private key

Proxy server

Public key

RDBMS

RealAudio

RealVideo

Shopping agent

Spider

SQL

Wi-Fi

Wireless

XHTML

XML

Exercises

Review Questions

1. What are the advantages of using Java, dynamic HTML, JavaScript, plug-ins, and XHTML?

2. How and why do e-marketers use database marketing technologies?

3. What are the four types of computer viruses?

4. How do consumers and e-marketers use shopping agents?

5. What is bandwidth and how does it affect the delivery of multimedia content over the Web?

6. What is content filtering and why is it important to some Internet users?

7. How are e-marketers addressing concerns about transaction security?

8. What are some advantages and limitations of using proxy servers and cookies as technologies for online advertising?

Discussion Questions

9. Both CSS and XML separate a document's content from its presentation. Why is this an important goal?

10. Which solution(s) would you recommend for content filtering to a local elementary school? Why?

11. Why would a company pay a hacker to break into its site? What ethical issues are involved in this type of decision?

12. Many Internet users are concerned about privacy issues. Should sites that are in the DoubleClick network be required to publicly disclose this to visitors? Support your position.

13. Why is customization more difficult to implement than personalization?

14. As a rule of thumb a company should use off-the-shelf CRM solutions. Yet, Amazon wrote most of its own software. Why did Amazon break the rule?

2

c h a p t e r

5

e t h i c a l
a n d   l e g a l   i s s u e s

l e a r n i n g   o b j e c t i v e s

The main goal of this chapter is to explore the ethical and legal issues that e-businesses face in marketing online. You will learn about the current and emerging issues that have caused concern among a variety of stakeholders, including e-businesses and consumers.

After reading this chapter, you will be able to:

- Compare and contrast ethics and law.
- Discuss the implications of ethical codes and self-regulation.
- Identify some of the main privacy concerns within traditional and digital contexts.
- Explain some of the important copyright, patent, trademark, and data ownership issues related to the Internet.
- Highlight key ethical and legal concerns related to online expression.

The biggest infraction of privacy actually occurs when people post their own e-mail addresses in public places on the Net.

patricia
seybold
customers.com

Have you ever broken the law while sitting at your computer? Most people would probably say no—not recalling the times they installed computer software that they didn't purchase. Software piracy occurs when people loan software CDs to others or companies install computer software for which they have no software licenses. Counterfeiting occurs when illegally copied software is duplicated and distributed on a large scale. Both piracy and counterfeiting violate U.S. copyright laws and are illegal.

So what's the big deal? Suppose you spent months writing a best-selling novel and then learned that thousands of people were copying it instead of buying it. That copying would cut into your income and reduce your enthusiasm for writing more novels. Software piracy creates a similar situation. The firms creating the software use the income to pay for innovative upgrades and new products; they can't do as much if they lose income. Also, software marketers must raise the price paid by legitimate buyers to replace income lost to piracy.

Amazingly, 40% of all software worldwide was pirated in 2001, resulting in a US$10.7 billion loss for firms. In addition, 840,000 Internet sites sold counterfeited software misrepresented as the real thing. The main culprit in 2000 was Vietnam, where 97% of all software is pirated. China (94%), Indonesia (89%), Ukraine (89%), and Russia (88%) follow closely in piracy rates (U.S. piracy is 25%).

What can companies do? Microsoft, one of the main victims, uses several methods: It proposes intellectual property legislation, files civil lawsuits, and creates antipiracy technologies such as holographic images embedded in software CDs. A few years ago Microsoft tried a system of sniffing out users' hard drives while they were online, but privacy advocates objected. In the end, Microsoft believes that education is the best weapon. Many people who use pirated software don't know they are stealing, and it is not against the law or out of the cultural norms in many countries. For example, executives in some countries believe that if they buy one copy of the software they can use it as they please, as with other products. To support its educational goal, Microsoft created a Web site about piracy (www.microsoft.com/piracy). Piracy and counterfeiting are huge problems for the software industry—problems that are unlikely to be solved for a long time.

Dave Bowman:
Open the pod bay doors, HAL.
HAL 9000:
I'm sorry, Dave. I'm afraid I can't do that.

arthur c. clarke 2001: a space odyssey

Authors' Note: This chapter was contributed by Dr. Brian M. O'Connell, a lawyer and computer science professor at Central Connecticut State University.

Overview of Ethics and Legal Issues

The study of ethical and legal issues is often treated as being about separate, often unrelated subjects. In reality, ethics and law are closely related. As we will see, **ethics** frequently concerns itself with the values and practices of professionals and others who have an expert knowledge of a specific field. Ethics is also a general endeavor that takes into account the concerns and values of society as a whole.

Law is similar to ethics in the sense that it, too, is an expression of values, but while ethics may be directed toward individual or group endeavors, laws are normally created for broader purposes, with the goal of addressing national or sometimes international populations. In the Anglo-American tradition, law is made by legislatures such as Congress or Parliament, enforced by executives or agencies, and interpreted by the courts. In all these instances, it is a public endeavor. This is reflected in the fact that law is often the result of political and social compromise. Additionally, law attempts to be consistent in both time and place so that citizens will be familiar with their rights and obligations.

Since law is the result of combinations of interests, beliefs, and goals, the processes that lead up to the making of laws are often slow and complex. The effects of lobbying, political contributions, and other special influences have been the focus of criticism and calls for reform. Similarly troubling, even when agreement is reached, there often remain many questions about the meaning of the law or about details concerning specific provisions. Thus, the courts are frequently called upon to evaluate laws or determine their effect upon individual conflicts, presented in the form of lawsuits. Administrative agencies such as the Federal Trade Commission (FTC) are also concerned with making laws responsive to particular situations and do this by promulgating rules and opinions within the sectors of their expertise. Throughout these efforts, it remains true that progress in the law can be slow, and this is particularly so within the new and often unfamiliar context of digital communication.

Ethics makes important contributions to legal developments—sometimes by influencing legislators, judges, and other lawmakers, and other times, by being directly sought out by these groups for opinions and advice. Likewise, the law's ability to sift through arguments and arrive at practical and acceptable conclusions can aid ethical inquiry. In the area of digital marketing, the role of ethics is particularly important since the experiences and practices of those who work in the field are particularly helpful to those who are charged with regulation and legal decision making.

Ethics and Ethical Codes

The study of ethics has been in existence for over 2,500 years. Its central focus is the analysis and description of such basic concepts as what is right and wrong and how we go about judging the differences. An important dimension of this investigation concerns the types of conduct that comprise ethical behavior. These tasks necessarily involve the examination of responsibilities, rights, and obligations. Ethical inquiry is not limited to purely theoretical boundaries. Rather, questions are studied at all levels of human interaction and often appear as political, legal, and commercial issues. Consequently, the scope of ethics is virtually as wide as its subject matter. Similarly, there are many types of ethical positions that compete against each other for acceptance.

A particularly important aspect of ethical inquiry involves the study of professional activities. Traditionally, groups of individuals possessing special skills or knowledge have established codes and systems of fair practice. A classical example is the Hippocratic Oath of physicians. Ethical standards work both externally and internally. They help to communicate consistency and trustworthiness to the community at large while also assisting in maintaining stability and integrity within the profession. In these ways, ethics are both pragmatic tools and essential elements of professional identity.

Documents such as the American Marketing Association's (AMA) Code of Ethics [1] reflect the recognition of a commitment to the exercise of honesty, integrity, and fairness within all professional transactions. In addition to articulating overall values, professional codes provide members with guidelines that are specific to their pursuits. They are often products of the combined experiences of practitioners and scholars that are passed along to the entire membership and published to the public. Historically, codes have been interpreted or revised to respond to changed circumstances and new issues. In the past, these processes have been relatively gradual with modifications often coming in conservative degrees. Today, this situation has been fundamentally transformed.

Modern technology presents a radical challenge to marketing ethics as well as to those of other professions. The extent of this demand is perhaps best reflected in the revolutionary features of the computer itself. When compared with other major technical advances such as the printing press, telephone, or automobile, digital media is arguably unique in its capacity for speed, ubiquity and versatility. Computers serve as data collectors, compilers, and disseminators. They represent the fastest-growing form of communication and, through the Internet and similar systems, forge global links of unprecedented proportion.

These factors have created vacuums in ethical policy. Although they do not directly challenge such general ideals as fairness or honesty, digital processes and potentialities are so new that ethics, like many other social endeavors, is only beginning to adapt itself to the *computer revolution*. Currently, a number of critical issues are confronting those who work within electronic environments. These include the ownership of intangible data, often termed, *intellectual property*; the role of privacy in a virtual world without walls, locks, or doors; the extent to which freedom of expression should be allowed; the uses of data, including methods of collection; and the special status of children who log into digital networks.

Easy solutions are seldom achieved within ethics or law and, in electronic contexts, progress is complicated by a lack of comparative historical situations. Likewise, the ability to analogize computers to objects or institutions with which society has had greater experience is often questionable. Is the computer network more like a broadcast station or a printing press or a public library? Our current lack of experience in these matters makes it difficult to say for certain. Finally, the fact that electronic spaces are global in nature accentuates the earlier observation that ethical positions are by no means agreed upon. What is accepted in Europe may be rejected in Asia or America.

The seemingly limitless opportunities afforded by computers also suggests the need for the constant assessment of their implications. Each participant in electronic marketing is given not only the responsibility to adhere to professional codes but also, in a very real sense, the unique opportunity to contribute to these standards in a meaningful way.

The Problem of Self-Regulation

Although law and ethics are frequently directed toward the same goals and often provide mutual assistance in the examination of complex problems, one emerging area of conflict involves the role of formal law in the regulation of online conduct. Throughout its tenure, the Clinton administration expressed a position that the development of the Internet should be largely left to the free operation of the market. Within such a system, the proper behaviors of participants are typically set forth in ethical codes developed by trade associations, commercial standards groups, and the professions.

Supporters of the **self-regulation** model point to the private sector's ability to rapidly identify and resolve problems specific to its areas of competence, particularly when compared to the seemingly confusing, contradictory, and lengthy processes of the law. According to this view, problems encountered within technological environments are particularly amenable to the expertise possessed by market actors. Once consensus is reached, uniformity is achieved through members' compliance with ethical codes as well as by ongoing education of providers and consumers. Although the law cannot normally force participation in these codes, many believe that improved consumer confidence and, consequently, enhanced economic opportunities will ensure voluntary compliance.

Critics of self-regulation argue that its incentives are insufficiently compelling. They note that perpetrators of such activities as fraud and deception frequently benefit from schemes of short duration and are rarely interested in the long-term gains offered by adherence to ethical codes. On a broader level, it has been suggested that commercial self-interest and pressures to maximize profits compromise the private sphere's ability to police itself and that, absent the type of sanctions that only the law can provide, true deterrence will not be achieved.

Although the resolution of this debate is far from over, recent policy-making activities indicate that governments are asserting themselves at least in the area of fraud prevention and in issues involving children's privacy. The Australian Bureau of Consumer Affairs has, for example, stated that a law enforcement role in the prevention of fraud is essential to consumer security. The FTC in the United States has likewise targeted detection and suppression of domestic and international fraud as a priority (Exhibit 5 - 1).

While heightened governmental involvement appears to be an increasing response to many online issues, it is significant to note that lawmakers in the United States and elsewhere have entered into a close dialogue with private entrepreneurs, public interest groups, and commercial associations. Such arguably unprecedented instances of cooperation and sharing of resources suggest that future regulation will take the form of "networked responsibility" among many participants.

Privacy

The concept of **privacy** encompasses both ethical and legal aspects. It is also relatively new to both disciplines. Perhaps more than any other legal or ethical issue, privacy is a product of the twentieth century. While many cultures have possessed customs establishing social boundaries, detailed consideration of this subject did not come about until 1890 when Samuel Warren and future Supreme Court Justice Louis Brandeis published an article that urged the recognition of a right to privacy within American law. This protection was defined as the "right to be left alone" [2]. Significantly, many of the justifications of this new idea were reactions to the phenomena of a maturing industrial and technological age, including the mass distribution of newspapers, the development of listening devices, and the widespread use of photography. In essence, privacy's young tradition has always been about information and the means of its delivery.

Although it has been the subject of constant debate since the Warren and Brandeis article, privacy has proven to be an elusive concept, both ethically and legally. One reason for legal confusion is the lack of any specific privacy provision within the Constitution. This situation was recognized in the U.S. Supreme Court's 1965 decision of *Griswold v. Connecticut* [3], which held that privacy in the use of contraceptives could be inferred from a number of elaborated Constitutional rights, including those of association, freedom from illegal searches and seizures, self-incrimination, and the quartering of soldiers. Later, in the 1973 opinion of *Roe v. Wade* [4], the Court found a privacy right in a woman's reproductive decision making. Through the Fourth Amendment to the United States Constitution, the privacy of the home has been established against governmental agencies that are required to obtain warrants before entering upon and searching a dwelling. This

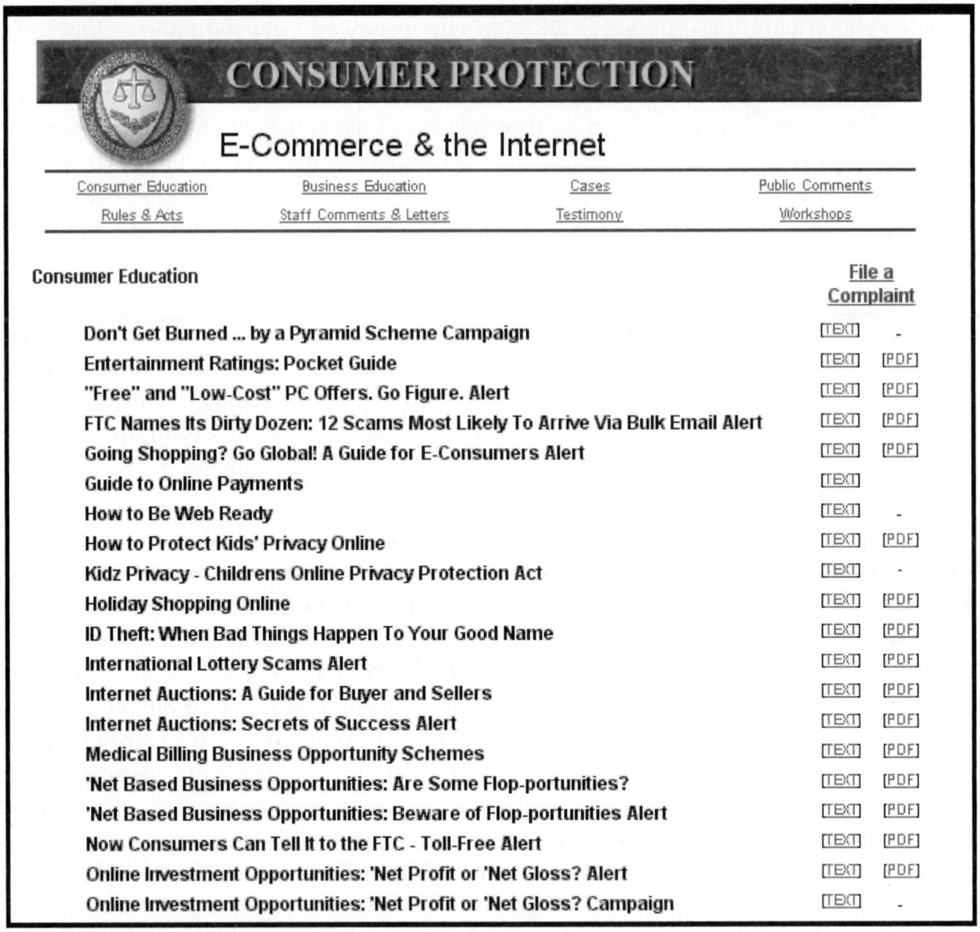

CONSUMER PROTECTION

E-Commerce & the Internet

Consumer Education | Business Education | Cases | Public Comments
Rules & Acts | Staff Comments & Letters | Testimony | Workshops

Consumer Education	File a Complaint	
Don't Get Burned ... by a Pyramid Scheme Campaign	[TEXT]	-
Entertainment Ratings: Pocket Guide	[TEXT]	[PDF]
"Free" and "Low-Cost" PC Offers. Go Figure. Alert	[TEXT]	[PDF]
FTC Names Its Dirty Dozen: 12 Scams Most Likely To Arrive Via Bulk Email Alert	[TEXT]	[PDF]
Going Shopping? Go Global! A Guide for E-Consumers Alert	[TEXT]	[PDF]
Guide to Online Payments	[TEXT]	
How to Be Web Ready	[TEXT]	-
How to Protect Kids' Privacy Online	[TEXT]	[PDF]
Kidz Privacy - Childrens Online Privacy Protection Act	[TEXT]	-
Holiday Shopping Online	[TEXT]	[PDF]
ID Theft: When Bad Things Happen To Your Good Name	[TEXT]	[PDF]
International Lottery Scams Alert	[TEXT]	[PDF]
Internet Auctions: A Guide for Buyer and Sellers	[TEXT]	[PDF]
Internet Auctions: Secrets of Success Alert	[TEXT]	[PDF]
Medical Billing Business Opportunity Schemes	[TEXT]	[PDF]
'Net Based Business Opportunities: Are Some Flop-portunities?	[TEXT]	[PDF]
'Net Based Business Opportunities: Beware of Flop-portunities Alert	[TEXT]	[PDF]
Now Consumers Can Tell It to the FTC - Toll-Free Alert	[TEXT]	[PDF]
Online Investment Opportunities: 'Net Profit or 'Net Gloss? Alert	[TEXT]	[PDF]
Online Investment Opportunities: 'Net Profit or 'Net Gloss? Campaign	[TEXT]	-

Exhibit 5 - 1 Consumer Protection at the FTC
Source: www.ftc.gov.

provision is however, only applicable to officials or those acting on their behalf and not against private individuals.

In addition to Constitutional developments, privacy has been addressed in the *common law.* This term refers to decisions, presumptions, and practices that have traditionally been embraced by Anglo-American courts. The common law has established a series of privacy violations that, individually and together, form the basis of invasion of privacy lawsuits. They are arranged into four categories: unreasonable intrusion into the seclusion of another, unreasonable publicity of another's private life, the appropriation of another's name or likeness, and the publication of another's personal information in a false light. These elements are codified in many state statutes and appear in the influential Restatement of Torts [5].

Despite these developments, much disagreement remains as to what privacy entails. Attributes that have been identified as central fall into three general areas. The first is the Warren and Brandeis concept of a right to be left alone, often referred to as the *seclusion* theory. Privacy within this perspective is the ability to remain isolated from society. This model encourages laws and ethical standards that are oriented toward maintaining personal distance and punishing those who cross the limits set by individuals. An intermediate viewpoint, known as *access control*, does not presume isolation as a norm but places its emphasis upon laws and standards that enable persons to reasonably regulate the information that they are giving up. Expressions of this model can be found in laws and standards that empower individuals to protect personal material from unauthorized release.

While both seclusion and access-control models provide measures of protection, their focus is concerned more with how information is released and less with what actually constitutes private data. A third theory, known as the *autonomy* model attempts to provide such a definition. It does so by identifying private matters as those that are necessary for a person to make life decisions. This entails freedom from the coercive use of personal information as well as the ability to be alone when reflection is necessary.

In addition to difficulties in definition and scope, privacy exists as one value among many. Within society, privacy interests routinely compete against concerns of personal and public safety, economics, and even the social and psychological need for association with others—a process that can require the divulging of sensitive information. The ways in which these interests are coordinated involve complex balances that can result in difficult choices. Often people are willing to give up personal information for benefits that they perceive to be worthwhile—credit cards, frequent flyer mileage, and security precautions in airports are but a few of these situations. In such cases, ethics and law attempt to provide guidelines in the final decision by critically examining definitions, priorities, and implications.

Privacy Within Digital Contexts

Information plays a pivotal role in the concept of privacy as well as that of marketing and electronic commerce. It is, therefore, not surprising that conflicts about how data should be collected and used have developed. A starting point for this discussion is the AMA Code of Ethics for Marketing on the Internet. This states that "information collected from customers should be confidential and used only for expressed purposes." This principle is concise and straightforward in general terms, but it must be applied to the Internet's many information-gathering mechanisms.

In the spring of 2000, the attention of the media, the government, and the public was captured by reports that DoubleClick, an online advertising firm, was engaged in an effort to collect and compile large amounts of personal consumer information. Within the relatively brief history of Internet marketing, DoubleClick has achieved success by establishing a system of over 11,000 Web sites that carry advertising that, when clicked, enables users to visit product sites. The system also records the responses, known as **clickstreams**, within its own databases. Clickstream information is then available to form a user profile, allowing the transmission of individually targeted advertising. Users are not required to give their active consent to this collection. At the time, DoubleClick had reportedly accumulated 100,000 online profiles.

Although privacy advocates had already voiced concern about the system's potential for abuse, the controversy reached a new height when DoubleClick acquired a second company, Abacus-Direct, which specialized in the acquisition of offline consumer data, and had amassed an electronic list that included the names, addresses, and buying histories of a large percentage of American households. With the merger, plans were reported to be underway to integrate data, providing a premium subscription service that would link for the first time these *real-life* identities to DoubleClick's online personalities. Pursuant to this news, an FTC complaint was filed by a coalition of privacy, civil rights, and consumer groups in an effort to prevent the tying of the Abacus information to online profile data and to enjoin the registration of users to the new database without first obtaining each subject's consent.

The most common means by which this type of data is obtained is through the use of cookies. These are packets of data that are created within the hard drive of a user in response to instructions received from a Web page. Once stored, they can be retransmitted from a user's computer to a pertinent Web site. Cookies serve many purposes. For example, they may handle online information, creating such features as shopping baskets to hold purchases. They may recall stored sales information to remind users of items already ordered or to suggest new products. Significantly, other data that may be collected by cookies include full name, email and postal addresses, phone numbers, a computer's geographic location, and time logged online.

Although cookies may be configured within a browser to run only with explicit permission, they are normally automatically executed without any user action. Cookie packets may be combined with other digital information and may be transferred between servers or sold to anyone with the capacity to read computer-generated data. User tracking occurs when cookies are appended and examined in the course of a user's online travels. The result is an ability to pinpoint an individual's online behavior. With the integration of offline data, this tracking will take on a more encompassing and, to some, a more troubling dimension.

The DoubleClick controversy illustrates several significant aspects of the online privacy controversy. Perhaps the most basic reflects the unsettled nature of privacy itself. Many people value privacy as a closely guarded right unto itself. According to this view, the ability to remain secluded from unwelcome intrusion as well as the capability to control the disclosure of personal data must be strongly presumed. This position advocates the implementation of policies that allow individuals to be explicitly informed of any data collection event and to have collection take place only if there is an affirmative decision to participate or opt-in. Supporters of systems such as DoubleClick's argue an opposite presumption that most users wish to receive the benefits of targeted advertising. This position reflects the view that privacy is only one of many values to be balanced. It generally supports an opt-out policy, which presumes that data collection will take place but allows users to withdraw consent by a variety of methods, including sending e-mail to collectors requesting removal from their databases.

Critics of opt-out presumptions point to the fact that most users have no significant knowledge of how computers operate or process data. They question whether the average person will take the steps necessary to withhold data and suggest that many opt-out routines have been found to be confusing and are, thus, unlikely to be successfully accomplished. Proponents of opt-out solutions emphasize consumer surveys that reveal a preference for targeted advertising and argue that the data necessary to provide this service should be collected unless otherwise denied. Although several Congressional bills are pending, no law yet exists to resolve the debate. Similarly, industry has not developed a widely accepted solution to the challenge. Presently, many firms and associations are emphasizing notification as the best approach. Others, such as Real Media Corporation, have developed routines that do not allow the sharing of its visitors' information with other Web Sites.

The DoubleClick matter was partially resolved by the withdrawing of the database integration plans within months of the initial announcement. Attention continued to be focused on the company, and in 2001, pursuant to an investigation, the FTC concluded that no privacy violations had been committed by the company. In the spring of 2002, a remaining group of state and federal class-action privacy suits were settled. The preliminary terms of this agreement are likely to provide a template for contemporary industry standards in consumer privacy. They include the obligation to provide clear notice of data collection, a ban on combining existing data with personal information unless explicit (opt-in) permission is obtained. Moreover, data obtained from cookies will be routinely deleted and new cookies will be programmed to deactivate at five-year intervals. Finally, DoubleClick will initiate an extensive program of consumer privacy education and submit to regular, independent audits. Critics of the settlement point to the relative brevity of its two-year term of enforcement and to the overly generous lifespan given to cookies.

While agreement on the parameters of data collection remains elusive, a recent study indicates that there is a trend toward the reduction of these activities. According to the 2002 report, practices of 100 major commercial sites and 300 sites with lesser traffic reflect a decrease in the collection of personal information as compared with that found two years ago. The study suggests that the decrease can be in part attributed to the greater prominence of privacy policies, more extensive use of opt-in routines, and the recognition within the industry that privacy is a significant consumer concern [6].

In addition to issues of collection, the problem of access to data is of fundamental significance within the context of online privacy. In this area, the status of sensitive information is not only a matter of hardware security but also one of administrative policy. This fact was recently reiterated when, with only an informal request, the United States Navy was able to obtain from America Online the personal user data of a serviceman who was suspected of violating military rules concerning homosexual conduct. The resulting prosecution was later terminated after a court found that the Navy's request had likely violated federal privacy law [7]. An apology and compensation from AOL resulted, but the incident illustrates the risks involved after data leave the control of a user.

The majority of privacy-related debates have focused upon traditional methods of data processing and the recently developed but already well-established use of cookies. Beyond these technologies, there exist cutting-edge applications which promise to gain popularity and to raise additional issues.

Java is a Web-friendly programming language that allows the downloading and running of programs or *applets* on individual computers. These applications are increasingly used to provide such enhancements as dynamic animation, Web-based simulations, and other useful additions to plain hypertext. Java may also be used to design programs known as hostile applets, which can be used to surreptitiously access and transmit data on hard drives, including e-mail addresses, credit card records, and other account information.

Intelligent agents are a growing topic of interest within Web marketing and computer science research. The products of developments in artificial intelligence, **agents** are programs that, once released by a user, can function autonomously within the Web to make electronic decisions. Some potential tasks include the searching of sites or the buying of products that conform to an individual's tastes or interests. Critics of agents worry that the preferences they hold may be chosen or controlled by entities other than their "owner." Such a situation would limit the individual's privacy-linked ability to make autonomous decisions and could create an incentive to distribute personal information contained in the agent applications.

Cookies, Java applets, and intelligent agents are *ubiquitous* **applications;** that is, they are able to function in the course of nearly any online session, without a user's knowledge or control. The ease of their operation can be a persuasive factor in favor of failing to inform a user that data are being collected. This attitude is objectionable when it places technological ease above ethical principles. Similarly, since much of the information is not of an explicitly confidential character, it may be tempting to disregard privacy implications. This argument ignores the fact that even innocent data may, when combined, result in very specific information.

In addition to application-based collection, sites often gather information through online forms and electronic mail. Often, this is done in exchange for browsing privileges or other benefits and with the full disclosure of the terms of use. Regardless of how elicited, the use of information as a form of currency has raised ethical questions, particularly in light of the fact that most average users (as well as information experts) are understandably uncertain of the ultimate value of the data. Although such valuation may indeed be unattainable at this stage of Internet development, consumer education about all uses of revealed data has been suggested as a solution that will at least increase the ability to make informed judgments in this area. Information may also be gathered through explicitly fraudulent methods—an approach that has unambiguous ethical and legal implications.

A particularly active area of study involves the collection of material from children. A 1998 report of the FTC indicates that 89% of the children's sites surveyed collected identifiable user data and 46% of these sites did not reveal their policies of collection or use. Merely 10% of the surveyed sites contained provisions for parental control [8].

In response to research, reports of abuses and lobbying from parents and other advocates, Congress passed the Children's Online Protection Act (COPPA) [9]. This statute requires that Web sites and other online media that knowingly collect information from children 12 years of age or under (1) provide notice to parents; (2) obtain verifiable parental consent prior to the collection, use, or disclosure of most information; (3) allow parents to view and correct this information; (4) enable parents to prevent further use or collection of data; (5) limit personal information collection for a child's participation in games, prize offers, or related activities; and (6) establish procedures that protect the "confidentiality, security, and integrity of the personal information collected." In addition, the FTC has, as required by Congress, enacted specific rules to govern and enforce the act [10] and, in its second year of administration, has instituted a total of six COPPA enforcement actions.

While federal laws relating to Internet privacy remain in debate, many explicit offenses can be addressed by conventional criminal statutes. Sanctions for misuse of consumer data are present in the Fair Credit Reporting Act [11] and the Electronic Communication Privacy Act (ECPA) [12]. Additionally, organizations such as the Direct Marketing Association have developed comprehensive guidelines for Web privacy [13].

The problem of privacy within electronic mail remains an unsettled aspect of online interaction. Under U.S. law, users who operate e-mail accounts on private services are generally assured of their legal privacy through service agreements with their ISP. In addition, the ECPA has been held to address the privacy of ISP clients, with certain exceptions, including situations in which e-mail is inadvertently discovered through system maintenance. The opposite condition applies to employees who use their organizations' computers or networks to communicate. Here, the current law generally extends no expectation of privacy to workers, particular those employed by nongovernmental entities. Many companies emphasize this status in memoranda of policy, but even when such notices are absent, the employee's wisest course of action is to assume that all material that passes through workplace facilities is monitored. Ethical questions remain as to whether strict surveillance policies adequately reflect values of personal autonomy and integrity. The fact that other property such as employer-owned phone systems or dressing rooms cannot be subjected to unlimited monitoring suggest that as computer-based communication develops, pressure will be applied to reevaluate worker's electronic privacy in light of social practices.

International Privacy Issues

On an international level, privacy issues have received close attention. On October 15, 1998, the European Union's (EU) Data Protection Directive [14] took effect, requiring its member states to enact national laws to protect "fundamental rights and freedoms of natural persons, and in particular their right to privacy with respect to the processing of personal data." Among its provisions, the directive requires that subjects be apprised of how their data are used and be given opportunities to review and correct information; that data use be restricted to the announced purpose; that the origin of data be disclosed, if known; that procedures to punish illegal activities be established; that consumer collection contain opt-out capabilities; that sensitive data collection cannot be accomplished without explicit permission and that any international transfer of data be executed only with countries possessing adequate privacy protection laws.

In March 2000, after extensive negotiation, the U.S. Department of Commerce and the European Commission reached agreement that U.S. organizations would submit to a series of **safe harbor** provisions for the protection of EU citizen data. These provisions essentially reflect the directive's emphases upon notice about collection, purpose, and use; choice in ability to opt-out of disclosure and third-party dissemination—including a requirement of affirmative permission in matters involving sensitive personal data; third-party transfer protection; and provisions for security, data integrity, redress, and enforcement [15]. Companies participating in data transactions with the EU can fulfill the safe harbor provisions by allowing the U.S. government to monitor compliance, by affiliating with a self-regulatory group under FTC supervision, by reporting directly to EU data protection agencies, or if not currently online, by promising to work with a EU privacy panel. A criticism of this plan focuses upon its reliance upon private compliance. Critics are particularly worried that without active governmental supervision, the aims of the safe harbor plan may largely be unfulfilled. In 2002, the European Commission issued a report on the safe harbor agreement process, affirming the establishment of required procedures, but expressing concern that some U.S. corporate policies and dispute resolution processes have failed to meet expectations [16].

Although approaches to the electronic privacy challenge vary and promise to remain debated far into the future, the following norms, identified by the FTC [17] appear to represent the present consensus regarding the minimum requirements essential to the ethical use of consumer information (Exhibit 5 - 2):

1. **Notice**: Users should be aware of a site's information policy <u>before</u> data are collected.

2. **Consent**: Users should be allowed to choose participation or exclusion from the collection.

3. **Access**: Users should have the ability to access their data and correct them if erroneous.

4. **Security**: Policies to ensure the integrity of data and the prevention of misuse should be in place.

5. **Enforcement**: Users should have effective means to hold data collectors to their policies.

Exhibit 5 - 2 FTC Monitors Online Privacy
Source: www.ftc.gov.

Digital Property

A primary function of law is to define ownership and here the law's goal of consistency is currently being challenged by digital technology. Traditionally, the law has protected intangible or intellectual property through three basic mechanisms. **Copyright** addresses the realm of ideas—specifically, the right to publish or duplicate the expressions of these ideas. *Patent* law is centered upon inventions and the ability to reproduce or manufacture an inventor's product. **Trademark** is concerned with images, symbols, words, or other indicators that are registered with the government and have become positively associated with a product's identity in the market. It is important to note that these categories have never been inflexible and often the boundaries between them have been modified by legislation and the courts. In addition, international treaties can redefine both distinctions and protections.

Computer-based communication has posed particularly difficult problems for intellectual property. For instance, the electronic medium by which messages are carried can properly be thought of as inventions that would classically be protected by patent law. On the other hand, the messages are also expressions of ideas—the subject of copyright law. Similarly, graphical and animation objects are both inventive creations and expressive. They may also reasonably be deemed to be associated with a commercial entity and trademark becomes a consideration.

Copyright

At this comparatively early stage of online legal development, it appears that copyright has been established as the primary means of protecting most expression on the Internet, including text and other data. In the conventional world, copyright has protected expressions of ideas in such formats as books, recordings, and film. Under American law, it is derived from the Constitution as a protection that is established for the benefit of the public and, within jurisprudence, it has been applied with certain limitations that have been created for the public's benefit. Chief among these are the doctrines of fair use and of first sale [18]. Fair use consists of the ability to copy without cost reasonable portions of protected material for purposes relating to such public activities as education, news reporting, and editorial comment. Under conventional law, the doctrine of first sale limits the ability of a copyright holder to obtain profit from the sale of his or her work after the initial time at which the material is sold. Purchasers are subsequently given the ability to transfer or otherwise dispose of their copy. The first sale doctrine is viewed as benefiting such institutions as public libraries and can also increase access to intellectual material through discounts such as those offered by used bookstores.

In 1997, President Clinton signed the **No Electronic Theft Act** [19]. The **NET Act** confers copyright protection for computer content and imposes sanctions when infringement is committed for commercial or private financial gain or by the reproduction or distribution of one or more copies of copyrighted works having $1,000 or more in retail value. Punishment under this provision may include criminal prosecution. While proponents believe that the NET Act will encourage innovation by protecting material placed on the Internet, critics believe that the definition of *infringement* has been made problematically broad by shifting its traditional meaning, which is normally associated with permanent or semipermanent reproduction (known as fixing), to now include electronic distribution without reproduction. It is argued that such acts could include the mere perusal of digital material through a Web browser and, thus, make criminal activities that have hitherto been protected by the First Amendment. Additional criticism has been directed to the use of criminal sanctions, particularly at a time when there is great debate about the economic value of electronic material.

A related law, enacted in 1998, is the **Digital Millennium Copyright Act** [20]. The **DMCA** is a complex piece of legislation that contains several provisions. It grants Internet service providers (ISPs) protection from acts of user infringement as long as certain procedures are followed, including the prompt reporting and disabling of infringing material. Supporters of this legislation claim that the DMCA will free ISPs from liability for its users' illegal actions and, thus, encourage industry growth. Critics believe that the reporting and disabling requirements may cause innocent behavior to be presumed infringing and wrongfully censored.

The DMCA also criminalizes the circumvention of software protections and the development or distribution of circumvention products [21]. As with the NET Act, DMCA supporters believe that this law will increase commercial willingness to place material on the Internet by deterring online piracy. Although some exceptions exist for educational and scientific activities, critics maintain that the DMCA goes well beyond this goal by banning the development of innocent and useful applications that may have minor circumvention capabilities, giving copyright holders a veto over any development that they perceive as a challenge to their profits [22].

The DMCA was enacted in part to comply with the World Intellectual Property Organization's (WIPO) Copyright Treaty and the WIPO Performances and Phonograms Treaty [23]. These documents set forth international standards for copyrighted material and were recently ratified by the United States. Treaty proponents argue that in a global networked environment international consensus regarding ownership, protection, and transfer of digital property is essential. As with the DMCA, critics worry that the specific laws required by the treaties will unfairly favor copyright owners.

Trademarks

Trademark law is concerned with the ownership of intellectual property that identifies goods or services. Under the federal **Lanham Act** [24], trademarks may be registered with the government, but whether registered or not, they may be protected under the act. In order to pursue an infringement case, claimants must prove that the mark is *protectable*. Generally, the more distinctive the mark, the greater the strength of this claim. The act also prohibits **dilution**—the diminishment of the ability to identify or distinguish a good or service.

Trademark law has recently been applied to the Internet naming system. Domains are unique configurations of letters or numbers that are used to route data. The most familiar examples of domains are addresses of Web sites, for example, www.someplace.com. In addition to designating Web sites, domain names are also used in e-mail addresses. As the primary means to reach commercial destinations, the significance of these identifiers is obvious.

Although the creative application of language provides for many distinctive names, it is inevitable that some similarity will occur. For example, "General Signpost" can plausibly be thought to resemble "General Sign," but traditionally trademark law has been able to allow such similarities because, among other factors, it looks to the type of business, product, and geographic locality. When there is enough dissimilarity within these factors, a certain redundancy is permitted. In the online world, however, geography is not a factor and name similarities may not be as easily distinguishable. Thus, on the basis of trademark infringement, the owner of the mark eToys.com successfully obtained a court order restraining the operation of etoy.com, a site set up by performance artists who parody corporate behavior. The suit was subsequently settled before the continuation of litigation.

Another type of trademark violation is known as **cybersquatting.** This activity involves the registration of domains that resemble or duplicate the names of existing corporations or other entities. The initial registrants are typically unrelated to the institution at issue. The domain is then offered for sale at a price set significantly higher than that originally paid. On November 29, 1999, President Clinton signed the Anticybersquatting Consumer Protection Act [25]. Under this law, a person is liable to suit if in bad faith, he registers, traffics, or sells a domain bearing a name that is identical or confusingly similar to a protected mark or would dilute the worth of the mark. As a national law, the act makes it easier to place notoriously elusive cybersquatters under the control of the court system and allows for swift possession by a successful complainant of the disputed domain name. Heralded by trademark holders, the Act has received criticism similar to that lodged against the DCMA, specifically, that the swiftness of the transfer of contested domain names may unfairly deprive a defendant of a proper hearing and due process.

Metatags are HTML statements that describe a Web site's contents. They are not normally displayed by browsers. They allow search engines to identify sites relevant to topics of their inquiries. Accordingly, these tags can provide a valuable means of attracting users to a site. Since metatags are defined by HTML authors, it is possible to insert words or phrases that are calculated to provide optimal attractiveness, including material protected by trademark. In a matter involving Playboy Enterprises, Inc., the defendant included in its metatags the protected words "Playboy" and "Playmate." In the subsequent suit, the court found that the intent of the site was to profit from a false association with Playboy and prohibited the inclusion, stating that dilution of the trademarks had occurred as a result [26]. This outcome should be contrasted with another recent matter in which a former Playmate of the Year included similar terms within her site, albeit repeatedly noting that she was not presently associated with Playboy Enterprises. Here, the use was upheld, with the court holding that trademarks may be fairly cited when applied in good faith, as in the accurate description of goods or identity [27].

A variation of the metatag problem is found in the practice of assigning **keywords** within search engines. In one case, the cosmetic manufacturer, Estee Lauder, sued Excite and others, alleging that the entry of its trademarked name at the Excite Shopping Channel would direct users to the site of a specific, unlicensed dealer [28]. In addition to deception, Estee Lauder claimed that the practice diluted its trademark. The case was subsequently settled with Estee Lauder reacquiring control over its name. The selling of trademark-protected keywords has also been claimed to occur at other Web portals where these words or phrases trigger banner advertising that is not sanctioned by or directed to the trademark holder.

In addition to word appropriation, trademark has been implicated in matters involving use of hyperlinks. Although the Web has flourished with its abilities to seamlessly transfer information from site to site, some entities have become concerned that links that take users to areas other than their introductory page may cause confusion or deprive the target sites of revenue obtained through the selling of advertising. Such *deep linking* was the subject of litigation when Microsoft's Seattle Sidewalk created deep links to city-specific event sales within a site run by Ticketmaster. Here, Ticketmaster claimed that the practice diluted Ticketmaster trademarks and constituted unfair competition. Microsoft countered that the placement of any material within public areas of the Web would make it open to access. These contrasting theoretical positions were never subjected to final court ruling as the case was ultimately settled with Microsoft agreeing to link only to Ticketmaster's primary entry page [29].

Related to linking is the practice of *framing,* a process in which a Web browser is instructed to divide itself into two or more partitions and load within a section material obtained from another Web site through the execution of an automatic link. In *Washington Post v. TotalNEWS, Inc.*, suit was filed over the use of a collage of frames, some linked to the *Post*, within a page dedicated to a sampling of news on the Web. Among other things, the *Post* alleged that the unattributed displays diluted trademarks, appropriated copyrighted material, and deprived the *Post* of advertising revenue [30]. The matter was settled before decision with TotalNEWS agreeing to use only nonframed, attributed textual links to the *Post*.

Patents

The application of patent law to computing is an uncertain but developing field. Under conventional American law, **patents** are granted by the U.S. government for inventive processes or steps [31]. Grounded in English legal foundations and the heritage of conventional invention, the law is tailored toward industrial or mechanical concerns. Currently, creators of software are attempting to make use of its protections. A primary motivation for this preference may lie in the fact that unlike copyrighted matter, during its duration, patented material is not subject to acquisition through the doctrines of fair use or first sale; however, like copyright, American patent powers are derived from constitutional concerns and, thus, public access to patented material is assured after the term of the patent has expired and the patent itself is always on file with the government.

The inclusion of software under patent law is largely based upon the assertion that programs describe inventive processes. A contrary opinion holds that software at its root consists of algorithms—formulas that are generic in nature and, therefore, cannot be owned by anyone. A similar criticism states that programs are merely schemes or plans that machines actually execute. The details of both sides' arguments are complex and promise to be the subject of much future debate, litigation, and, perhaps, Congressional action. An area of current Internet focus centers upon the use of *business patents* that describe such activities as marketing approaches and methods for conducting commerce. Presently, patent protection is being claimed for reverse online auctions, secure credit card processing, and incentive-based methods for reading Web site advertising.

An example of the attempted enforcement of a software patent is found in the claim that secure digital time-stamping is a unique and protected process. Critics fear that if this assertion is upheld, the majority of online encryption routines will be affected. Similarly, in *Amazon.com v. Barnesandnoble.com*, the plaintiff relied upon a patent to allege that it alone had the ability to use *1-Click* ordering routines—a now common practice within the Internet [32]. The matter was settled in 2002, without final judicial resolution and with the details of the terms left undisclosed.

The U.S. Patent Office has recently decided to increase the rigor with which it reviews applications for software-related protection (Exhibit 5 - 3). Likewise, both courts and Congress are being called upon to carefully examine whether historical data support the inclusion of software and business practices within a patent's ambit. Advocates of inclusion argue that the granting of patents in these areas will encourage productivity and innovation. Critics argue the opposite, stating that both the encryption matter as well as the unanswered issues of the *Amazon* case point to the potentially stifling and monopolistic effects of patent law's strong protections.

Licenses

An increasingly popular method of intellectual property protection involves the use of **licenses**. These instruments consist of contractual agreements made between consumers and software vendors, which allow the buyer to use the product but restrict duplication or distribution. Since laws related to licenses are derived from the commercially oriented law of contract, rather than through the constitutionally related realm of copyright or patent, public policy exceptions have traditionally played a less important role in its development. Moreover, because it is assumed that parties to contractual agreements bargain under conditions of informed self-interest, licenses may contain waivers of many protections normally found in consumer transactions.

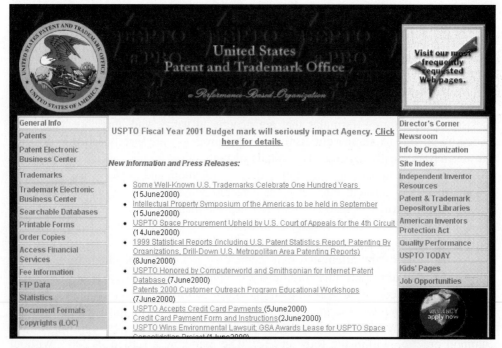

Exhibit 5 - 3 United States Patent Office Reviews Patent Applications
Source: www.uspto.gov.

Within the computer environment, a great deal of attention has been paid to the validity of licenses appearing upon or within software. Variations of this format are often known as **shrinkwrap** or *break-the-seal* licenses (when appearing outside of software) and **clickwrap** licenses when a user is required to click a button within a program to demonstrate acceptance of terms. While common to conventional business situations, the extent to which licenses with noncommercial purchasers will be enforced by the courts is not entirely clear. This is primarily due to the lack of bargaining that takes place between the user and the seller. Normally, a contract requires that an agreement can be demonstrated and it is not certain that average buyers agree to or even read the fine print that appears on their diskettes, boxes, installation routines, or software manuals.

The legal trend seems to favor enforcement of software licenses. In a recent case, a court upheld a shrinkwrap term that limited the vendor's liability for errors within the program [33]. In another case, a court found enforceable a clickwrap term that dictated the state in which a suit against the vendor could be brought [34].

A broad effort to enforce the terms of software licenses comes in the form of the **Uniform Computer Information Transactions Act (UCITA)**. If adopted by the states, this model would govern all legal agreements pertaining to software transactions, including sales. Supported by the majority of software manufacturers and publishers as a measure of legal uniformity, critics argue that UCITA will enforce license provisions including those restricting copying and resale of material, liability for damages incurred from defective software, and, it has been suggested, the ability to criticize software performance. Because UCITA applies to any material in computer-readable form, including electronic books and other reading matter, librarians and educators fear it will effectively remove the public policy protections of copyright and patent, making online information expensive and restricted.

To date, only Virginia and Maryland have adopted UCITA. In 2001, the attorneys general of 32 states and two territories stated their opposition to the act and in 2002 a task force of the American Bar Association issued a call for its redrafting. As the debate continues, it will be important to consider that, while intellectual property laws can act as incentives to create useful material, they can also work to restrict the data exchange that has contributed to the Internet's popularity. The achieving of a balance between both concerns will be an important and continuing task for digital law and ethics.

Trade Secrets

The field of trade secrecy has taken on new proportions with the advent of online technology. The federal Economic Espionage Act of 1996 [35] was enacted in part to address digital advances and now makes it a criminal offense to divulge trade secrets, which are broadly defined to include such areas as commercial, scientific and technical endeavors. Trade secrets can include, but are not restricted to, formulas, market data, algorithms, programs, codes, and models. They may be stored online or in tangible formats. Significantly, computer-based disclosures such as e-mails, downloads, Web publication, and similar means are within the ambit of the act.

Employees possessing trade secrets may be prohibited from engaging in similar businesses for a period of time. In one notable case, a court determined that an employee's particular skills in Web marketing were sufficiently protected under a noncompetition agreement with a former employer to prevent him from working for a competitor within a one-year period following his departure from a company [36].

Data Ownership

It is not overstatement to say that the online world runs on data. Not surprisingly, access and ownership questions relating to data and databases animate current legal and ethical debate. As the electronic market becomes more competitive, measures are being increasingly undertaken to obtain the advantages that control of information can provide.

Until recently, much data relating to such technical issues as Web site usage have been easy to access and, under informal practices, have often been shared among site owners, marketing professionals, advertisers, and consumers. Currently, a new technology is being introduced that would make information collected from banner advertisements invisible to site owners and their clients. These *click data* have been important in determining such factors as site content and marketing strategy. Protective technologies, thus, raise new issues concerning the ownership of information that is both a necessary element of online interaction and of extreme value in itself. Particularly significant will be the question of whether the *fencing in* of data will achieve the same status as that achieved through the more formal means of copyright, patent, trademark, or licensing laws. In the process, also challenged is a model of cooperation that has in the past been a characteristic of online dynamics, and arguably, a primary reason for the success of the interactive digital medium.

Another complex issue involving online data is an activity known as **spidering**. This process involves the use of software applications known as *robots* to enter targeted Web sites and obtain data for the use of its owner. In a recent matter, the online auction site, eBay, instituted an action against Bidder's Edge, which operated a service that presented comparative auction information through spidering. The information collected from eBay was unprotected by copyright. Advocates of eBay's claimed state that the use of the data generated by their efforts constitutes unfair competition and dilutes the worth of their business. They also maintained that the spidering activity constituted a trespass to property, creating the potential for impairment to the eBay system. Proponents of Bidder's Edge expressed concern that if data are cordoned off from the rest of the online community, the presently information-rich Internet will increasingly become a *gated community* where actions in trespass will become the predominant means of enforcing boundaries. The matter was settled before judgment on the merits. Significantly, the court sustained eBay's request for a preliminary injunction of Bidder's Edge activity based upon the trespass claim [37].

A final area of consideration is that of the special protection of data relating to facts. As previously noted, American copyright law protects *expressions* of ideas but not the ideas themselves. This is due to the public policy emphasis of protecting the raw material of free expression and national learning. For similar reasons, copyright cannot be used to protect facts. Since electronic databases often contain arrangements of facts, there is a movement within the law to offer protection for specially compiled or *sui generis* data.

The Trade Related Intellectual Property Rights (TRIPs) Agreement of 1995 is part of the World Trade Organization's (WTO) program of international treaties. Provisions exist within this Agreement to afford sui generis protection. Likewise, the EU's Database Directive [38] includes protection for compiled facts. Currently, Congress has not adopted a sui generis law; however, pressure is mounting to bring American law within this paradigm.

The foundation for arguments favoring sui generis protection revolve around the belief that this type of protection will afford an incentive for database vendors to create more of their products by assuring producers that their investments will be recouped and that their product will not be copied or diluted. In the long run, it is believed that society will be benefited by the increase and that it would result in a consequent decrease in the price of information.

Critics of these laws argue that there is no economic proof that such incentives will produce an increase in databases or that, with an increase, prices would necessarily come down. Instead, they state that worries about copying and dilution can be addressed through encryption and similar methodologies. In the balance, they claim that sui generis protection could stifle innovation by the erection of legal barriers and lead to a monopolization of the basis for all education and learning. Also troubling is the fact that many current proposals allow a virtually infinite term under which data could be kept out of the public domain. Under American law, the settlement of these issues will necessarily involve a close examination of the reasons underlying the Constitutional aversion to the ownership of facts, and in so doing, will raise ultimately ethical questions about whether facts are merely commodities or are so valuable that exclusive control can never be granted to one individual.

Online Expression

The mass distribution of unsolicited electronic mail or **spam** has been the subject of much complaint within the online world. The practice has been criticized on many levels. Internet service providers point to the burdens that spamming places upon network resources. As spam is, by definition, unrequested, users complain of unwanted intrusion into their affairs. Privacy-related worries are not restricted to transmission alone. Much spam is derived from mailing lists that are collected from e-mail addresses posted to such locations as Web bulletin boards or the USENET without any intention to participate in mass mailings. Similarly, many users are disturbed to find that information given to individuals or entities for one purpose may be collected and sold for mass distribution. The frustration with spam is further compounded by the fact that often these messages are sent without valid return addresses or other contact information.

Although spam has been the subject of much justified criticism, there is also some reason to approach its regulation with caution. Primary to this concern is the fact that the topic implicates freedom of expression, which in America is a right protected under the First Amendment to the Constitution. A recent statement by the Direct Marketing Association's President and CEO H. Robert Wientzen acknowledged that most reputable marketing professionals reject spam as an inappropriate means of consumer contact but also voiced concern that ill-conceived, blanket restrictions on bulk e-mail could pose a threat to expression and endanger the future of more sophisticated, responsibly targeted electronic messages.

The AMA Code of Ethics for Marketing on the Internet also addresses the spam problem by stating that "the expressed wishes of others should be respected with regard to the receipt of unsolicited e-mail messages." Disagreement remains between those who believe that participation in mass e-mails should be restricted to those who voluntarily agree to receive mailings and those who advocate an opt-out-only approach. Currently, the DMA has established such an opt-out list for those who seek to avoid mass emailings. While certainly a progressive step, critics point to the fact that only DMA members are obligated to respect this list and also worry that, like other opt-out systems, complexity and difficulty will prevent many average users from participation.

Within the law, spam has become a major issue. In the case of *Cyber Promotions, Inc. v. America Online, Inc.* [39], the court held that a spam producer had no First Amendment right to send its product to AOL subscribers and that consequently, the ISP could block its messaging activity. Similarly, a court has ruled that spamming activity violated the federal Computer Fraud and Abuse Act [40]. On the state level, Washington has enacted antispam legislation, which targets deceptive bulk messages directed to the state's residents or originating from a computer located within the jurisdiction. Washington's highest tribunal has upheld the statute's constitutionality. In an action likely to encourage antispam legislation in other states, the United States Supreme Court has recently declined to review this decision [41].

Criticism of products or industries has also been addressed within and without the spam context. In one case, a court prohibited an individual from sending mass e-mails to a corporation's employees complaining of employment violations. The trial court reasoned that corporate e-mail does not resemble traditional places of commentary and should, therefore, not be treated as public forums. The decision was affirmed by a California appellate court on the basis of trespass to property, but the matter continues to be litigated as the state supreme court has recently agreed to review the matter [42]. Less specific mailings may also be restricted through terms of service agreements. A recent Canadian decision has enforced such a contract that prohibited spam activity by the ISP's users [43].

Since the inception of ISPs, a question has arisen about the liability of network owners for defamatory messages posted on its bulletin boards or other public areas. Although most courts have adopted the view that like publishers, ISPs are not normally susceptible to suit, Congress has resolved the problem by placing this immunity within federal law [44]. The primary reason for this provision has been identified as a fear that if liability were at issue, a provider would be required to actively monitor and censor activity within its service, thus decreasing the level of free expression. The significance of this policy has been poignantly demonstrated when a court determined that an ISP could not be held liable for negligently publishing anonymous, allegedly false and defamatory statements concerning an individual's profiteering from the Oklahoma City bombings [45]. In contrast, an English decision has held that ISPs are indeed liable for defamatory material when notice of the defamatory content exists [46]. Commentators worry that within the United Kingdom, increased censorship will be a result if this position is left unchanged.

The issue of expression directed to children remains a highly visible issue within online law and ethics. In 1996, the federal Telecommunications Act of 1934 was amended to include the Computer Decency Act (CDA), which in relevant part made it a criminal act to send an "obscene or indecent" communication to a recipient who was known to the sender to be under 18 years of age. An additional provision made it an offense to use an interactive computer service to present material that "depicts or describes, in terms patently offensive, as measured by contemporary community standards, sexual or excretory organs" in a context available to minors. In 1997, in the case of *Reno v. American Civil Liberties Union* [47], the U.S. Supreme Court found that these provisions were unconstitutionally vague, prohibiting, among other things, the exchange of information about such subjects as AIDS and reproductive decision making. It further noted that the provisions would hinder or *chill* adult speech through the placement of undue burdens.

Although the broad regulatory attempts of the CDA failed, there are a number of efforts underway to provide more narrowly tailored regulations for children's content. In addition, the use of filtering models has been considered. Perhaps the best- known program is the Platform for Internet Content Selection Rules (PICS). This application allows the filtering of sites that are deemed to be inappropriate for minors. Advocates claim that PICS will place control into the hands of parents and schools. Some civil rights groups are concerned that this device, which works behind the scenes, presents a subtle but powerful means of censorship.

In December 2000, Congress passed the Children's Internet Protection Act (CIPA). The legislation links federal funding to libraries with the use of filtering software in public Internet terminals. In May 2002, after hearing extensive evidence, a federal judicial panel invalidated the act, stating that blocking software cannot adequately guarantee that only material harmful to minors would be screened [48]. The decision is being directly appealed to the United States Supreme Court.

These examples strongly suggest that the boundaries of expression will continue to be challenged by the Internet. While specific outcomes remain open to question, it appears that expression will be protected when the courts and the legislatures realize the purpose and importance of electronic communication. Education of all parties involved may prove to be the best security for the continued flourishing of online speech.

Emerging Issues

Along with the more conventional problems of online dynamics, a number of issues have arisen that are particularly unique to the Internet at its current stage of development. Based upon the astounding success of digital communication, the responses to these challenges will require the same levels of imagination and creativity demonstrated in the Internet's creation.

Online Governance and ICANN

In 1998, the U.S. Department of Commerce called for the creation of a private, non-profit regulatory body that would be responsible for the administration of the Internet name and address system. In response, the **Internet Corporation for Assigned Names and Numbers (ICANN)** was formed. Ideally, the purpose of ICANN revolves around the resolution of conflicts that surround the assignment and possession of domains. Today, ICANN is comprised of a governing board that currently faces substantial criticism for operating under secrecy and for failing to represent the broad range of online users. While many of these problems may be attributed to the newness of this endeavor, there remain many questions concerning the ability of any private regulatory organization to enforce its decisions within the online community. Along these lines, it has been suggested that parties to serious disputes will attempt to bypass ICANN or other arbitration arrangements in favor of the conventional enforcement abilities of legal forums, through such vehicles as trademark infringement suits.

Jurisdiction

The establishment of ICANN reflects the growing awareness that online controversies transcend physical boundaries. **Jurisdiction** is the legal term that describes the ability of a court or other authority to gain control over a party. Jurisdiction is traditionally based upon physical presence, but within the online world commonality of physical location is never assured. Similarly, attempts to exercise jurisdiction within the geographic territories of other nations or states will most likely be rebuffed.

The majority of cases decided within the United States have focused upon the character and quality of contacts with the forum state; generally, the more active the involvement, the more likely that jurisdiction will be conferred. Thus, jurisdiction over online activity was found where the court determined that an out-of-state defendant had knowingly and purposefully done business within the state of suit [49]. In contrast, another court has found that mere advertising within a state will not, without more, subject the advertiser to jurisdiction [50]. A similar decision held that the ability to access a Web site within a particular state does not subject the site owner to jurisdiction [51]. As previously mentioned, digital licensing agreements that have defined the jurisdiction in which suit may be brought have been upheld.

In addition to conventional legal tribunals, such mediation-oriented programs as **Virtual Magistrate** [52] have been developed to resolve online disputes. These programs often attempt to tailor their procedures toward the special circumstances of the Internet. Advocates of these approaches argue that their online orientation will encourage users to work out difficulties within a nonconfrontational framework. Critics voice concerns that online arbitration cannot adequately ensure enforcement or recognition of their judgments.

The previously mentioned cases have dealt exclusively with American jurisdictional questions. Although difficult problems are presented, they are arguably of less complexity than those involving international disputes. One method aimed at achieving a level of international cooperation is through the mediation of organizations. For example, the WIPO Arbitration and Mediation Center [53] exists to resolve commercial disputes relating to intellectual property.

Supranational organizations such as the EU may also regulate disputes between their members. Likewise, treaties may provide for international resolution and enforcement. The Model Law on Electronic Commerce by the United Nations Commission of International Trade Law (UNCITRAL) has been established to provide for global uniformity in digital commerce. This developing collection of laws addresses such matters as digital signatures, electronic documentation, sales of digital goods, contracts, exchanges of information, and credit records. The force of such model laws can be felt through their actual adoption or through the pressure that they can exert upon national legislatures and other organizations to conform their activities to international standards. Although acceptance of jurisdiction cannot be forced upon noncooperating countries, the existence of international agreements concerning key questions weighs heavily in favor of the mutual enforcement of obligations.

Fraud

The use of deception and false claims to obtain profit is, of course, not unique to the Internet. However, the nature of online dynamics has introduced several factors which impact upon prevention efforts. The first general factor relates to the technical nature of networked communication. The average person is not in a position to understand exactly how information is displayed, transferred, or stored and this lack of knowledge provides opportunities for novel deceptions. Included within this category are the use of e-mail or Web sites to impersonate individuals or corporations. This activity, known as **spoofing,** is often used to extract sensitive information by leading a user to believe that a request is coming from a reputable source, such as an ISP or credit card company. Other common swindles have involved the use of programs that secretly dial long-distance locations for the purpose of sharing in the resulting fees paid by the unknowing user or the use of false login pages that record account information.

A second factor involves the psychology of digital environments. The media is full of stories concerning technological advances and opportunities for profit. Unfortunately, many people are unable to differentiate genuinely worthwhile endeavors from those presented by mere opportunists. Messages originating from the online world are likely to be viewed by some as having an air of authority, solely due to their association with the digital revolution. Many investment opportunities make use of this rhetoric, often promoting breakthrough technologies and applications.

The problem of consumer **fraud** is being addressed on several dimensions. Federal agencies such as the FTC and the FBI have increased their efforts to track and prosecute fraudulent conduct (Exhibit 5 - 4). Likewise, many state agencies have begun to prosecute criminal activity within their borders. The range of sanctions available includes stipulated lifetime bans in the conduct of Internet commerce, civil judgments, forfeiture of property, and referrals for criminal prosecution. A recent FTC action report lists 140 cases pursued against over 490 companies involving the Internet and other online services [54]. Similar initiatives have been undertaken by authorities of other countries.

Although the establishment and prosecution of laws are necessary responses to the problem of fraud, it remains true that the Internet's global reach frustrates even the most comprehensive of enforcement plans. While law must frequently play a reactive role, conditions intrinsic to online dynamics create unique opportunities for marketing professionals to affect potential victims of fraud through education and certification.

The basis of fraud is usually incomplete or false information. A consumer's ability to evaluate online material is, thus, of primary importance. Promotion and adherence to codes of ethics, such as those promulgated by the AMA, are one means of inspiring consumer confidence. Codes may include requirements that members refrain from doing business with questionable clients or third parties. Many online and real-world businesses, particularly those within the finance and credit industry, require that their licensees follow strict legal and ethical protocols and may withdraw affiliation in cases of violation.

As previously discussed, a weakness of purely private regulation is the potential for conflicts of interest or less than rigorous enforcement of rules. Recent revelations of unpunished violations by members of eTrust, the Internet's largest non-governmental privacy watchdog, have caused many to wonder if industry-based enforcement is truly possible.

Another method of particular relevance to ethical online transactions is the encouragement of general consumer education. Professional associations have particular abilities to establish sites that outline and explain minimum standards and consumer protections. They may also serve as clearinghouses, reporting unethical or illegal conduct. Even within the information-rich environment of the Internet, online knowledge continues to be a need without limits.

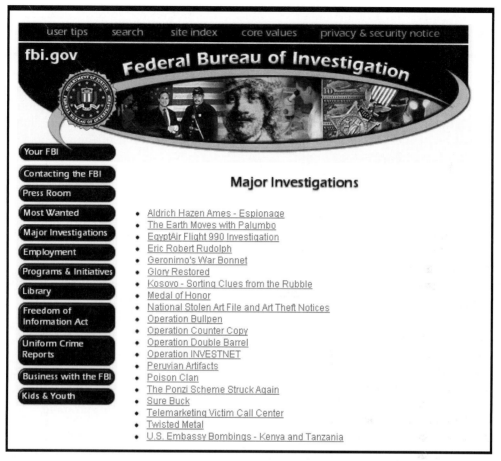

Exhibit 5 - 4 FBI Investigates Online Fraud
Source: www.fbi.gov.

Conclusion

Changes within the ethical and legal framework of networked communication are occurring with a swiftness equal to the technical, economic, and social transformations that this medium has brought about. As critical participants within the online world, marketing professionals will not only be required to remain well informed of regulations and accepted practices but also will be increasingly called upon to contribute to the global dialogue about electronic spaces.

Summary

Ethics is concerned with the values and practices of professionals and experts as well as the concerns and values of society. Law is also an expression of values but created for the broader goal of addressing national or even global populations. Groups of individuals with special skills or knowledge have established ethical codes over the years. Differing views exist of the role of law and self-regulation in ethical online behavior.

Privacy emerged during the twentieth century as a key ethical and legal concern. Key aspects include seclusion, access control, and autonomy. Online privacy issues in the United States and other countries relate to how data should be collected and used. U.S. firms can participate in a safe harbor plan to protect data from European Union Internet users. The FTC set forth five norms for ethical use of consumer information, including provisions for user notice, consent, access, security, and enforcement.

Intangible or intellectual property is protected through three basic legal mechanisms: copyright (covering ideas), patent law (covering inventions), and trademark (covering images, symbols, words, or other indicators associated with a product's market identity). Companies can license their products to allow their use while restricting duplication or distribution. Companies are concerned about legal protection for trade secrets and about the ownership of information such as Web site content, usage data, and facts. Online expression issues include concerns about spam, criticisms of products or industries, and expression directed to children. Three emerging legal and ethical issues are online governance, jurisdiction, and fraud.

Key Terms

Agents	Licenses
Clickstreams	Metatags
Clickwrap	No Electronic Theft Act (NET)
Copyright	Patents
Cybersquatting	Privacy
Digital Millennium Copyright Act (DMCA)	Safe harbor
Dilution	Self-regulation
Ethics	Shrinkwrap
Fraud	Spam
Internet Corporation for Assigned Names and Numbers (ICANN)	Spidering
Jurisdiction	Spoofing
	Trademark

Keywords	Ubiquitous applications
Lanham Act	Uniform Computer Information
Law	Transactions Act (UCITA)
	Virtual Magistrate

Exercises

Review Questions

1. Define ethics and law and show how they are different and similar.
2. What are some of the threats to Internet user privacy?
3. According to the FTC, what are the minimum requirements for ethical use of consumer information?
4. How does copyright differ from patent and trademark law?
5. What does it mean to clickwrap a license?
6. What are the NET Act and the DMCA?
7. What is the doctrine of first sale? How should it be applied online?
8. What is the doctrine of fair use and how should it be applied online?
9. What is safe harbor and why is it important for U.S. companies doing business in Europe?

Discussion Questions

10. Is it better to regulate industry via laws or let industry self-regulate? Support your claim.
11. Which is more ethically problematic: attacking a former employer via online discussion or making the same attack by e-mailing current employees?
12. Deep linking takes place regularly over the Internet. Anytime you make a Web page that links to another site and bypasses the home page of that site you are deep linking. Should this be allowed? Explain your position.
13. Framing takes place regularly over the Internet. To see an example of framing, look up information at AskJeeves (www.ask.com). Should framing be allowed? Support your claim.
14. The CEO of Amazon has publicly questioned the advisability of granting patents for business processes such as his company's 1-Click ordering process. Do such patents put a chilling effect on the expansion of e-commerce? Justify your position.
15. What court should have jurisdiction over the Internet? Why?

Practitioner Perspective

Past, Present, And . . . Perfect

Krishna Narayanan program manages strategic projects for the worldwide operations division of Sun Microsystems Inc., in California. He is a "Black Belt" in Six Sigma-based management tools. He has an M.B.A. and both master's and bachelor's degrees in engineering. He was a student of one of the authors of this book, Dr. Judy Strauss.

E-mail: nk1800@yahoo.com

Companies once able to compete based on an established and easily defined set of industry rules now find it difficult to keep pace in a world wrought with social, cultural, technological, economical, and regulatory changes. Consumers have become more sophisticated in their buying behavior, new products quickly become obsolete, technology life cycles become shorter, and new entrants bring better, leaner, and highly competitive products and services to the market. As a result, in the past few years we have seen many different management techniques, business tools, and strategies used; some succeed, some bust—here is one I bet will stay: *Six Sigma!*

Six Sigma—*New name to an old game?*

Six Sigma is a data-driven business concept that answers customers' demand for high-quality and near-perfect business processes. This is achieved by defining the problem from a customer's perspective, systemically analyzing the root causes (whether it is in manufacturing, marketing, sales, service, design, and so on) and solving it. Most of you might ask, "Sounds good. So, what's new?" If I could over simplify—probably, very little. That's one of the reasons, I bet Sigma is here to stay! Read on.

Sigma is the Greek letter statisticians use to represent the standard deviation of a population—a measure of variation. Most of the tools and techniques used are time tested, best practices borrowed from many different methodologies, blended and melted to form a unique recipe that can be easily customized to any occasion!

When these tools, and more, are combined with the following, it results in a genie called Six Sigma:

- strong management support
- performance metrics
- customer-focused culture
- financial results
- employee training like never before

With Six Sigma, the common measurement index is "defects per unit or opportunity." For example:

I.   Every minute of downtime for a retail Web site during holiday shopping season could be a *defect* and take a hit against your Sigma target.

II.   A customer waiting more than 15 seconds for a representative to begin a chat could be a defect when measuring a customer service response time for an online technical services Web site.

III. Delivery performance could be measured by number of orders delivered beyond the committed date for an online book retailer.

Defect is defined as anything outside of customer specifications and can be easily converted to Sigma allowing a companywide comparison of performance. Six Sigma is generally the goal, which means products and processes will experience only 3.4 defects per million opportunities or 99.999966% good. This reliance on customer-centric metrics, coupled with statistical analysis, eliminates the fluff found in many other quality strategies.

Six Sigma—*Perfect*

Six Sigma can be used for a major business transformation, strategic improvement, or a narrowly focused problem-solving technique. In any case, Sigma is about making money—period! Most of the companies decrease their cost of quality from 25 to 40% of sales revenue to about 1% or less with a corresponding 3 to 6 Six Sigma jump. Even though these numbers are seen to slightly vary depending on factors such as industry type and Sigma implementation effectiveness, most companies, big or small, in any industry, can yield significant competitive gains by using these tools.

There are two types of Six Sigma submethodologies in general use: DMAIC and DMADV. The DMAIC process (define, measure, analyze, improve, control) is an improvement system for existing processes falling below specification and needing an incremental improvement. The DMADV process (define, measure, analyze, design, verify) is an improvement method used to develop new processes, products, or services. It can also be employed if the existing process requires more than just an incremental improvement. Let me briefly outline the steps of the widely used DMAIC process:

- **Define.** Clearly identify a project based on business objectives, customer identified critical to quality (CTQ) requirements and feedback.

- **Measure.** Collect data to gain knowledge about the problem, process, customer, or organization.

- **Analyze.** Determine with repeated why(s) the root cause(s) and identify key variables.

- **Improve.** Confirm key variables and quantify their effects on CTQs. Modify the process to stay within the acceptable range and implement a permanent solution.

- **Control.** Ensure the key variables remain within the maximum acceptable ranges for the long term with right procedures and management statistics to "control."

Sounds, simple and logical? Absolutely! This is one reason Sigma is popular among business leaders and practitioners. Effective execution of these principles is possible in almost any situation or industry type by a team of trained Six Sigma Green Belts, Black Belts, and Master Black Belts. Just like in karate, the color of the belt signifies the expertise level in using Sigma techniques.

Late 1990s saw the dot-com rage! I wrote in the last edition of this book, "any crazy idea even remotely related to dot-com was immediately funded." Many decisions during those times were made quickly and without sufficient supporting data. In hindsight, many of these decisions were terrible mistakes—but could Six Sigma have made a difference even when the industry was an uncharted territory? I certainly think so! It's still not too late for some.

Note: The opinions set forth in this article are those of the author and do not represent those of Sun Microsystems, Inc.

Practitioner Perspective

Trust Me. Have I Ever Lied to You?

Don Peppers and Martha Rogers, Ph.D., are co-founders of Peppers and Rogers Group, the management consulting firm that focuses on customer-based business strategy. Recognized in 2001 by the World Technology Network as having played a significant role in developing the field of CRM, Don Peppers and Martha Rogers are the co-authors of the revolutionary The One to One Future *and a series of business books that further develop the unique one-to-one methodology espoused by their firm.*
Web site: www.1to1.com

For years, we've adamantly contended that, in the age of interactivity and customer relationships, acting in your customer's interest was becoming an essential business practice. To create sustainable and profitable customer relationships, you must first look at your company from the customer's perspective. Of course, we've been saying all along that acting in the customer's own interest is not just something likely to be good for business; it is also simply "good." It's the right thing to do. It's a moral imperative. These days, the ethical aspect of this business philosophy comes more and more to mind. Think of some recent headlines generated by companies that have violated the trust placed in them:

- Arthur Andersen's auditing business owes its very existence to a mandate from the federal government that requires publicly held companies to have their books and records audited by professionals charged with protecting the interests of investors, by applying generally accepted accounting standards. Now it seems, at least in the Enron case, that Andersen's professionals weren't acting in the public's interest at all.

- Merrill Lynch, Salomon Smith Barney, and other stockbrokers make money from clients who buy stocks on the recommendations of their analysts. But, apparently, some of these analysts were publicly recommending stocks to their clients at the same time they were deriding them to their own colleagues as "dogs" and "garbage," in a series of e-mail messages unearthed by New York Attorney General Eliot Spitzer.

- According to an April 23 article in *The New York Times*, Children's Health Corp. of America gives its seal of approval to medical products used in children's hospitals. But it only gives that seal to companies that pay for it, in the form of commissions and equity. It does no testing, even though it maintains that it only endorses "good" products. The CEO is quoted in the article as saying "if they don't pay, they don't get the seal."

To us, these stories represent more than just slimy corporate anecdotes. They paint a picture of a corporate world consumed by short-term self-interest to the point that it is not disciplined much by a sense of ethics or moral purpose. What these companies have in common is that they abuse the trust placed in them by our society, by their constituents, and by our legal infrastructure. One result is that some of them are now on the "endangered companies" list.

Free and unfettered markets, while they brutally punish inefficient competitors, can nevertheless generate immense prosperity and economic value over the long term. Companies competing against one another will, over time, produce better products and services for all of us. Over the past couple of decades, the world economy has benefited greatly from a public attitude that such business ambition is generally a good thing, that despite the short-term frictions and dislocations, free-market business competition produces cheaper, better, more abundant products and services for society in general.

The problem now is that the Andersen-Enron scandal and similar horror stories of corporate greed threaten to undermine society's cautious tolerance of free markets and unfettered competition. You can already see it in the stock market. Investors—a group of customers for the organizations they invest in—worry that they are being sold a bill of goods, that the companies they are investing in are not respecting investors' interests at all, painting the rosiest possible picture, even if inaccurate, just to get their money. Many companies are revising their financial statements now, trying as best they can to dissociate themselves from the kind of financial legerdemain that brought both Enron and Andersen down.

The Relationship Imperative

Maintaining individual customer relationships is now made possible by new technologies and is mandated by competition. In short, it is an imperative. As more companies execute customer-driven business strategies, forming true "partnerships" with individual customers, a firm's reputation for always acting in its customer's interest will become increasingly important. No customer will want to maintain a relationship with a firm that can't be trusted—trusted to provide products and services of reasonable quality, trusted to protect the customer's privacy, and trusted generally not to take undue advantage of the customer through deception or connivance. Because of this imperative, generating and maintaining trust are activities that must be high on every company's priority list. And, as we are learning from a variety of positive and negative examples, ethics and trust are compatible with profitability.

Conversely, any damage to your company's reputation for acting in the customer's interest—any erosion in the trust that you've built up—can be exceedingly costly. A large manufacturing firm with plants and inventory all over the world may require decades of growth to achieve success, and in the mass marketing era it wasn't necessary even to "know" many customers individually. Its customers were anonymous, so relationships were nonexistent, but that was OK because all its competitors were in the same boat.

Nevertheless, such a company can suffer a financial reversal and still be buoyed by the value of its physical assets, which can be used to sell products to other anonymous customers. Today, however, a company that achieves success largely through leveraging its brand reputation and its relationships with customers or investors can grow much more quickly, achieving longer-term profit by locking its high-value customers into lifetime relationships, based on individualized treatment. For such a company, however, one big betrayal of trust could cause it to sink without a trace in an economic nanosecond.

One of the most important preconditions for becoming a successful manager of customer relationships is the "attitude adjustment" involved. Anticipating customer needs and treating different customers differently require what amounts to a change in the philosophy of doing business. This means that, rather than asking how we can use new databases and interactive technologies to sell our customers more stuff, we should be asking how we can use these new technologies to make our customers' lives better—delivering a better, faster, or cheaper product, based on individual customer needs.

Culture Shift Required

This attitude adjustment is difficult to achieve. It means educating and training not just customer-contact people but also middle management. It means adopting a completely new set of metrics to gauge progress and financial success. It probably also means adopting a different organizational structure, with different accountabilities, to be able to manage the firm's treatment of different individual customers. Companies can buy and install all the CRM technologies they want, but the corporate attitude adjustment has to be separately negotiated, and a big part of it will only come from instilling a culture that says "we always act in the customer's interest."

In truth, many of the problems we see in the headlines today may have a structural explanation: It just might not be a good idea to allow a company charged with auditing the books of a publicly held corporation to earn large fees helping the same company structure its financial dealings. And maybe it's not a good idea for a stock market analyst to be paid for his or her "objective" assessment of a company that is simultaneously giving the analyst's employer millions of dollars in fees for investment banking services.

But structure aside, imagine that any one of these firms has actually gone to the trouble of making this profound attitude adjustment with respect to its business philosophy. Imagine that your firm has inculcated a culture of always acting in the customer's interest—a culture in which you treat each customer the way you would like to be treated if you were the customer. You can't consider building value in your firm until your firm becomes valuable—in a trustworthy, sustainable way—to one customer, and another and another. In that case, the success or failure of your firm would hinge on your ability to maintain and grow the trust your own customers place in you.

Somehow, we just can't see a company with this kind of culture stooping to the kind of betrayals that are making headlines today. Call us crazy, but in our opinion the relationship imperative just now getting under way promises to be one of the best things that could happen for corporate ethics. And it is coming none too soon.

Originally published in Inside1to1®: *Privacy on June 27, 2002; reprinted with permission from Peppers and Rogers Group. Copyright © 2001 Peppers and Rogers Group / Marketing 1to1, Inc.*

S a v v y   S i t e s

American Civil Liberties Union (ACLU) www.aclu.org/	This is the place to learn about legal issues affecting the Internet's users. The ACLU provides information about "Cyber-Liberties" such as privacy and censorship.
Builder.com builder.com	This site from CNET Networks provides articles, discussions, and tips for Web site design, management, and more.
Electronic Frontier Foundation www.eff.org	Here is another site dedicated to protecting civil liberties, such as free expression in the digital environment.
The Global Internet Project www.gip.org	The Global Internet Project is an international group of senior executives committed to spurring the growth of the Internet worldwide. The site focuses on the Internet's impact on society, globalization, laws, and so on.
Oracle www.oracle.com	As leading provider of enterprise software solutions, the company provides database software, tools, and application products, along with consulting and support services.
SAP www.sap.com	SAP provides e-business solutions for all types of industries.
Search Engine Watch www.searchenginewatch.com	This is a great site to learn all there is to know about search engines. It provides searching tips,

reviews, ratings, and news about search engines. It even provides submission tips if you have a Web site.

TechWeb www.techweb.com	TechWeb provides the latest news and information on business technology.
U.S. Patent and Trademark Office www.uspto.gov	Here you can find out about patents and trademarks.
webmonkey hotwired.lycos.com/webmonkey/	As they say, this site is a "Web developer's resource." It is really incredible!
World Intellectual Property Organization (WIPO) www.wipo.org	Here one can learn about international copyright law.
World Wide Web Consortium www.w3.org	This site is dedicated to an open forum discussion about the Web in order to develop common protocols and ensure the growth and interoperability of the Web.

Activities

1. Look for the cookies file(s) on your hard drive (on a Microsoft PC, use the *find file* function and search for *cookie*). Do you see sites there that you have never visited? Is DoubleClick on the list?

2. Download and install a free trial version of the Intermute software (www.intermute.com). What do you notice about the quantity and type of material filtered? What does this mean for Web site companies?

3. Visit GreatDomains at www.greatdomains.com. Do you see any names represented there that could be interpreted as cybersquatting?

4. Visit kazaa, or gnutella, two music file sharing Web sites following in the defunct Napster's footsteps. Do you think that its service is ethically problematic? Is it legally problematic?

5. Visit DoubleClick at www.doubleclick.com. Do you find any of its services ethically objectionable? Why or why not? Note that at the time of this writing, DoubleClick was being courted by MaxWorldWide, so things may be

changing—if this happens, why do you think the ad serving industry is in trouble?

6. Visit the FTC site at www.ftc.gov. What cases is it currently reviewing that relate to the Internet? Describe several and give your opinion about how the agency should rule.

7. Visit www.epinions.com and www.amazon.com, and review their privacy policies. What sorts of things do they cover? Which one has a better policy in your opinion?

Internet Exercises

Internet Exercise: Online Store

In this exercise you are going to build your own online store. Yahoo! Store is a comprehensive solution for small businesses seeking to establish an online storefront. Visit Yahoo! Store at store.yahoo.com. Go ahead and create a free online store (it expires in 10 days). You can sell anything you want at your store—but don't worry, no one can place a real order. Looking for ideas? How about some stuff you have lying around your room? Once you have created the store, make a printout of the home page and give it to your professor along with the URL. The URL will read like this: store.yahoo.com/yourusername. Now complete the following chart listing the retail functions provided by Yahoo! Store.

Function	Provided by Yahoo! Store (Y/N)?
Web store design	
Web store hosting	
Order processing	
Electronic shopping cart	
Secure order form	
Credit authorization	
Warehouse notification	
Order fulfillment	
Merchandising	
Relationship marketing	
Data warehousing and data mining	
Customer service	

Discussion Questions:

1. What type of retail operation defines your store (e.g., department store)? Explain in terms of amount of service and product line.
2. Who is your target market and what position will you occupy for this store?
3. What is the cost of running a store on Yahoo! Store?
4. Who are some of Yahoo! Store's more prominent clients?
5. What steps would you take to advertise your store?
6. Yahoo! Store domain names are store.yahoo.com/mystore. For an additional charge you can register a domain name such as www.mystore.com. Which approach would be better for your business? Why?

Internet Exercise: Prospecting Online

One interesting way to build a prospect list online is to find out which Web sites are linked to your site. By placing a link to your site the business has demonstrated an interest in your product and, therefore, is a potential customer. The AltaVista search engine (www.altavista.com) provides a feature that automatically constructs this list. Herman Miller, Inc. sells office furniture and systems to businesses, and it might use this feature to develop leads for the salespeople. In the AltaVista search box type link:www.hermanmiller.com to find out which sites are linked to Herman Miller's home page. From that list, select four sites that might be good prospects and explain why you chose them.

Company	Web Address	Reason for Inclusion

For Discussion

1. How could Herman Miller use the same search feature to find out which prospective customers have an interest in competitive office furniture stores? Would these constitute good prospects for Herman Miller? Why or why not?
2. What is the next step after building the prospect list?
3. How could Herman Miller identify prospects directly on its own Web site?
4. How could Herman Miller use e-mail to move prospects closer to purchase?

Internet Exercise: Spamming

Spamming refers to the bulk distribution of unsolicited, and often unwanted, e-mail messages. Because e-mail carries no postage cost, this form of direct marketing has grown rapidly in the past few years. Used properly, online direct marketing can inform consumers of products or updates of interest to them. When abused, spamming becomes at best an annoyance to Internet users and at worst patently offensive—for example, adult sites that spam to underage users. There are two ways for consumers to stop spam. Technological solutions filter the spam either at the Internet service provider (ISP) level or right on the user's PC. Spam can also be controlled by industry self-regulation and government legislation. Marketers that want to build customer relationships and positive brand equity will only add customers to e-mail lists with their prior consent. Customers, thus, opt-in rather than having to opt-out of the list. Complete the following table—leave blank any items for which the organization does not offer a position.

Item	Direct Marketing Association www.the-dma.org	American Marketing Association www.ama.org	Federal Trade Commission www.ftc.gov
Support opt-in lists only			
Support requiring spammers to reveal their return address			
Support consumer's right to be removed from lists			
Provide tips on how to be removed from lists			

For Discussion

1. Do these organizations promise to stop direct marketing entirely or just filter it to the items that you want?

2. If marketers were doing their job correctly, would consumer filtering be necessary? Explain why or why not.

3. A particularly venal form of spamming disguises the sender's e-mail address so as to make it impossible to request removal from the list. Do you believe that this practice should be allowed?

4. Many e-mail programs now allow you to block mail coming from specific addresses. Is this an effective way to stop spamming?

1. A service called BrightMail (www.brightmail.com) helps to remove spam at the ISP level. How does this service work?

chapter

6 marketing
knowledge

learning objectives

The main objective of this chapter is develop an understanding of why and how e-marketers turn marketing research into marketing knowledge. You will learn about the three categories of Internet data sources, consider the ethics of online research, look at key database analysis techniques, and explore the use of knowledge management metrics.

After reading this chapter, you will be able to:

- Identify the three main sources of data that e-marketers use to address research problems.
- Discuss how and why e-marketers need to check the quality of research data gathered online.
- Explain why the Internet is used as a contact method for primary research and describe the main Internet-based approaches to primary research.
- Contrast client-side data collection, server-side data collection, and real-space approaches to data collection.
- Highlight four important methods of analysis that e-marketers can apply to information in the data warehouse.

Knowledge is like money: to be of value, it must circulate, and in circulation it can increase in quantity, and, hopefully, in value.

louis l'amour

Nestlé Purina PetCare Company knows with certainty that Purina Web sites and online advertising increase off-line buying. How? Through a carefully conducted study that integrated online and off-line behavioral data.

Switzerland-based Nestlé S.A purchased the Ralston Purina Company in December 2001, gaining a full line of dog and cat care brands such as Friskies, Alpo, Purina Dog Chow, and Fancy Feast. The firm manages over 30 branded Web sites serving the following markets: consumers, veterinarians/veterinary schools, nutritionists/food scientists, and breeders/other enthusiasts. Nestlé started its inquiry with three research questions:

- Are our buyers using our branded Web sites?

- Should we invest beyond these branded Web sites in online advertising?

- If so, where do we place that advertising?

Combining comScore's representative panel of 1.5 million Internet consumers and the Knowledge Networks frequent grocery shopper panel of 20 million households revealed 50,000 consumers belonging to both panels. Researchers created three experimental cells from survey panel members, two receiving Purina O.N.E. banner advertising as they naturally surfed the Internet: a control cell (no ads), a low-exposure test cell (1 to 5 exposures), and a high-exposure test cell (6 to 20 exposures). Banner ads were randomly sent as exposure cell subjects viewed Web pages anywhere on the Internet. Next, the firm surveyed all cell members to assess Purina brand awareness, purchase intent, and advertising awareness. Finally, the researchers compared survey results with off-line buying, as measured in the Knowledge Network panel.

Nestlé's marketers were very interested in the study's findings. First, banner clickthrough was low (0.06% on average). Second, when study participants were asked *When thinking of dog food, what brand first comes to mind?* 31% percent of both exposure cell subjects mentioned Purina. In contrast, only 22% of the no-exposure subjects mentioned the brand; this clearly showed an advertising effect. Further, 7% more of the subjects in the high-exposure group mentioned the brand compared with those in the low-exposure group. Next, researchers reviewed the Internet panel's Web site viewing habits for those who purchased Purina products and determined that home/health and living sites receive the most visits from these customers. This helped the firm decide where to place banner ads. Among those, www.petsmart.com and about.com enjoy heavy usage and would be great ad buys (www.comscore.com and Moore and Hunter speech at the Advertising Research Foundation Annual Convention and Research Infoplex, April 2002).

There's a long way from data to knowledge. clifford stoll

Data Drives Strategy

Information overload is a reality for most consumers and marketers alike. This is an especially difficult problem for marketing decision makers as they gather survey results, product sales information, secondary data about competitors, and much more. The problem is compounded by automated data gathering at Web sites, brick-and-mortar points of purchase, and all other customer touch points. What to do with all the data? Purina marketers sorted through lots of consumer data to build a road map for their Internet advertising strategy.

Exhibit 6 - 1 displays an overview of this process. Data are collected from a myriad of sources, filtered into databases, and turned into marketing knowledge that is then used to create marketing strategy. This chapter discusses Internet data sources, describes important database analysis techniques, and most importantly, examines the purposes and payoffs for all this work—beginning with current thought about the *learning organization* and *knowledge management*. Most of these techniques are well grounded in marketing practice; however, new technology has led to new applications that are both helpful and confusing for marketing planners.

This chapter discusses the grayed areas in Exhibit 6 - 1; Chapters 8 and 9 focus on tier 1 e-marketing strategies of segmentation, targeting, differentiation, and positioning. Tier 2 strategies are covered in Part IV; because performance metrics

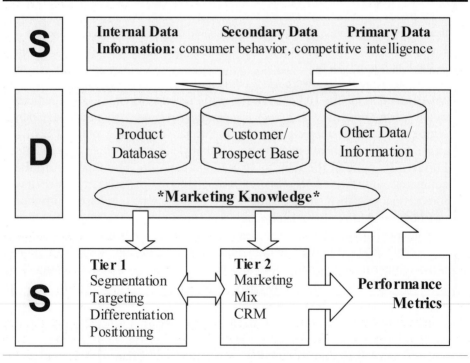

Exhibit 6 - 1 From Sources to Databases to Strategy (SDS Model)

permeate each of these processes, the relevant metrics are described in most chapters.

The Learning Organization

A **learning organization** is one that uses internal and external data to quickly adapt to its changing environment, creating organizational change that improves both its competitive position and employee satisfaction. Learning organizations recognize the importance of employee empowerment and development, cross-functional teams for brainstorming, and risk taking for breakthrough ideas. Learning organizations benefit from improved product quality and innovation, better customer relations, shared visioning, process breakthrough improvements, and stronger competitiveness through team effort.

The idea of a learning organization has been around for decades, but information technology advances and the rapid growth of the Internet have made the process even more important. This is because change is occurring very rapidly, so marketers cannot simply gather data to solve a certain problem and move on. Now they must ponder what they learned about this and similar problems—and make changes to prevent such problems from recurring in the future.

Marketing learning occurs in every area, but one of the most important has been dubbed the *learning relationship*. The more marketers can learn about their customers, the better they can serve them with appropriate marketing mixes. Imagine, for example, that an American Airlines frequent flier indicates on the www.aa.com Web site that she'd like to receive a short text message on her cell phone two hours before a flight with information about its actual departure time, gate number, and baggage claim location in the destination city. This is commonly done today, but it must be entered anew for each leg of each flight. Now imagine that American could go a step further, asking the customer via Web page or e-mail: *Would you like us to notify you this way for each flight you book with us?* Here, American would be learning what the customer wants, confirming it, and then delivering it—all automatically. Exhibit 6 - 2 gives a hypothetical scenario for a computer company that is learning from its customers as a whole and using the information to improve products.

From Data to Knowledge

Data are the lubricant for a learning organization, and organizations are drowning in it. Exhibit 6 - 3 shows that data growth rates are about 80% a year, necessitating an increasing amount of storage hardware space (e.g., data warehouses). This is an information technology manager's problem, and e-marketers must determine how to glean insights from these billions of bytes.

The Purina research vignette is a good example of how a firm sorts through hundreds of millions of pieces of data about 21.5 million consumers, collects even more data, and makes decisions (Exhibit 6 - 4). Organizations must do this with all the data they collect, or their data will be a bunch of facts and numbers that overwhelm.

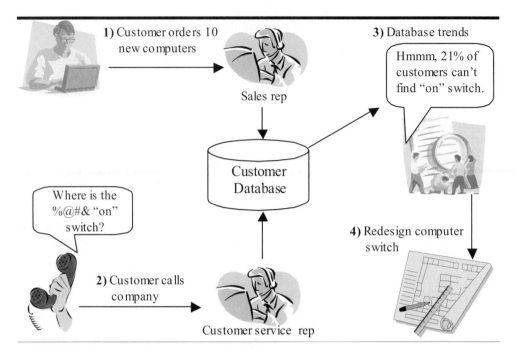

Exhibit 6 - 2 E-Marketers Learn from Customers
Source: Adaptation of ideas from Brian Caulfield (2001), "Facing up to CRM" at www.business2.com.

Marketing insight occurs somewhere between information and knowledge. Knowledge is more than a collection of information but something that resides in the user, not the computer. It can be compared to the difference between teaching and learning. A professor might spout information in a lecture or from a textbook, but it is not usable unless the student ponders it, relates it to other pieces of information, and adds insights that result in acquired and useful knowledge. People, not the Internet or computers, create knowledge; computers are simply learning enablers.

Marketing Knowledge Management

Knowledge management is the process of managing the creation, use, and dissemination of knowledge. Thus, data, information, and knowledge are shared with internal marketing decision makers, partners, distribution channel members, and sometimes customers. When other stakeholders can access selected knowledge, the firm becomes a learning organization and is better able to reach desired ROI and other performance goals.

Marketing knowledge is the digitized "group mind" or "collective memory" of the marketing personnel and sometimes of consultants, partners, and former employees as well. Sometimes the knowledge management technology even allows marketing staff to chat in real time for problem solving, which is why the system also includes contact information. For example, a Context Integration consultant working on an e-commerce problem at the client's offices can enter a "911" help call into the

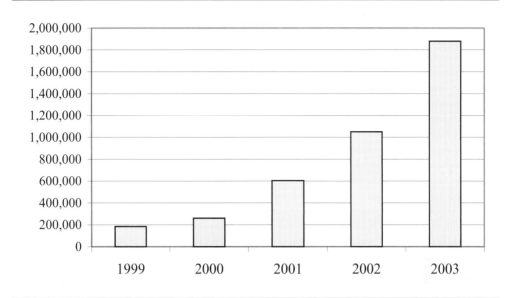

Exhibit 6 - 3 Terabytes of Corporate Data: Growth Rate from 1999 to 2003
Source: Data from International Data Corp (www.idc.com).

Exhibit Note: A character, such as the letter A, is 10 bits of data or 1 byte; a kilobyte (1 KB) of data is about 1,024 bytes; a megabyte (MB) is about 1 million bytes; a gigabyte is about 1 billion bytes; a terabyte is a thousand billion bytes (or 1,000 gigabytes); and petabytes and exabytes are, well, a lot more data.

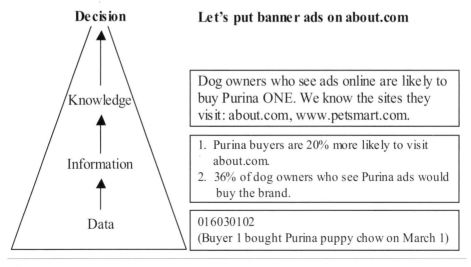

Exhibit 6 - 4 From Data to Decision at Nestlé Purina PetCare Company

Context Integration knowledge management Web page and immediately chat with other internal experts to solve the problem. A complete marketing knowledge database includes all the data about customers, prospects, and competitors, the analyses and outputs based on the data, and access to marketing experts, all available 24/7 through a number of digital receiving appliances. Consider these examples, and those in Exhibit 6 - 5:

- A large retailer of electronic products with 5,000 stores in the United States sends online weekly sales reports to all managers so they can identify what products are selling well in various locations. This information helps managers identify opportunities in their own stores.

- An insurance firm with 200 independent agents allows them access to claim data from over 1 million customers. This allows the agents to avoid high-risk customers as well as to compare claim data with their own database of customers.

- i-Go, a catalog marketer and online retailer, integrates incoming customer service calls with Web purchases, e-mail inquiries, and FAX and postal orders. This allows customer service representatives to have up-to-date information when talking with customers.

- Context Integration maintains a $10 million knowledge management system that serves daily customized electronic newsletters to its 200 marketing consultants, provides a searchable database of previous projects and experts, and allows online chats with experts and employees.

Use in the Telecom Industry	Representative Firm
Scanner Check-Out Data Analysis	AT&T
Call Volume Analysis	Ameritech
Equipment Sales Analysis	Belgacom
Customer Profitability Analysis	British Telecom
Cost and Inventory Analysis	Telestra Australia
Purchasing Leverage with Suppliers	Telecom Ireland
Frequent-Buyer Program Management	Telecom Italia

Use in the Retail Industry	Representative Firm
Scanner Check-Out Data Analysis	Wal-Mart
Sales Promotion Tracking	Kmart
Inventory Analysis and Deployment	Sears
Price Reduction Modeling	Osco/Savon Drugs
Negotiating Leverage with Suppliers	Casino Supermarkets
Frequent-Buyer Program Management	W. H. Smith Books
Profitability Analysis	Otto Versand Mail Order
Product Selection for Markets	Amazon.com

Exhibit 6 - 5 Uses of Knowledge Management in Two Industries
Source: Adapted from Kalakota and Robinson (1999).

The Electronic Marketing Information System

A **marketing information system** (MIS) is the *process* by which marketers manage knowledge. The MIS is a system of assessing information needs, gathering information, analyzing it, and disseminating it to marketing decision makers. The process begins when marketing managers have a problem that requires data to solve. The next step is to gather the data from internal sources, from secondary sources, or by conducting primary marketing research. The process is complete when these managers receive the needed information in a timely and usable form. For example, Web advertisers need audience statistics prior to deciding where to purchase banner ad space (the problem). They want to know how many people view various Web sites to evaluate the value of Web ads versus TV and other media ads, and they need to know whether an ad on a particular site will reach their target market (information need). One way to get this information is through secondary sources such as Media Metrix. Such firms rate Web sites by researching the Internet usage habits of large panels of consumers. Web advertisers use the data to make effective and efficient Web media buys.

In the past, marketers with a problem asked information technology or information systems personnel what software they had on the shelf. Today, however, e-marketing actually drives some technology change—it is this interdisciplinary activity that helps organizations learn. E-marketing changed the MIS landscape in several ways. First, many firms store electronic marketing data in databases and **data warehouses**. These enable marketers to obtain valuable, appropriate, and tailored information anytime day or night. Second, marketers can receive database information in Web pages and e-mail on a number of appliances in addition to the desktop computer: pagers, FAX machines, PDAs such as the PalmPilot, and even cellular phones. Third, customers also have access to portions of the database. For example, when consumers visit Amazon.com, they can query the **product database** for book titles and also receive information about their account status and past book purchases: all at the click of a mouse. Business customers, channel members, and partners often have access to customer sales data to facilitate product planning. Customer inquiries are usually automated, with personalized Web pages created instantaneously. Finally, most firms recognize that data and information are useless unless turned into knowledge to increase profits. Therefore, cutting-edge firms make one employee's project reports, proposals, and data analyses available to other stakeholders in the MIS network. In sum, all the data, output from their use, and stakeholder contact information that exist in an MIS comprise a firm's marketing knowledge.

The Internet and other technologies have greatly facilitated marketing data collection. Internal records give marketing planners excellent insights about sales and inventory movement. **Secondary data** help marketers understand competitors, consumers, the economic environment, political and legal factors, technological forces, and other factors in the macroenvironment affecting an organization. Marketing planners use the Net, the telephone, product **bar code scanners**, and other technologies to collect **primary data** about consumers. Through online e-mail and Web surveys, online experiments, **focus groups**, and observation of Net user discussions, marketers learn about both current and prospective customers.

Source 1: Internal Records

One important source of marketing knowledge is internal records. Accounting, finance, and production personnel collect and analyze data that provide valuable information for marketing planning. The marketing department itself collects and maintains much relevant information about customer characteristics and activities. For example, logistics personnel track product shipment through distribution channels, information that can help marketers improve the order-to-delivery and payment cycles. This is especially important in an electronic environment where customers expect quick response after online orders. The ability to make products as they are ordered also helps increase profitability. Just-in-time inventory systems, enhanced by channel member and other customer electronic ordering, allow a firm to minimize inventory costs while meeting customer demand in a timely manner.

Nonmarketing Data

The accounting department generates data about sales, cash flow, marketing expenses, and profitability that e-marketers can use to evaluate marketing effectiveness. For example, a firm introducing a new product on its Web site will want immediate feedback on its sales. The firm will also want to track its advertising spending and response from various media during the introductory period. In a digital environment, advertising adjustments are easy to make in a frequent and timely manner.

Sales Force Data

Sales information systems, often using *sales force automation* software, allow representatives to input results of sales calls to both prospects and current customers into the MIS. Remarkably many sales reps access the product and customer databases both for input and review of customer records while on the road from their laptop computers. For example, one office products firm has salespeople from different divisions calling on the same large customer. When the customer has a complaint, the sales rep must enter it into the database and other reps review the customer record prior to making a visit to the same customer. This firm has a rule: If four reps record the same complaint, a warning is issued and they must immediately visit the customer as a team and solve the problem. Sales reps are also instrumental in entering competitive and industry information gained in the field. For a few cutting-edge firms, marketers enter proposals, reports, and papers written on various topics into the MIS.

Customer Characteristics and Behavior

Perhaps the most important internal marketing data involve individual customer activity (refer to Exhibit 6 - 2). At a minimum database entries include an electronic list of customers and prospective customers, along with their addresses, phone numbers, and purchase behavior. Firms have used this technique for many years, but new storage and retrieval technologies, and the availability of large amounts of electronic information, have recently escalated its growth. For example, visitors to Expedia are asked to register before using its services. This firm has a large database that includes e-mail addresses, customer characteristics, and surfing and purchase behavior. Each customer file in a database might also include a record of calls made to customer service reps, product service records, specific problems or questions related to various products, and other data such as coupon and other promotional offer redemption. A complete customer record will include data from every customer touch point (contact with the company), including Internet orders and e-mail interaction, and product purchases and coupon redemption at the grocery store. Data on in-store behavior are gathered through scanning **universal product codes** (bar codes) on products. Firms use the data in customer databases to improve sales rep effectiveness, refine the product mix, identify optimum pricing for individual products, assess promotion effectiveness, and signal distribution opportunities. For example: Have you ever wondered why the local retailer asks for a zip code when you make a purchase? The retailer adds this information to the marketing database and uses it to decide whether or not a new store location might be profitable.

Many firms with Web sites track user movement through the pages and use these data to improve site effectiveness. By knowing how long users spend on each page, how long they are at the site, and what path they take through the site, Web developers can reorganize pages and content frequently and in a timely manner. In addition, firms can identify the Web site users visited immediately before and after the firm's site. This information provides competitive insights, especially if a user is reviewing particular products. These data are all generated automatically in the *Web site logs* and can be part of a firm's marketing databases.

Federal Express is especially adroit at gathering customer information automatically using electronic networks. Through its Web site, customers can dispatch a courier for package pick-up, locate drop-off points, track shipments, obtain shipping rates, prepare shipping documents, and request a signature proof of delivery in many different languages. All this information can be analyzed by FedEx's marketers for planning purposes. FedEx maintains an extranet for frequent shippers, providing them individualized rate books and other special services. In addition, FedEx maintains an intranet hub that serves 20,000 visitors a month for human resource management and workplace and marketplace integration—a thorough system of internal data input for effective marketing knowledge management.

Source 2: Secondary Data

When faced with a need for specific information not available in company or partner databases, the e-marketer first looks for secondary data, which can be collected more quickly and less expensively than primary data—especially on the Internet, where up-to-date information from over 200 countries is available 24/7, from home or work, delivered in a matter of seconds.

On the other hand, secondary data may not meet the e-marketer's information needs, because they were usually gathered for a different purpose than the one at hand. Another common problem is the quality of secondary data. Marketers have no control over data collection procedures, so they should always evaluate the quality of secondary data. Finally, secondary data are often out of date. The U.S. Census provides lots of population statistics; its heavy data collection periods occur only every 10 years, and results will not appear on the Web site until a year or two later. A marketer using data at www.census.gov must read the fine print to see when the data were collected.

Marketers continually scan the firm's macroenvironment for threats and opportunities. This procedure is commonly called **marketing intelligence.** What type of information do marketing managers need? An environmental scan seeks market information about the following:

- Demographic trends
- Competitors
- Technological forces
- Natural resources
- Social and cultural trends
- World and local economies
- Legal and political environments

One of the Internet's major benefits is access to secondary data about environmental factors and trends. For example, a firm wanting to understand the characteristics and behavior of the Generation Y demographic group can visit the U.S. Census site, read appropriate articles in online magazines and newspapers, and monitor Web sites such as MTV and www.gurl.com that target this group. The following sections present examples of public and private sources of data about the firm's macroenvironment. Look for more in the Savvy Sites boxes at the each end of each part in this book; also use your nearest search engine to identify more sites.

Publicly Generated Data

Most U.S. agencies provide online information in their respective areas. The U.S. Patent Office home page can explain how to apply for a patent and research pending trademarks. Many global organizations, such as the International Monetary Fund (www.imf.org), are also good sources of data for environmental scans involving countries other than the United States. Generally speaking, however, U.S. agencies collect and disseminate a great deal more data than do governments in other countries. In the not-for-profit category, most universities provide extensive information through their libraries, and many faculty post their research results

Web site	Information
Stat-USA www.stat-usa.gov	U.S. Department of Commerce source of international trade data.
U.S. Patent Office www.uspto.gov	Provides trademark and patent data for businesses.
World Trade Organization www.wto.org	World trade data.
International Monetary Fund www.imf.org	Provides information on many social issues and projects.
Mohanbir Sawhney www.mohanbirsawhney.com	An academic who generously publishes all of his work on his Web site.
Securities and Exchange Commission www.sec.gov	Edgar database provides financial data on U.S. public corporations.
Small Business Administration www.sbaonline.gov	Features information and links for small business owners.
University of Texas at Austin advweb.cocomm.utexas.edu/world	Ad World with lots of links in the ad industry.
Federal Trade Commission www.ftc.gov	Shows regulations and decisions related to consumer protection and antitrust laws.
U.S. Census www.census.gov	Provides statistics and trends about the U.S. population.

Exhibit 6 - 6 Public Sources of Data in the U.S.

online. Finally, industry- or profession-specific information is available at the sites of professional associations such as the American Marketing Association (www.ama.org). Most of this information is free and available to all Internet users. A sampling of important public sites is displayed in Exhibit 6 - 6.

Privately Generated Data

Many firms and individuals put timely information on Web sites. Company Web sites provide a great overview of the firm's mission, products, partners, and current events. Individuals often maintain sites with useful information about companies as well. Politicians and other public figures create sites containing commentary about issues close to their hearts (and political goals).

Another good resource is large research firms, such as comScore and Forrester Research, which put sample statistics and press releases on their sites as a way to entice users to purchase full research reports. Media Metrix, NetRatings, and PCData post the top Web sites or banner ads in a survey period. Several large research firms now also offer e-mail newsletters that are sent automatically to subscriber desktops. For e-business information, free newsletters from NUA Surveys (www.nua.ie) and CyberAtlas (www.cyberatlas.com) are especially helpful. While often incomplete, these tidbits of information are generally useful in an environmental scan and help marketers decide whether to purchase the full report.

Infomediaries are another important source of privately generated information. News aggregators, one type of infomediary, are firms that monitor a number of media sources, presenting selected stories to users either by "pushing" stories to the user's desktop via e-mail, or by allowing users to "pull" it from a specially tailored Web site. Thanks to news aggregators, the Internet has made scanning the world for news less effort than clicking a mouse. MyYahoo! (PC) and AvantGo (wireless) now perform this function by offering users free personal Web pages populated with specific news of interest. See Exhibit 6 - 7 for a sample of these sites.

Online Databases

Commercial online databases contain publicly available information that can be accessed via the Internet. Thousands of databases are available online covering news, industry data, encyclopedias, airline routes and fares, Yellow Page directories, e-mail addresses, and much more. Instead of going to the library to access such records, marketers can simply download articles and records into their marketing knowledge databases (as long as copyrights allow). Note that many of these databases are not available on Web pages but are simply electronic versions of articles and other information ordinarily found in the library. Some databases are free but others charge a fee for access.

Web Site	Information
AC Nielsen Corporation www.acnielsen.com	Television audience, supermarket scanner data, and more.
The Gartner Group www.gartnergroup.com	Specializes in e-business and usually presents highlights of its latest findings on the Web site.
Information Resources, Inc. www.infores.com	Supermarket scanner data and new-product purchasing data.
Arbitron www.arbitron.com	Local market and Internet radio audience data.
The Commerce Business Daily www.cbd.savvy.com	Lists of government requests for proposals online.
Simmons Market Research Bureau www.smrb.com	Media and ad spending data.
Dun & Bradstreet www.dnb.com	Database on more than 50 million companies worldwide.
Dialog library.dialog.com	Access to ABI/INFORM, a database of articles from 800+ publications.
LEXIS-NEXIS www.lexis-nexis.com	Articles from business, consumer, and marketing publications.
Dow Jones Interactive bis.dowjones.com	In-depth financial, historical, and operational information on public and private companies.
Hoovers Online www.hoovers.com	Business descriptions, financial overviews, and news about major companies worldwide.

Exhibit 6 - 7 Sampling of Sources of Privately Generated Data in the United States

Competitive Intelligence Example

Competitive intelligence (CI) involves analyzing the industries in which a firm operates as input to the firm's strategic positioning and to understand competitor vulnerabilities. According to Fuld & Co., 40% of all firms regularly conduct CI activities (www.fuld.com). Specialists at Fuld suggest the following intelligence cycle:

1. Define intelligence requirements.
2. Collect and organize information.
3. Analyze by applying information to the specific purpose and recommending action.
4. Report and inform others of the findings.
5. Evaluate the impact of intelligence use and suggest process improvements.

The Fuld & Co. Web site includes a thorough review of software to aid in CI activities as well as seminars on the topic. Astutely they note: "Technical tools without the right processes become shelfware!"

A few sources of CI include competitor press releases, new products, alliances and co-brands, trade show activity, and advertising strategies. The Internet simplified CI. Firms can observe competitive marketing strategies right on competitors' Web sites and can sometimes catch announcements of new products or price changes prior to media reports about them.

Marketers should be sure to check the Web sites linked to competitors' pages. To do this, simply type link:companyname.com at Yahoo!, AltaVista, or other search tools offering this protocol. The result is a list of links that may provide insight: Why are these sites linking to the competitor? Another technology-enabled CI activity is to analyze a particular firm's Web site log to see what Web page users visited immediately prior to and after the site. If, for example, Honda marketing managers noticed that a user visited the Toyota Echo Web page prior to checking out Honda models, they would gain a consumer perspective on competitive models.

Third-party, industry-specific sites can also provide timely information about competitive activities. An airline will monitor online travel agents to watch competitive pricing and route changes (e.g., Expedia and Travelocity). Company profiles for public firms are available in the SEC's online EDGAR database as well as at many investment firm sites (e.g., E*Trade). MyYahoo! and others will push relevant stories to users, and research firms will send e-mail notification of industry report availability.

Another valuable source of CI comes from user conversation, as will be discussed in the primary data collection section later. Liszt directs users to more than 90,000 e-mail lists on every imaginable topic. Most of the list members are professionals in their industries and combing through the many e-mail queries and responses can yield insights. A list called ELMAR, for instance, sends weekly edited e-mails from marketing educators discussing research, teaching, and job openings at universities worldwide. Google Groups offers Web access to over 35,000 bulletin board postings by Web users, and firms can often find consumer conversation about competitive product strengths and weaknesses via keyword searches.

Information Quality

Secondary and primary data are subject to many limitations; thus, marketers should approach the information with caution. It is advisable to be as objective as possible when reviewing data and to be somewhat skeptical before using information in decision making—especially before using Internet-based information. Why? Because anyone can easily publish on the Web without being reviewed by a publisher or being screened for accuracy or appropriateness. Special care is needed when dealing with secondary data from international sources because of cultural and data collection differences.

E-marketers should not be seduced by good design: The best-designed sites may not be the most accurate or credible, and vice versa. For example, the Securities and Exchange Commission publishes reports filed by public companies in simple text, spending no taxpayer money to make them pretty. Two librarians at the University at Albany, SUNY (library.albany.edu/briggs/addiction.html) created a fake Web page to show just how easy it is to get fooled (Exhibit 6 - 8). The following steps can be taken to evaluate the quality of secondary data collected online (some of this information is from the Albany site):

- Discover the Web site's author. A site published by a government agency or well-known corporation has more credibility than one by an unknown author. Sometimes discerning the difference is quite tricky: For example, there are usually several sites for the same musical group—some official and some published by individual fans. A search in AltaVista for "Rolling Stones" yielded over 67,000 results. Which of these are authorized by the group?

- Try to determine if the site author is an authority on the Web site topic. For example, an economist from Harvard University or Merrill Lynch might have more credible information about interest rates than a politician. Furthermore, the university's Web site may be more objective than the financial firm's site.

- Check to see when the site was last updated; don't just accept the automatic date function on the home page. Many Web sites change every day, but some have not been maintained for years. Obviously, the more current the information is, the more useful it will be for decision making. Check the hyperlinks. Although most sites contain occasional broken links, a site with many inoperative links is a site that has not been updated recently.

- Determine how comprehensive the site is: Does it cover only one aspect of a topic, or does it consider the broader context?

- Try to validate the research data by finding similar information at other sources on the Internet or in hard copy at the library. If the same statistics are not available elsewhere, look for other ways to validate the data. For example, one validation of the number of people with Internet service providers might be to check the

---

UNIVERSITY AT ALBANY
STATE UNIVERSITY OF NEW YORK

Psychosocial Parameters of Internet Addiction

Rudolph G. Briggs, Ph.D.
Department of Psychotechnology

- Internet Addiction Disorder (IAD) is characterized by seven basic diagnostic criteria, among them increasing tolerance of long online hours, withdrawal, and unsuccessful efforts to control Internet use.
  Ferris, Jennifer R. *Internet Addiction Disorders: Causes, Symptoms, and Consequences.* http://www.chem.vt.edu/chem-dept/dessy/honors/papers/ferris.html

- College officials are increasingly concerned about the growing number of students who are unable to control and amount of time they spend with their computers. These students are being called 'Internet vampires' because they emerge from computer laboratories often at dawn.
  DeLoughry, Thomas J. "Snared by the Internet: College Officials Debate Whether Students Spend Too Much Time On Line." *The Chronicle of Higher Education,* March 1, 1996, 42 (25), A25.

- Alcoholics Anonymous is considering setting up a separate division of their organization to work with people addicted to browsing the Internet.
  Press Release.

Exhibit 6 - 8 A Real Web Page?
Source: Laura B. Cohen and Trudi E. Jacobson, http://library.albany.edu/briggs/addiction.html.

number of people with computers (the latter should be larger). In general it is also a good idea to compare sites that cover the same topic.

- Check the site content for accuracy. If it has lots of errors or if the numbers don't add properly, this is a sign that the data cannot be trusted.

Don't stop looking when the first good screen full of hyperlinks appears. Remember that this is only one of many potential sites to research, and the list of related hyperlinks is provided as a service—so these are not necessarily the best sources for the topic.

Source 3: Primary Data

When secondary data are not available to assist in marketing planning, marketing managers may decide to collect their own information. Primary data are information gathered for the first time to solve a particular problem. They are usually more expensive and time-consuming to gather than secondary data; on the other hand, the data are current and more relevant to the marketer's specific problem. In addition, primary data have the benefit of being proprietary and, thus, unavailable to competitors.

This section describes two electronic sources of primary data collection: the Internet and **real space**. Primary data collection techniques on the Net include traditional approaches of experiments, focus groups, observation, **in-depth interviews (IDI)**, and survey research. Computer networks facilitate data collection and offer other advantages as well. An increasingly popular survey research method on the Internet entails single-source research via **online panels**. Nontraditional technology-enabled approaches include **real-time profiling** at Web sites and computer **client-side or server-side automated data collection**. Real-space primary data collection refers to technology-enabled approaches to gather information offline that is subsequently stored and used in marketing databases. The most important real-space techniques are bar code scanners and credit card terminals at brick-and-mortar retail stores, although computer entry by customer service reps while talking on the telephone with customers might also be included here. Whether collected on the Internet or offline, all electronic data gathered at any customer touch point (e.g., e-mail, telephone, Web site, grocery store purchase, store kiosk) end up in a marketing database and become part of the marketing knowledge to be used for effective planning.

Each primary data collection method can provide important information, as long as e-marketers understand the limitations. Remember that Internet research can only collect information from people who use the Internet, which leaves out a huge portion of the U.S. population, and many more in other countries. As a review, we present the steps for conducting primary research, and then discuss each approach along with its particular uses, strengths, and weaknesses.

Primary Research Steps

A primary data collection project includes five steps (Exhibit 6 - 9):

1. *Research problem.* As with secondary data, specificity is vital. Exhibit 6 - 10 shows some typical e-marketing research problems that electronic data can help solve.

2. *Research plan.*
   - *Research approach.* On the basis of the information need, researchers choose from among experiments, focus groups, observation techniques, in-depth interviews, and survey research, or nontraditional real-time and real-space techniques.
   - *Sample design.* At this stage researchers select the sample source and number of desired respondents.
   - *Contact method.* Ways to contact the sample include traditional methods such as the telephone, mail, and in person as well as the Internet and other technology-enabled approaches.

Exhibit 6 - 9 Primary Research Steps

Online Retailers	Web Sites
Improve online merchandising	Pages viewed most often
Forecast product demand	Increase site "stickiness" (stay longer)
Test new products	Test site icons and organization
Test various price points	Path users take through the site—is it
Test co-branding and partnership	efficient?
effectiveness	Site visit overall satisfaction
Measure affiliate program effectiveness	

Customers and Prospects	Promotions
Identify new market segments	Test advertising copy
Test shopping satisfaction	Test new promotions
Profile current customers	Check coupon effectiveness
Test site customization techniques	Measure banner ad clickthrough

Exhibit 6 - 10 Typical Research Problems for E-Marketers

- *Instrument design.* If a survey is planned, researchers develop a questionnaire. For other methods, researchers develop a protocol to guide the data collection.

3. *Data collection.* Researchers gather the information according to plan.

4. *Data analysis.* Researchers analyze the results in light of the original problem. This step includes using statistical software packages for traditional survey data analysis or data mining to find patterns and other information in databases.

5. *Distribute findings/add to the MIS.* Research data might be placed in the MIS database and be presented in written or oral form to marketing managers.

Internet-Based Research Approaches

The Internet is fertile ground for primary data collection. One reason is declining cooperation from consumers using traditional research approaches. Telephone survey refusal rates are between 40% and 60%, and an estimated 40% didn't answer the mailed 2000 U.S. Census. According to Fred Bove of Socratic Technologies, "Telemarketers ruined the telephone-interviewing enterprise" (Thompson 1999, p. 70). Conversely, with an increasing number of consumers online, conducting research using this inexpensive and quick method makes sense. In North America, 71% of all research firms use various online methodologies (Exhibit 6 - 11). Here are three examples of successful online research:

- *Creative test.* Leo Burnett, the advertising agency, built a panel of 50 elementary schools for the purpose of testing advertising directed to the "kid" market. Burnett put some advertising posters online and sent e-mails directing students to the Web pages displaying the posters. After viewing the posters, students completed a survey to select the best one. In this test, over 800 kids helped decide the best creative approach for the poster.

- *Customer satisfaction*. British Airways posted a questionnaire on its Web site to gather opinions of company services among Executive Club members. Over 9,000 people completed the questionnaire within nine months.

- *Product development*. The University of Nevada, Reno posted a questionnaire on the marketing program Web site, inviting practitioners and academics to give opinions about what should be included in e-commerce programs at the university level; 140 respondents helped to shape new courses.

Now marketers are learning how to combine online and offline data effectively and efficiently, as in the Purina example and as done by some brick-and-mortar retailers that also conduct e-commerce. This involves merging data from older legacy systems, incoming call centers, retailer bar code scanners, government statistics, and many other places that are difficult to integrate. In one example, Media Metrix installed PC meters on the computers of several thousand Information Resources, Inc. (IRI) Shoppers Hotline panel members. Web data include exposure to ads, sites visited, and surfing and purchasing frequency and patterns. These data are combined with offline panel data: actual packaged goods purchased at brick-and-mortar grocery stores, as well as volume purchased, timing of purchases, promotional effectiveness, and brand loyalty.

In addition, primary data are collected online using experiments, focus groups, observations, in-depth interviews, and survey research, as discussed in the following sections.

Online Experiments

Experimental research attempts to test cause-and-effect relationships, as in the Purina example. A researcher will select subjects, randomly put them into two or more groups, and then expose each group to different stimuli. The researcher then measures responses to the stimuli, usually in the form of a questionnaire, to determine if differences exist among the groups. If the experiment has been carefully controlled (only the experimental stimuli have been varied), group differences can be attributed to the stimuli (cause and effect). Of course, these effects must be tested in other situations and with other subjects to determine their degree of generalizability.

Marketers can easily test alternative Web pages, banner ads, and promotional offers online. For example, a firm might send e-mail notification of two different pricing offers, each to one half of its customer database. If a hyperlink to two different Web pages at the sponsoring firm's site is included in the e-mail, it will be quickly apparent which offer "pulls better."

Online Focus Groups

Focus group research is a qualitative methodology that attempts to collect in-depth information from a small number of participants. Focus groups are often used to help

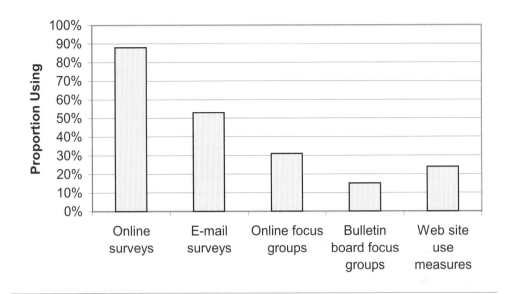

Exhibit 6 - 11 Proportion of 200 Firms Using Online Primary Research
Source: "Big Bytes" (2001).

marketers understand important feelings and behaviors prior to designing survey research.

Between 15% and 30% of advertising agencies and market research firms use the Internet to conduct online focus groups. This contact method provides some advantages over traditional focus groups, where all participants are in one room. First, the Internet can bring together people who do not live in the same geographic area, such as a focus group with consumers from five different countries discussing online shopping experiences. Second, because participants type their answers at the same time, they are not influenced as much by what others say ("groupthink"). Finally, by using the Web, researchers can show participants animated ads, demonstrate software, or use other multimedia stimuli to prompt group discussion.

On the other hand, online focus groups can accommodate only four to eight participants at a time while traditional groups generally host 10 to 12. The reason is that it is difficult to manage simultaneous, overlapping conversation online. Some researchers avoid this problem by using online bulletin boards and keeping focus groups going on for weeks (15% use this method according to the survey in Exhibit 6 - 11). Also, nonverbal communication is lost online—in offline groups facial expressions can be very revealing in a way that typed smiley faces do not match. Another disadvantage of online groups is the authenticity problem. Without seeing people in person, it is difficult to be sure they are who they say they are. For example, it is quite common for children to pose as adults online. This can be solved by verifying **respondent authenticity** and requiring password entry to the group. Technical problems can also stall an online group. Finally, one study compared face-to-face, telephone, and online focus groups and found that subjects used stronger positive and negative words online than in other modalities—typing is different from speaking (Ponnaiya and Ponnaiya 1999). Nevertheless, focus groups are quicker and less expensive to operate than offline versions.

King, Brown and Partners, a San Francisco research firm, conducts online focus groups for its clients (www.kingbrown.com) using this procedure:

- Contact potential participants via e-mail, asking them to go to a Web site and answer screening questions (e.g., the market may be teenagers in Europe who buy Levis).
- Send e-mail messages to qualified users, offering them money to participate in the group.
- Have clients and four to eight participants appear at an online site at the appointed time and day and have all greeted electronically by the moderator.
- Split the screen into two vertical portions: On the right, the moderator types questions and the participants type responses. Multimedia can also be presented on the right side. The left side is a "back room" where clients can communicate with each other and the moderator through their keyboards as the group progresses.

Online Observation

Observation research monitors people's behavior by watching them in relevant situations. For example, retailers videotape shoppers to see the pattern they choose in moving through the store and to monitor other shopping behaviors. Some researchers believe that actions speak louder than words, making customer observation stronger than surveys that record people's statements about what they believe and do. Of course, as a qualitative approach, observations of a small number of people cannot be used to describe how all people might act.

An interesting and very important form of observational research, available only on the Internet, involves monitoring consumer chatting and e-mail posting through chat rooms, bulletin boards, or mailing lists. The **Usenet** consists of over 35,000 newsgroups, each a forum for public discussion on a specific topic. People post articles to newsgroups for others to read. Discussions range from the meaningful to the absurd, but marketing planners can learn about products and industries by monitoring discussions. Some firms will, for a fee, monitor the Usenet and notify corporations of any bad rumors circulating about them. This enables the companies to quickly post a response and dispel rumors. A highly specialized search engine called Deja.com developed a system of indexing all postings to the Usenet, thus, proving a great service to the Internet community—since then Google Groups has taken over the index. To get an idea of the value of consumer observation, see Exhibit 6 - 12 for part of a discussion about the Palm VII. Such information is extremely important for both PalmPilot and its competitors. Other ways to monitor customer chat are to provide space on the firm's Web site or to subscribe to e-mail lists on product-related topics.

Online In-Depth Interviews (IDIs)

This technique involves semistructured conversation with a small number of subjects. Generally the interviewer develops a set of questions and encourages the subject to speak at length on particular issues through careful probing techniques. Many large companies conduct Web site usability studies to watch users as they click through the firm's Web site. In this case, the subject and interviewer are in the same room while the subject performs specified tasks on the computer. In a seminal study, Sun Microsystems tested Web site icons for communication effectiveness with only three users. Individual subjects looked at Sun's Web site, pointed at icons they wanted to click on, and did a "think aloud," indicating what information they thought would be on the page (Nielsen and Sano 1994). Through this research Sun was able to find icons that had appropriate meaning for users.

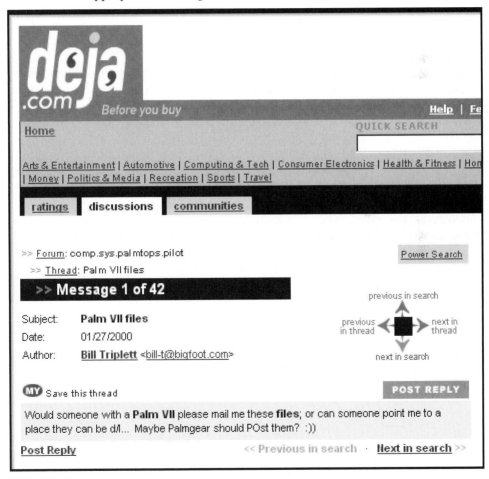

Exhibit 6 - 12 Consumers Discussing Product in the Usenet
Source: www.deja.com.

IDIs are better conducted in person; however, e-mail can facilitate communication when subjects live far from the researcher. For example, marketers could query a few experts about the future of Internet advertising by sending an initial set of e-mail questions, then compiling the results and sending the summary along with more questions to these same experts. Using several rounds of e-mail messages, researchers can probe for more information in desired areas.

Online Survey Research

E-marketers conduct surveys by sending questionnaires to individuals via e-mail or by posting a survey form on the Web or an electronic bulletin board. The latter is not recommended unless the bulletin board is owned by the organization: Netizens do not react favorably to companies posting commercial messages on the Usenet. BizRate is a good example of a firm that has built its business using online survey research. BizRate presents Web questionnaires to a random sample of shoppers at client sites for the purpose of helping the sites improve marketing efforts.

E-Mail Surveys   To prepare an e-mail survey, an organization can draw a sample of e-mail addresses from its database, purchase a list, or gather e-mail addresses from the Web or Usenet newsgroups. The firm wants to exercise control over who gets the electronic questionnaire, so it will select a specialized and representative group to research. After sending a questionnaire, the researcher can easily and inexpensively send e-mail reminders to participants who have not yet responded. Perhaps because of this capability, response rates are just as high for e-mail surveys as for traditional contact methods. As with all methodologies, the percentage of the sample responding depends, in part, on the participants' interest in the survey topic.

One problem with e-mail survey research is that many consumers do not have the technical skill to put the incoming e-mail questionnaire into a "reply and edit" mode to type their answers in the appropriate places. Respondents who know how to do this are often sloppy, placing their answers in any location near the question, thus increasing the chance of tabulation error. In 1995 FIND/SVP, a large market research firm, tested a way to solve this problem by placing two asterisks (* *) after each question and asking respondents to place their responses between them. The company developed computer software that would select responses in that location, minimizing time and tabulation error.

In general, e-mail survey research is diminishing in use as a contact method in favor of Web-based surveys. E-mail surveys are still preferable in countries where users pay by the hour for Internet connection because e-mail may be answered offline whereas a user must be online to complete a multipage Web form survey.

Web Surveys   Many companies post questionnaires on their Web pages. Respondents type answers into automated response mechanisms in the form of radio buttons (users click to indicate the response), drop-down menus, or blank areas. One of the authors conducted a Web survey with Ted Mitchell at the University of Nevada, Reno to determine what topics should be taught in e-commerce programs.

Exhibit 6 - 13 displays question types from the Web survey. Sometimes the purpose of these questionnaires is to gather statistics about a site's visitors (e.g., Web site registration); sometimes it is more formal survey research. For example, New Balance asks random Web site visitors to rate the importance and performance of various site features: customer service, navigation ease, product selection and prices, site security, and shopping. Through this process it learned that customers are willing to pay for shipping, which is why the firm added that element to the pricing structure.

When not sampling Web site users, researchers will post a Web survey and then send e-mail and use other forms of publicity to direct respondents to the Web site. The best response rates come from members of e-mail lists because they usually have a special interest in the topic. Customers and prospects on e-mail lists are also good sample sources. Finally, advertising on electronic bulletin boards or via banner ads and links from other Web sites will drive a very small amount of traffic to a Web survey. For example, one firm placed a banner ad on Yahoo! and received only 1% clickthrough, although this totaled 826 respondents. In general, response rates to online surveys are as good as or better than surveys using traditional approaches, sometimes reaching as much as 40%.

Online survey research has many advantages and disadvantages over traditional contact methods. Some are discussed in the next paragraphs; Exhibit 6 - 14 contains a more extensive list.

Online Survey Research Advantages   Online survey research is fast and inexpensive, especially when compared with traditional survey methodologies (Miller 2001), perhaps its most important advantage. Questionnaires are delivered nearly instantaneously worldwide over the Internet without paying for postage or an interviewer. Web surveys are converted to HTML files and do not need lengthy printing, collating, and mailing time. Those who complete the questionnaires generally do so in the first three days, making the entire process very quick. It is also easy to send multiple reminders if using e-mail invitations. Also, some researchers believe that Web surveys reduce errors. For example, contingency questions are those that the computer automatically presents depending upon responses to previous questions. If a respondent answers "c" to question 9, the software can immediately skip three questions and present question 12. This technique reduces the complexity and time involved for respondents. In addition, respondents enter their answers, which eliminates data entry errors found in traditional methods when converting answers from paper questionnaires. In addition, some researchers have discovered that respondents will answer questions more honestly and openly on a computer than when an interviewer is present—and will answer sensitive questions about private matters over the Net. The reason may be that the computer is impersonal and no one is watching what the respondent types.

Online Survey Research Disadvantages   Sample representativeness and measurement validity are the biggest concerns of market researchers today (Miller

7. Each course makes specific contributions to a program of study. For example, some may feel that a major contribution of their course is in the learning of HTML and Java. Others may feel that major contributions are in project management or measuring advertising effectiveness. What are some of the key contributions your course would make if it were part of a program in E-commerce and Internet Marketing?

8. In what field is your highest degree?

Open ended

9. For which of the following do you have substaintial experience, training, or education? (Please check all that apply.)

☐ Advertising   ☐ Marketing Management
☐ Journalism   ☐ Management of Information Systems
☐ Computer Science   ☐ Graphic Design

11. What is your gender?   ⦿ Male ○ Female

Radio buttons: Choose one

At which University or College are you teaching? (optional)

In-sourcing or outsourcing Web site functions

There are many different combinations of servers, databases, and programming support that can be used to maintain a web site, and these functions can be done either in-house or be outsourced. Please answer question 9, pertaining to your current situation, and question 10, your anticipated site support in the near future. You may check both in-house and outsource categories if appropriate.

| | Question 9 | | | Question 10 | | |
| | Currently | | | Future | | |
	Don't Know	In-house	Outsource	Don't Know	In-house	Outsource
Web server	☐	☐	☐	☐	☐	☐
Listserv server	☐	☐	☐	☐	☐	☐
DNS server	☐	☐	☐	☐	☐	☐
E-mail server	☐	☐	☐	☐	☐	☐
Database computer	☐	☐	☐	☐	☐	☐
Site programmers	☐	☐	☐	☐	☐	☐
Page developers	☐	☐	☐	☐	☐	☐
Graphic designers	☐	☐	☐	☐	☐	☐
Internet marketing strategy	☐	☐	☐	☐	☐	☐
Web ad sales staff	☐	☐	☐	☐	☐	☐
Site and log evaluation staff	☐	☐	☐	☐	☐	☐

Radio buttons: Choose all that apply

Exhibit 6 - 13 Mitchell and Strauss Web Survey

2001). Marketers cannot draw a scientific probability sample because no list of Internet users currently exists—unless the sample is only from a firm's customer list, they all use the Internet, and the firm has all the e-mail addresses. In contrast, researchers employing in-person or mail contact methods have population lists and can draw probability samples. Although no public lists of all telephone numbers exists, random digit dialing technology solved the probability problem for this contact method. Without the ability to draw a random sample, researchers cannot

Advantages	Disadvantages
Fast and inexpensive	Sample selection/generalizability
Diverse, large group of Net users worldwide to small specialized niche	Measurement validity Self-selection bias
Computer entry reduces researcher data entry errors	Respondent authenticity uncertain
Honest responses to sensitive questions	Frivolous or dishonest responses
Anyone-can-answer, invitation-only, or password protected	Duplicate submissions
Electronic data are easy to tabulate	Steep learning curve
Less interviewer bias	

Exhibit 6 - 14 Advantages and Disadvantages of Online Survey Research

generalize results to the entire population being studied. What this means is that researchers can send e-mail questionnaires to samples of respondents or put a Web survey online, but they must be very careful when interpreting the results. What does it mean when 15,000 online survey participants click off the products they've shopped for online? How does the result relate to all Web users? This is the generalizability problem. Some firms, such as Bizrate.com, compensate for sampling problems by offering the questionnaire to every "nth" visitor at a Web site. This works well if the firm wants information from a good sample of site visitors.

Online research entails several measurement issues. First, because there are many different browsers, computer screen sizes, and resolution settings, researchers worry that colors will look different and measurement scales will not display properly online. On some computers, a scale from one to five might not have equidistant spaces between them, creating the image of different values. Second, a comparison study between telephone and online surveys found that online users were less likely to use the two extreme scale points on a five-point scale (i.e., the one and five were clicked less frequently) (Miller 2001).

Some researchers believe that most differences among the various survey methodologies are due to demographic and other differences between online and offline populations; although differences like these exist, researchers have not yet found proof to support this explanation. Weighting is one way of handling this and other survey sampling problems—the responses of underrepresented groups in the survey are multiplied by a specific number to bring it closer to the number in the overall population. Still, according to Andy Kohutt of the Pew Research Center, "The traditional corrections that we make in survey research adjust for small imbalances, not for large groups of people who have no chance to play the game" (Thompson 1999, p. 68). Some believe that the Internet will not be a good vehicle for survey research until 80% of the population are online, but others believe that gaining large numbers of respondents, weighting, and comparing online and offline results are enough. For example, Harris Interactive's Poll Online predicted the results of 21 out of 22 election races accurately in the United States in 1998, and Avon Products found mall intercept surveys in 17 cities to correlate highly with online surveys—so it dropped the mall methodology (Thompson 1999).

Another problem with Web surveys and questionnaires posted on bulletin boards is that the firm has no control over who responds. Whereas the person receiving an e-mail generally keeps it private and responds personally, anyone can answer a Web survey if the address is published. This possibility creates a self-selection bias that is difficult to measure.

A closely related concern is respondent authenticity. This is a problem in any self-administered survey methodology, but it seems particularly acute on the Internet. Surveys have found that anywhere from 20% to 50% of Web users have posed as the opposite sex on the Internet, and children often pose as adults online. This situation is not easy to correct and obviously biases survey results. Many researchers are attempting to screen out nonlegitimate or flippant respondents. One way is to watch for frivolous results such as responses that form a pattern (e.g., each response is increased by one: 1, 2, 3, 4, and so on).

Another problem concerns duplicate responses to online surveys. GVU put e-mail address screening into its second user survey and found that 709 (3.8%) of its 18,503 completed questionnaires were multiple submissions from the same address (gvu.gatech.edu/user_surveys). Some respondents simply make a mistake and submit a questionnaire more than once, and perhaps others want their opinion counted heavily!

Finally, note that survey forms are not nearly as easy to create as most other types of Web pages. Also, in order to make the form interactive, developers must place a special program on the Web server (CGI or Perl script) that "tells" the server what to do with the respondent information. A few enterprising firms have created software to assist in this process. SurveySolutions software allows researchers to create a Web form survey nearly as simply as other Web page authoring tools or word processing software. Researchers then put the Web page on their site, and all the interactivity work is done on the SurveySolutions server. Survey responses are e-mailed back to the researcher who uses the software to turn e-mails into data tables appropriate for analysis in spreadsheet or statistical software.

Online Panels

More researchers are using online panels to combat sampling and response problems. Also called **opt-in** communities, they include a panel of people who have agreed to be the subject of marketing research. Usually they are paid and often receive free products, as well. Panel participants complete extensive questionnaires after being accepted, so that researchers have information about their characteristics and behavior. This way, when panel members are asked to test product, are given questionnaires to complete, or are sent coupons and other promotions, researchers can correlate results with already collected demographic data. In turn, the research firms can use shorter questionnaires, thus increasing response rates (i.e., no need for demographic questions). An advantage to large panels such those in the Purina opening story are that smaller groups of members can be targeted based on behavior or demographics. Conversely, panel access is usually more expensive for client firms than traditional methods of sample generation. Finally, since research firms sometimes recruit panel members in nonscientific ways, the generalizability of survey results from panels is questionable. Large numbers of respondents and high response rates minimize this problem, however. Greenfield Online has a 1.2 million member panel that includes both consumers and businesses and receives a 70% response rate for most surveys (see www.greenfield.com). Other firms with large online panels include Nielsen//NetRatings, NPD Group, Harris Interactive, and Digital Marketing Services (DMS).

Ethics of Online Research

Almost everyone conducting marketing research on the Web has considered its "gift culture" and decided to give something to respondents as appreciation for participating. With traditional research, respondents are frequently offered a nominal fee (e.g., $5.00) to complete a questionnaire, which increases the response rate. Firms can even send money online using services such as PayPal (www.paypal.com). Some researchers draw names of those who submit responses, offering free products or cash. Others donate money to charities selected by respondents (e.g., $3.00 to one of three charities listed on the Web page for each questionnaire submitted). Many post the entire results in downloadable form, and most provide at least some results on the Web sites after the survey period is completed.

Marketers face several other ethical concerns regarding survey research on the Internet.

1. With e-mail surveys, respondents are increasingly upset at getting unsolicited e-mail requesting survey participation.

2. Some researchers "harvest" e-mail addresses from newsgroups without permission (e.g., from Google.com). Perhaps this practice is analogous to gathering names from a telephone book, but some people object because consumers are not posting with the idea of being contacted by marketers.

3. Some companies conduct "surveys" for the purpose of building a database for later solicitation. Ethical marketers clearly mark the difference between marketing research and marketing promotion and do not sell under the guise of research.

4. Privacy of user data is a huge issue in this medium, because it is relatively easy and profitable to send electronic data to others via the Internet. Farhad Mohit, CEO at BizRate, notes that many others want the data they collect. According to Mohit, guarding respondent data privacy is central to the success of BizRate.

These and other concerns prompted ESOMAR®, the European Society for Opinion and Marketing Research, to include guidelines for Internet research in its International Code of Marketing and Social Research Practice. ESOMAR has over 4,000 members in 100 countries (www.esomar.nl).

In spite of serious shortcomings, the Net is useful for conducting primary research and will be used increasingly in the future, especially as the Net population grows. However, when using any primary or secondary data, marketers must evaluate their quality carefully and apply it accordingly.

Other Technology-Enabled Approaches

The Internet is an excellent place to observe user behavior because the technology automatically records actions in a format that can be easily, quickly, and mathematically manipulated for analysis. Computer client-side and server-side automated data collection are two nontraditional technology-enabled approaches deserving of special emphasis. Real-time profiling at Web sites is one particularly powerful server-side approach. These techniques are especially interesting and unusual because they did not exist prior to the Internet, and because they allow marketers to make quick and responsive changes in Web pages, promotions, and pricing.

Client-Side Data Collection

Client-side data collection refers to collecting information about consumer surfing right at the user's PC. One approach is to use cookies when a user visits a Web site. Cookie files are quite helpful, and even necessary, for e-commerce and other Internet activities. Some cookies track user surfing and help marketers present appropriate promotions and Web pages to individual users. However, the use of cookies can be controversial, as noted in Chapter 4.

One client-side data collection method that is not controversial involves measuring user surfing patterns by installing a PC meter on the computers of a panel of users and tracking the user **clickstream**. This approach is similar to the A.C. Nielsen "people meter" used on TV sets to determine ratings for various programs. We discuss this technique more thoroughly in other chapters.

Server-Side Data Collection

Web site log software generates reports on numbers of users who view each page, location of site visited prior to the firm's site, and what users buy at a site. For example, because of its online registration requirement, Expedia can track visitors' ticket purchases, browsing patterns, and how often they visit the site. It uses the information to send special offers to customers as well as to offer services such as the fare watcher. Amazon, through collaborative filtering software, keeps track of books ordered by customers and makes recommendations based on customer trends in its database. These observational data help firms improve online marketing strategies, sell advertising, and produce more effective Web sites.

Increasingly firms use server-side data to make frequent changes in Web pages and promotional offers. Real-time profiling occurs when special software tracks a user's movements through a Web site, then compiles and reports on the data at a moment's notice. Also known as "tracking user clickstream in real time," this approach allows marketers to analyze consumer online behavior and make instantaneous adjustments to site promotional offers and Web pages. Real-time profiling is not cheap—one estimate puts the software at $150,000 to start and $10,000 a month thereafter. The ability to predict future behavior based on past behavior and, thus, offer customized Web pages to appropriate customers while they are visiting a Web site can pay off handsomely, however. See Chapter 14 for more on these techniques.

Real-Space Approaches

Real-space primary data collection occurs at offline points of purchase. Offline data collection is important for e-marketing because these data, when combined with online data, paint a complete picture of consumer behavior for individual retail firms. Smart card and credit card readers, interactive point of sale machines (iPOS), and bar code scanners are mechanisms for collecting real-space consumer data. While the universal product code (UPC), also known as the bar code, has been in grocery stores since 1974, its use has grown to the point where such codes are now scanned billions of times a day. Product sales data gathered by scanning the UPC at retail stores is currently used primarily for inventory management. As UPC data go from the cash register into the computer, the software reduces accounting inventory levels automatically and sends communication to suppliers for replenishment of physical goods. This immediate inventory updating is quite efficient for retailers, wholesalers, and manufacturers.

Catalina Marketing uses the UPC for promotional purposes. This firm places small machines next to grocery store cash registers to generate coupons based on each customer's purchase. For example, if a customer buys Smucker's jam, the machine might spit out a $0.50 coupon for Knott's Berry jam. When the consumer redeems the Knott's coupon, the bar code scanner records it. In the process, Catalina Marketing and the retailer are building huge databases of customer purchases and responses to various offers. If consumers only redeem a small proportion of the Knott's coupons, Knott's Berry Farm might choose to increase the coupon size to $0.75. While not common practice, it is now possible to combine data collected at the brick-and-mortar retail store with that of the online version of the store. The Sharper Image retailer amasses a huge amount of data by combining server-side data from its Web site with telephone and mail orders from the catalog and UPC real-space data from the brick-and-mortar stores. This gives its customer service representatives a complete customer record from the database whenever needed.

Marketing Databases and Data Warehouses

Regardless of whether data are collected online or offline, they are moved to various marketing databases, as shown in Exhibit 6 - 1. Product databases hold information about product features, prices, and inventory levels; customer databases hold information about customer characteristics and behavior. **Transaction processing databases** are important for moving data from other databases into a data warehouse (Exhibit 6 - 15). Data warehouses are repositories for the entire organization's historical data (not just marketing data). They are designed specifically to support analyses necessary for decision making. In other words, marketers cannot apply the data in product or consumer databases to marketing problems as well as they can apply information in a data warehouse. Sometimes the data in a warehouse are separated into more specific subject areas (called data marts) and indexed for easy use. These concepts are important to marketers because they use data warehouse information for planning purposes.

Because Web sites are now so complex, often including tens of thousands of pages from or for many different corporate departments, content management is a hot new area. Many software vendors, including Microsoft, are attempting to solve the Web site maintenance problem with its software. These programs have features such as press release databases that automatically put the newest stories on a designated page and archive older stories, deleting them on a specified date.

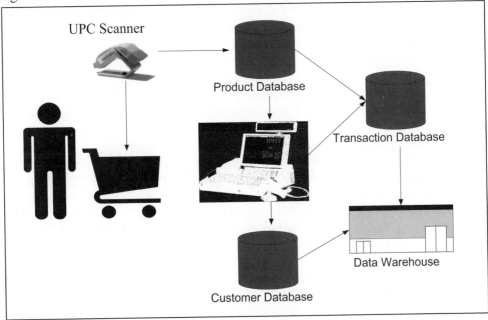

Exhibit 6 - 15 Real-Space Data Collection and Storage Example

Data Analysis and Distribution

Data collected from all customer touch points are stored in the data warehouse, ready for analysis and distribution to marketing decision makers. Four important types of analysis for marketing decision making include **data mining**, **customer profiling**, **RFM analysis** (recency, frequency, monetary), and report generating.

Data mining involves the extraction of hidden predictive information in large databases through statistical analysis. Here, marketers don't need to approach the database with any hypotheses other than an interest in finding patterns among the data. For example, a marketer might want to know if a product's heaviest users tend to purchase more during particular months, or if most buy extended warranties. Patterns uncovered by marketers help them to refine marketing mix strategies, identify new-product opportunities, and predict consumer behavior. Using data mining helped Fingerhut, the $2 billion catalog retailer, discover that customers who move their residence triple their purchasing in the 12 weeks after the move. Data mining also revealed that movers tend to buy furniture, telephones, and decorations but not jewelry or home electronics. Fingerhut used this information to create a special "Mover's Catalog," selecting appropriate products from among the 15,000 items it sells. In addition, it stopped sending other specialty catalogs to movers during the 12-week window.

Customer profiling uses data warehouse information to help marketers understand the characteristics and behavior of specific target groups. Through this process, marketers can really understand who buys particular products and how they react to promotional offers and pricing changes. Some additional uses of customer profiling include:

- selecting target groups for promotional appeals;
- finding and keeping customers with a higher lifetime value to the firm;
- understanding the important characteristics of heavy product users;
- directing cross-selling activities to appropriate customers; and
- reducing direct-mailing costs by targeting high-response customers.

RFM analysis scans the database for three criteria. First, when did the customer last purchase (recency)? Second, how often has the customer purchased products (frequency)? Third, how much has the customer spent on product purchases (monetary value)? This process allows firms to target offers to the customers who are most responsive, saving promotional costs and increasing sales. For example, an online retailer might notice that the top customer segment pulled 32% of the sales with a $69 average order value (AOV), or $22 of sales per thousand exposures to a banner ad on Yahoo! Now the retailer can estimate the value of this type of advertising and take steps to reach the top customer segment as directly as possible.

Individual marketing personnel can perform all data mining, customer profiling, and RFM analyses at any time through access to the data warehouse and distribute the results to other staff members involved in a particular decision. Report generators, on the other hand, automatically create easy-to-read, high-quality reports from data warehouse information on a regular basis. These reports may be placed in the marketing knowledge database on an intranet or extranet for all to access. Marketers can specify the specific information that should appear in these automatic reports and the time intervals for distribution, as in the earlier example of a retailer that sends online weekly sales reports to all managers.

Back Web Technologies (www.backweb.com), HotOffice (www.hotoffice.com), and many similar firms provide collaborative software that automatically integrates data from both the firm's macroenvironment and its microenvironment. For example, when a marketing manager working on a marketing plan saves it, the system can automatically put the file on the server for other managers to access. Internal data are seamlessly integrated with the firm's Web site, external Web sites, newsgroups, and databases—all with search capabilities. Such software helps firms distribute the results of database analyses.

Knowledge Management Metrics

Marketing research is not cheap. Marketers often weigh the cost of gaining additional information against the value of potential opportunities or the risk of possible errors from decisions made with incomplete information. They are also concerned about the storage cost of all those terabytes of data coming from Web site logs, online surveys, Web registrations, and other real-time and real-space approaches. Two metrics are currently in widespread use:

- **ROI.** Companies want to know why they should save all those data. How will they be used, and will the benefits in additional revenues or lowered costs return an acceptable rate on the storage space investment? For hardware storage space, ROI usually means total cost savings divided by total cost of the installation (Gruener 2001). Notably, companies use ROI to justify the value of other knowledge management systems as well.
- **Total Cost of Ownership (TCO).** Largely a metric used by information technology managers, this includes not only the cost of hardware, software, and labor for data storage but also other items such as cost savings by reducing Web server downtime and labor requirements.

For example, Galileo International offers travel reservations and maintains 102 terabytes of data—schedule, fare, and reservation information for 500 airlines, 47,000 hotels, and 37 car rental companies (Radding 2001). The company booked 345 million reservations in 2000, sometimes handling 10,000 requests a second! Galileo's ROI is simple: According to its owner, Frank Auer, every bit of the firm's $1.6 billion in revenue is a return on its data storage system.

In another example, trucking company Schneider National had enough data to fill ten 53-foot trailers with floppy disks. But it still could not easily figure out why it cost $0.20 a pound to deliver cars to a Ford Dealership in Texas and only $0.17 elsewhere. The firm spent an estimated $2 million to purchase business intelligence software that allowed employees to get quick answers to marketing problems and realized a $2.5 million return on that investment within two years (25% ROI) (Brown 2002).

Summary

E-marketers need data to guide decisions about creating and changing marketing mix elements. These data are collected from a myriad of sources, filtered into databases, and turned into marketing knowledge that is then used to develop marketing strategy. Knowledge management is the process of managing the creation, use, and dissemination of knowledge. A marketing information system (MIS) is the process by which marketers manage knowledge, using a system of assessing information needs, gathering information, analyzing it, and disseminating it to decision makers.

Marketers can tap three sources of marketing knowledge: (1) internal records (nonmarketing data such as cash flow, sales force data, and customer data), (2) secondary data (publicly and privately generated, from online databases, and for competitive intelligence), and (3) primary data (gathered for the first time to solve a particular problem). Competitive intelligence (CI) involves analyzing the industries in which a firm operates as input to the firm's strategic positioning and to understand competitor vulnerabilities. Marketers must evaluate the quality of data before relying on them to solve research problems.

Primary data may be collected on the Internet and in real space. The steps to conduct primary research are (1) define the research problem, (2) develop a research plan, (3) collect data, (4) analyze the data, and (5) distribute results. Internet-based research may include any of the following activities conducted online: experiments, focus groups, observations, in-depth interviews (IDI), and surveys. Surveys may be conducted either via e-mail or on a Web site or electronic bulletin board. Advantages to online surveys are that it is fast and inexpensive, has broad reach, reduces errors, elicits honest responses, can be restricted to authorized participants, and is easy to tabulate. Disadvantages include poor generalizability of results due to poor sample selection, self-selection bias, inability to confirm the respondent's authenticity, frivolous or dishonest responses, duplicate submissions, and a steep learning curve to create the online surveys.

Online panels are increasingly being used to combat sampling and response problems of online surveys. While some of these panels are small, others contain millions of participants. Some ethical concerns of online research include unsolicited e-mail, harvesting e-mail addresses from newsgroups, selling under the guise of research, and privacy of user data.

Marketers use technology to observe user behavior on the user's computer (client side) via cookies and PC meters or the server (server side) via the use of log files and real-time profiling. Real-space data collection takes place at offline points of purchase such as smart card and credit card readers, iPOS machines, and bar code scanners. The data can be used for inventory control and to target promotions.

Data warehouses are repositories for the organization's historical data. Data marts are subsections of the warehouse categorized by subject area. Data from all customer touch points are stored in the warehouse. Four types of analysis are conducted with the data—data mining, customer profiling, RFM (recency, frequency, monetary) analysis, and report generation. Data mining extracts hidden predictive information from the warehouse via statistical analysis. Customer profiling helps marketers understand the characteristics and behavior of specific target groups. RFM allows firms to target offers to customers who might be most responsive. Sophisticated report generation tools can automatically schedule and publish reports.

Key Terms

Bar code scanner	Opt-in
Clickstream	Primary data
Client-side data collection	Product database
Customer profiling	Real space
Data mining	Real-time profiling
Data warehouse	Respondent authenticity
Focus groups	RFM analysis
In-depth interviews (IDI)	Secondary data
Knowledge management (KM)	Server-side data collection
Learning organization	Total cost of ownership (TCO)
Marketing information system (MIS)	Transaction processing databases
Marketing intelligence	Universal product codes (UPC)
Online panels	Usenet

Exercises

Review Questions

1. What are the three main sources of data for solving marketing research problems?
2. Contrast primary with secondary data and explain the advantages and disadvantages of each.
3. What is competitive intelligence and what are some sources of online CI data?
4. Why and how do e-marketers evaluate the quality of information on a Web site?
5. What are the strengths and weaknesses of the Internet for primary and secondary data collection?
6. How do marketers turn marketing data into marketing knowledge?
7. What is a learning organization?

8. What is real-space data collection? Why is it important?

9. Is data mining possible without a data warehouse? Why or why not?

10. Give an example of how data mining uncovers new knowledge.

11. Identify the steps in a primary marketing research project.

Discussion Questions

12. What online research method(s) would you use to test a new-product concept? Why?

13. What online research method(s) would you use to test the brand image of an existing product? Why?

14. Of the ethical issues mentioned in the chapter, which are you most concerned about as a consumer? Why?

15. Can you think of a marketing research technique that could not be supported online? Explain your answer.

16. What are the current limitations for undertaking market research on the general population on the Net? How might these be overcome now and in the future?

17. Given that the cost of sending an e-mail questionnaire to 10,000 people is no higher than the cost of sending it to 10 people, why would market researchers bother devising samples if they were planning to undertake some research online?

7 consumer behavior

learning objectives

The primary objective of this chapter is develop a general understanding of the online consumer population. You will learn why billions of consumers do not use the Internet and explore the context in which online consumer behavior occurs, the characteristics and resources of online consumers, and the outcomes of the online exchange process.

After reading this chapter, you will be able to:

- Discuss general statistics about the Internet population.
- Identify the social, cultural, technological, legal, and political issues that explain why people do not use the Internet.
- Describe the Internet exchange process and the technological, social, and cultural context in which consumers participate in this process.
- Outline the broad individual characteristics and consumer resources that consumers bring to the online exchange.
- Highlight the five main categories of outcomes that consumers seek from online exchanges.

Many people believe that we have entered the age of the Internet. Actually, it's more accurate to say that we're living in the age of the customer.

anne busquet
american express

Four million customers annually buy through 12 different catalogs and associated Web sites—that's the customer base managed by Hanover Direct. Its brands include The Company Store and International Male. The firm has been online since 1996, and 10% of all sales come from the Web sites.

Hanover COO Richard Hoffman notes that 99% of all telephone customers complete the call with an order. Conversely, only 2% of all visitors, on average, actually buy during a visit to an online catalog retail site. One of the problems contributing to this low conversion rate (percentage of buyers among site visitors) is shopping cart abandonment—Web site visitors who start to buy online but somehow drop out of the purchasing process before paying. Not satisfied with this metric, Hanover conducted a survey of site visitors, held focus groups, and hired BizRate.com to conduct exit surveys with its Web site visitors. The purpose was to discover what consumer differences existed between catalog and Web channels that resulted in so many lost sales.

Hanover found that technical difficulties are usually the reason for an aborted sale. For example, the consumer gets booted off the Internet before the final order screen or the Web page doesn't load. The company also learned that some consumers are indecisive when they get to the final check-out page online and want someone to help them through the process. As a result, Hanover arranged to incorporate contact with customer service reps as part of the online buying process. When the Web server detects a customer returning to the order screen several times, a pop-up window appears offering help via chat box, phone call on the Web site, or phone call via telephone. The firm offers help only after observing this kind of consumer behavior because it wants to avoid undirected consumer chat and focus customer service personnel at the point of purchase where they can make a difference.

Additional changes to better meet consumer needs include getting rid of Web page jargon—instead of asking if the user wants to *modify* or *update* the shopping cart, the text asks if he wants to *change* the cart contents. Hanover also added pictures of the products in the shopping cart to more closely simulate an off-line shopping experience.

When Hanover began monitoring online customer behavior, its goal was to increase conversion rates by 50%. So far, the firm has achieved a one-third improvement (Wellner 2001)—and is well on its way to the goal.

Time is the only commodity worth anything anymore. Consumers will pay you to save them time. The Internet saves people time.

scott reamer s.g. gowen

Consumers in the 21st Century

Internet usage is still growing. From its inception until 1998, organizations scrambled to measure the number of users online and to make predictions about how fast those numbers would grow. Since then, Internet usage in developed nations has reached a critical mass and marketers such as Hanover Direct have turned their attention to practical questions such as whether a firm's target market is online, what these customers do online, what determines whether they'll buy from a site, and how much of the marketing effort should be devoted to online channels.

This chapter touches on the numbers and then investigates four important consumer behavior issues: the cultural, social, and technological context for consumer online behavior; individual user characteristics and resources; the online exchange process; and exchange outcomes. Understanding online consumer behavior helps marketers design marketing mixes that provide value and, thus, attract and retain customers. This chapter is a companion to Chapter 8, which expands on many potentially profitable online market segments. Also see Chapters 15 and 16 for more specifics about Internet users and issues outside the United States.

The Numbers

The Internet population was very small during the 1980s, experiencing a slow but steady growth until 1994 due to an increasing number of text-based users (e.g., those using e-mail and file transfer functions). Then, with the introduction of the World Wide Web and subsequent multimedia content expansion, the number of Net users exploded. In fact, the Internet has grown much more quickly than any other medium in history. In 2002, 531 million people had access to the Internet, representing 8.5% of the global population. Exhibit 7 - 1 presents the Internet's distribution by region. Recall from Chapter 1 that developed nations hold only 15% of the world's population but account for 88% of all Internet users (see www.weforum.org). In these countries, adoption rates range from 40% to 60%.

Where Are the Other 5.5 Billion People?

Not online. In one 30-country survey of non-Internet users, 40% said they have no need for the Internet (Pastore 2001). Some people in developing countries see no compelling reason to buy a computer or access the Internet. E-marketers have adjusted well to this disturbing news, recognizing that consumers—not companies—must decide what they want. This is one reason that e-marketers have shifted their attention from counting online eyeballs to digging deeper for a more thorough understanding of consumer preferences online and offline (Exhibit 7 - 2).

Social, cultural, technological, legal, and political issues are the main reasons why consumers do not use the Internet. Without major shifts some countries may not achieve high levels of Internet adoption among individual consumers for many years.

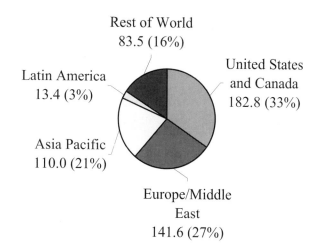

Exhibit 7 - 1 Millions of People with Home Internet Access by Region in 2002
Source: Data from Nielsen//NetRatings.

In these countries the B2B market will lead consumers to the Net, unlike in the United States, where a fast-growing consumer market enticed businesses online.

Social and Cultural Issues

In many countries, such as Egypt and Mexico, consumers are accustomed to touching merchandise before buying. These and other similar countries do not have a tradition of direct mail, and few people order from catalogs. In Arab countries and many other nations, the marketplace (bazaar) is a social meeting place that provides many benefits and would be hard to replace. In addition, consumers often have security and privacy concerns.

Payment also is a problem in many countries, especially where the credit card

Reason	%	Reason	%
No need for it	40	Content not of interest/relevance	2
Don't have a computer	33	Not my choice/decision at work	2
Not interested in it	25	Content not in my language	1
Don't know how to use it	16	Cost for ISP/access cost	1
Cost (general)	12	Cost for local telephone and toll	1
Not enough time to use it	8	service charges	
Don't know how to get it	3	Other	4
Current PC can't access Web	2	Unsure	2

Exhibit 7 - 2 Biggest Reasons for Not Using the Internet
Source: Pastore (2001) citing Ipsos-Reid study.

processing infrastructure is weak. Most consumers in such countries have no credit cards or bank accounts, and local retailers accept only cash. In Mexico, for example, many affluent consumers visit companies to pay cash for their phone or other bills; this is a way of life. Also, lack of Internet education is a problem in many countries. When PC penetration and Internet adoption rates are low, schools do not teach students how to use the Net. Although some firms in developing countries are using the Internet for transactions (especially travel and tourism-related firms), B2C e-commerce is not in the near future for such areas.

Technological Issues

One of the biggest barriers to Internet adoption is low PC penetration in some countries (33% in the survey). Communications infrastructure problems are an even bigger barrier. Arab countries, for example, have only 49 telephones per thousand people versus 133 phones per thousand people worldwide, and telephone callers frequently experience unreliable connections. Internet connections, where they exist, are often slow and unreliable. Also, in contrast to the U.S. norm, phone companies in many countries levy a per minute charge for *local* calls. This charge is in addition to what the ISP charges for Internet access. To solve these problems, some countries are turning to satellites and wireless information appliances to receive Internet and other communications.

Postal services are not reliable in many countries. Recently we heard one Mexican businessman state that the product he'd ordered on the phone was not delivered because someone robbed the delivery truck. Along with cultural patterns, this is one reason that direct marketing via mail is not used in many countries—and why e-commerce may develop slowly in these nations.

Legal and Political Issues

Other events that slow Internet adoption are government censorship and regulation. The Chinese government authorizes Web sites for citizen access and keeps a tight rein on Internet cafés. Some Egyptian government agencies block Internet ventures due to fear of losing tax money on direct sales to customers outside the country. Other barriers to exporting, such as tariffs and costly extended distribution channels, are slowing the adoption of e-commerce in some countries.

Despite these barriers, a global community connected by the Internet should emerge over time, fueled by the benefits of connecting multinational businesses, the lure of B2B e-business activity, and increasing consumer demand led by the younger generation (see Part V).

Inside the Internet Exchange Process

Many stimuli, characteristics, and processes explain consumer buying behavior. Stimuli that can motivate consumers to purchase one product rather than another include marketing communication messages and cultural, political, economic, and technological factors. Individual buyer characteristics such as income level and personality also come into play, along with other psychological, social, and personal aspects. Finally, consumers move through a variety of decision processes based on situational and product attributes. Marketing knowledge about consumer behavior is quite complex, and while we make many generalizations, individual differences are also important.

To create effective marketing strategies, e-marketers need to understand what motivates people to buy goods and services, both in the short and long term (i.e., develop brand loyalty). Recall from Chapter 1 that part of the e-marketing definition includes ". . .creating exchanges that satisfy individual consumer and organizational customers' objectives." **Exchange** is a basic marketing concept that refers to the act of obtaining a desired object from someone by offering something in return. When consumers purchase a product, they are exchanging money for desired goods or services. However, many other types of marketing exchanges can be made, such as when a politician asks citizens to exchange their votes for his services.

This chapter discuss only some of the many consumer behavior factors surrounding the exchange process that have been shown to be important in explaining Internet behavior. Bear in mind that many other basic motivating factors may also influence the consumer, as previously discussed.

Exhibit 7 - 3 summarizes the basic Internet exchange process. Individuals bring their own characteristics and personal resources to the process as they seek specific outcomes from an exchange. All of this occurs within a social, cultural, and technological context.

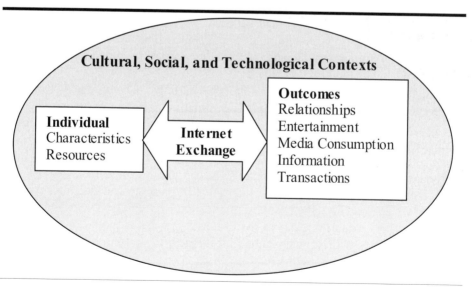

Exhibit 7 - 3 The Online Exchange Process

Context

Broad technological, social, and cultural forces affect online consumer behavior. Earlier chapters have discussed a variety of environmental factors affecting e-marketers; the following sections look at the consumer's environment or context and how they influence the purchasing process.

Technological Context

The Internet has moved from novelty to utility in the United States and most developed nations. Arranging for ISP services is like getting telephone services: slightly more than half of all consumers consider this routine. Chapter 4 discussed the current state of the ever-changing Internet technology. With regard to online consumer behavior, e-marketers need to consider home connection speeds and the changing landscape of digital receiving devices such as cell phones.

About 20% of Americans connect to the Internet with broadband (fast) Internet service, and these consumers exhibit different online behavior than do those accessing from a narrowband mobile handheld device or 56k modem in a PC. Broadband users enjoy more multimedia games, music, and entertainment because these download quickly. At the other extreme, those accessing with handheld devices such as Palm or Handspring personal digital assistants (PDAs) tend to access news, weather, stock quotes, and other data services that are low in graphics. As a practical example, the College of Business at the University of Nevada, Reno has found that students often access its Web site from home using slow modem speeds from computers with older operating systems. As a result, the school designs Web pages that download quickly and can be read by early versions of Netscape and Internet Explorer. This is more important to student customers than a flashy Web site that they cannot access from home. Chapter 8 discusses access speed market segments in detail.

E-marketers must remember that the PC is only one of many ways to communicate with customers using digital information. The key is to learn which devices a firm's customers and prospects own and prefer to use for various purposes, from communication through purchase and postpurchase service. Firms send data to customers' digital receiving devices such as the PC, electronic pager, fax machine, iTV (interactive TV), voice mail, handheld PDA, cell phone, and a other devices. For example, users can now access stock prices, FedEx package tracking information, airline schedule changes, weather, and more over their PalmPilot devices while in a taxi on the way to a client meeting or the airport. Wireless devices are much more important in countries with poor telephone infrastructures and other barriers to easy Internet access.

Social and Cultural Context

The days of marketers holding consumers captive for the 30 seconds of a TV commercial are quickly coming to a close. The Web is training individuals and organizations to help themselves to information, products, and virtually everything they want when and where they please. Thus, power is shifting to consumers, as mentioned in Chapter 1. For example, consumers walk into brick-and-mortar car dealerships with printed information sheets on automobile options and pricing. In addition, the following U.S. trends are affecting online exchanges:

- **Information overload** overwhelms consumers. It creates an **attention economy**— the idea that there is infinite information but the demand for it is limited by human capacity. This serious problem is compounded by the Internet and is one reason why consumers have little tolerance for spam (unsolicited e-mail).

- **Bunkering** means people are staying at home more (Hanson 2001). It is defined as ". . .the preparation and use of the home as a stronghold against assaults." In this climate, people want to be close to their nuclear family, buy products to fix up the nest, and stay in touch via e-mail and the telephone.

- **Security and privacy** are major concerns. A computer network open to 531 million people—and affected by frequent viruses and reports of Internet fraud— has consumers worried. Even a signature to receive a package from United Parcel Service on the digital pad gives the company a copy for the database. Consumers are not sure they can trust businesses with their personal information. Consumers want the Internet's benefits but are a bit leery about the downside.

- **Home and work** boundaries are dissolving. Many U.S. Internet users have access to the Internet both at home and at work. Fourteen percent report spending more time working at home because of the Internet (see www.pewinternet.org). Also, comScore MediaMetrix found that many U.S. workers make travel arrangements, purchase products, and handle other personal tasks online while at work. The home has become more like a center of life and home office for many; this trend will increase as more Americans telecommute (work and live in different cities and rarely visit the physical office).

- **Anywhere, anytime convenience** is critical for busy people. One study reported that 72% of American consumers ranked convenience as the most important factor affecting their decision about where to shop ("E-Commerce Numbers. . ."2001). They want to shop or pay bills anytime of the day or night, 24/7, from any geographic location, and receive deliveries when convenient for them, not for the firm or package delivery service.

- **Time poverty** creates multitasking and speeds up normal processes. Consumers want to find relevant information and products quickly and receive purchased goods as quickly as possible. Customers don't want to spend time looking up passwords to enter Web sites or helping firms correct account errors through repeated communication. Time poverty also contributes to a stressful environment in which consumers are ready to react badly if transactions don't go smoothly.

- **Demanding** expectations. The Internet has created a fierce competition to court consumers, and consumers know this. If a customer service rep has a bad attitude, the firm doesn't answer an e-mail quickly enough, or the Web page takes too long to download, consumers are ready to move to the competition. Consumers don't want their time wasted by unresponsive companies. And they know what to do about it, too: Many post complaints on epinions.com and send e-mails to everyone in their e-mail address books.

- **Self-service** is required. Customers want to log on, find information, make purchases, track package shipments, check their accounts, and make inquiries anytime, 24/7. Furthermore, they want to do this on a computer via e-mail, on the Web, or on a telephone, PDA, or fax machine—and they want all methods to produce identical information. It is an interesting contradiction: Consumers want to help themselves when they feel like it and be pampered by firms at other times.

- **Sophisticated consumers** know they are in control and have choices. For example, when consumers get sick, they often go online to learn more about the illness so they can help their medical doctors make treatment decisions.

- **Personalization** is becoming expected. Consumers want firms to remember who they are. This saves time and avoids the need to repeat information—an especially important consideration when an impersonal computer sits between consumers and the company. Furthermore, customers want to be treated as if they were important to the firm, particularly if they are loyal customers and place large orders.

- **Easy** does it, especially when it comes to the frustrations of technology. Consumers do not want to be forced to learn special software or elaborate instructions simply to order from a Web site or pay bills online. Also, people like *polite* computers—that is, error messages and thank-you screens with a friendly tone. How many times has the Microsoft message irritated you when the computer crashes through no fault of your own, and the opening reboot screen reminds you to *shut down properly next time?*

- **Multiple channel shopping** has become the norm. Eighteen percent of Internet users say that as a result of the Internet they spend less time shopping in brick-and-mortar stores (www.pewinternet.org). Consumers sometimes visit a store to see the product and then order it online or through a catalog; at other times they search for appropriate products online and then buy them offline.

Individual Characteristics and Resources

Because the demographics of U.S. and Canadian Internet users tend to mirror those of the general population, most consumer behavior research will apply to online exchanges, with some unique exceptions—due to the distinctive characteristics and individual resources consumers bring to the online exchange.

Individual Characteristics Affecting Internet Exchanges

Internet users have several characteristics that do not often exist in nonusers. The first is a positive attitude toward technology. Internet users who purchase products online tend to hold the attitude that technology helps make their lives richer and easier. (Forrester Research created a market segmentation scheme using this variable, as described in Chapter 8.) Second, online skill and experience play an important role in the exchange process. Consumers who have been online for over three years tend to be more adept than are new users at finding information and products quickly, resulting in less frustration and less shopping cart abandonment (this is about one-third of all users). Third, gender affects attitudes toward use of technology: Women have more positive attitudes about catalog and store shopping, whereas men are more positive about Internet shopping (Alreck and Settle 2002).

Another important characteristic involves language. Although only 1% of global users mentioned lack of local language content as a reason for not using the Internet, many experts think the Internet would be more useful if it had more content in the local languages of various countries (see Exhibit 7 - 2). As discussed in Chapter 8, 42% of the Web is still in English. On the other hand, in the United States, nearly 8 million Hispanics online access the Web using the Spanish language.

Next, two researchers found that online shoppers tend to be more goal oriented than experience oriented while shopping (Wolfinbarger and Gilly 2001). Goal-oriented behavior often includes going to a specific Web site with a purpose in mind, or searching for the lowest price for a particular product. Experience orientation relates to having fun, bargain hunting, or just surfing to find something new. Goal-oriented individuals like the idea that they don't have to deal with salespeople or crowds in the online environment, and they appreciate the online product selection, convenience, and information availability. When consumers are looking for experiential shopping, it makes sense that they would find this more often in brick-and-mortar stores than online.

Similarly, Forrester Research found that 70% of online shoppers have one of two traits: convenience or price orientation (Whelan 2001). Thirty-six percent of all online shoppers are price conscious and willing to buy from an unknown online retailer if the price is low. Another 36% won't turn down a bargain but won't change their favorite online retailer to find one. For these shoppers, convenience and trust are paramount, and they don't mind paying extra for these benefits.

Finally, McKinsey researchers reported differences in the outcomes sought online based on family life cycle (Mazur 2001). For example, mothers with small children have different interests and needs online than do teenagers. This seemingly obvious observation reinforces that family life cycle is an important influence on purchasing patterns online as well as offline and helps e-marketers to design Web sites and products that meet the needs of entire demographic groups.

Consumer Resources

Chapter 2 introduced the value equation showing that consumers perceive value as benefits minus costs. These costs constitute a consumer's resources for exchange: money, time, energy, and psychic costs.

Monetary Cost

Clearly, consumers need enough discretionary income to exchange for the goods and services they want—and to afford a computer and ISP connection for Net access. What makes the Internet exchange different, however, is that consumers usually can't pay cash or write paper checks for online transactions. Instead, consumers can pay by credit card, debit card, electronic check, or smart card. Most consumers in developed nations use credit cards. However, not everyone is able to acquire or wants a credit card. This is a big problem for e-marketers targeting the huge teen market online and for those targeting consumers in countries with low credit card availability. Consumers with bank accounts can use debit cards or pay by electronic check. **Electronic checks** work this way: The consumer sets up an account and authorizes a third-party Web site (such as PayPal) to pay a specified amount and withdraw funds from the user's checking account. Finally, smart cards are becoming popular in the United Kingdom. Also called Splash Plastic, smart cards have an electronic chip that can be coded to hold a certain amount of funds, payable by the bank or a depository company. The advantages are that anyone with the cash can get one and the limit of potential fraud is the amount of money coded into the card.

Time Cost

As previously mentioned, time poverty is a problem for today's consumers, so they want to receive appropriate benefits for the time they spend online. Exhibit 7 - 4 shows that, worldwide, the average user spent nearly 10 hours online every month in 18 sessions of 32 minutes and she moved fairly quickly, spending less than a minute per page. Did this user get what she wanted for the time she invested? The burden is on Internet firms to be sure their sites are well organized and easy to navigate so users can quickly find what they want. Search engines and shopping agents can help consumers find what they want to leverage their brief forays online.

The Internet's property of time moderator, discussed in Chapter 1, helps consumers manage their scarce time. This is because users can shop, e-mail, or perform other activities anytime, 24/7—a big advantage for working parents who can only find the time to shop late at night after the kids are in bed.

Time resource is a critical topic because online attention from consumers is a desirable and scarce commodity. The clutter of Web sites now parallels that of other

Metric	Quantity
Number of sessions for the month	18
Number of domains visited	48
Page views for each session	43
Time spent online for the month	9:50
Time spent per session	0:32
Duration of page viewed	0:00:44

Exhibit 7 - 4 April 2002 Global Internet Usage
Source: Data from www.Nielsen//NetRatings.

media—with some differences. Some researchers believe that consumers pay more focused attention to Web sites than to the content in any other medium. When in front of a television, consumers are easily distracted by other people or activities in the environment. The same holds true for the passivity of radio listening. Consumers seem to pay more attention to print media but may still flip pages quickly. Hoffman and Novak at Vanderbilt University applied the concept of **flow** from psychology to Web navigation behavior (www2000.ogsm.vanderbilt.edu). They define flow as:

> the state occurring during network navigation which is: (1) characterized by a seamless sequence of responses facilitated by machine interactivity, (2) intrinsically enjoyable, (3) accompanied by a loss of self-consciousness, and (4) self-reinforcing.

According to this concept, consumers are 100% involved and not easily distracted when they are online. Whether they are in a goal-oriented or experiential shopping trip online, they are focused. Therefore, once e-marketers can capture a pair of consumer eyeballs or earlobes, they can make a big impression in a short time as long as the Web site is enjoyable, self-reinforcing, and engaging. What is enjoyable for one segment may be different for another, however, which is good news for marketers trying to cut through the clutter of commercial messages on traditional media.

Energy and Psychic Costs

Closely related to time are energy and psychic resources. Sometimes it is just too much trouble to turn on the computer, log onto the Internet, and check e-mail. This accounts for the rising popularity of short text messaging (SMS) via cell phones and handheld mobile devices. All the user has to do is type a message on the phone, dial a phone number, and send the text. Incoming messages are announced by a phone ring. SMS use and marketing opportunities are discussed in Chapter 13.

Consumers apply psychic resources when Web pages are hard to figure out or when facing technological glitches. Such is the case with 44% of all online shoppers who

Reason Given	%	Reason Given	%
Page took too long to load	48	Returned the product	10
Site was confusing/couldn't find product	45	Site wouldn't accept credit card	9
Product not available/in stock	32	Tried/failed to contact customer service	8
Got logged off / system crashed	26	Site made unauthorized charge to my credit card	5
Had to contact customer service	20	Ordered product but never came	4
Product took too long to arrive	15	Wrong product arrived and couldn't return it	4

Exhibit 7 - 5 Most Common Reasons for Failed Online Purchases
Source: Boston Consulting Group Study as reported in Wellner (2001).

abandon online shopping carts at one time or another due to technical problems and other issues—buying just gets to be too much trouble (Wellner 2001). Some of these technical problems are presented in Exhibit 7 - 5. The bad news for e-marketers is that 65% of all online shopping carts are abandoned and 28% of these users never return to the site to shop.

Internet Exchange

This is the actual moment when exchange occurs. Browser bookmarks help consumers quickly jump to their favorite online retailer when looking for a product or making a purchase. In addition, e-mail messages from firms often contain hyperlinks to bring consumers directly to specific information, news reports, or advertised specials. The Internet has the added feature of automation to facilitate exchange. For example, CNN.com sends one sentence e-mails several times a day or week with breaking news for those who sign up for the service—the full story is a click away. Also, Amazon.com sends consumers a link to a new book by a previously purchased author. These automated e-mails facilitate the exchange process.

Exchange Outcomes

Just what benefits do consumers get by exchanging all that money, time, and energy? The Pew Research Center conducts continuing research entitled *Internet and the American Life*. Along with comScore MediaMetrix and other audience measurement firms, Pew has built a rich understanding of what American consumers do online and how the Internet has changed the way people behave. Using these data, the myriad of online activities can be categorized by the following general outcomes: relationships, entertainment, media consumption, information gathering, and transactions. Each is ripe with marketing opportunity.

Relationships

Internet users spend 43% of their precious online time handling e-mail or other communication-related activities; nearly all Internet users send e-mail ("Online Shopping Promises. . ."2001). This is true worldwide, as well as in the United States. Consumers communicate online because it is an inexpensive way to keep in touch, and because it is usually text based so it can be easily accomplished with a slow modem or over a wireless handheld device. In addition, consumers form new relationships with the people they meet online that sometimes carry over to the physical world. (As an example, of the 25 or so bylined contributors to this book, we've only met six in person—the rest are virtual relationships.)

Consumers also spend time in chat rooms, use the Internet to make phone calls, and visit online dating sites (Exhibit 7 - 6). Some of this communication takes place in communities of interest—for example, many people with serious diseases gain great comfort from participating in online support groups. Consumers exchange time and energy to build relationships with friends and family, and even to work out problems with companies.

E-mail popularity explains the success of Web-based e-mail services, such as Hotmail (Microsoft), AOL, and Yahoo! These sites consistently receive the most traffic as evidenced by May 2002 U.S. figures (www.Nielsen//NetRatings.com):

- AOL reached 61% of the Internet population with 65.2 million visitors.
- Microsoft reached 60% with 64.3 million visitors.
- Yahoo! reached 57% with 61.0 million visitors.

Clearly these sites attract users for other purposes as well, but e-mail services are an important part of the traffic draw. By offering a service based on the most important online activity, these companies bring a lot of eyeballs to their sites. They exchange these eyeballs for commissions on products sold at the site and on advertising revenues. Note that while the paying customers are retailers and advertisers, these sites are exchanging free services with consumers.

Web sites that offer virtual postcards also capitalize on consumer desires to use the Internet for relationship building. For example, two high traffic sites are AmericanGreetings.com (21.6 million visitors) and Hallmark.com (15.1 million visitors) ("Consumer Packaged Goods. . ."2002).

Entertainment

Many consumers use the Internet for entertainment (Exhibit 7 - 7). Over half browse for fun, sometimes on experiential shopping trips, as previously mentioned. One of the Internet's big promises, however, is audio and visual entertainment. Although 51% of U.S. users currently watch video online and 37% listen to music, these activities are difficult without a fast broadband connection. In this catch-22 situation, only 20% of all users have broadband at home; until more do, firms won't produce much of this type of online entertainment. Conversely, until more entertainment is available, mass audiences won't be lured into paying for broadband. We believe that a convergence is coming. First, all television content will be transmitted digitally within five years by federal mandate. Second, more devices such as the TiVo system will allow TV programs to be delivered on demand. Third, consumers will adopt broadband as part of their cable TV service. As this happens, online entertainment content will grow considerably and become just one of the choices for consumers

Outcome	%	Outcome	%
Send e-mail	95	Chat in online discussion	23
Send instant message	48	Make Internet phone call	12
Share files with others (music, video, games)	37	Check e-mail on cell phone or PDA	10
Visit online support group	36	Visit dating Web site	9

Exhibit 7 - 6 Proportion Performing Relationship Activities Online in the United States

Source: Data from www.pewinternet.org.

Outcome	%	Outcome	%
Surf for fun	64	Listen/download music	37
Watch video or audio clip	51	Play a game	37
Download games, videos, pictures	41	Visit adult Web site	14

Exhibit 7 - 7 Proportion Performing Entertainment Activities Online in the United States
Source: Data from www.pewinternet.org.

deciding how to spend time online. In the meantime, streaming media and improved compression techniques give more consumers access to online entertainment.

Media Consumption

Consumers are accessing news, weather, sports scores, and radio broadcasts over the Internet (Exhibit 7 - 8). E-marketers have known for some time that consumers only have a limited amount of time to exchange for media consumption and that the Internet takes away from offline media time. For example, Internet users watch 4.5 hours less television a week than nonusers (Conhaim 2002). One study by MSNBC, however, found that 65% of Internet users use the Web for news, 76% use cable television, and 89% use network television (Conhaim 2002). Thus, it appears that consumers use whatever medium is handy when they want news, including a handheld PDA—another indication that the Internet has morphed from novelty to utility.

Arbitron, the audience measurement firm, also studied online and offline media consumption. In its study, 33% of Internet users mentioned watching television less often, 25% read magazines less frequently, and 23% read newspapers less often. In addition, 16% listen to the radio less frequently because of the time they spend online (Rose and Rosen 2001).

This switch to online media consumption is why all the major media disseminate information on their Web sites. The challenge is making it pay off in profits. Thus far, most have used the advertising model, but the returns are not paying the bills. Some, like the *Wall Street Journal*, charge for subscriptions. Others have tried this with no success—and even worse—it appears that the Web site may be cannibalizing offline subscription sales and viewership. We see online media firms at a crossroads where they must decide what strategic purpose their Web site investment serves.

Outcome	%	Outcome	%
Get news	70	Political news / information	40
Check the weather	64	Sports scores	38
Listen to music from radio station, music store, recording artist	37		

Exhibit 7 - 8 Proportion Performing Media Consumption Activities Online in the United States
Source: Data from www.pewinternet.org.

Some, like MSNBC, believe the site draws a younger demographic to their network channels, but does this justify the cost?

Information

Second to e-mail, consumers spend much of their time gathering research and information online. Exhibit 7 - 9 displays the type of information they seek. This activity is especially acute during holidays and special events. For example, in February 2002, africana.com saw an 81% spike in traffic due to Black History Month, and more than 82 million users worldwide visited a variety of sports sites during that month's Olympic games (www.comscore.com). Additional opportunities for e-marketers (www.pewinternet.com) arise from these statistics:

- Seventy-three million Americans use the Internet for health information, and 61% claim it has improved the way they take care of their own health.
- Fifty-two million Americans use the Internet to find job information.

How do Internet users find information? Eighty-five percent have used search engines, and 29% use them on a typical day. Queries range from the ridiculous ("how many times does my name come up on Google?") to the sublime ("Where was Buddha born?") to the heartbreaking ("My mom has breast cancer—I need information fast") ("Search Engines Are. . ."2002).

Google.com is the most popular search engine: Visitors spend 25.9 minutes per month there. Users spend 10.8 minutes a month on Yahoo! and 6 minutes at MSN. This search activity is another reason Yahoo!, Microsoft, and AOL have such a large reach among consumers. Google's revenue model is entirely advertising based, unlike other search engines, and it has drawn a larger user base partly because it does not crowd the home page with offers, as do the other engines.

Buy and Shop for Products

In another use of the Internet for research, 75% of all Internet users seek information online prior to buying products. Sometimes they use this information to purchase on-

Outcome	%	Outcome	%
Hobby information	80	Find phone number /address	53
Map or driving directions	79	Research for school/training	53
Travel information	66	Financial	44
Books, movies, leisure activities	63	A job	37
Health/medical	61	A place to live	29
Government site	57	Religious/spiritual	28
Research for job	54	Family history/genealogy	20

Exhibit 7 - 9 Proportion Performing Information Consumption Activities Online in the United States

Source: Data from www.pewinternet.org.

line, and sometimes they purchase at a local brick-and-mortar store—15% of all global consumers purchased outside of the Internet based on information they got online (Global Key Report Findings 2002). In total, U.S., consumers spent 79% of their shopping dollars in brick-and-mortar stores, 15% online (estimates range from $32.6 to $64 billion), and 6% on catalog sales. Exhibit 7 - 10 shows the online shopping landscape for U.S. consumers.

Many people believe that consumers will never spend more than this proportion of their shopping dollars online for a number of reasons. First, 5.5 billion people are not Internet users, and even a large proportion of nonusers in developed nations have no drive to get connected. Second, the Internet does not provide the social experience found in the physical world, especially at shopping malls and bazaars. Third, consumers may not shop for most products online unless they are motivated by dissatisfaction with offline retailers. Fourth, some people do not trust the Internet enough to enter personal and credit card information on Web pages.

A final consideration involves the types of products appropriate for online and offline consumption. Some marketers suggest there are three types of products: search, experience, and credence goods (Coupley 2001). Search goods can be evaluated by reading about them; for example, items such as software, automobiles, and computers can be evaluated easily at a Web site (such as Dell.com for computers). We recently bought a laser printer in 20 minutes by reading online reviews, selecting the best one for our needs, and then using a shopping agent to find

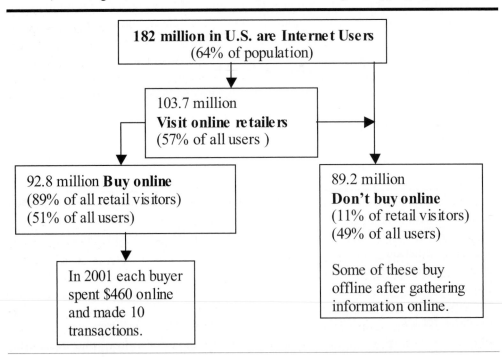

Exhibit 7 - 10 Slightly Over Half of All U.S. Internet Users Buy Online
Source: Data from www.bcg.com.

Outcome	%	Outcome	%
Research product before buying	75	Groceries	8
Buy a product	56	Charity donation	7
Buy/make travel reservation	42	Gamble	5
Bank online	23	Take class for college credit	5
Participate in online auction	20	Take any online class	5
Buy/sell stocks, bonds, mutual funds	12		

Exhibit 7 - 11 Proportion Performing Transaction Activities Online in the United States
Source: Data from www.pewinternet.org.

the lowest price from a reputable online store. Experience goods can only be evaluated through product use (examples are clothing and flowers). Although these types of goods are purchased online, consumers more often purchase them in a brick-and-mortar retailer if they have had no previous experience with the brand. Credence goods are items that are difficult to assess without someone else's opinion, such as expensive wine or even a book. Of these three product types, search goods are the most appropriate for online purchasing, although experience and credence goods might be appropriate to a lesser extent.

Despite all these issues and concerns, consumers do buy online, as shown in Exhibit 7 - 11. According to this study, 56% of consumers buy online, compared with the BCG research in Exhibit 7 - 10, which concluded that 51% of Internet users are buyers. This is typical of Internet research—online behavior can be difficult to measure with precision, which is why this book contains some inconsistent statistics. Nonetheless, a 5% difference demonstrates fairly good validation that at least half of all users buy online.

Summary

The Internet has grown more quickly than any other medium in history. In 2002, 531 million people had access to the Internet, representing 8.5% of the global population. Yet 5.5 billion other people are not online, due to social and cultural issues (such as traditional marketplace behaviors and cash payment habits), technological issues (such as communications infrastructure problems and telephone usage fees), and legal and political issues (such as government censorship and regulation).

The basic marketing concept of exchange refers to the act of obtaining a desired object from someone by offering something in return. Individual consumers bring their own characteristics and personal resources to the process as they seek specific outcomes from an exchange. All of this occurs within a technological, cultural, and social context. Among the U.S. trends affecting online exchanges are information overload, bunkering, security and privacy, blurring of home and work boundaries, anywhere/anytime convenience, time poverty, demanding expectations, self-service requirements, consumer sophistication, personalization expectations, consumer expectations of ease and courtesy, and multiple channel shopping.

Internet users tend to have a more positive attitude toward technology and be more adept and experienced with Internet usage. Gender affects attitudes toward use of Net technology, and language can also affect Net usage. Online shoppers tend to be more goal oriented and be either convenience or price oriented. Finally, family life cycle accounts for differences in the outcomes sought online.

The four main costs that consumers exchange for benefits are money, time, energy, and psychic costs. The Internet exchange can be facilitated by browser bookmarks, e-mail messages with hyperlinks, and automated e-mails from Web sites seeking to attract visitors. The main consumer activities online can be categorized by these general outcomes: relationships, entertainment, media consumption, information gathering, and transactions. Each outcome represents a marketing opportunity for savvy e-marketers.

Key Terms

Attention economy	Exchange
Bunkering	Flow
Electronic checks	

Exercises

Review Questions
1. What are some of the social, cultural, technological, and legal issues that slow Internet adoption in some nations?
2. What is an exchange?
3. What are some of the trends affecting online exchanges in the United States?
4. What individual characteristics influence online behavior?
5. What are the four costs that constitute a consumer's resources for exchange?
6. How can e-marketers facilitate Internet exchange?
7. What are the five main categories of outcomes sought by Internet users?

Discussion Questions

8. Why would a growing B2B market lead consumers onto the Internet in countries where penetration was previously low?

9. Can an attention economy exist in countries where Internet penetration is low? Explain your answer.

10. What might e-marketers do to accommodate consumers who are experiential shoppers?

11. Do you consider the concept of flow an explanation for what some observers call Internet addiction? Explain your answer.

12. How might e-marketers capitalize on consumer interest in relationships as an outcome of Internet activity?

chapter

8

targeting market segments and communities

learning objectives

The main goal of this chapter is to examine the various bases for market segmentation, the classifications and characteristics of market segments and communities, and the main coverage strategies for targeting selected segments. You will also gain a better understanding of the size and growth of various market segments and communities on the Internet.

After reading this chapter, you will be able to:

- Explain why and how e-marketers use market segmentation to reach online customers.
- List the most commonly used market segmentation bases and variables.
- Outline five types of usage segments and their characteristics.
- Discuss the role of occasionalization in Internet marketing.
- Describe the four coverage strategies e-marketers can use to target online customers.

If segmentation theorists had a god to worship, it would be the Internet.

roger d. blackwell
customers.com

Where on the Internet can teenage girls play "Virtual Boyfriend," take fun quizzes, chat, and send e-cards to friends? The answer is MyKindaPlace.com, a Web property targeted to 11- to 18-year-old girls that has attracted 1 million visitors since its opening in 2000. According to the marketing director, the site draws traffic because its interactive content and visual design were created specifically for the target market. The site sports bright pink, blue, and purple—colors popular with teen girls—as well as age-appropriate language. For example, link names on the site are labeled *showbiz, chill in, cringe, work it, agony, fun*, and more. In addition, site managers monitor chat rooms so parents don't pull the plug.

MyKindaPlace derives its revenue from sponsorship and merchandise sales. Ten of the site's channels are sponsored by brands targeting teens; this source brought in £1.5 million during 2001 (more than US$2.3 million). The site also sells merchandise online, accepting Slash Plastic payment cards, smart cards, and parents' credit cards—solving the big problem that teens don't have their own credit cards

Understanding the need to be honest and avoid gimmicks with the teen market, MyKindaPlace uses the database only for fun promotions. For example, site sponsor L'Oréal ran a survey seeking feedback about its Maybelline brand, offering participants the chance to win one of 100 lipliners. In just one weekend, 3,000 site visitors responded. This valuable feedback cost the company nothing but £34 for the free products. MyKindaPlace clearly understands its female teen market and uses a marketing mix that appeals to this market—a winning strategy.

Marketers are hunters—following the tracks of consumers and scattering promotional bait to lure elusive dollars out of hiding places.

jim
nail
media and
entertainment
research

Segmentation and Targeting Overview

MyKindaPlace.com clearly understands the needs and behavior of its teen target market. To do this, a company must have in-depth market knowledge and devise a savvy segmentation and targeting strategy. As explained in Chapter 3, e-marketing strategic planning occurs in two highly interrelated tiers. The first involves segmentation, targeting, differentiation, and positioning, topics covered in this and the following chapter. Second-tier strategies involving the 4P's and CRM are discussed in Chapters 10 to 14.

Marketers make informed decisions about segmentation and targeting based on internal, secondary, and primary data sources (see Exhibit 8 - 1). **Marketing segmentation** is the process of aggregating individuals or businesses along similar characteristics that pertain to the use, consumption, or benefits of a product or service. The result of market segmentation is groups of customers called market segments. We use the word *groups* loosely here. A market segment can actually be any size from one person to millions of people—an important point because the technology of Internet marketing allows companies to easily tailor market mixes for targeting individuals. It is also important to note that segments are worth targeting separately only when they have bigger differences between them than within them. For example, if Internet users behave differently at work than at home, marketers can capitalize on these differences by targeting each as a separate segment—otherwise why bother separating these users into two segments?

Targeting is the process of selecting the market segments that are most attractive to the firm and selecting an appropriate segment coverage strategy. Some criteria companies use for selecting segments to target include accessibility, profitability, and growth (among other criteria). Segment coverage strategy involves the development of marketing mixes and associated budgets to reach each target segment.

Market Segmentation Bases and Variables

Marketers can base their segmentation of consumer markets on **demographics**, geographic location, **psychographics**, and behavior with regard to the product. Within each base, there are many segmentation variables (see Exhibit 8 - 2). For example, McDonald's demographic segmentation uses the variables of age and family life cycle to target adults, children, senior citizens, and families. One way to look at this is that segmentation bases are a few general organizing categories, and segmentation variables include numerous subcategories.

Companies often combine bases and focus on categories such as **geodemographics** (geography and demographics). Similarly, they can build segments using any combination of variables that makes sense for their industry. The important thing to remember is that marketers create segments based on variables that can be used to identify and reach the right people at the right time.

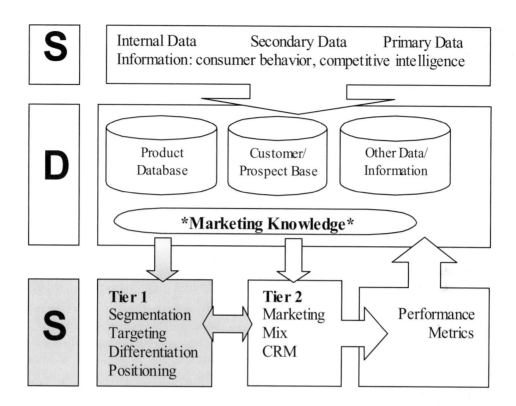

Exhibit 8 - 1 Sources, Databases, and Strategy: Tier 1 Strategies in Chapters 8 and 9

After using any of these four bases alone or in combination, marketers profile segment members using many other variables. For example, after a Web site such as iVillage.com creates a list of mothers who register at the site (segment basis), it can use primary and secondary research to develop profiles that describe these mothers. These profiles might indicate that a certain percentage of the mothers like to cook international dishes, another percentage generally prepares traditional meals, and another percentage seldom cooks at all. Marketers need to know which variables broadly identify the target segment and which simply further describe it because marketers use identification variables to enumerate and access the target. By this we mean that a firm can get mailing lists of mothers and discover which magazines reach them, but it is hard to figure out how to reach women who cook Italian food. If iVillage knows that only 5% of its target (mothers) cooks Italian food, and 60% does not cook at all, it will help them to design site products and content. Thus, marketers use profile variables to refine the marketing mix, including Web site content and advertising.

Bases	Geographics	Demographics	Psychographics	Behavior
Identifying /	City	Age	Activities	Benefits
Profiling	County	Income	Interests	sought
Variable	State	Gender	Opinions	Usage level
Examples	Region	Education	Personality	Brand loyalty
	Country	Ethnicity	Values	User status

Exhibit 8 - 2 Segmentation Bases and Examples of Related Variables

The next sections describe geographic, demographic, psychographic, and behavior segments on the Internet. Given the changes in Internet user profiles and the evolution of new segmentation schemes, marketers should consult the key sources of information cited in these sections to obtain more information when planning segmentation and targeting strategies.

Geographic Segments

Although the geographic location of computers in cyberspace is not important to users accessing Web sites, it is very important to organizations with an Internet presence. The reason is that most firms target specific cities, regions, states, or countries with their product offerings. Even the largest multinational firms usually develop multisegment strategies based on **geographics**. For example, McDonald's serves beer in its German restaurants and sake in its Japanese restaurants. Conversely, a restaurant in San Francisco may use a niche strategy by targeting only local residents.

Product distribution strategy is a driving force behind geographic segmentation. A consumer goods company such as Kraft will want to reach only customers in countries where it distributes products. Similarly, firms offering services online will only sell to geographic areas where they can provide customer service. Before an organization decides to serve the Web community, it must examine the proportion of Net users in its selected geographic targets. Consider Posadas, the leading hotel chain in Mexico, which targets tourists in Mexican and U.S. markets and, thus, maintains Web pages in Spanish and English (Exhibit 8 - 3). Posadas focused heavily on the U.S. market and built its first site for the United States because it recognized that Internet penetration was much higher in that country than in Latin American countries.

Important Geographic Segments for E-Marketing

The United States boasts the largest Internet usage in the world, with 182 million users (64% of population). Although this is the largest market in terms of absolute

Exhibit 8 - 3 Fiesta Americana Site in Spanish and English
Source: www.posadas.com.

size, 10 other country markets have more than 40% Internet penetration (Exhibit 8 - 4). Bear in mind that these figures represent one point in time during 2002, and that Internet usage statistics vary widely depending on who conducts the study. Nonetheless, these 11 countries represent good markets for new technology because they are quite Internet savvy. As previously mentioned, e-marketers using geographic variables for segmentation also evaluate online markets by region, city, urban area, and so forth. For instance, the entire North American and Scandinavian regions contain attractive markets, and most urban areas, such as Cairo, Egypt, are more wired than are rural areas. Marketers are also watching the People's Republic of China—it is poised to become a huge online market in the future.

Some research firms evaluate the quality of a country's market using additional criteria. IDC conducts an annual Information Society Index (ICI), evaluating countries on four infrastructure variables designed to predict their ability to access and absorb information technology: computer adoption, information, Internet, and social ("Sweden Remains the World's. . ." 2001). In 2001, Sweden and Norway held

Rank	Country	Percent of Population Internet Users
1	United States	64.0
2	Iceland	60.1
3	Hong Kong	54.2
4	Sweden	49.4
5	Norway	48.9

Rank	Country	Percent of Population Internet Users
6	United Kingdom	48.7
7	Switzerland	46.6
8	Canada	44.9
9	The Netherlands	42.5
10	Finland	41.3
11	Japan	40.5

Exhibit 8 - 4 Country Markets with over 40% Internet User Penetration

the top two positions as the world's dominant information economies, with the United States in fourth place. In part, this is because the two countries have quite high mobile Internet access. Many factors indicate market viability for e-commerce and other e-business activities, as explained in Chapters 15 and 16.

English is no longer the language of most Web pages and online bulletin boards, a major change from just two years ago. One study revealed the following top Internet languages: English (42%), Japanese (9%), Chinese (9%), Spanish (7%), and German (7%) (Exhibit 8 - 5). These findings obviously have huge implications for e-marketers desiring to reach global markets via the Internet; until more online text appears in local languages, users in those countries will not able to participate in e-commerce or other online activities. Unfortunately, Web developers in many Asian and Middle Eastern countries face technical challenges because local languages require double-byte character sets (versus single byte for romance languages) and, therefore, need more database and transaction customization and complicated search algorithms. These and other barriers to Internet adoption discussed in Part VI of this book can affect marketers' segmentation strategies.

Demographic Segments

In the Internet's early years, the typical user was a young male, college educated, with a high income—except for gender, the description of a typical innovator. This picture is generally repeated in countries with low levels of Internet adoption. In developed nations, users look more like the mainstream population, from a demographic perspective. According to *Insight Express,* 76% of U.S. users are 18 to

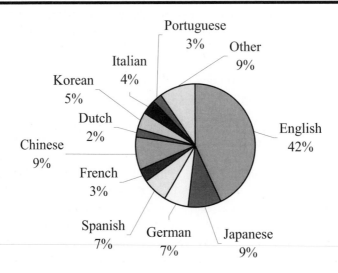

Exhibit 8 - 5 Less Than Half of Web Users Access in English
Source: Adapted from Cutitta (2002).

49 years old, and 25% are over 50. The annual average household income of a user is about $50,000 and the population is almost equally divided by gender, with 51% female (Pastore 2002a). According to Nielsen//NetRatings, the Internet population among its measured countries is predominately male, with the exception of the United States and Canada.

Knowing that U.S. Internet users mirror the population, marketers need to identify attractive demographic niches. The following sections describe a few market segments that have recently caught the attention of e-marketers.

Occupation

In just a few short years, the Internet has changed from a place for the technologically and financially savvy to a place where U.S. residents from all professions find something of use. This has huge implications for e-commerce and advertising, and big changes are still taking place. For example, blue-collar workers are currently the fastest-growing online occupational group in the United States, jumping 52% in home usage from 2000 to 2002 (Pastore 2001). Nearly 10 million laborers and factory workers spent 11 minutes online during March 2002 and visited 698 Web pages. That statistic tells marketers that this group is busy surfing and exploring, unlike folks who have been online longer and who tend to repeatedly visit their favorite sites—that is, the average U.S. user spent 31 minutes online and visited 47 Web sites in May 2002 (see www.nielsen-netratings.com). The blue-collar market represents a major marketing opportunity because segment members have not yet developed site loyalty and have some different product and entertainment needs from users in other professions. Other fast-growing occupational groups include homemakers (49% since 2000), service workers (37%), and salespeople (34%). E-marketers can use such facts about occupational segments online as information and then knowledge to drive e-marketing strategy.

Teens and Children

In the United States, approximately 75% of 14- to 17-year-olds and 65% of 10- to 13-year-olds use the Internet ("Web Still Growing. . ." 2002). Dubbed "The Net Generation" and Generation Y, this remains one of the fastest-growing online niches: 77 million are expected globally by 2005 ("Meeting Generation Y" 1999). Young U.S. users aged 12 to 17 send e-mail (81%); send instant messages (70%); play games; and purchase music, tickets, and videos (Jarvis 2002). Fifty-eight percent use the Internet for homework, and teens' repeated requests for online access is sometimes what leads families into computer and ISP purchases. Driving future growth in this market is the fact that 95% of all U.S. schools now have Internet access. Interestingly, over half of 18- or 19-year-olds and 39% of 12- to 17-year-olds use the Internet more than the telephone for communication (Fetto 2002). Jupiter Communications estimates that U.S. youth will spend $1.3 billion online by 2003.

This market is not impressed with brand names online; instead, these consumers want utility and particular activities. If marketers can entertain teens with something humorous, or an audio file or photo, the teens will spread the news through online word of mouth (viral marketing). A full 38% of teens share these types of things with friends several times a week—a great marketing opportunity. One big problem for marketers targeting this segment is payment. Teens and children do not typically have credit cards for online purchases, which is why only 12% have purchased online. Some youths are allowed to use their parents' credit cards and those over 16 years of age can obtain a debit card. However, innovative approaches such as Splash Plastic prepaid cards (as in the MyKindaPlace story) or "cyber allowance" accounts deposited at designated online retailers have emerged.

Other important characteristics of this market include the need to be honest about marketing tactics, such as revealing the motives behind asking for personal information. Up-front marketers will find teens eager to play online games, download music and movies, and sign up for sales promotion premiums and free samples. Incidentally, teens are heavy users of cell phones and just may be the group that moves the United States closer to Europe and Japan with mobile commerce.

Ethnic Groups

African Americans remain one of the largest and most quickly growing ethnic groups online in the United States, with 4.9 million users and a 31% annual growth rate ("Online Habits. . ." 2000; "Web Still Growing. . ." 2002). Internet users in this group tend to be younger, more highly educated, and more affluent than African Americans not using the Net. In addition, unlike the other Net users, users in this group are heavy purchasers of music online and buy less clothing and travel. They are more likely than other Net users to go online from academic and public locations and are less likely to register at Web sites.

Hispanics are a huge segment with 14.5 million Internet users and a 19% to 26% growth rate, depending on the study ("Study Reveals Previously. . ." 2002; "Web Still Growing. . ." 2002). Over half of this market (55%) uses the Spanish language when online, and the remainder use English, making this a market with unique needs in the United States (Greenspan 2002). Using a geodemographic segmentation basis, marketers note that Miami–Fort Lauderdale, Florida, is the Fifteenth largest market over all, but third largest for Hispanic Web users. Hispanics who use the Internet outspend those nonusers by a margin of 7%, a statistic that has caught the eye of marketers. In fact, in one poll, 20% of Hispanics said they would feel devastated if they couldn't use the Web, and they would rather give up their televisions (Greenspan 2002).

Chinese Americans living in the United States and Canada are also active online. More than half have Internet access and 65% of those are online everyday (Pastore 2002b). Chinese Americans purchase books, computer products, and electronics online and enjoy a large purchasing power—the average income is $69,000.

Differently Abled

Called by some "the Internet's next niche," Web users with disabilities spend an amazing 20 more hours a week online than other Internet users (Wellner 2000). Fifty-four million U.S. consumers have disabilities, health problems, or handicaps that prevent full participation in work, school, or housework. According to the World Wide Web Consortium (W3W), Web accessibility guidelines to accommodate disabled people include making alternative text for images, providing strong contrast between foreground and background, and expansion of text acronyms. This is because many disabled users have problems with highly complex and animated visuals on Web sites. In addition, the disabled and aging prefer large text. (See Chapter 10 coverage of assistive technologies for more about how Web developers are making accommodations for the blind, hearing impaired, and others.) This segment is a demographically diverse group and tend to have low incomes—thus, making them difficult and undesirable targets for some firms.

Why do marketers target this segment, despite its low income and accessibility challenges? Social values of full accessibility and potential legal action aside, marketers who make site accommodations can draw a larger consumer audience. In addition, the huge baby boomer group is headed for some of these problems as they reach age 65 and older; the sooner Web sites can solve such site design issues, the better poised they will be to effectively target and serve this market. Further, some evidence shows that this market can be a productive target. WeMedia.com Webcast the 2000 Paralympic Games from Australia last fall and experienced good traffic. Most importantly, a market consisting of 54 million Americans has a great deal of purchasing power.

Psychographic Segments

User psychographics include personality, values, lifestyle, activities, interests, and opinions (AIO). *Personality* characteristics are traits such as other-oriented versus self-oriented and habits such as procrastination. *Values* are deeply held convictions such as religious beliefs. *Lifestyles* and *activities* as psychographics refer to non-product-related behavior such as playing sports or eating out. For example, users say that their Web surfing takes time away from these other activities: reading (39%), sleeping (23%), socializing (14%), and working (12%) (www.intelliquest.com). *Interests* and *opinions* are attitudes and beliefs people hold. As an example, some people believe that the Web is a waste of time and others think they could not exist without e-mail.

Attitudes and Behaviors

How do attitudes and behavior differ? Attitudes are internal evaluations about people, products, and other objects. They can be either positive or negative, but the evaluation process occurs inside a person's head. Behavior refers to what a person physically does, such as talking, eating, watching an infomercial on television, writing for a free videotape, calling a 1-800 number to order, shopping, or purchasing a product. However, marketers do not include product-related behaviors in psychographic segmentation. This is because product behaviors are such a vital segment descriptor that they form an entirely separate category (see the next section).Thus, when marketers discuss psychographics, they mean the general ways that consumers spend time.

Psychographic information helps e-marketers define and describe market segments so they can better meet consumer needs. It is especially important for Web page design. For example, Japanese users do not like the flippant and irreverent tone at some U.S. sites. Japan's Web sites are more serious and do not include content such as political satire. This type of attitudinal information is increasingly available about Web users.

Attitudes Toward Technology

Most marketers believe that demographics are not helpful in predicting who will purchase online. Although they need to know if a particular demographic target is indeed online, it is the segment's attitudes toward technology that determine whether or not these users will buy when they surf the Web.

Forrester Research measures consumer and business attitudes toward technology with a system called **Technographics™**. In 2002, Forrester surveyed 380,000 consumers, with nearly one-third of those interviews held offline. Technographics works by combining three specific variables (Modahl 2000). First, the researchers ask questions to determine if a person is optimistic or pessimistic toward technology. Next, they measure a user's income level because this is an important determinant of online shopping behavior. Finally, they query users about their primary motivation for going online. After nearly two years of collecting data, Forrester identified 10 consumer technographics segments in the United States. Exhibit 8 - 6 displays these segments along with the proportion existing in the United States. According to Forrester, the following is an example of how each segment uses technology:

- Fast Forwards are the biggest users of business software.
- New Age Nurturers are the most ignored group of technology consumers.
- Mouse Potatoes love interactive entertainment on the PC.
- Techno-Strivers have the highest proportion of PC ownership of all low-income groups.
- Digital Hopefuls are a strong potential market for low-cost PCs.
- Gadget Grabbers buy low-cost, high-tech toys such as Nintendo.
- Handshakers aren't into technology for their business dealings.
- Traditionalists use VCRs but not much more.
- Media Junkies love TV and are early adopters of satellite television.

		Motivation for Using Internet		
		Career	**Family**	**Entertainment**
Technology Optimists 52%	**High Income (>$40,000)**	Fast Forwards 12%	New Age Nurturers 8%	Mouse Potatoes 9%
	Low Income (<$40,000)	Techno-Strivers 7%	Digital Hopefuls 7%	Gadget Grabbers 9%
Technology Pessimists 48%	**High Income**	Handshakers 7%	Traditionalists 8%	Media Junkies 5%
	Low Income	Sidelined Citizens 28%		

Exhibit 8 - 6 Consumer Technographic Segments and Proportion in the United States
Source: Adapted from Modahl (2000).

- Sidelined Citizens are technology laggards (see adopter categories).

Forrester's research revealed some interesting findings. First, technology optimism declines with age. Older users tend to have a more negative attitude toward technology. However, their attitudes may less negative if they use a PC at work or live in one of the largest 50 U.S. cities. Men tend to be more optimistic, and peer pressure can increase optimism in all demographic groups. That is, when friends discuss e-mail and Web sites, pessimists often rethink their positions. With regard to income, 40% of high-income citizens are optimistic, and certain low-income groups such as college students and young families are also optimistic about technology.

How do these findings translate to online purchasing? First, twice as many high-income optimists shop online (19%) compared with other groups. Only 2% of low-income pessimists shop online and, therefore, are not a good target for e-commerce firms. Second, combining Technographics with adopter categories, Forrester found that early adopters are high-income technology optimists, thus identifying the first consumers to shop online. Conversely, laggards are low-income pessimists who will be last to shop online. Finally, firms can use Technographic segments to profile customers who shop online and to determine where to allocate resources to attract more of the same. Starbucks used technographics and discovered that 47% of its customers are early adopters (Fast Forwards, New Age Nurturers, and Mouse Potatoes). It further found that 22% are career oriented with Fast Forwards using the Internet for self-advancement. These findings confirm that Starbucks will likely have good success selling online.

Forrester also maintains a database for its business Technographics. It conducts over 2,500 interviews with senior managers of North American companies with more than $1 billion in annual revenues.

Behavior Segments

Two commonly used behavioral segmentation variables are benefits sought and product usage. Marketers using **benefit segmentation** often form groups of consumers based on the benefits they desire from the product. For example, a Harris Survey reports that "70% of online shoppers can be segmented into two groups: bargain hunters and convenience shoppers. Bargain hunters consist of smaller segments: Hooked, Online & Single (16%), Hunter-Gatherers (20%). Convenience includes Time-Sensitive Materialists (17%), Brand Loyalists (19%), E-Bivalent Newbies (5%), and Clicks & Mortars (23%)" (Whelan 2001).

Product usage is applied to segmentation in many ways. Marketers often segment by light, medium, and heavy product usage. As a hypothetical example, heavy Internet users might be those who go online daily, medium users those who go on once every few days, and light users those who connect only once every week or two. Companies must research to determine actual usage and decide how to split surfers into appropriate user categories. Another approach is to categorize consumers as brand loyal, loyal to the competitive product, switchers (who don't care which brand they use), and nonusers of the product. Next we discuss some of these variables as they apply to the Internet (i.e., what do people do online and what do they get out of it?).

Benefit Segments

The Internet had 147.3 million servers worldwide in January 2002, many of which hosted multiple Web sites (see www.isc.org). Clearly, there is something for everyone: information, entertainment, news, social meeting places, and more. If marketers can form segments based on the benefits sought by users, they can design products to meet those needs. This approach is often more practical than simply forming demographic segments and trying to figure out what, say, professional women in Iowa want from the Web. In fact, marketers will use all segmentation bases to define, measure, and identify target markets, but benefits sought is the key driver of marketing mix strategy.

What better way to determine benefits sought than to look at what people actually do online? To do this, marketers can check which Web sites are the most popular. Several sites report each month on the top online properties—Exhibit 8 - 7 displays the top Web site parent companies for one week in 2002. AOL, MSN, and Yahoo! are consistently among the top sites in most countries. The exhibit demonstrates that many people search, use MSN (probably for downloads and Hotmail), participate or watch auctions, and so forth.

Here are just a few of the most commonly used segmentation variables:

- **E-mail.** Called the killer application, there are 8 billion e-mails flying over the Internet worldwide. User segments can also be formed by the communication benefits of online chatting, instant messaging, and posting on bulletin boards. As previously discussed, the demographics of an instant messaging segment would be high in the 12–17 age group.

- **Shop.** E-commerce comprises another segment in which marketers are intensely interested.

- **Information search.** Whether searching for product information or a homework assignment, this is one of the biggest uses of the Web.

- **Online stock trading and online banking.** While online banking has not achieved as high a usage as initially predicted, online stock trading is quite active. For example, 70% of Chinese Americans trade online an average of nine times a month (Pastore 2001).

- **Streamies.** An ad for an online broadcaster boasted, "Forget eyeballs. It's about earlobes." Streamies are a growing segment of people who listen to online audio. As bandwidth and compression techniques improve, the number of online listeners will increase.

Usage Segments

Effective targeting depends on more than user characteristics such as demographics. Internet users can be segmented according to how they use the medium. To visualize the difference between usage-based segmentation and user-based segmentation, consider that sometimes when you watch TV, you switch from channel to channel; at other times, you watch one show continuously for an hour or more. The same applies when users shop online: Sometimes they browse aimlessly, but sometimes they have a specific goal.

Rank	Parent Company	Millions of Visitors	Percentage Reach of All Users
1	Microsoft	39.4	50.7
2	AOL Time Warner	37.2	47.9
3	Yahoo!	33.8	43.5
4	Google	10.9	14.0
5	eBay	9.0	11.5
6	Terra Lycos	8.0	10.3
7	About-Primedia	7.3	9.4
8	Amazon	7.1	9.2
9	The Gator Corporation	6.0	7.6
10	USA Network	5.3	6.8

Exhibit 8 - 7 Top Web Properties as of June 30, 2002
Source: Data from www.nielsen-netratings.com.

In this case, e-marketers identify segments according to how users behave on the Internet. Then they further profile the segments by user characteristics, geographical location, and so on. This section discusses some key usage segments: home versus work access, access speed, time spent online, industry specific usage, and usage occasion.

Home and Work Access

Many companies segment by whether users access the Net from home or work. Access point is important because home and work segments tend to have different needs on the Web. In general, 80% of home users have slower connection speeds than those who enter the Net from work, making large graphics and other files undesirable on sites frequented from home. Another characteristic of the home market is that a small but growing number of households have more than one PC and are networking them within the home. The market for home networking is expected to grow to over $5.7 billion by 2004 ("Home Networking. . ." 2000).

One study found that 42 million U.S. users access the Internet from work ("Internet Usage at Work. . ." 2001). Nielsen//NetRatings researched at-work access in the United States, Australia, France, and Italy, and found some consistent and significant differences from home segments. One key finding is that people who access from work spend nearly twice as much overall time online than those who access only from home. For example, U.S. work users spend about 19.25 hours a month online, while at home users spend about 11.1 hours—a pattern that held for all countries in the study. In addition, the audiences in all countries are much more heavily male for the at-work segment. The most popular sites for U.S. at-work access follow:

1. Telecom or Internet services (29.7 million visitors)
2. Finance, insurance, or investment (21.2 million visitors)
3. Travel (18.4 million visitors)
4. Corporate information (14.6 million visitors)
5. Special occasions such as greeting cards, gifts, or flowers (14.1 million visitors)

E-marketing strategists can use such information to target their Web site offerings. Strategies might include special products, the language in sites, and the amount of interactivity and multimedia possible for work users.

Access Speed

Clearly, the type of Internet connection and the information receiving appliance can both affect usage behavior. Faster connections at work allow users to receive larger data files filled with multimedia content. The same is true for broadband users accessing from home, while the reverse is true for those using 56k modems or handheld wireless devices.

Approximately 20% of the U.S. population has broadband Internet access from home (21.9 million) versus 25.5 million office broadband users (60%). Home users are connected through ISPs offering cable modems and DSL (satellite). While cost is still a barrier for many home users, broadband penetration is nearly high enough to reach the critical mass needed for true video and audio program delivery on demand. This will certainly change the face of the Web. Think about the look of CNN, the 24-hour news channel on television, which is poised for Internet delivery with its mixture of text and video. In the future, users will be able to receive this type of programming on a computer and click on text boxes for more information or even delay the video delivery if desired.

Broadband users operate differently from narrowband users online. They play audio CDs (75%), play online games (60%), download music (48%), and watch streaming video or DVDs (Pastore 2002c). This market grew 67% in 2001, arousing the interest of e-marketers.

At the other extreme, mobile wireless users have very small screens (except for PC users) and slow access speed. About 200 million wireless devices were in use during 2001—a segment that is hard for marketers to resist. By comparison, 13.1 million PDAs (personal digital assistants) shipped in the United States in 2001. So what are the other 187 million devices? Of course, some are PDAs, but the majority are cell phones. U.S. wireless penetration reached 44% of all individuals in 2001, compared with European penetration of 72% and Japanese penetration of 56% (see www.displaysearch.com). In the wireless market, some have said that the Europeans are 18 months ahead of the United States, and the Japanese are 18 months ahead of the Europeans.

Wireless users do a lot more than talk on their cell phones. They send and receive data—anyplace, anytime. Exhibit 8 - 8 presents the kinds of data mobile users worldwide will access and send in 2002 on their devices. As expected, the biggest use is for e-mail and voice mail. However, online banking, information dependent upon the user location, and Internet access are also important uses. Wireless users currently track information on package shipment, stock quotes, airline schedules and changes, and news. Notably, wireless devices cannot access typical Web pages on their tiny screens, which is why many site developers now have a mobile viewing mode and a regular viewing mode. The mobile mode is 100% text and serves precise information on demand. For example, Zagat, the worldwide restaurant guide, allows mobile users to search its database for restaurants by city when they are traveling, and it charges a subscription fee for the service. The mobile wireless segment creates huge opportunities for firms wanting to produce wireless portals: a customized point of entry to the Net where subscribers can access Web sites and information in text format.

Big technical problems face global e-marketers, so marketers must be clever to provide users with desired services. At the same time, the market is unstoppable and will grow considerably, as discussed in Part IV. We also recommend Newell and Lemon's book, *Wireless Rules*, for more information.

Activity	Data Service %	Activity	Data Service %
E-mail, fax, voice mail	30	Mobile office	7
Online banking	15	Telemetry	5
Location-dependent information services	15	Games	3
Internet access/surf	13	Payments	1
Simple info services	10	Telematics (in car)	1

Exhibit 8 - 8 2002 Predicted Revenue Proportion on Mobile Devices Worldwide
Source: Fichter (2001).

Time Online

Although the Internet has been growing, not all the people with access are as active logging on as others. For example, about 57% of all users worldwide logged on during April 2002 (see www.nielsen-netratings for monthly statistics). On average, they visited 21 Web sites and viewed 34 pages, staying less than a minute on each page. Using Nielsen, Jupiter Media Metrix, and other data, researchers are finding big differences in online usage and have created some very useful segmentation schemes.

In one such study, McKinsey and MediaMetrix identified six user segments based on the active user's time online, pages, domains accessed, and the amount of time spent per Web page:

- **Simplifiers** want end-to-end convenience. They want to make their lives easier with quick, quality service. These are long-time Internet users, making half of all online purchases. They spend a total of 7 hours online per month.

- **Surfers** want what's new. They view up to four times as many pages as the average user. They move really quickly, always searching for new experiences. Sites capturing surfer loyalty need to be on the cutting edge with design, features, assortment of products and services, and continual updates; above all, they must have a strong online brand.

- **Connectors** are novelty seekers. They are "relative novices" that look for reasons to use the Internet. Their main purpose is to build relationships with others through chat rooms and e-mail. Sites wanting connector traffic need to have a strong presence offline to attract these beginners.

- **Bargainers** look for deals. They spend the least amount of time online. Sites appealing to bargainers satisfy their emotional and rational levels, thus luring them back to search for more deals—a good example is eBay.com.

- **Routiners** want something special. They search news and financial sites very carefully. They also spend a long time looking at Web sites, hoping to get something special through superior content.

Segment	Important Facts	Online Time
Simplifiers	50% of total online purchases. 49% have been online for over five years. Longest online tenure.	7 hours per month.
Surfers	8% of active user population. 32% of online time usage—far more than any other segment.	More than the average of 9.8 hours per month.
Connectors	36% active user population. 40% have been online under two years. 42% have made online purchases.	Less than the average of 9.8 per month.
Bargainers	8% of active user population. 52% are eBay users.	Less than the average of 9.8 per month.
Routiners	6% have purchased online. They visit fewer domains.	9.8 hours per month.
Sportsters	4% of active user population.	7.1 hours per month.

Exhibit 8 - 9 User Segments Based on Online Viewing Behavior
Source: Adapted from McKinsey and MediaMetrix study.

- **Sportsters** desire highly interactive content. They are a lot like Routiners, except that they visit colorful, exiting sports and entertainment sites. Sites offering free information will likely lead Sportsers to eventually pay for information.

These segments are likely to overlap because people use the Internet for different purposes at different times—such as research, e-mail, chat, work, and so forth. Nonetheless, marketers should examine segment differences in light of the firm's target markets. Exhibit 8 - 9 presents profiles that can aid marketers in determining how to develop strategies for reaching these segments.

Industry-Specific Usage Segments

Segmenting by usage may vary from one industry or business type to the other. For example, research from Forrester and comScore indicates that visitors to car sites behave differently than visitors to other e-commerce sites (see www.forrester.com and www.comscore.com). Even serious car buyers tend to visit car sites only a few times—64% of all buyers complete their online research in five sessions or fewer. Further, about 25% buy a car within three months of visiting a car site. Forrester identified these three visitor segments for car Web sites:

- **Explorers** are the smallest group, but almost half buy their new vehicle within two months of visiting a car site. They want a convenient, explicit buying process.

- **Off-roaders** tend to do a lot of research online and, subsequently, are very likely to purchase in an offline showroom.

- **Cruisers** visit car sites frequently but only 15% buy a car in the short term. Still, they have a strong interest in cars and heavily influence the car purchases of others, making them important visitors.

Targeting by Usage Occasions

In this very interesting segmentation scheme, called **occasionalization**, marketers identify segments based on how consumers are using the Web *at particular moments*. These different behavior patterns are called "usage occasions." Nielsen//NetRatings collects clickstream data by monitoring the route users take as they click from page to page. Using six months of data collected from 186,797 individual user sessions, researchers identified four key variables for defining discrete clusters of online behavior (Rozanski, Bollman, and Lipman 2001), which, in turn, combine to define seven usage occasions.

- **Session length**—the time a user stays online.
- **Time per page**—the average time a user spends on each page during a session.
- **Category concentration**—the percentage of time a user spends at sites belonging to the most frequented category. For example, if in a 10-minute session, a user spent five minutes at sports sites, three minutes at news sites, and two minutes at entertainment sites, the category concentration for sports sites would be 50 percent.
- **Site familiarity**—the percentage of total session time a user spends at familiar sites, defined as those previously visited four or more times.

Occasionalization Segments   **Quickies** occasions are typically under one minute in length and concentrate on visits to two or fewer familiar sites. Users spend about 15 seconds per page, extracting specific bits of information (sports scores, stock quotes) or sending e-mail. Sites requiring a longer time commitment such as entertainment, shopping, and communities are not on the itinerary for this type of session.

Just the Facts occasions involve users looking for specific information from known sites. At nine minutes, these occasions are longer than *Quickies* occasions but similar in that both involve rapid page views (30 seconds each). In *Just the Facts* sessions, users find and evaluate bits of information from related sites. For example, a woman seeking a certain type of shoe would move quickly from Web site to Web site, checking for the right style, size, and price, until she found just the right pair. These sessions typically include visits to transaction-oriented or time-consuming sites such as shopping, travel, and sports sites. *Just the Facts* occasions are less likely to involve sites best enjoyed at leisure, such as entertainment.

Single Mission occasions involve users who want to complete a certain task or gather specific information, then leave the Internet. At 10 minutes, the average session is about the same length as that of *Just the Facts*, but the 1.5-minute page views indicate the occasion involves more reading than in *Quickies* and *Just the*

Facts sessions. When on *Single Missions*, users venture to unfamiliar sites and concentrate on sites within one category (e.g., sports, portals/search engines, entertainment, real estate). In a sample occasion, a man seeking information about his high school reunion would start by finding his school at a search engine, click around to find the reunion page, learn about the logistics and registration for the gathering, and log off.

Do It Again occasions are 14 minutes long and notable for the lingering two-minute page views. The name reflects the strong focus in these sessions on familiar sites—users spend 95% of the session at sites they've previously visited four or more times. These users repeatedly go to favorite sites for auctions, games, and investments. Typical activities include completing bank transactions, downloading MP3 files, and participating in chat sessions. These occasions rarely involve searches, since users know exactly where they want to go.

Loitering occasions are leisurely visits to familiar *sticky sites,* such as news, gaming, telecommunications/ISP, and entertainment sites. They average 33 minutes in duration with two-minute page views. A typical visit might involve reading about favorite TV shows and celebrities on a TV network site. In this type of session, users make a few visits to sites that offer quick, practical bits of information, such as weather and shopping sites.

Information Please occasions average 37 minutes and are used to build in-depth knowledge of a topic. For instance, a user might research all aspects of buying a car, finding the most appealing model, computing trade-in value, finding a dealer, or arranging a loan. Unlike *Single Mission* users, *Information Please* users are gathering broad information from a range of sites. *Information Please* sessions tend not to concentrate on a single type of site or on familiar sites; instead, users go far afield from their usual destinations. These occasions are heavy on travel and automotive Web sites but light on telecom and portals/search engine sites. Users tend to jump among linked sites without resorting to a search engine.

Surfing occasions are by far the longest, averaging 70 minutes, with few stops at familiar sites—users hit nearly 45 sites in a typical session. Time per page is a minute or more, suggesting wide, but not deep, exploration. Users gravitate to sites that grab their attention immediately, such as shopping, online communities, and news, and spend little time at portals/search engines and education sites. Since these sessions are not concentrated in any one category, they appear to be random. One user in the sample, for example, checked e-mail, then read soap opera updates, and finally checked prices on amusement parks.

Online behavior usually entails multiple usage occasions. For example, 44% of the sample exhibited, at one time or another, all seven patterns. Fully two-thirds showed up in five or more session types and only 12% engaged in one session type at all times. How, then, can marketers profitably use these segments?

Why Use Occasionalization in Targeting?   None of the session types was dominated by a single demographic group. Girls ages 12 to 17 are just as likely to engage in a *Loitering* session as are professional men ages 30 to 50. Thus, by combining both usage occasion data and demographics, online marketers will raise the odds of communicating with their target consumers at a time when those consumers are most likely to pay attention to and be influenced by the message. Similarly, online retailers can tailor their environments in real time to meet the interests of not only the user but also the occasion.

By examining how the four session variables (session length, time per page, category concentration, and site familiarity) define the different segments, a marketer can identify behavioral patterns that can help in the creation and placement of communications. *Loitering* and *Surfing* sessions, for example, both involve visits to sites with which users are already very familiar. But occasion category concentrations—66% for *Loitering* and 26% for *Surfing*—show people in *Loitering* sessions are far more highly focused on a discrete set of categories, whereas people in *Surfing* sessions engage more in seemingly pointless meandering, skimming through a number of different topics but not getting deeply involved in any one subject. Based on these differences in the pace and breadth of sessions, some people will tend to be open to a range of messages; others will pay attention only to highly targeted messages; and others will whiz by anything not directly related to the purpose of their session.

Occasionalization on the Internet allows marketers to reach a larger number of users more effectively by pinpointing when they are most likely to be receptive to the specific message—based both on the relevance of its content and on user potential to become engaged in that content. For example, Web users in a *Quickies* session find banner ads a nuisance. In those cases, marketers should leave users alone and apply company resources to those occasions when users are likely to be more responsive. In three usage occasion types—*Loitering, Information Please*, and *Surfing*—online customers were more likely to shop than others. These occasions share an interesting relationship and are the lengthiest sessions, ranging from 33 to 70 minutes, enough time for users to be exposed to different messages. Marketers have their best shot at connecting during these sessions because the users are not in a hurry, usually go to familiar sites, and move across categories depending on their interests.

Reaching Users During Sessions   During occasions when users will be exposed to messages for a relatively long time, such as in the case of *Loitering, Information Please,* and *Surfing* sessions, marketers may want to post messages to generate click-throughs to their own sites as a way to build brand awareness. *Surfing* occasions may seem like a long shot for marketers because user behavior suggests impatient, impulsive clicking. However, if a site or message seems interesting, a user will likely pursue it. Boldly designed or worded messages, then, could appeal to impulse users attracted to novelty.

The other usage occasions—*Quickies, Single Mission, Just the Facts*, and *Do It Again*—are a mixed bag for marketers. The sessions are shorter over all (14 minutes or less), but the page views can be lengthy, depending on the dynamics of the session (from 15 seconds for *Quickies* to two minutes for *Do It Again*). Users in these occasions are less inclined to buy than are those in the three other sessions, so click-throughs should be the goal only in very specific situations.

How can marketers identify usage sessions? Cookie files are the answer for many companies. As discussed in earlier chapters, cookies are small bits of text placed on user hard drives that allow Web sites to identify them. When a Web server detects a *Loiterer* based on length of time at the site, it can send appropriate advertising messages and Web pages immediately on the next click. All this is automatic and nothing new for Web sites. Site developers have only to write programming to detect users by session and generate appropriate responses.

Targeting Online Customers

After reviewing many potential segments, marketers must select the best for targeting. To do this, they review the market opportunity analysis (see Chapter 3), consider findings from the SWOT analysis, and generally look for the best fit between the market environment and the firm's expertise and resources. Sometimes this is as easy as discovering a new segment that visited the company's Web site and then experimenting with offers that might appeal to this group. Other times it is a lengthy and thorough process. To be attractive, an online segment must be accessible through the Internet, be sizable and growing (if possible), and hold great potential for profit.

Next, e-marketers select a targeting strategy. E-marketers may select from among four different approaches for segment coverage:

- **Mass marketing**, also called **undifferentiated targeting**, occurs when the firm offers one marketing mix for the entire market. Wrigley's gum uses this strategy. On the Internet, many firms use an undifferentiated strategy. For example, banner ads that appear on portal site home pages (e.g., Yahoo!) tend to appeal to the entire market.

- **Multisegment marketing** occurs when a firm selects two or more segments and designs marketing mix strategies specifically for each. Most firms use a multi-segment strategy.

- **Niche marketing** occurs when a firm selects one segment and develops one or more marketing mixes to meet the needs of that segment. Amazon adopted this strategy when it targeted Web users exclusively. Cyberdialogue/findsvp (now Fulcrum) calls the Internet "a niche in time," indicating its ripeness for niche marketing (Clemente 1998). This strategy has real benefits but can be risky because competitors are often drawn into lucrative markets and because markets can suddenly decline, leaving the firm with all its eggs in one falling basket.

- **Micromarketing**, also known as **individualized targeting**, occurs when a firm tailors all or part of the marketing mix to a very small number of people. Taken to its extreme, this can be a target market of one person.

The Internet's big promise, one that is currently being realized by many firms, is individualized targeting. Amazon.com builds a profile of each user who browses or buys books at its site. It tracks the books that its customers read and makes recommendations based on their past purchases. Amazon also sends e-mail notifications about products that might interest particular individuals. This is the marketing concept at its finest: giving individual consumers exactly what they want at the right time and place. The Internet technology makes this mass customization possible in ways that were unimaginable 10 years ago.

Targeting Communities on the Internet

The Internet is ideal for gathering people with similar interests and tasks into communities. GVU's *Eighth User Survey* examined community membership and found that survey respondents join communities to feel connected with others who have the following common interests: 44.8% with folks who share their hobbies; 31.5% with other professionals; 27.2% with family members; 15.7% in support groups; 9.5% chatting about politics; and 6.9% in religious groups. One particularly interesting trend is the formation of communities consisting of former employees from a particular firm. One example is the large network of former Microsoft employees who use e-mail and a private bulletin board to discuss Microsoft gossip and to network for professional purposes.

Targeting can be achieved by building community through online chat rooms, discussion groups, bulletin boards, and online events. When folks with similar interests gather at the virtual watering hole to discuss issues, the value they receive in both information and social bonding keeps them returning. If a firm builds and maintains the watering hole, it can present products and messages customized to the group's interests. There are numerous examples of opportunities for targeting online college students through studentclub.com and collegeclub.com, women executives through RealSimple.com, and wine connoisseurs through wine.com.

Two of the most publicized consumer community sites include Yahoo! GeoCities and the numerous groups at www.google.com. Yahoo! GeoCities has many themed "neighborhoods," including everything from *magic* to *Christianity*. Members build Web pages that Yahoo! hosts for free and also join in chats and bulletin board postings (see geocities.yahoo.com). Google groups provides Web access to the Usenet with over 35,000 special-interest bulletin board discussion groups and 700 million community messages. Finally, Epinions.com has received quite a bit of attention as a consumer community because it allows consumers to post personal opinions about brands.

Although consumer communities are the most visible, business communities also play a big role in B2B commerce. Most professionals subscribe to discussion groups containing information in their field, and many Web sites promote community. For example, the PaperExchange is the leading online exchange for the pulp and paper industry—a $500 billion industry worldwide (www.PaperSpace.com). It has over 3,000 members worldwide. The Web site includes many features of value to members, including editorial content about the industry. In another example, Sap.com maintains a large community at its SAP user community portal, including many Web pages of "best practices" for the 12,000 companies and 10 million professionals using SAP software (CRM and SCM applications).

As another example, Exhibit 8 - 10 displays the Yahoo! mini-chat room at the bottom of the chessboard permitting users to converse while they play. More sophisticated chat rooms, such as Microsoft's Comic Chat, allow users to assume visual identities known as avatars. In discussion groups, users feel part of the site by posting their own information and responding to other users. Also, Amazon allows users to write their own book reviews and read the reviews of others. These kinds of

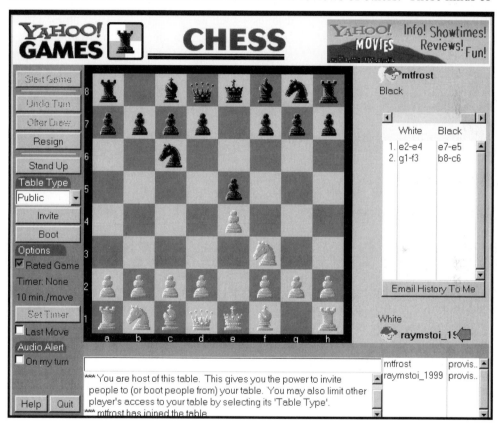

Exhibit 8 - 10 Yahoo! Games: Chess

Source: www.yahoo.com. Reproduced with permission of Yahoo! Inc. © 2000 by Yahoo! Inc. YAHOO! and the YAHOO! logo are trademarks of Yahoo! Inc.

Web sites encourage users to return again to see their cyber friends are discussing and doing online.

S u m m a r y

Marketing segmentation is the process of aggregating individuals or businesses along similar characteristics that pertain to the use, consumption, or benefits of a product or service. This results in groups of customers called market segments. Targeting is the process of selecting market segments that are most attractive to the firm and choosing an appropriate segment coverage strategy.

The four bases for consumer market segmentation are demographics, geographic location, psychographics, and behavior with respect to the product. Each basis is further refined into segmentation variables—such as age and gender variables within demographics. Currently e-marketers are targeting a number of demographic niches, including consumers identified by occupation, teens and children, ethnic groups, and people with disabilities. Different strategies are used to target each segment.

User psychographics include personality, values, lifestyle, attitudes, interests, and opinions. An important segmenting variable to predict online purchase behavior is attitude toward technology. Two behavioral segmentation variables commonly used by e-marketers are benefits sought (based on the benefits customers desire from the product, such as e-mail or shopping) and product usage (based on how customers behave on the Internet).

User segments can be divided according to home or work access, access speed, time online, industry-specific usage segments, and targeting by usage occasion (how consumers are using the Web at particular moments). Occasionalization allows marketers to reach a larger number of Net users by pinpointing when users will be receptive to the specific message—based both on the relevance of its content and on user potential to become engaged in that content.

Marketers use four coverage strategies to reach the segments: (1) mass marketing (undifferentiated targeting), (2) multisegment marketing, (3) niche marketing, and (4) micromarketing (individualized targeting). The Internet holds out tremendous promise for effective micromarketing, in particular. It is also an excellent way to gather people with similar interests and tasks into online communities for effective targeting.

K e y   T e r m s

Benefit segmentation	Multisegment marketing
Demographics	Niche marketing
Geodemographics	Occasionalization
Geographics	Psychographics
Individualized targeting	Targeting

Marketing segmentation

Mass marketing

Micromarketing

Technographics

Undifferentiated targeting

Exercises

Review Questions

1. Define the four main segmentation bases and list at least two segmentation variables for each.

2. Why do e-marketers need to measure attitude toward technology? What measures are available?

3. What benefits do consumers seek online?

4. How do benefit segments differ from usage segments?

5. What is occasionalization and why is it important for effective e-marketing?

6. How does micromarketing differ from multisegment marketing, niche marketing, and mass marketing?

7. Why would an e-marketer want to create or nurture a Web site for building a community?

Discussion Questions

8. Underdeveloped countries tend to have sharper class divisions than exist in the United States. It is not uncommon for 2% of the population to control 80% of the wealth. As a marketer, how would you use this knowledge to develop a segmentation strategy for targeting consumers in these countries?

9. Booz-Allen and Nielsen//NetRatings suggest that successful e-tailers will change their approach from one size fits all to a series of parallel sites targeted to appeal to multiple usage occasions. The challenge for e-tailers, they say, is to use technology to detect which occasion a user entering the site may be in and to use that information to trigger an interface geared to that occasion. Do you agree? Defend your position.

10. Many parents are upset that some Web sites specifically target children and young teens. Outline the arguments for and against a company such as MyKindaPlace.com (featured in the opening vignette) using this segmentation and targeting strategy. Which side do you support—and why?

11. Some company managers forbid employees from using the Internet for non-work-related activities. What are the implications for e-marketers that segment their markets using the variable of home and work access?

chapter

9 differentiation and positioning strategies

learning objectives

The main objective of this chapter is to provide an overview of how and why e-marketers use differentiation and positioning. You will learn about the differentiation strategies used by online businesses and the bases for positioning or repositioning companies, products, and brands on the Internet.

After reading this chapter, you will be able to:

- Define differentiation and positioning and explain why they are important.
- Identify six important Internet-specific differentiation strategies.
- Discuss how companies can position or reposition themselves on the basis of attributes, technology, benefits, user category, relation to competitors, or integrator capabilities.

The only way a company can survive is to differentiate. This is true even more on the Internet where business competitors are not limited by driving distance, but encompass all the similar Web sites in the site owner's country and, to a smaller degree, all the similar Web sites in the world.

ralph f. wilson
differentiate or die

The J. Peterman Company is a classic example of successfully combining clever differentiation with powerful positioning. This is evident when visitors to its Web site, www.jpeterman.com, read J. Peterman's statement of philosophy.

"People want things that are hard to find. Things that have romance, but a factual romance, about them." J. Peterman romances the customer in these first few words of company philosophy. He proceeds to establish his company as a breed apart from its ordinary competitors: "I think that giant American corporations should start asking themselves if the things they make are really, I mean really, better than the ordinary. Clearly, people want things that make their lives the way they wish they were."

Every clothing and accessory item offered comes complete with a rambling narrative setting the stage in the customer's mind for romantic travel. For example, the preamble for the *Out of Africa!* collection demonstrates a unique product positioning:

"Between the years 1906 and 1939, a trickle, then a light rainfall, then a downpour of Englishmen, Germans, Scots, and some remarkable women, began to fall upon the immense gorgeous plateau of East Africa. Some came for a year, and stayed a lifetime. Some came to farm; or make a fortune; or to put something awful far behind. Don't ask what. All came to start life over again. Fresh. Discovered they hadn't been expelled from a Garden of Eden after all, but were just now entering one. That first night they lay awake listening, hearing Africa, hearing for the first time how to hear. And how to read a flattened blade of grass: who or what had passed through here; and exactly how long ago. It was paradise. It lasted three decades. There will never be anything else like it again.

Out of Africa Skirt (No. 1085), in beautiful, softly washed 8 oz. cotton fine line twill, unlined; doesn't cling, doesn't reveal. Contour waistband with button and concealed side zip closure. Slant front pockets. Price: $58. Women's sizes: 4 though 16. Color: Khaki."

The future of electronic commerce is an implicit one-to-one negotiation between buyer and seller.

jerry kaplan
founder,
onsale, inc.

Authors' Note*: This chapter is contributed by Adel I. El-Ansary and a team of research associates: Ewa Charazinska, Sean Harrington, and Katherine Klement.. At the time of this writing all are enrolled in the M.B.A program at the University of North Florida while holding middle management positions. The contributions of the research team are based on reports from a research project on* Internet Marketing Strategies *Research Program of the Donna L. Harper Chair in Marketing, University of North Florida, 2002.*

Differentiation of Online Businesses

Differentiation is what a company does to the product. *Positioning* is what it does to the customer's mind, as demonstrated by J. Peterman. Differentiation strategies have evolved with the commercialization of the Internet. The keys to differentiating online businesses are the creation of a distinctive and superior customer experience and the development of one-to-one relationships with consumers. The real value added by the Internet is the enhanced ability to differentiate according to customer relationships and provide a unique experience for each customer.

Kotler defines "**differentiation** as the process of adding a set of meaningful and valued differences to distinguish the company's offering from competitors' offerings" (Kotler, 2003, p. 315). "A company can differentiate its market offering along five dimensions: product, services, personnel, channel, and image" (Kotler, 2003, p. 317). Traditional offline differentiation has usually emphasized the product dimension; the other areas have been used when little real difference exists between competing products. Companies still differentiate by product online. However, the Internet's effect is in the greater assortment of products that companies are able to offer and the ability to customize product offerings for individual customers while reducing interactions with company employees. The Internet also provides a powerful new avenue for differentiating by channel, services, and image. Exhibit 9 - 1 displays the relative importance of each dimension for online and offline businesses, showing how the Internet changes differentiation strategies. Note that this graphical representation is purely a conceptual and visual aid based on our views—not data.

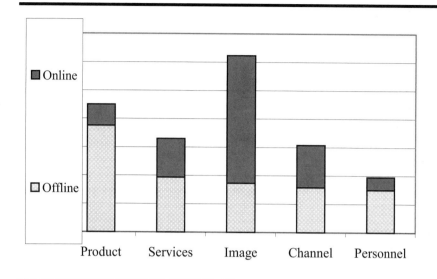

Exhibit 9 - 1 Relative Importance of Online and Offline Differentiation Dimensions

Channel Differentiation

The Internet is itself a distribution channel, a communication channel, and ultimately with individual customers. The Internet expands companies' (and consumers') geographic range (from local to global) and business hours (24 hours a day), as well as the assortment of products available. Customers may order a wider variety of products, at any time, day or night, for shipment to any location in the world, in contrast to the limited product assortment and limited business hours of traditional brick-and-mortar companies. This expands the scope of product distribution in time and space and gives the firm another channel through which it can reach customers, display a diversified assortment of offerings, and differentiate itself.

There are multiple levels of online channel differentiation. First, companies that provide product or service information on the Web have an advantage over companies with no Web presence by exploiting the Internet as a communication channel. Next, companies that conduct commercial transactions online have the advantage of the Internet's properties as a transaction and distribution channel. At a higher level is the differentiation of competitors' Internet-related service offerings. For example, in the banking industry, "one bank may provide a 'virtual pass book' facility, while another may transact on behalf of the client (e.g., digital signatures) and a third may actually provide interactive portfolio management services to key account holders" (Chakravarthy, 2000, p. 2).

Service Differentiation

Services can be effectively differentiated online in several ways. Customer service is enhanced by the ability to receive customer feedback through e-mail 24 hours a day, even if telephone operators and customer service personnel are not available—and the ability to respond more rapidly (in real time) to customer concerns. Another aspect of service differentiation is the distribution of products ordered online. Some companies, such as Peapod, specialize in the home delivery of products ordered online, thus differentiating their services from most traditional grocers. Other online services, such as online banking and securities trading, are becoming increasingly popular, differentiated both by the features they offer and the service consumption experiences. These services currently supplement traditional offline services, but as the world becomes more interconnected via the Internet, they may one day replace the traditional offline services.

Image Differentiation and the Customer Experience

Image differentiation will likely be most strongly affected by the Internet, as shown in Exhibit 9 - 1, through methods such as *experience branding*. Experience branding occurs when a company differentiates itself by creating a unique customer experience such as superior customer service. In turn, experience branding can increase customer loyalty and retention and produce referral business. Through experience branding, "firms can greatly improve their ability to retain customers, target key customer segments and enhance network profitability" (Vincent, 2000, p. 25). According to Karl Cluck of Razorfish, "online marketers must enhance the user's online experience in order to entice potential customers to buy" (Business Wire, 2000, p. 1).

Even the personal computer industry, long focused on product differentiation by computing speed, is now turning to image differentiation. For example, consider these perceptions about two computer industry firms, Gateway (which markets PCs) and Symantec (which markets system maintenance and protection software): "The perception is that *Gateway* is the vendor that will treat you right long term. *Symantec* has. . . fostered an image as the 'ambulance'. . . Differentiation has to be built upon the ability to create huge perceptual differences from . . . other aspects of the brand position" (Goldberg, 1999, p. 16).

The Internet's interactivity allows companies to respond more quickly to customer requests. Moreover, the ever-increasing speed of the Internet allows companies to communicate more quickly with current and potential customers, which is essential to retaining current customers and attracting new ones. Consider the pure-play home furnishings business iHome, which is "addressing customer requests to receive decorating help on a budget . . . iHome's ability to get download time under

30 seconds" is the key to iHome's growth rate." (Slott, 2000, p. 38). All of these benefits help to differentiate the image and customer experience of online firms.

Product Differentiation

Product differentiation includes customization and bundling—offering a combination of products or services that the individual consumer needs at prices that are attractive. Such differentiation supports one-to-one relationship building with each customer—critical for a company's long-term success on the Net.

Internet marketing is likely to have a major effect on product packaging. At present, marketers design most product packaging to appeal to consumers, be eye-catching, compete with other products on store shelves, and sell the product. As more commerce is conducted online rather than in retail stores, consumers might require products with more utilitarian packaging. Products purchased online will be shipped from the distributor directly to the consumer and, thus, never appear on retailers' shelves. As a result, these products will not need the expensive, colorful packaging that is necessary today for store display; nor will they need multiple layers of packaging (functional packaging inside the pretty display packaging). Instead, they'll only need a size and shape that is functional and useful for the consumer.

Packaging minimization will reduce waste and reduce packaging costs. The cost reduction obtained by converting to more minimalist packaging can be passed on to the consumer in the form of lower prices or could be reinvested in higher-quality, single-layer packaging enhancements, such as "better cook-in containers or easy-open or re-sealable freezer packs that also reduce in size as product is used up inside" (Du Bois, 2000, p. 25). Conversely, packages shipped to individual households will require additional packing materials not required in bulk case shipments to wholesalers and retailers.

Personnel Differentiation

In the past, personalized service and one-to-one relationships between merchants and consumers required the interaction of skilled personnel. Now, the Internet allows companies to "deliver their products and services through low-cost channels that automate the process and remove the expensive human element" (Wells, et.al. 2000, p. 32). By reducing a company's dependence on personnel to handle business transactions, the Internet leads to lower transaction and marketing costs, enabling a cost leadership advantage over offline companies. This "also results in cost reduction for the end user and at the same time acts as a differentiation by providing higher levels of service" (Chakravarthy, 2000, p. 2). However, as more companies offer products and services online, this cost advantage between online and offline operations will gradually shrink over time.

Customer Relationship

The Internet has made pricing information widely available to suppliers, customers, and competitors alike. This should have the effect of reducing price differences between suppliers, because customers can shop for a better price from any supplier in the world (see Chapter 11 for more on pricing). If this scenario develops, it would reduce the importance of price competition and increase the importance of differentiation (Neal, 2000). Thus, it is more important than ever for e-marketers to create brand loyalty and use the Internet to build one-to-one relationships with customers. "And when the dust settles, the real winners will be the brands that have built a strong emotional bond with consumers. (Shevack, 2000, p. 41)."

Businesses can "differentiate themselves by using the vast amounts of customer data that can be collected through their e-commerce activities, and then analyzed to better understand customer preferences and buying patterns" (Pravica, 2000, p. 15). Data mining is used to predict customer behavior and can be used to differentiate product and service offerings for individual customers as a way of fostering the one-to-one relationship with each. Sometimes, however, this can have the opposite effect of driving away customers who object to providing their personal preferences to companies online, or who unexpectedly find a completely different *customized* experience every time they visit a company Web site—an unpleasant experience that may result in the loss of valuable customers. The solution is to allow the customers the freedom to opt-out and remain anonymous or to provide personal information for customization purposes at each customer's discretion, allowing customers to control the online relationship and transactions. "The goal is simply to understand the customers' desires… and needs… so to better match the presentation and sales process to the right customer at the right time" (Wells, et.al. 2000, p. 33).

Product-Service Differentiation Strategies

In addition to the previously mentioned differentiation dimensions, Trout and Rivkin propose a concise list of specific differentiation strategies, many of which are particularly important in e-marketing initiatives (Wilson, 2000):

1. Being the first to enter the market.
2. Owning a product attribute or quality in the consumer's mind.
3. Demonstrating product leadership.
4. Utilizing an impressive company history or heritage.
5. Supporting and demonstrating the differentiating idea.
6. Communicating the difference.

These strategies are of particular importance on the Internet because the marketing strategy often revolves around the image and product information available on the Web. As the first Internet book retailer—and one of the pioneer online retailers in any category—Amazon.com captured an early lead in online book sales. The company has grown substantially since its inception in 1995; today Amazon is recognized as a leader on the Web. If a firm is first to provide the product or services, the "brand" can potentially become synonymous with the product as the best online provider. The Amazon.com brand is known around the world and has become associated with a variety of other products in addition to books.

This asset of a strong brand image can also help a company attain "ownership" of a product. Companies with a well-known brand still have an advantage despite the low entry barriers on the Internet. Customers are drawn to brands they trust, an attraction that is enhanced by a positive company history. Monster.com has essentially gained ownership of online job searches. The company offers a wide range of job-related information including job searches and résumé posting; it also includes special pages for high-level executives as well as graduating students. Monster.com's early entry into the market and its strong brand image have allowed the firm to become synonymous with the "product" of jobs.

Differentiation Strategies

Although the strategies discussed previously are more traditional, they still apply to e-marketing. Conversely, six differentiation strategies that are unique to marketing on the Web are presented in Exhibit 9 - 2, and discussed in the following sections.

1. Site Environment/ Atmospherics (Watson et al. 2000)	2. *Tangibilize* the Intangible (Watson et al. 2000)	3. Trust
▪ Look and feel of site ▪ User friendly ▪ Accurate portrayal of company and product	▪ Images ▪ Virtual tours ▪ Realistic descriptions	▪ Clearly state privacy policy ▪ Use encryption for secure transactions

4. Efficiency and Timeliness	5. Pricing	6. CRM
▪ Deliver what is promised to customers ▪ Deliver in a timely manner	▪ Be aware of competitor pricing ▪ Potential customer savings	▪ Customer tracking ▪ Seamless communication ▪ Greater relationship efficiency

Exhibit 9 - 2 Internet-Specific Differentiation Strategies

Site Environment/Atmospherics

Atmospherics refers to the in-store ambiance created by brick-and-mortar retailers. Similarly, Web sites can be differentiated by providing visitors with a positive environment to visit, search, purchase, and so forth. Visitors want a site that easily downloads, portrays accurate information, clearly shows the products and services offered, and is easily navigated. If customers view the home page and like what they see, they are more likely to view additional pages and ultimately become a paying customer.

Tangibilize the Intangible

An online product or service cannot be seen except by an image or description. Whether a company uses virtual tours, 3-D images, product image enlargements, trial downloads, or customer reviews, the goal is to make offerings seem more tangible by showing them in a realistic and customer-friendly manner.

Build Trust

Trust is a key issue on the Internet, especially when customers are expected to pay online or their information is tracked for personalized service or supply chain management. For this reason, trust building should be an integral part of a Web site's marketing strategy. In some instances trust may be built in as a by-product of strong brand recognition; however, a company site with lower brand recognition must project a secure environment. Detmer suggests that e-marketers must "take the time to clearly define your company's privacy policy, and make sure it is strictly enforced . . .Maintaining the balance between privacy and personalization will increase the comfort level your customers feel for your business" (Detmer, 2002). In addition to stating the privacy policy, e-commerce firms can reassure customers by using a safe and encrypted payment process for transactions. Trust is also important if customers should encounter problems on the Web site, require personal assistance, or need to exchange or return a purchase. Visitors may be more likely to buy from a site if they know a live person can be contacted.

Efficient and Timely Order Processing

One of the strongest motivators for customers who make Web-based purchases is the ease of ordering. Organizations must market their alliances and delivery timeliness as an important benefit. Furthermore, if the online company follows through on its promises, it is more likely to build customer loyalty and receive referrals from satisfied customers. Customer satisfaction or dissatisfaction can spread very quickly on the Internet with just a few keystrokes.

Pricing

Pricing as a method of differentiation has come under scrutiny, especially for Web marketers. When products were first offered on the Web, companies tended to offer price discounts as an incentive. Today, prices are relatively comparable on the Web, although some companies, such as Buy.com, offer lower prices. The majority of firms are choosing to differentiate themselves using methods other than pricing because pricing is easy to imitate and nonprice differentiation is more enduring for all but the price leaders.

Customer Relationship Management

As more firms shift away from price differentiation and as barriers to entry decrease on the Internet, customer relationship management (CRM) is becoming more predominant as a means of differentiation. Netflix, for example, forges long-term relationships with consumers who want the convenience of receiving movies on DVD by mail. Customers who subscribe to one of Netflix's monthly plans can set up personal lists of the movies they want to rent. Depending on the type of subscription they choose, customers can rent three or more DVD movies at one time—with no return deadlines or late return penalties. After viewing a movie, customers slip it into the prepaid return envelope to mail it back to Netflix; a few days later, they receive the next DVD on their list. Thus, Netflix builds customer relationships one at a time through customer-driven personalization (including a personal greeting on the Web site) and convenience.

Other Strategies

Another set of differentiation strategies is discussed in an "E-Marketing Opportunity Model" developed by Feeny (Feeny, 2001). This model helps companies define their customers and products in order to determine the degree of differentiation required. Feeny's methods of differentiation can be categorized as one of three e-marketing opportunities (Feeny, 2001, p. 45):

- Enhancing the selling process.
- Enhancing the customer buying process.
- Enhancing the customer usage experience.

In this model, firms use perceived product differentiation and frequency of purchase to choose the best strategies.

Positioning Strategies

Positioning strategies help to create a desired image for a company and its products in the minds of a chosen user segment. **Positioning** is the process of creating this image, and a **position** is the resulting view of the firm or brand from the consumer perspective (often two very different things). The concept is simple: To be successful, a company must differentiate itself and its products from all others and position itself among its competitors in the public's mind to carve out its own market niche. Firms can position brands, the company itself, or individual products. The positioning rule of thumb: "Mediocrity deserves no praise."

When firms don't include positioning strategies in their e-marketing plans, they have very little control over brand images. Ultimately a product position is in the eye of the customer, but marketing communication can help consumers see the brand in the way management wants it to be viewed. Without a company's positioning cues, customers may perform a competitive comparison using incomplete or even inaccurate information. Web sites such as www.compare.com, www.pricescan.com, and www.bizrate.com allow customer ratings and chat about products; firms do not want complaints at these sites to be the only input to customers' perceptions of brand image.

The e-marketer's goal is to build a strong and defensible position on one or more bases that are relevant and important to the consumer—and do it better than the competitors. How can a company do this?

Bases for Positioning on the Web

Firms can position on the basis of product or service attributes ("the smallest cell phone"), high-tech image ("our cell phones handle e-mail"), benefits ("fits in your pocket"), user categories ("best cell phone for college students"), or comparison with competitors ("our phone is less expensive than the Nokia"). Also, firms can take an integrator position ("a full range of electronic products and services"). Here are examples of these positioning bases online.

Product or Service Attribute

Attributes are product or service features such as size, color, ingredients, speed, and so forth. A patented product or process, such as Amazon's one-click check-out process, is an ideal basis for positioning. Other examples:

- iVillage allows users to build their own meal menus at its site using criteria such as ingredients and calorie counts (www.ivillage.com).
- Pillsbury adds value through ideas, recipes, and an advice service on its site (www.pillsbury.com).
- Kraft Foods offers *Interactive Kitchen* with tools such as *Your Recipe Box, Your Shopping List, Simple Meal Planner, Make It Now* (recipes suggestions based on what is in the fridge and cupboard), and *Party Planner*. Mothers, who are Kraft's main target, can find "real help in real time" (www.kraftfoods.com).
- Tylenol does not sell online but provides useful and entertaining one-to-one Web features such as Tylenol pain reliever and health information and Tylenol

greeting cards. The site provides links to stores where customers can buy the product (www.tylenol.com).

Technology Positioning

A type of attribute positioning, positioning on the basis of technology, shows that a firm is on the cutting edge—especially important for online marketers. Two examples are:

- At the Lands' End Web site, women can build virtual models based on their physical features such as hair color, skin tone, hair style, and face shape. Users can then see how Lands' End apparel would look on themselves by trying virtual outfits on the model. The model can be rotated for front, side, and back views (www.landsend.com).

- The American Airlines site offers various tools to allow customers to manage their flight arrangements: frequent flier account management, personalized travel planning, and personalized seat selection when booking flights. Customers can store user-profile information on preferred destinations, seating preference, companion travelers, and frequent flier rewards status and billing (www.aa.com).

Benefit Positioning

Benefits are the flip side of attributes—the customers' perspective of what the feature will do for them. Benefit positioning is generally a stronger basis for positioning because of its customer orientation in answering the question: *What will this do for me?* Examples include:

- The Polo Web site focuses on how its products shape an entire lifestyle. Its products are much more than a tie or a jacket—they are designed to help customers contemplate a dream world of adventure, style, and culture (www.polo.com).

- The Miller Lite Beer Web site offers a software package that can be downloaded and used as a social organizer for arranging meetings, mostly for entertainment. The Miller icon is then permanently present on the desktop, reminding the customer about the brand on a daily basis (www.milerlite.com).

- The Valvoline motor oil Web site has become a destination site for racing aficionados. It features schedules for NASCAR and other racing circuits, as well as results of recent races, driver photos, and interviews. Visitors can send racing greeting cards, buy official Valvoline racing gear, download a racing screensaver, and sign up for a weekly newsletter (www.valvoline.com).

- Kimberly-Clark's Huggies site has built a relationship with parents by offering help and advice on child care in a community format. In the "Happy Baby" section, parents can customize stories to include their child's name (www.huggies.com).

User Category

This type of positioning relies on customer segments. It is successful when the segment has some unique quality that ties product benefits more closely to the group than to other segments. Following are some Web examples:

- Kellogg's has set up an interactive Web site for children. They can register online and enter code numbers found on Kellogg's cereal packages, then use the codes as "money" on related Web sites or even earn interest in a "special" bank (www.kellogg.com).

- Yahoo! Geo Cities hosts Web user pages that are organized into neighborhoods based on specific interests. Consumers can connect with others who share the same interests, from Japanese anime videos to trucks (www.geocities.com).

- The Agent Provocateur-Lingerie online outlet appeals to men. The site provides sexy, downloadable screen savers and high-production retro "films noirs," which are meant to be tongue-in-cheek as well as sexy (www.agentprovocateur.com).

Competitor Positioning

Many firms position by touting specific benefits that provide advantages over competitive offerings. Online or offline companies often position themselves against an entire industry ("I Can't Believe It's Not Butter" margarine), against a particular firm (Amazon.com for toys), or according to relative industry position (AOL is the ISP connection leader and Earthlink a challenger). In the software business, Microsoft is the industry leader and lets everyone know it.

Integrator Positioning

Some companies want to be known for providing everything a consumer needs in a particular product category, industry, or even in general (e.g., Wal-Mart). This is a particularly important strategy online because busy consumers want convenience and one-stop shopping. For example:

- Martha Stewart's Web site brings together a wide spectrum of business units in one place. The site effectively communicates the core identity of the brand—improving the quality of living in the home and encouraging do-it-yourself ingenuity. Visitors to Martha Stewart's site are linked to Kmart's site, where Martha Stewart's branded domestics products are sold.

- Microsoft has created a veritable conglomerate through its own sites plus acquisitions and affiliations, such as Microsoft Expedia, Microsoft CarPoint, MSN, and others.

Repositioning on the Web

Positioning alone won't make a product successful. Marketers must also be sensitive to how the market perceives and subsequently views the company as well as the product. Based on market feedback, a company must be flexible enough to react to those opinions by enhancing or modifying a position. **Repositioning** is the process of creating a new or modified brand, company, or product position. Companies face a long-term challenge when attempting to use repositioning to change the way customers perceive their brands. Fortunately, companies can easily check on progress by tracking customers' preferences and habits on the Internet, as discussed in Chapter 6.

As one repositioning example, Yahoo! started life as a network of Internet guides: Yet Another Hierarchal Officious Oracle! Soon it sought to attract new customers, keep them coming back to the site, and be perceived as the first place to go when looking for anything online. To do this, the firm repositioned from online guide to Web portal. That's why Yahoo! is making content from its site and its partners downloadable not only on home PCs but also to PDAs and other wireless devices. Further, it invites users to set up customized Web pages through My Yahoo! Other features to draw traffic include Yahoo! chat, and Yahooligans! Its brand messages, distribution arrangements, and content partnerships combine to position the site as the most reliable portal, content-information provider, and shopping spot on the Internet.

Similarly, Amazon has repositioned itself within the last few years. Originally Amazon was positioned as the world's largest bookstore. Today it promises the "Earth's biggest selection" of a variety of products from music to electronics and more.

S u m m a r y

Differentiation is what a company does to the product. Positioning is what it does to the customer's mind. The proliferation of information, products, and services available on the Internet means companies must find ways of differentiating their products and services in order to attract customers and build long-term relationships.

Many traditional differentiation methods can be applied to an e-marketing strategy, including early market entry, product ownership, product leadership, impressive company history, and the ability to demonstrate and communicate the differentiation strategy. Although these methods are effective in an Internet strategy, e-marketing requires some additional and unique differentiation strategies focusing on site/environment atmospherics, "tangibilizing" the intangible, trust, efficiency, pricing, and customer relationship marketing.

Marketing strategies online and offline depend on the position that the brand, company, or product holds in the minds of customers. In today's environment, where information is easily accessible and consumers hold the power of choice, positioning needs to be focused on customers' desires and personalized to individuals rather than focusing on the product. Any position must answer the customer's question: "What's in it for me?"

Traditional product or service positioning strategies also apply to the Internet. However, e-marketers can use Internet-specific strategies such as positioning on the basis of technology, benefit, user category, competitor, or integrator. Repositioning is the process of creating a new or modified brand, company, or product position. Companies, offline and online, face a long-term challenge when attempting to use repositioning to change the way customers perceive their brands.

Key Terms

Atmospherics	Positioning
Differentiation	Repositioning
Position	

Exercises

Review Questions

1. How does differentiation differ from positioning?
2. What levels of online channel differentiation exist as options for companies?
3. What is the goal of experience branding?
4. How do site atmospherics affect online differentiation?
5. Why should e-marketers try to tangibilize the intangible?
6. Why is benefit positioning so powerful?
7. Why would an e-marketer choose to use competitor positioning? Integrator positioning?

Discussion Questions

8. Why is a company able to directly control the differentiation of its brand but not its positioning?
9. The positioning rule of thumb states that "Mediocrity deserves no praise." What does this mean? Do you agree with this statement? Explain your answer.
10. How might an online company react if a rival embarks on competitor positioning in an unflattering way?

11. Are customers likely to be confused by an integrator positioning that suggests a Web site sells anything and everything? What are the advantages and disadvantages of this positioning?

3 e-marketing strategy

resources and exercises

Practitioner Perspectives

At-Work Internet Usage: A Double-Edged Sword of Controversy and Opportunity

Mr. Hess leads industry analysis and marketing efforts at comScore Networks. As one of comScore's earliest employees, Mr. Hess previously held senior positions in the company's business development organization. With experience across a variety of major industries, Mr. Hess is frequently interviewed and quoted by global media on issues of importance to marketing and financial firms. Prior to joining comScore, Mr. Hess held various leadership roles throughout 10 years at Information Resources, Inc., the largest marketing research company in the United States, where he consulted with industry-leading consumer marketing firms in the analysis and development of marketing and sales strategies. As senior vice president of IRI's e-commerce division, Mr. Hess launched the first service to link online behavior with offline sales activity. E-mail: press@comscore.com

Research continues to unveil insights into Internet usage in the workplace. The truth—if at times painful—is that Americans do rely on the Internet during the workday as a discreet gateway *out* of the workplace for a variety of tasks, not the least of which is shopping.

What many employers undoubtedly fear as an enormous productivity gap offers a substantial opportunity for others, especially marketers. comScore Networks conducted the industry's first analysis of the daily and hourly dynamics of at-work shopping behavior, and the conclusions paint a vivid picture of this conflicted reality.

Considering that employees often are faced with longer workdays, more responsibilities, and increased performance expectations, it can be a relatively small concession to allow *some* latitude for staff to fulfill personal needs with the convenience of the high-speed connection that so many workplaces offer. Such an allowance can represent a valuable employee benefit as more companies set limits on at-work Internet use.

Numerous comScore studies suggest significant opportunities for marketers and advertisers in the targeting of online ads and other promotions—particularly for direct-response campaigns—at specific times and places that offer consumers with the greatest purchase propensity. Moreover, additional opportunities exist to employ offline advertising to increase awareness as consumers reach for their virtual wallets. Let's take a look at a few specific metrics, detailing these dynamics of online shopping behavior.

Peak Shopping Days

Through years of analysis of online consumer behavior, we've consistently observed a high level of workplace shopping activity, with a concentration of online sales during the workweek. In fact, sales tend to explode on Monday morning and continue building through Wednesday of each week. During the holiday shopping seasons, it is common for shopping to peak as late as Thursday, due to increased demand.

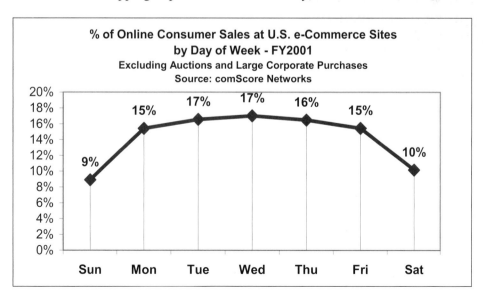

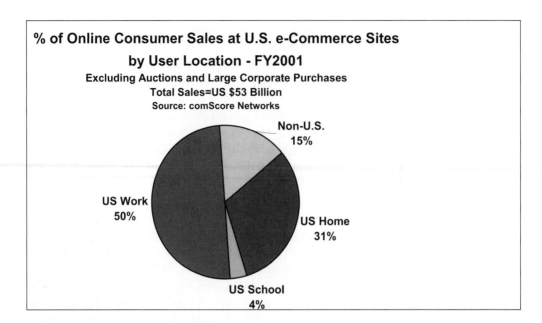

% of Online Consumer Sales at U.S. e-Commerce Sites by User Location - FY2001
Excluding Auctions and Large Corporate Purchases
Total Sales=US $53 Billion
Source: comScore Networks

Non-U.S. 15%
US Work 50%
US Home 31%
US School 4%

Contribution of At-Work Shopping

In our 2001 annual e-commerce review, we reported that 50% of online dollars spent at U.S. sites originated from consumers using PCs at work in the United States. Since non-U.S. buyers contributed 15% of sales at U.S. sites (an equally enlightening discovery), the workplace share of sales actually translates to approximately 60% of the total online dollars spent by U.S. buyers. By contrast, at-work PCs comprise just 44% of the total universe of domestic Web-enabled computers.

Shopping by Time of Day

Our initial findings intrigued us enough to conduct an analysis of the distribution of U.S. online sales by local time of day. The results were more dramatic than we expected. The online sales trend of an average day is not unlike that of an average week, with minimal spending during prework hours, a burst of activity commencing between 8:00 and 9:00 a.m. as the workday begins, and a steady build through 11:00 a.m. (just before lunchtime). Spending declines around lunch hour (a humorous twist, to be sure) to a level that is more or less maintained until the final hours of the workday.

The subsequent shift to home buying is unmistakable, with sales picking up just after the likely dinner hour and lasting until Americans head off to sleep around 11:00 p.m.

Where to Target At-Work Surfers?

How do marketers and advertisers leverage these findings? First, we must identify online media that are likely to deliver the highest share of users in the desired location(s)—such as homes, workplaces, or even universities. The following table details a few sites that might be highly attractive to a marketer seeking to reach a disproportionately high at-work audience.

But is a large at-work visitor audience enough? Despite the skew of online buying to the workplace, not all workplace Web users are buying online at the same rate. We can prove this by examining the Buying Power Index (BPI) of each site. This comScore-developed measure benchmarks dollars spent by the average visitor to a given site—that is, across the entire Internet, not just at that site—relative to the Web-wide spending of the average Internet user. BPI data clearly show that sites with the highest composition of at-work visitors don't necessarily attract visitors who spend the most money online.

Clearly, not all sites are created equal when actual buying power is added to the mix. Although newhomesource.com attracted a modest audience of 317,000 unique visitors in February, its impressive BPI of 495 means that those visitors spend an average of nearly five times as much as the average Web user. Weighting newhomesource.com's raw audience by its BPI validates that it wields the buying power of an average site with nearly *1.6 million* visitors. By contrast, choiceradio.com has an even higher share (71%) of at-work visitors, but its BPI of 81 tells us that those users spend almost 20% less online than the average surfer.

Targeting Audiences in the Future

For even greater precision, various online ad-serving technologies and media publishers are promising the delivery of ads to Web users by time of day and probable geographic location. Of course, any marketer needs to assess the total return offered by investments in such services, but as these become more accurate and cost-effective they will doubtless become an important component of a well-stocked marketing arsenal.

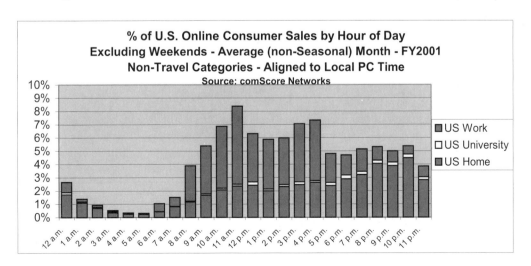

Source: netScore				
February 2002	Total U.S. Unique Visitors (000)	% of U.S. Audience at Work	Buying Power Index (BPI)	Total U.S. Audience Weighted by BPI
Total Internet	131,230	44%	100	131,230
virtuallythere.com	489	71%	515	2,521
choiceradio.com	183	71%	81	148
loopnet.com	220	71%	321	706
newhomesource.com	317	67%	495	1,567
inc.com	193	67%	165	319

Finally, it would be myopic to overlook the many ways in which audience behavior data can improve the efficiency of offline marketing efforts. For example, if online cash registers start ringing in a given product category between 8:00 and 9:00 a.m., a marketer would be wise to test share-boosting campaigns on morning TV and drive-time radio.

Conclusion

Savvy marketers have long used accurate information on consumer buying behavior to guide the design of more effective and efficient marketing plans. With increasing consumer Internet continuing developments in online measurement and intelligence, marketers can design and deploy strategies on an equal footing with offline platforms. In 2001 consumers spent $53 billion online at U.S. sites alone, and spending promises to rise in the future. The benefits to companies of using relevant and timely data to gain their fair share—or more—of this growing pie are simply too great to ignore.

Practitioner Perspective

How Good Customer Relationships Go Bad

Author: Martha Rogers Ph.D.

Don Peppers and Martha Rogers, Ph.D., are co-founders of Peppers and Rogers Group, the management consulting firm that focuses on customer-based business strategy. Recognized in 2001 by the World Technology Network as having played a significant role in developing the field of CRM, Don Peppers and Martha Rogers are the co-authors of the revolutionary The One to One Future *and a series of business books that further develops the unique one-to-one methodology espoused by their firm.*
Web site: www.1to1.com

Just how important is being a Trusted Agent for your customers? How vital is it that your employees provide a one-to-one, brand-name-enhancing experience across customer value tiers? Before you answer, consider these unfortunate events from the annals of the customer service "Hall of Shame":

- Mirroring the national ad campaign, a Radio Shack employee is wearing a button that says "You've Got Questions? We've Got Answers." Our shopping companion asks, "Excuse me, do you have a controller that will work with my TV, my stereo, my DVD player, and my satellite system?" The agent thinks for a moment, then says, "Gee dude, we don't carry Dish Network stuff. I don't know, you can look."

- This time, we're online looking for a Sony Digital Camcorder. With all of the options available, we decide to speak with a live customer service rep. Now on the phone, we've agreed on a price and handed over our credit card information. But for some reason, the salesperson begins insisting we take additional options. "You need this lens, that battery, and this case," he asserts. Ultimately, we're so unnerved we end the transaction; but to our astonishment, the salesperson puts us on hold to delay our cancellation. Ten minutes later, we finally get confirmation of our request along with a sarcastic "Hear that? I'm tearing up your order."

The moral here: Live customer service can be sublime or abysmal. You strive for the customer-focused company, but your face to the customer is manned by individuals who just don't "get it." Your customers don't make distinctions between your ad campaigns, Web site, or call center; they use unique interactions to form a single opinion of your company. So no matter how grandiose management's CRM vision, it's ultimately the frontline employees who have the most contact and influence with your customers. So how do you get them to consistently provide the right experiences?

Attacking the "Hey Dude" syndrome

According to Mark Olson, sales planning Vice President at Radio Shack, the "big challenge" is providing the right motivation, training, and tools that bring the one-to-one vision all the way to the customer. Olson wasn't pleased with the preceding experience, but says his company is working diligently to transform individual employees into Trusted Agents. "We want to be known as a trusted place to go," says Olson.

Within 14 days of being hired, new employees must complete four core certifications: customer service, selling intangibles, retail selling skills, and wireless communications. Radio Shack also offers 10 more certifications and rewards employees who complete all 10 with higher pay. To date, "Seventy percent of employees are fully certified," says Olson. While the "Hey Dude" syndrome can never be fully eradicated in retail—which, Olson admits, is "something that keeps me awake nights"—Radio Shack's goal is to "do our best to ensure that customers have an above average experience in our stores."

On the tools side, the retailer is rolling out a high-speed Internet site for its stores, Radio Shack online. In consumer electronics, "There are so many products and so much change, training itself could be a full time job," says Olson. The high-speed, retrieval-based system "gives the sales associate a tool where he can find the information he needs to get the customer's questions answered." Radio Shack intends to equip 95% of its 5,000 stores with the online tool this year.

Experiences like those mentioned previously may be the exception, but they can undermine the best CRM plan and seriously hurt your bottom line. Your line employees are the closest link you have to your customers. They are the agents of your brand name and the face of trusted agency.

Originally published in Inside1to1® *on January 7, 2002; reprinted with permission from Peppers and Rogers Group. Copyright © 2001 Peppers and Rogers Group / Marketing 1to1, Inc.*

Practitioner Perspective

Behavior of Internet Users

Mr. Fulgoni is the chairman and cofounder of comScore Networks, Inc. He brings more than 30 years of leadership in innovation and market success to the comScore Networks team. From 1981 to 1998 he served as president and CEO of Information Resources, Inc., where over an 18-year period he grew the company's revenues at an annual compound rate of 40%. Under Mr. Fulgoni's leadership, IRI grew from a start-up into the largest market research company in the United States. Mr. Fulgoni has long been involved in the growth of successful technology companies, having served on the Boards of US Robotics and Platinum Technology prior to their acquisition by 3Com and Computer Associates in multibillion dollar transactions. Educated in the United Kingdom, Mr. Fulgoni holds a master's degree in marketing and a B. Sc. in physics.
E-mail: press@comscore.com

To facilitate the growth of online marketing, marketers need a proven objective and comparative means of measuring audiences on the Internet. Insights are needed on users' unique page- and media-viewing habits, as well as the relationship of these figures to key demographic characteristics such as age, gender, household income, household size, education level, and spending. Companies that are equipped with the right market intelligence to understand their target audiences are in a better position to make smarter business decisions. Since it is impossible to measure the behavior of the entire Internet population, including users of proprietary online services such as AOL and Juno, a representative sample must be assembled.

comScore Media Metrix, a division of Reston, Virginia–based comScore Networks, Inc., uses a sample size of more than 120,000 individuals for its core U.S. syndicated digital media ratings—long recognized as the currency in online media measurement among financial analysts, advertising agencies, publishers, and marketers.

The comScore Media Metrix Monitoring Technology

comScore Media Metrix measures online behavior through use of its advanced monitoring technology, which provides continuous reporting of all Internet behavior, including usage of Web sites and proprietary networks like AOL, usage of Internet applications like instant messaging and multiple-player games, and online buying and other transaction behavior. When an Internet user agrees to join the comScore Media Metrix panel, a small applet is downloaded to the user's browser in a matter of seconds and configures the browser so that it unobtrusively routes the panel member's Internet connection through comScore's network of 500 servers, without requiring any further action on the part of the individual. The technology allows comScore to capture the complete detail of all the communication to and from each individual's computer—click by click, page by page, minute by minute. Moreover, all individuals can be identified through their unique user IDs. As such, a comScore-configured computer being used by three people in a household can be monitored so that the Internet usage of each of those three people is separately measured.

Building the Sample

comScore Media Metrix establishes the population characteristics of each of its reported segments of users—including home, workplace, and university—by conducting weekly telephone interviews of each segment. These interviews capture information such as the size of each segment and its demographic characteristics.

comScore Media Metrix recruits at-home panelists through a process called random digit dialing (RDD)—media researchers' preferred sampling framework. Prospects are determined based on randomly generated numbers from working telephone exchanges and then are called using stringent call-back guidelines to ensure random selection. However, since many heavy online users access the Internet through their household's sole phone line, it is often difficult to reach some prospects. Consequently, comScore Media Metrix has enhanced its recruiting methodology by recruiting prospects *both* by phone and by mail to ensure the highest possible cooperation rate. This recruiting methodology is the most effective and rigorous panel-recruitment process in the industry today.

Measuring At-Work and University Samples

Measuring Internet usage at work and among university students is critical for a variety of reasons. First, a substantial amount of personal online usage and buying occurs in the workplace and among university members. Second, usage patterns can differ from those at home due to the faster Internet connection speeds prevalent in the workplace and the younger demographics of the university audience. Moreover, many online marketers and advertisers are interested in targeting at-work and university audiences precisely because of their purchasing propensity. (See additional comScore case study on workplace audiences on page 254.)

While measuring work and university audiences is critical, these groups are more challenging to recruit and measure. Based on several years of experience, comScore Media Metrix has devised a rigorous at-work and university measurement methodology using special incentives—such as free server-based virus scanning—that has successfully recruited more than 35,000 people under measurement within each segment.

Expanded Reporting for Global and Local Geographies and for Measuring Online Spending

Supplementing comScore Media Metrix's core RDD-based digital media ratings are additional capabilities based on the company's opt-in "mega panel," which accurately measures the online browsing and buying behavior of 1.5 million representative participants globally. This panel provides total worldwide data based on users in over 200 countries, while also offering the industry's only detailed and accurate Internet usage data for the top 78 U.S. Designated Market Areas (DMA).

Finally, the unique capabilities of comScore's measurement technology—which actually captures the details of panelists' online buying, including what was bought and how much was spent—allows comScore to provide its clients with an Internet Buying Power Index (BPI). The BPI measures the total dollars spent online (across all sites) by the average member of a site's audience. For example, visitors to a site with a BPI of 100 spend an average amount across the Web, while a site with a BPI of 200 draws visitors that spend twice as much online as the average Internet user. This metric is particularly valuable for buyers and sellers of online advertising.

Measuring Internet Usage in the Future

Marketers have an immediate need for online media planning tools that are consistent with those used in the offline world. As a result, we are in the process of developing "reach and frequency" planning systems that use the comScore Media Metrix data and that will help marketers better integrate the Internet into their multimedia marketing plans.

comScore Media Metrix is also well poised for the continued development of its monitoring methodology. Since we capture all online activity through comScore's proxy-server technology, new monitoring instructions can be easily added as new Internet technologies and media emerge.

S a v v y   S i t e s

American Demographics www.demographics.com or www.inside.com (site owner)	*American Demographics* is a monthly publication geared toward marketers. The online edition contains the full edition of this publication—and archive—that features articles, trends, and "marketing tools," but only subscribers have access.
CyberAtlas cyberatlas.internet.com	*CyberAtlas* provides a wealth of marketing information from a variety of sources. Everything from demographics and geographics to understanding business markets such as advertising and finance. The free weekly newsletter is great.

eLab
ecommerce.vanderbilt.edu

eLab is produced by the Owen School of Management at Vanderbilt University. The site is devoted to topics about marketing on the Internet. It has become one of the premier research centers for studying e-commerce. There are plenty of excellent scholarly publications to be found here and a nice assortment of relevant links with descriptions.

Electronic Privacy Information Center
www.epic.org

EPIC is a public interest research center that focuses on emerging civil liberties issues.

Federal Trade Commission
www.ftc.gov

The FTC is a U.S. government agency that regulates monopolistic trusts and protects customers from unscrupulous business practices, including deceptive advertising. The FTC has a major impact on U.S. Internet regulations.

Forrester Research
www.forrester.com

Some free information about information technology issues can be found here.

Gartner
www3.gartner.com/Init

Gartner is a consulting firm that analyzes trends and technologies. The site offers access to news and some free research.

GPO Access
www.access.gpo.gov

GPO Access is a service of the U.S. Government Printing Office that provides free electronic access to a wealth of important information products produced by the federal government. This includes important business materials such as *Commerce Business Daily* (CBDNet).

comScore Media Metrix
www.comscore.com and www.jmm.com

comScore Media Metrix is a leader in marketing information services. The company provides analysis and measurement tools to businesses.

Nielsen//Net Ratings
www.nielsen-netratings.com

Nielsen Media Research and Net Ratings have joined forces to provide Nielsen//Net Ratings. This site provides the latest information in audience measurement, Internet marketing, e-commerce, and more. The first page even provides some useful "Hot off the Net" stats. The Nielsen//Net Ratings Reporter provides the latest information weekly via e-mail.

NUA Internet Surveys www.nua.ie	This is a good source of international information about the Internet. NUA also reprints results of other research about Net users and electronic commerce.
Pew Internet & American Life Project www.pewinternet.org	This nonprofit initiative of the Pew Research Center for People and the Press conducts research on the impact of the Internet on children, families, communities, the workplace, schools, health care, and civic/political life.
Securities and Exchange Commission www.sec.gov	The Securities and Exchange Commission (SEC) site contains all the financial report filings from public companies in its EDGAR database.
Stat-USA www.stat-usa.gov	This site is a service of the Department of Commerce. It is for businesses as well as the economic and trade community.
Survey-Net www.survey.net	A good source for dynamic, up-to-the-second information, opinions, and demographics from the Net community!
The U.S. Census Report www.census.gov	The U.S. government publishes all its demographic, social, and economic data at this site.
Thomas thomas.loc.gov	Thomas is the official site for U.S. legislative information; it contains up-to-the-minute text and news on current bills.

Activities

1. Customers face many barriers when purchasing online. It has been estimated that as many as 65% of all purchases are abandoned midstream. Working in groups, try to develop ways that online retailers can help more site visitors be converted to buyers.

2. In groups, try to come up with a list of characteristics that describe those in the group who have purchased online and those who haven't. What are the differences?

3. Watch a friend surf for 10 minutes and record the clickstream. (Netscape records sites visited in its history list; Internet Explorer records sites visited using the drop-down arrow by the back button.) List each site, page within, and how long

your friend spends on each page. Can you make any determination about your friend's attitudes, interests, and opinions based on the clickstream?

4. Conduct a survey in your class to determine what benefits each student looks for online. Categorize the benefits under the headings used in this chapter and then tally your answers to determine percentages.

5. You have been given the difficult task of researching online marketing communication practices in the soft-drink industry. Do some online searching and list sources that you discover to help with this problem.

6. Toyota has asked you to test the effectiveness of its new banner ad using four primary research techniques. Design these tests.

7. Find information on the U.S. Census and Nielsen TV ratings, either online or in the library. What methodology does each use? Evaluate their strengths and weaknesses based on what you've learned about research methods in this chapter.

8. Top-of-Mind positioning example (Developed by Eleas Wilson)

    a. Pick a number between 1 and 10.
    b. Multiply that number by 9.
    c. Add digits together (e.g., 4 x 7 = 28→ 2+8).
    d. Subtract 5 from that number.
    e. Pick a letter in the alphabet that corresponds with that number (1=A, 2=B, 3=C).
    f. Think of a country that starts with that letter.
    g. Think of an animal that starts with the last letter of that country.
    h. Think of a color that starts with the last letter of that animal.
    (see explanation after question 9)

9. Positioning by association example (Developed by Eleas Wilson)

    a. Complete the following math exercises:
        1 + 13 =
        23 − 9 =
        4 + 10 =
        7 + 7 =
        8 + 6 =
    b. Think of a vegetable and say it out loud!
    (see explanation below)

Explanation to question 8:

Do you really think there are orange kangaroos in Denmark?

   If the math is done correctly the ending number will always be four. Hence, the letter in the alphabet that corresponds to four is D. The most well-known country that starts with a D is Denmark. Usually, the animal that people choose is kangaroo. And finally, the first color that comes to peoples' minds is orange. The reason this usually works is because Denmark, kangaroo, and orange have the foremost position (in relation to other possible choices) in most people's minds. Holding the foremost position is very important in building brand equity. What kind of car comes to your mind when you hear the word safety? Most people think of Volvo. This association is a very significant asset. Volvo has positioned itself in a way that alleviates consumers' perceived physical risk.

Explanation to question 9:
Was the first vegetable you thought of a carrot? An overwhelming majority of people do. The next choice is usually tomato. What is the association between 14 and carrot, or 14 and tomato? It is not exactly known. Some suggest that there is an association between 14 and "karat"; however, this has not been proven. Why is the second choice usually tomato? No one really knows.

I n t e r n e t   E x e r c i s e s

Internet Exercise: Psychographic Classification of Consumers

SRI Consulting, through the Business Intelligence Center online, features the Values and Lifestyles Program (VALS^{TM}). Many marketers who wish to understand the psychographics of both existing and potential customers use this market segmentation program. Companies and advertisers on the Web can use this information to develop their sites. Visit SRI at www.sric-bi.com and follow the links under "Consulting Services" to the VALS^{TM} questionnaire. Take the survey to determine your type and then read all about your type. Use this information for the questions following the table. Also of interest to marketers in the global economy are the psychographic differences among cultures. SRI created two other segmentation programs: Geo-VALS^{TM} and Japan-VALS^{TM}. Complete the following table about the Japan-VALS^{TM} segments and characteristics as they are presented on the site.

Japan-VALS Type	% of Population	Characteristics

For Discussion

1. What is your VALS2^{TM} type? Does it describe you well? Why or why not?

2. How do the U.S. based VALS2™ segments differ from Japan-VALS™ segments? What does this say about consumer differences between the two cultures?

3. Why do you think SRI designed a separate typology for Japanese consumers?

4. How can marketers use information from Japan-VALS™?

Internet Exercise: Online Target Marketing

As the Internet becomes more mature, Web sites will focus to serve very specific target markets. College students are often surprised to learn that one of the most active groups online is older adults. ThirdAge is a Web site dedicated to this market segment. Visit ThirdAge and check out its media kit (www.thirdage.com). How does it characterize the demographic and psychographic profiles of its users? Now visit www.ign.com (at the other end of the age spectrum) and complete the table for its users. You may also find useful information on these two market segments at *American Demographics* (www.demographics.com).

Statistic	Profile of a ThirdAge User	Profile of a IGN User
Age		
Income		
Online purchase behavior		
Online investing		
Time spent online		
Online activities		
Psychographic characteristics		

For Discussion

1. Who are some of the sponsors of the ThirdAge Web site? Of IGN?

2. Browse around the sites—what types of products seem to appeal to ThirdAge users? To IGN users?

3. Look at the list of the site's sponsors. Do any of the brands that you find on the ThirdAge site also target the IGN demographic? Give some examples.

4. In general, how do the articles differ in content for each market?

5. Based on questions 1–5, write a one-sentence positioning statement for each site.

6. What segmentation variable(s) is ThirdAge using for defining its target market?

7. How is the site designed to appeal to the target audience?

Internet Exercise: Online Databases

Many business-to-business (B2B) marketers use the services of firms that provide information on other companies through their databases. Dun & Bradstreet is popular and has a fine reputation for both its paper and online company profiles. The Yellow Book, founded in 1930, also provides information for businesses seeking suppliers or other contacts. Finally, AskAlix Directory serves a niche market for businesses wanting a particuiar type of information. In this exercise you will visit all three online firms, check out their services, and evaluate their appropriateness for various business situations. Start by completing the table.

	Dun & Bradstreet www.dnb.com	Yellow Book www.yellowbook.com	AskAlix Directory www.askalix.com
Database size			
Geographic coverage			
Cost for using the database			
Specific company profile information in database			
Three important services			
Useful for a supplier search?			
Useful for a supplier selection?			
Useful for finding prospective business customers?			
Database includes government market?			
Competitive edge			

Discussion Questions:

1. If your firm was looking for an office supply company in Manhattan to replace its current supplier, which of the three databases would you use? Explain.

2. If you wanted to quickly find the phone number of an office supply firm in Tampa, Florida, which database would you use? Why?

3. Which database offers the broadest range of services? Explain.

4. Under what circumstances would the AskAlix business database be useful to a company?

5. If you were a salesperson for IBM and prospecting for new business customers, which database would you use? Why?

6. Over all, which database company is the best in your opinion? Explain.

7. If you were going to start an online database firm to serve the B2B market, what would you do differently than these three firms?

learning objectives

The primary goal of this chapter is to analyze the development of consumer and business products that capitalize on the Internet's properties and technology by delivering online benefits through attributes, branding, support services, and labeling. You will become familiar with the challenges and opportunities of e-marketing enhanced product development, Internet product classifications, and new-product trends.

After reading this chapter, you will be able to:

- Define product and describe how it contributes to customer value.
- Discuss how attributes, branding, support services, and labeling apply to online products.
- Outline some of the key factors in e-marketing enhanced product development.
- Identify the six categories of new-product strategies and the six classifications used to a suggested Internet product taxonomy.
- Highlight some of the important new-product trends that create digital value.

There are many choices for news, but the fact is, there really is only one Bugs Bunny. And when you have franchises like a Bugs Bunny or a Mickey Mouse, or the products that the networks have, there is only one place you can go to get that.

jim
moloshok
bros. online

Classmates.com joins the small group of profitable dot-coms that is quite alive and well. The company began in 1995 as a place for people to look up former high school and college classmates. The site had about 5 million registered customers in 2000, and 29 million just two years later—plus 1.5 million new registrations each month. One reason for this amazing growth was Classmate's huge Internet advertising campaign, launched in 2001 when ad prices were low. The privately held company generated $35.6 million in revenue in 2001 and reaped $500,000 in after-tax profits. Best of all, the firm has been profitable since October 2001.

This company is successful because it capitalized on a consumer need in the 30-plus age bracket, used the Internet's properties to create a new product, and designed a successful e-business model. Classmates.com tapped into the mass market's need to reconnect with people from the past and with individual needs to learn if, for example, a former girlfriend has a BMW or gained weight. What better place than the Internet, with its networking and communication strengths? CEO Michael Schutzler sees the Internet as a direct-marketing medium and notes that there's no business if customers are not willing to pay. Thus, the firm adopted a subscription model for revenues, selling content not advertising. Its sampling promotional approach allows people to register for free and read profiles, but they must pay to communicate with others. Eighty-five percent of the firm's revenue comes from 2 million subscribers paying $36 a year, and the subscriber base is adding 185,000 members a month. In addition to having full database access, subscribers receive an e-mail notification when someone from their school registers.

Moving beyond schools, customers can also register as alumni of their former places of employment or as ex-military. Thus, the firm has outgrown its brand name. Schutzler says he would use a different name if his company was just starting up, but discarding the existing brand equity makes no sense at this point. By now, Classmates.com has proven that a new product can be successful on the Internet, even in a difficult economic climate.

Convenience for the consumer drives the digital household.

robert pittman
former COO
aol

Many Products Capitalize on Internet Properties

The success of Classmates.com demonstrates how a new and purely online product can use the Internet's properties to build a successful brand. A **product** is a bundle of benefits that satisfies the needs of organizations or consumers and for which they are willing to exchange money or other items of value. The term *product* includes items such as tangible goods, services, ideas, people, and places. All of these can be marketed on the Internet, as the Classmates.com example shows. Products may also be classified by the purpose for which they are purchased. Consumer products are those purchased by an individual for personal consumption. Businesses sell products to consumers in the business-to-consumer (B2C) market, and consumers sell products to one another in the consumer-to-consumer (C2C) market. Industrial products are used in the operation of an organization, as components for manufacture into final product, or for resale (B2B market).

Some new products such as search engines are unique to the Internet while other products such as books simply use the Internet as a new distribution channel, often adding unique technology-enabled services. With the Internet's properties of market deconstruction, customer control, and other e-marketing trends, product developers face many challenges and enjoy a plethora of new opportunities while trying to create customer value using electronic marketing tools. This chapter focuses on both consumer and industrial products capitalizing on Internet properties and does so within the rubric of time-tested, traditional product and branding strategies.

To create new products, organizations begin with research to determine what is important to customers and proceed by designing strategies to deliver more value than do competitors. In line with the Sources, Databases, and Strategy model discussed in Part III, tier two strategies involve the marketing mix 4P's and customer relationship management (CRM). Because the process of designing these strategies is closely tied to the tactics used to implement them, Part IV presents strategies and tactics together in five chapters. As shown in Exhibit 10 - 1, the marketing mix (product, price, distribution, marketing communication) and customer relationship management (CRM) work together to produce relational and transactional outcomes with consumers. Assumed in the model is the parallel idea that this occurs in all markets—that is, marketers want the same outcomes with government and business customers (especially those in the supply chain). The present chapter begins this discussion by describing how information technology affects product and brand-name strategy and implementation.

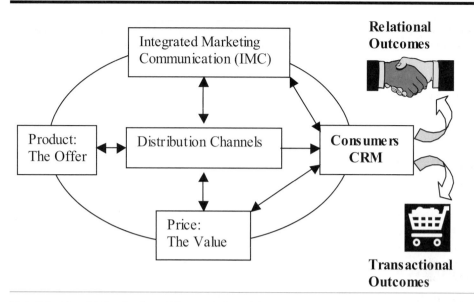

Exhibit 10 - 1 Marketing Mix and CRM Strategies and Tactics for Relational and Transactional Outcomes

Creating Customer Value Online

Never has competition for online customer attention and dollars been more fierce. To succeed, firms must employ strategies—grounded in solid marketing principles—that result in customer value. Recall from Chapter 2 that customer value = benefits – costs. But what exactly is value? First, it is the entire product experience. It starts with a customer's first awareness of a product, continues at all customer touch points (including the Web site experience and e-mail from a firm) and ends with the actual product usage and postpurchase customer service. It even includes the compliments a consumer gets from friends while driving that cool car, or the fun she has bragging via e-mail to friends about her new Samsung cell phone with the PalmPilot operating system. Second, value is defined wholly by the customer. Regardless of how favorably the firm views its own products, it is the customer's perceptions that count. Third, value involves customer expectations; if the actual product experience falls short of their expectations, customers will be disappointed. Fourth, value is applied at all price levels. Both a $0.05 micropayment for an online article in a newspaper archive and a $2 million e-commerce computer application can provide value.

The Internet can increase benefits and lower costs, but it can also work in reverse. The next sections explore the value proposition online.

Online Benefits

Along with Internet technology came a new set of desired benefits. In Chapters 7 and 8 we discussed many of the benefits customers seek online. Web users also want effective Web navigation, quick download speed, clear site organization, attractive and useful site design, secure transactions, privacy, free information or services, and user-friendly Web browsing and e-mail reading. Thousands of new products and Web sites were quickly created to fill these and many other user needs. As Internet technology evolves, user needs change, and the opportunities expand.

Marketers must make five general product decisions that comprise its bundle of benefits to meet customer needs: attributes, branding, support services, labeling, and packaging (Kotler and Armstrong 2001). Except for packaging, all of these can be converted from atoms to bits. Here we will discuss the first four in terms of the online benefits they provide to customers and their associated e-marketing strategies.

Attributes

Product attributes include overall quality and specific features. With quality, most customers know "you get what you pay for." That is, higher and consistent quality generally means higher prices, thus maintaining the value proposition. Product features include such elements as color, taste, style, size, and speed of service. Benefits, on the other hand, are the same features from a user perspective (i.e., what will the attribute do to solve problems or meet needs and wants?). For example, Yahoo! provides a list of Web site categories (attribute), which helps users find things quickly online (benefit). Product benefits are key components in the value proposition.

The Internet increases customer benefits in many remarkable ways that have revolutionized marketing practice. The most basic is the move from atoms to bits, one of the Internet's key properties. This opened the door for media, music, software, and other digital products to be presented on the Web. Perhaps the most important benefit is product customization. Tangible products such as laptop computers can be sold alone at rock-bottom prices online or bundled with many additional hardware and software items or services to provide additional benefits at a higher price. The same is true for intangible products, some offering tremendous flexibility for benefit bundling. For example, online research firms can offer many different business services in a variety of combinations; similarly, music retailers can create CDs to order, combining songs from many different artists as desired by customers. It is important to realize that information products can be reconfigured and personalized very easily, quickly, and cheaply, as compared to manufactured products. Consider that changing an auto design takes years, and one model may be offered in only a few versions. In contrast, changing and customizing some software can be very much easier.

While this type of benefit bundling occurs offline as well as online, the Internet offers users the unique opportunity to customize products automatically without leaving their keyboards. For example, Blue Nile, the profitable online jewelry retailer (www.bluenile.com), allows Web users to select from among many gemstone features (e.g., stone type, clarity, size) and pick a ring setting to match.

User personalization is another form of customization. Through Web site registration and other techniques, Web sites can greet users by name and suggest product offerings of interest based on previous purchases. For instance, as you saw in Chapter 1, a returning customer to Amazon.com gets a tabbed menu item with his name on it: "Sam's Store." Clicking on the tab reveals a list of items that Sam might be interested in examining, based on his previous purchases from Amazon.

Branding

A **brand** includes a name (McDonald's), a symbol (golden arches), or other identifying information. When a firm registers that information with the U.S. Patent Office, it becomes a trademark and is legally protected from imitation. According to the U.S. government, "a trademark is either a word, phrase, symbol or design, or combination of words, phrases, symbols or designs, that identifies and distinguishes the source of the goods or services of one party from those of others" (source: www.uspto.gov). Similarly, a brand is the public's "perception of an integrated bundle of information and experiences that distinguishes a company and/or its product offerings from the competition" (Duncan 2002). Many marketers have noted that a brand is a promise to customers. Delivering on this promise builds trust, lowers risk, and helps customers by reducing the stress of making product switching decisions.

A product's brand name and its image are often part of the benefits a user desires. This is because customers generally want to know they can trust the firm they are doing business with. What better way than to use either well-known brands or brands with which they have had good experiences? This is especially important online, because of concern over security and privacy issues and because firms and customers are often separated by large distances. Brand names such as Microsoft and Yahoo! generate consumer trust. Note, however, that trustworthy brand names add to customer-perceived benefits and, thus, can command higher prices from consumers. That's how the value proposition operates. Some customers will prefer a value proposition that includes paying lower prices and using less well-known brands. Of course, some brands, such as Wal-Mart in the United States or Aldi food stores in Germany and Australia, have a brand name synonymous with low prices and fairly good quality. The value proposition is preserved in these cases because the products provide fewer benefits (e.g., a smaller set of features or fewer services).

Customers and prospects develop brand images based on every brand contact. Some contacts are through one-way media such as advertising and packaging, and others are through two-way communication such as conversations with the firm's customer service or salespeople on the phone, at trade shows, on Web sites, or in company-initiated e-mail. When using the Internet, a firm must be sure that its online messages and employee e-mails convey a positive brand image that is consistent with messages from all other contact points. This is particularly difficult because Internet users often receive brand messages about the brand from sources that the company has not planned and managed, such as consumer online bulletin boards and consumer e-mail among friends (see Chapter 13 for more detail). According to Jim Gregory (2002), there are seven components for building a great global brand:

- **Research your corporate constituencies.** Information is critical for global brand building.
- **Understand your business.** Set guidelines based on global objectives.
- **Advance the vision.** Decide on the desired reputation, create a strategy to support it, and develop a strategic positioning document.
- **Release the power of communications.** All company communication should work together to promote the brand.
- **Set up your communications infrastructure.** Build a communication council with the firm's advertising, public relations, investor relations, and human resource specialists, both inside and outside the firm.
- **Include your employees in the message mix.** This is especially important in a time of PR crisis.
- **Measure performance.** Track progress toward goals and determine communication effectiveness.

Companies creating new products for online sale face several branding decisions: whether to apply existing brand names or create new brand names for new products; whether to lend their brand name as a cobrand with other firms; and what domain name to use for the Web site.

Using Existing Brand Names on the Web

Firms can use existing brand names or create new brands for their new products. An existing brand name can be used for any new product, and doing this makes sense when the brand is wellknown and has strong brand equity (value). For example, Amazon added music CDs, videos, software, electronics, and more to its product mix. It is beneficial for Amazon to use its well-established Web brand name for these other offerings rather than launch a new electronic storefront with another name. Similarly, when products with offline sales introduce online extensions, many choose to use the same brand name (e.g., *The New York Times*). In fact, the dot-com crash showed that the strength of brick-and-mortar brands carried over to the Internet is what gave many Web sites their enduring power.

Some firms may not want to use the same brand name online and offline, for several reasons. First, if the new product or channel is risky, the firm does not want to jeopardize the brand's good name by associating with a product failure. Entering the online publishing business tentatively, *Sports Illustrated* did not want to use its brand online and instead created an extension, naming it Thrive (www.thriveonline.com). The *Sports Illustrated* affiliation was not mentioned online. The thriveonline name was subsequently sold to Oxygen Media.

Also, a powerful Internet success might inadvertently reposition the offline brand. Most Internet products carry a high-tech, "cool," and young image, and this will carry over to offline branded products. For example, NBC (the television network) serves an older market than does MSNBC online. Because the network hoped to bring younger viewers from MSNBC on the Internet to its television network, it made a decision to stick with the brand name—thus intending to reposition the offline brand image. In such situations, firms must ensure that online brand images will have the desired effect on the offline versions and that overextended product lines do not create fuzzy brand images. Finally, sometimes the firm wants to change the name slightly for the new market or channel, as a way of differentiating the online brand from the offline brand. For example, *Wired* magazine changed the name of its online version to *HotWired* to convey a high-tech image and perhaps to position the two publications differently.

Creating New Brands for Internet Marketing

If an organization wants to create a new Internet brand, a good name is very important. Good brand names should suggest something about the product (e.g., www.WebPromote.com; www.Classmates.com), should differentiate the product from competitors (e.g., www.gurl.com), and should be capable of legal protection. On the Internet, a brand name should be short, memorable, easy to spell, and capable of translating well into other languages. For example, Dell Computer at www.dell.com is much easier than Hammacker Schlemmer (www.hammacker.com), the gift retailer. As another example, consider the appropriateness of these search tool names: Yahoo!, Excite, Lycos, AltaVista, InfoSeek, HotBot, WebCrawler, GoTo, Google, and LookSmart. Which ones fit the preceding criteria?

Cobranding

Cobranding occurs when two different companies put their brand names on the same product. This practice is quite common on the Internet and is a good way for firms to build synergy through expertise and brand recognition. For example, *Sports Illustrated* now cobrands with CNN as CNNSI. Even the Web site address displays the cobrand: sportsillustrated.cnn.com. Yahoo! is a good place to look for cobranded services. In the past it has joined with *TV Guide* and then Gist to provide TV listings; it has also offered the Yahoo! Visa Shopping pages. As a second example, EarthLink, the largest independent ISP, joined forces in early 1998 with Sprint, the telephone company, to form a cobranded business with a new EarthLink–Sprint name and logo. They used the cobrand to provide ISP services to Sprint customers and to pursue AOL customers (source: www.spiderline.com).

Internet Domain Names

Organizations spend a lot of time and money developing powerful, unique brand names for strong brand equity. Using the company trademark or one of its brand names in the Web address helps consumers quickly find the site. For example, www.coca-cola.com adds power to Coca-Cola brands. This is not always possible, however. There are many considerations when it comes to domain names.

Anatomy of a URL

A **URL (Uniform Resource Locator)** is a Web site address. It is also called an **IP address** (Internet Protocol) and **domain name**. This is a clever categorization scheme, similar to telephone area codes, that helps computer users find other computers on the Internet network. URLs are actually numbers, but because users can more easily remember names, a domain name server translates back and forth. A domain name contains several levels as depicted here.

http://www.dell.com			
http://	**www.**	**Dell**	**com**
hypertext protocol	world wide web	second-level domain	top-level domain

The *http://* indicates that the browser should expect data using the hypertext protocol—meaning documents that are linked together using hyperlinks. Sometimes URLs start with FTP:// (file transfer protocol), which means that an FTP server will send a data file to the user (most likely a Microsoft Word file or another document that is not an HTML page). The *www* is not necessary and most commercial sites register their name both with and without it. Firms are advised to register with the *www* because browsers vary in their ability to recognize sites without it.

When firms purchase a domain name, they must first decide in which top-level domain to register. Most businesses in the United States want *.com*, because users usually type in the firm name.com as a best guess at the site's location. Other countries have top-level domains such as .mx for Mexico or .uk for the United Kingdom. Thus, Amazon in the United Kingdom is www.amazon.co.uk. Exhibit 10 - 2 displays the largest top-level domains, ranked by number of hosts. A host is a computer connected to the Internet and may contain multiple IP addresses. For this and other technical reasons, these numbers represent the minimum number of possible IP addresses in each domain.

An interesting wrinkle on the country domains designation is that firms and marketers outside those nations sometimes want the name. For example, many doctors registered in Moldavia to obtain the .md extension. Another interesting example comes from the Pacific Island nation of Tuvalu (.tv). DotTV agreed to pay

Domain Designation	Top Level Domain Name	Number of Hosts (millions)
net	Networks	47.8
com	Commercial	44.5
edu	Educational	7.8
jp	Japan	7.1
ca	Canada	2.9
de	Germany	2.7
uk	United Kingdom	2.5
au	Australia	2.3
it	Italy	2.3
us	United States	2.1

Exhibit 10 - 2 Largest Top-Level Domain Names in January 2002
Source: Data from Network Wizards (www.isc.org).

Tuvalu $50 million in revenues for the right to sell .tv extensions. Will we see www.cbs.tv or www.nypdblue.tv rise in importance in the coming years? So far most of the networks have chosen to brand through their .com Web sites. However, there are many other possible top level domains from which to choose. The Internet Corporation for Assigned Names and Numbers (ICANN) is a nonprofit corporation that operates like a committee of experts to make decisions about protocol and domain name assignment, registration, and so forth. It approves all new top-level names such as the latest: .biz, .info, .pro, .name, .coop, .aero, and .museum.

Registering a New Domain Name

VeriSign, along with many other sites, provides domain registering services for a mere $70 for two years per name (www.verisign.com). One of the problems is that with more than 97% of words in the dictionary already registered as domain names, the online name a firm desires may not be available. A dictionary name is not necessarily the best option because it already has a meaning attached to it that is generic for the product category, making it difficult to build a competitive advantage. Thus, it is more difficult to build a unique brand identity for a wine firm called wine.com than for something like gallo.com, a well-known brand name.

What happens if the firm name has been registered by someone else? For example, DeltaComm, a software developer and ISP in North Carolina, was the first to register www.delta.com, preempting Delta Airlines (originally www.delta-air.com) and Delta Faucet (www.deltafaucet.com). These firms were forced to come up with alternative names. Another solution is to buy the name from the currently registered holder, and that is what Delta Airlines eventually did. In another example, Grupo Posadas, the large Mexican hotel chain owner, negotiated for 18 months to buy www.posadas.com.mx from a local family with the same last name. The company paid for the name with a free condo, many nights of free hotel stays, and *mucho dinero*. Many creative Netizens register lots of popular names and offer them for sale at prices of up to millions of dollars. GreatDomains.com allows users to buy and sell popular domain names (see Exhibit 10 - 3). As you read in Chapter 5, cybersquatting—which occurs when a domain name registrant takes an already trademarked brand name—is illegal. The same is not true, however, for dictionary or personal names. A "whois" search at VeriSign.com reveals domain name owners.

Incidentally, when registering a name, firms would be well advised to also purchase related names to keep them out of the hands of others. For example, Compaq Computer Company paid $3 million to develop the AltaVista search engine site (www.altavista.com) only to find that www.alta-vista.com was already in operation as an adult site with sexual material. Fortunately, the search engine outlasted the adult site and this has been remedied. Also, many individuals publish Web sites that include criticisms and comments from disgruntled customers about a company, calling them www.companyname.sucks.com. To combat this, some companies have begun buying their own www.companyname.sucks.com to preempt their detractors. Posadas, the Mexican hotel firm, purchased domain names for over 17 different spellings of its various hotels to make things easier for customers.

Picking the right domain name can make a huge difference when trying to entice users to the site and to build consistency in the firm's marketing communications. For example, Time Warner's Pathfinder was a Web site containing online versions of its many successful magazines: *People, Time, Fortune, Money,* and *Entertainment Weekly.* Dan Okrent, editor of *New Media* for Pathfinder, claims that the biggest error the firm initially made with the online division was selecting the name *Pathfinder* for the site. Pathfinder lacks the name recognition of its well-established magazine brands and, thus, the firm failed to capitalize on the value of its brands. Furthermore, according to Okrent, *Pathfinder* has little meaning to users. Type www.pathfinder.com today and you will be immediately presented with a page that links to all the firm's magazines.

Support Services

Customer support—during and after purchases—is a critical component in the value proposition. Customer service representatives should be knowledgeable and concerned about customer experiences. Sites that care about developing relationships with their customers, such as Amazon.com, place some of their best people in customer support. In the early days, Amazon's billionaire founder and CEO Jeff Bezos even answered some of the e-mail messages himself. Some products need extra customer support. For example, when a user purchases software such as SurveySolutions to design online questionnaires, technical support becomes very important. Customer service reps help customers with installation, maintenance problems, product guarantees, and service warranties, and in general work to increase customer satisfaction with the firm's products.

CompUSA Inc., the largest U.S. computer retailer, astutely combines online and

Exhibit 10 - 3 Have an Extra $1.5 Million to Spare? Buy www.ad.com.
Source: GreatDomains.com.

offline channels to increase support services. At www.compusa.com, customers can enter their zip code to check the availability and pricing of any product at the five nearest brick-and-mortar stores. Customers can also check the status of items left for repair at the store, searching the Web site by status or product serial number. Customer service as a product benefit is an important part of customer relationship management.

Labeling

Product labels identify brand names, sponsoring firms, and product ingredients, and often provide instructions for use and promotional materials. Labels on tangible products create product recognition and influence decision behavior at the point of purchase. Labeling has digital equivalents in the online world. For online services, terms of product usage, product features, and other information comprise online

| | All Products | Support | Search | microsoft.com Guide |
| | *Microsoft* |

Home | Images | Software | Text | International | Trademarks |

Copyright Permission

About Microsoft copyrights...

The following links will provide information regarding permission to use specific copyrighted materials such as **images**, **software**, and **text** which are owned by Microsoft Corporation.

A form of legal protection for the expression of an idea (not the idea itself) of an original work.

Obtaining Permission:
Find out when you should obtain written permission from Microsoft, and who to contact with regard to your request.

Images

Software

Do you need permission?
While many uses of Microsoft copyrighted materials do require written permission, some uses do not require written permission. The first step is to go here to find out if you need written permission.

(select from list)

Text

More Information

Use of Images
Check here to find out if you need to obtain special written permission to use Microsoft copyrighted images.

Exhibit 10 - 4 Microsoft Terms of Use Label

Source: www.microsoft.com. Copyright © 2000 Microsoft Corporation, One Microsoft Way, Redmond, Washington 98052-6399. All rights reserved.

labeling at Web sites. For example, when users download RealAudio software for listening to online broadcasts, they can first read the "label" to discover how to install and use the software. In addition, many firms have extensive legal information about copyright use on their Web pages. Microsoft, for instance, allows firms to reproduce product images without permission, but any images on its Expedia.com site must receive special permission before being copied and used in printed materials such as this book (see Exhibit 10 - 4). Online labeling can serve many of the same purposes on the Web as offline. Many brick-and-mortar businesses display the Better Business Bureau logo on their doors to give the customer a sense of confidence and trust. Similarly the BBB offers the BBBOnLine logo to its members. Another validating label is the TRUSTe privacy shield. If firms agree to certain terms of use regarding privacy of customer information collected at their site, they may register at TRUSTe, download the TRUSTe seal, and affix it to their Web sites as part of a label.

E-Marketing Enhanced Product Development

The move from atoms to bits adds complexity to online product offers. Developers must now combine digital text, graphics, video, and audio, and use new Internet delivery systems. They must integrate front-end customer service operations with back-end data collection and fulfillment methods to deliver product. This creates steep learning curves for traditional firms. E-marketers, therefore, need to consider several factors that affect product development and product mix strategies with new technologies.

Customer Codesign

The power shift to buyers, when combined with the Internet's global reach and the death of distance, allows for many unusual business partnerships and for both business and consumer collaboration. Partners are forming synergistic clusters to help design customer products that deliver value. For example, after Dell Computer contractually gave one supplier 25% of its volume requirement for computer monitors, the supplier assigned engineers to work with Dell's product development team (Ghosh 1998). These engineers stood beside Dell employees when new products were introduced to help answer customer questions.

Internet technology allows this type of collaboration to occur electronically across international borders as well. For example, software developers commonly seek customer input. After releasing Netscape Navigator 2.0 in 1996, the firm immediately began work on version 3.0. Netscape set objectives for improving the browser and then created Beta 0 for internal testing (Exhibit 10 - 5). When the browser was good enough, Netscape allowed Internet users to download it at the Web site and encouraged user feedback. After five months of creating new iterations with customer input, the next version was released. This old example is typical of the current practices of most software firms.

One study of over 300 research and development vice presidents found that customer interaction in the early and late stages of product development can actually

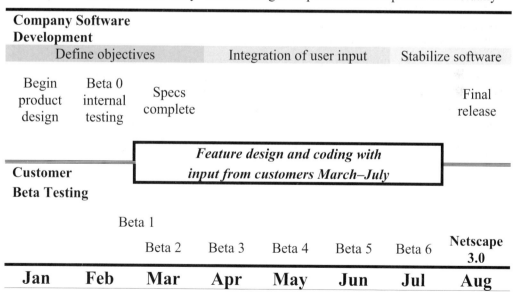

Exhibit 10 - 5 Customer Codesign of Netscape Navigator 3.0
Source: Adapted from Iansiti and MacCormack (2001).

increase product success (Gruner and Homburg 2000). This is especially true when product codesign occurs with what is called the "lead user" of a product. This is a key person who uses the product and often innovates himself to solve product use problems as they occur.

Electronic Input

Good marketers look everywhere for customer feedback to improve products. With the increase of Web sites inviting customer product ratings, the proliferation of e-mail "word of mouse," and the speed and reach of the Net, customers are quick to spread the word about product strengths and weaknesses. In this environment, savvy firms monitor customer input electronically and refine products to meet customers' needs. In what has been dubbed "passive feedback," companies hire electronic *clipping services*—firms that scan the Internet looking for company and product discussion. This is the electronic version of traditional clipping services that read print media and clip out articles mentioning the firm and its brands. Using this service, Mrs. Field's Cookies caught wind of false rumors spreading on the Internet that had caused offline sales to drop 1% in a short time period.

In another example, we put draft copies of this book online and asked faculty adopters and our students to review it and give us feedback prior to the final draft. Simon and Schuster did this when it offered Stephen King's 66-page novella, *Riding the Bullet,* as a text download for a low price at various online book retailers (Li 2000). Barnesandnoble.com offered the book for $2.50 and claimed that readers purchased a copy every 2.5 seconds after the first day: 400,000 copies were sold by all online booksellers in just one day. This experiment drove Simon and Schuster and other publishers to speed up the digitizing of their book lists.

The electronic input process is similar to the use of marketing research to support product development; however, the scale is much larger because many customers worldwide can be involved and provide quick feedback. Incidentally, Random House, HarperCollins, and other book publishers have partnered with Microsoft to develop ClearType, a technology that makes reading online much easier on the eyes—another example of partnering to codesign products that add value.

Web Content Development

It has been said that on the Web "content is king." Customers visit Web sites for information, entertainment, and to buy products. The success of Classmates.com rests on the strength of its database—if it does not have up-to-date and plentiful information on school alumni, users will not benefit. Content attracts users and keeps them returning—well-organized content, that is. Vicki August (2001) offers these five tips for "screaming content:"

- **Stay fresh.** Update the site every day and at least once on the weekend. That takes a huge commitment!
- **Be relevant and unique.** Deliver highly focused content that is differentiated from competitive site content.

- **Make it easy to find.** Users want to find information or products immediately. Also, don't include hyperlinks to other sites for content because users don't often return after they leave.

- **Serve a smorgasbord of content.** Integrate current news and facts with longer features and commentary. Include interactive material relevant to the site, such as quizzes, calculators, searches, and so forth. Vary the format to include multimedia.

- **Deliver content everywhere.** This includes Web sites, wireless devices, and special networks.

Two trends are worth mentioning here. First, a new breed of syndicated content providers has emerged to serve Web developers. This business is parallel to the Associate Press that feeds news to local and national newspapers and magazines. Syndicated content includes stock quotes, breaking news, sports updates, weather information, and more—in all formats from text to video. Forrester Research predicts the value of this industry will be more than $3.5 billion in 2005 (August 2001).

Another interesting trend involves users who want text-based content only. An apparently small but growing group of Web users does not want the distraction of video, sound, animation, and other nontext items; instead, they favor simple text information. These people block advertising content with special software and know exactly what they want online. They do not like HTML e-mail. This trend is important because mobile handheld devices use mostly text content, which means Web content providers might consider how to pare down the features in special areas for these users—and charge a subscription fee for the content.

Internet Properties Spur Other Opportunities

Market deconstruction created a disaggregation and reaggregation of product and service components to form unusual new products and firms. The AutoMall Online is only one example. Another is the Lending Tree, a firm that offers online searches for the best prices for mortgages and other types of loans. These firms provide bundles of benefits difficult to achieve before the Internet. Because they also represent a new type of intermediary, these firms are discussed more thoroughly in Chapter 12 and in examples featured later in this chapter.

The Internet is a great information equalizer, which means fierce competition, lots of product imitation, and short product life cycles. Online auctions are a perfect example. Not long after eBay came online, Amazon.com and others began offering auctions; now one restaurant in San Francisco is even auctioning meals to draw patrons during slow times. Most search engines are starting to look very similar. In this environment, product differentiation is the key to keep from becoming a price-driven commodity industry.

Taking short product life cycles to an extreme, Direct Hit Technologies Inc., the firm that sells Internet search engine software, has been known to launch six new product versions within a few days (King and Hoffman 1999). In another example, when Frank Sinatra died, BMG's five-person new-product development team created a lifetime tribute and a series of product offerings for the Web site in six short hours. The firm would have needed four months to produce this in a paper catalog. Firms must respond quickly to new technology or lose. As one astute pundit said, "eat lunch or be lunch." Despite the dot-com crash, innovation online is still rewarded.

New-Product Strategies for E-Marketing

Many new products, such as Netscape, Yahoo!, and Classmates, were introduced by "one-pony" firms. This means that the firm was built around the first successful product. Other firms, such as Microsoft, added Internet products to an already successful product mix. This section explores product mix strategies to aid marketers in integrating offline and online offerings.

Product Mix Strategies

How can marketers integrate hot product ideas into current product mixes? Companies can choose among six categories of new-product strategies (Lamb, Hair, and McDaniel 2002). Discontinuous innovation is the highest-risk strategy, while me-too lower-cost products are the least risky. Firms will select one or more of these strategies based on marketing objectives and other factors such as risk appetite, strength of current brand names, resource availability, and competitive entries.

Discontinuous innovations are new-to-the-world products never seen before. Music CDs and television were discontinuous innovations when introduced. On the Internet, the first Web authoring software, cell phone/PDA combination, shopping agent, and search engine fall into this category. A recent example is body scanning hardware and software, made popular by the Levi's Personal Pair product. This is a great idea for customers who can't find clothing with a proper fit and who want more influence on its design. It also helps manufacturers and retailers increase customer loyalty, lower inventory costs, and avoid seasonal cost reductions. There are many discontinuous innovations yet to come on the Internet. Although this strategy is quite risky, the potential rewards for success are great. E-marketers planning discontinuous innovations must remember that their customers will have to learn and adopt new behaviors—things they have not done before. The company faces the risk that customers will not change unless the new behavior is easy and they perceive that the benefits are worthwhile.

New-product lines are introduced when firms take an existing brand name and create new products in a completely different category. For example, General Foods applied the Jell-O brand name to pudding pops and other frozen delights. Microsoft created a new line when it introduced its Internet Explorer Web browser. Because the Netscape browser was already available, Microsoft's entry was not a discontinuous innovation.

Additions to existing product lines occur when organizations add a new flavor, size, or other variation to a current product line. *The New York Times Direct* is a slightly different version of the hard-copy edition, adapted for online delivery. It is yet another product in *The New York Times* line, which includes the daily paper, weekly book review, and others. GTE's SuperPages is an interactive line extension to its Yellow Page directories (superpages.gte.net). Many banks have begun offering banking over the Internet. Stockbrokers such as Schwab have also opened up Internet operations. Realtors now offer online listings for many communities throughout the United States. In an interesting twist, E*Trade is adding brick-and-mortar offices to complement its online trading business.

Improvements or revisions of existing products are introduced as "new and improved" and, thus, replace the old product. For example, Web-based e-mail systems improved on client-based e-mail systems such as Eudora or Outlook because users could check and send e-mail from any Web-connected computer. One provider, Web2Mail.com, allows users to pick up e-mail from an existing account without even registering—a different service from Hotmail or Yahoo! Web mail. On the Internet, firms are continually improving their brands to add value and remain competitive.

Repositioned products are current products that are either targeted to different markets or promoted for new uses. Yahoo! began as a search directory on the Web and then repositioned itself as a portal (an Internet entry point with many services). By so doing, Yahoo! positioned itself against the leader, America Online. MSNBC repositioned its news organization for younger viewers.

Me-too lower-cost products are introduced to compete with existing brands by offering a price advantage. When America Online and other ISPs were charging per hour rates for Internet access, several other providers introduced unlimited use at flat rate pricing for $19.95 per month. Firms such as EarthNet were able to grab significant share until America Online followed suit and won back customers. The Internet also spawned a series of free products with the idea of building market share so the firm would have a customer base for marketing its other products. For example, Eudora Light, the e-mail reader software, and Netscape, were two early entries with this strategy.

A Word About ROI

Part I of this book discussed the need for performance metrics as feedback so firms can assess the success of their e-marketing strategies and tactics. This is especially important when introducing new products, online or offline. Marketers generally forecast the expected product revenue over time, deduct marketing and other expenses, and generate a return on investment estimate for new products prior to launch. Usually brand managers compete for the firm's resources by showing that their products will generate either a higher ROI or payout in shorter time frame. By *payout* we mean that the R&D and other initial costs will be recovered at a particular date based on projected sales. In the process, they calculate a break-even date when the product is projected to start making a profit. How long is acceptable? In 2002, some managers were saying that Internet projects had to break even within three months or they would not get funded. Of course, the exact timing varies by industry—Boeing does not expect most new aircraft to pay out for 20 years!

Nonetheless, ROI and break-even are important metrics for selling new-product ideas internally and for measuring their success in the market.

A Taxonomy for Internet Products

Thousands of products based on Internet technologies have been introduced. These can be classified according to the customers to whom they appeal. In Exhibit 10 - 6 each column represents a group of customers; each row in the exhibit represents a type of product. The first two columns represent the B2B market. Businesses provide content and build out the Internet infrastructure. Their top concerns in both these endeavors are features, performance, and cost savings. The third column represents B2C and C2C markets. The rows in the exhibit divide products by hardware, software, and services. This matrix is helpful because it displays areas of new-product opportunity. For example, application service providers (ASPs) assist B2B content providers with many useful value chain services.

While the B2C market gets most of the attention, marketers must know about cutting-edge products and trends in both the B2C and the B2B markets, as discussed in the next section.

New-Product Trends

Cutting-edge products and the technologies that make them work create digital value, thus using the Internet's properties to best advantage. These products apply concepts mentioned earlier: Each represents a new brand, a new-product line, a discontinuous innovation, or a technology improvement. This section will cover a wide range of products from wireless end user appliances to B2B software. Some of these products are in the early stages of the product life cycle. Their success will depend on how well they deliver customer value by offering desired benefits or by lowering costs.

Many new products are largely unseen by the final consumer. Yet they form the engine that drives electronic commerce. The importance of these enabling products was brought to light in April 2000 when Cisco Systems, a company many consumers had never heard of, briefly became the most valuable company in the world. Cisco makes the hardware and software that powers computer networks.

This chapter offers just a taste of the incredible variety of new products available. Cisco's managers note that new technologies accelerate product change—for example, wireless and broadband open the door to lots of new products. According to Cisco executives, the most important technologies in 2002 include wireless/mobile

	Content Provider	Internet Infrastructure	End User
Hardware	Server farm, high-speed switch	Router, satellite, fiber-optic backbone	Modem, PC, Web TV, PDA, assistive technologies, convergence products
Software	Web authoring, encryption, audio/video digitizing enabling software	Protocols, TCP/IP, DNS	Web browser, e-mail client, decryption, audio/video player software
Services	E-commerce consulting, Web development, Web design, application service providers	ISP, backbone service provider, Web hosting	Web-based virus scan, auto updates, calendaring, e-mail

Exhibit 10 - 6 Product Taxonomy

computing, distributed content delivery and local caching, digital imaging, clustering and parallel computing, high-scale interoperability, and universal network storage.

Seven new-product trends are of particular interest. The first four are in the B2B market, with the potential to improve efficiency and effectiveness in marketing functions such as sales, distribution, supply chain management, and marketing research:

- **Value chain automation**. Software products in the B2B market enable businesses to perform important marketing functions, including specific value chain functions. Here, the value chain refers to all businesses involved in moving product from supplier to consumer.

- **Outsourcing**. Many businesses look outside their corporate boundaries to providers of key value chain functions. Application service providers (ASPs) perform marketing functions on behalf of other businesses.

- **Information sharing**. Once a closely guarded asset, organizations now share internal information with selected value chain partners on an unprecedented scale. OBI and XML, two variations on electronic data interchange (EDI), support information sharing.

- **Centralizing information access**. Organizations realize enormous cost savings and increases in effectiveness if they can reduce information search times for their employees. Corporate portals provide a single integrated interface to all of a company's data stores.

The next three trends operate primarily in the B2C market and have the power to open up new markets.

- **Multimedia**. Gains in network performance will finally enable Internet multimedia to come of age. Some of the products in development are fascinating—from video on demand to Webisodes.

- **Assistive technologies**. Clever developments allow for computer access by persons with a wide range of disabilities. These same technologies are also used for everyday applications such as listening to one's e-mail while driving.

- **Convergence of media**. The much talked about convergence of media is now happening. Expect the biggest initial improvements in the corporate market with gains in consumer markets close behind.

Value Chain Automation

The primary benefits of automating the value chain are improvements in efficiency and effectiveness of operations among suppliers, manufacturers, and the entire distribution channel. Value chain automation products automate existing business processes, such as order execution, as well as enabling processes not previously feasible, such as data mining to uncover consumer behavior patterns. These products help firms solve some of the challenges mentioned previously and lower costs that can be passed on to customers as lower prices.

Although some businesses try to produce their own enabling software, this is generally a mistake. Business can enjoy at least six benefits by purchasing off-the-shelf software solutions. These include rapid deployment, relatively bug-free rollout of systems, integrated solutions, large number of features, compatibility with business trading partners, and cost savings.

First, the business can rapidly deploy technology already developed. The vendor often provides an installation team and after-sale support services. The vendor also helps the business integrate its existing (legacy) systems with the new technology.

Second, most bugs have already been worked out of commercially available software. As a result, the service quality of the business improves when it introduces the new technology—an important consideration for customer retention.

Third, some of the **enabling technologies** are integrated solutions that help with multiple functions in the value chain. Customers typically prefer integrated solutions, and this is one example.

Fourth, because these are competitive markets, the features offered by different vendors are constantly improving.

Fifth, since one of the key benefits of the Internet is the ability to integrate computer systems with those of a firm's trading partners, anything that a business can do to make sure its internal systems conform to industry standards will enhance its position in systems integration.

Sixth, infrastructure products save both time and money, two very important

Company	Core Business
Commerce One	Value chain management B2B portals
Redback Networks	Broadband access solutions
Vignette	E-relationship management through customized content
F5 Networks	Internet traffic and content management—load balancing traffic across servers
Vitria Technology	Value chain management
Exodus	Scalable Web-hosting services
E.piphany	Customer relationship management

Exhibit 10 - 7 Internet Enabling Companies
Source: Adapted from Pegasus Research.

costs in the value equation. Businesses save in time-to-market and in day-to-day efficiencies. They are often able to lower their personnel costs through automation. Consumers save in time and aggravation (psychic costs).

Enabling products are expensive, sometimes costing more than $1 million, not including additional setup and maintenance fees. However, properly installed and managed, they can bring millions of dollars to the bottom line through new market opportunities or cost savings.

The number and sophistication of enabling products has grown dramatically in recent years (see Exhibit 10 - 7). All are new brands based on new-product opportunities emerging from Net technology. The following is an overview of marketing functions and the enabling products that have been developed to assist them (many of these ideas are adapted from Sawhney 2000).

Promotion

Companies can buy enabling products to help manage four key promotional activities on the Net: affiliate programs, targeted advertising, personalized promotions, and sales.

Affiliate Programs

Many sites now offer affiliate marketing programs. These sites pay their affiliates referral fees to help to drive traffic to the affiliate sponsor, just as manufacturers pay commissions to selling agents. Affiliate marketing is a relatively low-cost way to acquire customers. This is why the Amazon logo is splashed over the Web sites of some 600,000 Amazon affiliates (which Amazon calls "associates"). If each associate referred just 10 customers, the total would be 6,000,000 customers! Anyone who clicks through on the logo and buys merchandise from Amazon generates revenue for the associate. Even if Amazon were to lose money on the sale by paying the referral fee, it could make it up on repeat business by some of the referred customers.

Keeping track of the click-throughs and properly crediting the affiliates is a complex programming task. Companies such as BeFree and Commission Junction sell software that automatically monitors and credits all followed links resulting in a sale.

Targeted Advertising

Contrary to what some consumers believe, marketers have no interest in placing an ad in front of an unreceptive audience. In fact, marketers go to great lengths to target ads to appropriate demographic and psychographic segments.

But what if marketers could learn about individual users and their surfing habits? Assuming that "you are what you view," user surfing patterns form an excellent basis by which to target ads. DoubleClick sells services to target ads based on users' surfing habits. DoubleClick can follow the user from site to site around the Internet and target ads accordingly. DoubleClick also allows its clients to monitor the success of their advertising campaigns in real time and make immediate changes.

Personalized Promotions

Web site content becomes more valuable when it is highly customized for the user. Thus, many sites now create custom Web pages for each user, targeting specific promotions for each user's individual preferences. However, dynamically creating Web pages is a formidable programming task. Therefore, many companies have turned to enabling firms such as Vignette that automate dynamic creation of Web pages. Using such software, firms can cross-sell and up-sell in real time.

Sales

In the B2B market, National Semiconductor uses enabling software to maintain relationships with its corporate clients. Software by Vignette gives customers instant access to pricing information, product availability, and order lead time.

One of the more attractive e-business models is a manufacturer's representative, also known online as a catalog aggregator (see Chapter 12). The online manufacturer's rep takes information from multiple vendor databases and distills it into a single database available for search by the end user. Aggregating data into a single database is quite a complex endeavor, in part because each vendor tends to use a different file format. Enabling companies help automate the aggregation process.

Product Configuration

One of the more difficult tasks in the sale of high-tech products is proper component configuration. Many companies employ a well-trained sales force to properly configure products for the end user. However, many end users prefer to configure their own products online—both for the sake of convenience and to speed delivery of the product. Those users view self-service as a product benefit.

To automatically configure a product requires a software program known as an expert system, which is a difficult program to write and requires a thorough understanding of the knowledge domain being modeled. PeopleSoft sells enabling software to guide users through the process of product configuration based on their needs. Clients include companies in the communications, health care, and high-tech manufacturing industries, where configurations for equipment and services are often complex.

Brokerages

Web auction sites are all the rage in the B2B, B2C, and C2C markets. While it is difficult to write the software to support an online auction, it takes even longer to test and debug such software. Furthermore, reliability is essential in auction markets. Moai makes software that supports B2B auctions. Web-based B2B auction software represents a discontinuous innovation. Companies in the airline, food, gas, and water industries use Moai's reverse auction software to drive down prices for products purchased from their suppliers.

Payment/Financing

One of the barriers to trading in the B2B market is in processing credit for purchases. Enabling software that automates the task of providing, verifying, and processing credit must be very reliable. ECredit makes software that supports B2B payments and financing as well as customer credit approvals. Gateway Financial Services (Gateway Computer) uses Ecredit's software to automate the Gateway Your☺Ware program's credit application and checking process.

Customer Service

Since the dawn of e-commerce, businesses have, on the whole, not responded very promptly to e-mail inquiries and complaints. Ideally all messages should be acknowledged right away and should receive a personal response within 48 hours. However, employee costs for e-mail customer service can be prohibitive. Furthermore, businesses prefer to develop a consistent response to similar problems.

EGain makes enabling software that helps route and respond to e-mail customer inquiries. The software immediately acknowledges the customer's e-mail and promises a response within a fixed time frame. EGain software then analyzes the e-mail text, scanning for keywords and phrases that can assist in routing the message to the appropriate customer service representative. The software can also call up any previously related messages and account information to help form a context for the inquiry. The software can even compose a personalized response to the e-mail using artificial intelligence! The customer service representative can accept the eGain-generated response, choose from a list of canned responses, or compose an entirely new response.

Using eGain's software, companies are able to double the productivity of their e-mail response teams. EGain's software was used by online job placement company Monster.com to field the high volume of e-mail traffic following its January 2000 Super Bowl television commercial.

Interestingly, EGain has been shifting its focus to call center management, with e-mail comprising just one aspect of a call center. Other channels include telephone and live Web chat, because e-marketers need to ensure that customers receive a consistent level of service no matter which channel they elect to use.

Distribution

Value chain management is one of the more difficult tasks that companies face. The goal is **just-in-time (JIT) delivery** of products to avoid carrying excessive amounts of inventory. However, the coordination that JIT requires is difficult to achieve. I2 makes enabling software that supports value chain management. Sun Microsystems uses i2's software to coordinate all interactions in its value chain, a particularly arduous task for Sun because it does not make any of the components that go into its computers. Rather, Sun coordinates the activities of its suppliers and its suppliers' suppliers to ensure continued viability of the entire value chain.

Relationship Marketing

Data mining customer information can often reveal important marketing opportunities. Verbind makes enabling software that automates the task of profiling customers. Reel.com used Verbind's software to discover that 33% of its customers made a second purchase and most of them (71%) bought within 30 days. Using Verbind's software, Reel was able to target e-mail promotions to first-time buyers during the time when they would be most receptive to a second purchase. Verbind's software also offers real-time profiling of consumer behavior and dynamic site configuration in response to that behavior.

Outsourcing

Application service providers (ASPs) perform value chain functions for their client businesses—but do it off-site. ASPs allow businesses to disaggregate business functions and outsource them to separate providers. As a simple example consider a business that decides to outsource its payroll. The manager logs onto the ASP's Web site, enters the hour totals for each employee, hits submit, and voilà—a courier delivers the checks the next day!

The key distinction between application service providers and the enablers previously discussed is the location of the software and support. In the enabler case,

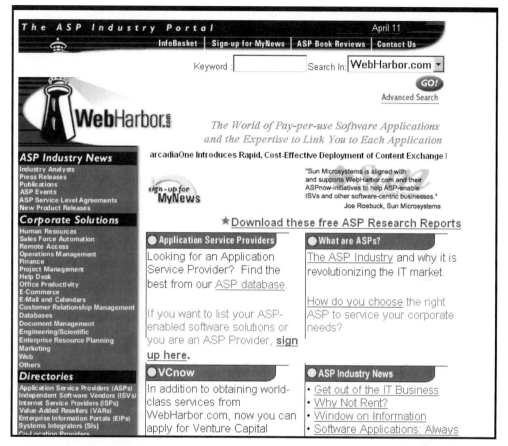

Exhibit 10 - 8 Application Service Provider Database
Source: WebHarbor.com.

the business licenses software from the enabler but installs, configures, and maintains the software on-site. In the ASP model the software resides at the ASP's site. The business accesses the application remotely via a Web browser.

Advantages of the ASP model include lower start-up costs, lower or no information technology staff costs, and lower switching costs. These advantages are particularly attractive for small businesses.

Disadvantages of the ASP model include lack of control over key customer data and business processes. A business customer is literally putting its reputation in the hands of another business. WebHarbor.com is a site that maintains a database of many application service providers for services ranging from payroll processing to procurement. See Exhibit 10 - 8.

Some ASPs can run an entire business. These aggregate almost all of the value chain functions for the client businesses. Companies such as Digital River and Yahoo! Store provide integrated outsourced solutions. Other ASPs focus on a single value chain function such as payroll or customer service. These ASPs go to great lengths to make sure that their modules will integrate smoothly with the business's other computer operations. A by-product of this interoperability is that the business can select best-of-breed ASPs for each value chain function that it chooses to outsource.

Information Sharing

Some of the enabler and ASP models discussed earlier rely on the exchange of data between separate businesses. Today businesses are sharing information with their value chain partners in unprecedented ways. *Electronic data interchange (EDI)* is a generic term that refers to the exchange of data between businesses in digital form. The most obvious benefit is that consistent standards mean the data do not need to be rekeyed by the receiving business. Clearly, exchange is easier if the businesses agree on a common format for exchanging data. This is complicated because most businesses store data in proprietary formats.

Two clever solutions to this problem have been developed on the Internet—both representing discontinuous innovations. One solution, open buying on the Internet (OBI), requires each business to translate its data to a common format for exchange. The other solution, XML, allows each business to keep its own format while sending the instructions for translation to the receiving business. Open buying on the Internet is the older of the two technologies and is more limited in its functionality.

Extensible Markup Language (XML) is the newer technology that, in principle, has unlimited functionality. Extensible means that the language can be extended by the user to accommodate new types of data. XML has strong support: It is built into Internet Explorer, Netscape Navigator, the MS-Office suite, and many other products. Furthermore, a number of industry standards groups base their content definitions on XML. As an example, RosettaNet standardizes how part numbers are defined and sets a basic template for procurement forms. Such standards facilitate interoperability of computer systems among businesses. However, until standards such as RosettaNet are finalized, businesses can still use XML to encode information for easier exchange.

To better understand XML, consider that a cook who is baking a cake needs both an ingredient list and a recipe to be successful. The ingredient list corresponds to a company's data; the recipe corresponds to XML formatting instructions. The company receiving the information must have both in order to decode the communication.

Peregrine Systems is a company that offers solutions in value chain integration, e-commerce fulfillment, and Net markets. Peregrine has made excellent use of XML to create systems allowing businesses to rapidly exchange time-sensitive data with their business partners.

Centralizing Information Access

One of the hottest new areas in the knowledge management field is **corporate portals**. Corporate portals use Web-based technology to create sites specifically for a particular company's employees. Corporate portals are an extension of an earlier concept, the intranet, which is also a site for internal consumption. Intranets typically publish corporate information such as news, policies, and procedures. However, corporate portals do more than just serve as brochures. They are linked to a wide variety of corporate information stores—such as sales data, groupware documents, and calendars. The portal translates data from all of the information stores into a common interface for presentation to the employee. Plumtree, the founder of the corporate portal market, likens the portal to the my.yahoo service provided by Yahoo! In both cases users can customize the screen display to include categories of information that they find useful. Corporate portals have the potential to save businesses millions of dollars by reducing the time that their employees spend searching for information.

Extranets are corporate portals that value chain partners are allowed to access. For example, EDS developed its Renasence system to order products from its many suppliers. EDS then opened up the system to its own buyers so that they could enjoy the same selection and price. At the extreme end of extranets is the one at Sun Microsystems. Sun's suppliers have nearly complete access to Sun's production information and use that access to plan their own production schedules.

Groupware products such as Lotus Domino are used to coordinate and share information among work teams. Collaboration software represents a brand extension strategy for Lotus, which began as a company making electronic spreadsheet software. Most groupware products support threaded discussion groups. Each thread represents a separate topic. Users add to the thread by responding to one of the topics. In this way the entire dialogue and any posted documents are maintained. Other groupware applications include e-mail and calendaring. Most corporate portals either integrate with existing groupware products or imitate their functionality.

Multimedia

Real-time multimedia—sound and video—are currently of fairly low quality when viewed or heard on a computer over the Net. The limiting factor for multimedia adoption is lack of sufficient bandwidth—the number of bits per second that can flow through a communications channel. The quality of transmission is directly proportional to the bandwidth of the communications channel. Lower-bandwidth channels lead to choppy audio and/or video because the detail must be omitted from the signal to compress it through the channel. In technical terms, the sampling rate and the precision of each sample are reduced.

Most users still connect to the Internet with modems operating at 56K or slower. Nonetheless, there is growing penetration of high-speed access via cable modems, DSL modems, and wireless technologies. Furthermore, Cisco Systems and other networking companies are working on technologies for increased bandwidth at lower prices. In spite of the bandwidth limitations, a number of multimedia technologies are available today. They include:

- Conferencing software
- Webcams
- Streaming audio
- CD-quality audio
- Streaming video
- Internet telephony VoIP

Conferencing software allows users to hold text, audio, or video conferences over the Internet. For example, users can simultaneously work on shared whiteboards using Microsoft NetMeeting.

The hardware device that transmits a real-time video image over the Web is called a Webcam. Webcams can be used for Internet conferencing or may just be fixed on a target such as a university quad. Two popular Webcam devices are the Logitech QuickCamera and Intel's PC Camera.

Streaming audio is the delivery of either live audio or stored audio on demand over the Internet. Steaming differs from traditional file downloading in that streaming users can start hearing the audio very shortly after clicking on the file. With traditional downloading, users must wait until the entire file is downloaded before playing it. Because audio and video files are quite large, streaming technologies created quite a breakthrough. RealNetworks is the pioneer and market leader for encoding software that streams audio and video data. Sites such as Yahoo! Broadcast use its products to rebroadcast radio, TV, and music over the Internet.

There has been an explosion of interest in CD-quality audio over the Internet. The de facto standard for CD-quality audio is MP3. Interestingly MP3 began almost as a renegade movement that has now become mainstream. WinAmp was one of the first players to decode MP3 files. Today almost all computers and many CD and DVD players can play MP3 files. Diamond Rio was the first company to offer a Walkman-like device that could store and play MP3 files. Apple's iPod stores 2,000 songs on a handheld device. But how does the user find the files online? Napster was the first major service that allowed users to share MP3 files from their computers with the entire Net community in a peer-to-peer fashion. Napster maintained a database of MP3 availability but did not actually provide the music. Legal battles with the recording industry finally forced Napster into bankruptcy. At the time of this writing Napster was still hoping to reemerge from bankruptcy under the auspices of its partnership with Bertelsmann AG. However, Napster may have trouble winning back market share from the hundreds of MP3 search tools and services such as Morpheus that have sprung up in the wake of its demise.

Streaming video requires many times more bandwidth than does streaming audio. As a result streaming video is even more heavily constrained by the lack of bandwidth online. Nonetheless, many observers see a bright future for live video and video on demand. A number of industries could be threatened by the development of streaming video, including the broadcast industry and the video rental business.

SonicBlue's ReplayTV, a competitor to Sony's TiVo, allows users to record broadcast video and then share it over broadband Internet connections with other SonicBlue users. For example, if someone forgets to record an episode of a favorite TV show, a friend who recorded it could send the episode over the Internet using a cable modem. At the time of this writing, the broadcast industry was battling SonicBlue in court over copyright infringement.

Internet telephony relies on the Web to transmit phone calls, thus eliminating long-distance charges. **Voice over Internet Protocol (VoIP)** is the term for this revolution. Again the major constraint is bandwidth. At times the voice quality is quite good, but it is not reliable. Yet because it requires less bandwidth than streaming video, Internet telephony is an attractive business proposition. Companies such as Net2Phone cash in on this market with products that can complete long-distance calls off the Net. Net2Phone is even bundled with Internet Explorer. These services represent a clear threat to long-distance phone companies—especially for international calls. The long-distance companies are taking the threat very seriously as evidenced by AT&T's acquisition in April 2000 of a 39% voting share in Net2Phone.

Assistive Technologies

Assistive technologies were designed to help people with disabilities operate their computers. Millions of people are potential customers for these products—not just people with disabilities. A product that reads e-mail aloud has market potential for anyone driving a car. Nonetheless, assistive technologies do allow persons with certain disabilities to productively enter the workforce. These include:

- **Voice-activated computers**. A voice-activated computer can be completely controlled by voice commands. Voice-activated computers allow even a quadriplegic person to control a computer system. Another use for voice-activated computers is in call centers where the caller interacts with the computer by speaking commands.

- **Large-type screen displays**. Large-type screen displays help people with poor vision see and navigate on their computer screens.

- **Type-to-speech or braille**. Even people who are blind can interact with a computer using type-to-speech or type-to-braille technologies. A clever application of this technology reads Internet pages aloud. One product in this category is IBM's Home Page Reader (see Exhibit 10 - 9). Type-to-speech technologies are also being built into automobiles such as GM's OnStar system, so drivers can listen to e-mail messages and stock quotes while driving. Type-to-speech technologies have important implications for Web page design. In particular, designers should avoid embedding text in graphics since the technology can only read text that is represented as text.

- **Speech-to-text telephony**. The telecommunications device for the deaf (TDD) converts speech to text, allowing deaf people to hold telephone conversations or conference online.

- **Eye gaze-to-type technology**. Even people who are completely paralyzed can still control a computer using eye gaze-to-type technologies. The user controls her computer by staring at control buttons on the screen.

Three Types of Convergence

The marketing opportunities in **media convergence** are tremendous. Three types of convergence are attracting attention today—(1) voice, video, and data on corporate networks, (2) wireless devices and the Web, and (3) the Web with broadcast media.

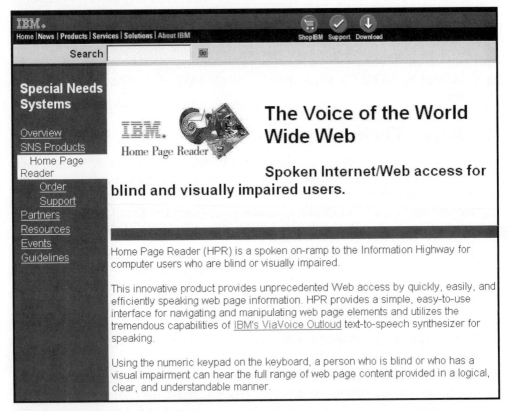

Exhibit 10 - 9 Home Page Reader

Source: www-3.ibm.com/able/hpr.htm.

Voice, Video, and Data on Corporate Networks

The first type of convergence is that of voice, video, and data on corporate networks. This will allow corporations to have a single switch for voice, video, and data communications rather than three separate systems. Cisco is leading the charge in this market, supporting both the infrastructure and end user appliances such as IP telephones.

Wireless Devices and the Web

The second convergence of media is the convergence of wireless devices—cell phones and **personal digital assistants (PDAs)**—with Web access and sometimes a global positioning function as well (GPS). There is a race to see whether cell phones or PDAs will become the preferred platform for wireless Internet access. Many people think these devices are likely to merge, although the Gartner Group does not think this will happen until 2006. In that scenario, a single device would serve as a combination cell phone, PDA, and Web browser. For example, the Samsung cell phone powered by Sprint uses the Palm Computing platform and can receive e-mail and other data from the Net.

The major limitation for browsing the Web is the screen size of PDAs. Cell phones have even smaller screens. Yet even the tiny cell phone screen can be used to check e-mail and retrieve weather, news, and stock quotes. However, mainstream Web content is designed for color on much larger displays. Nonetheless, many Web sites are starting to create content for the **Wireless Access Protocol (WAP)** so that it displays correctly on these tiny screens. Companies such as AvantGo and Foliage Software produce graphical browsers for the PDA platform. One interesting application that runs on a PDA is Auctioneer, used to track eBay auctions.

A second limitation to Web browsing on wireless devices is bandwidth. Wireless networks are, with few exceptions, much slower than land line networks. In spite of these limitations the market is growing rapidly. One technology to watch is that of WiFi networks built on the Ethernet 802.11b standard. Also on the horizon are 3G wireless cell phone networks.

Outside of the United States, the current and potential market for wireless Web access is even greater, because mobile phone communications have a much higher penetration rate in those countries. Why? As discussed in detail in Part V, telephone companies in other countries usually charge by the minute for local calls. Many users conclude that if they are going to be charged by the minute anyway, they might as well have the additional benefit of wireless access. Also, consumers in many countries have to wait years for a telephone line to be installed—at a high price. Small wonder that in Japan, DoCoMo's i-mode service has attracted millions of users who check weather forecasts, sports scores, maps, stock trading, banking, concert tickets, train timetables, recipes, and horoscopes on their cell phones. In northern Europe, Nokia users can make purchases from vending machines with their cell phones.

According to the Peppers and Rogers Group, wireless mobility of the future will have six components (Exhibit 10 - 10) (Peppers and Rogers Group 2001):

1. **Content providers.** These firms create wireless versions of current Web content. This might include sites such as travelocity.com (where users can search airline

flight information) and B2B services such as sales force automation (offering interactive access to customer information stored in company databases).

2. **Portal software.** These firms—such as Yahoo!, AOL, and Microsoft—will provide a higher level of personalization, maintaining user preferences for a wide variety of content.

3. **Data aggregation agent.** Companies such as Yodlee, Acxiom, and Microsoft keep track of a user's login and password information for quick mobile access to banks, stock brokerage accounts, and so forth—a boon to business travelers.

4. **Infrastructure.** These firms provide wireless Internet access, parallel to non-mobile ISPs.

5. **Transaction providers.** American Express, Visa, and others will serve online retailers by processing payments.

6. **Mobile devices.** This includes both cell phones and PDAs, or some convergence of the two platforms, allowing the user to send and receive data.

Broadcast Media and the Internet

The third type of convergence is between broadcast media (television and radio) and the Internet, sometimes called iTV (interactive TV). This convergence will result in a single appliance that receives broadcast content over the Internet. The major obstacle is lack of bandwidth to support full-motion video. However, cable modems, DSL modems, and fixed wireless access to the home may provide more bandwidth to overcome that obstacle.

Initial forays into the Web/TV convergence include MSN TV and Enhanced TV. MSN TV users simply browse the Web on a TV screen. This has not been a very successful model due to the low resolution of TV screens and the fact that consumers are not used to reading on a TV screen. ABC's Enhanced TV requires users to log onto ABC's Web site while they are watching a TV program. Users can get more information about the current broadcast, play games with other users, and participate in polls and chats. Interestingly, when promoted on ABC's show, *Who Wants to Be a Millionaire*, 97% of users who signed on to Enhanced TV reported that they would return!

When the bandwidth does become available, it is unlikely that the Web will be used only to serve TV and audio on demand. A taste of the future can be seen at BrilliantDigital. BrilliantDigital produces multipath movies in which viewers take a

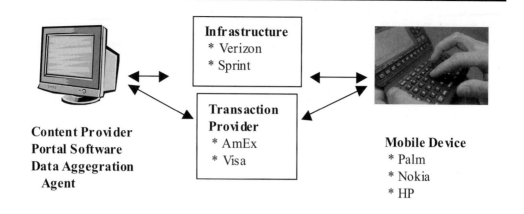

Exhibit 10 - 10 Six Components of Mobile Communications
Source: Information from Peppers and Rogers Group (2001).

more active role. For example, in one BrilliantDigital production, viewers can choose whether Superman saves Lois or Jimmy. It also has a product under development that will allow users to appear in their own Webisode. The product captures the user on video in the studio, performs voice-overs, and then places the user in the program.

Many of the preceding products depend heavily on the telecommunications industry. The startling collapse of the telecommunications industry since mid-2000 deserves some mention. Over a two-year period the industry lost nearly $2 trillion in valuation and suffered numerous high-profile bankruptcies. Like the Web itself, the industry was overhyped. Markets were flooded with products and services driving prices down below profitable levels. Many of the after-effects were felt in third world countries that provide manufacturing facilities for the industry.

The products that survive in the long term will be those that best deliver customer value. We'll end by discussing a product that didn't make it. The Iridium project was designed to place low earth orbit satellites to enable worldwide satellite phone access. It had wonderful corporate backing. Unfortunately, while it was being developed, the customer need evaporated as existing cell phone networks dropped in price while improving in quality. Customers were reluctant to spend $2,300 for an Iridium phone and $4/minute for a call. Even after slashing phone prices to $1,000 and call prices to $3/minute the company went bankrupt in 1999. Reflecting on what happened, interim chief executive John A. Richardson said, "We've got the hard stuff [the technology] right," and added, "We're a classic MBA case study in how not to introduce a product. First, we created a marvelous technological achievement. Then, we asked the question of how to make money on it." Iridium was left with 88 orbiting satellites.

Summary

A product is a bundle of benefits that satisfies the needs of organizations or consumers and for which they are willing to exchange money or other items of value. A product can be a tangible good, a service, an idea, a person, a place, or something else. The entire product experience provides value to the customer, is defined by the customer, involves customer expectations, and applies at all price levels.

Of the five general product decisions that comprise a bundle of benefits for meeting customer needs, four (attributes, branding, support services, labeling) apply to online products. Companies creating new products for online sale must decide whether to use existing brand names or create new brand names for new products; whether to cobrand; and what domain name to choose. Customer support—during and after purchases—is a critical component in the value proposition. Online labeling is the digital equivalent of product labeling and can serve many of the same purposes as offline labeling.

When developing new online products, e-marketers can turn to customer codesign, invite electronic input, work on Web content development, and use Internet properties to spark other opportunities. They can choose among six categories of new-product strategies (discontinuous innovations, new-product lines, additions to existing product lines, improvements/revisions of existing products, product repositionings, and me-too lower-cost products) and are generally required to estimate revenues, costs, and ROI or payout for management review and approval. Internet products can be classified into a taxonomy using the categories of hardware, software, and services (as the rows) and content provider, Internet infrastructure, and end user (as the columns).

Among the seven key new-product trends, four are in the B2B market (value chain automation, outsourcing, information sharing, centralizing information access) and three operate in the B2C market (multimedia, assistive technologies, convergence of media). However, only the products that best deliver customer value will survive for the long term.

Key Terms

Application service providers (ASPs)	Media convergence
Assistive technologies	New-product lines
Brand	Outsourcing
Cobranding	Personal digital assistant (PDA)
Corporate portals	Product
Discontinuous innovations	Streaming audio
Domain name	Streaming video

Enabling technologies

Extensible Markup Language (XML)

Internet telephony

IP address (Internet Protocol)

Just-in-time (JIT) delivery

URL (Uniform Resource Locator)

Value chain automation

Voice over Internet Protocol (VoIP)

Wireless Access Protocol (WAP)

Exercises

Review Questions

1. What are the arguments for and against using existing brand names on the Web?

2. List six new-product strategy categories and provide Internet examples of each.

3. Why is value tied to the entire product experience?

4. What are some important criteria for Internet domain naming?

5. How does labeling work on the Internet?

6. What techniques can e-marketers employ to enhance new-product development?

7. Why do e-marketers need to forecast revenue, expenses, ROI, and payout for new products under consideration?

8. What are the advantages to buying B2B software off the shelf?

9. Why are technology standards like RosettaNet important?

10. What is the major limitation to the use of multimedia over the Net?

11. What are assistive technologies?

Discussion Questions

12. Of the three types of convergence, which do you think has the greatest market opportunity? Why?

13. How can automating the value chain increase customer value?

14. Under what circumstances would it make sense to take an existing brand name online? When would it not make sense?

15. Why do e-marketers often have difficulty estimating the revenues, costs, and payout or ROI of a new product under development?

16. What are some of the consumer privacy issues related to enabling products for online promotional activities such as targeted advertising and personalized promotions? How would you, as an e-marketer, respond to these privacy issues?

17. Do you agree with the CEO of Classmates.com, who says his firm has outgrown its brand name but should not make a change because of the strong existing brand equity? Defend your position.

11 price

learning objectives

The primary goal of this chapter is examine how Internet technology is influencing pricing strategies. You will gain an understanding of both the buyer's and the seller's perspectives of pricing online, consider whether the Net is an efficient market, and learn about fixed pricing as well as the return to dynamic pricing.

After reading this chapter, you will be able to:

- Identify the main fixed and dynamic pricing strategies used for selling online.
- Discuss the buyer's view of pricing online in relation to real costs and buyer control.
- Highlight the seller's view of pricing online in relation to internal and external factors.
- Outline the arguments for and against the Net as an efficient market.

All too often, corporate strategists overlook one of their best weapons: improved pricing strategies.

robert
doctors
principal
Booz Allen &
Hamilton, Inc.

What can a company do when revenues start to slow in a maturing market? This is the situation facing AOL Time Warner's America Online unit. Internet growth has slowed in the United States, slowing AOL's subscription growth. Although it boasts 33 million dial-up subscribers, 2001 growth was only 24%, compared with 30% and 36% in the previous two years—not a pretty trend. In addition, average revenue per subscriber dropped due to lower U.S. advertising revenues in 2001. Note that the $24.37 figure includes both total subscriber fees and all advertising revenue, divided by the number of subscribers.

AOL has tried spurring growth by expanding internationally, but that has not worked well. Now it wants to build more *share of wallet* from current customers by adding new products such as interactive entertainment, communication services, and information products to the basic ISP product. In fact, it plans to pry $159 from that customer wallet every month, up from $19.95 today, by adding these services:

Revenue/Subscriber		Service
2001	Future	
	$15.00	Games and entertainment
	$20.00	Voice services
	$20.00	Mobile services
	$20.00	Music
	$30.00	Multiple devices
	$30.00	Broadband access
$24.37*	$24.00	Narrowband subscription
	$159.00	**Total Monthly Revenue**
		* including advertising

The first step is to move subscribers to broadband connectivity, which is more costly for AOL than its current telephone line narrowband. The firm plans to price this service at $30 to entice adopters and build quick market share. This price would yield a much smaller profit margin than current narrowband services but attract customers because it is much lower than competitive offers. AOL executives believe they can lead customers from broadband to other services, one at a time: first, $20 more for adding other household computers to the service; $20 for downloading music into the stereo of the future's hard drive; $20 to access the Net from cell phones, PDAs, and laptops while traveling; $20 for long-distance telephony over the Internet; and $15 more so the kids can play online games with other AOL users.

AOL has a lot of experience with pricing strategy. In its early days it charged a small flat fee for limited time online plus an hourly fee for overage. In 1997 it moved to flat pricing of $15, and has slowly pried more money from each subscriber while significantly expanding the customer base. But will customers pay as much as $159 per month for a multitude of AOL services?

Price goes by many names. philip kotler

The Internet Changes Pricing Strategies

In the narrowest sense, **price** is the amount of money charged for a product or service. More broadly, price is the sum of all the values (such as money, time, energy, and psychic cost) that buyers exchange for the benefits of having or using a good or service. Throughout most of history, prices were set by negotiation between buyers and sellers, and that remains the dominant model in many emerging countries. Fixed price policies—setting one price for all buyers—is a relatively modern idea that arose with the development of large-scale retailing and mass production at the end of the nineteenth century. Now, one hundred years later, the Internet is taking us back to an era of **dynamic pricing**—varying prices for individual customers. This chapter explains why.

In the past, most marketers touted the Internet for marketing communication and distribution channel benefits; only a few thought it had a huge but unrealized potential to change the face of pricing. Current e-marketing practices show that those few folks were right—information technology *is* changing pricing strategy. In this chapter we discuss both the buyer's and seller's view of price and explain why Erik Brynjolfsson, codirector of the E-business Center at MIT, says, "We're moving toward a very sophisticated economy. It's kind of an arms race between merchant technology and consumer technology (in the form of shopbots). If consumers are not sophisticated they can be soaked. If managed intelligently, the tools are there to create a revolution." This chapter discusses some of those tools.

The Internet properties, especially in the role of information equalizer, allow for **price transparency**—the idea that both buyers and sellers can view all competitive prices for items sold online. This feature would tend to commoditize products sold online, making the Internet an efficient market. But is it? We'll explore the Internet as an efficient market in this chapter, using the economist's view as a guide.

Buyer and Seller Perspectives

The meaning of *price* depends on the viewpoint of the buyer and the seller. Each party to the exchange brings different needs and objectives that help describe a *fair* price. In the end, both parties must agree or there is no sale.

Buyer View

Recall that buyers define value as benefits minus costs. In Chapter 10 we discussed the benefit variable, explaining that the Internet creates many benefits important to consumers and business buyers alike. Here we'll explore the cost side of the formula: money, time, energy, and psychic costs.

The Real Costs

Today's buyer must be quite sophisticated to understand even the simple dollar cost of a product. This is because the seller's price may or may not include shipping, tax, and other seemingly hidden elements—hidden in the sense that these costs often are not revealed online until the last screen of a shopping experience. For example, think of the last time a long-distance telephone company promoted a new pricing scheme. Many of these deals are complex and difficult to understand, which is why some carriers advertise "$0.07 a minute, period." As another example, Exhibit 11 - 1 displays the five different prices for AOL's ISP services. These are fairly clear yet complex, and the burden is on the consumer to understand his or her needs and translate those into the best price.

How about the time, energy, and psychic costs that add to a buyer's monetary costs? Sometimes the Net is slow, information is hard to find, and other technological problems cause users to spend more time and energy, thus becoming frustrated (psychic cost). Shopping agents will find the lowest prices online, but the search adds to the time cost. For example, when buyers search for the lowest airfare at Orbitz.com or Travelocity.com, the search time is minimal compared to the dollar savings, but the same may not be true for a book price search—it all depends on the time it takes to search, the savings as a percentage of the item cost, and how much familiarity and experience the buyer has with the search engine (making an easier search process). The Internet is far from perfect, but as bandwidth increases, technology evolves, and firms develop better online strategies, some of these costs will decline.

1. $23.90 per month standard plan providing access to AOL and the Internet, without hourly fees.*

2. $19.95 per month ($239.40 one year prepaid subscription) providing access to AOL and the Internet, without hourly fees, for members who pay in advance for one year.*

3. $14.95 per month "bring-your-own-access" plan providing unlimited access to thousands of unique AOL features,* including access to the Internet, for individuals who already have an Internet connection or access through the work or school environment.

4. $4.95 per month light usage plan providing three hours of AOL, including the Internet, with additional time priced at just $2.50 per hour.*

5. $9.95 per month limited usage plan providing five hours of AOL, including the Internet, with additional time priced at just $2.95 per hour.*

* Pricing plans do not include premium services, which carry additional charges.

Exhibit 11 - 1 AOL ISP Fee Schedule in July 2002
Source: See www.aol.com.

In contrast, buyers often enjoy many online cost savings:

The Net is convenient. It is open 24/7 so that users can research, shop, consume entertainment, or otherwise use the Web's offerings anytime. E-mail allows asynchronous communication among users at any location and prevents "telephone tag" with sellers (both parties don't need to be online simultaneously to communicate).

The Net is fast. Although it might take more time to download a Web page than users would like, they can visit a site such as iGo.com, order a laptop battery, and receive it the following day—even while on a business trip.

Self-service saves time. Customers can track shipments, pay bills, trade securities, check account balances, and handle many other activities without waiting for sales reps. In addition, technology allows users to request product information at Web sites and receive it immediately. Of course, all these activities take time to perform.

One-stop shopping saves time. Market deconstruction opened the door for firms to increase customer convenience through one-stop shopping. AutoMall Online has partnered with a number of firms to provide automobile price comparisons, research about various models and manufacturers, financing and insurance information, and service options. This firm also offers instant online pricing from a large network of auto dealerships and gives customers a "purchase certificate" guaranteeing that the price quote will be honored at the dealership. AutoMall Online's track record proves that customers receive value: Over 50% of its users purchase a car within 45 days of using the service, and 90% do so within six months.

Integration saves time. Web portals such as Yahoo! and AOL allow users to quickly find many things they want online. Some sites allow users to create individualized Web pages with news, stock quotes, weather, and other customized information. One of the authors had the experience of purchasing a unique backpack online only to find out, via e-mail, that the firm was out of business. No problem—it forwarded the order to another e-commerce company, which filled the order in a day.

Automation saves energy. Customers value simplicity and ease; because the Net makes some activities more complex, technology can help. For example, functions that allow customer computers to keep track of passwords for Web sites and to track previous purchases at Web sites save time and energy.

Note that not everyone wants to save money in online transactions. Customer needs and their view of the value proposition vary as each individual weighs the desired and perceived benefits against all the costs. For example, some people prefer to order books from Amazon.com with overnight delivery, knowing full well that Amazon prices are often higher than other online booksellers, that the book is in stock at a local bookstore, and that overnight delivery costs quite a bit more and only shaves one day from the delivery time. Nevertheless, the Amazon brand name is trustworthy, these customers have had excellent previous experiences with Amazon, and they are familiar with the site and can quickly find what they need. Thus, those benefits and time/energy-saving features overcome the higher expense.

Another interesting example of the value equation trade-offs relates to online auctions. In what has been called "the winner's curse," some people actually pay a higher price for auctioned products than they would pay an online retailer. In the B2B market, one study found that car dealers pay significantly more for used automobiles online than they do offline. In the B2C market, researchers evaluated the winning bids for new surplus computer items at Egghead.com and compared prices for the exact items sold on the retail portion of the Egghead site (Pellegrino, Amyx, and Pellegrino 2002 working paper). They found that 20% of winning bidders overpaid. Perhaps the entertainment benefit of an online auction keeps the value equation in balance, but just as likely, buyers do not realize they've overpaid.

Buyer Control

The change in power from seller to buyer affects many e-marketing strategies, not the least of which is pricing. In what is known as a **reverse auction**, buyers set prices for new products and sellers decide whether or not to accept these prices. A good example of this is Priceline.com. In the B2B market, buyers bid for excess inventory at exchanges and for products at firms such as General Electric and Caterpillar. In the B2G market, government buyers put out a request for proposal for materials and labor needed for a particular project, and businesses bid for the work. The government buyer selects the lowest price, in effect having control over the exchange.

Buyer power online is based largely on the huge quantity of information and product availability on the Web. As a result, online buyers are becoming more sophisticated—as they must be, considering the AOL pricing options as one example (Exhibit 11 - 1). To repeat Brynjolfsson: "If consumers are not sophisticated they can be soaked."

Finally, sellers are more willing to negotiate, thus giving power to buyers in the exchange. Perhaps it is easier for U.S. consumers to negotiate from behind an impersonal computer, as compared with standing face-to-face with the seller. Also, sellers realize that information technology can help them better manage inventories and automate frequent price changes.

Seller View

Sellers view price as the amount of money they receive from buyers, unless they are making a barter exchange. Seller costs for producing the good or service represent the pricing floor, under which no profit is made. Above that floor, marketers have the freedom to set a price that will draw buyers from competing offers. Between cost and price is profit.

The seller's perspective on pricing includes both internal and external factors affecting pricing levels. Internal factors are the firm's strengths and weaknesses from its SWOT analysis, its overall pricing objectives, its marketing mix strategy, and the costs involved in producing and marketing the product. External factors that affect online pricing in particular include the market structure and the buyer's perspective, as discussed earlier.

Internal Factors: Pricing Objectives

Marketers begin by setting overall pricing objectives from among those that are profit oriented, market oriented, or competition oriented. The most common **profit-oriented objective** for pricing is current profit maximization, which focuses on current financial results rather than long-term performance. When using this objective, companies first estimate what demand and costs will be at different prices and then choose the price that will produce the maximum current profit, cash flow, or return on investment. Online research firms such as Forrester and Gartner Group are using a profit-oriented approach when they charge $1500 to $4500 and more to download current e-business research reports. Cost-plus pricing and other cost-based approaches are generally profit-oriented.

Companies can also select among various **market-oriented objectives**. Building a larger customer base may lead to lower costs and higher long-run profit. Low prices generally build market share. For instance, AOL wants to price its broadband Internet connection services quite low to take market share from other cable modem and DSL suppliers (see the chapter-opening vignette). Another market-oriented objective is product-quality leadership, which calls for charging a high price to cover higher performance quality and the high cost of R&D. Negotiation and bidding are also market-oriented approaches. For example, Circus Circus Reno seeks bids for room nights at its Web site.

The objective of **competition-based pricing** is to price according to what competitors charge for similar products, paying less attention to the company's own costs or to demand. As an example, after one airline drops prices, its competitors usually follow suit. The Internet's pricing transparency gives firms quicker access to competitive price changes.

Internal Factors: Marketing Mix Strategy

Successful companies use an integrated and consistent marketing mix strategy. For example, Volvo sells relatively high-priced automobiles through dealerships, supported by a Web site and offline marketing communication that convey its upscale brand image. Volvo marketers know that more than 80% of its customers shop online (Greenberg 2001). Highly educated men who live in urban areas are the most likely to configure a new Volvo on the firm's Web site, price it, and then talk to dealers via e-mail. Dealers say they close about 10% to 15% of these leads. Thus, Volvo uses the Internet to generate sales leads, knowing that its customers are not likely to buy a high priced item directly from the Internet.

The Internet is only one sales channel and must be used in concert with other marketing mix elements. Marketing managers must carefully consider how to price the same product for sale in both online and offline channels. There are no proven rules or standard practices at this point—only experimentation.

Internal Factors: Information Technology Affects Costs

Information technology can be expensive, but once it is running smoothly it can create tremendous cost efficiencies—putting both upward and downward pressure on prices.

The Internet Puts Upward Pressure on Prices

Many dot-coms failed because they added expensive customer relationship management or other software that did not help to generate enough new revenue to cover the sites' costs. Following are some of the factors that put upward pressure on Internet pricing:

- **Distribution**. Online retailers face hefty distribution costs for their products: each product must be shipped separately to its destination. Called "the last mile" problem, this is similar to the catalog marketer's cost structure. Most retailers pass shipping costs on to their customers and reveal it only at the conclusion of the order entry process. Some vendors even inflate the shipping cost to recoup some of the discount they offered on items purchased. Not surprisingly, some customers are offended by the shipping costs they see added only at the last minute.

- **Affiliate programs**. Many Web sites pay a commission on referrals through affiliate programs. Affiliate sponsors reward the referring Web sites by paying a 7% to 15% commission on each reference that leads to a sale. This commission, like all channel intermediary costs, has the effect of inflating the price of the item or lowering company profits if referral fees are absorbed.

- **Site development and maintenance**. Web site development and maintenance is not cheap. Forrester Research estimates the cost for a "conservative" site to be $10,000 to $100,000, while an "aggressive" site costs $1 million or more—and that is just to develop the site. Maintenance can be quite expensive, especially with hardware, software, and monthly Internet connection costs.

- **Customer acquisition costs (CAC)**. The cost of acquiring new customers online is quite high; this was the downfall of many dot-com firms. For example, the average CAC for online retailers is $82. How many orders must a firm receive to recoup that cost, and at what price? In addition, many customers are not nearly as brand loyal online as offline.

The Internet Puts Downward Pressure on Prices

The Internet also allows marketers to shave costs, translating into lower prices and ultimately higher value for customers. When lower costs lead to higher prices, profit increases—a win either way. The following are a few ways firms can save costs using Internet technology:

- **Order processing—self-service.** Since customers fill out their own order forms, firms save the expense of order entry personnel and paper processing. These expenses can be considerable. The average cost of producing and processing an invoice electronically is $10, compared with $100 in offline transactions. An average retail banking transaction costs $0.15 to $0.20 online versus $1.50 offline. Cisco Systems, the world's largest manufacturer of networking equipment, invites Web-based orders from customers. The paperwork reduction it reaps from its Web site saves hundreds of millions of dollars each year.

- **Just-in-time inventory**. Some manufacturers use electronic data interchange (EDI) to drive down costs in the digital channel by coordinating value chain activities and allowing for just-in-time (JIT) delivery of parts and reduced inventories. Some online retailers and offline retailers do not even hold inventory, saving considerably on financing costs. Instead, they acquire the inventory in response to customer orders or have partners drop-ship products directly to customers.

- **Overhead**. Online storefronts can lower their overhead costs since they do not have to rent and staff expensive retail space. Amazon's physical warehouses are considerably less expensive to rent and staff than the retail space of a trendy shopping mall. Furthermore, these warehouses can be located in areas with low rents, low wages, low taxes, and quick access to shipping hubs.

- **Customer service**. Customer service requests average $15 to $20 in an offline call center versus $3 to $5 when customers help themselves on the Internet.

- **Printing and mailing**. Online sellers do not incur mail distribution and printing costs for their product catalogs. Once the catalog is placed online, access carries little or no incremental costs. The same holds true for e-mail promotions.

- **Digital product distribution costs**. Distribution costs for digital products are extremely low in the Internet channel. Conversely, the Internet channel has high distribution costs for tangible products because they are sent to individuals in small quantities instead of in larger lots to brick-and-mortar intermediaries.

External Factors Affecting Online Pricing

The competition, market factors, price–demand relationship (i.e., elastic or inelastic), and customer behavior all affect a firm's pricing strategies online and offline. The buyer's viewpoint was covered earlier; online behavior affecting pricing was covered in Chapter 7. In this section we examine two important market factors in the online environment: market structure and market efficiency.

Market Structure

The seller's leeway to set prices varies with different types of markets. Economists recognize four types of markets, each presenting a different pricing challenge.

- **Pure competition.** This market consists of many buyers and sellers trading in a uniform commodity such as corn. Product differentiation and marketing communication play little or no role, so sellers in these markets do not spend much time on marketing strategy.

- **Monopolistic competition.** This market consists of many buyers and sellers who trade over a range of prices rather than a single market price. A range of prices occurs because sellers can differentiate their offers to buyers.
- **Oligopolistic competition.** This market consists of a few sellers who are highly sensitive to each other's pricing and marketing strategies. If a company drops its price by 5%, buyers will quickly switch to this supplier.
- **Pure monopoly.** This market consists of one seller whose prices are usually regulated by the government.

This market structure distinction is extremely important for online sellers because if *price transparency* eventually results in a completely efficient market, sellers will have no control over online prices—the result will be pure competition as depicted in Exhibit 11 - 2. One example of a nearly efficient market is the stock market. If other products follow suit, the Internet will have a profound effect on pricing strategy. Note that online stock trading firms operate in a monopolistic competition because they compete based on trade commission prices, not actual security selling prices. Next we examine what comprises an efficient market and discuss whether the online market is approaching efficiency.

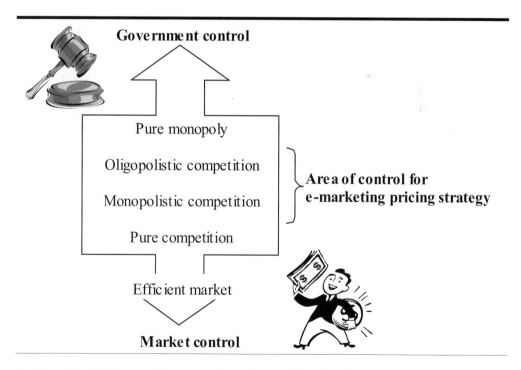

Exhibit 11 - 2 Efficient Markets Mean Loss of Pricing Control

Efficient Markets

Economists have long theorized about consumer behavior in **efficient markets**. Such markets would experience perfect price competition. A market is efficient when customers have equal access to information about products, prices, and distribution. In an efficient market one would expect to find lower prices, high **price elasticity,** frequent price changes, smaller price changes, and narrow **price dispersion**—the observed spread between the highest and lowest price for a given product (Smith 1999). As previously mentioned, the closest example of an efficient market is the stock market. Commodity markets came close to being efficient until the government intervened with controls. However, the Internet is probably as close to a test ground for efficient markets as has ever existed because it exhibits so many of the appropriate characteristics. Interestingly, the behavior of consumers on the Internet does not bear out all of the economists' predictions.

Is the Net an Efficient Market?

Many people believe that the Internet is an efficient market because of access to information through corporate Web sites, shopping agents, and distribution channels. Products sold online exhibit lower prices, high price elasticity, frequent price changes, and smaller price changes: all symptoms of efficient markets. But do these factors actually make the Net an efficient market?

Lower costs can result in lower prices for consumers; technology enables buyers to evaluate and demand appealing prices. With respect to price, the best-studied products online are books and CDs (among the earliest products to be marketed online). Research shows that online prices for books and CDs are indeed lower by 9% to 16%. In another study, brick-and-mortar retail prices for 21 of 24 computer and consumer electronic products were higher than online prices. Does that mean that all prices online are lower? Further study is needed to provide solid proof. For example, in the pharmaceutical industry, 60 capsules of the prescription drug Allegra are $53.50 at retail pharmacies, $49.66 from mail-order houses, and $51.60 online ("Rx.com. . ." 2000). Nonetheless, we can identify many factors that place a downward pressure on Internet prices, contributing to efficiency.

Shopping Agent Site	Millions of Visitors
Dealtime.com	7.4
Bizrate.com comparison shopping	5.7
Mysimon.com	2.7
Pricegrabber.com*	2.2
All other search sites combined	0.2
Users of One or More Comparison Shopping Sites	**18.2**
Monthly Users of the Internet	**119.5**
* Represents an aggregation of commonly owned/branded domain names.	

Exhibit 11 - 3 Retail Shopping Comparison in July 2002
Source: Data from comScore Media Metrics.

- **Shopping agents**. Shopping agents such as PriceScan (www.pricescan.com) facilitate consumer searches for low prices by displaying the results in a comparative format. Exhibit 11 - 3 displays the top shopping agents mid-2002. Slightly over 15% of Internet users visited shopping agents in July 2002, an increase of 6% from six months earlier—a positive trend, but still small usage among Internet users. See Exhibit 11 - 4 for an example of a VCR search at mySimon.com. Since the results are listed in order with the lowest price first, outlets that are not price competitive risk being left off of the first screen and might as well be invisible.

- **High price elasticity**. Price elasticity refers to the variability of purchase behavior with changes in price. As an example, leisure travel is a very elastic market: When the airlines engage in fare wars, consumers snap up ticket inventories creating huge demand. For many products such as books and CDs, the online market is more elastic than the offline market, so we would expect Internet users to be very sensitive to price changes.

- **Reverse auctions**. Reverse auctions allow buyers to name their price and have sellers try to match that price. This pits sellers against one another and usually drives prices down.

- **Tax-free zones**. Since most online retailing takes place across state lines, buyers often pay no sales taxes on purchases, reducing total out-of-pocket expenditures by as much as 5% to 8% per transaction. Although states and foreign governments have challenged the Internet tax-free zone, the U.S. government continues to support a moratorium on taxes for Internet purchases.

- **Venture capital**. Many Internet companies are financed through venture capital or angel investors. Many investors take a long-term view and are willing to sustain short-term losses (up to five years, in some cases) to let those companies grow by establishing brand equity and grabbing market share. These companies can price lower because they do not have a profit-maximization pricing objective. However, changes are coming, partially because of the dot-com crash, and partially because the five-year time frames are over for many early Net firms.

- **Competition**. The competition online is fierce and very visible. Furthermore, competitors such as AOL are willing to set prices that return little or no short-term profits to gain brand equity and market share.

- **Lower costs**. Lower costs in the Internet channel can result in either higher profits or lower prices, as noted earlier; this puts downward pressure on Internet pricing.

- **Frequent price changes**. The online market experiences more frequent price changes than the offline market because (1) online suppliers must jockey with competitors to attract price-sensitive consumers; (2) shopping agents give consumers excellent comparative information about prices and vendors may frequently alter their pricing to place higher on the results; (3) sellers can easily change prices in a computer-controlled environment; (4) in a computerized environment firms can offer volume discounts in smaller increments than in an offline environment (the way FedEx creates millions of different rate books based on shipping volume for posting on Web pages for individual clients); (5) experimentation is easy online, allowing firms to change prices frequently, see how demand changes, and then adjust as competition and other factors emerge.

- **Smaller price change increments**. In one study, the smallest offline price change was $0.35 whereas the smallest online price change was $0.01. Some of the same factors that encourage frequent price changes may play a role here as well. First, price-sensitive consumers may respond to even a small price advantage with respect to the competition. Second, shopping agents rank their results by price—even a $0.01 advantage will earn a higher ranking than the competition. Third, because it is difficult to change prices offline, retailers may wait until the need for a price change is even greater.

Is The Net an Inefficient Market?

While the Web exhibits many characteristics of an efficient market, it does not act like an efficient market with respect to narrow price dispersion. Prices tend to equalize in commodities markets, because sellers cannot easily differentiate one

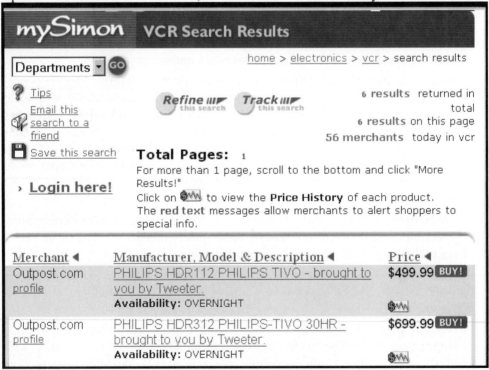

Exhibit 11 - 4 MySimon Shopping Agent Search Results
Source: www.mysimon.com.

bushel of peas from another. With perfect information for all, one would expect narrow price dispersion. With perfect information online, one might expect the prices to differ among sellers of the exact same PalmPilot organizers. Interestingly, this expectation does not hold on the Net, due to online retailer branding and other benefits that justify price differences in the minds of customers.

In at least two examples greater spread was found between high and low prices online versus high and low prices offline for the same items. The online price dispersion is 33% for books and 25% for CDs. One possible explanation may be that the online channel is still not completely mature—many buyers do not know about or use shopping agents, for example. Perhaps as businesses and consumers become more Net savvy we would expect the price dispersion to narrow.

However, more interesting explanations for the price dispersion relate to the way goods are priced online as well as delivery options, time-sensitive shoppers, branding, differentiation, switching costs, and second-generation shopping agents.

- **How goods are priced online**. Offline most goods are offered at fixed prices. By contrast, on the Web the same good is often available for a fixed, a dynamically updated, or an auction price on different sites at the same time—and the prices among them may vary widely. In addition, products are bundled with shipping and special services in different ways, confusing shoppers who want to compare like products.

- **Delivery options**. The same product delivered under differing conditions (time and place) may have considerably different value to the consumer. For example, a beer served at a bar has more value than one bought at a supermarket. Similarly, a product delivered to the door may have considerably more value for some consumers than one that is bought at the store. Online grocery shopping follows this value model. Some marketers would argue that groceries delivered to the door are not the same product as the same groceries picked up at the store. By this argument the additional benefits actually differentiate the product. Normally, the consumer has to wait longer for a product delivered to the door, but that may be changing. Amazon offers one-hour delivery of popular books and music in some metropolitan areas and other firms may follow suit.

- **Time-sensitive shoppers**. Time-sensitive shoppers may not wish to invest the time and energy required to track down the best price. Also, some sites may be so complex that consumers need more time to navigate and complete the transaction.

- **Branding**. In spite of the proliferation of Web sites, brand is still a sought-after benefit. Research shows that the top Web sites get most of the traffic. Consumers will even show a preference for brand when using shopping agents. Many consumers will pick a well-known merchant brand from the search results even if that brand does not offer the lowest price. Because of the importance of brand, the best-branded Web sites spend millions of dollars to attract customers. Amazon spends 24% of revenues or $29 per customer on promotion. By contrast, Barnes & Noble spends just 4% of revenues to promote its offline stores. The brand-loyal customer base allows Amazon to charge 7% to 12% more than bargain online retailers.

- **Differentiation**. One result of strong branding is perceived or real product differentiation, which enables marketers to price their products differently (see Chapter 9).

- **Switching costs**. Customers face switching costs when they choose a different online retailer. Some customers are not willing to incur those costs and, thus, stick with a familiar online retailer. If an Amazon customer shops at another retailer he loses access to a familiar interface, personalized book recommendations, and the one-click ordering that Amazon has patented. Switching costs are even higher in the B2B market. Many organizations have found that it is more effective to build relationships with a limited number of suppliers rather than offer all items out for bid. These organizations readily pay a slight premium to enjoy better service and support.

- **Second-generation shopping agents**. Second-generation shopping agents guide the consumer through the process of quantifying benefits and evaluating the value equation. If the consumer ranks certain benefits very highly, she may be willing to pay more to receive those benefits. BizRate allows consumers to evaluate merchants based on ratings compiled from previous customers. PriceScan and DealTime allow consumers to set filters so that merchants delivering the desired benefits will rise in the rankings.

Is the Internet an efficient market? The answer is no, not yet. However, it has all the features to move toward efficiency in the future. This would have devastating effects for e-marketers wanting control over pricing strategies; thus, marketing planners should watch this trend closely.

Pricing Strategies

Price setting is full of contradictions. It has become nearly as much art as science, with lots of data needing insightful interpretation for best application. If the price is too low profits will suffer, yet if it is too high sales may decline. And that is just the short-term view. In the long run, an initial low price that builds market share can create economies of scale to lower costs and, thus, increase profits. Also, *how* marketers price is as important as *how much* they charge. Look back at the AOL vignette and Exhibit 11 - 1 to see how much thought this firm has put into deciding *how* to price its various products, using an array of flat and hourly pricing schedules.

Another contradiction is that information technology has complicated pricing in some ways while making it easier in other ways. Sellers can easily change prices at a moment's notice or vary them according to each individual buyer's previous behavior. Technology makes all this possible, but it is a steep learning curve and in general, today's online sellers are nowhere near the downhill slope. In addition, pricing objectives produce very different results. For example, a low price will build market share at the expense of maximizing profit. Next, buyer value perceptions vary between rational and emotional, and not everyone reacts the same way. For example, some high-income customers enjoy walking into the Volvo dealership with a printed Web page detailing what they want and how much it should cost, while others enjoy the emotional relationship with a favorite salesperson and return every three years for the latest model, trusting that "Joe will take care of me." One of these customers may buy the Volvo for safety and another for the image it projects. Finally, firms using multichannel delivery systems must consider the varying costs of each channel and buyers' differing value perceptions about purchasing on the Internet versus the brick-and-mortar store. Pricing is a tricky business, guided by data, experience, and experimentation.

In general, marketers can employ three types of pricing strategies offline and online: fixed pricing, dynamic pricing, and barter.

Fixed Pricing

Fixed pricing (also called *menu pricing*) occurs when sellers set the price and buyers must take it or leave it. With fixed pricing, everyone pays the same price. This is the model most brick-and-mortar retailers use. Even when wholesalers and manufacturers offer quantity discounts, the price levels apply to all businesses that purchase the required amount. The basic pricing principles every marketer uses offline also apply online. Two common fixed pricing strategies used online are price leadership and promotional pricing.

- **Price leadership**. A price leader is the lowest-priced product entry in a particular category. In the offline world, Wal-Mart is a price leader, setting the pace for other retailers. With shopping agents on the Web, a price leader strategy is sweet indeed. To implement this strategy, however, marketers must shave costs to a minimum. This can be done through Internet marketing cost efficiencies described earlier, but a firm must do it better than the competition. Often the largest producer becomes the price leader because of economies of scale, but on the Internet an entrepreneur operating out of a basement constantly challenges the large producer. This is a productive strategy on the Internet, although competition is fierce and **price leadership** is often fleeting. Of course, the second-lowest-priced item will also gain sales, especially if it offers advantages over the price leader. On the Net, Buy.com is a price leader in many different categories, selling many items below market value and recouping losses through advertising revenue from the Web site.

- **Promotional pricing**. Many online retailers have turned to **promotional pricing** to encourage a first purchase, encourage repeat business, and close a sale. Most promotions carry an expiration date that helps create a sense of urgency. Promotional pricing on the Internet can be highly targeted through e-mail messages and research shows high customer satisfaction with Internet purchases.

Dynamic Pricing

Dynamic pricing is the strategy of offering different prices to different customers. Firms use this strategy to optimize inventory management and to segment customers by product use or other variables. Airlines have long used dynamic pricing software to price air travel. Now Web-based technology and database marketing have made this pricing strategy much more practical for companies to apply to segments of any size. For example, online music retailer CDNow offers lower prices on selected products to targeted segments in its customer database, such as particularly loyal customers. These customers receive an e-mail message directing them to a special Web page to view and buy these featured products. With the right technology, segments as small as one can be targeted with different prices—changed daily or even hourly—depending on changes in demand, supply, competition, costs, or other factors. See Exhibit 11 - 5 for an example of dynamic pricing by customer type, showing how Networksolutions.com practices segmented pricing in domain name registration.

XML and other technologies make dynamic Web page serving possible. As described in Chapter 4, this technique allows database information ("cake ingredients") to be consolidated in a recipe for a Web page. As a result, marketers can update product databases instantly and continuously as new-product features are developed and as they decide on price adjustments. Dynamic pricing means that Internet users receive up-to-date price information on demand from product databases—information that may change with the time and with the user.

Dynamic pricing can be initiated by the seller or the buyer (as compared with fixed pricing, which sellers always initiate). There are two types of dynamic pricing. The first is **segmented pricing**, where the company sells a good or service at two or more prices, based on segment differentiation rather than cost alone. The second is **negotiation**, where the company negotiates prices with individual customers, who comprise segments of one. Segmented pricing involves a one-time price, which may be different for different customers, the price in negotiation may change many times before buyers and sellers agree on the final price. Also, negotiation is more often initiated by the buyer, while segmented pricing is usually set by the seller.

Segmented Pricing

Segmented pricing uses the Internet properties for mass customization, automatically devising pricing based on order size and timing, demand and supply levels, and other preset decision factors. With segmented pricing online, the firm uses decision rules to set pricing levels for segments of customers all the way to a segment of one person— that is, any customer that is X or does X gets Y price. For example, any person who books a flight within seven days of departure is quoted the full price (no discount). Segmented pricing has its roots in traditional marketing, as when theaters lower prices for consumers attending afternoon movies. Pricing according to customer behavior segments is becoming more common as firms collect an increasing amount of electronic behavioral information.

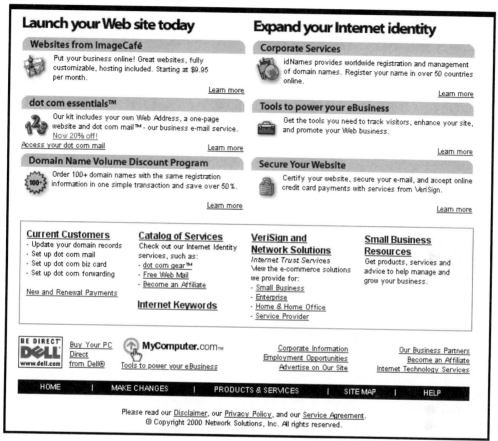

Exhibit 11 - 5 Network Solutions Practices Segmented Pricing for Services
Source: www.networksolutions.com. Reprinted with express permission. Copyright © 2000 Network Solutions, Inc. All rights reserved.

Segmented pricing at the individual level is easier online because sophisticated software permits firms to set rules and make price changes in a *nano* second—even as a buyer is clicking on a Web page (e.g., e.piphany). This is what all the excitement is about—the Internet's ability to customize prices, marketing communication, and products to the individual level. Using cookie files, online sellers recognize individuals and experiment with offers and prices to motivate transactions. Sometimes these individuals are particular customers, as when Amazon.com recognizes the customer and presents customized recommendations. Other times individuals are part of a larger segment, such as those logging in from a particular geographic location or those exhibiting a behavior such as abandoning a shopping cart. Sellers define the segment and then customize prices following preset decision rules when an individual member of the segment visits the site. For example, an online retailer can lower the price by small increments on each subsequent visit to see if the buyer will buy. Also, online firms can build loyalty programs, like frequent flyer programs, to offer special prices to individuals who return and purchase often.

Segmented pricing can be effective when the market is segmentable, the different prices reflect real differences in each segment's perceptions of the product's value, and the segments show different degrees of demand. It is also appropriate when the costs of segmentation and segmented pricing do not exceed the extra revenue obtained from the price difference. In addition, the firm must be sure that its segmented pricing meets legal and regulatory guidelines. Finally, the firm must take care not to upset customers who learn they are getting different prices than their neighbors. Amazon.com created an uproar when customers learned of its segmented pricing for individual customers; for some reason, airline passengers have accepted this practice but not book buyers. Thus, e-marketers employing segmentation must use customer-accepted reasons such as giving discounts to new or loyal customers or adjusting shipping fees for purchases sent to outlying locations.

Internet users can be segmented using many variables, as discussed in Chapter 8. Two variables that are particularly important to online pricing strategies are geographic segmentation and value segmentation.

Geographic Segment Pricing

With **geographic segment pricing**, a company sets different prices when selling a product in different geographic areas. An online seller often knows where the user resides because server logs register the user's IP address, and the top-level domain name typically indicates country of residence (e.g., a Japanese user will have a .jp designation). Geographic pricing can help a company better relate its pricing to country-by-country or regional factors such as competitive pressure, local costs, economic conditions, legal or regulatory guidelines, and distribution opportunities. For example, a computer priced at $1,000 in Los Angeles may be priced at £1,000 in London. This is because the manufacturer faces price escalation and must price to reflect the higher costs of transportation, tariffs, and importer margins, among other costs involved in selling in another country. Given the Internet's worldwide reach, marketers also may display a special Web page to those coming in from markets it does not serve. This helps to build goodwill for the firm's brand.

Value Segment Pricing

With **value segment pricing**, the seller recognizes that not all customers provide equal value to the firm. The well-known **Pareto principle** states that 80% of a firm's business usually comes from the top 20% of customers. As represented in Exhibit 11 - 6, a firm's A+ customers comprise a small group that contributes disproportionately to the firm's revenues and profits (Pitt et al. 2001). These tend to be the most loyal customers who may become brand advocates to their friends and acquaintances: The frequent flyers who always go first class, the casino high rollers who return repeatedly, or the high-volume package shippers who use the FedEx Web site to automate all services. These customers are also brand-loyal frequent customers who provide significant value to the seller. When A+ or A customers appear at the Web site, they will be recognized and receive special attention. These customers may not be price sensitive because they perceive that the brand or firm offers greater benefits (like free upgrades and special treatment) and has earned their loyalty.

The large group of type C customers may be price shoppers or infrequent users of the product category, not accounting for much of the seller's revenue. Type B customers are also price sensitive and probably use the product category more than do C customers.

Market factors tend to drive customers to the C level, whereas moves such as competitive offerings and price cuts attempt to lure A and B customers away. The seller's goal is to keep A customers brand loyal and to move all groups up to a higher level of value. Pricing strategies can help. For example, A customers might be allowed to bid on surplus inventory before others get a chance. Giving high-value customers the first shot at discounts will reinforce their loyalty. Conversely, B and C customers will seek the lowest price, so discounts do not have the same effect—because if they are not moved up the pyramid they will remain brand switchers. These customers might enjoy e-mail blasts with fixed prices so they can be informed of the firm's prices. The seller can use this technique to build a database for moving customers up in value. See Chapter 14 for more about value segmentation and marketing communication techniques for building customer relationships.

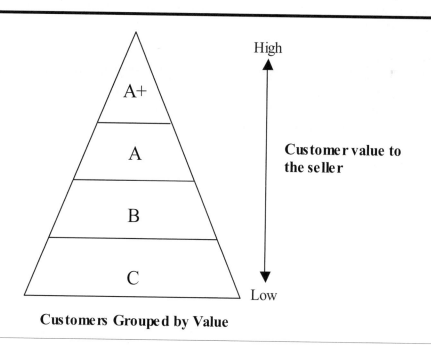

Exhibit 11 - 6 Customer Value Segments from Low (C) to High (A+)
Source: Adapted from (Pitt et al. 2001).

Negotiated Pricing

While sellers usually set pricing levels when using segmented pricing, buyers usually initiate pricing when bidding for items online. Through negotiation the price is set more than once in a back-and-forth discussion—a major difference from all other pricing strategies. Haggling over price is common in many countries; however, with a few exceptions U.S. consumers have shied away from such bargaining. The Net is changing this, as evidenced by the spectacular growth of online auctions. Many consumers enjoy the sport and community of an auction while others are just looking for a good deal. Auctions in the B2B market are a very effective way to unload surplus inventory at a price set by the market.

Bartering

With bartering, goods or services are exchanged for other products rather than cash. Buyers and sellers have practiced this since the beginning of time. Users may enjoy tax benefits, but otherwise this is not a particularly profitable pricing strategy. We present it here, not only to be complete, but also because consumers exchanging or auctioning used items online can hurt sales of new products. Such is the case with MP3 music file swapping, although this is not entirely an exchange-type barter. Switchouse.com once operated as a place for buyers and sellers to swap used goods, but it went out of business due to the lack of a viable business model.

S u m m a r y

Price is the amount of money charged for a product or service. More broadly, it covers the sum of all the values (such as money, time, energy, and psychic cost) that buyers exchange for the benefits of having or using a good or service. Fixed price refers to one price set for all buyers. Dynamic pricing means varying prices for individual customers. Internet technology has prompted mass customization and a return to dynamic pricing—especially negotiation and pricing for segments as small as a single buyer. This is creating huge opportunities for marketers to optimize pricing strategies, including changing them daily or more often. However, the Internet is also facilitating price transparency, the idea that both buyers and sellers can view all competitive prices for items sold online.

From the buyer's perspective, the cost of a product purchased online may be higher than offline (due to seemingly hidden elements such as shipping costs and the time and effort needed to search out and compare prices). Yet buyers may also enjoy online cost savings due to the Internet's convenience, speed, self-service capability, one-stop shopping, integration, and automation. Moreover, online buyers have more control through strategies such as reverse auctions, the availability of information and products, and negotiation opportunities.

From the seller's perspective, any price above the cost of producing the good or service has the potential to return profit. The seller's perspective on pricing covers internal factors such as pricing objectives, the marketing mix strategy, and information technology. Beyond the buyer's perspective, the market structure and the efficiency of the market are key external elements affecting online pricing.

A market is efficient when customers have equal access to information about products, prices, and distribution. Efficient markets are characterized by lower prices, high price elasticity, frequent and smaller price changes, and narrow price dispersion. The Web exhibits many characteristics of an efficient market except narrow price dispersion. Because the Internet could become a more efficient market in the future, marketers that want to maintain control over pricing should differentiate their products on bases other than price, create unique product bundles of benefits, and consider the role of customer perceptions of value when determining pricing levels.

Key Terms

Competition-based pricing	Price elasticity
Dynamic pricing	Price leadership
Efficient markets	Price transparency
Fixed pricing	Profit-oriented objective
Geographic segment pricing	Promotional pricing
Market-oriented objectives	Pure competition
Monopolistic competition	Pure monopoly
Negotiation	Reverse auction
Oligopolistic competition	Second-generation shopping agents
Pareto principle	Segmented pricing
Price	Value segment pricing
Price dispersion	

Exercises

Review Questions

1. How does fixed pricing differ from dynamic pricing?
2. What is price transparency and why is it an important concept for e-marketers to understand?
3. List the main factors that put downward pressure on prices in the Internet channel.
4. List the main factors that put upward pressure on prices in the Internet channel.
5. From the buyer's perspective, how does the Internet affect costs?
6. What is an efficient market? What makes the Internet an efficient market and what indicates that it is not an efficient market?

7. How do e-marketers use geographic, value segment, and negotiated pricing online?

Discussion Questions

8. Near perfect access to pricing information is a problem that airlines have faced for years. How have airlines responded to this problem? Should Internet businesses adopt similar strategies?

9. Which of the online cost-saving factors do you think has the greatest effect on price? Why?

10. Which pricing strategy would you use to introduce a new product for wireless Web access? Why?

11. Internet technology allows a company to price the same product differently for different customers. What do you think would be the advantages and disadvantages of Amazon offering the same book at one price to a professor and at a different price to a student?

12. As a buyer, how do you think price transparency affects your ability to develop an appropriate bidding strategy for new products auctioned by companies through eBay?

13. As a seller, how do you think price transparency affects your ability to obtain as high a price as possible for used products you auction through eBay?

chapter

12 the internet for distribution

learning objectives

The key objective of this chapter is to develop an understanding of the Internet as a distribution channel, identify online channel members, and analyze the functions they perform in the channel. You will learn how the Internet presents opportunities to alter channel length, restructure channel intermediaries, improve the performance of channel functions, streamline channel management, and measure channel performance.

After reading this chapter, you will be able to:

- Describe the three major functions of a distribution channel.
- Explain how the Internet is affecting distribution channel length.
- Discuss trends in supply chain management and power relationships among channel players.
- Outline the major models used by online channel members.
- Highlight how companies can use distribution channel metrics.

The art of getting rich consists not in industry, much less in saving, but in a better order, in timeliness, in being at the right spot.

ralph waldo emerson

Michael Dell dropped out of college at age 19 to start a computer company, and it paid off big time. He owns 14% of Dell Computer, a firm with more than $31 billion in annual revenues. What does it take to be the number-one PC maker in the world?

Dell sells about $40 million a day online, representing nearly half of its sales. This *direct-distribution model* offers Dell several competitive advantages. First, it eliminates wholesalers and retailers, allowing complete control over inventory levels and distribution costs. Dell turns its inventory every 10 days, minimizing costs and obsolescence. And by avoiding an extensive intermediary network, Dell can directly monitor its customers' needs.

Dell is well known for outstanding *customer service*—despite handling 10,000 daily customer communications from corporations, government agencies, medical and educational institutions, small businesses, and individual consumers. Dell's huge customer database supports its marketing communication and customer service efforts. When a customer calls or e-mails with a technical problem, Dell responds quickly with an appropriate solution. It also maintains 60,000 custom Web storefronts for major corporate buyers.

Dell fully utilizes the Internet's properties for *mass customization* by allowing online customers to build their own computer systems for speedy delivery. Dell offers an extensive menu of product components and lets the market decide their relative importance—the marketing concept at its best. The company analyzes what customers order and uses this information to guide new-product development.

Finally, Dell has a *tightly coordinated supply chain*. Suppliers work closely with Dell engineers to keep R&D costs low and keep products flowing to customers as ordered. Dell manages supply and demand in a way that leaves both suppliers and customers satisfied—a tricky job when selling in 140 country markets. And what does Michael Dell say about all this? "I'm having a great time. This is fun."

If I'm selling to you, I speak your language. If I'm buying, dann mussen Sie Deutsch sprechen (then you must speak German).

willi brandt former chancellor, germany

Distribution Channel Overview

Marketers are concerned about distribution because it determines how the customer actually receives a product or service. A customer's experience in gaining access to the product often colors her brand image. Dell, for example, maintains complete control of its distribution, so its customers buy directly from the manufacturer. Marketers help their companies set strategies for availability, access, and distribution service. A **distribution channel** is a group of interdependent firms that work together to transfer product and information from the supplier to the consumer. It is composed of the following participants:

- **Producers**, manufacturers, or originators of the product or service;
- **Intermediaries**—the firms that match buyers and sellers and mediate the transactions among them; and
- **Consumers,** customers, or buyers who consume or use the product or service.

Each channel member performs some of the marketing functions needed to get the product from the point of origin to the point of consumption. In addition to matching buyers and sellers, intermediaries exist in the channel to perform some of these functions perhaps more effectively and efficiently than other channel participants. Some benefits of intermediaries include mediating transactions between parties, as well as providing cost savings in the form of lowered search, monetary, transaction, and energy costs.

The structure of the distribution channel can either make or impede possible opportunities for marketing on the Internet. For example, when a consumer purchases online, he must perform the search function himself, and if the transaction is automated he could save money by performing some distribution functions himself. Four major elements combine to form a company's channel structure:

1. Types of channel intermediaries.
2. Length of the channel.
3. Functions performed by members of the channel.
4. Physical and informational systems that link the channel members and provide for coordination and management of their collective effort to deliver the product or service.

The next sections introduce channel intermediaries and discuss channel length.

Types of Intermediaries

Channel intermediaries include wholesalers, retailers, brokers, and agents.

- **Wholesalers** buy products from the manufacturer and resell them to retailers.

- Both brick-and-mortar and online retailers (sometimes called e-tailers) buy products from wholesalers and sell them to consumers.

- **Brokers** facilitate transactions between buyers and sellers without representing either party. They are market makers and typically do not take title to the goods.

- Agents usually represent either the buyer or seller, depending upon who hires and pays them. They facilitate transactions between buyers and sellers but do not take title to the goods. **Manufacturer's agents** represent the seller whereas purchasing agents represent the buyer.

For some digital products, such as software, the entire distribution channel may be Internet based. When a consumer buys software online, the supplier often delivers it over the Internet to the buyer's computer. In most cases, however, only some of the firms in the channel are wholly or partially Web enabled. For example, nondigital products such as flowers and wine may be purchased online but must be delivered via truck. Nonetheless, the exact location of that shipment can be tracked using a Web-based interface (the informational role of distribution).

Distribution Channel Length and Functions

The length of a distribution channel refers to the number of intermediaries between the supplier and the consumer. The shortest distribution channel has no intermediaries—the manufacturer deals directly with the consumer, the way Dell Computer sells directly to customers. This is known as a **direct-distribution channel**. Most distribution channels incorporate one or more intermediaries in an **indirect channel**. A typical indirect channel includes suppliers, a manufacturer, wholesalers, retailers, and end consumers. Intermediaries help to perform important functions (described in the next section).

Originally, it was predicted that the Internet would eliminate intermediaries, thereby creating disintermediation in distribution channels. **Disintermediation** describes the process of eliminating traditional intermediaries. Eliminating intermediaries can potentially reduce costs since each intermediary must add to the price of the product in order to profit. Taken to its extreme, disintermediation allows the supplier to transfer goods and services directly to the consumer in a direct channel. Complete disintermediation tends to be the exception because intermediaries can often handle channel functions more efficiently than producers can handle them. An intermediary that specializes in one function, such as product promotion, tends to become more proficient in that function than a nonspecialist.

Much of the initial hype surrounding the Internet focused on disintermediation and the possibility that prices would plummet as the Internet eliminated costly intermediaries. This line of reasoning failed to recognize some important facts. First, the U.S. distribution system is the most efficient in the world. Second, using intermediaries allows companies to focus on what they do best. Third, many traditional intermediaries have been replaced with Internet equivalents. In many cases the online intermediaries are more efficient than their brick-and-mortar counterparts. Consider the online storefront. Online retailers do not have to rent, maintain, and staff expensive retail space in desirable shopping areas. An inexpensive warehouse provides an acceptable storage location for goods sold online. On the other hand, online stores incur the costs of setting up and maintaining their e-commerce sites; while these charges can be significant, however, they do not outweigh the savings realized by eliminating the physical store.

The Internet has added new intermediaries that did not exist previously. For example, Yahoo! Broadcast aggregates multimedia content. Yahoo! and Yahoo! Broadcast together are like a record store, audio bookstore, radio broadcaster, and TV broadcaster all rolled into one. Other new intermediaries include shopping agents, buyer cooperatives, and **metamediaries**. Exhibit 12 - 1 shows CNET Shopper.com (shopper.cnet.com), a shopping agent geared toward the purchase of computer products.

Functions of a Distribution Channel

Many functions must be performed in moving products from producer to consumer, regardless of which intermediary performs them. One Internet property is market deconstruction—removing distribution channel functions from the players that normally perform them, and reconstruction—reallocating those functions to other intermediaries in novel ways. For example, online retailers normally hold

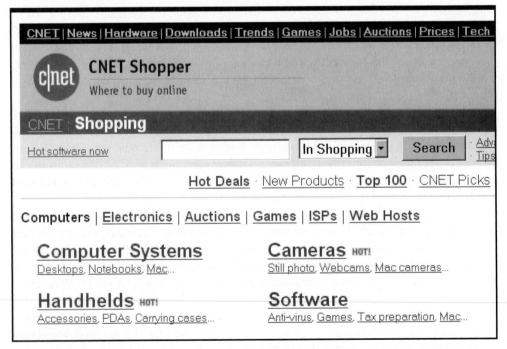

Exhibit 12 - 1 CNET Shopper Helps Users Find Computer-Related Products
Source: www.shopper.com.

inventory and perform the pick, pack, and ship functions in response to a customer order. In an alternative scenario, the retailer might outsource the pick, pack, and ship functions to a logistics provider such as UPS. Here, the retailer forwards the order to a UPS warehouse where the product waits in storage. UPS picks, packs, and ships the product to the consumer. Distributors perform many value-added functions. The functions can be broadly characterized as transactional, logistical, and facilitating (Lamb, Hair, and McDaniel 2002).

Transactional Functions

Transactional functions refer to making contact with buyers and using marketing communication strategies to make them aware of products. They also include matching product to buyer needs, negotiating price, and processing transactions.

Contact with Buyers

The Internet provides a new channel for making contact with buyers. Forrester Research calls the Internet the fourth channel after personal selling, mail, and the telephone; retailers see it as the third channel after brick-and-mortar stores and catalogs. The Internet channel adds value to the contact process in several ways. First, contact can be customized to the buyer's needs. For example, the Honda site (www.honda.com) allows customers to find a dealer in their area where they can buy Honda vehicles (see Exhibit 12 - 2). Second, the Internet provides a wide range of referral sources such as search engines, shopping agents, newsgroups, chat rooms, e-mail, Web pages, and affiliate programs. Third, the Internet is always open for business, 24 hours a day, seven days a week.

Marketing Communications

Marketing communication encompasses advertising and other types of product promotion (discussed in Chapter 13). This function is often shared among channel players. For example, a manufacturer may launch an ad campaign while its retailers offer coupons. Cooperative advertising is another example, with manufacturers sharing advertising costs with retailers. These communications are most effective when they represent a coordinated effort among channel players.

The Internet adds value to the marketing communications function in several ways. First, functions that previously required manual labor can be automated. When American Airlines sends out a promotional message to millions of its registered users, there are no papers to fold, no envelopes to stuff, no postage to imprint—its marketers simply click Send to distribute the message. As another example, promoting a Web site to the search engines can be automated by services such as Submission Pro (www.submission-pro.com) and MoreVisiblity (www.morevisibility.com). These firms study how the search engines rank Web sites and then optimize their clients' Web sites to achieve a higher ranking.

Second, communications can be closely monitored and altered minute by minute. DoubleClick, for instance, allows its clients to monitor the click-through rates of their banner ads in real time and quickly make substitutions for poorly performing ads.

Third, software for tracking a user's behavior can be used to direct highly targeted communications to individuals. Engage Technologies (www.engage.com) can anonymously track user behavior online and target ads to individual users.

Finally, the Internet enhances promotional coordination among intermediaries. Firms e-mail ads and other material to each other, and all firms may view current promotions on a Web site at any time. In contrast, companies in the brick-and-mortar world would sometimes run promotions that retailers would not know about until consumers began asking for the special deals.

Matching Product to Buyer's Needs

The Web excels at matching product to buyer's needs. Given a general description of the buyer's requirements, shopping agents can produce a list of relevant products. **Shopping agents** such as MySimon (www.mysimon.com) and PriceScan (www.pricescan.com) allow consumers to quickly compare prices and features within product categories. Online retailers can also help consumers match product to needs. Gap (www.gap.com) lets consumers mix and match clothes to create outfits. Exhibit 12 - 3 shows the Land Rover site (www.landrover.com) where consumers can custom-configure vehicles. Of particular interest are **collaborative filtering**

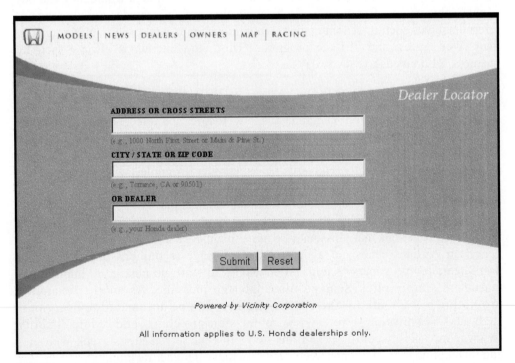

Exhibit 12 - 2 Honda Dealer Locator
Source: www.honda.com.

agents, which can predict consumer preferences based on past purchase behavior. Amazon uses a collaborative filtering agent to recommend books and music to customers. Once the system is in place, it can handle millions of users at very little incremental cost. The effectiveness of the collaborative filtering agent actually increases as consumers are added to the database. Note that all of these services scale well because they are automated. By contrast, efforts to match product to buyer needs in the brick-and-mortar world can be very labor intensive and are quickly overwhelmed as volume increases. Salespeople in retail outlets attempt this chore, but the Internet improves on this function by being on call anytime and by matching buyers with products across retailers. Of course, this puts a burden on electronic retailers to compete on the basis of price or to differentiate their products in a way that is meaningful to the market.

Negotiating Price

True price negotiation involves offers and counteroffers between buyer and seller such as might be conducted in person, over the phone, or via e-mail—a two-way dialogue. Even so, shopping agents implicitly negotiate prices downward on behalf of the consumer by listing companies in order of best price first. Bidding, on the other hand, is a form of dynamic or flexible pricing in which the buyer gives

Exhibit 12 - 3 Land Rover Allows Customers to View Options Online
Source: www.landrover.com.

suppliers an equal opportunity to bid. Many businesses currently conduct bidding online. There are consumer market auctions such as those held by eBay and Amazon. Businesses such as General Electric also solicit online bids from their suppliers. Online bidding has the effect of widening the supplier pool, thereby increasing competition and lowering prices. Many auction houses allow buyers to program an agent to represent them in bidding against other buyers or their agents.

Process Transactions

Studies have shown that electronic channels lower the cost to process transactions dramatically. The National Association of Purchasing Management places the cost of manually processing an average purchase order at $79—mainly due to labor costs.

Logistical Functions

Logistical functions include physical distribution activities such as transportation and inventory storage, as well as the function of aggregating product. Logistical functions are often outsourced to third-party logistics specialists.

Physical Distribution

Most products sold online are still distributed through conventional channels. Yet any content that can be digitized can be transmitted from producer to consumer over the Internet: text, graphics, audio, and video content (see Exhibit 12 - 4). Products currently delivered over the Net include television and radio programs, magazines, books, newspapers, software, videos, and music. Trisenx can transmit digital smells and tastes over the Web (www.trisenx.com)! Distribution costs are significantly lower online. The alternative, physical distribution of digital product, is comparatively expensive. Physical distribution first requires the costly step of embedding the content in a medium such as newsprint, plastic-coated paper, a CD, or a diskette. The medium must then be packaged and shipped to the consumer, further increasing costs.

Aggregating Product

In general, suppliers operate more efficiently when they produce a high volume of a narrow range of products. Consumers, on the other hand, prefer to purchase small quantities of a wide range of products. Channel intermediaries perform the essential function of aggregating product from multiple suppliers so that the consumer can have more choices in one location. Examples of this traditional form of aggregation include online category killers such as CDNOW (www.cdnow.com), which offers thousands of compact disks from multiple suppliers. In other cases the Internet follows a model of virtual aggregation, bringing together products from multiple manufacturers and organizing the display on the user's computer. In the case of shopping agents, the unit of aggregation is the product page at the online store. A

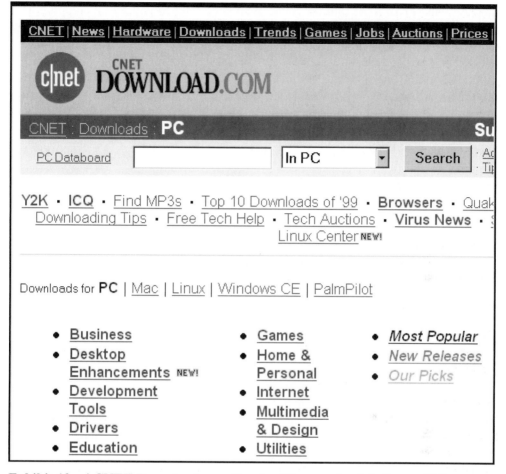

Exhibit 12 - 4 CNET Download.com Carries Thousands of Software Titles
Source: download.com.com.

search for a particular product will produce a neatly arranged table with comparative product information and direct links to the vendor pages.

Third-Party Logistics—Outsourced Logistics

A major logistics problem in the B2B market is reconciling the conflicting goals of timely delivery and minimal inventory. One solution for many companies is to place inventory with a **third-party logistics** provider such as UPS or FedEx. Taking logistics one step further, third parties can also manage the company's supply chain and provide value-added services such as product configuration and subassembly. The logistics providers will even handle the order processes, replenish stock when needed, and assign tracking numbers so customers can find their orders. Alcatel, for example, uses UPS to manage orders and distribute cellular phones in Europe.

In the B2C market a major logistics problem is product returns (reverse logistics), which can run as high as 15%. Customers frequently complain about the difficulty and expense of returns. Some Web sites offer to pay return shipping. But even with a credit for return shipping, the customer still has to weigh the package, pay shipping fees up front, and schedule pickup (or deliver to a shipping location).

The U.S. Postal Service (USPS) has introduced a clever program to ease the return process. Merchants can install software on a site that allows them to authorize customers to download and print postage-paid return labels. The customer simply boxes the item, slaps on the label, and leaves it by the door for the letter carrier. Even if a Web site does not participate in the USPS program, customers can still weigh their packages at home and download appropriate postage onto a laser-printed label using a service from eStamps.

In the C2C market, eBay has formed a partnership with brick-and-mortar Mailboxes Etc. After auctions close, sellers take their items to Mailboxes Etc. to be packaged and shipped.

The Last Mile Problem

One big problem facing online retailers and logistics managers is the added expense of delivering small quantities to individual homes and businesses. It is much less expensive to send cases of product to wholesalers and retailers and let them break the quantities into smaller units for sale. There are two other problems: 25% of deliveries require multiple delivery attempts, thus increasing costs, and 30% of packages are left on doorsteps when no one is home, opening the way for possible theft (Laseter et al. 2001). With 2.3 billion packages delivered in the United States in 2000 (an average of 13.4 packages per household) e-marketers are looking for ways to shave costs and solve this *last mile problem.*

Innovative firms are trying three solutions. First is a smart box, such as produced by Brivo. The consumer buys a 2.5 foot tall steel box that comes with a numeric keypad connected to the Internet via a two-way modem. Delivery people, such as Federal Express or the USPS, receive a special code for each delivery and use it to open the box and leave the shipment. This activity is sent via the Internet and recorded in the Brivo database. The consumer uses his own code to open the box and receive the delivery—also recorded at Brivo. This is an efficient and secure solution if consumers are willing to pay the hefty box fee.

A second solution involves a retail aggregator model. Consumers can have packages shipped to participating retailers, such as local convenience stores or service stations, then consumers pick up the package—not as convenient as the current method. In Japan, NTT DoCoMo customers can use their Web-enabled cell phones to order goods for shipment to local Seven-11 stores. The third solution calls for special *e-stops,* storefronts that exist solely for customer drive-through and package pick-up.

Facilitating Functions

Facilitating functions performed by channel members include market research and financing.

Market Research

Market research is a major function of the distribution channel. The benefits include an accurate assessment of the size and characteristics of the target audience. Information gathered by intermediaries helps manufacturers plan product development and marketing communications. Chapter 6 explored market research in detail, and Chapter 7 examined Internet user behavior. This section will look at the costs and benefits of Internet-based market research.

The Internet affects the value of market research in five ways. First, much of the information on the Internet, especially government reports, is available for free. Second, managers and employees can conduct research from their desks rather than making expensive trips to libraries and other resource sites. Third, information from the Internet tends to be timelier, as when advertisers monitor interactions with banner ads. Fourth, Web-based information is already in digital form, so e-marketers can easily load it into a spreadsheet or other software. Finally, because so much consumer behavior data can be captured online, e-marketers can receive detailed reports. For example, comScore Media Metrix (www.jmm.com or www.comscore.com) produces a site interaction report that details to what extent a site shares audience with another site—showing exclusive and duplicated audience.

Nonetheless, there is no free market research. Even free government reports require a significant investment of human resources to distill the material into a useful form for making decisions. Furthermore, many firms need access to costly commercial information such as comScore Media Metrix's reports, which sell for about $50,000 each.

Financing

Financing purchases is an important facilitating function in both consumer and business markets. Intermediaries want to make it easy for customers to pay in order to close the sale. Most online consumer purchases are financed through credit cards or special financing plans, similar to traditional store purchases. However, as noted in Chapter 4, consumers are understandably concerned about divulging credit card information online—resulting in safeguards that probably make online purchasing the most secure channel for consumers.

Online merchants have a major concern as well: How do they know that they are dealing with a valid consumer using a legitimate credit card? The major credit card companies have, therefore, formed **Secure Electronic Transactions (SET)** as a vehicle for legitimizing both the merchant and the consumer as well as protecting the consumer's credit card number. Under SET the card number goes not to the merchant but to a third party with whom the merchant and consumer communicate to validate one another as well as the transaction. The communication occurs automatically in the background and places no technical burdens on the consumer. However, SET is so technical that most consumers do not appreciate its subtleties. Furthermore, most merchants do not want to pay for costly upgrades to an SET system.

Still, SET has been successful outside the United States, in part because of legislative protections: U.S. consumers have a maximum $50 liability for purchases made with a stolen card. The card issuer usually waives the $50 in order to retain customers, and some issuers now advertise $0 liability for online purchases. However, that legal protection does not exist in some countries and consumers may be liable for all charges on their card up to the time they report it stolen.

In the B2B market, brokers and agents often extend lines of credit to buyers to facilitate purchases. These lines of credit significantly speed the buying process and make the online channel more attractive.

Distribution System

The distribution channel is actually a system, when viewed by the flow of products, information, and finances along the channel—a unified system of interdependent organizations working together to build value as products proceed through the channel to the consumer. This perspective recognizes that a channel system is stronger when its participants compete in a unified way with other channel systems.

There are three ways to define the scope of the channel as a systems:

1. The first is to consider only distribution functions that are downstream from the manufacturer to the consumer, the traditional definition of the distribution channel.

2. The second is to consider only the supply chain upstream from the manufacturer working backward to the raw materials, the traditional definition of the **supply chain**.

3. The third view is to consider the supply chain, the manufacturer, and the distribution channel as an integrated system called the **value chain** (a more recent name for the value chain is *integrated logistics)*. Many refer to the supply chain *as* the value chain. By this definition the supply chain includes upstream and downstream activities as well as processes internal to the firm. See Exhibit 12 - 5, in which the circles represent firms in a network of suppliers, manufacturers, and intermediaries.

Redefining the supply chain to include the entire value chain is somewhat controversial, but it reflects what a great number of practitioners mean when they talk about supply chain management. Thus, value chain, integrated logistics, and supply chain are equivalent terms.

The more inclusive definition of the supply chain is used to describe the emerging field of **supply chain management (SCM)**. Supply chain management (SCM) refers to the coordination of flows in three categories: material (e.g., physical product), information (e.g., demand forecast), and financial (e.g., credit terms) (Kalakota and Robinson 1999). The word *flow* evokes the image of a continuous stream of products, information, and finances flowing among the channel members much as blood and nerve impulses flow through an organism. The most important flow is

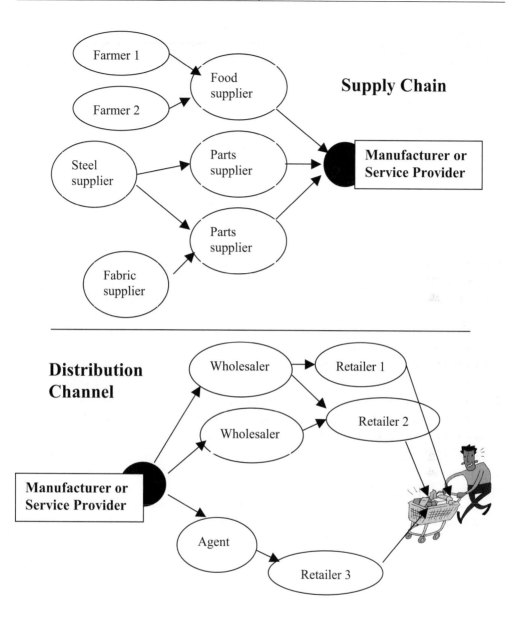

Exhibit 12 - 5 Supply Chain + Distribution Channel = New Definition of Supply Chain

information since creation of the physical product and the financing depend on the information.

The Holy Grail in supply chain management is "scan one, make one—and deliver it fast." This is known as **continuous replenishment**. For more complex products such as computers, the goal is to build to order and deliver quickly. Both continuous replenishment and **build to order** help to eliminate inventory. In turn, this reduces costs because inventory is expensive to finance; it also increases profits by avoiding unsold inventory going stale and being sold at a discount. The cost savings may be passed onto the customer in the form of lower prices, which improve the value proposition for the customer. However, creating product in response to demand almost always results in some delay in delivery. The customer's value is only increased if the increased delays are acceptable. Today's customer wants it all— lower prices, quick delivery, and custom configuration. The only way to provide these benefits is to tightly coordinate the activities of upstream suppliers, the inner workings of the firm, and the downstream distribution channel—a formidable task that would have been impossible before the information age.

A difficult problem in SCM is deciding which participant should manage a channel composed of many firms. For example, Sun Microsystems designs computers but doesn't build any of them—yet Sun manages the entire supply chain, even the suppliers, of its contract manufacturers. The coordination is made possible by sophisticated supply chain management software from i2, which operates over the Web. Interestingly, the coordination is cooperative rather than dictatorial. Sun makes customer demand information visible to the suppliers who then indicate what portion of the demand they can handle. Supply chain management allows for coordination of all supply chain functions into a seamless system, made possible by Internet technology.

Interoperability is especially important in SCM since many of the participants in modern supply chains have **enterprise resource planning (ERP)** systems to manage their in-house inventory and processes. If the individual ERP systems can seamlessly share information with the SCM system, coordination is greatly facilitated in real time. See Exhibit 12 - 6.

Channel Management and Power

Once a channel structure is established, its viability requires a certain measure of coordination, communication, and control to avoid conflict among its members. A powerful channel member must emerge to assume the leadership and institute these

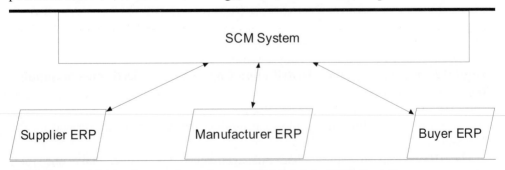

Exhibit 12 - 6 SCM System Interfaces with Multiple ERP Systems

required measures, the way Sun coordinates its supply chain participants. Increasingly, market competition is between entire supply chains, which is why e-marketers need to understand power relationships among channel players.

Whenever new information technology is introduced into a distribution channel, it can potentially alter the power relationships among existing channel players. Nowhere has this effect been more evident than with the Internet. In many cases the power of the buyer has been significantly increased at the expense of the supplier. In other cases the power of the supplier has come out on top. Wal-Mart gained power over its channels when it introduced electronic systems to notify suppliers of needed product. This was a major power upheaval in channels where giant manufacturers such as Procter & Gamble had previously been in control. A classic source of power for retailers and distributors has been geographic location. Retailers have built power on the place (location) utility and restricted access to manufacturers. The Web neutralizes the importance of location and offers new sources of supply for purchasing.

Just as the Internet has increased the power of buyers by providing access to more information and to more suppliers, it has increased the power of suppliers, as well. First, the supplier that takes the early lead online will receive business from consumers and firms eager to shop in this channel. But even in cases when multiple firms are online, suppliers can gain power by establishing structural relationships with buyers. For example, Amazon establishes structural relationships with its customers using its one-click ordering and collaborative filtering technologies. Amazon customers switching to another site would have to reenter their billing information and, more important, would lose access to Amazon's recommendations.

A type of business-to-business commerce known as **electronic data interchange (EDI)** is particularly effective for establishing structural relationships between businesses. Electronic data interchange is the computerized exchange of information between organizations, typically used to eliminate paperwork. A buyer logs onto the supplier's computer system and types in an order. The order is electronically conveyed to the supplier and the buyer receives an electronic bill.

The Internet has put a new face on EDI with the advent of open standards and interoperable systems. First, the Internet replaced expensive proprietary networks, yielding tremendous cost savings. Second, business can use the same computer to interface with multiple suppliers. Third, networks of suppliers and buyers can more easily exchange data using a Web-based interface.

Thus, EDI is based on three key variables: the openness of the system, the transport method (Internet or non-Internet), and the type of technology used for implementation. Combining these variables in different ways shows the five flavors of EDI most commonly used today (see Exhibit 12 - 7).

Openness	Transport	Technology
Proprietary	Non-Internet	Traditional EDI
Open system	Non-Internet	Standards-based EDI (X.12)
Proprietary	Internet	Application Program Interface (API)
Open system	Internet	Open Buying on the Internet (OBI)
Open system	Internet	Extensible Markup Language (XML)

Exhibit 12 - 7 Flavors of EDI

The goal is to create a standards-based open system that runs over the Internet so all suppliers and buyers can seamlessly integrate their systems. The technology with the greatest promise to meet this goal is Extensible Markup Language (XML), as discussed in earlier chapters.

Classifying Online Channel Members

A good way to classify online intermediaries is according to their business model. Many e-business models have new names, but how many of them are really new? On closer inspection most e-business models turn out to be variations on existing marketing concepts—which is fortunate since it allows for a clear organizational scheme. Exhibit 12 - 8 shows the overall classification scheme for the discussion that follows.

The first two models, content sponsorship and direct selling, are particularly important ways that producers sell directly to customers using e-marketing. The third model, infomediary, is in some ways a combination of content sponsorship and direct selling. The fourth model involves intermediaries in the distribution channel. These include brokers and agents, who position themselves between producers and retailers, as well as online retailers who sell to consumers.

Content Sponsorship

In this model, firms create Web sites, attract a lot of traffic, and sell advertising. Some firms use a niche strategy and draw a special interest-audience (e.g., iVillage.com). We include this model in the e-commerce chapter because content

1. Content sponsorship
2. Direct selling
3. Infomediary
4. Intermediaries

    Broker: Online exchange
                Online auction
    Agent: Agent models representing seller
                    Selling agent (affiliate program)
                    Manufacturer's agent (catalog aggregator)
                    Metamediary
                    Virtual mall
            Agent models representing buyer (purchasing agent)
                    Shopping agent
                    Reverse auction
                    Buyer cooperative
    E-tailer: Digital products
                Tangible products

Exhibit 12 - 8 E-Business Models

sponsorship generates revenues for firms selling advertising to other firms. The product, of course, is ad space on a Web site. This model has its roots in traditional media, where television, magazines, and other media sell space and airtime. In c Chapter 13 we discuss the other side: firms that buy advertising space as a way to communicate with stakeholders.

Some very valuable Web properties utilize the content sponsorship model including all the major portals: AOL, Yahoo!, MSN, and so on. Many online magazines and newspapers also use this model; indeed, much content on the Net is ad supported.

The **content sponsorship** model is often used in combination with other models to generate multiple revenue streams. For example, Buy.com, an online retailer, sells ads on its site to generate additional revenue, which in turn allows it to lower prices. Similarly, while most online newspapers offer their current edition for free, they will usually charge about $2 to retrieve an archived article.

Direct Selling

The manufacturer sells directly to the consumer or business customer in this model, as does Dell Computer. To the extent that the firm no longer needs the services of wholesalers and retailers, this creates disintermediation. This practice is commonly used in offline selling; however, the Internet made it much easier for producers to bypass intermediaries and go directly to consumers or business customers.

Direct selling has been successful in some B2B markets—sometimes saving millions of dollars in sales-related expenses for personnel, product configuration, and order processing. Expert systems built into some online sales systems assist the customer in configuring the product with compatible components, the way Dell's system helps customers order online.

Direct selling also has been successful in the B2C market with sales of digital products, such as software and music, that require no inventory and no pick, pack, and ship logistics. Perishable products such as flowers and fresh food are also well served by disintermediated channels. As one example, Proflowers.com delivers flowers fresh from the grower. Since the flowers don't pass through an intermediary, they tend to be fresher, last longer, and are in many cases less expensive.

Even subscription services can be considered a form of direct selling. While the subscription model has not been very successful for content providers, some, such as the *Wall Street Journal Online* and Classmates.com, are able to sell content in this manner.

Disintermediation saves customers money by avoiding the middleman; sometimes it leads to more rapid delivery of the product. Benefits to the manufacturer include the ability to claim a piece of the middleman's margin. The major costs of direct selling for the customer include higher search costs to locate individual manufacturers and the time costs of transacting with each manufacturer.

Infomediary

An **infomediary** is an online organization that aggregates and distributes information. One form of infomediary is a market research firm. Usually the infomediary compensates the consumer for sharing information. For example, a comScore Media Metrix panel member is paid; however, some intermediaries cull the information covertly and without compensation (e.g., DoubleClick uses cookies to track users as they surf the Web).

Another type of infomediary is a variation on the content sponsorship model. Using permission marketing, the firm pays the customer to buy space on her computer screen. The payment might be money, points toward shopping, or free Internet service. Here, the consumer is really selling space on her screen, but more importantly she is selling her attention—the scarcest commodity in cyberspace. The infomediary then generates revenue by reselling the screen space to advertisers. To receive payment, the consumer must share demographic and/or psychographic information with the permission marketer (although individual identities are usually not disclosed to advertisers). The consumer is also required to install software on her system that gives the infomediary a permanent window in which to run ads. So the consumer sees two sets of ads—the ads on the Web site and the ads in the infomediary window.

In addition, the consumer benefits by receiving ads targeted to her specific interests. Indeed the original idea behind the infomediary model was to give consumers more control over how they receive marketing messages (Hagel and

Singer 1999). The benefit to the infomediary is that the consumer information increases the value of its ad inventory. The benefit to advertisers is that they can market to very highly targeted audience that has expressly opted-in to the system. Permission marketing allows advertisers to do something never before possible—advertise while the consumer is on a competitor's site! See Chapter 13 for more on this strategy.

Intermediary Models

Three main intermediary models are in common use on the Internet: brokerage models, agent models, and online retailing.

Brokerage Models

The broker creates a market in which buyers and sellers negotiate and complete transactions (Rappa 2000). Brokers typically charge the seller and/or buyer a transaction fee, but they don't represent either party for providing exchange and negotiation services. Some brokers also charge listing fees. Brokers provide many value-added services to help attract customers and facilitate transactions. Brokerage models operate Web site exchanges in B2B, B2C, and C2C markets. The best example in the offline world is a stockbroker who brings buyers and sellers together at the NYSE or other exchanges. Exchanges and auctions are the most popular online brokerage models.

The primary benefits to the buyer are convenience, speed of order execution, and transaction processing. Cost savings to the buyer come in the form of lower prices, decreased search time, and savings of energy and frustration in locating the appropriate seller. The primary benefit to the seller is the creation of a pool of interested buyers. Cost savings to the seller come in the form of lowered customer acquisition costs and transaction costs.

Online Exchange

E*Trade, Ameritrade, and a host of other online brokerages allow customers to place trades from their computers without phoning or visiting a broker. These brokerages pass along the cost savings to the buyer in the form of lower transaction fees. They also provide the benefits of executing trades very quickly, providing reference resources, and allowing for program trading. Some newer services catering to day traders bypass the Web entirely and connect traders straight to the market. One such service is TradeCast.com, which started out by taunting users with the tag line, "You still trading stocks on the Web, sissy boy?"

Carpoint.msn.com, AutoByTel, and other online brokers allow customers to receive bids from qualified dealers on vehicles available in their area without first phoning or visiting the dealer. The dealers offer a no-hassle price quote through the service. Thus, the customer avoids the potentially unpleasant task of negotiating price with a dealer.

The B2B market has spawned a number of very successful brokerages. Converge is the leading anonymous exchange for the global electronics market (www.converge.com), aggregating supply and demand from thousands of component, original equipment and contract manufacturers, distributors, and resellers. The model is very similar to a stock exchange. Customers contact a Converge trader on the floor of the exchange with their request (e.g., an order for 100,000 transistors). The trader locates a supplier, completes the purchase, and pockets the spread between the buy and sell price. Additional revenue comes from other fixed fees. The exchange is anonymous: Suppliers ship to an Converge quality control warehouse where the goods are inspected and then forwarded to the buyer. Converge guarantees the quality of the products and has a no-questions-asked return policy. Converge online services include personal buy-and-sell portfolios, chatlike communication with traders, and multiple methods for issuing requests including uploading a list of items or searching for items individually.

PaperExchange is the leading online exchange for the pulp and paper industry—a $500 billion industry worldwide. It has over 4,000 members in more than 80 countries, serves as a marketplace for buyers and sellers to negotiate deals, and offers benefits such as logistics, credit, and editorial content. PaperExchange represents a hybrid business model since it is also a catalog aggregator, and auction house, and even supports customized storefronts in addition to the exchange.

Online Auction

Auctions are challenging the fixed price model, which has been the norm for the last 100 years. Auctions are available in the B2B, B2C, and C2C markets. While some merchants choose to host their own auctions, many more auction their surplus through auction brokers such as uBid. When merchants auction items on their own Web sites, they become direct sellers using dynamic pricing. Third-party auctioneers are broker intermediaries.

Sellers benefit by obtaining the market price for goods and unloading surplus inventory. Buyers benefit by obtaining a good deal and, in many cases, enjoying the sport of the auction. The downside is that the buyer can waste a lot of time monitoring the auction. Although buyers can use services to automatically proxy bid buyer, studies show that many repeatedly visit auction sites to check on bids.

Some auction houses offer a broad range of products. Ubid hosts a B2C auction for products ranging from computers to travel. Other auction houses specialize in niche markets. Industry giant eBay hosts C2C auctions in thousands of product categories. EBay has rolled out a number of innovative services to benefit the customer and facilitate the auction process, including escrow, electronic payment, and appraisal services.

Agent Models

Unlike brokers, **agents** *do* represent either the buyer or the seller depending on who pays their fee. In some cases they are legally obligated to represent the interests of the party that hires them. In the brick-and-mortar world, real estate agents who are hired to list a property must represent the interests of the seller.

Agent Models Representing Sellers

Selling agents, manufacturer's agents, metamediaries, and virtual malls are all agents that represent the seller.

Selling Agent   Selling agents represent a single firm, helping it sell its products; these agents normally work for a commission. For example, **affiliate programs** pay commissions to Web site owners for customer referrals. Normally the referral must result in a sale in order to qualify for the commission. Some affiliates demand a share of the lifetime value of the customer as opposed to just a piece of the first sale. Amazon.com pioneered one of the first affiliate programs.

Manufacturer's Agent   Manufacturer's agents represent more than one seller. In traditional marketing, they generally represent only firms that sell complementary products to avoid conflicts of interest, but in the virtual world they often create Web sites to help an entire industry sell its products. In e-marketing, manufacturer's agents are often called seller aggregators because they represent many sellers on one Web site.

Almost all of the travel reservations Web sites qualify as manufacturer's agents since their commissions are paid by the airlines and hotels they represent. Expedia, Travelocity, Orbitz, and many other online travel sites allow customers to make travel reservations without phoning or visiting a travel agent. In some cases the traveler can get a better deal online but often the greatest benefit is simply convenience.

In the B2B market manufacturer's agents are often called catalog aggregators. Each of the sellers these firms represent generally has a broad catalog of product offerings. Picture a purchasing manager in a small room surrounded by hundreds of catalogs—this suggests the origin of the term. The challenge for the aggregator is to gather the information from all of these catalogs into a database for presentation on the Web site. Normally the catalog aggregator offers software that seamlessly interfaces with the suppliers' internal database systems. The task is made significantly easier when the suppliers use industry standard software such as Arriba, CommerceOne, Concur, or Alliance to manage their catalogs. Furthermore the catalogs must be constantly maintained as product availability and prices change.

The more advanced manufacturer's agents support catalog customization and integration with the buyer's enterprise resource planning (ERP) systems. The customized catalogs display prenegotiated product offerings and prices. Some will even maintain spending limits for particular employees and automatically forward big-ticket orders to the appropriate officer for approval. Additional services include recommending substitutions, notifying buyers of production lead times, processing orders, and tracking orders.

With this model, the buyer gains substantial benefits, including shorter order cycles, reduced inventories, and increased control. Order processing costs are lowered through paperless transactions, automated request for proposal (RFP) and request for quote (RFQ), and integration with ERP systems.

The College Source (www.collegesource.org) is a catalog aggregator for the college market where students can search over 21,000 catalogs at one site. Google is also testing a catalog search site (catalogs.google.com) and may soon have a large inventory of online versions for mail-order catalogs. Another player is www.catalogs.com.

Metamediary   As noted in Chapter 2, an agent that represents a cluster of manufacturers, e-tailers, and content providers organized around a life event or major asset purchase is called a metamediary (Sawhney 1999). Mohanbir Sawhney coined this term to reflect a practice that is quite stable online. Metamediaries solve four major consumer problems—reducing search times, providing quality assurance about vendors, facilitating transactions for a group of related purchases, and providing relevant and unbiased content information about the purchase. Metamediary business partners benefit by having traffic directed to their sites as well as cobranding with the metamediary.

Metamediaries receive commissions for referrals. Sometimes commissions are contingent on a completed transaction. The key to a metamediary's success is consumer trust. Therefore, these sites must carefully select the sellers they will represent. Some metamediaries avoid accepting ads so their recommendations will not be perceived as tainted.

Edmunds is a metamediary for the car-buying market, providing information about new and used automobiles and advice on negotiating deals. It also refers interested customers to a car-buying service, financing information, aftermarket parts, and insurance alternatives. TheKnot is a metamediary for the bridal market, offering information about planning, fashion, beauty, grooms, maids and moms, and so forth. It also has tools such as a gown finder, registry, checklist, and guestlist. In addition TheKnot provides sponsored content such as the guide to invitations by OurBeginning or the guide to bridal showers by GiftCertificates.

Virtual Mall   **Virtual malls** host multiple online merchants in a model very similar to a shopping mall. Hosted merchants gain exposure from traffic coming to the mall. The mall gains through a variety of fees: listing fees, transaction fees, and setup fees.

Although brick-and-mortar malls provide a desirable collection of stores in one location, are easily accessible from major highways, and have ample free parking, none of these benefits apply online. Nonetheless, virtual malls may provide six customer benefits. The first is branding—consumers may be more comfortable buying from a store listed on Yahoo! Store than buying from one that is not. The second benefit is availability of digital wallets. Digital wallets allow customers to register their shipping and billing information just once and retrieve that information when purchasing at any participating store, simplifying the order process. The third benefit is availability of frequent shopper programs that reward consumers for shopping within the mall. The fourth is a gift registry that operates across multiple stores. The fifth benefit is a search facility to locate products in mall stores. The sixth is a recommendation service such as suggestions for Mother's Day gifts.

Yahoo! Store hosts a number of large merchants including Toys "R" Us and Target, as well as a number of smaller retailers. It offers a free digital wallet that can be used to shop at many of its listed merchants, has a frequent shopper program, a gift registry, product recommendations, and a search facility.

Agent Models Representing Buyers

Purchasing agents represent buyers. In traditional marketing, they often forge long-term relationships with one or more firms; however, on the Internet they represent any number of buyers, anonymously in many cases. Shopping agents and reverse auctions help individual buyers obtain the prices they want, while buyer cooperatives pool buyers for larger volume buys and, thus, lower prices.

Shopping Agent As discussed in Chapter 11, when shopping agents were first developed, many feared that they would drive prices on the Internet down to impossible margins. That has not happened because price is not the only factor consumers consider when making a purchase. Newer shopping agents can now measure value and not just price; these are called second-generation shopping agents. PriceScan and DealTime are two firms offering this service.

Consumers who desire a quantitative performance evaluation of a merchant can shop through BizRate.com. BizRate rates online merchants based on customer feedback. BizRate posts a report card of past consumer experiences with the merchant (generated from thousands of customer surveys) and shows the merchant's stated business policies. BizRate also offers a rebate program for customers who buy from participating merchants.

Reverse Auction A reverse auction occurs at a Web site serving as purchasing agent for individual buyers. In a reverse auction the buyer specifies a price and sellers bid for the buyer's business. The buyer commits to buying at a specified price and the seller either meets the price or tries to get close enough to make the sale. Priceline was the first major player in reverse auctions.

The benefit to the seller is in unloading excess inventory without unduly upsetting existing channels—a valuable benefit for sellers with perishable inventory such as airline seats or hotel rooms. The benefit for the buyer comes in the form of lower prices and the satisfaction of being able to name one's price. However, buyers have fewer choices of brand, suppliers, and product features. The reduced choice feature sufficiently differentiates the product in most cases to avoid conflict with the supplier's existing channel partners.

Buyer Cooperative   The **buyer cooperative** (also known as a buyer aggregator) pools many buyers together to drive down the price on selected items. The individual buyer, thus, receives the price benefit of volume buying. The more buyers that join the pool, the lower the price drops, usually in a step function. For example, one to five buyers pay $69 each; six to ten buyers pay $58 each, and so on. The step function encourages buyers to recruit their friends to help push the price down to the next step. Buyers can make their bid contingent on the product reaching a specified price point.

Mercata, MobShop, and other promising buyer's cooperatives were not able to build profitable business models online and closed. The remaining online co-ops represent more traditional brick-and-mortar buyer's co-ops such as the Solar and Renewable Energy Cooperative (www.soarenergy.org). Nonetheless, we believe that the Internet is capable of supporting this model.

Online Retailing

Online retailing is one of the most visible e-business models. Merchants set up online storefronts and sell to businesses and/or consumers. Digital goods may be delivered directly over the Internet while physical goods are shipped via a logistics provider such as UPS, USPS, or FedEx. Firms selling physical goods online can make any level of commitment from pure play to barely dabbling. Well-known electronic storefronts include CDNOW (www.cdnow.com) and Dell Computer (www.dell.com).

While a pre-Internet presence carries brand equity, it does not guarantee online success. Often the pure plays are free from the cultural constraints of the established businesses and can innovate more quickly in response to customer needs. Now some Internet pure plays are establishing brick-and-mortar operations to enhance branding through additional exposure and an additional channel for customers to experience their products. Two of the more prominent examples are E*Trade and Gateway Computer, which both extended their brick-and-mortar presence in recent years.

Digital Products

One great hope for the Internet is to serve as a medium for the physical distribution of goods and services. Although great strides are being made, there is still a way to go. Yet, as mentioned earlier, content that can be digitized can be transmitted over the Internet. *The New York Times* (www.nytimes.com) digitally distributes an online version of its newspaper; thousands of radio stations broadcast live programming over the Internet; software has a long history of online distribution. Clearly, distribution costs are significantly lower for digital products, compared with physical distribution.

Tangible Products

Many products sold online are still distributed through conventional channels. For example, most major record labels will not allow their music to be distributed online.

The Internet consumer may make the purchase online but the CD will arrive via the Postal Service, UPS, FedEx, or some other carrier. This type of distribution is relatively inefficient: Rather than deliver 100 copies of a CD to a record store in a single shipment, the UPS truck must make deliveries to 100 customers. Consumers pay a premium for this service, which may outweigh the cost savings of purchasing online.

Furthermore, local regulations sometimes impede the direct distribution of product. For example, Wine.com (the former Virtual Vineyards at www.wine.com), a wine distributor, has been forced by some state regulations to operate through local intermediaries—which lengthens its distribution channel.

Distribution Channel Metrics

Does online commerce work? To answer this question, firms must consider its effectiveness in terms of reaching target market segments effectively and efficiently.

B2C Market

Regardless of a 20% growth from 2000 to 2001, online retailing is only a tiny fraction of all retail sales. For example, U.S. consumers spent $32.6 billion online in 2001, while catalog sales in 2001 were $72 billion. According to the U.S. census, overall U.S. retail sales in 2000 totaled $3,059 billion. In one large global study of 37 countries, 15% of Internet users purchased online in 2001; however, another 15% purchased offline based on information they got on the Web (the study found 34% users in study countries) ("Global Key Report. . ." 2002). Authors Blackwell and Stephan (2001) suggest that online sales are unlikely to ever reach more than 10% of all retail sales. This is because consumers are fairly satisfied with brick-and-mortar shopping; until they become dissatisfied, they will not be motivated to switch to the Internet in a big way. What remains, then, is for firms to analyze which customers prefer which sales channels for specific products. Online, catalog, and brick-and-mortar retail operations each have their place, not the least of which is to move traffic to the other channels. (Chapter 7 discusses online shopping behavior in more detail.)

What are U.S. consumers buying online? Exhibit 12 - 9 shows that computer hardware, toys, apparel, and travel (air tickets, hotels, car) are important products for online shopping. Apparel and toy purchases have gained in sales over the past two years. Total spending for the month of November 2001 was $4.9 billion with an average spending of $293 per person—which may be a bit higher than other months due to holiday shopping. In the global study previously mentioned, 47% of shoppers spent less than € 100 in the four weeks prior to the survey and 6% spent over € 1000 (at this writing 1 Euro = US$0.99).

In one global study of online retailers, McKinsey and Company researchers found that two strategies are particularly effective online.

- A high-reach strategy of accumulating large numbers of customers with cost-effective conversion rates (visit the site and buy) for high-frequency purchases of low-margin products and services such as CDs and books. This describes Amazon.com.

- A niche strategy with narrow focus on a particular product or service category such as luxury items or apparel. This describes Dell.com.

For all others, the best use of online retailing is as a complement to offline channels. As Daryle Scott of Venus Swimwear says, "When your customers have the opportunity to purchase your products through *any* channel *they* choose—bricks and mortar, the Internet, or traditional catalogs—that's true customer service."

Amazon is now profitable with its CD, book, and music lines. Other firms also report profits, but many could not sustain their heavy losses due to high customer acquisition, fulfillment, and other costs. Chapter 2 presented many performance metrics to aid e-marketers in evaluating online retailing and supply chain management. A few of the more important include revenues (as just mentioned), ROI, customer satisfaction levels, customer acquisition costs, conversion rates, and average order values. The following are additional measures recommended by NetGenesis, an e-metrics firm:

- Which affiliations deliver the most users? This is a measure of affiliate program effectiveness.
- What is happening to users referred from an affiliate site?
- When and how do customers arrive at a Web site?
- How long do users stay at a Web site?
- How is buyer behavior different from other users who do not buy?
- How frequently are visitors converted to customers?
- Which channel partners deliver the most profitable customers? The most loyal ones?

B2B Market

The B2B market is big business. While it is impossible to measure the amount of dollars that exchange hands in supply chains, Gartner Group estimates $400 billion globally in 2001 and $1 trillion for 2002 (see www.thestandard.com). The Internet has proven to be a much more efficient way for firms to order from each other, spurring growth in e-procurement. Businesses use the Web to search for suppliers, but more often they simply facilitate current relationships throughout online ordering, shipment tracking, and more.

In the B2B market, as in B2C, e-marketers should select metrics that relate to their e-marketing goals. It is critical to understand how e-commerce fits into the overall marketing strategy, what the firm expects to accomplish through it, and whether or not it is working. For B2B, metrics may look at time from order to delivery, order fill levels, and other activities that reflect functions performed by channel participants.

Category	Average Spent	Total Dollars (000)
Small-ticket items:		
Apparel	$ 76.07	$ 405,439
Toys/video games	$ 66.98	$ 306,298
Books	$ 36.52	$ 192,183
Music	$ 32.97	$ 177,935
Software	$ 48.35	$ 165,020
Videos	$ 34.22	$ 135,211
Office supplies	$ 57.34	$ 131,110
Jewelry	$ 73.90	$ 116,796
Health and beauty	$ 39.45	$ 116,064
Linens/home decor	$ 58.68	$ 106,548
Footwear	$ 58.92	$ 100,055
Sporting goods	$ 67.08	$ 94,742
Flowers	$ 46.83	$ 74,805
Small appliances	$ 62.58	$ 70,494
Tools and hardware	$ 64.70	$ 52,220
Garden supplies	$ 31.73	$ 21,336
Total small-ticket items		$ 2,266,257
Big-ticket items:		
Air tickets	$ 313.56	$ 690,635
Computer hardware	$ 194.12	$ 388,402
Hotel reservations	$ 199.99	$ 339,609
Consumer electronics	$ 161.01	$ 316,731
Food/beverages	$ 95.31	$ 153,837
Car rental	$ 157.76	$ 135,276
Furniture	$ 168.72	$ 70,919
Appliances	$ 236.48	$ 55,664
Other	$ 120.33	$ 513,884
Total big-ticket items		$ 2,664,958
Total average spent	$ 293.28	
Total monthly online sales		$ 4,931,215

Exhibit 12 - 9 Forrester Online Retail Index: Consumer Online Retail Expenditures November 2001

Source: Data from CyberAtlas, www.cyberatlas.com.

Summary

A distribution channel is a group of interdependent firms that work together to transfer product and information from the supplier to the consumer. The transfer may either be direct or through a number of intermediaries that perform certain marketing functions in the channel between suppliers and customers. By specializing, intermediaries are able to perform functions more efficiently than a supplier could.

Channel intermediaries include wholesalers, retailers, brokers, and agents. The length of a distribution channel refers to the number of intermediaries between the supplier and the consumer. The shortest distribution channel has no intermediaries; the producer deals directly with customers. Indirect channels include one or more intermediaries. Disintermediation describes the process of eliminating traditional intermediaries. Eliminating intermediaries can potentially reduce costs but functions must be performed by someone. Although the Internet was expected to lead to disintermediation and lower prices, new intermediaries are emerging instead.

Three broad types of value-added functions performed in the channel are transactional, logistical, and facilitating functions. Transactional functions refer to making contact with buyers, using marketing communication strategies to raise awareness of products, matching product to buyer needs, negotiating price, and processing transactions. Logistical functions include physical distribution such as transportation and storing inventory and aggregating product; e-marketers often outsource these to third-party logistics providers. Facilitating functions include providing marketing research about buyers and providing financing. The last mile problem is the added expense of delivering small quantities to individual homes or businesses.

The distribution channel is a unified system of interdependent organizations working together to build value as products proceed through the channel from producer to consumer. This perspective recognizes that channels are stronger when they compete in a unified way with other channels. Supply chain management is the coordination of flows of material (e.g., physical product), information (e.g., demand forecast), and financial (e.g., credit terms).

The Internet has increased the power of buyers and suppliers. It has also changed the way electronic data interchange is used to establish structural relationships between suppliers and buyers. The major business models used by online intermediaries can be categorized as content sponsorship, direct selling, infomediary, or intermediary.

Key Terms

Affiliate programs	Indirect distribution channel
Agents	Infomediary

Brokers

Build to order

Buyer cooperative

Collaborative filtering agents

Content sponsorship

Continuous replenishment

Direct distribution channel

Direct selling

Disintermediation

Distribution channel

Electronic data interchange (EDI)

Enterprise resource planning (ERP)

Facilitating functions

Logistical functions

Manufacturer's agents

Metamediaries

Secure Electronic Transactions (SET)

Shopping agents

Supply chain

Supply chain management (SCM)

Third-party logistics

Transactional functions

Value chain

Virtual malls

Wholesalers

Exercises

Review Questions

1. What is a distribution channel?
2. What are the types of intermediaries in a distribution channel?
3. What are the three major functions of a distribution channel?
4. What is supply chain management (SCM) and why is it important?
5. Why are e-marketers concerned with the last mile problem?
6. What is disintermediation? Give an example.
7. What is an infomediary? Give an example.
8. What is a metamediary? Give an example.
9. How do brokers and agents differ?
10. What types of distribution channel metrics are used in the B2C market?

Discussion Questions

11. How does the value of distribution channel functions change when they become Internet based?
12. Do you agree with the more inclusive definition of the supply chain to include the entire value chain? Support your position.
13. Although direct selling often results in lower prices, does it have disadvantages for buyers?

14. Each intermediary in the channel has to mark up a product's price to make a profit. Some retailers sell products for almost double the wholesale cost. What would a retailer have to do to add enough value to justify such a markup?

15. How would you suggest e-marketers solve the last mile problem?

chapter

13 e-marketing communication

learning objectives

The primary goal of this chapter is to understand the Internet as a tool for efficiently and effectively exchanging marketing communication messages between marketers and their audiences. You will learn how each marketing communication tool can carry messages over the Internet and how marketers buy and use promotional space on the Net as a communication medium.

After reading this chapter, you will be able to:

- Define integrated marketing communication (IMC) and explain the importance of the hierarchy of effects model.
- Discuss how marketers use the Internet for advertising, marketing public relations, sales promotions, and direct marketing.
- Describe the characteristics of the major media and the Internet's media characteristics.
- Differentiate among broadcast, narrowcast, and pointcast electronic media.
- Outline the main methods for buying media and vehicles and for evaluating an IMC campaign's effectiveness.

All the great programming in the world won't help you if you can't express yourself online. It's about the words, dummy.

seth godin
permission marketing

The Internet has become a sweet medium for eDietShop, which manufactures sugar-free products and a variety of gourmet diet foods for a target market of 15 million diabetics. To draw this audience to his retail Web site, founder Steven Bernard has devised a detailed online advertising plan. He arranged banner ad exchanges with other sites and sponsored e-mail newsletters for groups such as DiabeticGourmet.com. He also used keyword advertising on search engines such as GoTo.com, so that users saw his banner ad when searching using the terms "sugar free" and "low fat." Bernard negotiated pay-for-performance advertising pricing to ensure that he only paid for visitors who clicked on the search engine ad to visit eDietShop.com. In late 2001, he spent $10,000 a month on online advertising to generate $150,000 in sales: a nifty 1500% return!

More recently, Bernard has purchased advertising time on the cable TV Food Channel—a move that dramatically increased traffic and site transactions. Now the company's revenues are 10 times higher than they were two years ago. This example illustrates how carefully targeted online advertising combined with messages in traditional media can build awareness, drive traffic, and boost sales for an online retailer.

Firms that are truly customer driven will build 1 to 1 technologies into every corner of their firm and will link their networks to many other networks.

bruce kasanoff

accelerating 1 to 1

Overview of E-Marketing Communication Issues

As the opening example of eDietShop demonstrates, Internet marketing is a powerful way to start and strengthen relationships with customers. However, online marketers must be increasingly clever to design and deliver brand messages that capture and hold audience attention—because on the Internet, users are in control. They can delete unwanted incoming e-mail and impatiently click away when Web sites don't quickly deliver desired information or products. Also, the Internet allows consumers to widely disseminate their own attitudes and brand experiences via e-mail and Web postings, shifting the balance of control over brand images from companies to consumers. Marketing communication (MarCom) tools that use technology to provide convenience, in conjunction with value-added product experiences, are the keys to capturing attention and winning long-term customer relationships. And as a bonus, technology lowers the costs: According to Forrester Research, companies spend about $33 to serve a customer over the phone, $9.99 through e-mail, and $1.17 using automated Web-based support.

Integrated Marketing Communication (IMC)

Integrated marketing communication (IMC) is a cross-functional process for planning, executing, and monitoring brand communications designed to profitably acquire, retain, and grow customers. IMC is cross-functional because every contact that a customer has with a firm or its agents helps to form brand images. For example, a Sharper Image customer might buy and use a product from the Web site, then e-mail or call the 1-800 number to complain about a problem, and finally return the product to the brick-and-mortar retail store. Every contact with an employee, a Web site, a magazine ad, a catalog, the physical store facilities, and the product itself helps the customer form an image of the firm. The best advertising can be undermined if these online and offline contact experiences do not communicate in a unified way to create and support positive brand relationships with customers. In addition, the product experience, its pricing level, and its distribution channels enhance the firm's marketing communication in a variety of online and offline media to present a strong brand image.

Profitable customer relationships are key to a firm's existence. Successful firms recognize that not all customers are equally valuable—some, such as frequent flyers or buyers, are more important than others. Using technology, firms can monitor profits customer by customer and, based on this analysis, pay more attention to high-value customers. Databases and the analysis techniques described in Chapter 6 allow firms to differentiate customers by value and track the results of company MarCom campaigns.

IMC strategy begins with a thorough understanding of the target stakeholders, the brand, its competition, and many other internal and external factors. Then marketers select specific MarCom tools to achieve their communication objectives.

After implementation, they measure execution effectiveness, make needed adjustments, and evaluate the results. Although strategic IMC entails a coordinated marketing mix and cross-functional participation, this chapter focuses on the promotion mix elements (also called marketing communication tools), the core of a firm's marketing communication plan.

Marketing Communication Tools

MarCom consists of both planned and unplanned messages between firms and customers, as well as those among customers. Companies use planned messages when trying to inform or persuade their target stakeholders. Unplanned messages include things such as word of mouth among consumers and publicity in media. However, because consumers have more control over communication on the Internet, it is nearly impossible for companies to directly manage unplanned messages. Thus, firms should concentrate on creating positive product experiences so that unplanned messages will be positive. In fact, some firms have experienced tremendous growth almost entirely based on unplanned e-mail (e.g., Hotmail).

In this chapter, we approach Internet MarCom from the perspective of the traditional promotion mix, discussing advertising, sales promotions, marketing public relations (MPR), and direct marketing. The fifth traditional tool, personal selling, by definition takes place face-to-face and is, therefore, inappropriate for use online. Nonetheless, the Internet can effectively generate leads for salespeople. Using innovative technologies, e-marketers can enhance the effectiveness and efficiency of traditional MarCom in many interesting ways. Important technologies include text and multimedia messages carried via Web pages and e-mail; databases to store information; new Web development, browsing, and e-mail software to facilitate Internet communication; and a plethora of digital receiving devices from PCs to cell phones for viewing multimedia messages.

Hierarchy of Effects Model

The traditional **AIDA model** (awareness, interest, desire, and action) or the "think, feel, do" **hierarchy of effects** model guides marketers' selection and evaluation of MarCom tools for use on the Internet. Both the AIDA and hierarchy of effects models suggest that consumers first become aware of and learn about a new product (think), then develop a positive or negative attitude about it (feel), and ultimately move to purchasing it (do) (Ray 1973). The thinking, or cognitive, steps are awareness and knowledge. The feeling, or attitude, steps are liking and preference. Consequently, e-marketers must select the appropriate IMC tools—which may vary from one stage to the other, depending on the desired results. For example, e-marketers may opt to use traditional IMC tools of sales promotion, such as giving away free T-shirts or mouse pads, to create awareness; television advertising to create interest and desire; and direct selling by telephone to get the desired action (buying).

The think, feel, do model is well accepted for high-involvement product decisions (those that are perceived as being high financial, emotional, or social risk). This is so because consumers spend some amount of time gathering information and considering alternatives prior to buying such products. Conversely, for low-involvement decisions, consumers often just hear about a product, give it a try, and then decide if they like it. Exhibit 13 - 1 presents this classic model and its low-involvement adaptation.

If a firm wants to build its brands and inform customers, it will operate at the cognitive and attitude levels of the hierarchy of effects, perhaps utilizing information publishing, Web advertising, e-mail campaigns, and other promotional techniques. When Ourbeginnings.com spent over $4 million on Super Bowl TV ads in 2000, it was trying to build awareness of the Web site—and it was so eager to achieve this goal that it spent four times its annual revenue on the campaign. This turned out to be a poor strategy, which is why only the strongest firms, such as E*Trade, purchased Super Bowl advertising in 2002. If a firm wants to encourage online transactions (behavior), it needs more persuasive communication messages that tell how to complete the transaction on the Web site, over the telephone, and so forth. Postpurchase behavior doesn't appear on the commonly accepted hierarchy, yet many MarCom strategies seek to build customer satisfaction after the purchase. E-mail is especially well suited for this goal.

The hierarchy of effects model is important because it helps marketers understand where consumers stand in relation to the purchase cycle so the firm can select appropriate communication objectives and strategies that will move consumers closer to purchase and loyalty. Bear in mind that some MarCom tools are more appropriate for building awareness and brand attitudes (advertising, public relations) and others are more suited for encouraging transactional behavior (direct marketing, sales promotions, personal selling). Nevertheless, all can be used at each level. Understanding the desired effects in each target market is the first step to building an effective IMC plan and establishing benchmarks for applying performance metrics to measure the plan's success.

High Involvement		Low Involvement	
Awareness	Cognitive	Awareness	Cognitive
Knowledge	(think)	Knowledge	(think)
Liking	Attitude	Purchase	Behavior
Preference	(feel)	Conviction	(do)
Conviction	Behavior	Liking	Attitude
Purchase	(do)	Preference	(feel)

Exhibit 13 - 1 Traditional Media Hierarchy of Effects for High- and Low-Involvement Product Decisions

Branding Versus Direct Response

Marketing communication can be used to build brand equity or to elicit a direct response in the form of a transaction or some other behavior (such as Web site registration or e-mail inquiry). The goal of **brand advertising** online is to put the brand name and product benefits in front of users. "Brand advertising creates a distinct favorable image that customers associate with a product at the moment they make buying decisions" (Doyle et al. 1997). Marketing public relations also aims to build brands, while sales promotion, direct marketing, and personal selling primarily attempt to solicit a direct response. **Direct-response advertising** seeks to motivate action. Brand communication works at the awareness and attitude levels of the hierarchy of effects model (heads and hearts), while direct-response communication primarily works at the behavioral level (do something).

Although every contact with a firm helps to create brand impressions in the heads and hearts of consumers, marketers tend to focus on only one type of strategy in each IMC campaign. Why, then, is all marketing communication not direct response? Marketers hope that all communication will contribute to sales in the long run, but consumers must first be made aware of a product before they will buy it. For high-involvement products, consumers must develop positive attitudes prior to purchase. Marketers must keep these principles in mind when selecting among IMC tools.

Internet Advertising

Advertising is nonpersonal communication of information through various media, usually persuasive in nature about products (goods and services) or ideas and usually paid for by an identified sponsor. All paid space on a Web site or in an e-mail is considered advertising. Internet advertising parallels traditional media advertising, in which companies create content and then sell space to outside advertisers. This can be confusing, especially when a **house banner** appears on a firm's own Web site. The key is exchange: If a firm pays money or barters with goods for space in which to put content it creates, the content is considered advertising. In Chapter 12 we discussed how firms create revenue streams from selling advertising space, but this and later sections discuss the flip side: buying advertising space from someone else to reach a firm's stakeholders. These specific definitions are meaningless to consumers (who view all commercial messages as advertising), but they are important to marketers because various MarCom tools help to accomplish different goals.

Trends in Internet Advertising

Internet advertising in the United States began with the first banner ads on Hotwired.com in 1994, reached $1 billion in 1998, grew to $8.2 billion in 2000, and dropped 12.3% in 2001 (Exhibit 13 - 2). This decline reflected the global economic

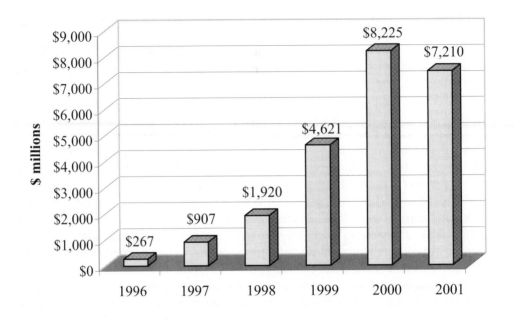

Exhibit 13 - 2 U.S. Internet Advertising Expenditures 1996 to 2001
Sources: PricewaterhouseCoopers IAB Internet Advertising Revenue Report (2002), "eMarketer Designates Interactive Advertising Bureau. . ." (2002), and "A Classic Scenario. . ." (2002).

recession and dot-com bankruptcies and is on par with the drop in U.S. advertising expenditures for all media ("No surprise: total. . ." 2002).

To understand the context of advertiser spending on the Internet, consider that total advertising expenditures in the United States alone during 2001 reached $99.8 billion ("No surprise: total. . ." 2002), compared with more than $400 billion worldwide in 1996. In other words, in 2001 Internet firms with space to sell only captured 7.2% of advertiser dollars (Exhibit 13 - 3). Contrary to the lofty predictions of the recent years, this proportion has remained constant: A Forrester survey of 50 traditional and Internet marketers revealed that companies responding spent 8% of their advertising budgets in 1999 on the Internet. Yet averages can be misleading— the Internet is actually an important advertising medium for particular industries and firms but not for all. This may change when a majority of consumers have high-bandwidth connections at home and can receive television programming over the Internet.

Which industries are advertising online? According to the Internet Advertising Bureau (IAB), most ad spending came from the following product categories in 2001:

- consumer related (30%)
- computing (18%)

- financial services (12%)
- media (12%)
- business services (9%)

This represents an increase in consumer-related, media, and financial service expenditures over time. Note that retailers comprise 50% of consumer related online advertising.

Internet Advertising Formats

E-mail, wireless content sponsorship, and Web sites are the three major vehicles for Internet advertising. E-mail and wireless advertising are most often text-based, tagging along on a consumer's incoming content from a third party. Conversely, Web advertising usually includes multimedia content. Still, Web site advertising can be as small as a line of text with an embedded hyperlink to the advertiser's site, and e-mail advertising can include graphics. However, based on the definition of advertising, note that HTML and multimedia e-mail messages sent from a firm directly to Internet users are direct marketing, not advertising.

As displayed in Exhibit 13 - 4, most advertising expenditures in 2001 were for banner ads, with sponsorships a close second, classifieds next, and then slotting fees, keyword search, and e-mail (www.iab.net). This reflects a 20% decline in banner ads since 1999 in favor of classifieds and new forms of advertising. Expenditures on e-mail, sponsorships, and interstitials has remained constant over the past three years.

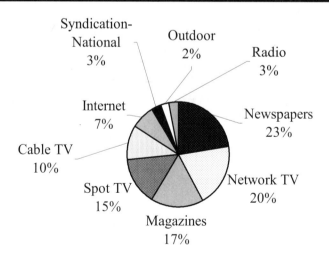

Exhibit 13 - 3 Proportion of Spending for Various Media of $99.8 Billion in 2001
Source: Data from "A Classic Scenario. . ." (2002).

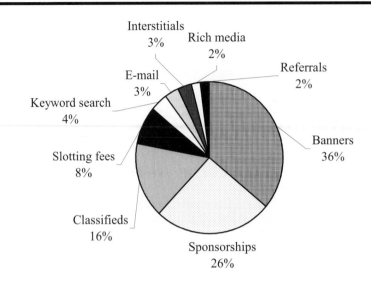

Exhibit 13 - 4 Proportion of Advertising Dollars by Format in 2001
Source: Compiled from data at www.iab.net.

E-Mail Advertising

By far the least expensive type of online advertising, **e-mail advertising,** is generally just a few sentences of text embedded in another firm's content. Advertisers purchase space in the e-mail sponsored by others (e.g., Hotmail). Exhibit 13 - 5 displays an e-mail ad that CDW purchased to accompany e-mail discussion among community members using the former Listbot service (now Microsoft List builder). As another example, firms sponsor e-mail newsletters such as those sent by eDietShop (see opening example). Exhibit 13 - 6 displays an ad for the *E-Mail Marketing Handbook* that helps to sponsor an interesting newsletter about marketing communication online from WordBiz.com. Despite a trend toward more HTML and rich media e-mail such as this ad, many users still prefer text-based e-mail due to its faster download time. As a result, before purchasing e-mail advertising, firms must be sure that their recipients closely match their own target markets.

Wireless Advertising

Forward-thinking marketers are closely watching developments in the mobile device market. As mentioned in Chapter 10, 6.5 million PDAs were purchased worldwide in 2002. Cell phones and laptop computers have even better penetration, with cell phones being the primary Internet device in many countries (see Chapter 15). Four

```
Date: Wed, 12 Apr 2000 16:59:34 -0700 (PDT)
From: "Lyzel C." <XXX@scs.unr.edu>
To: mgrs_324@listbot.com
Subject: Marketbyte

[message deleted]

_____

To unsubscribe, write to mgrs_324-unsubscribe@listbot.com
------------------------------------------------------------------
Advertisement:
Workstation with Monitor under $800!
So, you just heard that you need to add how many new workstations by
the end of next week? Check out the bundle below. It includes
everything you need to get everyone up and running quickly. http://www.listbot.com/links/cdw5
```

Exhibit 13 - 5 Embedded Text Advertisement in E-Mail Message

promising marketing communication techniques for mobile devices are discussed in this chapter: free mobile content delivery (marketing public relations), content sponsored advertising, and two direct marketing techniques—location marketing and short message services (SMS). In practice, the line between these techniques is blurred.

Content sponsored advertising for mobile devices is the wireless version of banners and other ads that sponsor Web content. Mobile ads employ the *pull* model of advertising: Users pull content from mobile Web sites and ads come along for the ride. Companies such as Microsoft and AvantGo offer free news and other content to mobile users, sponsored by a third-party advertiser (Exhibit 13 - 7).

Mobile ads are a new area with great promise and many unanswered questions. An important current debate involves whether mobile users would rather pay for content or receive advertising sponsored content. This is analogous to television—the audience can pay for cable TV programming with no commercials or receive advertising sponsored programming from stations. One survey of 3,300 mobile users in 11 global markets found users receptive to mobile ads, although 86% said there should be a clear benefit to them (Pastore 2002). In a study by Cahners In-Stat Group, 64% of respondents said they would not embrace mobile advertising unless they could decide whether or not to receive messages.

Several major issues may affect the future of mobile advertising. First, wireless bandwidth is currently small, so additional advertising content interferes with quick download of the requested information. Second, the smaller screen size of cell phones and PDAs greatly limits ad size. Third, it requires different techniques to track advertising effectiveness, although AvantGo does track page views and advertising click-throughs for content partners. Finally, most mobile users must pay their service provider by the minute while accessing the Internet—and many do not want to pay

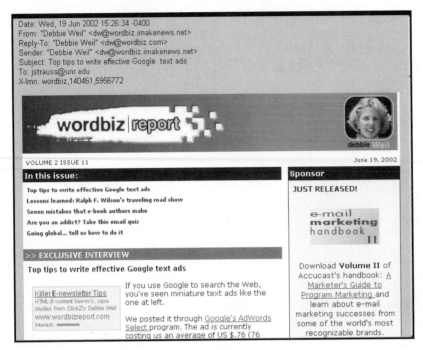

Exhibit 13 - 6 Advertisement in E-Mail Newsletter

for the time it takes to receive ads. In spite of these issues, content sponsored advertising on mobile devices is likely to increase in the future.

Web Site Advertising Formats

Anything goes with Web advertising: text—from a sentence to pages of story—graphics, sound, hyperlinks, or the Energizer Bunny hopping through a page. The following section discusses each commonly used format. By the time this book is in print, however, entirely new forms may have emerged, given the fast pace of Internet advertising.

Interactive Formats

Banners, buttons, skyscrapers, and other interactive formats occupy designated space for rent on Web pages. This is similar to the print advertising model used by magazines and newspapers, except on the Net there are video and audio capabilities in that few square inches of space. Buttons are square or round and banners are rectangular. The Interactive Advertising Bureau (IAB) and the Coalition for Advertising Supported Information and Entertainment (CASIE) have proposed standard dimensions for what they call *interactive formats*. Exhibit 13 - 8 displays the standard full banner—the most common banner size today (468 by 60 pixels)—along with two other popular sizes. A monitor set to standard VGA resolution has screen dimensions of 640 horizontal pixels by 480 vertical pixels, and a pixel is one

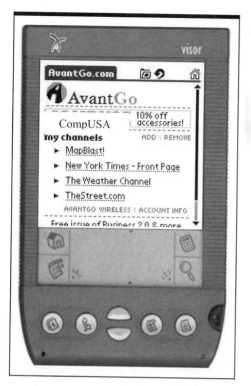

Exhibit 13 - 7 Content Sponsored Advertising on Visor PDA
Source: AvantGo, Inc: AvantGo Mobile Internet (www.avantgo.com).

dot of light on a computer or television screen. The newest look for interactive formats: skyscrapers (160 x 600 pixels) and large rectangles (360 x 300 pixels).

Some observers thought that the industry would eventually standardize online ad sizes, as in traditional media, to smooth the way for Web sites selling space and agencies designing ads. That hasn't happened because newer sizes and formats break through the online clutter and grab user attention better than do standard banners. In fact, DoubleClick reported serving over 8,000 different ad sizes in May 2002 alone ("DoubleClick Ad Serving. . ." 2002). Nonetheless, the IAB now suggests the following ad sizes in its attempt to create industry standards:

- Five differently sized rectangles and pop-ups
- Seven banners and buttons
- Two skyscrapers

All ads in this category are interactive, at least offering click-through. By clicking on the ad, the user is transported to the advertiser's Web site, where the transaction or other objective is actually achieved. Some banners enhance the interactivity by sensing the position of the mouse on the Web page and animating faster as the user approaches. Other banners have built-in games. Still other banners have drop-down menus, check boxes, and search boxes to engage and empower the

Click Here Now

480 X 60 Pixels

No, Here!

120 X 60 Pixels

Here!

88 X 31 Pixels

Exhibit 13 - 8 Three Most Common Banner Sizes: Full Banner, Button 2, and Microbar

user. Exhibit 13 - 9 displays a banner ad that allows users to interact by selecting items from a drop-down menu.

One downside of animated and highly interactive banners is that they tend to require more bandwidth. Keeping banner file sizes small reduces the time that they take to load. Ads under 9K in size usually appear before most content on a given Web page. Therefore, the ad is spotlighted on the user's screen if only for a split second. Users may not wait for large banner ads to download, but instead follow a hyperlink to leave the page before the ad loads—effectively making the ad invisible. With increased bandwidth and high-speed Net delivery to most homes, these interactive banners may become more important in the future.

How effective is banner advertising? Some say not at all, yet the advertising dollars pour in. E-marketers should measure results against the banner's objective to determine effectiveness. Research shows that Web banners help build brands and generate a small click-through (on average less than 0.5%). We'll return to this topic later in the chapter.

Sponsorships

Sponsorships integrate editorial content and advertising—something traditional publishers abhor. Most traditional media clearly separate content from advertising; women's magazines are an exception. Food advertisers usually barter for recipes that include their products in these magazines, and fashion advertisers get mentions of their clothing in articles. This practice pleases advertisers because it gives them additional exposure and creates the impression that the publication endorses their products. This blending of content by two firms is becoming increasingly adopted by Web sites: It now comprises 26% of all Web advertising expenditures.

Sponsorships are important on the Web as banners are easily overlooked by users and as more firms build synergistic partnerships to provide useful content. Sponsorships are particularly well suited for the Web because, in essence, the commercial side of the Web consists of a series of firms clamoring after similar targets. Traditional publishers such as NBC (www.msnbc.com) and *People* magazine are only two of the many companies selling advertising online. Another reason that

Exhibit 13 - 9 BuyComp Interactive Banner
Source: www.buycomp.com.

sponsorships are an increasing source of advertising revenues for Web sites is the interactive possibilities. See Exhibit 13 - 10 for the Candystand Web site, sponsored by Life Savers candy. Each link at the site leads to a game sponsored by one of the Life Savers candies.

Note that in Exhibit 13 - 10 the sponsor is clearly identified. Consumers know that this content is brought to them by Life Savers in conjunction with Candystand. Some people worry about the ethics of sponsorships when consumers cannot easily identify the content author(s). Perhaps this is not a problem because many users view the entire Web as one giant advertisement, but when advertising is passed off as locally generated content, it can potentially lower user trust in the Web site and hurt brand image. Addressing this important issue, the IAB recently established a panel to set standards for sponsor disclosure in this type of advertising.

Slotting Fees

A **slotting fee** is "a fee charged to advertisers by media companies to get premium positioning on their site, category exclusivity or some other special treatment" (Glossary on www.IAB.net). Slotting fees have been charged for many years but the IAB just began measuring them in 2001. Special positioning comprises 8% of all advertising formats online. It is important because many search engines charge for the top few positions in search query return page, and in the attention economy a

Exhibit 13 - 10 Life Savers Sponsorship at Candystand
Source: www.candystand.com. Used with permission of Nabisco, Inc.

better ad or hyperlink position has a better chance of being seen. These position fees parallel traditional print advertising practices. For example, magazine publishers charge a premium for an ad on the back cover. Incidentally, it is no coincidence that this term was coined for online advertising positioning: It is analogous to the slotting fee charged by retailers for an advantageous shelf position.

Interstitials, Superstitials, and Other Rich Media Ads

Interstitials are Java-based ads that appear while the publisher's content is loading. They represent only 3% of all Web advertising expenditures. Interstitials held great promise when they were first introduced, but their number has not increased for the last few years. One reason is that they are hard to execute properly; another is that they give the impression of lengthening user waiting time, which is not good.

The next iteration of interstitials is called superstitials. Created by Unicast, these feature videolike ads timed to appear when a user moves her mouse from one part of a Web site to another (www.unicast.com). Superstitials look like mini videos, using Flash technology and Java to make them entertaining and fast. The advantage of superstitials over interstitials is that the former loads behind the scenes and doesn't appear until it is fully loaded on the user's computer. Thus, a superstitial doesn't slow page download time, nor does the user have the impression that it does. Agency.com, a dot-com ad agency, designed a superstitial for British Airways that created an amazing 20% click-through. Of course, anything new on the Web draws attention.

An important variation of interstitials is **daughter windows** or *pop-ups*. These ads usually appear in a separate window that overlays the current browser window. To find an example, simply visit Geocities. Many people are irritated by daughter windows because users must close them.

The **Shoshkele**, created by United Virtualities (also called a floater ad or screen interrupt) is a five-to-eight second Flash animation that runs through a Web page to capture user attention. The Energizer Bunny was among the first Shoshkeles, creating a lot of excitement as it hopped through and interrupted the page text. A recent Shoshkele appeared at Speedvision.com. After arriving at the page, the screen slowly darkened to the point of making the text unreadable, and then a hand emerged at the lower left corner and sparked up a Zippo lighter to illuminate the page again before disappearing. These ads are enjoyable to some and invasive to others because they can't be stopped. Web technology allows for many interesting multimedia advertising formats. The novelty of new formats such as Shoshkeles captures consumer attention, but the traditional rules persist: Marketing communication success is about reaching the right audience with the right message at the right time.

Marketing Public Relations (MPR)

Public relations (PR) consists of activities that influence public opinion and create goodwill for an organization. PR is used to create goodwill among a number of different publics including company shareholders and employees, the media, suppliers, and the local community, as well as consumers, business buyers, and many other stakeholder groups. **Marketing public relations (MPR)** includes brand-related activities and nonpaid, third-party media coverage to positively influence target markets. Thus, MPR is the portion of PR directed to the firm's customers and prospects in order to build awareness and positive attitudes about its brands. For example, during the week of the ninth MTV Music Awards, MTV.com site traffic increased by 48% to 1.1 million visitors as people logged on to learn more about the stars nominated for awards (Carr, 2000). MPR activities using Internet technology include the Web site content itself, online community building, and online events.

Web Site

Every organization, company, or brand Web site is an MPR tool because it serves as electronic brochure, including current product and company information. According to the Direct Marketing Association, "As marketers gain a better understanding of their ROI, they have begun to allocate more resources to online site development than to promoting their Web sites as the way to increase their profitability. Improving the customers' experience online is now a priority (see www.the-dma.org)." For example, Butterball's site (www.butterball.com), which features cooking and carving tips, received 550,000 visitors in one day during Thanksgiving week. Although it costs the firm money to create such a Web site, it is not considered advertising (paid for space on another firm's site). **Brochureware** is used to describe sites that exist only to inform customers about products or services. The term has its roots in the early days of the Web when all sites were exclusively brochureware.

In addition to this Web content, firms usually include press releases about brands on their Web sites and send them electronically via e-mail or the Web to media firms for publishing. The resulting brand publicity is part of most company MPR strategies.

There are several advantages of using the Web for publishing product information. First, the Web is a low-cost alternative to paper brochures or press releases sent in overnight mail. Second, product information is often updated in company databases so Web page content is always current. Finally, the Web can reach new prospects who are searching for particular products.

What Do Web Users Want?

Many books discuss how to create effective Web sites. The most important point is to create a site that satisfies the firm's target audiences. Web sites can entertain (games and electronic postcards), build community (online events, chat rooms, and e-mail discussion groups), provide a communication channel with the customer (customer feedback and customer service), provide information (product selection, product recommendation, retailer referrals), and assist in site navigation (search buttons, drop-down menus, and check boxes). In general, this is what most users want (partially from Frost and Strauss 2002):

- **Value.** Users want information, entertainment, or to accomplish other goals such as buying merchandise at Web sites. If a Web site doesn't quickly give users what they want—or if the information is outdated—they'll go elsewhere.

- **Information acquisition.** Some people acquire and organize information visually, while others prefer aural or tactile cues. Web developers should include graphics and video for visual learners, consider sound for aural learners, and provide plenty of clicking or play action for tactile types. Also, some users go straight for the text links and others look for visual cues. It is safest to provide information in many different formats to accommodate all styles. A great example of this is the Microsoft site that on the same page allows users to search four different ways! Users can click on a product type from the navigation menu, search for keywords using the Find It button, select from an alphabetical list of products from a drop-down menu, or click on a popular product family. See Exhibit 13 - 11.

- **Information overload.** Everyone suffers from this, but it becomes acute when Web surfers face the plethora of online treasures. Developers can help users by providing good site organization with page design that draws readers through the graphics and text in a meaningful way.

- **Short attention span.** Unless highly motivated by content, users will only wait 7 to 10 seconds for a page to download. They will scan a page quickly, trying to find what they want, and move on immediately if they don't find it. Developers can use page layout, navigation, and other principles covered in this chapter to assist users.

- **Lost in cyberspace.** It is easy to get lost within or among Web sites. Search tools, indexes, and good organization of pages and page elements all help.

- **Content anywhere, anytime.** The wireless Web sends content to users with PDAs, cell phones, and other mobile devices. Due to small screen sizes, mobile users cannot access regular Web sites, which is why firms create special sites for these devices. For example, Travelocity.com allows users to enter flight number, airline, and day of travel into a handheld device and receive database information about the exact departure time and gate number for the flight. Similarly, **telematics** is a communication system in an automobile that uses a global positioning system (GPS) for interactive communication between firms and

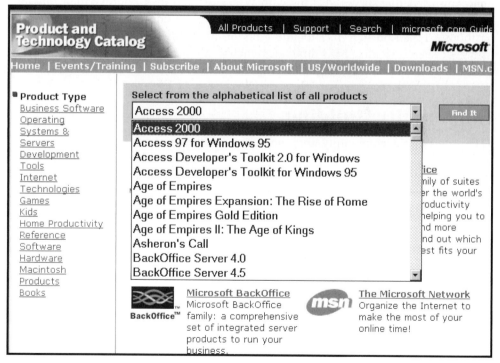

Exhibit 13 - 11 Microsoft Provides Multiple Ways to Search for Products

Source: www.microsoft.com. Copyright © 2000 Microsoft Corporation, One Microsoft Way, Redmond, Washington 98052-6399. All rights reserved.

drivers. This system allows drivers to receive directions and Internet content or send for emergency help.

Search Engine Optimization (SEO)

Web sites can attract traffic using a variety of online and offline marketing communication techniques. However, one is unique to the online environment: **Search Engine Optimization (SEO)**. According to Jupiter Media Metrix, nearly 47% of Web users surveyed said that the most common way they find products or online stores is through search engines. Because the top 10 results to a search query get 78% more traffic than subsequent listings, many firms use SEO to be sure their site is high on the list. To do this, firms first register with the top and niche search engines for their industry. Although search engine robots are constantly looking for new Web pages, registration accelerates the process. Next, firms use keywords that describe their sites in hidden HTML tags located by search engines (metatags). They also carefully craft the text and titles on their pages to reflect these topic areas, even purposefully including different spellings of keywords that users might type into the search engine (e.g., email and e-mail). Exhibit 13 - 12 shows these and other important ways that surveyed firms with Web sites said they improve their rankings at search engines. Remember that many search engines charge a slotting fee for top positions—13% said they pay for the links or clicks-throughs. To stay high on the listing of search results, SEO strategies change almost daily. As soon as one firm finds a way to come out on top, others imitate and kill the leader's advantage.

Community Building

Many sites build community through online chat rooms, discussion groups, and online events. Amazon allows users to write their own book reviews and read and rate the reviews of others. To the extent that Web sites gather folks with similar

Method	Percent
Changing metatags	61
Changing page titles	44
Reciprocal linking	32
Purchasing multiple domain names	28
Multiple home pages (doorways)	21
Hiding keywords in background	18
Paid links/pay per click	13
None of the above	13

Exhibit 13 - 12 Methods Used to Improve Search Engine Rankings

Source: Adapted from www.iconocast.com.

interests, users will keep returning to see what their cyber friends are discussing and doing online. Online interest communities from diverse geographic locations are one of the Net's big promises that is being fulfilled for users and capitalized upon by marketers. This includes business communities as well as consumer groups.

Online communities form the basis of bulletin boards and LISTSERV e-mailing. A bulletin board or newsgroup is an area where users can post e-mail messages on selected topics for other users to read. The largest public newsgroup forum is the Usenet, which has 35,000 groups (accessed at groups.google.com/) and contains lots of community discussion about product experiences, among other topics. A LISTSERV is an e-mail discussion group with regular subscribers. Each message that members send to the LISTSERV is forwarded to all subscribed members. LISTSERVs push content to the e-mailboxes of subscribed users, whereas bulletin boards require users to visit the page and pull content.

An interesting new development is the use of offline events to spark online communities. For example, WOW Entertainment representatives take digital pictures of female wrestling stars with their fans at events. Using an assigned number, the fan can access the picture online, turn it into an electronic postcard, and send it to friends ("Female Wrestling Co. . ." 2001). Chapter 14 discusses the many ways that online community building develops relationships with customers.

Online Events

Online events are designed to generate user interest and draw traffic to a site. In a highly publicized event, Amazon let users contribute to a story started by the author John Updike. Each year Land Rover sponsors the Camel Trophy race through exotic regions of the world. Land Rover allows users to receive updates from the race at its Web site. Perhaps the most memorable commercial online event occurred in 1999 when Victoria Secret held a Web-based fashion show. The firm announced it in advertisements in the *New York Times*, Super Bowl football game, and other traditional media. The event drew 1.2 million visitors, an 82% increase in Web traffic and the firm's Web servers could not handle all the traffic. The tradition continued in subsequent years, although in 2001 Victoria Secret televised the show and put only highlights on the Web site. As bandwidth problems disappear, expect more online multimedia events.

Companies and organizations can hold seminars, workshops, and discussions online. A publisher might encourage people interested in a new book to chat with the author at an online forum. Companies use forthcoming events as legitimate reasons to e-mail potential clients as well as their existing clients. Holding online events in which clients get to "talk to" senior or prestigious people may be seen as one more valuable reason for being a client of a particular organization. It also saves considerable time and cost compared to holding or attending a physical seminar.

Sales Promotion Offers

Sales promotions are short-term incentives of gifts or money that facilitate the movement of products from producer to end user. Sales promotion activities include coupons, rebates, product sampling, contests, sweepstakes, and premiums (free or low-cost gifts). Of these, coupons, sampling, and contests/sweepstakes are widely used on the Internet. The Direct Marketing Association predicts that Internet promotions will comprise 70% of the worldwide $170 billion dollar promotional market in 2004, up from 15% in 1999 (www.investors.com). This is because sales promotion works. Marketers report three to five times higher response rates with online promotions than with direct mail. Whereas most offline sales promotion tactics are directed to businesses in the distribution channel, online tactics are directed primarily to consumers. As with offline consumer sales promotions, many are used in combination with advertising. Sales promotions are popular banner ad content and are also good for drawing users to a Web site, enticing them to stay, and compelling them to return. Online sales promotion tactics can build brands, build databases, and support increased online or offline sales.

Coupons

Coupons are big business online. Coolsavings.com and Valuepage.com are the top two Web sites offering online coupons from a myriad of online and offline clients; however, many coupons are delivered via e-mail. E-coupon firms also send e-mail notification as new coupons become available on the Web, attempting to build brand loyalty. One study found that 55% of online users prefer to receive e-mail coupons, as compared with 30% preferring newspapers and 18% preferring snail mail ("e-Consumers prefer eMail. . .," 2001).

H.O.T! coupons is in the top 10 among the many firms offering electronic coupons. It provides local coupons, allowing consumers to search the database by zip code (Exhibit 13 - 13). H.O.T! coupons has its roots in a 350-franchise direct-mail distribution system. According to Jeff McIntosh of H.O.T! coupons, most postal mailings result only in a 1% to 2% coupon redemption, but H.O.T! coupons can add value by putting coupons on the Web site as well as in a traditional mail package. When retailers drive customers to the Web site through point-of-purchase or traditional advertising, coupon redemption increases substantially.

Retailer J. Crew sends electronic coupons to customers via e-mail. Following is an excerpt of e-mail written in response to a customer complaint sent by e-mail via a feedback button at the J. Crew Web site.

> As an expression of our sincere regret for the inconvenience you have experienced, we have attached a Merchandise Certificate for use with your next catalog order. We hope you will consider giving us another opportunity to serve you.
> MERCHANDISE CERTIFICATE $20.00

Exhibit 13 - 13 H.O.T! Coupons Distributes Coupons in Most Local Areas
Source: www.hotcoupons.com.

> MERCHANDISE CERTIFICATE TOWARD YOUR NEXT PURCHASE FROM THE J. CREW CATALOG. BE SURE TO MENTION #12345 TO YOUR ORDER CONSULTANT OR INCLUDE THIS CERTIFICATE WITH YOUR MAIL ORDER.

Interestingly, the customer does not have to clip the coupon but merely has to give the number included in the e-mail to a telephone staff member or type it into the Web site order form when placing an order. CDNOW also sends out coupons periodically to customers.

Sampling

Some sites allow users to sample digital product prior to purchase. Many software companies provide free download of fully functional demo versions of their software. The demo normally expires in 30 to 60 days, after which time users can choose to purchase the software or remove it from their system. Online music stores allow customers to sample 30-second clips of music before ordering the CD. Market research firms often offer survey results as a sampling to entice businesses to purchase reports. For example, Jupiter Media Metrix posts the results of its monthly survey of top Web sites on the Web site for prospects to see, use, and, thus, perhaps discover a need for more in-depth data.

Contests and Sweepstakes

Many sites hold contests and sweepstakes to draw traffic and keep users returning. Contests require skill (e.g., trivia answer) whereas sweepstakes involve only a pure chance drawing for the winners. Just as in the brick-and-mortar world, these sales promotion activities create excitement about brands and entice customers to visit a retailer. They persuade users to move from page to page on a Web site, thus increasing site stickiness. If sweepstake offers are changed regularly, users will return to the site to check out the latest chance to win. According to Jupiter MediaMetrix, online sweepstakes appear to be growing in popularity: In early 2001, 36% of the most successful new Web sites were sweepstakes sites. Freestuff2000 does an excellent job of consolidating sales promotions from many Web sites (see Exhibit 13 - 14).

Orbitz.com entered the online travel agent market in mid-June 2001 after competitors Travelocity.com and Expedia.com were well established. Nonetheless, the site drew 1.9 million customers in its first month, partly because of a huge

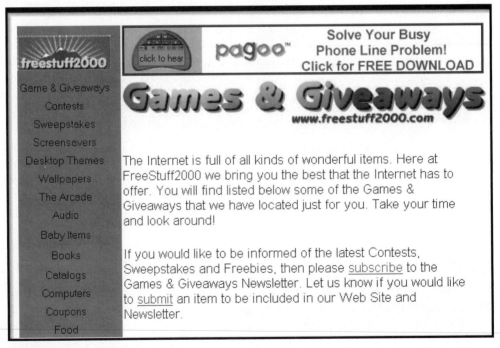

Exhibit 13 - 14 Freestuff2000.com Consolidates Sales Promotions from Many Web Sites
Source: www.freestuff2000.com.

sweepstakes featured in radio advertising. Every visitor who registered on the site was eligible for the free round-trip ticket given away every hour, 24/7, for six weeks (Orbitz, 2001).

Direct Marketing

According to the Direct Marketing Association, **direct marketing** is "any direct communication to a consumer or business recipient that is designed to generate a response in the form of an order *(direct order)*, a request for further information *(lead generation)*, and/or a visit to a store or other place of business for purchase of specific a product(s) or service(s) *(traffic generation)* (source: www.the-dma.org/)." It includes such techniques as telemarketing, outgoing e-mail, and postal mail—of which catalog marketing is a big part. Targeted banner ads and other forms of advertising and sales promotions that solicit a direct response are also considered direct marketing. For simplicity, and because e-mail is the Internet's "killer app," we focus our discussion of direct marketing communication on this application and its wireless offspring, **short message services (SMS).** In Chapter 14 we discuss e-mail's customer relationship building implications.

E-Mail

With 8 billion e-mails a year flying over the Internet worldwide, the typical user spends over one-third of all time online managing e-mail. Marketing related e-mail is 22% of a typical Internet user's in-box, of which half is unwanted spam (Mardesich 2001).

E-mail has several advantages over postal direct mail (Exhibit 13 - 15). First, there are no postage or printing charges. The average cost of an e-mail message is less than $0.01, compared to $0.50 to $2.00 for direct mail. Second, e-mail offers an immediate and convenient avenue for direct response; in fact, e-mail ads often direct users to Web sites using hyperlinks. Third, and perhaps most important, e-mail can be automatically individualized to meet the needs of specific users. For example, Exhibit 13 - 16 displays one author's monthly e-mail from MCI regarding American Airlines frequent flyer miles earned via long distance calls. Finally, e-mail is quicker than postal mail.

Conversely, e-mail's disadvantages include **spam** (unsolicited e-mail) and difficulty in finding appropriate e-mail lists. Consumers are much more upset about spam than they are about unsolicited postal mail (more later on this topic). While many highly targeted and accurate direct-mail lists exist for postal addresses, e-mail lists are hard to obtain and maintain. Lists can be built any of three ways: generated through Web site registrations, subscription registrations, or purchase records; rented from a list broker; or harvested from newsgroup postings or online e-mail directories—though this practice is questionable, for reasons to be mentioned shortly. Only 15% of the 150 million U.S. postal addresses can be associated with e-mail addresses that identify particular individuals (as compared with about 75 million

	E-mail	**Postal Mail**
Delivery cost per thousand	$30	$500
Creative costs to develop	$1,000	$17,000
Click through rate	10%	N/A
Customer conversion rate	5%	3%
Execution time	3 weeks	3 months
Response time	48 hours	3 weeks

Exhibit 13 - 15 Metrics for Electronic and Postal Mail
Source: Jupiter Communications as cited in "E-Mail and the Different. . ."

phone numbers connected to postal addresses) ("The Value of. . .," 2001). Thus, although nearly 50% of the U.S. population has one or more e-mail addresses, at this time it is very difficult to match a list of these with individual customers and prospects in a firm's database. And as soon as a good list exists, individuals change their e-mail addresses—a problem because no forwarding system for e-mail addresses exists like the ones for telephone and postal addresses (a good business opportunity?). E-marketers must remember that e-mail is not simply postal mail minus the paper and postage. E-mail offers the chance for real dialogue with individual customers, as well as a way to develop broad and deep customer relationships instead of merely using it to acquire customers.

Firms can use outgoing e-mail to make announcements, to send promotional offers, or to communicate anything important and relevant to stakeholders. When Amazon tested free shipping on orders over $49 in 2001, CEO Jeff Bezos sent a message to Amazon's customers informing them of the new offering. Microsoft e-mails registered users when new software patches are available for download. Many firms send out periodic e-mail newsletters (refer to Exhibit 13 - 6), an excellent tool for communicating with clients; small wonder that 80% of U.S. online customers enjoy receiving them. E-mail newsletters are a growth area because they provide many benefits:

- Regularly and legitimately promoting the company name to clients.
- Personalizing the communication with tailored content.
- Positioning the company as an expert in a subject.
- Pointing recipients back to the company Web site.
- Being easy for clients to pass along to others.
- Paying for themselves by carrying small advertisements.

E-postcards are another alternative. Firms send e-mail to users informing them of a Web site address and claim number for viewing a digital postcard. Usually the firm uses its own site or a special fulfillment site because commercial sites such as Blue Mountain Arts do not allow postcards to be sent in bulk. IKEA sent e-mail postcards to promote its San Francisco store opening; Johnson and Johnson sent postcards to its target for the adolescent skin care brand, Clean & Clear. The postcards included audio, and kids could even record their own voices and send additional postcards to

Date: Mon, 14 Feb 2002 09:13:14 -0500
To: Judy Strauss <jstrauss@unr.edu>
From: MCI WorldCom <statement@email.mciworld.com>
Subject: Monthly Mileage Statement

Dear Judy Strauss,

Your monthly statement helps you keep track of the AAdvantage miles you're earning with the MCI/AAdvantage program.

MCI WorldCom Account Number: XXX
American Airlines Frequent Flyer Number: XXX

MCI AADVANTAGE MILES EARNED

ON YOUR LAST BILL:
PROGRAM TO DATE:

160
44785

See your miles online anytime. Go to Online Account Manager at
www.mci.com/service.

Aadvantage miles represented in this statement reflect your prior month's balance. These AAdvantage miles have been sent for posting to your American Airlines AAdvantage account. Please allow 6-8 weeks for AAdvantage miles earned to appear on your account.

Exhibit 13 - 16 Individualized E-Mail to Account Holder

friends, all with the Clean & Clear message, of course (thus initiating viral marketing).

Opt-In, Opt-Out

When renting e-mail address lists from list brokers, marketers should search for lists that are guaranteed to be 100% opt-in. This means that users have voluntarily agreed to receive commercial e-mail about topics of interest to them. NetCreations' PostMaster Direct is such a list broker, with over 50 million opt-in names and e-mail addresses, 13 million of which are segmented by 235 countries outside of the United States (www.netcreations.com/). Brokers rent lists rather than sell them because they prefer to charge a fee for each mailing. The cost to rent from NetCreations is about $0.15

per name ($150 CPM—cost per thousand) for B2C market lists, and $250 CPM for the B2B market. Compare this to a typical B2C postal mail list rental at $20 CPM.

Web users have lots of opportunity to opt-in to mailing lists at Web sites, often by simply checking a box and entering an e-mail address. Research shows that lists with opt-in members get much higher response than do lists without. Marketing messages to opt-in lists can generate response rates of up to 90%, quite good when compared to 0.05% click-through rates on banner ads. For instance, Ticketmaster reported a 90% click-through a mailing offering additional merchandise to Bruce Springsteen fans who had already bought a ticket for an upcoming concert. Opt-in lists may be successful, in large part, because users often receive coupons, cash, or products for responding. With this technique, marketers are shifting marketing dollars directly to consumers for rewards in lieu of purchasing advertising space.

Opt-out is similar to opt-in; however, users have to uncheck the box on a Web page to prevent being put on the e-mail list. Some marketers question this practice because users do not always read a Web page thoroughly enough to evaluate the meaning of checked boxes and, therefore, may be surprised and upset at receiving e-mail later. Some U.S. legislators have proposed laws banning opt-out e-mail.

Opt-in techniques are part of a bigger traditional marketing strategy called **permission marketing.** According to Seth Godin (1999), permission marketing is about turning strangers into customers. How to do this? Ask people what they are interested in, ask permission to send them information, and then do it in an entertaining, educational, or interesting manner. We expect opt-in techniques to evolve and grow considerably over the next few years.

Viral Marketing

Viral marketing is a bad name for a great technique. When individuals forward e-mail to friends, co-workers, family, and others on their e-mail lists, they are using what we like to call *word of mouse*. More commonly known as **viral marketing**, this is the online equivalent of word of mouth. Viral marketing works and it's free. Hotmail started with only a $50,000 promotion budget (as compared with the $50 to $100 million needed to launch a brand offline). The firm simply sent some e-mail telling folks about its Web-based e-mail service, and within six months the firm had 1 million registered users (Ransdell 1999). Eighteen months after the launch, it had 12 million subscribers and Microsoft acquired the firm for $400 million in Microsoft stock.

There are many other viral marketing success stories—among them, Dell Computer, the six month 0 to 50% MP3 adoption rate, and the *Blair Witch Project* film. Lions Gate films sent 16,000 people e-mail for 30 days prior to the 1999 opening of *American Psycho*. The twist that made it work as viral marketing is that the e-mails were from the film's main character, a serial killer. Recipients got a kick out of passing these notes to others.

Short Text Messaging (SMS)

Short text messages are 160 characters of text sent by one user to another over the Internet, usually with a cell phone or PDA. This is different from **instant messaging,** short messages sent among users who are online at the same time. SMS, which uses a store-and-send technology that only holds messages for a few days, is particularly attractive to cell phone users because they can communicate quickly and inexpensively. When users send short text messages, they are charged cell phone minutes, but the cost is minimal compared to using the phone for a conversation. In addition, SMS is easy because users do not have to open e-mail or other software to send or receive. Instead, they simply type the message on the phone keyboard. In Japan, consumers are reportedly so adept at this they have created what is called the "thumb culture" (because they rapidly type out messages using their thumbs).

By one estimate, 200 billion short text messages a month were flying between mobile phones worldwide by the end of 2002 (Silk, 2001). The Japanese are quite advanced with SMS use, and Europeans are not far behind. In the United Kingdom alone, SMS is the technology of choice for peer-to-peer communication, with users currently sending an estimated 1 billion messages a month.

How can marketers capitalize on SMS use? Most experts agree that marketers can build relationships by sending permission-based information to customers when and where they want to receive it. To be successful, the messages should be short, personalized, interactive, and relevant. Some customers might want to receive an SMS warning about pending natural disasters from their insurance firm, an SMS notification of an upcoming flight delay, or notification of an overnight shipment.

In one interesting example, Heineken, the global beer brand, used an SMS sales promotion to capitalize on the British pub tradition of quiz nights. Typically a quiz night consists of a loyal pub customer shouting out a series of questions to which other customers answer on paper score sheets. Winners receive free pints or meals. Using a combination of online and offline promotion, Heineken placed point-of-purchase signs in pubs inviting customers to call a phone number from cell phones or other mobile devices, and type in the word "play" as a text message (SMS). In response, the customer received a series of three multiple-choice questions to answer. Correctly answering all the questions scored a food or beverage prize to be redeemed by giving a special verifiable number to the bartender—and 20% of all players won. "Feedback was that it was a great promotion. . .consumers found it fun and sellers found it to be a hook," said Iain Newell, marketing controller at Interbrew, which owns the Heineken brand.

Location-Based Marketing

A few marketers have experimented with **location-based marketing:** promotional offers that are pushed to mobile devices and customized based on the user's physical location. The technology behind this is either a global positioning system (GPS) in a handheld device or automobile (telematics) or user address information stored in a database. Lycos spent $1.2 million in 2001 turning some Boston and New York taxicabs into animated billboards by sending relevant ads based on the cab's physical location. The GPS device sent physical coordinates to the ad server, which then returned financial ads when the cab was in the financial district, and so forth. In one study of 3,300 people in 11 countries, 88% said they would be receptive to getting coupons on their mobile devices for redeeming at a store near their physical location (Pastore 2002). Imagine receiving a short text message on your cell phone offering a free beverage while driving by your favorite restaurant!

Spam

Now for the dirty side of e-mail marketing. Netizens do not like unsolicited e-mail because it shifts the burden of selectivity from sender to recipient. Users developed the term *spam* as a pejorative reference to this type of e-mail. Marketers must be careful because viral marketing can work in reverse as well. Recipients of e-mail perceived as spam can vent their opposition to thousands of users in public newsgroup forums and to friends on e-mail lists, thereby quickly generating negative publicity for the organization. The Nike Corporation is so sensitive to spam that it published an antispam policy that reads as follows:

> Nike does not sell, trade, or otherwise transfer outside the company personally identifiable information that visitors voluntarily provide in any registration or contest submission. This information is used to better understand visitors' use of Nike's site and to support related transactions made on the site.
>
> However, this data in an aggregate form may be provided to other parties for marketing, advertising, or other uses. For example, the majority of visitors to Nike.com are boys age 8 to 18. Nike may also use e-mail addresses and other personally identifiable information to contact visitors who communicate with us. For example, we direct e-mail to visitors who provide us with their e-mail addresses for specific purposes such as receiving our e-mail newsletters or being notified if they have won one of our contests. Each e-mail newsletter always contains instructions on how to discontinue receipt of the newsletter. However, if a visitor at anytime chooses to no longer receive such information and opt-out from any future mailings, they should simply reply to any Nike e-mail sent to them and type UNSUBSCRIBE as the subject of their reply.

Spammers routinely harvest e-mail addresses from newsgroup postings and then spam all the newsgroup members. Spam lists can also be generated from public directories such as those provided by many universities to look up student e-mail addresses. Spammers often hide their return e-mail addresses so that the recipients cannot reply. Other unscrupulous tactics include spamming through a legitimate organization's e-mail server so that the message appears to come from an employee of that organization.

Incidentally, spam is a problem in the B2B market as well as the B2C market. Editorial staff from the media complain about getting spam from public relations personnel at firms. James Fallows, a journalist from *The Industry Standard,* gave an example of the typical note he receives from folks he has never met nor heard of:

> Subject: New Company Meeting
> From: Frankie@AcmePR.com
> Hi Jim,
> My client will be in the area on Wednesday, April 12, is there any way you could take a quick meeting? [blah, blah, blah about the company]. Please let me know ASAP for a meeting, thanks!
> Best, Frankie

Some measures have been put in place to limit spam. Many moderated newsgroups filter spam, and most e-mail programs offer users the option to filter spam as well. There have also been a number of suits filed by ISPs seeking to recover costs from spammers for the strain on their systems from the tremendous number of spam messages. Remember that all unsolicited e-mail is considered spam; still, as with direct mail, when the e-mail is appropriate and useful to the recipient, it is welcomed, unsolicited or not.

It is increasingly common for opt-in lists to remind users that they are not being spammed. Usually a disclaimer appears right at the beginning of the message, "You are receiving this message because you requested to be notified about...". The message also advises users how they can easily request to be removed from the list. This is important since many users do not realize that they opted-in—especially if they did so far in the past or in an unrelated context.

Privacy

Databases drive e-mail marketing. This requires collecting personal information, both online and offline, and using it to send commercial e-mail, customized Web pages, banners ads, and more. Astute marketers have found that consumers will readily give personal information to firms that use it to provide value and that do not share it with others unless given permission. For example, Amazon.com has implicit permission to collect customers' purchase information in the database and serve it collectively to others looking for book recommendations. Users don't mind this because they receive valuable information and their privacy is guarded on an individual level. Amazon also has permission to send customers e-mail notification of books that might interest each individual. When Amazon announced that it would share customer databases with partners, there was a huge media backlash. This proves, once again, that firms that desire to build customer relationships must guard the privacy of customer data. This topic is discussed more thoroughly in Chapters 5 and 14.

The Internet as a Medium

Up to this point we have been describing how promotion tools can be put to work on the Internet. Now we will focus on how marketers view the Internet as just one of many media to carry marketing communication messages. TV, radio, newspapers, magazines, outdoor (e.g., kiosks, bus cards, and billboards), and direct mail are all channels of communication, as is the Internet. Because the Internet is often compared with traditional media, marketers need to understand the major media's characteristics as well as the Internet's media characteristics so they can make appropriate choices when buying promotional space.

The Medium Is Not the Appliance

Marketers should understand that the medium is not the same as the receiving appliance. Messages are sent by content sponsors in electronic form via satellite, telephone wires, or cable, and then received by the audience through appliances (also called receivers) such as televisions, computers, radios, cell phones, PDAs, and so on. Bear in mind that the receiving appliance is separate from the media transmission because this mind-set allows for flexibility. For example, computers can receive digital radio and television transmissions, and television can receive the Web. Some appliances, such as radio and FAX machines, have limited receiving capabilities, while others are more flexible. Today the computer is the only appliance that allows all types of two-way digital multimedia electronic transmissions. This idea is both mind boggling and exciting because of the business opportunities. Separating the medium from the appliance opens the door to new types of receiving appliances that are also "smart," allowing for saving, editing, and sending transmissions. So, next time you think of television programming, remember that by the year 2008 it will be simply digitized video that can be sent several ways to a number of receiving devices.

Media Characteristics

Electronic media include network television, radio, cable television, the Internet, Fax machine, cellular phone, and pager. We present these media as broadcast, narrowcast, and pointcast on the basis of their capability to reach mass audiences, smaller audiences, or even individuals with different messages. Other traditional media competing for marketing communication dollars include print and direct mail.

Broadcast Media

Broadcast media (TV and radio) have a number of strengths and weaknesses, as reflected in Exhibit 13 - 17. TV penetration reaches over 98% of U.S. households, with one-third owning three or more sets. TV remains the only medium for advertisers wanting to reach large numbers of consumers at one time, but it is costly ($70,000 to $550,000 for 30 seconds of prime time in the United States). Radio's penetration

Criterion	TV	Radio	Magazine	Newspaper	Direct Mail	Web
Involvement	passive	passive	active	active	active	interactive
Media Richness	multi-media	audio	text and graphic	text and graphic	text and graphic	multi-media
Geographic Coverage	global	local	global	local	varies	global
CPM	low	lowest	high	medium	high	medium
Reach	high	medium	low	medium	varies	medium
Targeting	good	good	excellent	good	excellent	excellent
Track Effectiveness	fair	fair	fair	fair	excellent	excellent
Message Flexibility	poor	good	poor	good	excellent	excellent

Exhibit 13 - 17 Strengths and Weaknesses of Major Media

is also ubiquitous. Almost every household and car has a radio. Radio advertising time is inexpensive ($20 to $200 for 60 seconds) and has excellent local market coverage.

Narrowcast Medium

Cable TV (CATV) is a narrowcast medium. It is called *narrowcast* because cable channels contain very focused electronic content appealing to special-interest markets. For example, cable channels such as CNN or ESPN are networks in that they reach extremely large audiences worldwide, but they still have very specialized programming. CATV advertising tends to be less expensive than broadcast advertising, although there are exceptions.

Pointcast Media

The folks at www.pointcast.com, who brought individualized news service to every computer desktop, coined the term *pointcast*. **Pointcast media** are electronic media with the capability of transmitting to an audience of just one person, such as the Internet and the cell phone. Pointcast media can transmit either personalized or standardized messages in bulk to the entire audience of those who have the equipment to receive them, and these individuals can transmit a single message back to the sender using the same equipment. Receiving devices include pagers, cell phones, PDAs, computers, TV, Fax machines, and more. Fax machines are the only pointcast receiving device where unsolicited marketing communications are illegal. This is due to the cost of receiving messages.

From a media buyer's perspective, the strengths of the Internet include selective targeting with e-mail and Web content by using databases, ability to track advertising effectiveness, flexibility of message length and delivery timing, ability to reach global markets with one advertising buy (e.g., the Yahoo! portal), and interactivity. The Internet is the first electronic medium to allow active, self-paced viewing (similar to print media), and it is the first and best medium for interactivity. In fact, many say that with the Internet, users create their own content. The Internet's weaknesses include the inability to reach mass audiences, slow video delivery to most due to low broadband penetration, and incomplete audience descriptions. Many of the weaknesses of the Net are in the process of being remedied. Audience measurement was initially a weakness, though companies such as Jupiter Media Metrix and Nielsen//NetRatings have made major improvements in this area.

Print Media

Print media include newspapers (local and national) and magazines. The Net is often compared to print media because its content is text and graphic heavy, and because many traditional print media publishers maintain online versions. Unlike television and radio, print media allow for active viewing: Readers can stop to look at an ad that interests them, sometimes spending quite a bit of time reading the details. In general, magazine advertising space is much more expensive than newspaper space.

Direct Mail

Finally, like the Internet, direct mail allows for more selective targeting than any mass medium, can be personalized, gives good message and timing flexibility, and is excellent for measuring effectiveness because of response tracking capability. However, direct mail has a poor image (junk mail) and high costs for production and postage. Conversely, e-mail has low costs but limited market coverage compared with postal mail. This is changing as companies build extensive e-mail databases.

Which Media and Vehicles to Buy?

Marketers spent more of their 2001 media budgets on the Internet than on radio or outdoor, but much less than on television or newspapers (refer to Exhibit 13 - 3). This generalization is interesting but not very useful for media buyers who plan a combination of media to achieve marketing communication goals for a particular campaign and brand. Media planners want both effective and efficient media buys. *Effectiveness* means reaching and gaining the attention of the target market, and *efficiency* means doing so at the lowest cost.

Efficient Internet Buys

To measure efficiency before buying advertising space, media buyers use a metric called CPM (cost per thousand). This is calculated by taking the ad's cost, dividing it by the audience size, and then multiplying by 1,000 (cost ÷ audience x 1,000). Internet audience size is counted using **impressions**: the number of times an ad was served to unique site visitors. For example, in June 2002 a full banner ad at MediaPost.com, an advertising and media Internet portal, received 2.4 million impressions and cost $168,000 a month for a CPM of $70. (Incidentally, this firm charges an additional $10 CPM *slotting fee* for a specific position.) CPM is used because it allows for efficiency comparisons among various media and *vehicles* within the media (e.g., a particular magazine or Web site). If the audience for certain media vehicles matches the firm's target (*effective* buy), CPM calculations will determine the most efficient buy. Magazines are usually the most expensive media to reach 1,000 readers; radio is often the least expensive.

Typical Web CPM prices are $7 to $15 CPM (Hallerman, 2002). MediaPost is higher because it reaches a select target in the B2B market. According to eMarketer in March 2002, the CPM ranges between $75 and $200 for e-mail ads (refer to Exhibit 13 - 5), and between $20 and $40 for e-mail newsletter sponsorship (refer to Exhibit 13 - 6).

It is interesting to note that only 50% of Web site advertising is purchased using the CPM model (PricewaterhouseCoopers 2002). Unlike most traditional media, 13% of online advertisers pay based on performance, and the remainder use some combination of the two models. Performance-based payment, often called cost per action (CPA), includes schemes such as payment for each click on the ad, payment for each conversion (sale), or payment for each sales lead. This type of pricing is beneficial to advertisers but risky for Web sites that must depend partially on the power of the client's ad and product for revenues.

CPM, CPA, and other online advertising pricing models are only part of the measurement picture. As noted later in this chapter, marketers use many other metrics to evaluate the efficiency of their advertising while it is running.

Effective Internet Buys

Once a firm decides to buy online advertising (medium), it faces the question of which vehicle (individual site) to use. As noted earlier, media planners look for the Web site(s) and e-mail lists with audiences that closely match the brand's target markets. Beyond that important principle, marketers use many innovative technology strategies to reach narrowly targeted markets.

Advertisers trying to reach the largest number of users will buy space at the portals such as Yahoo! and AOL. Exhibit 13 - 18 displays the top Web properties worldwide in January 2002. While this is only a snapshot in time, AOL, Microsoft (MSN sites including Hotmail), and Yahoo! are consistently in the top five in most countries. Note that an advertiser buying all three sites worldwide cannot amass a million sets of eyeballs. This is further evidence that the Web is not very effective at reaching the masses but is better at reaching niche markets.

Ad servers track user click-streams via cookies and serve ads based on user behavior. One such firm, DoubleClick, served 55 billion ads to Web users along with client Web pages during May 2002. This represents multiple servings of the same ads, because Nielsen-Netratings reports only about 70,000 unique ads in April 2002. DoubleClick technology can detect a user at a client site who then goes to a second client site (click-stream), and serve the user an appropriate ad based on the user's interests. DoubleClick data from three months in early 2002 revealed that 43.8% of its ads were targeted by keywords or key values in this manner, while 5.5% were served to specific geographic areas and 1.3% by time of day ("DoubleClick Ad

Web Property	Unique Visitors in millions	
	Worldwide	U.S.
Microsoft Corporation	269.8	99.7
Yahoo Inc.	219.5	92.5
AOL Time Warner	169.6	88.0
Terra Lycos	143.1	51.1
Google Inc.	93.2	31.1
Amazon.com Inc.	79.0	37.5
CNET Networks Inc.	75.1	28.0
Primedia Inc.	72.1	31.6
U.S. government	56.1	38.6
eBay	55.9	32.9

Exhibit 13 - 18 Top Online Properties by Parent Company for January 2002
Source: Data from www.cyberatlas.internet.com.

Serving. . ." 2002). Many Web sites offer specific ad targeting by day, time, user geography or domain (e.g., .edu, .jp), and so forth.

Another targeting approach, **keyword advertising,** refers to search word buys at search engine sites. For example, advertisers can buy the word *automobile*, and when users search using that word, the advertiser's banner or message will appear on the resulting page. Usually keyword buys are more expensive because they deliver a more highly targeted audience. Google.com goes a step further by ordering the search query return page keyword banners by popularity. Thus, the most relevant ad tops the list of four or eight on the page. Google charges $8 to $15 CPM for placement on its keyword search (called AdWords). The amount an advertiser can spend at Google varies widely; depending on the popularity of the keywords, an advertiser might pay $10,000 to $500,000 per month.

IMC Metrics

Savvy marketers set specific objectives for their IMC campaigns and then track progress toward those goals by monitoring appropriate metrics. Exhibit 13 - 19 displays many of the commonly used measurements along with industry averages. Note that individual results vary widely; however, the following generalizations are based on research studies.

Effectiveness Evidence

When viewed as a direct-response medium, banner ads are generally ineffective: Only 0.5% of all users click on them. There are notable exceptions, however. DoubleClick statistics show that rich media ads receive an average 2.4% click-through ("DoubleClick Ad Serving. . ." 2002). Many individual firms have received stunning click-through results. For example, the Mexican Fiesta Americana Hotels got a 10.2% click-through by narrow targeting of Americans living in seven eastern

Metric	Definition/formula	Online Averages
CPM	Cost per thousand impressions CPM = [Total Cost ÷ (Impressions)] × 1000	$7 to $15 for banners[1] $75 and $200 for e-mail ads[2] $20 and $40 for e-mail newsletter[2]
Cost per message	Cost to send an e-mail Cost = Number of E-mails ÷ Total Cost	Less than $0.01[3]
Opt-out rate	Percent who opt-out of an e-mail list Rate = Opt-Out Number ÷ Total Number	Ranges between 0.2% and 0.5%[4]
Response time	Time between sending e-mail and click-through response	85% within 48 hours[3]
Site stickiness	Length of stay as tracked on Web site log	Varies 44 seconds per page[8]
Click-Through Rate (CTR)	Number of clicks as percent of total impressions CTR = Clicks ÷ Impressions	0.3% - 0.8% for banners[3,5] 2.4% rich media ads[5] 3.2% - 10% opt-in e-mail[3,9]
Visitors resulting from click-through	A pageview(s) on Web site resulting from a click Visitors = Impressions × Click-Through %	Varies widely
Cost per Click (CPC)	Cost for each visitor from ad click CPC = Total Ad Cost ÷ Clicks	Varies widely Google.com ranges from a few cents to a few dollars
Cost per lead (CPL)	Pay only for delivered leads from special offer CPL = Cost ÷ Number of Leads	25 cents to $2.50, B2B prices at the high end[1]
Conversion Rate	Percent of people who purchased from total number of visitors Conversion Rate = Orders ÷ Visitors	1.8% for Web sites[6] 5% for e-mail[9]
Cost per order equation (CPO)	Cost of each order resulting from click-through visit CPO = Total Ad Cost ÷ Orders	Varies widely
Customer Acquisition Cost (CAC)	Total marketing costs to acquire a customer	Varies by industry $82 for online retail pure plays; $31 for multi-channel brick and mortar retailers[7]

Exhibit 13 - 19 IMC Metrics and Industry Averages

Sources: [1]Hallerman (2002); [2]data from www.eMarketer.com; [3]Saunders (2001); [4]Gallogly and Rolls (2002); [5]"DoubleClick Ad Serving. . ." (2002); [6] data from shop.org; [7]data from www.computerworld.com; [8]data from www.nielsen-netratings.com; [9]PricewaterhouseCoopers, LLP (2002).

states who had just purchased an airline ticket to Cancun and who were online between 2 p.m. and 7 p.m. Monday through Wednesday (Strauss and Frost 2000). Also, AdRelevance found that 61% of its study participants who clicked on a banner ad purchased within 30 minutes of clicking, and 38% purchased within eight to 30 days later (Saunders 2000). Clearly, if users do click, they are likely to buy.

E-mail is a different story. E-mail receives a 3% to 10% click-through to the sponsor's Web site and an average 5% conversion rate (PricewaterhouseCoopers, LLP 2002; Saunders 2001). Catalog companies and retailers both realize over 9% click-throughs on e-mail campaigns run through DoubleClick ("DoubleClick Ad Serving. . ." 2002).

According to research, when banner ads are viewed as a branding medium, they increase brand awareness and message association, and they build brand favorability and purchase intent (see www.iab.net). In three studies, online ads that were bigger, were placed as interstitials, or contained rich multimedia delivered an even greater impact. For example, skyscrapers and large rectangles were found to be three to six times more effective than standard size banners in increasing brand awareness (Pastore, 2001). Further, research by DoubleClick and Information Resources, Inc. discovered that online advertising can increase offline sales by 6.6% for consumer packaged goods ("IRI and DoubleClick. . ." 2002).

There is increasing evidence that online and offline advertising work well together. When Unilever advertised its Dove Nutrium Bar, it found the Internet as effective for increasing brand awareness, brand attributes, and purchase intent as TV and print—but much more cost-efficient ("Internet Is Powerful. . ." 2002). The Dove study also revealed that an increase in online impressions from six to twelve during a six-week period resulted in a 42% branding effectiveness increase.

Metrics Example

To see how a firm evaluates the effectiveness of its Internet advertising buy, consider the actual Internet buy made by iGo, an online retailer selling batteries and small electronic devices by catalog and online (Exhibit 13 - 20). Many different forms of online advertising are represented in this buy, from a simple text link to buttons, banners, and content sponsorships at major portals (names removed to protect confidentiality). This spreadsheet shows estimated click-through percentage, conversion to people who might order, number of visitors that might visit the iGo site from the ad, number of orders expected, and cost of the ad. Exhibit 13 - 21 displays several effectiveness measures: average order value and more. Based on the annual profit and loss estimate from this campaign, it appears to generate over half a million dollars in profits as well as drawing nearly 3.5 million visitors to iGo.com—folks who may develop into long-term customers.

Type	Yearly Impressions	Est. Click %	Est. Conv.	# Visitors	# Orders	Cost @ $4.64 CPM
E-commerce text link	400,000,000	0.20%	0.60%	800,000	4,800	$1,856,000
Shopping Channel						
Computing - anchor	8,500,000	3.00%	2.00%	255,000	5,100	$39,440
Computing - sponsor	1,700,000	3.00%	2.00%	51,000	1,020	$7,888
Home page	10,000,000	1.10%	1.50%	110,000	1,650	$46,400
Computing Channel						
ROS	40,000,000	1.10%	1.50%	440,000	6,600	$185,600
Section front pages	3,500,000	1.10%	1.50%	38,500	578	$16,240
Home page	2,100,000	0.75%	1.00%	15,750	158	$9,744
Home page text link	7,200,000	0.75%	1.00%	54,000	540	$33,408
News Portal						
Selected sections	10,000,000	1.10%	1.50%	110,000	1,650	$46,400
Technology	5,000,000	1.10%	1.50%	55,000	825	$23,200
Shopping section	200,000	1.10%	1.50%	2,200	33	$928
ROS sticky ads	5,000,000	0.75%	1.00%	37,500	375	$23,200
ROS banners	11,000,000	0.75%	1.00%	82,500	825	$51,040
Portal (6.5 months)						
Home page - button	6,000,000	0.75%	1.00%	45,000	450	$27,840
Home page - text link	6,000,000	0.75%	1.00%	45,000	450	$27,840
Office computing	50,000	0.75%	1.00%	375	4	$232
Office computing	300,000	0.75%	1.00%	2,250	23	$1,392
BCentral ROS	6,000,000	0.75%	1.00%	45,000	450	$27,840
Link exchange	20,000,000	0.75%	1.00%	150,000	1,500	$92,800
Portal Co-Promotion						
Promo main page	75,000,000	1.10%	1.50%	825,000	12,375	$348,000
Sweepstakes						
Banners linked-sweeps	4,000,000	1.10%	1.50%	44,000	660	$18,560
Promo button	6,000,000	1.10%	1.50%	66,000	990	$27,840
Button on sweeps site	1,000,000	1.10%	1.50%	11,000	165	$4,640
Portal Package						
Transition Ads-1	2,000,000	1.10%	1.50%	22,000	330	$9,280
Mid page Ads-2	1,000,000	1.10%	1.50%	11,000	165	$4,640
Mid page Ads-3	5,000,000	1.10%	1.50%	55,000	825	$23,200
Mid page Ads-4	5,000,000	1.10%	1.50%	55,000	825	$23,200
A-column Ads-5	5,400,000	1.10%	1.50%	59,400	891	$25,056
	646,950,000	**0.54%**	**1.27%**	**3,487,475**	**44,255**	**$3,001,848**

Exhibit 13 - 20 iGo.com $3 Million Dollar Advertising Buy
Source: Adapted from information provided by Brian Casey, iGo.

Variables	
AOV	$140
Incremental Order (annual)	0.60
Gross Margin	0.36
Click Rate	0.54%
Conversion	1.27%
Annual P&L	
Revenue	$ 6,195,735
Incremental Revenue	$ 3,717,441
Total Revenue	**$ 9,913,176**
COGS	$ (6,344,433)
Advertising Cost	$ (3,001,848)
Total	**$ 566,895**
CPM	**$4.24**
Cost Per Order (CPO)	**$67.83**
Cost Per Click (CPC)	**$0.86**
Total Visitors	**3,487,475**

Exhibit 13 - 21 iGo Effectiveness Measures
Source: Adapted from information provided by Brian Casey, iGo.

S u m m a r y

Integrated marketing communication (IMC) is a cross-functional process for planning, executing, and monitoring brand communications designed to profitably acquire, retain, and grow customers. Marketers use specific MarCom tools (advertising, sales promotions, marketing public relations, direct marketing, and personal selling) to achieve their communication objectives. After implementation, they measure effectiveness, make any adjustments, and evaluate results. Marketers' use of the Net for MarCom can be understood in light of the AIDA (awareness, interest, desire, and action) model or "think, feel, do" hierarchy of effects model. These models suggest that consumers first become aware of and learn about a new product (think), develop a positive or negative attitude about it (feel), and then move to purchasing it (do).

Advertising is nonpersonal communication of information through various media, usually persuasive in nature about products and usually paid for by an identified sponsor. E-mail, wireless content sponsorship, and Web sites are the three major vehicles for Internet advertising. The least expensive type of online advertising is e-mail ads. Content sponsored advertising for mobile devices is the wireless version of banners and other ads that sponsor Web content, similar to commercials that typically support broadcast television programming. Web advertising covers interactive formats (banners, buttons, and skyscrapers); sponsorships integrating editorial content and advertising; slotting fees for premium positioning on a site; and interstitials, superstitials, daughter windows, and Shoshkeles that appear while content is loading.

Marketing public relations (MPR) includes brand-related activities and nonpaid, third-party media coverage to positively influence target markets. MPR activities using Internet technology include Web site content, online community building, and online events. Sales promotion activities include coupons, rebates, product sampling, contests, sweepstakes, and premiums. Coupons, sampling, and contests/sweepstakes are among the most widely used sales promotion activities on the Internet. Direct marketing covers techniques such as telemarketing, outgoing e-mail, and postal mail (including catalog marketing), as well as targeted banner ads and other forms of advertising and sales promotions that solicit a direct response.

Outgoing e-mail is a highly efficient and customizable form of Internet direct marketing with potential for maintaining a dialogue with targeted customers. Its disadvantages include the negative image of spam (unsolicited e-mail) and the difficulty in finding appropriate e-mail lists. Internet users dislike spam and, as a result, some measures are being enacted to limit it. Marketers using outgoing e-mail should search for address lists that are guaranteed to be 100% opt-in. Opt-in techniques are part of a strategy called permission marketing, which offers consumers incentives to willingly accept information in e-mail messages.

Individuals who forward e-mail to other people are using word of mouse, also known as viral marketing. Marketers are starting to use permission marketing to send short text messages (SMS) over the Net to cell phones and PDAs. Another emerging technique is location-based marketing, promotional offers that are pushed to mobile devices and customized depending on the user's physical location.

Because the Internet is often compared with traditional media, marketers need to understand the major media's characteristics as well as the Internet's media characteristics so they can make appropriate choices when buying promotional space. Electronic media include network television, radio, cable television, the Internet, Fax machine, cellular phone, and pager. It is helpful to view these media as broadcast, narrowcast, and pointcast based on their ability to reach mass audiences, smaller audiences, or even individuals. The Internet is often compared to print media because of its text and graphics content; print media allow for active viewing. Direct mail, like the Internet, allows for selective targeting, can be personalized, offers good message and timing flexibility, and is excellent for measuring effectiveness; however, it has a poor image and is costly (although e-mail is low cost).

When selecting advertising media and vehicles, media buyers look at CPM (cost per thousand) and, if available, CPA (cost per action or performance-based payment) or other pricing models. Media planners look for Web sites and e-mail lists that match the brand's target markets; they also use ad targeting techniques such as keyword advertising. Marketers can apply numerous metrics for measuring IMC campaign effectiveness.

Key Terms

Advertising

AIDA model

Banners

Brand advertising

Brochureware

Buttons

Click-through rate (CTR)

Conversion rate

Cost per click (CPC)

CPM

Customer acquisition cost (CAC)

Daughter windows

Direct marketing

Direct-response advertising

E-mail advertising

Hierarchy of effects

House banner

Impressions

Instant messaging

Integrated marketing communication (IMC)

Interstitials

Keyword advertising

Location-based marketing

Marketing public relations (MPR)

Permission marketing

Pointcast media

Search engine optimization (SEO)

Short message services (SMS)

Shoshkele

Skyscrapers

Slotting fee

Spam

Sponsorships

Telematics

Viral marketing

Exercises

Review Questions

1. What is integrated marketing communication and why is it important?

2. What is the hierarchy of effects model and how does it apply to high- and low-involvement product decisions?

3. What is the difference between brand advertising and direct-response advertising?

4. What are the three main vehicles for advertising on the Internet?

5. What are the advantages and disadvantages of using the advertising formats of banners, buttons, skyscrapers, interstitials, and superstititals?

6. What are some ways companies are using the Internet for marketing public relations, sales promotion, and direct marketing?

7. How does permission marketing differ from viral marketing?

8. List examples of broadcast, narrowcast, and pointcast media.

9. What are the strengths and weaknesses of the Web as an advertising medium?

10. Identify several ways to measure the Web audience, giving the strengths of each.

Discussion Questions

11. "The more successful list brokers are in selling their lists, the more they dilute the value of those lists." Do you agree or disagree—and why?

12. How effective is banner advertising compared with other media?

13. Is there a danger in letting sponsorship blend with content? Defend your position.

14. If you were running an online ad campaign for Nike, how would you allocate your ad budget? Why?

15. Why would manufacturers invite consumers to search for and print coupons from the Web? Might this encourage customers who were prepared to pay full price to simply use the Net to lower their costs?

16. Some U.S. sites draw one-third of their visitors from overseas. Do these users dilute the value of advertising at these sites? Why or why not?

17. "You should aim to be consultative not persuasive in the way you use the Internet for marketing communication." What does this mean? What is the reasoning behind this statement?

chapter

14 customer relationship management

learning objectives

The main objective of this chapter is provide an overview of the purpose and process of building a company's relationship capital through customer relationship management (CRM). You will learn about CRM's benefits, its three facets, and the seven building blocks needed for effective and efficient e-marketing CRM.

After reading this chapter, you will be able to:

- Define customer relationship management and identify the major benefits to e-marketers.
- Outline the three legs of CRM for e-marketing.
- Discuss the seven major components needed for effective and efficient CRM in e-marketing.
- Differentiate between relationship intensity and relationship levels.
- Highlight some of the company-side and client-side tools that e-marketers use to enhance their CRM processes.

We exceed our guests' expectations and they become our evangelists.

rebekah
salgado
disney

The Cisco Story

Cisco Systems, Inc. is a company that practices what it preaches. Cisco provides Internet networking systems for corporate, government, and education clients worldwide, ringing up $2.2 billion in annual revenues. Operating in the B2B market, Cisco turned a hefty $1.7 billion in profits in 2001 by solving its own networking problems and turning those solutions into products for customers. It offers products for transporting data, voice, and video within buildings and around the world. Cisco boasts that its solutions increase clients' revenue, decrease costs, increase productivity, empower employees, transform corporate cultures, and integrate core processes. What better way to prove it than to use its products to build relationships with its own clients?

At Cisco, the Internet plays a major role in acquiring, retaining, and growing customer business. With 2.5 million users logging onto the Cisco site

Relationship Task	Metric
Acquire/grow customers	90% of orders come through the Internet. $60 million in orders online each day. 366,754 registered users at the Cisco Web site.
Retain customers	82% of all customer questions handled online. Registered site user satisfaction is 4.26 on a 5.0 point scale.

each month, Cisco has become quite adept at online customer relationship management (CRM). The following demonstrates Cisco's success, using CRM metrics.

Cisco set a goal to migrate customers to the online channel, and it has: In early 1996 a mere 5% placed orders on the Web site. Further, Cisco was able to increase customer satisfaction from 3.4 in 1996 to its present 4.3. Such gains do not occur without a vision from the top and careful planning and execution throughout the company. Cisco's close attention to customer care includes a Web-to-live-agent contact center and a collaborative whiteboard so that customers and Cisco employees can work together on problems as visually displayed on their computers. Customer care agents operate several customer live chats simultaneously to help customers find what they need on the Web. Additionally, customers can contact the company via e-mail or even telephone for help.

Cisco's attention to CRM and monitoring of performance metrics have paid off. The firm saves $340 million a year in customer service costs due to automation. More important, Cisco gains considerable repeat business and sells products to customers who want to follow Cisco's lead by using technology to solve their own problems.

Building Customer Relationships, 1:1

Cisco develops long-term customers relationships one at a time (1:1), not unlike those developed by neighborhood retailers in the early 1900s—except that information technology allows Cisco to handle millions of these close relationships. A Cisco customer with an investment in software and high satisfaction is brand loyal and will not easily be enticed by competition. This customer will slowly spend an increasing amount of money on additional products and services and also refer others. According to *Harvard Business Review* authors Thomas Jones and Earl Sasser, "Increased customer loyalty is the *single most* important driver of long-term performance." Business 2.0 calls **relationship capital** the most important asset a firm can have ("Relationships Rule" 2000). In an environment of customer control, with attention a scarce commodity, a firm's ability to build and maintain relationships with customers, suppliers, and partners may be more important than a firm's land, property, and financial assets. It is this relationship capital that provides the foundation of future business.

This represents a major shift in marketing practice: from mass marketing to individualized marketing, and from focusing on acquiring lots of new customers to retaining and building more business from a smaller base of loyal high-value customers. Although many industrial firms have practiced customer relationship management for a long time, now firms in the consumer services market (e.g., the local hair salon), and even marketers of consumer packaged goods are considering how to build long-term customer relationships, 1:1. How can the maker of canned dog food profitably build relationships with each consumer? Internet technologies can facilitate relationship marketing in many new ways, yet many firms that purchase and install relationship management technologies are losing money on them. This chapter explains the process, identifies key Internet tools, and presents the case for a consumer-centric customer relationship management focus throughout the entire supply chain.

Relationship Marketing Defined

Marketers dubbed this customer focus *relationship marketing* (also *1:1 marketing*.) As originally defined, **relationship marketing** is about establishing, maintaining, enhancing, and commercializing customer relationships through promise fulfillment (Grönroos 1990). Usually firms try to build profitable, mutually beneficial relationships in the long term (versus the short term); Chapter 2 noted the balanced scorecard customer focus was created from this very idea. Promise fulfillment means that when firms make offers in their marketing communications programs, customer expectations will be met through actual brand experiences. For example, the author recently ordered some tea from the Stash Tea Web site. An offer on the home page promised a free box with the purchase of three but the order page did not confirm this offer, and the total quantity shown on the final order was three. If four did not arrive, the customer would consider buying tea from competitor Twinings next time. Ultimately, four boxes arrived in the shipment but the suspense eroded some of the customer's trust in the firm. Similarly, good relationships are built when company personnel meet the promises made by salespeople and promotional messages.

Today relationship marketing involves much more than promise fulfillment. It means two-way communication with individual stakeholders, one at a time (1:1). How can a firm understand an individual customer's needs without asking what they are? Also, a firm using relationship marketing focuses on share of mind, often called **share of customer** or share of wallet, rather than share of market. It also differentiates individual customers based on need rather than differentiating products for target groups. It will be more profitable for Cisco to identify its best customers, get to know them individually, and suggest additional products based on their needs than to spend all its efforts acquiring new customers. If Cisco is successful, clients will eventually buy all their networking products and services from the firm. Cisco saves on promotion and price discounting expenditures by spending time on customer retention versus customer acquisition. Exhibit 14 - 1 displays a summary of these ideas, comparing mass marketing to relationship marketing.

Few firms fall on either end of the continuum but instead use varying strategies for different products and markets. For example, Procter & Gamble must differentiate its brands of laundry detergent for sale to the masses; however, it tries to build relationships with mothers who will buy increasing numbers of P&G products over the years, from Ivory powder for washing baby clothes and Pampers diapers to Crest toothpaste for the family and Olay cosmetics for themselves.

Stakeholders

Most firms also use relationship marketing techniques to build mutually supportive bonds with stakeholders other than consumers, such as employees and suppliers. Firms can establish and maintain relationships with many different stakeholder groups. The four most affected by Internet technologies are:

1. **Employees**. It is difficult for a firm to persuade buyers when employees are not happy. The University of Nevada at Reno features employee accomplishments on its Web site and also includes lots of information such as how to put an individual home page on the site from a remote location. Employee relationship building is often handled by the human resources department as part of internal marketing. Because many employees are instrumental in building relationships with customers, it is critical for them to have training and access to data and systems used for relationship management. In fact, some observers say that many relationship management programs fail due to lack of employee training and commitment.

2. **Business customers in the supply chain**. Firms build and maintain relationships with other businesses for the purpose of buying and selling both upstream and downstream. First are business customers: the B2B market. Procter & Gamble works with numerous wholesale and retail intermediaries, using Internet

technologies to facilitate these relationships. Second are a firm's suppliers. General Electric uses the Internet to receive bids from its suppliers, a system that not only lowers transaction costs but also enhances competition and speeds order fulfillment.

3. **Lateral partners**. These are other businesses, not-for-profit organizations, or governments that join with the firm for some common goal but not for transactions with each other. CargoNet Transportation Community Network, a consortium of 200,000 shippers, handles 250 million trade-related documents a year for Hong Kong shippers at the world's busiest port. The Internet facilitates document tracking and customer service for manufacturers, ocean, rail, truck, and air carriers as well as banks, insurance companies, and governments associated with CargoNet (www.eds.com).

4. **Consumers**. These are the individuals who are end users of products and services. Marketers must differentiate between business customers and final consumers because different tactics are often employed in the B2C and B2B markets.

Customer Relationship Management (CRM)

Customer relationship management (CRM) is used to define the process of creating and maintaining relationships with business customers or consumers. CRM is a holistic process of acquiring, retaining, and growing customers. It sprang from the relationship marketing concept after the advent of the Internet and other

Mass marketing		**Relationship marketing**
Discrete transactions		Continuing transactions
Short-term emphasis		Long-term emphasis
One-way communication	←——————→	Two-way communication and collaboration
Acquisition focus		Retention focus
Share of market		Share of mind
Product differentiation		Customer differentiation

Exhibit 14 - 1 Continuum from Mass Marketing to Relationship Marketing

technologies but has now grown to include all online and offline relationship management. Increasingly, firms are recognizing that if they don't keep their customers happy, someone else will.

CRM Benefits

One key CRM benefit is its cost-effectiveness, as seen in the Cisco example. Consider the following:

- One study estimated that U.S. businesses saved $155 billion between 1998 and 2000 by using Internet technology for both CRM and supply chain management (interactive.wsj.com).

- A 5% increase in customer retention translates to 25% to 125% profitability in the B2B market.

- Customer defection rates are near 20% per year.

Most businesses spend more money acquiring new customers than they spend keeping current customers—but this is usually a mistake. The cost of acquiring a new customer is typically five times higher than the cost of retaining a current one, as shown in Exhibit 14 - 2 (Peppers and Rogers 1996). In this example, if a firm budgets $3,000 to acquire six customers, the cost of acquiring each will be $500. Because retaining customers costs one-fifth less (on average), that same $500 could be spent enticing five customers to stay at a cost of $100 each. If instead of spending $3,000 on gaining six customers, a firm spent $1,500 on three new customers and $1,500 on customer retention, it would be 12 customers ahead.

One reason that retention is less costly than acquisition is reduced promotion costs, both for advertising and discounts. Additionally, higher response rates to promotional efforts yield more profits. Also, sales teams can be more effective when they get to know individual customers well. Another reason CRM makes sense is that loyal customers are experienced customers. They know the products well, and they know who to call in the firm when they have questions. This means loyal customers cost less to service.

More customers leads to more sales. However, acquiring and retaining customers is only part of the equation. A firm must also attempt to increase the amount purchased by each customer. Amazon cross-sells by offering music, videos, and toys to its book customers. CDNow periodically e-mails special offers to its customers to encourage repeat business. Expedia™ and Travelocity e-mail customers when the airfare to a destination of interest to them drops.

In addition to buying more, satisfied customers recommend Web sites, stores, and products to their friends. Word-of-mouth communication among customers has been called the heart of CRM. Businesspeople commonly refer each other to bankers and other suppliers, just as consumers tell friends about product experiences. Positive word of mouth can attract many new customers but negative word of mouth can drive them away. One study reported that each dissatisfied customer tells 10 people about the unhappy experience, and 13% of dissatisfied customers each tell 20 people

Acquisition Emphasis		Retention Emphasis	
Gain 6 new customers ($500 each)	$3,000	Gain 3 new customers ($500 each)	$1,500
Retain 5 current customers ($100 each)	$ 500	Retain 20 current customers ($100 each)	$2,000
Total cost	$3,500	Total cost	$3,500
Total number of customers	11	Total number of customers	23

Exhibit 14 - 2 Maximizing Number of Customers
Source: Adapted from Peppers and Rogers (1996).

how bad the company and its products were (Sonnenberg 1993). The Internet magnifies this: "If you have an unhappy customer on the Internet, he doesn't tell his six friends, he tells his 6,000 friends," says Jeff Bezos, founder of Amazon.com. This is accomplished through e-mail, newsgroups, chat, and personal Web pages.

CRM's Facets

Many e-marketers, especially those focusing on CRM software capabilities, suggest that CRM has three facets: sales force automation, marketing automation, and customer service. The first occurs primarily in the B2B market, while the second and third are important in all markets. This is an emerging perspective on CRM; however, we present it so readers will gain familiarity with popular business terminology.

Sales Force Automation (SFA)

"Increase your sales, not your sales force." This is the claim of SFA software. Used primarily in the B2B market, **SFA** allows salespeople to build, maintain, and access customer records; manage leads and accounts; manage their schedules; and more. In relation to e-marketing, SFA helps the sales force acquire, retain, and grow customers by accessing customer and product data from the company's data warehouses, both while in the office and on the road. Salespeople can also send the results of sales calls and activity reports to the data warehouse for access by others. Up-to-date customer and prospect records help customer service representatives and others build customer relationships. As an example, Salesforce.com's software boasts the following benefits (source: www.salesforce.com):

- **Close more deals.** Teams across your organization can effectively work together to close accounts by scheduling events, assigning tasks, coordinating meetings, flagging new opportunities, and updating client files on every account.

- **Seize all sales opportunities.** Every lead is immediately recorded, automatically routed to the right person, and tracked through the pipeline in real time.

- **Update opportunities, accounts, and contacts offline.** When closing deals puts you on the road, on a plane, or in the lobby of your most important customer, you need to be able to work offline.

- **Enable collaborative and consistent customer management.** Real-time, company-wide access to detailed account data enables you to facilitate collaboration between sales, customer service and support, and marketing personnel. With instant access to all communication, including e-mail, notes, calls, resolutions, and more, you can collectively manage customer relationships across your entire organization.

- **Recognize "big picture" market trends.** It's so easy to review, "slice and dice," or otherwise analyze current and historical sales data that you immediately spot changes in customer behavior or shifts in key market indicators.

Marketing Automation

Marketing automation activities aid e-marketers in effective targeting, efficient marketing communication, and real-time monitoring of customer and market trends. It is "a disciplined approach to the capture, integration, and analysis of customer data [that] is needed to identify and leverage customer relationships and opportunities to their fullest. This emerging space, called marketing automation, forms the core of the knowledge engine which drives customer relationship management (CRM)" (Distefano 2000)." Marketing automation software usually takes data from Web sites and databases and turns it into reports for fine-tuning CRM efforts. Software solutions include e-mail campaign management, database marketing, market segmentation, Web site log analysis, and more. This is a very new and general term at this point (encompassing most CRM activities) and, thus, we discuss these techniques throughout the chapter—particularly in the CRM technology and metrics sections.

Customer Service

Customer service permeates every stage of customer acquisition, retention, and development practices, although most service occurs post purchase when customers have questions or complaints. Exhibit 14 - 3 reports on one study showing the proportion of customers in respondent firms who use the Internet for customer service. Mercedes-Benz takes customer service to a new level with its "teleweb" technology. The consumer types a question into a form on the Web site and receives an immediate phone call from a Mercedes representative. The consumer and representative can then discuss the question while viewing the same Web pages. In fact, software now allows customer service reps on the telephone with a customer to take control of the user's mouse and guide her around the company Web site. E-mail, customized Web pages, live Web chat, package tracking using PDAs: These and many more customer service techniques are described throughout this chapter. Regardless of technique, online or offline, customer service is critical to building long-term customer relationships.

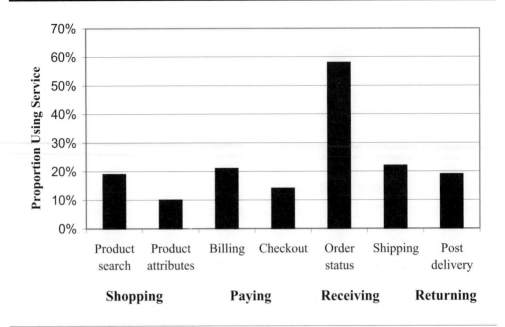

Exhibit 14 - 3 Customers Receive Service at Every CRM Point
Source: Forrester Research as cited in speech by Tod Famous at Internet World (2001).

CRM Building Blocks

Although firms understand CRM's benefits and are investing heavily in CRM software, as many as 70% lose money on this investment. Thus, businesses are trying to determine what works and what doesn't, knowing that the first businesses to get CRM right will win. These businesses agree with the CRM concept but want to know *how to do it effectively and efficiently*. This section focuses on the seven important CRM components used for effective and efficient e-marketing, based on a Gartner Group model of CRM (see Exhibit 14 - 4).

1. CRM Vision

Many firms purchase expensive CRM software just because everyone else is doing it. CRM is the hottest, newest thing on the block. It is no wonder that so many projects fail. Management must start with a vision that fits the company culture and makes sense for the firm's brands and value propositions. Some say that the main reason CRM projects fail is because firms do not realize how pervasive they are and underestimate the costs. For example, when a firm installs CRM software to integrate data from the Web site and brick-and-mortar retail operations, customer service reps need training and must be committed to the initiative. Some customer service reps bypass CRM software because it is easier to do it the old way. To be successful, the

1. CRM Vision: Leadership, value proposition	
2. CRM Strategy: Objectives, target markets	

3. Valued Customer Experience	**4. Organizational Collaboration**
Understand requirements	Culture and structure
Monitor expectations	Customer understanding
Maintain satisfaction	People, skills, competencies
Collaboration and feedback	Incentives and compensation
Customer interaction	Employee communication
	Partners and suppliers

5. CRM Processes: Customer life cycle, knowledge management
6. CRM Information: Data, analysis, one view across channels
7. CRM Technology: Applications, architecture, infrastructure
8. CRM Metrics: Value, retention, satisfaction, loyalty, cost to serve

Exhibit 14 - 4 Eight Building Blocks for Successful CRM
Source: Adapted from Gartner Group (www.gartner.com).

CRM vision must start at the top and filter throughout the company to keep the firm completely customer focused.

Another vision that should be clarified throughout the firm is the privacy policy. Marketers have access to lots of information about every customer and prospect, and that information is stored in a database and used for direct-marketing communications. "Big brother is almost here. His sister is the telemarketing operator who called you during dinner last night" (Peppers and Rogers 1996). One key aspect of this vision is how to guard customer privacy.

Guarding Customer Privacy

Using customer data is very tempting to marketers, yet this temptation must be balanced by the need to satisfy customers and not anger them. The burden is on marketers to use customer and prospect information responsibly, both for their own business health and for the image of the profession. In one study of 1,000 adult Internet users, 92% said they were concerned about online privacy, and this concern remains high on consumer lists today ("Consumers Wary..." 1999). Two-thirds said they were very concerned about misuse of personal information and did not want it shared with others unless they gave permission. Consumers are unaware of the extent to which real-time profiling and other techniques monitor their online behavior—and marketers must address this issue before regulators make them do it.

CRM is based on trust. Customers must believe that the information they give companies on Web forms, in e-mail, or in other ways will be used responsibly. This means using the information to improve the relationship by tailoring goods, services, and marketing communications to meet individual needs. It means allowing consumers to request removal of their information from databases, to opt-out of e-mail lists, and not sharing information with other companies unless permission is granted.

Another important privacy issue concerns intrusions into people's lives. Junk mail, spam, repeated telephone calls requesting a switch of long-distance provider are all examples of marketing messages that can upset consumers. Even the community classified ad newspaper that arrives on the doorstep each week is an assault on the privacy of some residents.

What's a marketer to do? The answer is twofold: build relationships through dialogue and through better target profiling. Firms must listen to customers and prospects and give them what they want. If a consumer wants to receive e-mail from American Airlines, great. If not, the firm should remove that customer from the list, perhaps checking once a year to see if the status has changed. Why? Firms know that retention and development of customer relationships are more profitable than one-time customer transactions, and that relationship capital is one of the firm's strongest assets. Second, marketers can use consumer information to build more precise target profiles. Instead of sending a mass e-mailing to everyone who visits the site, how about sending individual or small group e-mails to people who might really need a car for the flight they just booked at the site? Individuals do not get upset with firms who send valuable and timely information to them.

TRUSTe

To help Web sites earn the trust of their users, an independent, nonprofit privacy initiative named TRUSTe was created. TRUSTe provides its seal and logo to any Web site meeting its philosophies, as stated on the site (Exhibit 14 - 5). Note how well these and the following information requirements fit with good CRM practices.

- Adopting and implementing a privacy policy that factors in the goals of your individual Web site as well as consumer anxiety over sharing personal information online.
- Posting notice and disclosure of collection and use practices regarding personally identifiable information (data used to identify, contact, or locate a person) via a posted privacy statement.
- Giving users choice and consent over how their personal information is used and shared.
- Putting data security and quality, and access measures in place to safeguard, update, and correct personally identifiable information.

In addition, sites must publish the following information on their sites to gain the TRUSTe seal (source: www.truste.org):

- What personal information is being gathered by your site.
- Who is collecting the information.
- How the information will be used.
- With whom the information will be shared.

- The choices available to users regarding collection, use, and distribution of their information: You must offer users an opportunity to opt-out of internal secondary uses as well as third-party distribution for secondary uses.

- The security procedures in place to protect users' collected information from loss, misuse, or alteration: If your site collects, uses, or distributes personally identifiable information such as credit card or social security numbers, accepted transmission protocols (e.g., encryption) must be in place.

- How users can update or correct inaccuracies in their pertinent information: Appropriate measures shall be taken to ensure that personal information collected online is accurate, complete, and timely, and that easy-to-use mechanisms are in place for users to verify that inaccuracies have been corrected.

Other organizations also provide guidelines for Internet privacy. The American Marketing Association has a code of ethics for Internet marketing, dealing primarily with privacy and intellectual property. See Chapter 5 for more about the legal aspects of privacy.

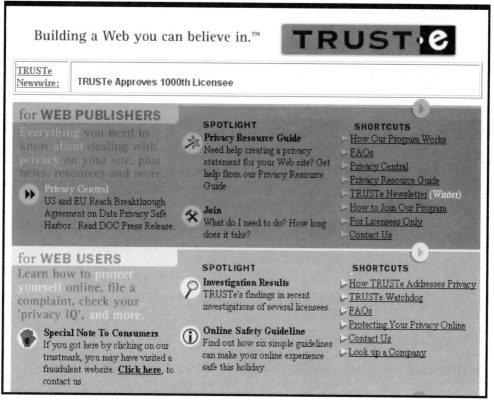

Exhibit 14 - 5 TRUSTe Builds User Trust
Source: www.truste.org.

2. CRM Strategy

E-marketers must determine what they want to accomplish before buying CRM technology. NetPerceptions, one of many CRM software suppliers, suggests the following goals for CRM projects (source: www.netperceptions.com):

- Increase order size through more effectively targeted cross-sell promotions.
- Build customer loyalty and repeat sales through consistently relevant and compelling offers.
- Expand wallet share by increasing the variety of products and categories that customers buy from you.
- Move overstocks by knowing which customers will buy them at list price to avoid deep discounting.
- Reduce costly returns by promoting products you know your customers want.
- Enable multichannel coordination of field sales, inside sales, e-commerce, and direct mail through consistent and relevant product recommendations for each customer interaction.

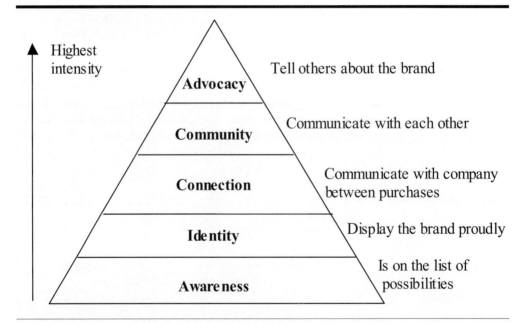

Exhibit 14 - 6 Levels of Relationship Intensity
Source: Adapted from Duncan (2002).

Relationship Intensity

Many of these CRM goals refer to customer loyalty. Most firms would be delighted if they had customers who proudly wore their brand name on clothing and tried to talk others into buying the brand—like customers of Harley Davidson and Apple Computer. Exhibit 14 - 6 displays the possible levels of relationship intensity. The pyramid shape indicates that fewer customers are at the highest level, where they have become advocates who tell everyone how great the brand is. Many people are advocates because of positive experiences with their MacIntosh computers or with eBay auctions. One student purchased the inventory of a bankrupt comic store and made $10,000 auctioning the comics on eBay—he became an eBay advocate. Thus, an important CRM strategy is trying to move customers upward in this pyramid.

Relationship Levels

Another CRM strategy involves building bonds with customers that transcend the product experience itself. Some experts suggest that relationship marketing is practiced on three levels (see Exhibit 14 - 7). The strongest relationships are formed if all three levels are used and if the product itself actually satisfies buyers. At level one marketers build a financial bond with customers by using pricing strategies. This is the lowest level of relationship because price promotions are easily imitated. CDNow sends periodic e-mail notification of price discounts to individual users. These can be timed and priced to build share of customer.

At level two, marketers stimulate social interaction with customers. This involves ongoing personal communication with individual customers and may include aggressive pricing strategies as well. According to eMarketer, nine out of ten interactions with customers are nontransactional communication, thus demonstrating this strategy. At level two customers are more loyal because of the social bond with the company or the salesperson. This stimulates customers to move to the *connected* level of the intensity pyramid previously mentioned.

Level	Primary Bond	Potential for Sustained Competitive Advantage	Main Element of Marketing Mix	Web Example
One	Financial	Low	Price	www.cdnow.com
Two	Social Build 1:1 relationships Build community	Medium	Personal communications	www.palmpilot.com
Three	Structural	High	Service delivery	my.yahoo.com

Exhibit 14 - 7 Three Levels of Relationship Marketing

Source: Adapted from Berry and Parasuraman (1991).

Level-three relationship marketing relies on creating structural solutions to customer problems. Structural bonds are formed when firms add value by making structural changes that facilitate the relationship. All of the major Web portals work to create structural bonds with their users. Services such as My Yahoo! allow consumers to customize their interface to Yahoo! so it lists local weather and movies, personal stock portfolios, and news of interest to them. Once consumers invest the time and effort to customize this interface, they will be reluctant to switch to another portal.

3. Valued Customer Experience

Most customers want brand loyalty as much as the firms they patronize want it. Being a consumer can be difficult because of constant bombardment by marketing communications and unlimited product choices. Jagdish Sheth (1995) wrote that, from a consumer's perspective, the basic tenet of CRM is choice reduction. This suggests that consumers want to patronize the same Web site, mall, and service providers because doing so is efficient. That is, consumers do not want to spend their days contemplating which brand of toothpaste to buy or how to find a good dentist. Many consumers are "loyalty prone," searching for the right product or service and then sticking with it as long as the promises are more or less fulfilled. For example, many customers buy from Amazon.com because of good previous experiences, the convenience of having personal preferences on file, the familiar interface, and the competitive prices (though not usually the lowest).

Customers generally like to patronize stores, services, and Web sites where they are treated like individuals with important needs and where they know those needs will be met, "satisfaction guaranteed." Users believe the company cares when they get an e-mail about nifty new uses of the PalmPilot that is addressed to them by name and refers to the exact product purchased. They feel more brand loyalty when Amazon sends an e-mail announcing a new book by an author they enjoy. Of course, firms must learn to answer e-mails sent from customers as well. Listening to hundreds of thousands of customers, one at a time, can be difficult and expensive but it satisfies customers.

Customer Preferences Vary

Customers' preferences for communicating with each company vary by individual as well as by situation and product type. Customers might want to call and speak with a live rep about an account problem, go to a Web site to research product information, use e-mail to complain about a service problem, and so forth. Exhibit 14 - 8 displays these options covering many technologies, using both automated and human intervention for both synchronous (simultaneous) and asynchronous communication. This exhibit reinforces the importance of the Internet in creating valued customer experiences and the idea that firms must be adept with many different technologies and processes, putting the focus on customers and their preferences, not the company's capabilities.

	Automated	**Human**
Synchronous	Web 1:1 self-service Online transactions Telephone routing	Telephone Online chat Collaboration tools
Asynchronous	Automated e-mail Short message services (SMS) Web forms Fax on demand	E-mail response Snail mail

Exhibit 14 - 8 Relationships over Multiple Communication Channels

Community-Building Principles

As noted in other chapters as well as in this chapter, community-building is an important way to forge relationships and strengthen loyalty (see Exhibit 14 - 6). Building a successful online community is not as simple as putting a link on a Web site and hoping folks will drop by. As with most e-business strategies, research and planning precede success. A book by Amy Jo Kim (2000) on this topic offers nine critical success factors (Exhibit 14 - 9); note how many follow good CRM principles.

4. Organizational Collaboration

E-marketers collaborate both within and outside of the organization. Within the firm, cross-functional teams joining forces to focus on customer satisfaction can create a CRM culture. Outside the firm, when two or more companies join forces, the results often exceed what each firm might have accomplished alone. This is true whether it is in the distribution channel or a nontransactional-type collaboration. In fact, some marketers believe that today's marketplace consists of supply chain competition, not individual firm competition. Amazon and Toys "R" Us have teamed up to form the online baby retail site BabiesRUs.com, as one example. Amazon's online retail expertise combined with the toy merchandising expertise of Toys "R" Us benefits both partners as well as the site's customers.

In the following sections we discuss two important collaboration techniques that capitalize on Internet properties: CRM-SCM integration and extranets.

CRM-SCM Integration

CRM usually refers to "front-end" operations. This means that firms work to create satisfying experiences at all customer touch points: telephone calls to customer service reps, in-person visits to stores, e-mail contact, and so forth. This is quite challenging because different employees and computer systems collect various information, and somehow it must be integrated into appropriate customer records. In one study sponsored by Jupiter Communications, three phone calls were made to *Forbes* magazine asking why two renewal offers were different. The interviewer got three different explanations. Fortunately several firms now provide software to address this issue. For example, the Aspect Relationship Portal assists CRM staff by integrating all customer contact media—phone, Fax, e-mail, and Web—with front- and back-office operations (www.aspect.com).

In the online environment of customer control, however, even consistently good customer service is not enough. With technological advances and interoperability, online retailers can seamlessly link the "back end" (e.g., inventory and payment) with the "front-end" CRM system and the entire supply chain management system (SCM). This means the entire supply chain can work together to single-mindedly focus on meeting consumer needs and make higher profits in the process. It all centers, of course, on information (Exhibit 14 - 10).

Imagine that a customer orders a particular shirt from a clothing retailer's Web site. Currently, if the shirt is out of stock, the customer might see a Web screen with that messagebut more likely the customer will receive a postcard or an e-mail after some time. With an integrated CRM-SCM system, however, the system can instantly

Define the community's purpose Construct a mission statement, identify the target market, and create a strong site personality	**Organize and promote cyclic events** Hold regular, hosted, themed events, conduct community surveys, and hold contests that reinforce the purpose
Create extensible gathering places Provide a good system overview or map, include rich communications features, and allow members to extend the environment	**Provide a range of roles** Offer newcomers a controlled experience, offer increased privileges to regulars, and recruit leaders and mentors from within
Create evolving member profiles Communicate the benefits of membership, make profile creation as easy and fun as possible, and keep the profiles up-to-date and evolving	**Facilitate member-created subgroups** Provide features that facilitate small groups and create events and contests for groups
Promote effective leadership and hosting Set up your program to grow, build some flexibility into the house rules, and set reasonable expectations for online support	**Integrate with the real world** Celebrate events that reinforce social identity, acknowledge important personal events, and encourage real-life meetings (when appropriate)
Define a clear yet flexible code of conduct Create and enforce your code of conduct and don't try to stifle all conflict	

Exhibit 14 - 9 Community-Building Design Principles
Source: Adapted from Kim (2000) at www.naima.com/articles/webtechniques.html.

check inventory levels at the retailer and then at the wholesaler or manufacturer to determine availability. Then the system could notify the customer during the ordering process and offer options: Wait two weeks for delivery from the manufacturer or consider a similar shirt currently in stock, for example. This could even be done with a daughter window pop-up featuring a live customer service rep helping the customer. Already, LandsEnd.com and iGo.com are two of many sites using LivePerson software, which offers Web site integration with live customer service reps in real time (www.liveperson.com).

Connecting customers with supply chain businesses provides several advantages. First, all firms will share transaction data so that inventories can be kept low. If producers and wholesalers constantly receive data about consumer orders, they can produce goods in a timely manner. Second, upstream firms can use the data to design products that better meet consumer needs (see codesigning discussion in Chapter 10). Third, if customer service reps have up-to-the-minute information about product inventories, they will be able to better help consumers immediately. Catalog firms are already fairly accomplished at thisbut the process breaks down when supplier firms are several levels upstream from the retailer.

As more firms integrate CRM and SCM activities, they will become more responsive to individual customer needs. For example, Levi's Personal Pair program used electronic scanners to send precise measurements directly to the factory for individualized jeans, and Dell Computers produces and ships customized computers within days. Conversely, this type of integration is quite difficult when a firm has

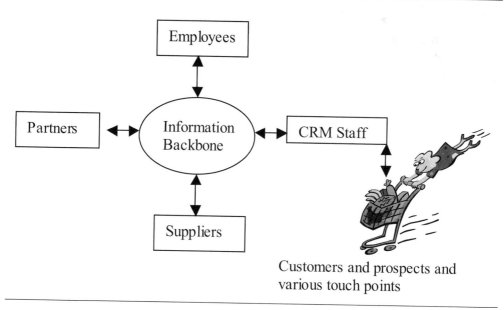

Customers and prospects and various touch points

Exhibit 14 - 10 CRM–SCM Integration

many different channels for its brands and when each firm uses different software and hardware to manage its internal systems. Nevertheless, the systems for integration are currently available and are helping firms become market winners.

Extranet

Extranets are two or more intranet networks that are joined for the purpose of sharing information. If two companies link their intranets, they would have an extranet. By definition, extranets are proprietary to the organizations involved. Companies participating in an extranet have formed a structural bond, the third and strongest level of relationship marketing. It is the use of extranets that allows CRM-SCM integration.

Electronic Data Systems (EDS) is a Dallas-based firm that provides enterprise-wide computer desktop services from procurement to network management for large clients. The word *enterprise* means that EDS focuses on all the computer desktops in an entire company, bringing them together in a network. In 1998 the firm managed over 736,000 desktops, both internally and externally, in 19 countries (Fernandes 1998). EDS created an innovative extranet called the Renasence Channel, which links desktops of its suppliers, clients, and employees into an electronic marketplace. Forty suppliers selling over 2,000 software products fund the private network, paying $25,000 to $100,000 each to display their products and services in a catalog-type format. Suppliers benefit because they have access to and can build relationships with lots of potential buyers. The buyers trust the suppliers because EDS selected them and they pay lower prices because suppliers' costs are lower in this channel: One vendor reported a drop in order-processing expenses from $150 to $25 per item. Buyers benefit by having desktop access to convenient product information, click-of-a-mouse purchasing, product delivery tracking, online training, and expedited delivery. The Renasence Channel both creates a barrier to entry for suppliers not part of the network and presents switching costs for companies using the channel's services. The Renasence Channel is a good example of relationship building in the B2B market using Internet technology.

5. CRM Processes

CRM involves an understanding of the customer care life cycle, as presented in Exhibit 14 - 11. Firms monitor and attract customers, both online and offline, as they progress through the stages: target, acquire, transact, service, retain, and grow. This begins with the e-marketing plan when companies select target markets. However, opportunities often arise when a new target group appears at the Web site—such as when Brooks Brothers noted a large number of Japanese users at the site. Thus, the cycle is circular in nature: for example, while servicing customers a new target may emerge. This important cycle is based on one central tenet of CRM—it is better to attract, retain, and grow customers than to focus only on customer acquisition. Of course, not all customers go through this process—some do less business with the firm or leave to transact with a competitor. Sometimes companies try to reacquire these companies,

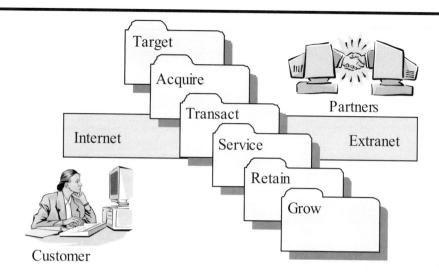

Exhibit 14 - 11 Customer Care Life Cycle
Source: Adapted from speech by Tod Famous, Cisco Systems.

as when AOL sends CDs to customers who have cancelled their accounts, with the line "We want you back. . . " and an offer of free service for a certain period.

Digging deeper into CRM techniques reveals that firms use the process shown in Exhibit 14 - 12 to focus on moving specific individual customers through the customer care life cycle.

Identifying Customers

Firms obtain prospect, business customer, and end consumer information through personal disclosure, automated tracking through the sales force, customer service encounters, bar code scanners at retailers, and Web site activity. Every piece of user information goes into a database that helps firms identify the best customers. *Best* is described many different ways, such as highest value, longest loyalty, highest frequency of purchase, and so on, as described next.

Differentiating Customers

Customers have different needs. The Internet allows firms to collect information to identify various benefit segments and individual similarities and differences and use this information to increase profits.

One very important way to differentiate is by customer value: Not all customers have equal value to a firm. One rule of thumb states that 20% of the customers provide 80% of the business's profits (recall the Pareto principle pyramid from Chapter 11). While this varies widely by industry and firm, CRM allows marketers to

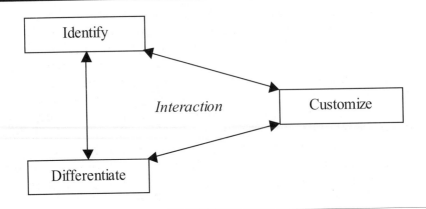

Exhibit 14 - 12 CRM Process
Source: Formulated from the ideas of Moon (2000) and Kasanoff and Thompson (1999).

leverage their resources by investing more in the most lucrative customers. The idea is not new but what is new is that technology allows firms to identify high-value customers and respond with offers in real time over the Internet. Value differentiation pays off: When a plastics firm focused on its most profitable customers, it cut its customer base from 800 to 90 and increased its revenues by 400% (Renner 2000). However, not all firms have high- and low-value customers. According to the Rogers and Peppers Group, differentiation by valuation is not profitable unless a firm can say that at least half of its profits come from 20% or fewer of its customers (the A and A+ customers in Chapter 11).

How can firms identify their high-value customers? By mining and profiling in customer databases and using real-time and real-space data collection techniques (for a review see Chapters 4 and 6). Many firms use RFM analysis (recency, frequency, monetary) to mine databases for customers who spend the most money and buy frequently and recently. They also evaluate sales growth per customer over time and determine service costs for individual customers.

Some customers call more often with questions and inquiries; some return products more frequently. Some customers are clearly not profitable and, thus, should be "fired" so that the firm can allocate resources profitably. For example, in the stockbrokerage business, clients trading small numbers of shares and calling often for information are clearly not profitable. Conversely, big traders can be offered personalized Web pages with account and investment information tailored to their portfolios. This is one reason for the huge success of online trading. Offline brokerage firms cannot operate profitably by offering low prices on small trades the way automated online firms can.

Customizing the Marketing Mix

Once a firm has identified prospects and differentiated customers according to characteristics, behavior, needs, or value, it can consider customizing offerings to various segments or individuals. Customer needs are paramount, and if the firm has done its homework it will have the data to make customization decisions. **Customization** occurs throughout the marketing mix, not just in the product offerings. Further, marketing communication messages can be tailored to individuals and delivered over the Internet in a timely manner (see Chapter 13); dynamic pricing is another option (see Chapter 11). These approaches were not possible before the Internet except with very high-priced products such as manufacturing equipment. Through customization firms can zero in on the precise needs of each prospect and customer and build long-term, profitable relationships. The mission statement for MatchLogic, Inc. puts the customization goal quite succinctly:

> To deliver the right marketing message, to the right person, with the right offer, at the right time, and know within seconds if that message was effective.

Some writers use the term *personalize* when referring to customization. **Personalization** marketing refers to such things as Web pages that greet users by name or e-mail that is automatically sent to individuals with personal account information. We use the term *customization* because it refers to much more than automated personalization: for example, product configuration at Blue Nile and dynamic pricing at FedEx—both customer initiated.

Interaction

Implicit in the MatchLogic statement is a feedback loop. Interaction with customers is what allows firms to collect the data necessary for identification and differentiation and to evaluate the resulting customization effectiveness on a continuous basis. Peppers and Rogers (1997, p. 15) call this a "learning relationship."

> A **learning relationship** between a customer and an enterprise gets smarter and smarter with each individual interaction, defining in ever more detail the customer's own individual needs and tastes.

The idea here is that both the firm and the customer learn from each experience and interaction. In a perfect relationship, this equates to increased trust, loyalty, and an increasing share of mind for the firm, with peace of mind for the customer. The Internet is uniquely positioned to deliver on this promise. When a company adopts this philosophy, it is a learning organization, as presented in Chapter 6.

6. CRM Information

Information is the lubricant of CRM. The more information a firm has, the better value it can provide to each customer and prospect in terms of more accurate, timely, and relevant offerings. Many firms entice customers to provide additional information over time. For example, Orbitz.com first requests a simple e-mail address from those who want information about discount offers and subsequently asks about vacation preferences so as to provide more relevant e-mailings. When a customer provides increasingly more personal information, she trusts the firm enough to invest in the relationship. Sometimes firms gather this type of information under the guise of entertainment. For example, Stolichnaya vodka gains valuable information about the preferences of site visitors by allowing them to mix their own drinks at its virtual bar, name the drinks, and submit their recipes (Moon 2000).

Firms gain much information from customers less intrusively by tracking their behavior electronically. Information technology allows companies to move beyond the traditional segment profiling (e.g., Generation X) to detailed profiles of individuals. For example, when product bar code scanner data collected at the checkout is combined with a store shopping card, the company can identify individual customer purchases over time. On the Internet, software tracks a user's movement from page to page, indicating how much time was spent on each page, whether the user made a purchase, the type of computer and operating system, and more. Firms can track which sites users visited before and after theirs, use this information to guess which competitive products are under consideration, and learn what about users' interests. Tracking user behavior is useful to both users and companies but it has its critics because of privacy considerations, as previously mentioned.

Retailers face the daunting task of gathering information from each channel and filtering it into a common database. The Sharper Image does this brilliantly. Now a customer can telephone the customer service representative to discuss a product purchased in the brick-and-mortar store last week, and refer to an e-mail sent yesterday, because the data are all in the database under one customer record. This is known as having a 360-degree customer view, or one view across channels. In her book, *Customers.com*, Patricia Seybold (1998) identifies eight critical success factors for building successful e-business relationships with customers. These factors are a good springboard to understanding how Internet technologies facilitate customer relationship management using e-marketing.

- Target the right customers—identify the best prospects and customers and learn as much about them as possible.
- Own the customer's total experience—this refers to the customer share of mind or share of wallet previously discussed.
- Streamline business processes that impact the customer—this can be accomplished through CRM-SCM integration and monomaniacal customer focus.
- Provide a 360-degree view of the customer relationship—this means that everyone in the firm who touches the customer should understand all aspects of her relationship with the company. For example, customer service reps should know all customer activity over time and understand which products and services might benefit that particular customer.
- Let customers help themselves—provide Web sites and other electronic means for customers to find things they need quickly and conveniently, 24/7.

- Help customers do their jobs—this refers to the B2B market, and the idea that if a firm provides products and services to help customers perform well in their businesses, they will be loyal and pay a premium for the help. Many supply chain management electronic processes facilitate this factor.

- Deliver personalized service—customer profiling, privacy safekeeping, and marketing mix customizing all aid in delivering personalized services electronically.

- Foster community—enticing customers to join in communities of interest that relate to a firm's products is one important way to build loyalty.

7. CRM Technology

Technology greatly enhances CRM processes. Incoming toll-free numbers, electronic kiosks, fax-on-demand, voice mail, and automated telephone routing are examples of technology that assist in moving customers through the life cycle. The Internet, however, is the first fully interactive and individually addressable low-cost multimedia channel—it forms the centerpiece of a firm's CRM abilities. Cookies, Web site logs, bar code scanners, and other tools help to collect information about consumer behavior and characteristics. Databases and data warehouses store and distribute these data from online and offline touch points, thus allowing employees to develop marketing mixes that better meet individual needs

Important tools that aid firms in customizing products to groups of customers or individuals include "push" strategies that reside on the company's Web and e-mail servers, and "pull" strategies that are initiated by Internet users. The difference is important, because firms have more control over push techniques.

Company-Side Tools

Exhibit 14 - 13 displays important e-marketing tools used by firms to push customized information to users. Users are generally unaware that marketers are collecting data and using these technologies to customize offerings.

Cookies

Cookie files are the reason that customers returning to Amazon.com get a greeting by name, and that users don't have to remember passwords to every site for which they are registered. Cookie files allow ad-server firms to see the path users take from site to site and, thus, serve advertising banners relevant to user interests. Finally, cookies keep track of shopping baskets and other tasks so that users can quit in the middle and return to the task later. Although there was some initial negative backlash against the use of cookie files, they have become ubiquitous and accepted by most.

Company-Side Tools (push)	Description
Cookies	Cookies are small files written to the user's hard drive after visiting a Web site. When the user returns to the site, the company's server looks for the cookie file and uses it to personalize the site.
Web log analysis	Every time a user accesses a Web site, the visit is recorded in the Web server's log file. This file keeps track of which pages the user visits, how long he stays, and whether he purchases or not.
Data mining	Data mining involves the extraction of hidden predictive information in large databases through statistical analysis.
Real-time profiling	Real-time profiling occurs when special software tracks a user's movements through a Web site, then compiles and reports on the data at a moment's notice.
Collaborative filtering	Collaborative filtering software gathers opinions of like-minded users and returns those opinions to the individual in real time.
Outgoing e-mail Distributed e-mail	Marketers use e-mail databases to build relationships by keeping in touch with useful and timely information. E-mail can be sent to individuals or sent *en masse* using a distributed e-mail list.
Chats Bulletin boards	A firm may listen to users and build community by providing a space for user conversation on the Web site.
iPOS terminals	**Interactive point-of-sale terminals** are located on a retailer's counter and used to capture data and present targeted communication.

Exhibit 14 - 13 Selected E-Marketing "Push" Customization Tools

Web Site Log

By performing **Web log analysis**, firms can do many things, not the least of which is to customize Web pages based on visitor behavior. Software, such as FlashStats, also tells which sites the users visited immediately before arriving, what keywords they typed in at search engines to find the site, user domains, and much more. See the AutoTrader.com opening story to Chapter 4 to understand how a firm makes sense of 25 million lines of Web logs on a daily basis.

Data Mining

Marketers don't need *a priori* hypotheses to find value in databases but use software to find patterns of interest. For example, Nissan used E.piphany software to increase its sophistication with up-selling and cross-selling. Prior to using the software,

Nissan would simply attempt to sell the same model of automobile as previously owned to a repeat customer. Using E.piphany data mining software, Nissan identified a group of affluent, loyal customers with children ages 19 to 24 living at home who purchased the Sentra model. Nissan used this information to cross-sell Sentras to other customers fitting the same profile. Even though Nissan did not use the Web, this is a great e-marketing application.

Real-Time Profiling

Customer profiling uses data warehouse information to help marketers understand the characteristics and behavior of specific target groups. American Express has done this for years: It sends bill inserts to groups of customers based on their previous purchasing behavior. What's new is that this can all be done online inexpensively via e-mail and customized Web pages. *Real-time profiling*, also known as tracking user clickstream in real time, allows marketers to profile and make instantaneous and automatic adjustments to site promotional offers and Web pages. For example, the software could be set to use the following rule: If a customer orders a Dave Matthews Band CD, display a Web page offering a concert T-shirt. TokyoPop.com, a site targeted to Generation Y, carries real-time profiling over to all its affiliate sites. Every time a TokyoPop registered member visits an affiliate site, it serves rule-based content, advertising, or offers. This builds relationships because members are presented with relevant and timely offers, which increases their business with TokyoPop.

Consumers visiting Greatcoffee.com are greeted with personalized Web content on the very *first visit*! The site doesn't know who users are because they have never entered information at the site nor been given a cookie file from Greatcoffee (Peppers 2000). So how is it done? The site uses real-time profiling to match a database of anonymous cookie files from Angara. This firm's e-Commerce Targeting Service purchased over 20 million anonymous cookie files with demographic and geographic data from firms such as Dell Computer (all personal information is removed first). When users surf to the Web sites at Angara's clients, such as Greatcoffee.com, this database is accessed and relevant Web page content served. For example, if Angara matches a new user's IP address and other easily obtained information and the database shows she lives in California, the site might display the greeting, "Drink our coffee, win free San Francisco Giants tickets." This happens in less than a half a second and has increased surfer-to-buyer conversion to twice the normal amount in some segments. In addition, the reorder rate at Greatcoffee.com is 60% versus 5% before using Angara's service.

Collaborative Filtering

In the offline world, individuals often seek the advice of others before making decisions. Similarly, collaborative filtering software gathers the recommendations of an entire group of people and presents the results to a like-minded individual.

BOL.com, an international media and entertainment store (owned by Germany's DirectGroup Bertelsmann), uses NetPerceptions collaborative filtering software to observe how users browse and buy music, software, games, and more at its site. The more time a user spends at the site, the more BOL.com will learn about her behavior and preferences, and the better able it will be to present relevant products ("learning relationship"). BOL.com notes that it realized increased revenues from using this software, and achieved a positive ROI within months. In its brochure, Net Perceptions claims that its "recommendation engines":

> Harness the collective knowledge of all your customers to make predictions for an individual. It is based on collaborative filtering technology, which automates word-of-mouth recommendations. . . The recommendation engine lets you generate online recommendations in real-time, and dynamically tailor content and advertising to [the user's] preferences. With every visit, the recommendation engine learns more and gets smarter.

To see how collaborative filtering works, check out Chapter 4.

Outgoing E-Mail

As discussed in Chapter 13, outgoing e-mail from firm to customer is the Net's "killer app." E-mail is used to communicate with individuals or lists of individuals (*distributed e-mail*) in an effort to increase their purchases, satisfaction, and loyalty. E-mail sent to distribution lists is redistributed to the entire subscription list. Many companies maintain e-mail distribution lists for customers and other stakeholders.

Permission marketing dictates that customers will be pleased to receive e-mail for which they have opted-in. MyPoints rewards consumers with points and gift certificates, all for reading targeted e-mail ads and shopping at selected sites (Exhibit 14 - 15). MyPoints client companies pay a fee for these e-mails, some of which go directly to customers as points. MyPoints advertises "responsible" e-mail messaging, meaning that consumers agree to receive commercial messages within their e-mails. Conversely, spam does not build relationships but instead focuses on customer acquisition. The Internet provides the technology for marketers to send 500,000 or more e-mails at the click of a mouse, and all for less than the cost of one postage stamp. Relationship-building e-mail requires sending e-mails that are valuable to users, sending them as often as users require, and offering users the chance to be taken off the list at any time. It means talking and listening to consumers as if they were friends.

Chat and Bulletin Boards

Firms build community and learn about customers and products through real-time chat and bulletin board/newsgroup e-mail postings at its Web site (for a government example see Exhibit 14 - 15: "My Government Listens"). Analysis of these exchanges is used in the aggregate to design marketing mixes that meet user needs. For example, if many consumers log onto a Caribbean Chat at Expedia, it might feature special tours o Caribbean islands during the next week (www.expedia.com).

Exhibit 14 - 14 MyPoints Rewards Members for Time Spent Online
Source: www.mypoints.com.

Expedia can also send e-mail notes to users who participate in the chats with offers of special tours. Lively and useful chat and bulletin boards increase repeat visits and site stickiness.

iPOS Terminals

These are small customer facing machines near the brick-and-mortar cash register, used to record a buyer's signature for a credit card transaction. They are important because they can gather survey and other data as well as present individually targeted advertising and promotions as well. Federated Department Stores installed 34,000 of these Web-enabled machines in 2001. The retailer has used signature data to see if women are buying their own clothing, as well as clothing for male family members, and it plans to use the terminals to send images and personalized messages—all generated from a database and sent over the Internet.

Client-Side Tools

Client-side tools come into play based on a user's action at her computer or handheld device. Although the tools generally reside on a Web server, it is the customer "pull" that initiates the customized response. See Exhibit 14 - 16.

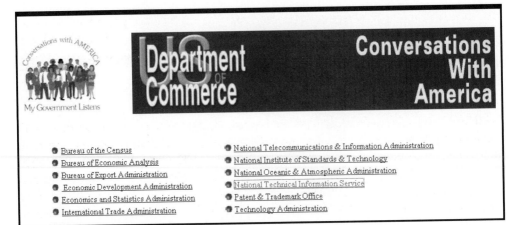

Exhibit 14 - 15 Chat Opportunities with the U.S. Government and Its Citizens
Source: www.commerce.gov.

Agents

Software agents such as shopping agents and search engines match user input to databases and return customized information. Agent software, such as Inference's k-Commerce products, often relies on more than one interaction. For example, a user might type in "computer" on the Dell site and then be presented with either laptop or desktop options. This process continues until the search is narrowed. Similarly, when

Client-Side Tools (pull)	Description
Agents	Agents are programs that perform functions on behalf of the user, such as search engines and shopping agents.
Experiential marketing	**Experiential marketing** gets the consumer involved in the product to create a memorable experience, offline or online.
Individualized Web portals	Personalized Web pages users easily configure at Web sites such as MyYahoo! and many others.
Wireless data services	Wireless Web portals send data to customer cell phones, pagers, and PDAs, such as the PalmPilot.
Web forms	Web form (or HTML form) is the technical term for a form on a Web page that has designated places for the user to type information for submission.
Fax-on-demand	With **fax-on-demand**, customers telephone a firm, listen to an automated voice menu, and select options to request a fax be sent on a particular topic.
Incoming e-mail	E-mail queries, complaints, or compliments initiated by customers or prospects comprise incoming e-mail, and is the fodder for customer service.

Exhibit 14 - 16 Selected E-Marketing "Pull" Customization Tools

visitors to Yahoo! use a keyword search, they often receive a banner or other ad based on the word they entered along with a customized Web page of Web site links. For example, if a user types "automobile" into the search box, an ad for Toyota might be returned along with the list of relevant sites.

Experiential Marketing

In the brick-and-mortar world FAO Schwartz's Chicago store is a cool playland, with a xylophone bridge and other attractions. On the Internet, Calvin Klein developed an interactive, experience-based campaign to promote CK One, the unisex fragrance (Moon 2000). CK One advertising included three characters, each with social dilemmas representative of those in the target market (e.g., hip jobs and new romances). The advertising invited viewers to e-mail campaign characters, and each e-mail received standard replies that developed the characters a bit more. This type of offline/online integration, when combined with customized experiences, builds positive relationships between customers and brands. The movie and sports industries are quite adept at creating online experiences. Some marketers predict that after all firms become adept at CRM, it will no longer be a differentiation factor and only product experiences will differentiate products. This is possible but probably not in the near future.

Individualized Web Portals

The Wall Street Journal's online edition allows individual customers to create a personalized Web page based on keywords of interest. This is particularly helpful for business readers who want to monitor stories about their competitors. *The Wall Street Journal* creates a structural bond with individual customers, thereby boosting loyalty—something that was unheard of prior to the Internet.

Individualized Web portals are more often used to build relationships in the B2B market than the B2C market. It is through these portals that supply chains access inventory and account information and track various operations. Webridge sells partner and customer relationship management software (PRM/CRM) that allows businesses to access all the data they need on demand. This is a huge improvement over the previous method, where buyers searched through piles of brochures, catalogs, and price lists that included many products not carried by channel partners and were constantly out-of-date. InFocus Systems used Webridge software to send offers of interest via e-mail to partners and then serve Web pages customized to display those featured products and prices when partners visited the site. Primedia, a health care training company, used Webridge software to create a site for hospitals, doctors, and other partners using its services. Differentiating customers, it offers four layers of entry to the site: visitor, registered user, member, and premier partner. B2B Web portals use extranets to access partner information.

Wireless Data Services

Wireless data services are included as a separate tool because of their rapid growth and distinctive features. These portals are remarkable because wireless users only want text data due to the screen size of wireless devices and download time for graphics. Services such as AvantGo.com offer users news headlines, sports scores, stock quotes, weather in selected cities, and more to users on pagers. Microsoft's wireless services even notify users when they've received a new e-mail in their Hotmail account (mobile.msn.com). As users customize this information, they give serving firms a better idea of how to better serve them and, thus, build relationship. In the future, watch for mobile data aggregators, as discussed previously in this book. Firms such as Yodlee.com allow mobile or desktop access to Web sites, online accounts, user data anywhere, anytime.

Web Forms

Many corporate Web sites sport Web forms, using them for a multitude of purposes from site registration and survey research to product purchase. In fact, many sites strive to build the number of registered users as a prelude to transactions. For example, the U.S. Federal Trade Commission (FTC) allows consumers to complain about questionable business practices and advertising via its Web site form. Regardless of purpose, the information gathered serves to help the firm build relationships and move users through the customer life cycle.

Fax-on-Demand

In the B2B market, firms often want information sent via fax machine. Services such as eFax.com allow Internet users to send and receive fax transmissions at their Web sites. Why would a user use this service as opposed to an e-mail attachment? This is appropriate when the document is not in digital form, a signature is needed, or Internet access is not available so the document cannot be sent as an e-mail attachment. Also, eFax is handy for users who do not want to leave their fax machines online constantly. EFax will notify users by e-mail if a fax is waiting and they can download it when convenient.

Incoming E-Mail

Post transaction customer service is an important part of the customer care life cycle. Normally the Web online channel consists of a feedback button or form that delivers an e-mail message to the corporation. Often an automated customer service program acknowledges the message via e-mail and indicates that a representative will be responding shortly. Research shows that firms are getting much better at responding to incoming e-mail. In one study, 100% of customer service departments responded to e-mail inquiries within one week: 26% responded within a day, and 51% responded the same day ("Vast Improvements in. . . " 2001). Companies should include feedback options online only if they have staff in place to respond: E-mail addresses on a Web site imply a promise to reply. Some firms, such as Apple

Computer, decide not to provide e-mail feedback from their Web sites, opting instead for automated telephone routing.

CRM Metrics

E-marketers use numerous metrics to assess the Internet's value in delivering CRM performance—among them are ROI, cost savings, revenues, customer satisfaction, and especially the contribution of each CRM tactic to these measures. Recall that all e-marketing performance measures assess specific tactics from different perspectives, and that the metrics of choice depend on the firm's goals and strategies (refer to the balanced scorecard in Chapter 2). Here we present a few of the common metrics used to track customers' progress through the customer life cycle Exhibit 14 - 17.

Armed with this and other information about what makes customers value the firm's products, firms attempt to increase conversion and retention rates, reduce defection rates, and build AOV and profits per customer over time (acquire, retain, grow). For example, FTD.com, the florist, worked hard in 2001 to improve its CRM metrics over those in 2000. In the second quarter, it successfully increased orders year-to-year from 514,000 to 624,000, increased AOV from $57.00 to $58.93, and reduced marketing costs 8%, from $8.30 to $7.67 (Cox 2002).

In addition to performance improvements, many firms use some of these methods to identify the least profitable customers and minimize interactions with them. The point is not to treat some customers poorly but to try to minimize the time invested in servicing low-profit customers.

One very important CRM metric deserves more discussion—customer **lifetime value (LTV),** shown in Exhibit 14 - 18, is an adaptation of an LTV calculation from the Peppers and Rogers Group. This calculation assumes that the firm has 1,000 customers in the first year, each spending an average of $35.90. In the second year, 60% of the customers are retained, and due to clever cross- and up-selling, they each spend $75.90 in that and subsequent years. The second to last column includes the net present value of each year's net profits, calculated at 15%. Finally, the 10-year LTV of each customer is displayed. The numbers may look smaller than expected because this calculation realistically discounts revenue to its present value. Note that the LTV increases after the fifth year due to a higher retention rate in later years. Even with this high retention rate assumption (60% to 80%), notice how few customers are left in year 10. This calculation demonstrates the benefits of retaining customers over time and the need for building share of wallet. It also shows that no matter how good a firm is at retaining customers, new customer acquisition is still an important activity.

Target
- Recency, frequency, monetary analysis (RFM)—identifies high-value customers.
- Share of customer spending—proportion of revenues from high-value customers as compared to low-value customers.

Acquire
- New customer acquisition cost (CAC).
- Number of new customers referred from partner sites.
- Campaign response—click-throughs, conversions, and more from Chapter 13.
- Rate of customer recovery—proportion of customers who drop away that the firm can lure back using various offers.

Transact
- Prospect conversion rate—percent of visitors to site that buy.
- Customer cross-sell rate from online to offline, and the reverse.
- Services sold to partners.
- Sales of a firm's products on partner Web sites.
- Average order value (AOV)—dollar sales divided by the number of orders for any given period.
- Referral revenue—dollars in sales from customers referred to the firm by current customers.
- Sales leads from Internet to closure ratio.

Service
- Customer satisfaction ratings over time (see Cisco opening story).
- Time to answer incoming e-mail from customers.
- Number of complaints.

Retain
- Customer attrition rate—proportion who don't repurchase in a set time period.
- Percentage of customer retention—proportion of customers who repeat purchase.

Grow
- Lifetime value (LTV)—net present value of the revenue stream for any particular customer over a number of years.
- AOV over time—increase or decrease.
- Average annual sales growth for repeat customers over time.
- Loyalty program effectiveness—sales increase over time.
- Number of low-value customers moved to high value.

Exhibit 14 - 17 CRM Metrics by Customer Life Cycle Stage

Year	Total Customers	Retention Rate	Total Revenue	Net Profit	NPV at 15%	10-Year LTV
1	1,000	60%	$35,900	$ 5,900	$ 5,900	$ 66.94
2	600	65%	45,540	27,540	23,948	118.12
3	390	70%	29,601	17,901	13,536	129.15
4	273	75%	20,721	12,531	8,239	138.35
5	205	78%	15,541	9,398	5,373	143.45
6	160	79%	12,122	7,330	3,645	145.55
7	126	80%	9,576	5,791	2,504	146.81
8	101	80%	7,661	4,633	1,742	146.81
9	81	80%	6,129	3,706	1,212	146.81
10	65	80%	4,903	2,965	843	146.81

Exhibit 14 - 18 Customer Lifetime Value (LTV)

Source: Adapted from Peppers and Rogers Group at www.1to1.com.

Summary

Marketers have practiced relationship marketing for some time; however, Internet technologies made it possible to manage relationships one at a time. In the move from mass marketing to relationship marketing, the emphasis has become long-term customer retention rather than many discrete transactions with new customers.

Customer relationship management is used to create and maintain relationships with employees, business customers in the supply chain, lateral partners, and final consumers. CRM's benefits include cost-effective acquisition, retention, and growth of current customers as well as word-of-mouth referrals. The three legs of CRM are sales force automation, marketing automation, and customer service. The Gartner Group model of CRM covers seven building blocks: CRM vision, CRM strategy, valued customer experience, organizational collaboration, CRM processes, CRM information, and CRM technology.

The CRM vision must include guarding of customer privacy and building user trust. CRM strategy starts by defining what the company wants to accomplish with CRM technology. Relationship intensity ranges from awareness (the lowest intensity) to advocacy (the highest intensity). Three relationship levels mark the bonds that e-marketers build with customers. The highest level of CRM involves creating structural bonds that raise switching costs and build loyalty. E-marketers need to think about the experience of their valued customers, how customers prefer to interact with companies, and how they can forge ties through community building.

An important trend in CRM is the integration with supply chain management (SCM). When the firm's front end, back end, and supply chain all focus on the consumer, value is delivered, satisfaction is increased, and the firm has a competitive edge. The customer care life cycle covers the stages of targeting, acquiring, transaction, servicing, retaining, and growing customers by identifying customers, differentiating customers, and customizing the marketing mix for targeted segments or individuals—customization. CRM depends on information and on technology using company-side tools (including cookies, Web site logs, data mining, real-time profiling, collaborative filtering, outgoing e-mail, chat and bulletin boards, and iPOS terminals) and client-side tools (including agents, experiential marketing, individuals Web portals, wireless data services, Web forms, fax-on-demand, and incoming e-mail). Then e-marketers use a variety of metrics to assess the performance and value of using the Internet for CRM.

Key Terms

Customer care life cycle

Customer relationship management (CRM)

Customization

Experiential marketing

Fax-on-demand

Interactive point of sale terminals (iPOS)

Learning relationship

Lifetime value (LTV)

Marketing automation

Personalization

Relationship capital

Relationship marketing

Sales force automation (SFA)

Share of customer

Web log analysis

Wireless data services

Exercises

Review Questions

1. Explain why relationship capital is the foundation of future business.
2. Define relationship marketing and contrast it with mass marketing.
3. What are the main benefits of CRM?
4. Why do companies use sales force automation and marketing automation?
5. What are the seven building blocks of CRM?
6. What are the five levels of relationship intensity and why do e-marketers strive to move customers to the top level?
7. Why do e-marketers see community building as an important aspect of CRM?
8. What are the advantages to CRM-SCM integration? Give an example.
9. What are the six stages in the customer care life cycle?
10. Explain how data mining, real-time profiling, collaborative filtering, and outgoing e-mail help firms customize offerings.

11. How are company-side and client-side customization tools different? Explain your answer.

Discussion Questions

12. Explain the difference between share of mind and share of market.

13. If good relationship marketing means firing a company's least profitable or most costly customers, suggest how this might be accomplished without causing them to criticize the company to their friends.

14. Explain how the customer benefits from SCM-CRM integration.

15. Do you agree with the statement that the customer's goal in relationship marketing is choice reduction? Are consumers really such creatures of habit? Why or why not?

16. Which tools do you think are more powerful for building relationships—company-side tools or client-side tools? Why?

17. Compare and contrast the concept of differentiating customers with that of differentiating products.

18. As a consumer, would you be more likely to buy from a Web site displaying the TRUSTe seal and logo than from a competing Web site without the TRUSTe affiliation? Explain your answer.

Practitioner Perspective

Home Page Copy Makeover Triples Conversion from Visitor to Customer

Debbie Weil is president of WordBiz.com, Inc. and publisher of WordBiz Report, an e-newsletter enjoyed for its cogent analysis of what makes words drive revenues online (www.wordbiz.com). She is also a longtime columnist for ClickZ.com on B2B Email Marketing and E-newsletter Strategies. Debbie has an M.B.A. from Georgetown University, a master's in journalism from the University of Wisconsin and a B.A. from Harvard in English.
E-mail: debbie@wordbiz.com.

What makes a home page convert your visitors into customers? Is it the copy, the design and layout, the navigation, the perceived value of your product or service? The answer is all of the above. But effective copy is a key element that propels a visitor to click for answers to his or her decision points and then take action on your site.

A before and after home page copy makeover offers some great lessons on how small changes in wording and design can yield significant business results. In this case, the number of solid leads generated by this small business site tripled from five to seven a month to 15 to 20 for the same time period. Here's how they did it.

Max-Effect (www.max-effect.com), a company that designs display ads for the Yellow Pages, had a frustrating problem: They were getting good traffic to their site through pay-per-click advertising with Yahoo! but visitors were not turning into leads. In other words, their home page wasn't "converting" clicks into customers. They consulted FutureNow (www.futurenowinc.com) "conversion rate" consultants who eliminate barriers preventing a visitor from taking the desired action on a Web site to convert to a customer, a subscriber or a qualified lead.

The *Before* Home Page Copy

Max-Effect's old site   http://www.max-effect.com/oldsite was "not that bad," according to FutureNow's CIO Bryan Eisenberg. The 800-number (i.e., the call to action) is displayed prominently. Still, the home page in particular had some obvious problems. Light-colored text on a dark background was hard to read. A bright red logo was hard to decipher. It was not clear where to start and it wasn't clear where to go next (hence, few conversions to sale). Key copy points were buried in italics below a noninspiring headline. The most prominent bit of copy was a purple scrawl that expressed a negative spin on what MaxEffect offers: "eliminate yellow page advertising hassles forever." Max-Effect agreed that FutureNow would rewrite three key pages (home page, ad samples page, and contact us page) to make them friendlier and to encourage visitors to pick up the phone and call to place an order.

Simple Design on a White Background

The design was changed from a dark to a white background and kept deliberately simple. Colors were modified from the rather jarring purple and red to a warmer blue and orange. A new logo is more up-to-date looking. The overall effect is to make the home page more cheerful and inviting.

Reorganized Copy Elements

The somewhat randomly placed blocks of copy on the old home page were re-organized so that your eye is immediately drawn to the central headline: "Maximize your investment." It's short, positive, and plays off the company name.

Precise, Specific Language Replaces Generic Phrases

Underneath it, the central copy points are listed again as a series of bullets but they've been completely rewritten. Generic phrases like "save you money, save you time, eliminate frustration" have been replaced with more precise examples of MaxEffect's value proposition: "Your customers will…be drawn to your yellow page ad more

Before: http://www.max-effect.com/oldsite

strongly than anything else on the page…Recognize that you are the solution to what they've been looking for."

Good Copy Propels a Visitor to Click for More Information

A formula for call-to-action copy on a Web page:

- Make the text scannable by bolding key phrases. Although this may not be appropriate for every site, it seems to work on the new Max-Effect home page.
- Use interesting, informational headlines and subheads.
- Follow the AIDA principle (engage attention and interest, stir desire, stimulate action).
- Give the reader immediate satisfaction by anticipating and then answering his or her question.

How to Write an Effective Text Link

Use hypertext links strategically. A visitor looking to buy (or compare) always has questions. Make each text link "an imperative with an implied benefit," advises Eisenberg. In plain English, tell 'em what to do ("Find out more" is an imperative.) At the same time, imply that visitors will find the answer to their question as soon as

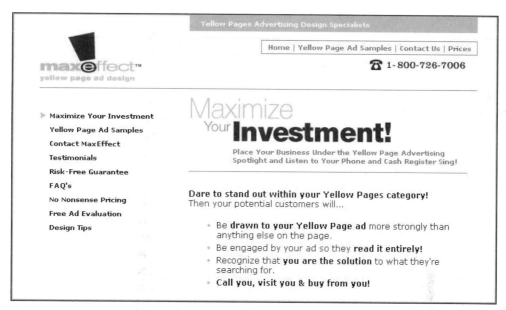

After: www.max-effect.com

they click on the text link. In this way, well-crafted copy can convert a reader into a buyer by anticipating and satisfying questions and by filling in the missing gaps at each step of the conversion process.

The take-home lesson: Good copy is integral to successful conversion. In addition, flaws or inefficiencies in design or navigation—or too many steps—can hamper conversion to sale.

Copyright 2002 WordBiz.com, Inc. with permission to publish in this book.

Practitioner Perspective

Migration of Direct Mail to E-Mail

Michael Hemphill, president/CEO of CSG Direct, Inc., has been in the direct-marketing industry since 1987. CSG Direct, Inc. is based in Reno, Nevada, and specializes in database marketing for gaming, tourism and nonprofit industries. Michael has also managed the installation, training, and maintenance of over 1,500 public, private, state, and federal mail processing facilities in his career. CSG Direct, Inc. was one of the first direct-mail facilities in the country to provide live job tracking over the Internet as well as direct e-mail services.
E-mail: home@csgdirect.com

Our clients are constantly pursuing better direct-marketing returns as well as programs that retain current direct-marketing returns in a growing, competitive marketplace. Marketing departments must continue to reinvent their approaches to reaching clients as old methods become outdated and slowly reduce themselves to ineffectiveness. Successful marketing campaigns grow as a diverse portfolio of branding and response-generating efforts that work to generate new business, as well as increase income from current business.

A sample marketing portfolio would include varying percentages of signage, newspaper, television, radio, direct mail, telemarketing, in-house sales, strategic alliances, broadcast faxing, event exposures, and one of the newest additions—e-mail marketing. This Marketing Portfolio will change with the marketplace, and each technique must produce its own sales, while still building on the successful message of your company brand. In this article I will be specifically addressing the migration of some direct-mail programs into e-mail programs.

Direct Mail's Primary Successes over Other Media

What direct mail offers that other marketing methods do not is the ability to reach a strategically targeted audience while accurately tracking the results. It also has the opportunity to deliver personalized offers tailored to customer buying habits, instead of the "one size fits all" promotions that traditionally come with signage, radio, newspapers, and television.

Direct mail is one of the best opportunities to interact with clients directly to gather information or take orders without the need to relate on a person-to-person basis. This allows us to have an ongoing relationship with *all* of a firm's clients instead of just the active ones. Customers develop loyalty to companies that successfully create a relationship with them and make them feel special or appreciated; this makes personalized offers an excellent solution to assist in the development of this relationship.

Direct Mail's Shortcomings

There are many mysteries left unanswered after a direct-mail campaign. What about the people who did not respond? What could we have changed to get a higher response with the same audience? What are the top five reasons that people didn't respond to our offer? Even with focus groups, firms are usually left somewhat unaware of the reasons for not responding. The most common fix for this is controlled experiments including multiple offers to the same demographics, but this only refines offers and still doesn't answer all of the questions.

Postage costs are also continuously on the rise. This year the United States Postal Service raised rates another approximately 7.7 percent. This means that companies will spend about 7.7 percent more for the same number of responses. Of course, this is multiplied by two for gathering information using surveys since the cost of return mail has increased as well. These postage rates do not decrease direct mail's effectiveness, but they can increase its cost per response.

E-Mail's Answers

E-mail has many advantages over direct mail:

- Instant delivery of message or offer—No mistakes planning delivery windows.
- Immediate changes, edits, and proofing—No costly reprinting at the last minute.
- *No* printing costs—A slow, expensive process.
- *No* postage costs—The largest cost in direct mail.
- Easily forwarded to friends—To grow customer referrals.
- Tracking of nonresponders—Now the customers can guide us.
- Instant feedback from surveys—*Live* data for event planning and inventory.
- Data collection directly from the audience—Direct data entry is more accurate.

E-mail offers an extremely reduced cost per response based on much reduced costs to produce. Additionally, e-mail introduces a new feature into the picture that gathers more information from your clients per contact than other marketing media. With the proper database in place, a company could dynamically save money on all marketing to current clients by shifting large portions from expensive media to an inexpensive direct e-mail relationship.

E-Mail Ties It All Together: The Common Thread

Billboards, radio, television, and other traditional marketing media help develop a brand reputation as well as build excitement for a firm's products. Direct mail and e-mail marketing are the means of direct contact with customers and an opportunity to ask for their business. E-mail provides the opportunity for customers to give input *before and during the sale* and to guide marketers in the right direction to *get the sale*. E-mail also continues to be the most inexpensive relationship *after the sale*.

Finally there is a method that allows firms the chance to talk to their customers and prospective customers *en masse* while also trying to sell to them. We now have the ability to inexpensively track and compile data on a campaign instantly and to change the campaign while it's in progress to ensure a higher response.

The Future Will Seem Familiar

Most traditional media will be around for a long time. However, we are also seeing new communication technologies every day. These new technologies will certainly change our marketing portfolios in the near future except for one factor—the database will continue to be the best way to communicate effectively with customers. Data based on behavioral patterns, shopping patterns, and requests for new products and services will continue to drive the most successful marketing campaigns.

Currently, the biggest challenge in our industry is managing the addition of all of these new high-tech "addresses" to the traditional databases that only cater to postal addresses. But that is another article.

Practitioner Perspective

Exploding the Web CPM Myth

Rick Boyce is a former ad agency executive and was head of sales for Wired Digital, and later Lycos, and was most recently president of IGN.com. Boyce now runs an Internet consultancy in San Francisco and can be reached on the Web at www.rickboyce.com.

Editor's Note: Rick had the foresight to write this article for the first edition of this book, and except for the numbers, it is still a visionary piece today.

As an ad guy since 1984, and an Internet ad guy since 1994, I humbly submit that I've learned a fair amount about media and media value. And I must say that I have never felt more strongly about the remarkable value Internet advertising offers to marketers. I honestly believe that the Internet is the most cost-effective medium for reaching young, educated, and affluent target audiences in America today. You may not believe this. Heck, many marketers and advertisers don't. Scarborough estimated that in 2001 the Internet represented 12% of all media consumption yet was allocated just 2% of all media spending. Incidentally, this level of spending still made U.S. Internet advertising an $8 billion industry in 2001, making it larger than outdoor or network radio.

While Internet advertising has many attributes, the focus of this article is to explore Internet cost-per-thousand (CPM) and demonstrate how Internet advertising is highly cost-efficient relative to television in delivering young, educated, upscale target audiences. Exploding the Web CPM myth, if you will. I will also elaborate on how Internet advertising makes a terrific complement to television campaigns by delivering light TV viewers and will illuminate several "small" benefits that are very important but often overlooked by buyers.

Exploding the Web CPM Myth

Since time immemorial (okay, since the mid-nineties or so) advertisers have complained that Web cost per thousand impressions (or CPM) was too high relative to other media generally and TV specifically. Even Morgan Stanley's landmark 1996 report on Internet advertising reported, "While CPMs on the Web vary widely, on average, they have been at higher levels than they are in most other media."

What is important to remember when looking at comparative CPMs is that TV is a mass-reach medium and when a target is refined by adding income and/or education screens, TV CPMs jump dramatically. The truth is that for reaching high-income, well-educated audiences, television CPMs are quite high, and Web advertising, in many cases, delivers significantly lower CPMs against the same profile.

The following exhibit explores the average CPMs for network TV and Web sites for sports, women's and business/investment content. Against broad target definitions of Men 18+ for sports content and Women 18+ for women's content, Web CPMs are

Sports Web Site vs. TV	Men 18+	Men 18+ and Any College	Men 18-49	Men 18+ and HHI $50,000+
Web Site Avg.	$25.62	$30.73	$34.01	$37.22
Network TV Avg.	$20.00	$51.22	$44.77	$51.19
Web vs. TV CPM Index	1.28	0.60	0.76	0.73

Women's Web Site vs. TV	Women 18+	Women 18+ and Any College	Women 18-49	Women 18+ and HHI $50,000+
Web Site Avg.	$13.63	$17.41	$17.93	$24.08
Network TV Avg.	$10.00	$30.60	$28.60	$32.01
Web vs. TV CPM Index	1.36	0.57	0.63	0.75

Investing and Business Web Site vs. TV	Adults 18+	Adults 18+ and Any College	Adults 18-49	Adults 18+ and HHI $50,000+
Web Site Avg.	$30.00	$34.48	$49.42	$40.27
Network TV Avg.	$50.00	$92.42	$95.57	$120.74
Web vs. TV CPM Index	0.60	0.37	0.52	0.33

Notes and sources:

1) Web site Total Audience CPMs supplied by Sportsline.com, iVillage.com, and CBSMarketwatch.com (June 2002) and represent the CPM average of all creative units offered by each.

2) Conversion factors applied to Total Audience Web site CPMs from @plan Summer 2002 Release.

3) 18+ Television CPMs based on industry estimates for :30 units. Conversion factors developed from Fall 2001 MRI.

actually higher than those offered by television. But, when the target audience is refined to include college education, or younger consumers or a household income of $50,000+, the Web CPM is actually lower and, in some cases, significantly so. For investing and business content, not only does Web advertising offer a superior CPM versus the broad target of Adults 18+, but also as you add the demographic filters of education, youth, or income, the Web CPM advantage becomes dramatic indeed.

Internet Advertising Complements TV Campaigns by Delivering Light TV Viewers

The preceding CPM comparisons demonstrate how well the Internet delivers young, well educated, and more affluent consumers and how TV actually delivers the opposite. Another tool for illustrating this is through a TV viewing quintile analysis like the one following that illustrates rating point distribution, on average, against a population of TV viewers (in this example, male viewers). What this chart demonstrates is that a network television schedule of 100 GRPs would deliver 68% of the weight to the two heaviest viewing quintiles and just 14% against the two lightest viewing quintiles. Looked at from this perspective television and the Internet are wonderfully complementary as TV provides mass reach (albeit with GRP distribution skewed to the heaviest TV viewers) while Internet advertising reaches the more upscale, light TV viewers. Thus, the two media combined in a single plan would result in more balanced media delivery across all viewing quintiles.

Quintile	% U.S. Population	Avg. Hours of Weekly Viewing	% of Total Viewing
Heaviest	20	44.7	42
Next	20	26.4	26
Next	20	18.4	18
Next	20	11.3	11
Lightest	20	3.3	3
Total	100%	104.1	100%
Average		20.8	

Source: Simmons (as published in *Media Planning. A Practical Guide* by Jim Surmanek, 1996).

Internet Advertising Offers Many "Small," Often Overlooked, Benefits

Internet advertising offers numerous "little" advantages versus other media that are often overlooked. Here are just four from my list.

1) **Extraordinary audience selectivity.** No medium can offer the target audience selectivity of the Internet. It is the ultimate vertical publishing medium and virtually any conceivable target audience is reachable online, often times with very little waste!

2) **Supershort close dates.** Want your ad to run tomorrow or maybe even later today? No other medium can get your ad up immediately (or darn close) and presented to a worldwide audience as quickly and as inexpensively as the Internet. If you have ever trafficked tapes to hundreds of stations or expressed camera-ready art to a hundred newspapers you know exactly what I'm talking about.

3) **Low cost ad production.** Even the most elaborate Internet ads utilizing Flash or other rich media technologies rarely cost more than a few thousand dollars to produce and .gif (graphical image file) ads can cost just a few *hundred dollars each.*

4) **The lean forward medium.** You literally cannot navigate the Web without high concentration and high attention levels and both are required for advertising to get noticed, remembered, and ultimately acted upon.

Internet Advertising Drives Brand Awareness and Purchase Intent

One of the biggest challenges faced by media planners has been to quantify the effectiveness of online relative to other media. This, of course, has made it difficult to rationalize an increase in spending in the medium or to add online to a plan in the first place. A 2002 research study for Unilever Home & Personal Care's Dove Nutrium Bar sponsored by the Interactive Advertising Bureau and designed by Rex Briggs of Marketing Evolution and conducted by Dynamic Logic reached these conclusions:

- Increases in online advertising spending result in increased key metrics, such as brand awareness, brand attributes, and purchase intent.

- Higher online frequency boosts branding effectiveness. Specifically, increasing the number of online impressions from six impressions to 12 impressions over six weeks increased Dove Nutrium Bar's overall branding effectiveness by 42 percent.

- TV, print, and online advertising are each effective at branding, yet online is generally more cost-efficient in terms of branding increases from the precampaign level.

"We've seen lots of proof that online advertising works, but this is the first time we have measured how online really stacks up to television and magazines," said Jim

Spaeth, president of ARF. "The results are a giant leap forward for the advertising industry, addressing a question it has long been pondering."

The Interactive Advertising Bureau, or IAB, considered these results so valuable that it secured participants for a Phase II study with more than 15 publishers and six major marketers. You can track the progress of this and other projects sponsored by the IAB at http://www.iab.net.

Parting Thoughts...

I sincerely hope that, like me, you find yourself hopelessly attracted to Internet marketing and advertising as both vocation and *advocation*. Even after eight plus years of existence, Internet advertising still fails to get the respect it deserves despite the fact that it represents an exceptional value. And sadly this lack of respect is more emotional than rational. I believe that if marketers were to look at Internet advertising objectively, they would be hard pressed to find good reasons for not adding Internet advertising to most media plans and that, my friends, is where you come in. Good luck!

S a v v y   S i t e s

1 To 1 **www.1to1.com**	This site comes from the Peppers and Rogers Group and includes interesting papers on CRM. It provides consulting services for firms that wish to have a 1-to-1 strategy.
Clickz www.clickz.com	This site provides articles on e-mail marketing, strategies, and more.
DealTime www.dealtime.com	This shopping agent is good all around. It has many categories from which to choose and it allows users to compare prices with many different online stores.
Direct Marketing Association www.the-dma.org	This is the largest trade organization for direct, database, and interactive marketing. A great source for e-commerce news and direct-marketing information.
DoubleClick www.doubleclick.com	DoubleClick is a firm that specializes in serving banner ads and closed loop marketing.

E.piphany
www.epiphany.com

A leading provider of CRM solutions. Users can sign up to receive their Catalyst Newsletter, which discusses the latest topics of interest in CRM.

Google Groups
groups.google.com

Read and post comments in a variety of Usenet discussion groups. This is the source for 700,000 archived messages since 1981.

H.O.T! Coupons
www.hotcoupons.com

This is one of many firms that offer electronic coupons. Consumers can search its database by zip code.

Interactive Advertising Bureau
www.iab.net

The Interactive Advertising Bureau is a nonprofit association entirely devoted to the coverage of advertising on the Internet. The site provides news, research materials, and membership information.

mySimon
www.mysimon.com

A great place to compare prices for just about anything you want to buy online. This site searches through other online stores, so users can find the best prices. It also provides product availability, shipping specifications, and more useful items. This is a great place to compare prices for textbooks.

NetCreations, Inc.
www.netcreations.com

NetCreations is an online firm that provides opt-in e-mail marketing services allowing direct marketers to reach prospects in a cost-effective way that respects the culture of the Internet. Its PostMaster Direct Response service is a list manager and broker for more than 1 million e-mail addresses that encompass over 3,000 topical categories. NetCreations also offers Web site promotion and per-inquiry lead generation services.

Net Perceptions
www.netperceptions.com

Net Perceptions offers CRM solutions for catalog retail, e-tail, distribution, and manufacturing clients.

NetPlus Marketing
www.netplusmarketing.com

This company provides strategic online marketing, e-mail marketing, and advertising consulting services. It provides a free newsletter, which offers Internet marketing news and tips.

PriceGrabber
www.pricegrabber.com

This shopping agent is good all around. It has many categories from which to choose, and it allows customers to compare prices with many different online stores.

PriceSCAN
www.pricescan.com

Very similar to mySimon, this site will also compare prices. This shopping guide lists product and pricing information gathered from magazine ads, catalogs, and information directly sent from vendors.

Topica
www.topica.com

This is the place to join a variety of e-mail lists.

Activities

1. Using a shopping agent such as Pricewatch, what is the very lowest price that you can find for a bare-bones notebook computer sold online? How is it configured? What is the highest price for the same computer?

2. Many companies use a new-product development process called *scenario* planning. For example, the Microsoft executives wonder what it would be like if you could search your computer for phone numbers, e-mail addresses, and both file names and document content all at once with one search word. Think of five scenarios that would make your life easier while using the Internet.

3. Clip an ad for electronic products from the newspaper. Pick a specific computer product and look up the product online using a shopping agent such as www.shopper.com or www.pricegrabber.com. Complete a table showing how the online prices compare with the local ad.

4. Survey 20 people. Ask them to rate their online purchase experience on a scale of 1 to 10, with 10 as the best. If they have never purchased online, try to find out what stops them. Summarize the results.

5. Find three banner ads that you think are particularly effective and three more that are ineffective. Explain your reasons, telling how you might improve the ineffective ads.

6. Identify a company, such as Microsoft, that advertises on TV, the Web, and one print medium. Make copies of ads from that firm and discuss the similarities and

differences among them. Is the firm following the IMC concept? Why or why not?

7. Go to www.couponsonline.com or www.hotcoupons.com and print a coupon for a retailer in your area. Visit the retailer and interview him or her about the effectiveness of the electronic coupons. How many are redeemed? How long has the offer been running? How often does the retailer change the offer?

8. Find a company online that you think does a poor job with relationship marketing. Suggest a strategy by which it could build in phases toward a structural relationship with its customers.

9. Working in small groups, discuss online shopping experiences and what companies did to meet group members' needs, including follow-up e-mail.

10. Register at two Web sites and see if you get e-mail. Identify the ways in which those sites attempt to build relationship with you: Evaluate the sites as well as the incoming e-mail.

I n t e r n e t   E x e r c i s e s

Internet Exercise: Elasticity of Demand

Airline tickets are a price-driven market for most customers. Many will trade off nonstop flights, preferred travel times, and choice of airline to get the lowest possible price. Therefore, airlines offer advance purchase discounts to make sure they fill as many seats as possible. Demand tends to be very elastic, as evidenced by the heavy reservation activity that takes place during fare wars. Notable exceptions include first-class travelers and business travelers. First-class travelers are easily segmented—they get a better seat; but business travelers often sit in coach. Ever wonder why you get a cheaper fare when you have a Saturday night stay? It's because the business traveler is willing to pay a premium to fly out and return home in the same workweek. Vacation travelers by contrast are willing to spend Saturday night. In this exercise we are going to plan a flight online in order to observe the price elasticity in this industry.

Expedia is a comprehensive travel site developed by Microsoft and then spun off as a separate company. The site allows consumers to book flights, reserve hotel rooms, and rent cars online. Sign onto the Expedia Web site at www.expedia.com. Register a new account; it's free. Then price a round-trip flight from New York (any airport) to Paris (any airport) traveling coach class, departing tomorrow, and returning one day after you arrive. Record Expedia's response in the following table. Then press the Search Again button and vary the criteria to complete the rest of the table.

Class	Departing	Returning After	Airline and Departure Flight	Price
Coach	Tomorrow	1 day		
Coach	Tomorrow	1 week		
Coach	Next month	1 day		
Coach	Next month	1 week		
First	Tomorrow	1 day		
First	Tomorrow	1 week		
First	Next Month	1 day		
First	Next Month	1 week		

For Discussion

1. What can you conclude from this example about the elasticity of demand for coach fares? For first-class fares?

2. Do you think the higher price for a first-class seat is justified by higher costs to the airline?

3. How do the prices differ for one-day versus one-week trips? How can you explain this?

4. For first class, do the prices differ for trips departing tomorrow versus next month? Why or why not?

5. What pricing approach(es) mentioned in the chapter might the airlines be using based on your research?

Internet Exercise: Hybrid Marketing Channels

Many companies have adopted multichannel distribution systems or hybrid marketing channels. This allows companies to reach different customer segments simultaneously. One segment that publishers would like to reach is college students. Traditionally, students have been reached through the campus bookstore, which is probably where you bought this book. But what if the bookstore was out of stock and you needed the text right away? You have alternatives. For example, you can purchase the book directly from Prentice Hall by phone, or you can order it online from a Web bookstore. Visit Prentice Hall at www.prenhall.com and others in the following table to explore these options. Get price quotes from at least three of the online retailers listed.

Retailer	Price	Shipping Charge	Shipping Time
Campus Bookstore			
Prentice Hall by phone			
Amazon **www.amazon.com**			
Barnes and Noble (online) **www.barnesandnoble.com**			
Varsity Books **www.varsitybooks.com**			
Bookstore at another college (online—specify)			

For Discussion

1. Which distribution channel offers the lowest prices (including shipping charges)?

2. Is the shipping time for the off-campus channels substantial enough to present a hardship for the college student segment?

3. Are there advantages to the campus bookstore that the off-campus channels cannot provide?

4. What are the advantages to the publisher for maintaining a multichannel distribution system? Disadvantages?

5. Why doesn't Prentice Hall display the text on its site and simply charge users for using and printing it?

Internet Exercise: Customer Satisfaction

In the highly competitive world of Internet content providers, customer satisfaction is key. Therefore, content providers must continuously innovate to meet or exceed customer expectations. Portals such as Yahoo! have added numerous services to their portfolios—many of them free in an effort to build lasting customer relationships. Visit Yahoo! and record five of its services that you would consider using. For each service you choose, find a competitor providing the same service and compare strengths and weaknesses. Finally, suggest Yahoo!'s competitive strategy for each service (e.g., market leader).

Service that interests you	Competitor providing the same service	Compare strengths/weaknesses	Yahoo! competitive strategy

For Discussion

1. In general, how would Yahoo! define and, thus, identify its competitors?

2. There is no charge for many Yahoo! services. What benefits does Yahoo! realize from providing these services?

3. Yahoo! has acquired some of its services through purchasing smaller Web companies. Is this a strategy you would recommend that it continue? Why or why not?

4. Is it important for Yahoo! to be the market leader in each service area? Why or why not?

5. One way that Yahoo! builds customer satisfaction is its consistently high ratings for speed of page downloads over the Internet. What are other ways Yahoo! builds relationships with customers?

chapter

15   e-marketing in emerging economies

learning objectives

The primary goal of this chapter is to examine the unique challenges and opportunities facing e-marketers that target or operate within countries with emerging economies. You will learn how consumer behavior and attitudes, payment methods, technological issues, and both economic and technological disparities within nations can influence e-marketing in less developed countries.

After reading this chapter, you will be able to:

- Define emerging economies and explain the vital role of information technology in economic development.
- Outline how e-marketers apply market similarity and analyze online purchase and payment behaviors in planning market entry opportunities.
- Describe how e-marketing strategy is influenced by computer and telephone access, credit card availability, attitudes toward Internet use, slow connection speeds, Web site design, and electricity problems.
- Review the special challenges of e-marketing on the wireless Internet in the context of emerging economies.
- Discuss the controversy related to the Digital Divide.

60% of the world's population has never made a phone call.

michael s. hart
project gutenberg

EthioGifts (www.ethiolink.com/ethiogift) is not an ordinary e-tailer. For one thing, it is located in Ethiopia—one of the poorest countries in the world. For another thing, customers can send sheep as a present if they so desire. Yes, sheep! Sheep are a traditional Ethiopian gift that folks can order through the EthioGifts Web site along with more "ordinary" gifts such as flowers, special cakes, and imported liquor. EthioGifts is an e-marketing success story, yet it illustrates many special challenges e-businesses face when they market goods and services in countries with emerging economies:

- How to deliver a package when street names and numbers are not used or are difficult to find? Solution: Call ahead and ask gift recipients to describe where they live.

- How to deliver a package when neither a mailing address nor a telephone are available? Solution: Ask for a very detailed description of the dwelling from the person who placed the order and ask for alternative delivery locations, such as at work or a friend's house.

- What happens when a package cannot be delivered? Solution: Give the buyer a refund, minus telephone and attempted delivery costs.

- How to get payment for an order if the customer has no credit card? Solution: Accept multiple payment methods, including checks and money orders.

EthioGifts has succeeded against the odds. In the midst of poverty (the average Ethiopian citizen earns about $100 a year), it is flourishing, in part, because it effectively applied key e-marketing principles. It understood its target market (Ethiopians living abroad who want to send presents to family and friends back home) and developed the right product mix (flowers, candy, cakes, liquor, and sheep) for that target. Just as important, EthioGifts used creativity to overcome some of the unique barriers of operating an e-business in an emerging economy. EthioGifts has its Web site hosted in Canada, conducts banking in Maryland, uses a California-based credit card verification service, and is registered as a U.S. business. One thing more: Gift givers can choose sheep in three sizes: small, medium, or large.

On the Internet, you can listen to a poem in Quechua with a translation. . .or get an update on the fight by the Ogiek people to keep their homes in the Mau Forest of Kenya where they have lived for centuries.

UNESCO public service applications of the internet in developing countries

Author's Note: This chapter was contributed by Al Rosenbloom, Associate Professor of Marketing at Dominican University in Illinois (arosenbl@pyro.net). In 2001, Al was a Fulbright Scholar and taught Internet Marketing to M.B.A. students in Nepal. This chapter is based on Al's experiences in a number of emerging economies with particular emphasis on Far Eastern nations, including Nepal, India, and China.

Overview of Global E-Marketing Issues

The EthioGifts example highlights some of the opportunities and challenges facing e-marketers outside the most industrialized nations. As another example, consider the ad that Accenture, the world's largest management and technology consulting firm, recently ran. The ad showed the silhouette of a Chinese fisherman atop his small boat at twilight. In the ad's right-hand corner was a headline that looked like it had been torn from a daily newspaper: "Chinese to be the number one Internet language by the year 2007." Beneath that were the words, "Now it gets interesting." This Accenture ad highlights one of the big changes online—users from other countries, speaking languages other than English, will increasingly dominate the Internet.

As shown in Exhibit 15 - 1, worldwide Internet use is projected to increase by 60% from 2002 to 2004. In 2002, one-third of all Internet users in the world lived in North America; however, by 2004, North American users will account for only a quarter of the world's active Internet users. By 2004, more Internet users will be living in Asia Pacific countries than in North America! Latin America, which will have just 6% of the world's active Internet users in 2004, will experience the greatest percentage increase in growth. Between 2002 to 2004, the number of Latin American Internet users will increase by a substantial 84%. Finally, by 2004, Europe is projected to be home to the largest number of Internet users in the world.

	Year				
	2000	2001	2002	2003	2004
North America	97.6	114.4	130.8	147.7	160.6
Europe	70.1	107.8	152.7	206.5	254.9
Asia/Pacific Rim	48.7	63.8	85.4	118.8	173.0
Latin America	9.9	15.3	22.1	31.0	40.8
Africa and Middle East	3.5	5.3	7.2	9.0	10.9
Worldwide Total	229.8	306.6	398.2	513.0	640.2

Exhibit 15 - 1 Active Adult Internet Users Aged 14+ Worldwide (in millions)
Source: Adapted from eMarketer (2000).

Changing usage rates will have a significant influence on Internet marketing. Geoffrey Ramsey, the statistician who compiled the data for the eGlobal Report 2000, noted: "The increasing number of non-US Internet users will have two important effects on the Internet. The Web's content and language will become more diversified as Internet companies catering to languages and tastes in other countries [to] provide unique local content. At the same time, a truly global Internet…is likely to accelerate the convergence of styles, tastes, and products" to create a more homogenous, global marketplace ("New eGlobal Report" 2000).

However, as with any global snapshot, important details are often hidden. One such detail is that Internet use varies greatly from country to country. Country size and population have little bearing on Internet use. Consider Russia, the largest country in the world, with 6,592,812 square miles and 145 million people spread across 11 different time zones. Despite its huge size and population, Russia has only 7.5 million Internet users (5% of the population). In contrast, Singapore, one of the world's smaller countries, is one of the most cyber-sophisticated. Covering an area of just 253 square miles with a population of 4.3 million, Singapore has 1.3 million Internet users (30% of all Singaporeans) ("The World's Online Populations" 2002). Lastly, there is the story of Bhutan, a small country in the Himalaya Mountains. It wasn't until June 2, 1999, that the 600,000 citizens of Bhutan even *had* access to the Internet. On that date, Jigme Singye Wangchuck, king of Bhutan, inaugurated Druk.net, the first and still only Internet Service Provider (ISP) in his country. The king gave Internet access as a gift to his country on the 25th anniversary of being crowned king (Long, 2000).

These brief country profiles suggest that as Internet access and use accelerates around the world, so, too, will e-marketing opportunities. Yet where will the greatest challenges lie? We believe they will be in countries with emerging economies—countries such as Russia, India, Nepal, the Czech Republic, and China, which present different and sometimes difficult decisions for e-marketers.

Emerging Economies

Countries vary in their level of economic development. Some countries, such as the United States, Canada, Japan, Australia, Great Britain, and Germany, have high levels of economic development. Economists classify these countries as *developed*. Developed countries include all of Western Europe, North America, Japan, Australia and New Zealand (Case and Fair, 2001). These countries are highly industrialized, use technology to increase their production efficiency, and, as a result, have a high gross domestic product (GDP) per capita. A high GDP means that citizens have enough discretionary income to buy items that will make their lives easier, richer, and fuller. Developed countries are, therefore, ideally suited for the broad range of e-marketing activities discussed in earlier chapters.

It is hard to find a single label to describe the rest of the world's economies. Rapid economic growth has brought some countries, such South Korea and Chile, much closer to developed economies. Yet most countries are struggling with—and working toward—improved standards of living for their citizens. We will call this broad, diversified group of countries **emerging economies**—those with low levels of gross domestic product (GDP) per capita that are experiencing rapid growth.

Countries with emerging economies can be found on every continent. In North America, Mexico has an emerging economy. All of the Central and South American countries have emerging economies. In Europe, all the countries in the former Baltic States (Latvia, Estonia, and Lithuania) and in Eastern Europe (Poland, Hungary, the Czech Republic, Slovakia, Romania, and all the states that made up the former Yugoslavia) have emerging economies. Russia, Belarus, and the Ukraine also have emerging economies, as do all the countries in Africa and in Central Asia (Afghanistan, Tajikistan, Uzbekistan, Kazakhstan, Uzbekistan), South Asia (India, Pakistan, Bangladesh, Nepal, and Bhutan), and Southeast Asia (Thailand, Vietnam, Cambodia, Myanmar and Laos). Finally, China, the world's most populous country, has an emerging economy.

Importance of Information Technology

Every country can improve its level of economic development through increased efficiencies in the production, distribution, and sale of goods and services. For countries with emerging economies, technology plays an especially important role. While technology can, in general, boost a nation's overall production capacity and efficiency, it is through the application of information technology that countries with emerging economies can really open up new, exciting, global markets. As is often noted, "The Internet accelerates the process of economic growth by speeding up the diffusion of new technologies to emerging economies" (Cateora and Graham 2002, p. 245). In the past, decades passed before many developing countries could benefit from railroads, electricity, and telephones. Today, the Internet, along with its supporting information technologies, can jump-start many national economies. For example, the prime minister of Malaysia, Mahathir Mohamad, has established a program to transform the country into Southeast Asia's premier high-tech, cyber corridor. The prime minister plans to spend more than $10 billion to achieve that goal. Whether he will succeed, only time will tell. What is not in question is that the Internet allows businesses in emerging economies to instantaneously tap a global marketplace. Successful marketing on the Internet can leapfrog a company from *nowhere* to *somewhere* overnight.

E-marketers from countries with emerging economies face a double challenge. Not only must they confront all the marketing issues and decisions described throughout this text, but they must also address some unique challenges related to the conditions of operating within a still developing nation. Some of the Internet marketing differences between developed and still developing countries were illustrated in a 1999 survey conducted by the International Telecommunications Union (ITU). When asked about the greatest obstacles to e-commerce, U.S. and

European respondents listed privacy concerns (31%), censorship (24%), navigation difficulties (17%), and taxes (9%). In contrast, respondents from countries with emerging economies listed slow connection speeds (29%), the costs of domestic phone calls (29%), Internet Service Provider costs (19%), lack of content in one's own language (10%), and lack of local content (10%) (Mannisto, 1999). In addition, businesses operating in emerging economies must deal with fewer computer users, limited credit card use, lack of secure online payment methods, and unexpected power failures. We will now look at these challenges in more detail.

Country and Market Opportunity Analysis

As noted in Chapter 3, an e-marketing plan guides the marketer through the process of identifying and analyzing potential markets. Astute global e-marketers must carefully balance two different analytical approaches. If they are operating *from* a country with an emerging economy and want to target markets *in* developed countries, they must understand **market similarity** (Exhibit 15 - 2). If, on the other hand, they are based in an emerging economy and want to market to their home (domestic) target market or if they are from a developed economy and want to target groups in an emerging economy, they must understand **market differences**—ways in which the two markets exhibit dissimilar characteristics, such as different languages, cultural behaviors, buying behaviors, and so forth.

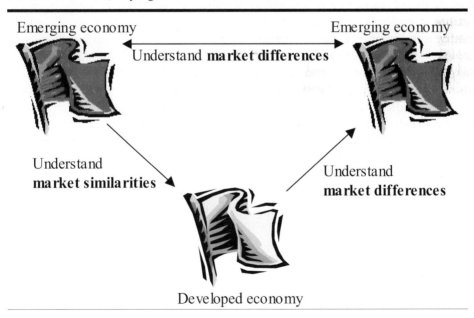

Exhibit 15 - 2 Market Approaches Between Emerging and Developed Economies

Market Similarity

According to the concept of market similarity, marketers will often choose foreign markets that have characteristics similar to their home market for initial market entry (Jeanette and Hennessey, 2002). Thus, a U. S.-based company would first target countries like Canada, the United Kingdom, and Australia before targeting countries like France, Japan, or Germany. Amazon.com has used this strategy as it expanded globally. It has international Web sites in the United Kingdom (www.amazon.co.uk), France (www.amazon.fr), Germany (www.amazon.de), Austria (www.amazon.at), and Japan (www.amazon.com.jp). While these markets share some similarities based on language (English for the U.S. and U.K. sites and German for the sites based in Germany and Austria), deeper similarities exist across each foreign market: All these countries have high literacy rates, high Internet usage rates, and clearly defined market segments willing to shop for books (and other products) online; in each country credit cards are widely used for purchases; each country has secure, trusted online payment mechanisms; and each country has efficient package delivery services. For Amazon.com, market similarity not only reduces (without eliminating) the risk of entry into foreign markets but also helps explain why it targeted these countries in the first place.

E-businesses in countries with emerging markets make parallel target market decisions. For example, Tortas Peru (www.tortasperu.com.pe) specifically targets Peruvians living abroad who would like to surprise friends and family living in Peru with homemade, traditional Peruvian cakes. All of the cakes are made in Peru for delivery to a Peruvian home market. Peruvian homemakers who need a second income to help support their families do all the baking. A similar Web site, www.munchahouse.com, offers a wide range of products that Nepalis living overseas can send to individuals back home. This site is presented online as a traditional retailer, which is appropriate because Muncha House is a famous department store in the main shopping center of Kathmandu.

Customers can pay for products on the TortasPeru and MunchaHouse sites by providing their credit card numbers using a secure server. At first glance, both sites could be mistaken for online retailing Web sites in developed countries, in part because the sites look and function like traditional retailers: They have a range of products for purchase, accept credit cards as payment, and process credit card purchases on secure servers (in these two instances the servers are located in the United States). These are all crucial marketing decisions. If, for example, the Muncha House marketer had targeted a domestic home market, his marketing situation would be completely different. One of the biggest differences between developed countries and countries with emerging economies is the limited use and acceptance of credit cards in underdeveloped countries.

Credit Card Conundrum

Convenience and ease of transactions are two of the Internet's greatest benefits. Credit cards and secure online payment systems make for seamless and easy Web-based transactions in developed countries. But in countries with emerging economies, things aren't so easy. Nepal, for example, is essentially a completely cash-based economy. Credit cards are scarce and of limited use and only issued to individuals with very high incomes. Even after someone obtains a credit card, he faces one more hurdle. Cards issued by a Nepal-based bank can be used in only two countries: Nepal and India (Minges, 2000).

The situation is similar in Bolivia, one of the poorest nations in South America. Fewer than 200,000 credit cards are in circulation within a country with a population of 8.3 million people. Only 2.3% of all Bolivians have a credit card (ITU, 2000a). Clearly, limited credit card use can severely restrict a target market's purchasing ability.

Consider the Rita's Pizza site (www.rita.lt) in Vilnius, Lithuania. This looks like a typical Web site for ordering pizza, sandwiches, snacks, and beverages online. The site is presented in two languages—Lithuanian and English—as befits the Lithuanian American who runs the restaurant. Even the graphics are bold and hip, with a sassy Lithuanian swagger. Yet the final screen for ordering indicates that Rita's is strictly a cash business. Customers either pay at the time of delivery (C.O.D.) or when they pick up the food at Rita's. The limited use and availability of credit cards in Lithuania limit what an e-marketer can accomplish.

Marketers must also analyze relevant buyer behavior within a market. In addition to knowing how many credit cards are in circulation, e-marketers working in emerging economies should understand consumer attitudes toward credit card purchases. Continuing with the e-marketing challenges Rita's Pizza faces in Lithuania, research indicates that local consumers are very reluctant to purchase products online. When surveyed, 37% said it was easier and more fun to buy goods and services in a store than online. Furthermore, 21% said it was more *secure* to buy goods and services in a store. In other words, most Lithuanians did not trust online buying. Limited credit card use, coupled with skeptical attitudes toward online purchases, may have prompted Rita's Pizza to make its site merely an online ordering mechanism. Nonetheless, the business understood one important thing: its target market. Twenty four percent of all current Lithuanian Internet users are under 20 years old, and 11% are between the ages of 20 to 25 (Taylor Nelson Sofres, 2001).

E-Commerce Payment in the Czech Republic

E-marketers in the Czech Republic face the same challenges of limited credit card use and consumer skepticism of online purchasing—but some have found innovative solutions. The Czech Republic (which is half of the former nation of Czechoslovakia) is a relatively small country in central Europe with a population of 10.2 million. Of these, 22% (2.2 million individuals) are Internet users ("The World's Online

Year	Average Monthly Sales (in Millions of Kronus)
Q1-99	5.9
Q2-99	9.9
Q3-99	18.2
Q4-99	25.6
Q1-00	28.0
Q2-00	30.0

Exhibit 15 - 3 Total Online Sales in the Czech Republic
Source: Adapted from American Chamber of Commerce… (2000).

Populations," 2002). Online purchasing has increased dramatically there in recent years, as Exhibit 15 - 3 indicates.

In 2000, most online purchases occurred in these categories: airline tickets (28%), appliances (17%), books (12%), consumer electronics (10%), videos (8%), music (6%), and computer hardware (6%) (American Chamber of Commerce…, 2000). These categories largely mirror shopping interests in developed countries. The Czech Republic has many online retailing Web sites such as www.obchodnidum.cz (a specialist in appliances, consumer electronics and mobile phones) and www.vltava.cz (a site where users can buy music, books, videos and software). The country also has specialized Web sites ranging from airline ticket agents (www.fractal.cz), wine (www.arvin.cz), and flowers (www.flowers.cz) to Czech classical music (www.musicabona.cz).

As in Lithuania, individuals in the Czech Republic still fear online shopping. In a recent survey, an astonishing 75% of the consumers interviewed said that it was more *secure* buying goods and/or services in a store than online. Sixty-five percent said it was *easier* and more *fun* to buy goods and/or services in a store, and 61% said "you don't know what you get when you shop online." Finally, 42% said they didn't trust online brands (Taylor Nelson Sofres, 2001). Savvy online marketers don't fight with their customers—they adapt their Web sites to the target market's needs and preferences. This is exactly what www.musicabona.cz has done. Recognizing that Czech consumers are hesitant to buy online, Musica Bona posts the following in its *About Security* section (www.musicabona.cz/info1/secuity.html):

When shopping at the Musica Bona store, you need have no fears about the safety of your personal data. Your personal data, including information about your payment card, is transmitted via the secure SSL encoded transfer system. If, during a purchase, you decide to become one of our registered customers, you needn't fill in your personal data and send it over the Internet at all upon subsequent purchases.

If, in spite of this, you do not think it is safe to send your personal data through the Internet, you can send your order in writing, by fax or mail. The link to the written order form is on the Shopping Basket page. If you don't want to disclose to us the number of your payment card, you can pay by cheque.

Online shopping faces many hurdles in the Czech Republic. Musica Bona understands this and gives its customers many different payment choices.

How *do* Czech consumers pay for their online purchases? Overwhelmingly, 31% make bank transfers, 28% pay cash on delivery (like customers of Rita's Pizza in Lithuania), 21% pay with a credit card, 9% make bank transfer through either a PC or mobile phone, and 8% pay with postal orders. As in other emerging countries, many Czech citizens are reluctant to use online payment methods. In addition, only 35% of all Czech adults have credit cards (American Chamber of Commerce... 2000).

An innovative solution to the credit card and online payment dilemma in the Czech Republic is found, though, in eBanka (www.ebanka.com). Established in 1998, eBanka is the oldest purely Internet bank in Central and Eastern Europe. The bank issues credit cards (Eurocard, Visa, and MasterCard) and handles secure and efficient online money transfer accounts for purchases at many Czech Web sites. A customer simply opens an eBanka account, deposits money, uses that money to make online purchases, and deposits more money when the account balance is low. This is the Czech version of digital cash. Convenient electronic transfers through eBanka can be conducted at the computer and software sites www.compucity.cz, www.ecity.cz, and www.patro.cz, as well as at the beauty and cosmetics site www.fann.cz.

Technological Readiness Influences Marketing

Solving the credit card payment conundrum is only one of several marketing challenges in emerging economies. E-marketers must also deal with daunting issues of basic technology: limited access to and use of computers and telephones, high Internet connection costs, slow Internet connection speeds, and unpredictable power supplies.

Computers and Telephones

Clearly, customers must have access to a computer and an Internet Service Provider (ISP) to use the Internet. For e-businesses operating in developed countries, this is not a problem. Individuals can use computers at home, at work, at school, or at libraries and other community institutions. For e-businesses and consumers in emerging economies, however, computer access is a big problem. Exhibit 15 - 4 shows the percentage of the population owning a personal computer in different countries.

The smaller the number in the last column of Exhibit 15 - 4, the fewer total number of computers in that country. The Ukraine has less than two computers for every 100 individuals, while a country like Colombia has about three and a half

Country	Estimated Total Number of Personal Computers in Country (in thousands)	Estimated Total Number of Personal Computers per 100 Inhabitants
Colombia	1,500	3.5
Ecuador	275	2.2
Guatemala	130	1.1
India	4,600	0.5
Jordan	150	2.3
Latvia	340	14.0
Lithuania	240	6.5
Mexico	5,000	5.1
Morocco	350	1.2
Nigeria	750	0.7
Pakistan	590	0.4
Philippines	1,480	1.9
South Africa	2,700	6.2
Thailand	1,471	2.4
Ukraine	890	1.8
United States	161,000	58.5
Zambia	70	0.7

Exhibit 15 - 4 Computer Ownership in Selected Countries
Source: ITU (2001a).

computers per 100 citizens. When compared to the United Sates, which has about 58 computers for every 100 citizens, it is apparent that computer access is unevenly distributed throughout the world. E-marketers should never underestimate the profound influence of limited computer access on Internet marketing. It directly limits market size. Exhibit 15 - 4 suggests that e-marketing faces some of its most basic challenges in countries like Pakistan, Nigeria, the Ukraine, and Ecuador.

Owning a computer is only the beginning. Individuals and businesses need to be connected to the Internet in some way. Generally, connections are made through telephone lines, although Internet connection patterns, as discussed in earlier chapters, are rapidly changing. Telephones are a common and prevalent commodity in developed countries like the United States. Most families have more than one telephone at home; many have multiple telephone lines; some even have several telephone numbers; and many may have both fixed and mobile phones.

In countries with emerging economies, however, telephones are both a scarce and expensive product. A startling statistic comes from Indonesia, the world's largest Muslim country. Muslims pray in mosques five times a day. In Indonesia, "Indonesians are closer to mosques than public phones" (ITU, 2002, p. 13). This means that while 80% of all Indonesians are less than 1 km (0.6 mile) from a mosque, only slightly more than 20% are that close to a single telephone. Forty percent of all Indonesians are more than 5 kilometers (3 miles) from a telephone (Kretek Internet,

2000). In a 1999 survey, Indonesia was reported to have only 2.9 phones for every 100 individuals. The same survey reported that India had 2.7 phones/100 people, the Philippines had 4.0 phones/100 people, Mexico had 11.2 phones/100 people, and South Africa had 13.8 phones/100 people (ITU, 2001). Finally, consider Thailand. The official Thai 2000 census reports that 91.5% of all Thais own a television, but only 27.7% own a phone. More than twice as many Thais own motorcycles (64.5%) as own telephones (27.7%) (Minges, 2001b).

In emerging economies, telephone access has a very different pattern than in developed countries. Online firms can't market to someone who has no computer or no means of connecting to the Internet, which leads to the next topic: Internet connection costs.

Internet Connection Costs

Countries with emerging economies often have higher Internet-related business costs—a concern because the Internet is essential for every e-business. Dial-up connection is the most common way of connecting to the Internet worldwide. A modem is the means through which one computer connects to and exchanges information with another computer. Dial-up connections use telephone lines. Dial-up connection costs vary quite considerably in emerging economies. Exhibit 15 - 5 compares the total access costs in various Arab countries.

The total price for 30 hours of Internet service is quite large in many countries. In Morocco, 30 hours of service costs slightly more than $70 per month; in Jordan, it costs almost $50; and in Tunisia, it costs slightly more than $40. Given the level of underdevelopment in each of these countries and their low GDP per capita, connecting to the Internet is very expensive. This situation illustrates one of the inescapable ironies of emerging economies. Although labor costs may be quite low, technology and other business costs can be quite high. Why? Two major explanations include government-owned telephone monopolies and the lack of competition among ISPs. When both of these constraints are loosened, Internet growth accelerates, creating a rapidly expanding domestic market for e-marketers.

The Egyptian government is both liberalizing and loosening its control on the telephone and ISP market. While Telecom Egypt (the government-owned state telephone company) still retains its monopoly on telephone land lines, the cellular phone market is booming in Egypt. As of April 2000, the country had 1.2 million cellular phone subscribers. In addition, the ISP market is very competitive. The two largest cities in Egypt—Cairo and Alexandria—have over 60 ISPs competing for subscribers. Egypt has an estimated 55,000 paying Internet subscribers and an estimated 250,000 Internet users, giving the country the fourth-largest number of Internet users in the Arab world, behind the United Arab Emirates, Saudi Arabia, and Lebanon (ITU, 2001b).

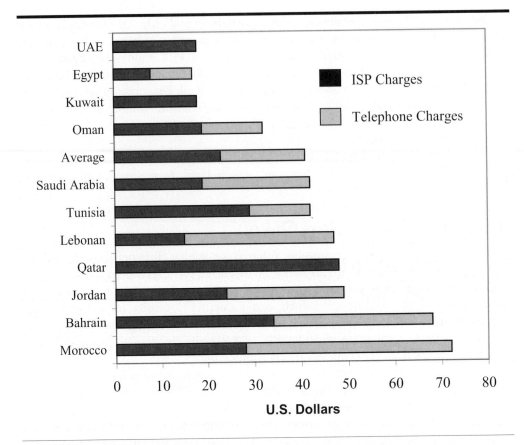

Exhibit 15 - 5 Total Internet Connection Costs in Selected Arab Countries
Source: Adapted from Gray (2001).

Slow Connection Speeds and Web Site Design

Another key issue for e-marketers in emerging economies is the relationship between connection speed and Web site design. Although most Internet connections around the world are through dial-up connections, a telephone line limits the speed at which data can be sent and received. The current maximum speed for a modem connection is 56 kbps (56,000 bits per second). As in developed countries, countries with emerging economies are seeking faster and better connections through broadband and ISDN, for example. In the meantime, download speeds in emerging economies may be much lower than 56 kbps—often 28.8 kbps or lower. This has significant implications for Web site design, especially the extent to which graphics are used.

The Web is quintessentially a visual medium, and users expect to see pictures, particularly complicated graphics and pictures that move, swirl, and morph into usual shapes. Web sites may also have sound. Yet each of these elements slows the download rate. This is especially true for home pages, which often attempt to *wow* the user. In countries with emerging economies, where connections speeds are slow and a user may be paying by the minute, download speed is a major consideration. Two points are important here. First, every e-marketer needs to understand how connection speeds influence download rates. Second, just because graphic designers *can* do something cutting edge on Web sites doesn't mean they *should*. In other words, just because a Web site *can* use flash graphics and incorporate lots of pictures doesn't mean that it should.

E-marketers must see the world from their target market's perspective. In the world of e-marketing, this means understanding the target market's total *experience* with a Web site. E-marketers are always selling an experience along with the site content. Users in developed countries experience extremely slow download times only occasionally. In developing countries, slow downloads are an everyday occurrence. Consider cite an experience that this chapter's author had while teaching in India. He wanted his students to explore the Amazon.com site, but each student had to wait more than five minutes for the home page to download! Multiply that by every hyperlink and query, and e-marketers can begin to understand the consequence of slow download speeds coupled with graphic-intensive Web page design. To avoid this problem, e-marketers need to understand the target market; consider the country's overall bandwidth; keep graphics simple; and limit the number of pictures, optimizing the site for speedy and smooth downloads.

Electricity Problems

Countries with emerging economies pose another challenge for e-marketers: sporadic electricity. Nepal is a good example. One of the poorest countries in the world, with an annual per capita income of less than $250, Nepal is rich in many natural resources, including water. Through the efforts of the United Nations and other international aid organizations, Nepal has built a series of hydroelectric dams throughout the country. Nepal needs these dams because only 15% of all households in Nepal have electricity. Most people living in Nepal's major cities of Kathmandu, Pokhara, and Nepalgrunj have electricity. Even so, households and businesses in these major cities are sometimes without electricity during the summer months. In the summer of 2001, for example, there were frequent rolling blackouts across the entire country. The Nepal Electrical Authority (NEA) could not generate enough electricity for the entire country. Electricity loss affected every business, including Internet-dependent businesses. All locally hosted Nepali Web sites went down when the electricity was cut.

Brazil, the largest and most populous country in South America, faces the same problem. When summer rains are not sufficient, electrical outages spread across Brazil. When lack of electricity forces an e-business offline, the business is effectively closed. Running an e-business in countries with electricity shortages can be challenging, to say the least!

Wireless Internet Access

Until recently, the technological problems noted previously—fewer fixed-line telephone connections, higher ISP fees, and costly dial-up connections—limited e-marketing activities in countries with emerging economies. Now mobile phones and the supporting technology have the potential to dramatically change the face of e-marketing around the world.

Many countries have reached the point where they have more mobile telephone subscribers than fixed-line telephone subscribers, as shown in Exhibit 15 - 6. Of these, Cambodia, Chile, Ivory Coast, Morocco, Paraguay, Philippines, Senegal, Uganda, and Venezuela are all countries with emerging economies.

Cambodia is an interesting case in point. In 1993, Cambodia became the first country in the world to have more mobile telephone subscribers than fixed-line telephone subscribers. Why? Price is part of the answer. Even in 1993, cell phones and the accompanying technology for mobile networks were less expensive than fixed-line telephones. But country history also provides a clue. Part of Cambodia's recent political history includes a long, very violent civil war (the movie *The Killing Fields* is about this war). During this conflict, the Khmer Rouge, one of the warring political parties, planted land mines throughout the country. The U.S. State Department estimates that "As a result of more than two decades of war…Cambodia has 4 to 6 million landmines in the ground" (U.S. State Department, 1998). The country is still littered with landmines, so digging up the ground to lay telephone cable is simply too risky. As a result, mobile phones and mobile phone networks found and satisfied a large, unmet need in Cambodia.

The case of Cambodia reminds international e-marketers that understanding country *history* is an important element in assessing foreign markets. "Executives

1993	1998	1999	2000	2001
Cambodia	Finland	Austria	Bahrain	Senegal
		Hong Kong SAR	Belgium	Singapore
		Ivory Coast	Botswana	Slovenia
		Israel	Chile	United Kingdom
		Italy	Greece	
		Paraguay	Iceland	
		Portugal	Morocco	
		Uganda	Philippines	
		Venezuela	Rwanda	

Exhibit 15 - 6 Selected Countries That Have More Mobile Telephones Than Fixed-Line Telephone Subscribers by Year

Source: Adapted from Minges (2001).

often underestimate the value of appreciating a country's history. Many developments that appear to be of a short-term political nature are driven by the longer-term historical experiences of a country" (Jeanette and Hennessy 2002, p. 269).

Exhibit 15 - 6 also demonstrates that, because mobile phone technology is an effective and relatively inexpensive path to telecommunications, countries with emerging economies can leapfrog industrialized countries in terms of usage. However, just having a cell phone does not eliminate the challenges of wireless e-marketing. E-marketers must still determine how to modify existing Web site content for the smaller screens on cell phone displays; how to resolve potentially cumbersome text entry using tiny keypads; how to develop new content that consumers will want; how to price services; and how to develop easy, secure payment methods. E-marketers also must understand that consumer behavior with the mobile Internet differs from consumer behavior with stationary desktop computers or even laptop computers.

Text messaging is a good example. On PCs, a user can write e-mail and send instant messages. E-mail length is not a problem with PCs. It is, however, a problem with mobile phones. The mobile phone counterpart to e-mail is short messaging service (SMS). As the name implies, SMS is the ability to send very short messages (up to 160 characters) to and from mobile devices (pagers, phones, PDAs, and so forth). SMS is very popular worldwide. Globally, in December 2000, users sent 15 billion SMS. The Philippines leads the world in SMS volume, with more than 18 million SMS sent daily within the country (Pastore, 2001).

Given its rising popularity, e-marketers must be creative in their use of SMS. Taking content developed for a Web browser and attempting to squeeze it onto the small screens of mobile phones will not work. To give a sense of just how short a message 160 characters can convey, this complete sentence contains 155 characters, including the spaces between words. New content and new marketing strategies must be developed for wireless Internet access.

During the 2002 World Cup finals, McDonald's developed a special SMS promotion for the China market. China is the world's largest mobile telephone market, with more than 160 million subscribers. McDonald's sent an SMS alert to selected mobile phone subscribers explaining how to download coupons for free ice cream, how to get a special McSmilie icon for their mobile phones, and how to download a McDonald's theme song as a special phone ringer. As a result, store sales increased because the free ice cream required the purchase of other food items. Also, every mobile phone with a McDonald's phone ringer promoted McDonald's every time the subscriber received an incoming phone call. In addition, McDonald's developed a special game for mobile phone subscribers during the 2002 World Cup. A couple of hours before certain matches, registered subscribers received an SMS asking them to predict the winning team for that match. Gamers earned points toward winning cash or soccer-related merchandise (Bolande, 2002). This success story shows how McDonald's identified and capitalized on an e-marketing opportunity by merging the anytime, anywhere capability of mobile phones with China's interest in soccer and its rapidly growing consumer economy.

The Digital Divide

In addition to the technical challenges they must overcome, e-marketers have to consider the social environment in which their e-businesses operate. Nations with emerging economies may be in different stages of economic development, which affects their social climate. The United Nations had developed a classification system to rank the economic development of countries. **Least developed countries** (LDCs) are those countries with the world's poorest economies. As the term implies, LDCs are economically underdeveloped. They also share one other common characteristic: excruciating poverty. Rather than use gross national product or gross domestic product as a way to describe the economic situation, Exhibit 15 - 7 lists the percentage of a country's population earning less than $2 per day. In these, the world's poorest countries, life is literally a war waged for survival.

Case and Fair (2001) describe the reality behind the numbers in Exhibit 15 - 7. In the least developed countries:

> Meager incomes provide only the basic necessities. Most meals are the same, consisting of the region's food staple—rice, wheat, or corn. Shelter is primitive. Many people share a small room, usually with an earthen floor and no sanitary facilities. The great major of the population lives in rural areas where agricultural work is hard and extremely time-consuming. Productivity…is low because household plots are small and only the crudest of farm implements are available. Low productivity means farm output per person is barely sufficient to feed a farmer's own family, with nothing left to sell to others. School age children may receive some formal education, but illiteracy remains chronic for you and old. Infant mortality runs 10 times higher than in the United States. Although parasitic infections are common and debilitating, there is only one physician per 5,000 people (pp. 434-35).

Life in an LDC is lived at its most basic and starkest level: survival. Of course, not every individual in these countries is poor. In fact, LDCs often contain population segments with much higher income levels. Many say this divides the country into *haves* and *have-nots,* a division that creates a **dual economy.** In practical terms this means that wealth is concentrated in a country's largest city, usually the capital. Capital cities look surprisingly the same everywhere in the world. Country capitals all have jet airports, world-class hotels, banks, department stores, movie theaters, new factories, and a middle and upper class. Outside the capital, life is similar to what Case and Fair described in the preceding quote. Two completely different economies exist side by side in an LDC. Although they may be geographically close to each other, these two economies are centuries apart in terms of economic and technological development.

Country	Percentage of Population Earning Below $2 a day
Bangladesh	77.8
Bolivia	38.6
Botswana	61.4
Central African Republic	84.0
China	53.7
Ecuador	52.3
El Salvador	51.9
Guatemala	64.3
Indonesia	86.2
Mali	90.6
Nepal	82.5
Nigeria	90.8
Senegal	67.8
Turkmenistan	59.0
Zambia	64.2

Exhibit 15 - 7 International Poverty Lines for Selected Countries
Source: Adapted from Table 4, World Bank (2000).

This disparity, especially as it concerns the ability of technology to raise both a person's and a whole country's standard of living, is called the **digital divide**. The Bridges Organizations (www.bridges.org) interprets digital divide to mean "that between countries and between different groups of people within countries, there is a wide division between those who have real access to information and communications technology and are using it effectively, and those who don't." The World Economic Forum, an organization that, like the Bridges Organization, is committed to closing the digital divide, posts this statement on its home page: "Industrialized countries, with only **15%** of the world's population, are home to **88%** of all Internet users" (emphasis in original document). Finland alone has more Internet users than the whole of Latin America (www.weforum.org/). As individuals who care passionately about the issue observe, and as noted in this chapter, the World W

ide Web is hardly *worldwide*.

The digital divide raises challenging questions for global policy makers, international businesses, and local entrepreneurs. What responsibilities, if any, do these different groups have for narrowing the gap between those that have and those that don't have access to technology? Should an e-businesses in Calcutta, India, be competitive with an e-business in Calumet City, Indiana? Global policy makers at the United Nations, the World Bank, and the G8 (leaders of the world's eight wealthiest countries who meet regularly to discuss common economic problems) believe the answer is yes. There are numerous initiatives around the world to bring Internet technology and e-commerce capabilities to LDCs.

Some e-marketers are successfully helping to close the digital divide. One example is the e-marketing effort in Robib, Cambodia, a group of six small villages in an inaccessible part of the country where only 128 families live. As might be expected, most of Robib's families are subsistence farmers and have no running water, electricity, or telephones. Annual family income is less than $40 per year. The village, though, has a Web site (www.villageleap.com) where village women successfully market traditional Cambodian silk weavings to overseas buyers. Money earned from Internet sales is reinvested in the local pig farm, the main form of livelihood for the villagers. Additionally, the communications linkages that make Robib's Internet site possible also allow villagers to send and receive medical information. This has greatly reduced the number of two-hour, bone-jarring trips, on deeply rutted roads, that villagers must take to the nearest hospital (Chandrasekaran 2001; Chon 2001). As this example shows, Internet technology has substantially improved the quality of life for villagers in Robib.

The success of Robib gives hope for closing the digital divide. Challenges for the e-marketer, though, still remain. The following message recently appeared on the Village Leap home page:

New Urgent Notice For Orders

After experiencing some initial problems of establishing e-commerce to remote Robib we feel confident we can now effectively place your orders. We are not yet Amazon.com but getting there. Your order forms are fed into an e-mail address: robibshop@yahoo.com. If you experience problems then please send the order directly to: robibshop@yahoo.com. If you would like to communicate or have questions, you may send them to: aafc@forum.org.kh.

To be able to fill orders more efficiently we have recently reduced the number of items in order to avoid disappointing customers who have to wait because of short supply. In the event an item is out of stock we will let you know and suggest a substitute. We hope you will cooperate. We are also reducing the shipping charge for orders to the U.S. and Japan (as we have volunteers there who will reship them, capitalizing on bulk shipments there).

Therefore, you may ignore the costly EMS postal charges for ORDERS TO THE U.S., CANADA AND JAPAN AND ADD ONLY $20.00 IN SHIPPING COSTS IF YOU ORDER ONE ITEM AND $5.00 ADDITIONAL FOR EXTRA ITEMS. For example, if you buy three items, regardless of weight, please add $30 for shipping. NO TAX. You may charge orders to a credit card or (preferably) you may send a U.S. dollar check, issued to *American Assistance for Cambodia* and you may mail the check either to Cambodia (the address on the order form) or to: Robib Project American Assistance for Cambodia Attn: Bernard Krisher P.O. Box 2716, GPO New York New York 10116 Yen are accepted in Japan.For information contact: bernie@media.mit.edu. Let us know by e-mail (to: robibshop@yahoo.com) when you have mailed the check (and enclose your order data with the check). The Robib villagers are deeply appreciative of your support.

Note that orders to the Robib collective must be sent by e-mail; there is no direct-order fulfillment mechanism as is there is on more dynamic retailing Web sites. Also, note how volunteers are helping to reduce overall costs. EMS is a global package delivery service and is quite expensive. Village Leap is trying to reduce total price to lower a barrier to purchase. Finally, note the remark about a reduced number of products. E-marketers know that it is better to underpromise and overdeliver than to overpromise and underdeliver. Customer satisfaction will always be the cornerstone of marketing, and Village Leap knows that. We hope they succeed.

S u m m a r y

Internet usage, which varies from country to country, is growing so rapidly outside the United States that users from other countries will increasingly dominate the Internet. This is creating opportunities and challenges for e-marketers to target or operate in countries that are less developed than the most highly industrialized nations. Emerging economies are those with low levels of gross domestic product (GDP) per capita that are experiencing rapid growth. Not only can technology generally boost a nation's overall production capacity and efficiency, but also information technology can help countries with emerging economies open up promising global markets.

In the course of analyzing country and market opportunities, e-marketers in emerging economies that target markets in developed countries must understand market similarity. E-marketers in emerging economies that market within their own countries or those in developed economies that want to target groups in an emerging economy must understand market differences. In general, e-marketers that target emerging economies must deal with a variety of challenges, including limited credit card use, lack of secure online payment methods, consumer attitudes toward online purchasing and payment, limited computer and telephone access, slow connection speeds that affect Web page download rates, and unexpected power failures. Enterprising e-marketers have reacted to these challenges with innovative solutions.

Many countries, including those with emerging economies, have more mobile telephone subscribers than fixed-line telephone subscribers. As a result, e-marketers must consider how to modify Web site content for small cell phone displays; how to handle text entry using tiny keypads; how to develop appropriate content for wireless Web users; how to price services; and how to develop appropriate payment methods. E-marketers also must understand how consumers behave with the mobile Internet.

Nations with emerging economies may be in different stages of economic development, which affects their social climate. Least developed countries (LDCs) have the poorest economies and, in many cases, a dual economy because the population has both higher-income citizens and poorer citizens. Capital cities in LDCs may have both a middle and an upper class, while the areas outside these cities are underdeveloped economically and technologically. This disparity, especially as it concerns the ability of technology to raise both a person's and an entire nation's standard of living, is called the digital divide. Many organizations and e-marketers are working to close this digital divide by bringing Internet technology and e-commerce capabilities to LDCs.

Key Terms

Digital divide

Dual economy

Emerging economies

Least developed countries (LDCs)

Market differences

Market similarity

Exercises

Review Questions
1. What is an emerging economy?
2. What use can countries with emerging economies make of information technology?
3. What is the concept of market similarity and how does it apply to companies that target foreign markets?
4. Why is credit card payment a conundrum in emerging economies?
5. How do computer and telephone ownership affect e-marketing in emerging economies?
6. Why must Web site designers consider connection speeds in emerging economies?
7. What are some of the electricity problems faced by e-marketers in emerging economies?
8. How is wireless Internet access likely to influence e-marketing around the world?
9. What is the digital divide and what does it mean for e-marketers?

Discussion Questions

10. Do you agree with the observation that the global Internet will drive styles, tastes, and products to converge and create a more homogenous, global marketplace? Why or why not?

11. What are the advantages to a business like Rita's Pizza in Lithuania of establishing a Web site where customers can order online but not pay for products?

12. Knowing that many consumers in emerging economies are wary of buying online, what would you do, as an e-marketer, to encourage them to change their attitudes and behavior?

13. What are the advantages and disadvantages of e-marketers creating fast-loading, low-graphics versions of their Web sites to accommodate slower connection speeds in emerging economies?

14. What responsibility do you think e-marketers should assume for helping to close the digital divide? Do you think consumers and governments should assume some responsibility as well? Explain your answers.

5

chapter

16 country profiles from the six continents

learning objectives

The primary objective of this chapter is to gain an understanding of the main country-by-country differences in Internet access, usage, and shopping as a foundation for segmenting and targeting specific markets. You will learn about some of the barriers to Internet adoption and e-commerce in selected countries and see how these barriers are being addressed.

After reading this chapter, you will be able to:

- Discuss overall trends in Internet access, usage, and purchasing around the world.
- Describe some of the key factors encouraging or discouraging growth in Internet access and usage in specific countries.
- Outline some of the government and commercial initiatives being used to support Internet usage, access, and purchasing in different countries.

Sweden has maintained its position as the world's dominant information economy.

2 0 0 1
IDC/world times
information
society index

Soccer has made history on the Internet. The Federation Intérnationalé de Football Association, better known as FIFA, recently partnered with Yahoo! to create and run the most popular sports Web site in history. According to Nielsen//NetRatings, FIFAworldcup.com was seen by 3.7 million people from 17 countries between May 1 and June 23, 2002—even before the final match between the German and Brazilian teams. That was a lot of eyeballs for World Cup 2002 official partners.

McDonald's, Mastercard, JVC, Budweiser, Fuji Xerox, FujiFilm, Avaya, Toshiba, Philips, Kt NTT, Hyundai, Coca-Cola, Gillette, and Adidas posted hyperlinked logos on the site. Also, thanks to Nielsen's excellent measurement system, sponsors could monitor site demographics. For example, the site was visited by more men than women; more people from Korea, the United Kingdom, and Denmark visited—with one-fifth of Korean visitors in the 2–11 age group; and the site received many more visitors on particular days. The French organization Handicapzéro even presented information for the visually impaired on the site.

Why was the site more successful than other sport sites with worldwide appeal, such as the Olympics? One answer is the worldwide passion for football (which U.S. fans call soccer). Also, spectators couldn't always catch the important games live on television because they were sleeping or at work when the games were played in Korea. Most importantly, the site offered continual updates of information, photos, and video highlights—giving users what they wanted in an easy-to-navigate format. Visitors found promotions, live polls, information on players and teams, data on previous World Cup matches, and FIFA merchandise for sale—priced in euros with a handy currency converter and convenient delivery to 190 countries. Interestingly, Yahoo! chose a subscription model, charging anywhere from US$4.95 to US$19.95 for video access, but the fee did not seem to deter visitors. FIFA World Cup action has come a long way from the 1950s, when fans had to visit local movie theaters to get news of their favorite teams.

*Industrialized countries, with only **15%** of the world's population, are home to **88%** of all Internet users.*

world economic forum

Overview of E-Marketing Around the World

FIFA and its partners are keenly aware of the global reach and impact of a good Web site. Firms can reach 530 million consumers worldwide in the B2C market. While this represents only 8.5% of the world's population, some countries have very high Internet usage. For example, the top 10 countries in 2002, in terms of absolute number of users, account for nearly 382 million Internet users (72.1% of all users). While these represent huge markets, some of the smaller countries, such as Iceland and Sweden, enjoy 50% to 60% Internet penetration in their populations (Exhibit 16 - 1). And in countries with small Internet penetration, users tend to be in the upper class or in a university.

Exhibit 16 - 2 shows Internet penetration estimates for 72 countries. These data represent a wide variety of studies and methodologies conducted over several years; thus, there may be differences between numbers in this exhibit and those in the country profiles; more up-to-date statistics may be found on the Web. Although this exhibit represents only a snapshot in time, it offers informative clues for marketing segmentation purposes. E-marketers should research the country's computer, information, Internet, and social infrastructures in more detail before selecting specific country targets (see www.idc.com for reports).

This chapter presents profiles for representative countries over five continents. Data about North America is contained throughout the earlier chapters in this book (representing the sixth continent mentioned in the chapter title). Each profile was written and generously contributed by someone who has lived in the country or who currently resides there. Each provides a rich understanding of Internet usage, barriers to adoption, and the unique characteristics of the country to aid in understanding its Internet industry. Following are profiles for Australia, Chile, Egypt, Germany, Guatemala, India, Northern Ireland, the People's Republic of China, Peru, Poland, Thailand, and Turkey.

Rank	Country	Number of Internet Users (millions)	Country	% of Population Internet Users
1	United States	149	Iceland	60.1
2	China	56.6	United States	53.6
3	Japan	51.3	Hong Kong	54.2
4	Germany	32	Sweden	49.4
5	United Kingdom	29	Norway	48.9
6	South Korea	16.7	United Kingdom	48.7
7	Canada	14.2	Switzerland	46.6
8	France	11	Canada	44.9
9	Italy	11	The Netherlands	42.5
10	France	11	Finland	41.3

Exhibit 16 - 1 Top 10 Countries in Number or Percentage of Internet Usage
Source: Data compiled from www.cyberatlas.internet.com.

Country	Population (millions)	% Net Users	Country	Population (millions)	% Net Users
Argentina	37.4	5.3	Malaysia	22.2	9.0
Australia	19.4	25.8	Mexico	101.8	2.3
Austria	8.2	32.9	Morocco	30.6	0.2
Bahrain	0.645	6.2	New Zealand	3.8	34.2
Belarus	10.4	1.0	Norway	4.5	48.9
Belgium	10.3	26.2	The Netherlands	16	42.5
Brazil	174.5	3.5	Oman	2.6	1.9
Bulgaria	7.7	5.5	Philippines	82.8	2.4
Canada	31.6	44.9	Poland	39	12.6
Chile	15.3	11.8	Portugal	10.1	30.3
China	1,300	4.4	Qatar	0.77	6.1
Colombia	40.3	1.7	Romania	22.4	2.8
Croatia	4.3	7.0	Russia	145	5.2
Cuba	11.2	0.5	Saudi Arabia	22.8	1.3
Czech Republic	10.2	21.6	Singapore	4.3	30.2
Denmark	5.4	29.6	Slovakia	5.4	13.0
Djibouti	0.461	0.2	Slovenia	1.9	21.1
Egypt	70	0.7	South Africa	43.6	3.4
Estonia	1.4	33.0	South Korea	47.9	34.9
Finland	5.2	41.3	Spain	40	17.5
France	60	18.3	Sri Lanka	19.4	0.3
Germany	83	38.8	Sudan	36	0.0
Greece	10.6	12.3	Sweden	8.9	49.4
Hong Kong	7.2	54.2	Switzerland	7.3	46.6
Hungary	10.1	7.2	Syria	16.7	0.1
Iceland	0.278	60.1	Taiwan	22.3	28.7
India	1,000	0.5	Thailand	61.8	7.4
Ireland	4	25.0	Tunisia	9.7	1.2
Israel	6	20.0	Turkey	66.5	5.6
Italy	57.7	19.1	UAE	2.4	38.3
Japan	126.8	40.5	Ukraine	48.8	1.5
Jordan	5.2	0.5	United Kingdom	59.6	48.7
Kuwait	2	3.2	United States	278	53.6
Lebanon	3.6	11.7	Vietnam	80	0.0
Libya	5.2	0.2	Venezuela	24	5.0
Lithuania	3.6	8.9	Yemen	18	0.1

Exhibit 16 - 2 Estimated Internet Penetration in 2002

Source: Population from CIA World Factbook; Internet usage data from www.cyberatlas.internet.com.

Australia

Carl Driesener
Research Associate
Marketing Science Centre
The University of South Australia, Adelaide,
Australia
E-mail:
carl.driesener@marketingsciencecentre.com
Web: www.MarketingScienceCentre.com

In keeping with its reputation as an adaptor of new technologies, Australia has one of the highest levels of Internet use in the world, behind Sweden and the United States, and Internet use in Australian households continues to grow strongly. Showing even stronger growth is the increase in online shopping, roughly doubling each year since 1998, from a 3% baseline. While household computer ownership is also increasing, the gap between the proportion of households owning a computer and those also accessing the Internet is shrinking. One factor spurring the growth of Internet usage is Australia's untimed local calls (a low, fixed fee irrespective of connection time), although this may change due to uncertainty about the 51% public ownership of Australia's telephone company. An issue for Australian Internet use is the lack of widespread broadband access. At the end of 2001, 96% of Internet users (including government and business) were using dial-up access (the vast majority of these analog).

Computer Ownership

By early 2001, 56% of all households reported having a home computer. This proportion was projected to rise to about 64% by the end of 2001, a healthy increase from the 48% of home computer ownership in 1999. Sixty-six percent of adults reported using a computer during 2000. Of these, 47% used a computer at home, 42% at work, and 40% at some other site (library, educational facility, or friend/neighbor/relative's house). In households without a computer, 36% of respondents said they had no need for a computer and 25% said they did not have one because of the expense. As a comparison to the household ownership of computers, 61% of households had at least one mobile phone.

Internet Usage

Household usage of the Internet is somewhat lower than computer ownership, with 37% of all households reporting Internet access at home (32% of nonmetropolitan households have Internet access, compared with 40% of metropolitan households).

Household Internet usage was predicted to rise to 50% by the end of 2001. Half of all adults reported using the Internet during 2000—some 6.9 million adults. Despite optimistic predictions about using noncomputer devices for Internet access (e.g., mobile phone or television set top boxes), by the end of 2000 only 0.4% of all households reported actually doing so. The strong growth in household Internet access (and to a lesser extent, home computers) is also seen in the growth of households with dedicated game machines (from 23% to 33% between 1998 and 2000) and pay TV (11% to 17%). Of the households without Internet access, about 25% cited lack of interest, and a similar number said they had no use for it. Nineteen percent stated that it was too expensive.

Uses of the Internet

Activities conducted online at home included e-mail or chat (68%), general browsing (57%), searching for information on goods or services (26%), and finding information for work-related purposes (36%). On average, households downloaded about 58 Mbs per month compared to 337 Mbs per month by businesses and the government (per ISP subscription).

E-Commerce

By the end of 2000, 10% of adults had purchased or ordered goods or services (for private consumption) via the Internet, showing continuing strong growth. Approximately 20% of household Internet users utilized it for purchases, the relationship holding for nearly all age groups (including 55+). The only age group that fell below this level was the 18–24-year-olds, for whom only about 15% purchased or ordered via the Internet. Eighty-two percent of Internet shoppers used a credit card online to pay for all or part of the purchase. Reasons given for not shopping on the Internet included no need (43%), security concerns (29%), or a preference to shop in person (17%). About 30% of shoppers spent more than $500 during 2000, and 74% made at least two purchases. The most commonly purchased items were books or magazines (36%), music (20%), and computer software (18%), with computer hardware accounting for another 10%. Compared to other forms of electronic financial transactions, Australian use of the Internet to pay bills or transfer money was relatively low. Thirteen percent of adults in 2000 reported using the Internet for this function as compared with 49% who used the telephone, 67% who used EFTPOS, and 74% who used an ATM. EFTPOS is an electronic funds transfer at point of sale, using a debit or credit card, that enables funds to be transferred directly from the account of the purchaser to that of the vendor, in near real time. Twelve percent of adults accessed government services using the Internet.

Chile

Felipe Lüttges
MBA Dominican University, River Forest, Illinois
Sales Manager BanChile Stock Brockers, Santiago,
Chile
e-mail: fluttges@manquehue.net

Carlos Jiménez
Economist, Gabriela Mistral University,
Santiago, Chile

Chile is the South American country with the highest overall Internet penetration rate. In 1999, Chile had approximately 700,000 Internet users; by 2001, that number had grown to 2,837,000 (Telecommunications Bureau, January 2000). This 305% increase in growth—in only two years—suggests that the Internet is rapidly gaining acceptance and use in Chile. Chile is a small country, dwarfed in size and total population by both Argentina and Brazil. However, in 2000, Chile had an Internet penetration of 16.6% as a percentage of total country population—the highest in South America. In contrast, Argentina had a penetration rate of 6.8% based on total country population, while Brazil had a penetration rate of only 2.9% (Telecommunications Bureau, January 2000).

According to the National Institute of Statistics, 17% of Chilean households own a computer, and 50% of households with computers also have an Internet connection. The most frequent users are 19– to 29–year-olds.

Two key factors help explain the Internet's explosive growth in Chile: the highly deregulated domestic telecommunication market and the low cost of fixed-line telephone charges. Although the Chilean telecommunication industry is being affected by several factors (a large number of competitors, substitution, lower prices and margins, and a constraint on demand), the cost of a fixed-line phone call for Internet access is US$0.01 per minute (ENTEL Chile 2002).

The insatiable demand for Internet access and faster connections have developed another quickly growing industry in Chile: the broadband market. In 2001, the broadband Chilean market had 61,000 users; by the end of 2003, total broadband user is expected to reach 195,700 (The Yankee Group, published on "Digital Economy 2001"). The broadband market in Chile includes all the modern technologies available and used so far: ADSL, Cable Modem, Dedicated and WLL (Wireless Local Loop).

E-Commerce

The Chamber of Commerce of Santiago (Chile) has released a study on the digital economy in Chile. Data collected by the chamber show the strong growth of e-commerce in many Chilean companies:

- Between 1999 and 2000, products offered online grew from 10,000 to 120,000 units.

- In 1999, Chilean online retailers sold US$2.6 million and in 2002 the market is expected to rise tenfold to US$25 million. Adding foreign sources sales the revenue climbs respectively to US$12.6 and US$45 million.

- In 1999, online B2B sales reached US$75 million; in 2001 B2B sales are expected to grow to US$262 million.

- The number of Internet domains grew 150% over the last year.

- Of the 123 Chilean companies interviewed in the survey, only one-third said that within five years e-commerce would represent more than 20% of their sales.

Government Role

Recognizing the potential benefits of IT, the Chilean government established a Communications and Information Technology Unit (UTIC) in 1998. The UTIC was given the mandate of coordinating, promoting, and advising the Chilean government on the development of IT in the areas of employment, informatio, and communications. One area of reform where the UTIC has been particularly successful is pushing forward comprehensive reforms of its procurement system. Chile's experience with e-procurement has made business opportunities with the Chilean government more transparent, reduced firms' transaction costs, increased opportunities for feedback and cooperation between firms and public agencies, and sharply reduced opportunities for corruption. In the relatively short period that this e-procurement system has been in operation, it has resulted in substantial savings, creation of a more perfect information market, and increased transparency and accountability.

Chile is making progress in its use of the Internet in B2B, B2C, and B2G markets. Yet Chile is not totally free of the natural fears and doubts generated by electronic commerce. Chilean users do not yet have complete confidence in current electronic methods of payment. This may soon change: A draft law regulating digital signatures is close to being passed by Congress. Should the law pass, e-marketing will likely accelerate throughout all sectors of the Chilean economy.

People's Republic of China

Dr. Wenyu Dou
Assistant Professor of Marketing
University of Nevada-Las Vegas, U.S.A.
E-mail: wenyu.dou@ccmail.nevada.edu

Internet access and use in (P. R.) China has been growing rapidly in recent years and the trend is projected to continue in the near future. The number of Chinese Internet users increased from about 10 million at the beginning of 2000 to about 33 million by the end of 2001. The latest Nilsen/NetRatings Report estimated that this number had reached 56 million by April 2002. Hence, China now has the biggest Internet population in Asia.

A few years ago, Chinese Internet users were primarily younger (18–35), better-educated males. But this situation is quickly changing as the Internet becomes increasingly mainstream, especially among urban residents in China. Female Internet users now account for 40% of the overall Internet population and Internet users with college degrees have dropped to only 30% of total users.

Whereas Internet access in the United States is almost evenly split between work and home, Chinese Internet users primarily access the Internet from either home (61%) or net café (15%) with work-related access accounting for only about 25%. Dial-up is most frequently for home access. The top two objectives for using the Internet among Chinese Internet users are "information" (46%) and "entertainment" (31%).

E-Commerce

Despite the fast growth of online users, online shopping is still relatively uncommon in China. Only 36% of the users have purchased anything from the Internet during the past year and the total number of online shoppers was only 3.5 million in 2001. Major obstacles to online purchasing by Chinese Internet users include security, vendor reputation, delivery, and payment. Among the products that were bought by Chinese Internet users, books were ranked number one with a 58% share followed by computer-related products and travel services.

Compared to the relatively small volume of Chinese B2C e-commerce (about $47 million in 2000), B2B e-commerce took the lion's share in China (about $9.3 billion in 2000). The biggest activities of B2B e-commerce came from manufacturing and IT companies with industrial powerhouses such as Haier Group leading the race. With China's entry into WTO and its rising status as "Manufacturing Center for the World," China's B2B e-commerce is expected to continue playing an important role.

Obstacles

While the number of Internet users in China looks impressive, the actual percentage of households using the Internet in China is still quite low (5%) compared to developed countries. Barriers to the continuing growth of Internet usage and e-commerce in China include low telephone penetration rate, high Internet access charges, few good Web sites in the Chinese language, government regulation of Web contents, and lack of convenient online payment systems.

Future

The future of the Chinese Internet market stills looks promising because of its huge potential market size. Noteworthy trends in the Chinese Internet market in the next few years will likely include e-government initiatives, broadband Internet access, and entry of multinational e-business companies.

Egypt

Sherif A. Elfayoumy, Ph.D.
Assistant Professor of Computer Science
University of North Florida
Jacksonville, Florida, U.S.A.
Elfayoumy@IEEE.org

According to the Egyptian ministry of communications and information technology (MCIT), Egypt had more than 1 million Internet users as of April 2002. This represents a 256% increase in the number of users since October 1999. A recent study by the Arab Advisors Group forecasts an increase to 2.6 million users by 2006. This steady growth in the number of Internet users is attributed to the improvements made to the communications infrastructure, the increase in public awareness, and the introduction of new regulation and legislation.

Communications Infrastructure

Telecom Egypt monopolizes the country's fixed phone operations and services. In 2000, a complete digital network with a fiber-optic backbone and ATM switches replaced the former copper-based network to provide more capacity for the constantly growing number of phone lines and services. The number of fixed phone lines grew from 6.4 million in October 1999 to more than 9.1 million by April 2002. Fixed phone subscribers are charged per minute for their phone calls; flat-rate plans are not offered. Two private sector companies, Menatel and NilePhone, are licensed to provide pay phone services. The number of pay phones has surged from 13,000 in October 1999 to more than 40,000 in April 2002.

MobiNil and Misrfone are the only companies licensed to provide GSM-based mobile phone services in Egypt; a third license is currently under consideration. Although mobile phone services are relatively new to the Egyptian market, the number of cellular phone subscribers grew from 7,000 in 1995 to 650,000 by October 1999. Thanks to reform and reorganization in the communication sector, this number had surged to about 3.8 million by April 2002. A recent study for the Arab Advisors Group projects the penetration of fixed phone lines will increase from less than 10% in 2002 to more than 14% by 2006, and GSM penetration will reach 17% by 2006.

Parallel to these fast developments in phone services, the country's Internet bandwidth increased from 20 Megabit/sec in October 1999 to 400 Megabit/sec in April 2002. The Information and Decision Support Center (IDSC) of the Egyptian cabinet accounts for 70% of the IP traffic and the remaining 30% is handled by Telecom Egypt. This bandwidth is being sold through more than 60 ISPs offering services ranging from dial-up connections and DSL for home users to DSL, ISDN, and leased lines for enterprises and governmental institutions.

Internet account sharing has been very common among Egyptian Internet users. Some studies estimate that the number of Internet users is eight times higher than the number of actual service subscribers where many users go online using their university or work accounts. Account sharing is expected to drop now that free dial-up Internet access became available in January 2002 and covers most of the country, although Internet users still have to pay for phone line time usage. Telecom Egypt sponsors the free Internet access by sharing the money collected from Internet users for their phone time with ISPs.

Public Awareness

Despite a high illiteracy rate (more than 50% among adults), Egypt ranks 17th in the world in the number of high school graduates. A small fraction of the educated population enjoys Internet surfing and the convenience of online services (Internet penetration is about 1% among Egyptians). The number of home-based Internet users is limited due to the relatively high subscription fee: approximately 60 Egyptian P pounds ($18 USD) for unlimited Internet access plus per-minute local phone charges. Another limiting factor is computer availability. The International Telecommunication Union (ITU) estimates a total of 1 million PCs in Egypt in 2001.

MCIT and Telecom Egypt have orchestrated efforts to elevate public awareness of the Internet and online services through (1) improving the local market for IT companies and creating new IT jobs, (2) enriching the local content of the Internet and creating more online services, (3) providing affordable IT training to students and fresh graduates, (4) reducing Internet access fees, and (5) increasing PC affordability for individuals. MCIT has many ambitious projects underway, such as E-Government, which aims to automate many government-provided services and provide them online for convenience use. Private sector companies are encouraged to participate in the development of these projects. An incubator project, another exemplary effort, seeks to provide incentives to attract investments in CIT, such as tax breaks, reduced land prices, and so on.

MCIT has forged training alliances with major IT players, such as Microsoft and IBM, to train college graduates on the cutting-edge IT technologies at reasonable fees (some competitive training programs are fully sponsored by the government and students are given stipend in many cases). These training programs pumped more than 7,000 certified professionals into the local market by April 2002, according to MCIT published numbers. Another 44,400 individuals received basic CIT training (word processing, spread sheets, presentation skills, data entry, etc.). These efforts contributed significantly to the third aspect.

The last two aspects were approached through various projects such as free dial-up Internet access and affordability projects to help households and university students finance the purchase of PCs at zero interest rate. Along the same lines 325 IT clubs (government-subsidized Internet cafes) were established in youth centers, public libraries, schools, and NGOs to offer members free Internet access; membership is usually free. Also the ministry of education plays a notable role in connecting the nation's schools to the Internet.

Regulations and Legislations

The CIT sector is participating in the country-wide economic reform toward progressive market liberalization. The creation of MCIT and Telecom Egypt was part of these efforts. New laws are facilitating this paradigm shift in the governing policies of CIT operations. A new bill that addresses the legality of e-signatures is being prepared for the parliament approval. If passed, the law will allow the government to provide true online services through the E-Government project, because most government forms require the requester's signature. Still more efforts are needed to overcome challenges related to taxation and customs issues.

E-Commerce Success Stories

One e-commerce success story in the B2C market is **www.otlob.com** (*otlob* is an Arabic verb that means "request"). This shopping site, founded in 1999, invites Internet users to order cooked meals for home delivery. Dozens of restaurants participate in this service. Users pay cash for the food on delivery, an appropriate payment mode for users living in a cash-based society. Users can also buy flowers, medications, and rent videotapes in addition to the original food delivery service.

Another B2C success story is **www.e-kotob.com** (*kotob* is the Arabic translation of the word "books"), an online Arabic bookstore launched in 2000. Users can search and buy from the site's catalog of 50,000 Arabic titles and even download Arabic books to read on their computers. The site accepts credit card and money order payments for deliveries to other countries, and credit card and cash-upon-delivery payments for domestic deliveries. The cash-upon-delivery option is expected to cover all deliveries to Arab countries soon.

CiraNET Pharma is the first Egyptian online B2B trade exchange targeted to all local players in the pharmaceutical industry. Launched in February 2001 to foster and facilitate trading relationships between pharmaceutical manufacturers, distributors, and pharmacies, this market exchange provides centralized order placement, billing, payment, and customer service. Egypt has a huge pharmaceutical market that meets over 90% of its 68 million inhabitants' needs for pharmaceutical products through more than 19,000 pharmacies.

Challenges for E-Commerce in Egypt

- **Modern financial system:** The Egyptian cash-based culture limits the volume of online transactions. The establishment of payment centers and collection agencies is expected to lessen the severity of the problem but will also add to overhead expenses incurred by online services.

- **Language barrier:** Most online service providers opt to provide bilingual interface for their sites to accommodate local and foreign customers. This increases costs and adds some technical challenges.

- **Lack of flat-rate phone plans:** Until now, dial-up Internet users have been charged per minute for phone use—an inconvenient arrangement for heavy Internet users. The introduction of free Internet access should relieve the burden for users looking for inexpensive Internet access. Also, reasonably priced DSL plans should accommodate users who want faster Internet access.

- **High illiteracy rate:** This limits usage of high-tech services of all kinds. Progressive governmental strategies are certainly needed to reduce the relatively high illiteracy rate.

- **Legislation and regulation:** New rules and laws are needed to address issues related to taxation, customs, privacy, security of electronic transactions, software piracy, credit card fraud, and online money laundering.

Germany

Stefanie Lohrmann
Graduate Student at University of Lüneburg/ Germany and Faculty of Applied Cultural Studies

The Internet has expanded rapidly in the last few years in Germany: An estimated 31.4 million adults (57% of Germany's 14–69-year-old population) had access to the Net by spring 2002, compared to 22.2 million (40%) in 2001 and 15.9 million (30%) in 2000 (GfK 2002/2000). According to research, the German market will reach a saturation point in the next few years and the number of nonusers is estimated to stabilize at about 50% of the total population (Eimeren 2001).

Today most users go online at home, whereas in 1997 most Germans accessed the Internet at work or an educational institution. Though the gender gap is slowly closing, men (58%) continue to outnumber women (42%) online (GfK 2001).

In 2001, about 29% of German private users purchased products and services online. The most popular products have been books, followed by software, music CDs, clothes, tickets, and gifts (GfK 2002). Even though market research found half of consumers not prepared to pay for online content, publishing houses are cautiously introducing paid content for exclusive parts of their media products (archives, title story, personalized news, SMS/Short Message Services, and so forth). Nevertheless, the majority of online content will remain free, according to research.

One recent barrier to Internet usage has been the relatively high cost of going online, because German telephone companies charge for local calls on a timed rate. Charges, however, are dropping. Although unmetered services are not common, flat-rates for heavy users are offered for about $50 a month. High-speed Internet access technology DSL is not yet available everywhere and is relatively expensive, but expansion is coming. By 2001 only 5% of the users accessed the Internet by DSL or Cable modem, while the majority (47%) logged on by standard modem, and 41% via ISDN (Integrated Services Digital Network) (Eimeren 2001).

Europe lags behind the United States in terms of accessing the Internet from a desktop computer, but it is ahead in wireless technology. The percentage of European mobile Internet users is higher than the percentage of U.S. mobile Internet users but slightly lower than in Asian countries such as Japan or Korea. In 2000, the large European wireless carriers agreed to spend a combined $150 billion on licenses to provide the third generation (3G) system UMTS (Universal Mobile Telecommunications System), to reach the market by 2003 or 2004. While most mobile operators are confident that 3G phones and services will be successful, some researchers doubt that consumers will be interested. Though WAP technology (Wireless Application Protocol) already allows cell phone owners to access some Internet information, most consumers stick to traditional voice calls and SMS messaging. Currently 54% of Germans are estimated to have Internet-enabled mobile devices, although only a minority use their cell phones to go online. The reasons for this restraint include lack of interest, lack of familiarity with the technology, and costs (NUA/The Age 2002).

Interestingly, German consumers are more willing to pay for content on their cell phones than on their PCs, where they seem to be more concerned about security issues. Ring tones, logos, news alerts on SMS, and e-cards dominate consumer interests.

As in the United States and many other markets, 2001 brought the end of the "Internet hype" and the consolidation of the market in Germany. Businesses involved with the Internet had to rethink and become realistic about their return on investment. Despite an uncertain future for profitable e-commerce, the Internet itself has become established as part of daily life for many Germans.

Guatemala

Douglas R. Keberlein Gutiérrez
Assistant Professor of History
Dominican University, Illinois, U.S.A.
e-mail: keberle@email.dom.edu

Guatemala, a small Central American country of 10 million inhabitants, has a rather brief history of Internet usage. In 1992, one of Guatemala's private universities, the Universidad del Valle, established the country's original UUCP. Public access to the Internet only became available in late 1995 when GUATEL (then the state-run telecommunications agency) created the first ISP. In April 1996 the government removed all monopoly restrictions. Approximately 20 new ISPs entered Guatemala's market for Internet users, and public and private usage grew at a moderate pace. By the end of 1996 Guatemala had an estimated 5,000 Internet users. The vast majority were academics and upper-class businessmen who lived and worked in the capital, Guatemala City. Since then, the number of regular users has expanded to approximately 75,000.

In comparison to the rest of Central America, Guatemala's experience with Internet usage is par for the course. According to the most recent statistics compiled by Fundación Accesso, Internet coverage ranges from a low of 0.3% in Honduras to a high of 3.9% in Costa Rica. In Guatemala, Internet coverage is 0.6%. This is more than the 0.4% rate for Nicaragua yet slightly less than the 0.7% rate recorded for El Salvador. Although Internet usage continues to expand, the poor state of the Guatemala's national telecommunications infrastructure continues to impede Internet access, particularly in areas outside the capital, Guatemala City. Telephone density in urban areas is 10.0% and in rural areas it is a paltry 1.0%. Quite often, families outside the capital must resort to cellular phones to make calls—even though cellular phone service is expensive. Rural people commonly rent out usage of their phones as an informal means of offsetting ownership costs and subsidizing their incomes. Moreover, Internet service fees in Guatemala average 6.0% of per capita income. Although this is a lower rate than any other Central American country other than Costa Rica (3.0%) and much lower than the 16.0% of per capita income recorded for Nicaragua, it nonetheless represents a significant expenditure for the average Guatemalan.

Yet where Internet access is available, especially in the capital, ISPs offer a complete range of services. In addition, although poverty is a significant obstacle, there are opportunities for growth in Internet-related commerce. Increasing numbers of teenagers and university-level students have begun using the Internet for education-related research. University students generally have Internet access on the various campuses in the capital city. Guatemalans have found that the Internet provides a valuable means of communicating with friends and family outside the country (especially in the United States), often at a lower cost than long-distance phone calls. Politicians regularly use the Internet to stay informed about international and domestic developments; the tourism industry uses the Internet to attract foreign travelers. Individuals also use the Internet for entertainment purposes such as keeping abreast of new music releases, films, and fashion. Although few Guatemalans have computers in their homes, Internet cafes are a regular feature in malls throughout Guatemala City and a handful more can be found in important tourist locations like Panajachel and Antigua.

Looking at future trends, dial-up access to the Internet has been, and probably will continue to be, a luxury rather than an everyday means of communication for the typical Guatemalan, because 40 to 70 percent of the population is living in poverty (based on income). Second, the vast majority of Internet users will be found among the roughly 3 million people who live in the capital. Third, Internet cafes and university-sponsored computer centers have the greatest potential for increasing the number of Internet users outside the capital. And fourth, buying products online most likely will not be significant. Guatemalans have a cultural preference for face-to-face negotiating over prices, and the Guatemalan postal service is less reliable than the telephone service, another obstacle for online shopping.

India

Nilesh Patel
Graduate Research Assistant
University of Nevada, Reno, U.S.A.
E-mail: Npatel4906@aol.com

Internet access and usage in India has grown rapidly in the past few years. Most of the usage has been in via e-mail and information access (Web surfing). According to AccessMedia, Internet markets and usage trends in India registered a 116.5% growth in the year ending March 2001 over the previous year. It is estimated that India will have more than 10 million subscribers before the end of 2004, and the corporate segment is expected to grow 40% over the next five years. Also, IDC (www.idc.com) projects growth from the current 4.4 million Internet subscribers to 37.5 million by the end of 2005. According to IDC, home and small business segments will drive the growth in the Internet user base. India is expected to be behind only China in terms of total number of Internet users by the end of 2005, because these countries are highly populated and are embracing Internet technologies very rapidly (the combined populations of India and China represent one-third of the world's population).

Barriers to Growth

While India's Internet adoption rate has been projected to grow rapidly, significant barriers limit the growth of future adoption and e-business. A recent report conducted by Nasscom and Boston Consulting group outlines the following barriers (Chand, 2001):

- PCs and other devices to access the Net for individuals are less than 1%.
- Telephone line penetration is limited to less than 3% of the population.
- Poor telecom and communications infrastructure for reliable connectivity.
- Internet connectivity is very slow and access costs are still very high.
- High legal and regulatory barriers.
- Safeguards to protect privacy of personal and business data not in place.
- Low penetration of credit cards.

E-Commerce

A recent survey carried out by the Internet research arm of Taylor Nelson Sofres ranked India 33rd in the world in terms of e-commerce and online shopping. Only 2 percent of its Internet users shop online. This survey also revealed that 10 percent of Internet users plan to buy or order goods or services online within the next six months (DQWeek).

Profile of an Indian Internet User

The following is a representation of a typical Internet user in India (Cheung 2001):

- Users are young and predominantly male.
- Internet usage is restricted mainly to members of middle class and above.
- Users are mainly educated, media-savvy urbanites who are willing to adopt to new technology.
- Cyber cafes are popular gathering places among young, novice Indian Internet user.
- E-mail is by far the most popular online activity among Indian users.
- Indian users do not seem to show a preference of local sites or foreign sites.
- Site loyalty seems to depend mostly on ease of access and richness of information.

Exhibit 16 - 3 displays these and other activities conducted online by Indian Internet users.

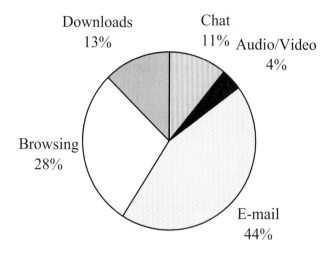

Exhibit 16 - 3 What Indian Users Do Online (2000)
Source: Net Sense (2000), as compiled at www.eMarketer.com.

Northern Ireland

Arthur McKeown
The Management Institute
University of Ulster

Northern Ireland has been slower and more cautious than other regions of the United Kingdom and the Republic of Ireland in addressing the opportunities and challenges presented by the Internet and related technologies. But the impact of such technologies, and their practical application, is beginning to make a significant contribution to the economic growth of Northern Ireland, especially as confidence in the peace process grows.

The Internet is becoming more integrated into an organization's overall business strategy, especially as organizations—public and private, large and small, new and long-established—seek to align their products and services more closely to their customers' and clients' expectations for online delivery.

Basic Adoption Rate and Trends

In the United Kingdom as a whole there continues to be a steady rise in expenditure on Internet hardware, software, and related services, from £3.59 billion in 2000 to (predicted) £4.97 billion in 2001 (*Internet Usage in Business*, Key Note, July 2001). In addition, in revenues from e-commerce and advertising are steadily rising, growing 59% in 2001 alone. Access costs continue to fall, and companies are recognizing Internet costs, both capital expenditure and operational costs, as a necessary business expense.

Recent changes to improve broadband access are expected to increase Internet adoption by organizations, especially SMEs. At the other extreme, WAP telephony has failed to deliver on its promises. Instead, text messaging, for both business and recreational purposes, has been enjoying great success, especially among young users. And many organizations are starting to develop innovative applications for PDAs and similar technology. Nonetheless, wireless access to the Internet is not yet available to businesses or domestic users in any significant form.

Net Adoption

Domestic Internet installation has continued to increase; now just over 50% of people in Northern Ireland have access at home. More people are spending more time online, especially on Sunday evenings (when they report that they are more relaxed). Schools, colleges, and universities are making considerable use of online media, both as a means of delivering elements in learners' programs and as a resource to complement and extend traditional book-based resources. Also, community and church organizations are increasingly aware of the potential benefits of the Internet. Finally, to bridge the "digital divide," local councils and other groups providing low- or no-cost Internet facilities in libraries and other public buildings. (See Chapter 15 for more on the digital divide.)

Shopping and Buying Behavior Online

Consumers have grown more confident in their use of the Internet for personal purchasing. They are aware of the increased choices available and are more confident in using trusted sites and sites that can assure the security of online transactions. Books, DVDs, CDs, and videos continue to be popular online purchases, but consumers are prepared to be more adventurous, and growing numbers report willingness to participate in online auctions. Some sectors (such as travel agencies, real estate agencies, and gambling) are finding their traditional activities displaced by the availability of the Internet. Budget airlines offer online booking facilities, so travel agents are focusing more on specialty or high-value holidays; real estate agents are advertising property at comprehensive Web sites that potential buyers can search before making contact with the agents; and bookmakers are finding that they can provide a greater range of things on which clients are willing to bet—and are facing up to the challenges presented by possible changes in how betting and gambling activities are taxed. Finally, online grocery shopping is enjoying reasonable success, especially in urban areas. This is likely to increase as more people experience its cost-effectiveness and convenience.

B2B Market

Large organizations continue to have the best links to the Internet and are making more use of both the Internet and their own intranets than are SMEs; however, SMEs are increasingly adopting Internet technology. Many organizations, which had established a prototype Web site in the closing years of the 1990s, are now in a strong position to make well-informed decisions about the suitability of the Internet for their activities; and many have developed more substantial sites in response to the real needs of their internal and external users. Online tendering for public contracts continues to grow in significance. More and more public organizations are adopting e-procurement, often in parallel with their traditional procurement procedures.

Future Predictions

The Internet is well on the way to becoming established as an integral part of how people in Northern Ireland and in every local community earn their living, learn at school, and manage many personal and social activities. The Internet adoption rate may slow, however, if the local economy fails to grow as quickly as projected.

Conclusion

Internet usage is increasing steadily, though cautiously in some areas. The momentum will increase as more and more users become more confident in their own skills and as organizations work, with government encouragement and support, to meet their users' expectations for increased online delivery of information and services.

Peru

Carla Olivieri
School of Business Director
E-Marketing Professor
Universidad Peruana de Ciencias Aplicadas,
UPC, Lima, Peru
E-mail: colivier@upc.edu.pe

At first glance, Peru does not seem to be an ideal location for e-business growth. The low salary rate per capita means most people have insufficient disposable income to purchase PCs—and they are not educated enough to incorporate technology into their lives. Also Peru has a poor infrastructure, a lot of red tape, and little technological investment. However, the Internet sector has contradictory indicators: Latin America shows an explosive growth in the Internet sector, innovative solutions have arisen, many dot-coms have been established (mainly copies of U.S. firms) and more establishments are migrating to the *bricks-and-clicks* model.

Why is the Internet growing in Latin America? The region has over 500 million inhabitants who mostly speak the same Spanish language (except for Brazil where Portuguese is spoken). Also, 60 percent of the population is under 30 years of age—an important point because the younger population is more eager to accept new technology. Also, in most Latin American countries, the population is concentrated in many small areas, which is appealing for e-commerce purposes. Internet penetration is still very low (less than 3% in the region) but is to grow to 19% by 2003. In Peru, approximately 2% of the population accounts for 60% of the country's purchasing power. Internet penetration in this economic group is 38%.

Some barriers to Internet usage in Peru include:

- People fear placing data on the Web (or anywhere!).
- Credit card penetration in Peru is less than 10%. Debit cards, in-store credit cards, and cash are the primary payment methods in retail stores.
- Telephone line penetration is one of the lowest in the region. By 1999, Peru had 1,637 telephone lines (6.5 per 100 persons, compared to 20.7 in Argentina). It is expected that by 2003 Peru will have 2,325 lines (8.7 per 100 persons, compared to 23.6 in Argentina).
- Broadband Internet connection is not available, and telephone use is still very expensive. In fact, people can buy special boxes to lock their phones so they can control who makes calls at home.
- Despite privatization efforts, telecommunications are still run by very few operators.

Internet usage in Peru is growing as privacy and security issues are addressed. One promising plan is the use of prepaid cards for online purchasing. Consumers buy these cards at banks or stores in designated amounts of money—US$10, $20, and so forth. Then they enter the number of the card when making a purchase online, so no credit card is needed. Many young people are using these cards to buy CDs, tickets, and more online. Also, the home pages of many banks feature virtual stores, and users can debit funds into their account for purchases through Web sites. Of course, online buyers can also arrange C.O.D. payment.

Another trend spurring Internet use is promotion. President Toledo's government has the "Plan Huascaran" to give every school in Peru Internet access and instruction as part of their curricula. Banks and firms have also mounted promotions to foster Internet usage. Banco de Credito, the leading bank in Peru, launched its Web site in 2000 (ViaBCP.com). Aware of Peru's low Internet use and PC penetration, it began a promotion offering special low prices for PCs.

A cultural factor that is helping to promote Internet use is "Internet cabins," which are not Internet cafes but public computer labs located in almost every street. Internet cabins started during Peru's recession as an alternative for people who were downsized from firms. Internet cabins offer Web access at a very low price (between US$0.75 and US$1 per hour). The price is so reasonable that even small firms give their employees money to use the cabins instead of installing an expensive dedicated line at the office.

Poland

Dorota Walerysiak
Alumna of the Warsaw University
(Faculty of Journalism and Political
Sciences) and *Logistics Specialist at Mint*
Electronics Ltd.

In 2001, about 7 million people used the Internet in Poland (Samuelson 2002). The number of host computers grew 800% since 1995, the year Polish Internet use began expanding beyond academic circles. The most growth occurred in 1999, when the number of users doubled (Zwierzchowski 2000). According to PriceWaterhouseCoopers, Poland will have almost 10 million Internet users by 2006 (Nua Surveys, 2002).

Internet usage is heavy in Poland: about half of the users log on daily and 35% at least once a week. E-mail and the Web are the most popular Internet applications. For 67% of users, the Internet is a crucial source of information, and for 30% it is a work tool. About 20% of the users work in companies that offer an Internet provider, and over 15% work in education. The Internet influences people's habits: 50% of Internet users reported watching less TV or sleeping less than they had before they started using the Internet (Krakow Economic Academy 2000).

The percentage of men using the Internet was 80% in 1999 but has since dropped to 63%. In 2001, 68% of Internet users lived in towns with populations over 100,000, and 70% were younger than 35 years of age. It is remarkable that 35% have college degrees, compared with 10% of the total population in Poland. Twenty-seven percent of Polish Internet users were still in school or in college. The fastest-growing group of Internet users is high school and college students. This trend will continue, as computers and the Internet are being introduced in schools and public libraries.

The Internet has already become the most up-to-date and comprehensive source of information for all aspects of life. Immediate access to information, such as weather and road condition forecasts and reports, is widely available through mobile phones. Television channels and radio stations invite the Internet audience to shape the content of their programs. All major national newspapers have an online version and offer Internet access to their archives (Kowalczyk [1], 2001). Although their presence on the Web is very important, none of these subsidiary Web sites has produced profits so far (Mielnik, 2002). The three largest Polish publishing houses maintain a Web site offering free access to over 200 dictionaries and encyclopedias online (Latek, 2002).

The digital divide phenomenon can be observed in Polish society. Over 30,000 public schools are not yet connected to the Internet, nor do they have at least one computerized classroom. National public fund-raising campaigns have so far managed to provide classroom and Internet access to only 7,000 schools (Kowalczyk [3], 2002). As a prospective European Union member (expected to join in 2004), Poland hopes to obtain significant funds to support its nascent information society (Augustyniak, 2002). Interestingly, in June 2002 several Polish universities launched the first long-distance learning project in the country: Polish Virtual University. This project takes advantage of Internet tools such as e-mail, discussion groups, and chat rooms (Wodecki, 2002).

In 2001 Poland had about 500 online shops, and over 500,000 customers purchased over $4 million dollars worth of goods online (Dygas, 2002). For most e-businesses, lower prices is the main marketing strategy and products are rarely customized. Therefore, online shoppers are mostly one-time shoppers. According to e-shop managers, the most important advantages to selling online are fast response to the client's needs, lower cost, and customers' convenience (Leszczynski, 2002). In 2001, only one-third of the operating e-shops were profitable. The goods sold in e-shops are on average 10% cheaper than the same products in traditional retail shops (Kowalczyk (2), 2002). Extensive cost savings draw customers to online travel and tourist services; travel Web sites' net income has grown steadily by 8 to10% since 1999 (Pisera, 2002). The first Polish auction Web site hosts about 3,500 transactions per day, with computers, VCRs, and audio equipment among the most frequently auctioned goods (Kowalczyk [2], 2002).

In August 2001, the Polish Parliament passed the Electronic Signature Bill. Increased safety of online transactions is expected to boost transactions in the B2B market, increase the popularity of e-banking, and facilitate communication between citizens and public administration in the first two years (Bonarowski, 2002; Iszkowski, 2002).

Most national supermarket chains do not yet consider e-mail an important means of communicating with customers; few answer customers' e-mail inquiries in a timely matter. Also over 50% of central/national public offices remain ignorant of the Internet's benefits in contact with citizens (Kowalczyk (2), 2002). Polish Internal Revenue Service, Central Customs, Office and Social Security Administration are the first central administration entities to adopt high Internet standards in public services (Siluszek, 2002).

The first two online virtual banks, M.-Bank and Intelligo, have gained enormous popularity since early 2001. This growth is mainly due to the relatively high interest rates offered on checking and saving accounts: 12 to 13% compared to 6 to 7% in regular banks (www.mbank.com.pl). Most other banks have introduced online services, and they also accommodate customers who use cellular phones. In 2001, over 11 million people in Poland used mobile phones; that number is expected to increase to 18 million by the 2004. Among other functions, users can check their account balances by sending SMS messages.

While shopping online is still in the early growth stages, B2B transactions generated more than half of the total value of all online transactions. In 2001 their net value amounted to $40 million dollars—$1 per capita, but still low compared with $30 per capita in the United States.

The high cost of Internet connection, as well as a highly regulated telecom market, are the most significant impediments to Internet growth. Polish Telecommunication Ltd., a former state monopoly, has had competition from new long-distance providers within the last two years, yet it still monopolizes the local communications market. Private households that use modems can obtain Internet connection only through this company's cables and they are charged the regular local phone call rate (10 cents per 3 minutes) for this service. Since 1999 several cable TV providers have also offered Internet access. The cost of cable installation varies from $100 to $200 and the monthly flat fee ranges from $20 to $40—a rather large investment when the average monthly salary per capita is only $430 (Piasek, 2001). Under these economic constraints, the wireless Wi-Fi technology becomes increasingly attractive: for as low as $600 users can purchase the equipment to build a simple wireless Internet network. The main barrier has been, again, complex licensing regulations (Stone and Levy 2002).

Amazing Thailand

Dr. Ellen Hertzberg
Dr. Supong Limtanakool
Bangkok University, Graduate School
E-mail: ellen@ehertzberg.com

Sitting in a cyber cafe in downtown Bangkok, we reflect upon the dramatic transformations in Thai culture while watching an elephant plod along the traffic-clogged street. Thailand was one of the first countries in Asia to go online, in 1987—but will the Internet totally reshape this culturally rich and diverse culture? The answer is a definite **no**. Even if it were possible, such a transformation will take years.

The chart in Exhibit 16 - 4 depicts Internet usage in Thailand. The academic sector is still the largest for Internet usage. Thailand's focus has been largely academic and educational in developing and using the Internet, resulting in "The Thai Cyber Child" project. This project is a school information action program aimed at developing young human resources to build information technology skills and future careers: the most important of Thailand's three pillars of information technology development (telecommunications, human resources, government). The

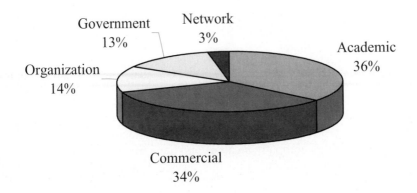

Exhibit 16 - 4 Internet Users in Various Segments in Thailand

Thai SchoolNet targets about 185 secondary schools within a network. Yet the typical Cyber Child's usage erodes Thai traditional values (avoidance of confrontation and emotional distance). Thai children today are becoming increasingly attached to the Internet and know much more than their parents. This threatens values of hierarchical society, particularly in the rural areas.

Thailand and E-Commerce

The Thai government's official e-commerce site follows. E-commerce began just a few years ago, but the Thais have flocked to use it. Both the private and government sectors have tried introducing universal e-commerce in all sectors. The following sections report on Thailand's e-commerce strengths, weaknesses, opportunities, and threats.

Strengths

Usage of computers per 1,000 persons is among the lowest in Southeast Asia. Thus, the rate of usage is in the developmental stage—but growth is likely to be very substantial. Commercial Internet usage is increasing, bringing gains to the B2B sector; as computer prices and the cost of Internet services drop, per capita usage of the Internet will increase.

Weaknesses

Thailand still lacks the proper infrastructure and legal framework to support e-commerce. As a result, most businesses operating in Thailand have been unable to take full advantage of the Internet's opportunities. Also, Internet and telecommunication services can be considered to be a quasi-monopolistic operation with very few players charging high rates as compared to South Korea, Japan, or Taiwan.

Credit card usage is still very low. Only about 4% of GNP is devoted to credit card expenditure in Thailand. This is the most crucial aspect of e-commerce operations, because online buying must be more convenient than conventional shopping if it is to gain a foothold here. E-commerce in Thailand suffers from a comparative and competitive disadvantage. With little effort Thai consumers can shop for whatever they want at flashy high-tech shopping malls and are less motivated to buy if they cannot feel or touch the merchandise or cannot make an instant purchase. In addition, shipping and handling are expensive, which wipes out any price advantage of e-commerce.

Opportunities

Another focus of the three pillars of IT development in Thailand is on investing in the National Information Infrastructure to expand telephone services to remote areas and to create an information superhighway. In addition, the use of middlemen or agents in service sectors in Thailand affects e-marketing. For example, in the insurance industry, savings on insurance premiums can be reduced by as much as 40% by eliminating agency fees or middlemen. Generations of Thai consumers will be much more prepared to use e-commerce services with readily available cyber money, cheaper computer networks and airtime, and more favorable attitudes about shopping on the Internet.

Threats

The product life cycle for new technologies changes so quickly that one miscalculation in operations can lead to a very bad situation. The most crucial factor necessary for the sustainable development of e-commerce in Thailand is good governance and better services for citizens.

About the Future

The development of electronic commerce is one of the keystones of Thailand's IT-2000 plan (Exhibit 16 - 5). In January 1999 the government approved a proposal

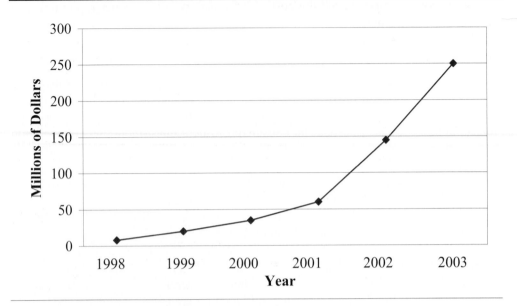

Exhibit 16 - 5 Estimated E-Commerce Revenues

to set up an Electronic Commerce Resource Center for e-commerce related information and training programs, particularly to SMEs. One goal of the center is to prepare SMEs to compete internationally via e-commerce as well as to defend themselves against foreign competition. Related initiatives include a smart card development program.

The first phase of many company e-commerce strategies in Thailand (e.g., Jay Mart) is to adopt a "cash on delivery" system to overcome logistics and payment problems. This reflects the saying in Thailand: There are three ways of doing things—the right way, the wrong way, and the "Thai way." Accordingly, companies are now introducing e-commerce, adopting a "cash on delivery" system, and using Tuk-Tuks (motorbikes) for delivery.

Turkey

Dr. A. Ercan Gegez
Asst. Professor of Marketing and
International Business
Marmara University, Istanbul, Turkey
E-mail: egegez@marmara.edu.tr

Despite economic crisis, Turkey is one of the fastest-growing and most promising markets for communications and technology products in the world. In the second half of the 1990s, fierce competition among newspaper publishers led to the free distribution of computers, and PC ownership in Turkey increased dramatically. A Roper survey in 2000 listed Turkey among the countries with the largest increase (26%) in home computer owners (www.nua.com/surveys). PC usage rate in small businesses is around 20%. (turk.Internet.com/haber).

Turkey is also among the fastest-growing markets for cell phones. According to recent research by CRC Consultancy and Research Center, 76% of the people in Turkey tend to connect to the Internet through cell phones. This suggests great opportunities for mobile commerce in Turkey.

The country has 4 million Internet users. According to Dr. Kircova (2002a), the digital divide is a big problem: Different income levels among geographic regions make the Internet available in medium- to high-income level regions only. In spite of this problem, low to medium-income level citizens are using Internet cafes for access. Internet cafes are the main places for Internet access (10% among the whole population or 49% among the Internet population). The second favorite place of access is home (5% among whole population or 25% among Internet population) (The Global E-Commerce Report 2002).

Despite current barriers posed by the digital divide, the Internet holds great expansion potential for the future. Increasing Internet usage might also create a more homogeneous population of Internet users in Turkey, at least in terms of income and education. For instance, the typical Turkish Internet user has a university-level education. More than half of users can speak a foreign language, and 82.5% of all foreign language speakers speak English. Additionally, more than half of all Internet users are single, living with their families, and Internet usage is higher among the younger age group (under 29 years of age).

According to the Global E-Commerce Report (2002), the percentage of Internet users in Turkey increased from 16% in 2001 to 20% in 2002, paralleling the recovery following Turkey's economic crisis in 2001. That 25% increase has moved Turkey from *Low Internet Penetration Country* status to *Medium Internet Penetration Country* status.

Turkey has approximately 49 Internet Service Providers (ISPs), but just two control more than half of the market. In 2000 alone, there was a 609% growth in Internet subscribers in Turkey creating a penetration rate of 5.5% (cyberatlas.Internet.com). Despite low consumer spending power, Turkish consumers are so open to technology that rapid adoption can occur in a short time.

Nevertheless, none of the Turkish ISPs are profitable at this point and no Turkish ISP is listed on any stock exchange. Revenues from e-commerce and advertising are currently low but analysts expect rapid growth in these areas. (www.nua.com/surveys). ISP revenues mostly come from dial-up connection charges, making the final price very high for consumers.

Following the rapid development of the Internet in Turkey in 1998, some big firms began e-commerce through their Web sites. The number of consulting companies serving Internet marketing has increased as well. Although recent online trade activities mostly focus on B2C sales, B2B and extranet activities will likely increase over time.

The Turkish banking sector leads those involved in Internet usage for many services, although some basic functional problems remain, such as slow operations and the need to repeat authorization requests due to security reasons (Kırcova 2002b: 220).

The Turkish e-commerce market stands at about $126 million including online banking and stock trading. The main product categories bought online are books and magazines, computer hardware and software, toys and gifts, and stationery. Online shoppers in Turkey make up only 4.1% of all Internet users. Global E-Commerce Report (2002) revealed that the number of online shoppers increased 200% in 2002 compared to 2001. Despite this rapid increase, the main barriers to online shopping in Turkey are difficulty/lack of knowledge (31%), insecurity (31%), and preference for buying goods and services in a store (26%). This is not surprising because Turkish consumers have traditionally taken a "see first, bargain, and buy" approach to purchases.

Some efforts are underway to develop a legal structure for the Internet. With great support and pressure from the government, organizations such as the Internet Higher Council and Electronic Commerce Coordination Council are taking important steps. However, probably the biggest barrier to the Internet in Turkey is economic, particularly in light of the economic crisis. Although subscriptions to ISP servers are still expensive for the many people, Turkey's Internet future has great potential.

Dr. A. Ercan Gegez thanks Superonline and CRC Research and Consultancy, Inc. for providing up-to-date information about the Turkish Internet market.

Summary

Within a worldwide B2C market of 530 million consumers, some countries have higher penetration of Internet access, usage, and shopping. Among the many factors affecting Internet penetration are income, infrastructure, computer ownership, telecommunication availability and pricing, social and cultural traditions, business attitudes, and wireless Web access.

Internet penetration is relatively high in countries such as Australia but relatively low in countries such as Egypt. In many nations, the government (and some businesses and educational institutions) are launching initiatives to increase Internet access and usage. Countries such as Poland and Turkey are also working to create an appropriate legal structure for e-commerce by passing electronic signature laws and other bills. Deregulation of the telecommunication industry has affected Internet access in some countries by allowing for more competition and lowering rates for dial-up access. Wireless Internet access is growing in some countries where dial-up and broadband access are quite expensive.

E-marketers must carefully research each country's current market conditions and environmental factors before selecting specific targets for entry.

E x e r c i s e s

Review Questions

1. How is deregulation of the telecommunication industry affecting Internet access and usage in different countries?
2. What are the main product categories purchased by online shoppers in different countries?
3. How are some e-marketers dealing with low penetration of credit cards in some countries?
4. How does literacy affect Internet usage in Egypt?
5. How do language barriers affect Internet usage in China?
6. What techniques are companies and governments using to spur growth in Internet usage and access around the world?
7. What cultural factors are affecting Internet shopping in some countries?

Discussion Questions

8. Would the Internet cabins used in Peru be a good solution for increasing Internet access in China? Explain your answer.
9. In countries that have just passed electronic signature laws, what types of online activities are likely to increase—and why?
10. The Cyber Child project is changing Thai children's attitudes toward traditional cultural values. What consequences do you foresee as a result of this change?

Practitioner Perspective

E-Commerce from Ghana

Cordelia Salter-Nour, founder of eShopAfrica, is originally from England and has lived in Africa since 1979. For most of that time she has worked in the IT sector. In 1998 she founded a Web studio specializing in high-quality Web sites with an African theme (www.cordelia.net). eShopAfrica.com is her first e-commerce project. eShopAfrica began in Spring 2001 and is based on Accra, Ghana.
e-mail: cordelia@cordelia.net

Although eShopAfrica.com is based in Ghana, we are marketing to the rest of the world so the fact that credit cards are hardly used in Africa does not affect us. Until there is an easy-to-use digital cash solution, any e-commerce in Africa would only be aimed at a very, very small minority. A possible solution to this is through mobile phones—which are already very popular in Africa.

I think all of us face the same problems when it comes to getting onto search engines these days—you have to pay to get to the top. We are considering paying to be listed, or paying to target advertise, but we have many doubts about how many serious purchasers would actually use search engines to find the kinds of products we have. We think a well-targeted, real-world marketing campaign may be a more effective use of our funds.

I have developed and run eShopAfrica in Ghana using dial-up phone connections since 1999. Connectivity in Ghana is really not at all bad—I used to live in Ethiopia where being connected was a big challenge! Since I took an office at BusyInterenet (www.BusyInternet.com), which has a VSAT and a 56k connection speed, I have been able to do much more online marketing. Dial-up speeds were often too slow or there was too much local congestion for online marketing to be worthwhile time wise before.

I think the main challenge we face is with perceptions of product prices. We find that those we target fall into two categories—either they know African products (or are African) or they don't. Those who know African products want to purchase from us at the same or less than they would pay if they came and bought it themselves. They seem very unwilling to recognize or pay for the costs of running the Web site or connectivity and just want rock bottom prices. Those who don't know Africa have a perception that Africa is very poor and expect to see our items cheaper than artifacts from other poor areas (such as India). However, if you know Africa, you know that in fact it is expensive here and that things are not cheap. Also, there are many Indian and Chinese copies of African products (particularly textiles) that make our genuine products look expensive. Many people outside have little idea of quality, and so again, just think we are overcharging.

Another problem that we have faced is that local artisans see the dollar prices on the Web site and then increase their own prices in expectation of getting that amount themselves. They have little understanding of the costs of running and maintaining a Web site. We have to take a lot of time and trouble explaining to them that the prices on the Web site include our overhead. Our heaviest cost is that of the payment service provider (in our case Worldpay). Being based in Africa puts us in the high-risk category so we pay the heaviest premiums. We can offer a further discount to people who don't mind paying by ordinary bank transfer in the old fashioned (non-e) method.

I think e-commerce in general is going through the doldrums—maybe it's disenchantment, or maybe a reality call. Who knows?

Banner Ad Targeting Increases Hotel Room Sales

Ana Maria Alvarez Bujalil is international marketing and CRM Director at Grupo Posadas, the leading hotel companies in Latin America. Grupo Posadas owns a number of hotel chains such as Fiesta Americana, Fiesta Inn, Caesar Park, and Caesar Business.

Customers are currently saturated with advertising, invitations, and other offers. This makes them reluctant to respond to the increasing flood of marketing messages. The most effective way for marketers to increase responses to their efforts is by offering their products and services directly to the people with the highest potential interest. The better directed, in terms of needs and interests, the greater the response of each effort. This means that customer demographics are not necessarily the most effective targeting criteria. Targeting customers based on interests was extremely expensive and difficult for marketers in the past. The Internet is now the best and cheapest way to do this efficiently and rapidly.

At Fiesta Americana we have some meaningful experiences with Internet targeting. We launched a banner ad campaign at Travelocity.com, a leading travel portal on the Internet. We thought that this site was the best for our hotels since its users are people interested in travel. However, being a bit more ambitious with our targeting, we asked DoubleClick, the company that sells banners for Travelocity, to show our banners only to people requesting information about the seven most popular destinations in Mexico. We started with three different banners. Studying the performance was very easy since DoubleClick has an online tracking system that allows clients to see the number of impressions and clicks for every banner, destination, time, day, and so forth. After doing some tracking, we realized that we could include more filters to increase the click-through rate, which was averaging 1%. Using trial and error, we narrowed the audience to people who met the following criteria: They had already bought an air ticket to Cancun, they were coming from the seven eastern United States, they were using only the latest version of Explorer or Netscape, and they were browsing only between 2 p.m. and 7 p.m. Monday through Wednesday. We used these criteria because each iteration increased click-through rates.

We continually experimented with the banners until we reached the one with the highest response rate from people wanting to stay in Cancun, Mexico. The result of this narrow targeting was an increase of 1,275% in the click-through rate: It jumped from 0.8% to 10.2%. This not only represented a greater number of people coming to our Fiesta Americana Web site, but these represented better prospects for purchasing hotel rooms. In fact, reservations increased 3% during the period of the optimized banner campaign. The effort turned out to be quite profitable, even though the highly targeted banners cost a bit more to run. They were especially effective as compared with conventional advertising, which is rarely profitable and is difficult to measure.

At Grupo Posadas, e-mail targeting is another successful form of direct marketing. We are constructing a database formed from the users at our Web site, those who actually made a reservation, frequent travelers, and other potential and current customers in both Mexico and the United States. This database has been used to select people with interests in certain kinds of trips or destinations. We send them e-mail with special offers, and the response to this program has been 367% greater than the response to our conventional mailing efforts with a cost of less than 20% of the conventional costs.

These two examples of direct marketing through the Internet are the first steps of an aggressive wave of customer relationship management (CRM). The Internet is definitely the best soil in which to sow the seeds of personalization, customization, and targeted services. Based on our experiences, I have no doubt that it will become the most used promotional media in the near future.

Savvy Sites

CIA World Factbook www.cia.gov/cia/publicatio ns/factbook/	The Central Intelligence Agency provides this comprehensive guide to the world with information on every single country.
ebusiness forum www.ebusinessforum.com	This site provides a wealth of information on global issues affecting the digital economy and even provides a section where users can find out how to do business in over 60 countries.
Europa – The European Union On-Line www.europa.eu.int	Provides information on the current state of the European Union.
International Data Corporation (IDC) www.idc.com	Some very useful and free information can be found at this site. The topics include information technology and data analysis in addition to a global perspective on IT trends.
Taylor Nelson Sofres www.tnsofres.com	This company provides market research and analysis for over 80 countries. Its 2002 Global eCommerce Report studies industry trends in 37 countries.

U.S. Department of Commerce www.doc.gov	This is a great source of information for exporters using information technology to expand into new markets. The site has a section dedicated to electronic commerce where users can read various publications and reports.
World Bank Group www.worldbank.org	The World Bank Group works in over 100 developing economies and provides assistance in a variety of areas. The site provides articles, research, and much more.
World Economic Forum www.weforum.com	The World Economic Forum is a nonprofit organization, which seeks to further economic growth and social progress. Here one can access their online magazine *World Link,* which covers issues of concern to global businesses.
World Trade Magazine www.worldtrademag.com	Get the latest industry news on world trade shipping and sourcing. Users can even access up-to-date articles from other regions of the world.
NetAid www.netaid.org	This is an organization dedicated to fighting poverty. We include it here in case readers want to become "online volunteers."

A c t i v i t i e s

1. Visit the Country-Code Top-Level Domain database at www.icann.org under the Resource section. Notice how Web sites originating in the United States do not have to append the ".us" root to the end of URLs. Which root names owned by these countries could be used for commercial purposes rather than differentiating country of origin? If you wanted to register a Web site ending in one of these country root names, what requirements do you have to meet? What country root names are already being offered through registrations sites like NetworkSolutions.com?

2. The World Wide Web is a borderless medium that spans the globe. Check out the Internet Law and Policy Forum at www.ilpf.org. What attempts have been made to regulate the Internet both domestically and overseas? What kind of problems may arise concerning jurisdiction and enforcement in a medium that spans the globe? Jurisdiction is typically based on the location of Web servers. What recourse do users have if they are wronged in activities such as gambling, if the

servers are physically located outside the United States? What of spam outside the United States?

3. More Web sites are providing pages in languages other than English. Visit Google.com and select language tools. What kind of services does Google provide for specific languages and countries? Try translating an entire Web page into a different language and view the results. What languages are compatible with these feature sets? What efforts is Google making to translate sites from languages that are currently unavailable?

4. Visit the "How Many Online" Survey found at www.nua.com. According to this survey, what percentage of the world is currently online? How has that changed since this book was written? Divided by region, which areas of the world show the highest percentage for online usage? In comparison to the United States, what are the usage patterns of those in Europe and Asia? What trends in Internet adoption and usage do you think will occur as the Internet continues to mature (see Chapter 16)?

5. Visit the UPS Web site at www.ups.com. If you wanted to deliver a package to Paris, France, what steps would you have to take to complete the transaction? How has UPS made the process easier? What languages other than English are available to UPS customers? What difficulties might you run into when delivering to an address that doesn't use English characters? How does UPS address these issues?

I n t e r n e t   E x e r c i s e s

Internet Exercise: "World Wide Web" Is Not a Misnomer

U.S.-based Web sites often offer different services and products in different markets. One fertile market for U.S. firms is Europe. Visit www.yahoo.co.uk and compare the services offered there with its U.S. branch counterparts. Complete the following table.

Service	Offered by Yahoo! U.K. but not by Yahoo! U.S.	Offered by Yahoo! U.S. but not by Yahoo! U.K.

Now visit www.amazon.co.uk and complete a similar table.

Service	Offered by Amazon U.K. but not by Amazon U.S.	Offered by Amazon U.S. but not by Amazon U.K.

For Discussion

1. What is the size of the U.S. Internet market versus the U.K. market? Visit CyberAtlas or nua to answer this question.

2. What proportion of the U.S. population is online? The U.K. population?

3. How are the ads different on Yahoo!'s U.K. site?

4. What different search option is available on Yahoo!'s U.K. site?

5. Why do you think Amazon offers fewer services in the U.K. market?

6. Yahoo! provides free Internet access in the U.K. market. Why doesn't it do the same in the U.S. market? Hint: Research a company called Freenet.

Internet Exercise: International Service Strategies

The core service in the airline industry is transportation. The "problem-solving" benefit for the customer is travel from one place to another. To differentiate their services, airlines provide many additional benefits. If you wanted to visit Europe, you might consider KLM, British Airways, or Lufthansa. Review the Web sites of these airlines and complete the table just to evaluate their services.

For Discussion

1. Which airline brand name best conveys a quality image to you?

2. How does each airline differentiate itself from the others: KLM? British Airways? Lufthansa?

3. If Lufthansa decided to expand by developing a tourist hotel, would you recommend a brand extension or a new brand? Justify your choice.

4. Which airline would you choose for your European travel? Why?

5. What services can an airline provide to make you a loyal customer?

	KLM Royal Dutch Airlines www.klm.com	**British Airways** www.british-airways.com	**Lufthansa** www.lufthansa.com
Many destinations?			
Attractive frequent flyer program?			
Other service features			
Evidence of service quality			
Evidence of competitive positioning strategy			
Ways customers can give feedback to company at site			

Appendices

Glossary

access   Users should have the ability to access their data and correct them if erroneous.

access control   Places its emphasis on laws and standards that enable persons to reasonably regulate the information that they are giving up.

action plan   One of the phases of the Internet marketing plan, in which the marketer identifies specific tactics to implement selected strategies.

ad click rate   The number of ad clicks as a percentage of ad views, or the number of times an ad is clicked on by users as a percentage of the number of times an ad was downloaded and viewed by users. **

ad clicks   The number of times a user "clicks" on an online ad, often measured as a function of time ("ad clicks per day"). **

adoption barriers   Sociological, cultural, technological, legal, and political issues that pose barriers to consumer use of particular products (in this case the Internet).

adoption curve   Representation of the adoption process, consisting of five decision-making steps consumers go through before buying goods or services: (1) unawareness, (2) awareness, (3) interest, (4) evaluation, and (5) trial.

ADSL (Asymmetric Digital Subscriber Line)   One variation of DSL, in which the information coming to the user's home is delivered faster than the information that the user sends upstream.

advertorial   A print advertisement styled to resemble the editorial format and typeface of the publication in which it runs. **

ad views   On the Internet, the number of times an online ad was downloaded by users, often measured as a function of time ("ad views per day"). The actual number of times the ad was seen by users may differ because of caching (which increases the real number of ad views) and browsers that view documents as text only (which decreases the number of ad views). **

affiliate program   Firms put a link to an e-tailer's Web site and make a commission on all purchases by referred customers.

affinity group   People with a common interest. On the Internet, typically a subject-oriented mailing list, a newsgroup, or a conference on a Web site. **

agent An intermediary representing either the buyer or the seller, not taking title to the goods, and making a commission for work completed.

aggregation The gathering of products from multiple suppliers so that the consumer can have more choices in one location.

AIO Activities, interests, and opinions of consumers.

animated GIF (Graphic Interchange Format) Files that consist of a series of frames each containing a separate picture. These are used to provide the animation for banner ads.

Application Service Provider (ASP) Allows businesses to outsource value chain functions to separate providers. The software resides at the ASP's site.

assistive technologies Help people with disabilities use their computers to communicate over the Net. These include voice-activated computers, large-type screen displays, type-to-speech or braille, speech-to-text telephony, and eye gaze-to-type.

atmospherics The in-store ambiance created by retailers.

attention economy The idea that there is infinite information but the demand for it is limited by human capacity.

attitudes Internal thoughts about people, products, and other objects. They can be either positive or negative, but the whole thing happens inside a person's head.

audience accumulation The net number of people (or homes) exposed to a medium during its duration (e.g., a half-hour broadcast program, or magazine issue). **

audience composition The demographic profile of a media audience. **

audience turnover The average ratio of cumulative audience listening/viewing to the average audience listening/viewing. **

automatic customization Tailoring of the content presented to the user based on information known about the user and the user's historical surfing behavior. See *mass customization.*

average audience (AA) In broadcast, the average number of homes (or individuals) tuned to a given time segment of a program. In print media, the number of individuals who looked into an average issue of a publication and are considered "readers." **

average order value (AOV) A calculation that reflects dollar sales divided by the number of orders.

bandwidth The data-transferring capacity of a system—how much information can be sent from one place to another in a given period of time. There are many ways to measure this—for example, the number of megabytes transferred per second.

balanced scorecard An enterprise performance management system that links strategy to measurement by asking firms to set goals and subsequent performance metrics in four areas: customer, internal, innovation and learning, and financial.

banner ad A rectangular space appearing on a Web site, paid for by an advertiser, which allows the user to click-through to the advertiser's Web site.

bar code scanner A real-space primary data collection technique by which information is gathered offline at brick-and-mortar retail stores and is subsequently stored and used in marketing databases.

barter The exchange of goods and services without the use of cash. Usually, the acquisition of media time or space by a media company in exchange for similar time/space in return. **

basic cable A "basic" service agreement in which a subscriber pays a cable TV operator or system a monthly fee. Does not include "pay" services that might be offered by the cable operator. **

benefit segmentation A variable in behavioral segmentation where marketers form groups of consumers based on the benefits they desire from the product.

bit vendor A type of e-tailer that sells digital products such as media, software, and music and delivers them via the Internet.

brand advertising Advertising that creates a distinctly favorable image that customers associate with a product at the moment they make buying decisions. †

brand loyalty Level of commitment customers feel toward a certain brand, expressed by their continued purchase of that brand.

brick and mortar An offline firm.

broadband High bandwidth required for the delivery of multimedia content over the Web.

brochureware A site that provides information about the company's products and services. Brochureware provides an excellent opportunity to brand as well as to develop a relationship with the consumer and other stakeholders.

broker An intermediary that brings buyers and sellers together but doesn't represent either side. Like agents, brokers are paid by either the buyer or the seller.

build to order A complex product is created as it is ordered. This helps to eliminate inventory and reduce cost.

bunkering People staying at home more (Hanson 2001). It is defined as ". . .the preparation and use of the home as a stronghold against assaults."

business intelligence The gathering of secondary and primary information about competitors, markets, customers, and more.

business model A method by which the organization sustains itself in the long term, which includes its value proposition for partners and customers as well as its revenue streams.

business-to-business (B2B) The marketing of products to businesses, governments, and institutions for use in the business operation, as components in the business products, or for resale.

business-to-consumer (B2C) The marketing of products to the end consumer.

button Like banners ads, buttons are paid for by an advertiser but are square or round instead of rectangular.

buyer cooperative (buyer aggregator) A type of online purchasing agent that brings buyers together for the purpose of buying in larger quantities and, thus, reducing prices.

cable modem Allows transmission of Internet traffic over the cable TV wire connected to the home. The speed of transmission over a cable modem ranges between 500 Kbps and 2.5 Mbps.

cable TV Reception of TV signals via cable (wires) rather than over the air (i.e., via a TV antenna). **

caching Phenomenon that occurs when access providers or browsers store or buffer Web page data in a temporary location on their networks or in their disk space to speed access and reduce traffic. Reduces the number of measured page views at the original content site. **

catalog aggregator Brings together many catalog companies, creating a new searchable database of products for buyers.

caveat emptor "Let the buyer beware." A slogan popular before the late 1930s when there was no regulation protecting consumer rights.

CDA (Computer Decency Act) In 1996, the federal Telecommunications Act of 1934 was amended to include this legislation, which made it a criminal act to send an obscene or indecent communication to a recipient who was known to the sender to be under 18 years of age.

chat room Virtual space where Internet users can communicate in real time using special software.

circulation In print media, the number of copies sold or distributed by a publication. In broadcast, the number of homes owning a TV/radio set within a station's coverage area. Or, in cable TV, the number of households that subscribe to cable services for a given network. In out-of-home media, the number of people passing an advertisement who have an opportunity to see it.[**]

click and mortar Stores with both offline and online selling.

clickstream A user's Web surfing patterns.

clickstream data Data that are recorded by software either on the user PC or a Web server. Includes every page that the user visits and the frequency with which the user returns to a page.

click-through Determined when a Web surfer clicks on a banner or other ad that is hyperlinked to the advertiser's site.

client-side Refers to activities that occur on the user's computer, such as writing and sending e-mail.

client-side data collection Information about consumer surfing is gathered right at the user's PC. One example of this is the cookie file.

closed loop marketing Tracks user with cookie files as long as the user remains in one of the Web sites on that loop or network.

cobrand The combination of two different companies' brand names on the same product.

collaborative filtering This software gathers opinions of like-minded users online and returns those opinions to the individual in real time.

common law Decisions, presumptions, and practices that have traditionally been embraced by Anglo-American courts.

communications and collaboration A part of Net commercialization, which includes gathering and processing information, communicating, collaborating, and publishing. All media that place their content online for subscription or as advertising fall into this category.

competitive intelligence (CI) The analysis of the industries in which a firm operates as input to the firm's strategic positioning and to understand competitor vulnerabilities.

concentrated targeting Also called *niche marketing*, a firm selects one segment and develops one or more marketing mixes to meet the needs of that segment.

consent When users are allowed to choose participation or exclusion.

consumer centric A Web audience measurement model similar to the Nielsen ratings for TV. A panel representative of the population is formed, its Web viewing actions are recorded, and the results are generalized to the population.

consumer-to-consumer (C2C) Business transaction from one consumer to another. Once limited to classified advertising and garage sales, C2C has now grown due to the popularity of online auctions.

content filtering A process by which Web users may block unwanted material.

content publishing (brochureware) Used by every firm that has a Web site. Content refers to any text, graphics, audio, or video online that informs or persuades.

continuous replenishment The concept of "scan one, make one—and deliver it fast." This helps to eliminate inventory and reduce cost.

cookie A persistent piece of information stored on the user's local hard drive, which is keyed to a specific server (and even a file pathway or directory location at the server), and is passed back to the server as part of the transaction that takes place when the user's browser again crosses the specific server/path combination.[**]

cookie file See *cookie.*

COPPA (Children's Online Protection Act) Requires that Web sites and other online media that knowingly collect information from children 12 years of age or under (1) provide notice to parents; (2) obtain verifiable parental consent prior to the collection, use, or disclosure of most information; (3) allow parents to view and correct this information; (4) enable parents to prevent further use or collection of data; (5) limit personal information collection for a child's participation in games, prize offers, or related activities; and (6) establish procedures that protect the confidentiality, security, and integrity of the personal information collected.

copyright Addresses the realm of ideas—specifically, the right to publish or duplicate the expressions of these ideas.

corporate portal A second-generation intranet. The goal of a corporate portal is to merge all of the employee's information and communication needs into a single interface, accessing internal documents, data warehouses, groupware, e-mail, and calendars, in addition to the Web.

cost per click Total advertisement cost divided by number of clicks on an ad or hyperlink.

cost per order Total ad cost divided by the number of orders.

cost per rating point (CPP) The cost of an advertising unit (e.g., a 30-second commercial) divided by the average rating of a specific demographic group (e.g., women, 1849).[**]

cost per thousand (CPM) The cost to deliver 1,000 impressions (associated with delivery of ad views on the Internet, and delivery to people or homes in traditional media).[**]

coverage   The percentage of a population group covered by a medium. Commonly used with print media to describe an average issue's audience within defined demographic or purchasing groups. Akin to rating.[**]

CPM   Cost of advertising per thousand people reached.

creative   The name given the art/design within an advertisement.[**]

cume (cumulative)   Rating the reach of a radio or TV program or station as opposed to the "average."[**]

customer profiling   Uses data warehouse information to help marketers understand the characteristics and behavior of specific target groups.

customer relationship management (CRM)   A holistic process of identifying, attracting, differentiating, and retaining customers. As it relates to e-business, it uses digital processes and integrates customer information collected at every customer touch point.

customization   The third step in the CRM process (identify, differentiate, and customize). It means that firms tailor their marketing mixes to meet the needs of small target segments, even to the individual level, using electronic marketing tools. It sometimes refers to technology that allows consumers to cater the Web site to suit their own needs.

cybersquatting   A type of trademark violation that involves the registration of domains that resemble or duplicate the names of existing corporations or other entities.

database management   For e-marketing, this includes collecting, analyzing, and disseminating electronic information about customers, prospects, and products in order to increase profits.

database marketing   Collecting, analyzing, and disseminating electronic information about customers, prospects, and products in order to increase profits.

data mining   Marketers extract hidden predictive information from the warehouse via statistical analysis in order to find patterns and other information in databases.

data warehouse   Repository for an entire organization's historical data (not just marketing data), designed specifically to support analyses necessary for decision making.

daughter window   Separate window that overlays the current browser window and contains content or advertisements. Sometimes called pop-up window.

decoding   Reading; receiving of the message transferred over the Internet.

demographics   The characteristics of populations.

differentiated targeting Also called *multisegment targeting*, exists when a firm carefully selects two or more segments and designs marketing mix strategies for each. Most firms today use a multisegment strategy.

diffusion of innovations The process by which new products are spread to members of the target market over time.

digital audio, video, graphics These are visual materials stored in a digital format for inclusion on Web pages and other electronic transmission over the Internet.

dilution The diminishment of the ability to identify or distinguish a good or service.

direct marketing Any direct communication to a consumer or business recipient that is designed to generate a response in the form of an order (direct order), a request for further information (lead generation), and/or a visit to a store or other place of business for purchase of specific a product(s) or service(s) (traffic generation) (source: www.the-dma.org/).

direct-response advertising Seeks to create action such as inquiry or purchase from consumers as a result of seeing the ad.

discontinuous innovations New-to-the-world products never seen before, such as were music CDs and the television at their introductions.

disintermediation The process of eliminating traditional intermediaries. Eliminating intermediaries has the potential to reduce costs since each intermediary must add to the price of the product in order to make a living.

distributed e-mail E-mail sent to distribution lists is redistributed to the entire subscription list.

distribution channel A group of interdependent firms that work together to transfer product from the supplier to the consumer. The transfer may either be direct or employ a number of intermediaries.

DMCA (Digital Millennium Copyright Act) A complex piece of legislation that contains several provisions, among them it grants Internet Service Providers (ISPs) protection from acts of user infringement as long as certain procedures are followed, including the prompt reporting and disabling of infringing material, and criminalizes the circumvention of software protections and the development or distribution of circumvention products.

domain name The unique name that identifies an Internet site, such as microsoft.com. A domain name always has two or more parts, separated by periods. A given server may have more than one domain name, but a given domain name points to only one machine. **

dot-com A firm engaging in e-commerce activities.

DSL (Digital Subscriber Line) Technology that refers to a family of methods for transmitting at speeds up to 8 Mbps (8 million bits per second) over a standard phone line. There are nine variations of DSL.

duration time The length of time between two events, such as successive requests to one or more Web pages (page duration) or visits to a given Web site (intervisit duration). **

dynamic pricing The strategy of offering different prices to different customers.

early adopters The next 13.5% to purchase the product, after the innovators, who comprise the first 2.5%. Early adopters are eager to buy new products, but they are more community minded than innovators and tend to communicate with others about new products.

early majority Consumers comprising the next 34% after innovators and early adopters. These consumers do not rush to try new products but collect information first, perhaps talking to opinion leaders, and purchasing only after thoughtful consideration.

e-business See electronic business.

e-business model A method by which the organization sustains itself in the long term *using information technology*, which includes its value proposition for partners and customers as well as its revenue streams.

e-business strategy The deployment of enterprise resources for capitalizing on technologies to reach specified objectives and ultimately improve performance and create sustainable competitive advantage.

e-commerce Uses digital technologies such as the Internet and bar code scanners to enable the buying and selling process. E-commerce is about transactions through distribution channels and e-tailing.

e-coupons Like traditional coupons, but Internet users "point and clip" these electronic coupons.

ECPA (Electronic Communication Privacy Act) As with the Fair Credit Reporting Act, this provides sanctions for misuse of consumer data.

EDI (electronic data interchange) The computerized exchange of information between organizations in order to avoid paper forms. The classic use of EDI is to eliminate purchase requisitions between firms.

effective frequency The level of exposure frequency at which reach is deemed "effectively" delivered. **

effectiveness Refers to choosing the right thing to do in order to maximize a company's competitive advantage.

effective reach The percentage of a population group reached by a media schedule at a given level of frequency.[**]

efficiency Generally refers to the relative costs of delivering media audiences.[**] See *cost per rating point* and *cost per thousand.*

efficient market A market in which customers have equal access to information about products, prices, and distribution.

electronic business (e-business) Includes all electronic activities conducted by organizations such as business intelligence, customer relationship management, supply chain management, e-commerce, and enterprise resource planning. This term and *e-commerce* are often used interchangeably.

electronic checks They work this way: The consumer sets up an account and authorizes a third-party Web site to pay an amount and withdraw funds from the user's checking account.

electronic commerce (e-commerce) Includes buying/selling online, digital value creation, virtual marketplaces and storefronts, and new distribution channel intermediaries. This term and *e-business* are often used interchangeably.

electronic marketing (e-marketing) The use of electronic data and applications for planning and executing the conception, distribution, promotion, and pricing of ideas, goods, and services to create exchanges that satisfy individual and organizational objectives.

e-mail advertising The least expensive type of online advertising, e-mail ads are generally just a few sentences of text embedded in another firm's e-mail content.

e-marketing strategy A marketing strategy using information technology.

enabling technology Electronic marketing products unique to the Internet that operate behind the scenes and assist in the creation of customer value.

encoding Creating messages or documents to be transmitted via the Internet.

enforcement Users should have effective means to hold data collectors to their policies.

enterprise knowledge management (EKM) A combination of the database contents and the technology used to create the system: the marketing information system (MIS) at a company-wide level. Marketing knowledge contributes to the EKM system through the MIS.

enterprise resource planning (ERP) Back-office operations such as order entry, purchasing, invoicing, and inventory control. ERP systems allow organizations to optimize business processes while lowering costs.

environmental factors The online legal, political, and technological environments that can greatly influence marketing strategies, alter the composition of the Internet audience, and affect the quality of material that can be delivered to them. These factors also affect laws regarding taxation, access, copyright, and encryption on the Internet.

environmental scan Continual task that includes economic analysis as well social and demographic trends.

e-tailer An intermediary firm that buys products and resells them online, just as traditional retailers do offline.

ethical code Developed by trade associations, commercial standards groups, and the professions, it outlines proper behaviors of participants.

ethics A general endeavor that takes into account the concerns and values of society as a whole.

evaluation plan System whereby the site is continually evaluated after it is created and published. This requires tracking systems that must be in place before the site is launched.

exchange A basic concept in marketing that refers to the act of obtaining a desired object from someone else by offering something in return.

experiential marketing This technique gets the consumer involved in the product to create a memorable experience.

Extensible Markup Language (XML) The next generation of HTML that allows Web browsers to pull information from databases on-the-fly and display in Web pages.

extranet Two or more networks that are joined for the purpose of sharing information. If two companies link their intranets, they would have an extranet. Extranets are proprietary to the organizations involved.

fax-on-demand Customers telephone a firm, listen to an automated voice menu, and through selecting options request that a fax be sent on a topic of interest.

fixed pricing Also called *menu pricing*, it occurs when sellers set the price and buyers must take it or leave it.

flow The state occurring during network navigation that is (1) characterized by a seamless sequence of responses facilitated by machine interactivity, (2) intrinsically enjoyable, (3) accompanied by a loss of self-consciousness, and (4) self-reinforcing. [‡]

focus group A qualitative methodology that attempts to collect in-depth information from a small number of participants.

framing A process in which a Web browser is instructed to divide itself into two or more partitions and load within a section material obtained from another Web site through the execution of an automatic link.

fraud The use of deception and false claims to obtain profit.

frequency The number of times people (or homes) are exposed to an advertising message, an advertising campaign, or a specific media vehicle. Also, the period of issuance of a publication (e.g., daily, monthly).[**]

frequency discount A rate discount allowed an advertiser that purchases a specific schedule within a specific period of time (e.g., six ads within one year).[**]

frequency distribution The array of reach according to the level of frequency delivered to each group.[**]

FTC (Federal Trade Commission) Administrative agency concerned with making laws responsive to particular situations by promulgating rules and opinions within the sectors of its expertise.

FTP (File Transfer Protocol) The procedure whereby files are transferred from the designer's computer to the Web server; used in the publication of Web pages.

geodemographics Combination of geography and demographics of consumer market segmentation designed to identify and reach the right people at the right time.

geographics Separation of large markets into smaller groupings according to country, region, state, city, community, or block divisions.

gross rating points (GRPs) The sum of all ratings delivered by a given list of media vehicles. Although synonymous with TRPs, GRPs generally refer to a "household" base. In out-of-home media, GRPs are synonymous with a *showing*.[**]

GUI Graphical user interface lets users interact with their computer via icons and a pointer instead of by typing in text at a command line.

hierarchy of effects model Device that attempts to explain the impact of marketing communication. It assumes that consumers go through a series of stages when making product decisions and that communication messages are designed to assist that movement.

high bandwidth See *broadband*.

hit Web-speak for any request for data from a Web page or file. Often used to compare popularity/traffic of a site in the context of getting so many "hits" during a given period. A common mistake is to equate hits with visits or page views. A single visit or page view is usually recorded as several hits and, depending on the browser, the page size, and other factors, the number of hits per page can vary widely.[**]

hop   Movement of a digital packet of information from one node to the next. In general the fewer the number of hops, the faster the packet arrives at its destination.

hostile applets   Programs that can be used to surreptitiously access and transmit data on hard drives, including e-mail addresses, credit card records, and other account information.

HTML (Hypertext Markup Language)   A simple coding system used to format documents for viewing by Web clients. Web pages are written in this standard specification.**

hyperlink   See *link.*

hypertext   Generally, any text on a Web page that contains links to other documents—words or phrases in a document that can be chosen by a user and that cause another document to be retrieved or displayed.**

ICANN (Internet Corporation for Assigned Names and Numbers)   Responsible for the administration of the Internet name and address system, resolving conflicts that surround the assignment and possession of domains.

IMC (integrated marketing communication)   See *integrated marketing communication.*

impressions   The gross sum of all media exposures (number of people or homes) without regard to duplication.**

in-depth interviews (IDI)   A semistructured conversation with a small number of subjects.

individualized targeting   See *micromarketing.*

infomediary   An online organization that aggregates and distributes information.

information architecture   The design of Web site organization, indexing, labeling, and navigation systems to support browsing and searching.

information publishing   Marketing communication with the goal of disseminating persuasive information to create awareness, knowledge (cognitive step), and positive attitudes (attitude step).

infrastructure   The equipment and communication lines that allow data to travel through a network.

inline discussion   A way to reach a wide audience that allows comments made about one site to be stored on an unrelated server.

innovators   The first 2.5% of consumers to purchase a product. They tend to be risk takers, eager to try new products (especially high-tech products), and with higher levels of education and income. They are very self-reliant, gaining information from experts and the press rather than from peers.

integrated marketing communication (IMC) A comprehensive plan of communication that includes advertising, sales promotion, public relations, direct marketing, personal selling, and the rest of the marketing mix to provide maximum communication impact with stakeholders.

interactive advertising Includes all forms of online, wireless, and interactive television advertising, including banners, sponsorships, e-mail, keyword searches, referrals, slotting fees, classified ads, and interactive television commercials. (IAB Glossary of Interactive Advertising terms: www.iab.net)

interactive banner The most advanced stage of the banner. Some banners sense the position of the mouse on the Web page and begin to animate faster as the user approaches. Other banners have built-in games. Still other banners have drop-down menus, check boxes, and search boxes to engage and empower the user.

interactive point of sale terminals Located on a retailer's counter, and used to capture data and present targeted communication.

intermediary A firm that appears in the channel between the supplier and the consumer. By specializing, intermediaries are able to perform functions more efficiently than the supplier could.

internal efficiencies Reductions in marketing and operations costs. A company going online usually realizes internal efficiencies.

Internet The global network of interconnected networks.

Internet business models A subset of e-business models that uses the Internet to add value and generate a revenue stream.

Internet marketing Use of the Internet and other network systems for marketing a firm's products. E-marketing may be replacing this term because it includes a broader range of technologies.

Internet telephony Use of the Internet to carry simultaneous digitized voice transmission.

interstitials Java-based ads that appear while the publisher's content is loading.

intranet A network that runs internally in a corporation but that uses Internet standards such as HTML and browsers. Thus, an intranet is like a mini-Internet but only for internal corporate consumption.

instant messaging Short messages sent among users who are online at the same time.

inventory Normally defined as the quantity of goods or materials on hand. On the Internet, a site's inventory is the number of page views it will deliver in a given period of time and is, thus, the amount of product that can be sold to advertisers. **

ISP (Internet Service Provider) Company that has a network of servers (mail, news, Web, and the like), routers, and modems attached to a permanent, high-speed Internet "backbone" connection. Subscribers can then dial into the local network to gain Internet access.

jurisdiction The legal term that describes the ability of a court or other authority to gain control over a party. Jurisdiction is traditionally based on physical presence, but within the online world commonality of physical location is never assured.

just-in-time inventory/delivery (JIT) A goal of value chain management in which carrying excessive amounts of inventory is avoided. Some retailers do not even hold inventory but rather acquire and ship it at the time of the order.

keyword advertising Presents banner ads or links on a search query return page based on the keywords the user enters at a search engine.

knowledge management The process of managing the creation, use, and dissemination of knowledge.

laggards The last 16% of buyers of new products. They are very traditional and generally of lower socioeconomic status. Often they adopt a product when newer products have already been introduced.

Lanham Act Trademarks may be registered with the government, but whether registered or not, they may be protected under the act.

late majority Consumers comprising the next 34% to adopt new products, after innovators, early adopters, and early majority. These folks are skeptical and generally purchase a product only after their friends already have done so. They adopt because of the desire to conform to group norms.

lateral partnerships Competitors, not-for-profit organizations, or governments that join with the firm for some common goal but not for transactions.

law An expression of values, normally created for broader purposes, with the goal of addressing national or sometimes international populations. Law is made by legislatures such as Congress or Parliament, enforced by executives or agencies, and interpreted by the courts.

learning organization Uses internal and external data to quickly adapt to a changing environment, creating organizational change that improves its competitive position and employee satisfaction.

license Consists of contractual agreements made between consumers and software vendors that allow the buyer to use the product but restrict duplication or distribution.

lifetime value (LTV) Net present value of the revenue stream for any particular customer over a number of years.

line extensions A lower-risk strategy for marketers introducing a new-product line.

link The path between two documents that associates an object, such as a button or hypertext, on a Web page with another Web address. The hyperlink allows a user to point and click on an object and thereby move to the location associated with that object by loading the Web page at that address.**

list broker Firm that sells lists. It does not usually hand over the list but will send a company's e-mail message to massive distribution lists.

LISTSERV A program that provides automatic processing of many functions involved with mailing lists. E-mailing appropriate messages to it will automatically subscribe the e-mailer to a discussion list or unsubscribe the person. A LISTSERV will also answer requests for indexes, FAQs, archives of the previous discussions, and other files.

location-based marketing Involves promotional offers that are pushed to mobile devices and customized based on the user's physical location.

log file In Internet server software, a feature that records every file sent by the server along with the destination address and time sent.

lower-cost products Products introduced to compete with existing brands by offering a price advantage. The Internet spawned a series of free products with the idea of building market share so the firm would have a customer base for marketing other products owned by the firm. For example, Eudora Light, the e-mail reader software, was an early entry with this strategy.

macroenvironment Consists of all stakeholders, organizations, and forces external to the organization.

manual customization Creating systems according to explicit *a priori* instructions from the user regarding preferred content categories. See *mass customization*.

manufacturer's agents (seller aggregators) Represent more than one seller. In the virtual world they generally create Web sites to help an entire industry sell product.

market deconstruction Removing distribution channel or other functions from the players that normally perform them.

marketing concept The idea that an organization exists to satisfy customer wants and needs while meeting organizational objectives.

marketing intelligence The procedure in which marketers continually scan the firm's macroenvironment for threats and opportunities.

Marketing public relations (MPR) Brand-related activities and nonpaid, third-party media coverage to positively influence target markets.

market opportunity analysis Analysis conducted by a firm upon reviewing the marketing environment, focusing on finding and selecting among market opportunities. A traditional market opportunity analysis includes both demand and supply analyses. The demand portion reviews various market segments in terms of their potential profitability. Conversely, the supply analysis reviews competition in selected segments that are under consideration.

marketing segmentation The process of aggregating individuals or businesses along similar characteristics that pertain to the use, consumption, or benefits derived from a product or service.

market skimming pricing Introduces new products at a high price that will only attract the innovators and early adopters. The company then steadily drops the price as it introduces newer high-end models.

mass customization The Internet's unique ability to individualize marketing mixes electronically and automatically to the individual level.

mass marketing See *undifferentiated targeting*.

metamediary An agent that represents a cluster of manufacturers, e-tailers, and content providers organized around a life event or major asset purchase.

metatags   HTML statements, which describe a Web site's contents, that allow search engines to identify sites relevant to topics of their inquiries.

metric Another word for a measurement number.

microenvironment Consists of stakeholders and forces internal to the organization.

micromarketing Individualized targeting.

MIS (marketing information system) The system of assessing information needs, gathering information, analyzing it, and disseminating it to marketing decision makers. In a separate context MIS also refers to management information systems—a field of study in many business schools.

MP3 Technology for the compression of audio multimedia, which can reduce CD recordings to one-tenth their original size. The compression helps alleviate the problem of low bandwidth.

multimedia The audio and video experience that is not prevalent yet on the Internet due primarily to lack of sufficient bandwidth for its transmittal.

multisegment targeting See *differentiated targeting*.

narrowcast An electronic media term referring primarily to cable channels because they contain very focused electronic content that appeals to special-interest markets.

NET (No Electronic Theft) Act Confers copyright protection for computer content and imposes sanctions when infringement is committed for commercial or private financial gain or by the reproduction or distribution of one or more copies of copyrighted works having $1,000 or more in retail value.

network A broadcast entity that provides programming and sells commercial time in programs aired nationally via affiliated or licensed local stations (e.g., ABC television network, ESPN cable network). On the Internet, an aggregator/broker of advertising inventory from many sites.[**]

networked applications Include distributed Internet applications, linked corporate and legacy data, Web-enabled and live applications, and object-oriented applications. These are database applications and methods for sharing information within an organization.

new-product lines Lines introduced when firms take an existing brand name and create new products in a completely different category. For example, General Foods applied the Jell-O brand name to pudding pops and other frozen delights.

newsgroup Communities of interest that post e-mails on electronic bulletin boards. One such example is Usenet, which is organized around topics or products.

niche marketing Occurs when a firm selects one segment and develops one or more marketing mixes to meet the needs of that segment.

notice Users should be made aware of a site's information policy before data are collected.

online auctions The auction-style sale of merchandise via the Internet.

online community Users who are widely dispersed geographically but come together in cyberspace based on similar interests.

online exchange Electronic forum in which buyers and sellers meet to make transactions.

online observation Monitors people's behavior by watching them in relevant situations, such as consumer chatting and e-mail posting through chat rooms, bulletin boards, or mailing lists.

online panel Called single-source data systems or opt-in communities, they include a panel of people who are paid to be the subject of marketing research.

open buying on the Internet (OBI) This electronic data interchange (EDI) supports the sharing of internal information with value chain partners.

opt-in List of users who have voluntarily agreed to receive commercial e-mail about topics that might be of interest to them by simply checking a box and entering an e-mail address. Also called permission marketing.

opt-out Similar to opt-in, however, users have to uncheck the box on a Web page to prevent being put on the e-mail list.

out-of-home media Those media meant to be consumed only outside of one's home (e.g., outdoor, transit, in-store media).[**]

outsource To contract services from external firms in order to accomplish internal tasks.

P3P (Platform for Privacy Preferences) Gives sites needed information to serve customers without compromising user privacy.

page An HTML (Hypertext Markup Language) document that may contain text, images, and other online elements, such as Java applets and multimedia files. It may be statically or dynamically generated.[**]

page interactivity Ability of a user to submit information to an organization from a browser and receive either standard or tailored responses including search tools, forms, purchase options, and e-mail.

page view The number of times a page was downloaded by users, often measured as a function of time ("page views per day"). The actual number of times the page was seen by users may be higher because of caching.[**]

paid circulation Reported by the Audit Bureau of Circulation (ABC), a classification of subscriptions or purchases of a magazine or newspaper based on payment in accordance with standards set by the ABC.[**]

parallel pull The technology that shopping agents employ in which what appear to the user as one shopping agent are actually multiple agents that simultaneously (in parallel) collect (pull) information from relevant Web sites located worldwide.

Pareto principle 80% of a firm's business usually comes from the top 20% of customers.

patent Centered on inventions and the ability to reproduce or manufacture an inventor's product.

penetration The percentage of people (or homes) within a defined universe that are physically able to be exposed to a medium.

penetration pricing The practice of charging a low price for a new product for the purpose of gaining market share.

perishability Characteristic whereby if service is not consumed when it is produced, it goes to waste.

performance metrics Specific measures designed to evaluate the effectiveness and efficiency of an organization's operations.

permission marketing Allows advertisers to present marketing communication messages to consumers who agree to receive them.

personal digital assistant (PDA) Handheld personal organizer that sometimes allows for wireless Web access.

personalization   Ways that marketers personalize in an impersonal computer networked environment. For example, Web sites that greet users by name, providing personalized information.

personalized Web page   Web page created with cookies that were put on the user's hard disk by the Web site. Cookies help companies to personalize Web pages by greeting the user by name or by listing previous purchases, thus building relationship with users.

PICS (Platform for Internet Content Selection Rules)   This application allows for the filtering of sites that are deemed to be inappropriate for minors.

pointcast   Electronic media with the capability of transmitting to an audience of just one person.

portal   A point of entry to the Internet such as Yahoo!, Lycos, and Excite.

price dispersion   The observed spread between the highest and lowest price for a given product.

price elasticity   Refers to the variability of purchase behavior with changes in price.

price leadership   The lowest-priced product entry in a particular category.

price transparency   The idea that both buyers and sellers can view all competitive prices for items sold online.

primary data   Information gathered for the first time to solve a particular problem. It is usually more expensive and time-consuming to gather than secondary data, but conversely, the data are current and they are generally more relevant to the marketer's specific problem. In addition, primary data have the benefit of being proprietary and, thus, unavailable to competitors.

privacy   Topic of much debate, including issues of the Warren and Brandeis concept of a right to be left alone, often referred to as the seclusion theory; access control, which places its emphasis on laws and standards that enable persons to reasonably regulate the information that they are giving up; and autonomy that identifies private matters as those that are necessary for a person to make life decisions.

probability sample   A sample selected in such a way that each item or person in the population being studied has an equal likelihood of being included in the sample.

product flow (systems perspective)   The distribution channel is viewed as a unified system of interdependent organizations in which intermediaries work together to build value as products proceed through the channel to the consumer.

product life cycle (PLC)   A model that describes the stages that a product or a product category passes through from its production to its removal from the market.

product line   Products grouped for sale in a specific market category.

product usage A variable in behavioral segmentation in which marketers group consumers based on how or when they use a product.

promotional pricing Special deals in price that retailers use to encourage a first purchase, to encourage repeat business, or to close a sale.

protocol A formal, standardized set of operating rules governing the format, timing, and error control of data transmissions and other activities on a network.

proxy server A system that stores frequently used information closer to the end user to provide faster access or to reduce the load on another server; it also serves as the gateway to the Internet.

proxy server caching The process that occurs when users access copies of Web sites rather than the site itself. Users accessing Web sites from proxy servers are not counted as new visitors.

psychographics Pertains to the identification of personality characteristics and attitudes that affect a person's lifestyle and purchasing behavior.**

pure play A business that began only on the Internet, even if it subsequently added a brick-and-mortar presence.

RADSL (Rate Adaptive Digital Subscriber Line) One variation of DSL, in which the information is sent at the maximum speed the line can handle under changing weather and interference conditions. This is similar to modems, which can adapt to different speeds depending on the quality of the phone line.

random digit dialing Telephone survey technique of calling people at random and asking specific questions.

rating The percentage of a given population group consuming a medium at a particular moment. Generally used for broadcast media but can by applied to any medium. One rating point equals 1% of the potential viewing population.**

reach The number of different homes/people exposed at least once to an impression (ad view, program, commercial, print page, etc.) across a stated period of time. Also called the cumulative or unduplicated audience.**

RealAudio Technology developed by RealNetworks for the compression of audio multimedia.

real-space data collection Takes place offline at points of purchase such as smart card and credit card readers and bar code scanners.

real-time chat Web users type messages to each other in real time at a Web site.

real-time multimedia Technology that offers opportunities such as distance learning and education, virtual reality, entertainment, and video/audio conferencing through live broadcasting from radio stations or online chatting and other real-time broadcasts.

real-time profiling Occurs when special software tracks a user's movements through a Web site, then compiles and reports on the data at a moment's notice.

RealVideo Technology developed by RealNetworks for the compression of video multimedia.

referral revenue Dollars in sales from customers referred to the firm by current customers.

relationship capital A firm's ability to build and maintain relationships with customers, suppliers, and partners: The total value of these relationships to a firm in the long term is its relationship capital.

relationship marketing The process of establishing, maintaining, enhancing, and commercializing customer relationships. It has a long-term customer orientation, involves ongoing interactive communication between a firm and selected stakeholders, and focuses on individual customers 1:1.

relevance ranking Search engine query results are often returned in order of relevance (i.e., the most likely to be the item that the user is seeking).

repositioned products Current products that are either targeted to different markets or promoted for new uses.

repositioning The process of creating a new or modified brand, company, or product position.

respondent authenticity A disadvantage of online research in which it is difficult to determine that respondents are who they say they are.

revenue streams Cash flows that may come from Web site product sales, advertising sales, and agent commissions.

reverse auction Allows individual buyers to enter the price they will pay for particular items at the purchasing agent's Web site, and sellers can agree or not.

revisions of existing products Products that are introduced as "new and improved" and, thus, replace the old product. On the Internet, firms are continually improving their brands to add value and remain competitive.

RFM analysis Scans the database for three criteria: recency, frequency, and monetary value. This process allows firms to target offers to the customers who are most responsive, thus saving promotional costs and increasing sales.

safe harbor Provisions for the protection of EU citizen data.

sampling   Users are allowed to sample a digital product prior to purchase. For example, software companies provide a free 30- to 60-day trial and online music stores give 30-second sound clips to customers.

SDSL (Symmetric Digital Subscriber Line)   One variation of DSL, in which the information is delivered at the same speed upstream or downstream. This option is appropriate for users who want to FTP Web pages or send other large files over the Net.

search engine   A Web site that scans the Web, searching for matches for the user's keywords, and returns a list of Web sites that might have the desired information.

seclusion   Warren and Brandeis theory outlining the concept of the right to be left alone.

secondary data   Information that has been gathered for some other purpose but is useful for the current problem; it can be collected more quickly and less expensively than primary data.

second-generation shopping agents   Shopping agents that measure value and not just price.

security   Policies to ensure the integrity of data and the prevention of misuse should be in place.

segmentation basis   The market can be segmented by the general categories of demographics, geographic location, psychographics, and behavior, each of which has a number of variables.

segmentation variables   Variables used by marketers to identify and profile groups of customers.

segmented pricing   The company sells a good or service at two or more prices, based on segment differentiation rather than cost alone.

self-regulation   The private sector's ability to rapidly identify and resolve problems specific to its areas of competence.

selling agent   Represents a single firm to help it move product and normally works for a commission.

server-side   Refers to activities that take place on an organization's Web server such as processing forms, streaming video, and accessing product databases for sending product Web pages to users.

server-side data collection   Information about consumer surfing that is gathered and recorded on the Web server.

session   A series of consecutive visits made by a visitor to a series of Web sites. **

SET (Secure Electronic Transaction) A vehicle for legitimizing both the merchant and the consumer as well as protecting the consumer's credit card number. Under SET the card number is never directly sent to the merchant. Rather a third party is introduced to the transaction with whom both the merchant and consumer communicate to validate one another as well as the transaction.

share Share of audience is the percentage of homes using TV (HUT) tuned to a particular program or station. Share of market is the percentage of total category volume (dollars, unit, etc.) accounted for by a brand. Share of voice is the percentage of advertising impressions generated by all brands in a category accounted for by a particular brand but often also refers to share of media spending.[**]

share of mind Refers to relationship marketing focusing on customer development in the long term: maintaining and enhancing. A firm using this kind of relationship marketing differentiates individual customers based on need rather than differentiating products for target groups.

shopping agents Programs that allow the consumer to rapidly compare prices and features within product categories. Shopping agents implicitly negotiate prices downward on behalf of the consumer by listing companies in order of best price first.

short text messages (SMS) 160 characters of text, using a store and delivery technology, sent by one user to another over the Internet, usually with a cell phone or PDA.

Shoshkeles Browser-driven, platform-agnostic, sound-enabled, free-moving forms that interrupt Web page content. This technology does not require plug-ins, and there is no discernable download time for users (adapted from www.unitedvirtualities.com).

site centric Audience measurement model in which user activity is tallied at the content provider's Web site to produce audience composition statistics, page views, and other statistics.

site stickiness A measure of length of time spent at a site.

situation analysis Review of the existing marketing plan and any other information that can be obtained about the company and its brands, examination of environmental factors related to online marketing, and development of a market opportunity analysis.

slotting fee A fee charged to advertisers by media companies to get premium positioning on their site, category exclusivity, or some other special treatment. It is similar to slotting allowances charged by retailers. (IAB Glossary of Interactive Advertising terms: www.iab.net)

snail mail Traditional mail delivered offline, so called because it is slower than online mail.

social bonding Stimulated social interaction between companies and customers resulting in a more personalized communication and brand loyalty.

spam Unsolicited e-mail, either sent to users or posted on an electronic bulletin board.

spam filter A program that has the capability of blocking unsolicited e-mails.

spider Automatic programs in search engines that search the Web from site to site, page by page, and word by word. They build up a massive index or database of all the words found, where they were found, how many times they appear on each page, and so on. It is this database that is actually queried when you type in a search term.

sponsorship Sponsorships integrate editorial content and advertising on a Web site. The sponsor pays for space and creates content that appeals to the publisher's audience.

spoofing Relies on the fact that the average person is not in a position to understand exactly how information is displayed, transferred, or stored. This lack of knowledge provides opportunities for novel deceptions and is often used to extract sensitive information by leading a user to believe that a request is coming from a reputable source, such as an ISP or credit card company.

spot Refers to the purchase of TV or radio commercial time on a market-by-market basis as opposed to network (national) purchases. Also the term is commonly used in lieu of *commercial announcement.* **

stakeholder Entity with a specific interest in a company—for example, an employee, stockholder, supplier, lateral partnership, and customer.

stakeholder communication Interaction with a stakeholder involving strategies, such as advertising, public relations, sales promotion incentives, and lead generation, that can help marketers to accomplish cognitive and attitude objectives, often at substantial cost savings over traditional methods.

strategic e-marketing The design of marketing strategy that capitalizes on the organization's electronic or information technology capabilities to reach specified objectives.

strategic planning The "managerial process of developing and maintaining a viable fit between the organizations objectives, skills, and resources and its changing market opportunities" (Kotler 2003 p. 64).

strategy The means to achieve a goal.

streamies An increasingly large number of people who listen to online audio.

streaming audio/video Content that is sent to the user's computer as it is viewed versus sending an entire file before the user can view it.

structural bonds Bonds created when firms add value by making structural changes that facilitate the relationship with customers and suppliers.

supply chain management (SCM) The behind-the-scenes coordination of the distribution channel to deliver products effectively and efficiently to customers. This process is also called integrated logistics.

switchers Consumers who do not care which brand they use—in other words, do not show any specific brand loyalty but go for the best price.

SWOT Strengths, weaknesses, opportunities, and threats analysis. The SWOT analysis objectively evaluates the company's strengths and weaknesses with respect to the environment and the competition.

syndicated selling Web sites paying a commission on referrals. Syndicated selling rewards the referring Web site by paying a 7% to 15% commission on the sale; commonly called affiliate programs.

syndication In broadcasting, a program carrying on selected stations that may or may not air at the same time in all markets. In newspapers, an independently written column or feature is carried by many newspapers (e.g., "Dear Abby"). In magazines, a centrally written or published section being carried by newspapers, generally in the Sunday edition (e.g., *Parade*).**

synergy Result that occurs when two or more firms join in a business relationship in which the results often exceed what each firm might have accomplished alone.

systems perspective See *product flow*.

TCP/IP Transmission Control Protocol/Internet Protocol, the most widely used protocol on the Internet. TCP/IP is a set of rules that each computer follows in order to enable communication. Only computers using the same protocol are able to communicate.

technographics Segments of online shoppers as identified by Forrester Research. Consumers fall into one of 10 groups based upon their attitude toward technology, income as an indicator of shopping behavior, and primary motivation to go online.

telematics A communication system in an automobile that uses a global positioning system (GPS) for interactive communication between firms and drivers.

third-party logistics Logistics is outsourced such that a third party manages the company's supply chain and provides value-added services such as product configuration and subassembly.

trademark Concerned with images, symbols, words, or other indicators that are registered with the government and have become positively associated with a product's identity in the market.

trailblazer page Also called an index page, helps marketers find relevant Web sites quickly. Trailblazer sites are those that contain long lists of links to outside sites on a particular topic.

transactional functions Include matching product to buyer needs, negotiating price, and processing transactions.

transaction-based online systems Systems that allow organizations not only to communicate with the consumer but to sell online as well.

transactive media Interactive channels of communication that are capable of carrying out product transactions.

TRIPs (Trade Related Intellectual Property Rights) This 1995 agreement is part of the World Trade Organization's (WTO) program of international treaties.

ubiquitous application One able to function in the course of nearly any online session without a user's knowledge or control.

UCITA (Uniform Computer Information Transactions Act) If adopted by the states, this model would govern all legal agreements pertaining to software transactions, including sales.

UNCITRAL (United Nations Commission of International Trade Law) Established the Model Law on Electronic Commerce to provide for global uniformity in digital commerce.

undifferentiated targeting Another term for *mass marketing*. In this case the firm offers one marketing mix for the entire market.

unique users The number of unique individuals who visit a site within a specific period of time. With today's technology, this number can be calculated only with some form of user registration or identification.**

unique visitors See *unique users*.

universal product code (UPC) Also called the bar code, this is scanned by retailers, wholesalers, and manufacturers for the purpose of inventory management.

universe The total population within a defined demographic, psychographic, or product consumption segment against which media audiences are calculated to determine ratings, coverage, reach, and so on.

URL (uniform [or universal] resource locator) The URL provides information on the protocol, the system, and the file name, so that the user's system can find a particular document on the Internet. An example of a URL is www.sholink.com/, which indicates that "Hypertext Transfer Protocol" is the protocol and that the information is located on a system named "www.sholink.com," which is the Sholink Corporation's Web server. This example does not show a particular file name (such as index.htm), since most Web servers are set up to point to a home page if no file name is used. **

Usenet Worldwide network of thousands of computer systems with a decentralized administration. The Usenet systems exist to transmit postings to special-interest newsgroups.

value Benefits minus costs.

value chain (integrated logistics) The supply chain, the manufacturer, and the distribution channel viewed as an integrated system.

Vertical Service Provider (VSP) An Application Service Provider (ASP) that runs an entire business because it aggregates almost all of the value chain functions for the client business.

viral marketing This is the online equivalent of word of mouth and referred to as word of mouse. It occurs when individuals forward e-mail to friends, coworkers, family, and others on their e-mail lists.

Virtual Magistrate Mediation-oriented program developed to resolve online disputes.

virtual mall A model similar to a shopping mall in which multiple online merchants are hosted at a Web site.

visitor A user who visits a site; however, this does not distinguish between one-time and repeat visitors.

Voice over Internet protocol (VoIP) The term used to refer to Internet telephony that relies on the Web to transmit phone calls, thus eliminating long-distance charges.

volume discount The price discount offered advertisers who purchase a certain amount of volume from the medium (e.g., pages or dollar amount in magazines). **

wearout A level of frequency, or a point in time, when an advertising message loses its ability to effectively communicate. **

Web form Technical term for a Web page that has designated places for the user to type information. Many corporate Web sites sport Web forms, using them for a multitude of purposes from site registration and survey research to product purchase.

Web page An HTML (Hypertext Markup Language) document on the Web, usually one of many that together make up a Web site. **

Web ring A number of independent Web sites that together build community among users and the products that interest them.

Web server A system capable of continuous access to the Internet (or an internal network) through retrieving and displaying documents and files via Hypertext Transfer Protocol (http). **

Web site The virtual location for an organization's presence on the World wide Web, usually made up of several Web pages and a single home page designated by a unique URL. [**]

Web site content The text, graphics, video, and audio that are displayed on a Web page. Can also include interactive features such as search tools, forms, purchase options, and e-mail.

Web site log Data about how long users spend on each page, how long they are at the site, and what path they take through the site, among other things.

Webisode An episode of a TV-like program where the viewer takes a more active role. The BrilliantDigital product captures the user on video in the studio, performs voice-overs, and then places the user in the program.

wireless Relies on towers to relay signals in a mode very similar to that of cell phones.

word of mouse See *viral marketing*.

World Wide Web The mechanism originally developed by Tim Berners-Lee for CERN physicists to be able to share documents via the Internet. The Web allows computer users to access information across systems around the world using URLs (uniform resource locators) to identify files and systems and hypertext links to move between files on the same or different systems. [**]

Notes

[**] Reprinted with permission from Dean Witter Morgan Stanley.

[*] Reprinted with permission from SRI.

[‡] Quoted from Hoffman/Novak Project 2000.

[†] Quoted from Forrester Research.

References

Note: References for Chapters 5 and 16 are displayed at the end of this list.

"About Amazon.com" (1998), Amazon (September). Internet: www.amazon.com.

"A Classic Scenario: Bad News, Good News," (2002), eMarketer (June 18). Internet: www.emarketers.com.

Afuah, Allan and Christopher Tucci (2001), *Internet Business Models and Strategies*. New York: McGraw-Hill/Irwin.

Alreck, Pamela and Robert Settle (2002), "Gender Effects on Internet, Catalogue, and Store Shopping," *Journal of Database Marketing* (January), 150–162.

"Amazon.com Talks to Andrew Sather" (1998), Amazon (July). Internet: www.amazon.com/exec/obidos/show-interview/s-a-atherndrew/002-5327610-3567040.

American Chamber of Commerce in the Czech Republic (2000), *E-Commerce in the Czech Republic*. Internet:www.amcahm.cz/downloads/e-commerce.pdf.

Aronica, Ronald and Peter Fingar (2001), "Ten Myths of the New Economy." *The Business Integrator Journal* (Fall), 14–22).

"Background of Datek Online Holdings Corporation" (1998), *Datek* (August). Internet: www.datek.com/marketing/about/abouthome.html.

August, Vicki (2001), "Feeding Time," *Internet World Show Daily* (December 11) 7, 35.

"Big Bytes" (2001), *Marketing News* (March 18), 3.

Barboza, David (1998), "Golden Boy? He's Dazzled Wall Street, But the Ghosts of His Company May Haunt His Future," *The New York Times on the Web* (May 10). Internet: www.nyt.com.

Barboza, David (1998), "The Markets: Market Place: Some Clouds Dim a Star of On-Line Trading," *The New York Times on the Web* (July 8). Internet: www.nyt.com.

"Barred for Life: UPC's at 25" (1999), *Chain Store Age Executive with Shopping Center Age* (December), 146.

Berinato, Scott (1998), "RealNetwork's Glaser Sings Praises of Streaming Media for Enterprises," *PC Week Online* (May 7). Internet: www.zdnet.com/zdnn/content/pcwo/0507/314557.html.

Berry, Leonard and A. L. Parasuraman (1991), *Marketing Services—Competing Through Quality*. New York: Free Press.

"Beyond Cool: Online Trading Goes Mainstream as Quality Rises and Commissions Plunge" (1998), *Barron's* (March 16).

Internet: www.datek.com/marketing/about/in_news/bar031698.html.

Blackwell, Roger and Kristina Stephan (2001), *Customers Rule!* New York: Crown Business.

Bolande, H. Asher (2002), "Shanghai Start-up Hopes Deal with McDonald's Scores Victory." *Wall Street Journal* (May 22), p. B7A.

Booker, Ellis (1997), "Microsoft Buys Stake in Progressive Networks," *Webweek* (July 28). Internet: www.internetworld.com.

Briggs, Rex and Nigel Hollis (1997), "Advertising on the Web: Is There Response Before Clickthrough?" *Journal of Advertising Research* (March/April), 33–45.

Broersma, Matthew (1998), "Yahoo!'s Yang: Web Is Now a 'Lifestyle Medium,'" *ZDNN* (March 12).
Internet: www.zdnet.com/zdnn/content/zdnn/0312/293987.html.

Brown, Eryn (2002), "Slow Road to Fast Data," *Fortune* (March 18), 170-172.

Carl, Jeremy (1995), "Bookseller's Online Ambitions," *Web Week* (October: Vol. 1, Issue 6). Internet: www.internetworld.com/print/ww-back.html.

Carr, Laura (2000), "Events Move Millions to the Net." *The Industry Standard*, (October 30), 190–191.

Case, K. E. and R. C. Fair (2001), *Principles of Economics.* Upper Saddle, NJ: Prentice Hall.

Cateora, P. R. and G. R. Graham (2002), *International Marketing*, 11th ed. New York: McGraw Hill.

Caulfield, Brian (1998), "RealNetworks' Newest Ally Is Affront to One of Its Oldest," *InternetWorld News* (February 2). Internet: www.internetworld.com.

Caulfield, Brian (1998), "Streaming Media Platform Updated," *InternetWorld News* (May 4). Internet: www.internetworld.com.

Caulfield, Brian (1998), "When Good Web-Page Design Comes Before the Customer," *InternetWorld* (January 12). Internet: www.internetworld.com/print/1998/01/12/index.html.

Chakravarthy, Srinivas (2000), "E-Strategy: Different Strokes." *Businessline* (October 4). 1–2.

Chandrasekaran, Rajiv (2001), "Life in Cambodian Village Transformed by Internet," *Seattle Times* (June 17). Internet: archives.seattletimes.nwsource.com/cgi-bin/texis.cgi/web/vortex/display?slug=wiredvillagesub17&date=20010617

Chon, Gina (2001), "Bernard Krisher: Healing the Killing Field," *Asia Week* (June 29).

"Company Profiles 'Pretty Good Privacy'" (1997), *The Red Herring Magazine* (February). Internet: www.redherring.com/profiles/0297/pretty.html.

Conhaim, Wallys (2002), "How We Use the Internet," *Information Today* (March/April).

"Consumer Packaged Goods Marketers Gain Sharper Visibility of Online Consumers and Competition Through CPG Scorecard" (2002), Press release at www.comscore.com.

"Consumers Wary of Online Profiling" (1999), *USA Today* (November 5), Internet: www.usatoday.com.

Cooper, Charles (1998), "The Guys Running Yahoo! Are Far from Yahoos," *ZDNN* (April 30). Internet: www.zdnet.com/zdnn/content/zdnn/0429/311279.html.

Coupley, Eloise (2001), *Marketing and the Internet.* Upper Saddle River, NJ: Prentice Hall.

Cowell, Alan (2000), "Europe Plays Internet Catch-Up. A Bewildering Choice of Portals, Most of Them Pricey," *New York Times* (March 11).

Cox, Beth (2002), "The Little Flower Company That Could," (January 22). Internet: www.internetnews.com.

"Creating Killer Interactive Web Sites" (1997). *Adjacency's Web Design Book.* New York: Hayden Press/Macmillan.

Cutitta, Frank (2002), "Language Matters," *Target Marketing* (February), 40–44.

Cutler, Matt (2001), Forrester Research Study as Cited in "NetGenesis Spotlight on ROI." Presentation at Internet World (December 9).

"CYBERsitter Now Blocks Web Site Advertising" (1998), *Business Wire* (February 12). Internet: www.solidoak.com/pr298.txt.

Detmer, Tom (2002), "Seeking the Complete Customer Experience: The Web as a marketing tool. *Customer_Inter@Ction_Solutions.* Volume 20, No. 11, p. 45.

Distefano, John (2000), "The Decisioning Frontier: Get Ready for Marketing Automation," *DM Review* (March). Internet: www.dmreview.com.

"DoubleClick Ad Serving Data Shows Rich Media Click-Through Rates Six Times Higher Than Standard Ads," (2002). Press release available at www.doubleclick.com.

Doyle, Bill, Bill Bass, Ben Abbott, and Kerry Moyer (1997), "Branding on the Web," Forrester Report: Media & Technology Strategies (August).

Dreier, Troy (1997), "Safeguarding the Web," *ZDNet* (October 2). Internet: www.zdnet.com/products/special/filter2.html.

Du Bois, Max (2000), "Why Brands Won't Be Bland in the E-World," *Marketing*, p. 25.

Duncan, Tom (2002), *Using Advertising and Promotion to Build Brands.* New York: McGraw Hill-Irwin.

"E-Commerce Numbers Add Up in December" (2001), Internet: cyberatlas.internet.com.

"eConsumers Prefer E-Mail Newsletters and Coupons" (2001), *eStatNews.* Available at: www.emarketer.com (Date of access: December 15, 2001).

Eitel-Porter, Ray (2001), "Competing in the Age of Electronic Time," (July) Internet: www.the-dma.org.

"E-Mail and the Different Levels Of ROI" (date unknown). Available at: www.boldfish.com (Date of access November 17, 2001).

eMarketer (2000), eGlobal Report. Internet: www.emarketer.com/about_us/ press_room/press_releases/032800_global.html

"eMarketer Designates Interactive Advertising Bureau/PricewaterhouseCoopers Quarterly Internet Ad Revenue Report as Its Benchmark Source for Online Ad Revenues," (2002), Internet: www.iab.net (Date of access April 25, 2002).

"Fast Forward Through the Ads?" (1996), *Netday News* (May 9). Internet: www.internetnews.com/96May/0509-ads.html.

"Female Wrestling Co. Using E-cards" (2001), Internet: www.digitrends.net.

Feeny, David. (Winter, 2001), "Making Business Sense of the E-Opportunity". *MIT Sloan Management Review,* p. 45

Fetto, John (2002), "Teen Chatter," *American Demographics* (April) 14.

Fichter, Martin (2001), "GPRS: The Trigger for Mass Mobile Internet Adoption in America." Speech at Internet World in New York (December).

Foust, Dean (1998), "New Kids on the Street," *Yahoo! Internet Life* (January: Vol. 4. No.1). Internet: www.zdnet.com/yil/filters/toc/tocv4n1.html.

"Free Enterprise Comes to Wall Street " (1998), *Forbes* as cited in *Datek* (April 6). Internet: www.datek.com/marketing/about/in_news/forbes0498.html.

Frost, Raymond and Judy Strauss (2002), *Building Effective Web Sites.* Upper Saddle River, NJ: Prentice Hall.

Gallogly, Jackie and Lynne Rolls (2002), "Response Metrics: How to Crunch the Numbers," Internet: www.clickz.com/.

Gardner, Elizabeth (1998), "Amazon Buys Three Companies to Move into European Market and Video Sales," *InternetWorld News* (May 4). Internet: www.internetworld.com/print/1998/05/04/news/19980504-amazon.html?InternetWorld+3808+Amazon.

Gardner, Elizabeth (1998), "Slower Pace, Cheaper Living Entices Net Workers to Midwest," *InternetWorld* (July 13). Internet: www.internetworld.com/.

Ghosh, Shikhar (1998), "Making Business Sense of the Internet," *Harvard Business Review* (March–April), 126–135.

Glave, James (1998), "InterMute Cleans Up Web-Site Clutter," Wired News (March 18). Internet: www.wired.com/news/technology/story/11012.html.

Global Key Report Findings (2002), TNS Interactive Global eCommerce Report. Internet: www.tnsofres.com

Godin, Seth (1999), *Permission Marketing.* New York: Simon and Schuster.

Goldberg, Aaron (1999), "Speed Kills." *MC Technology Marketing Intelligence.* Vol. 19. Issue 6. p. 16.

Gray, Vanessa (2001), "Barrier to Internet Penetration in the Arab Region." Internet: www.itu.int/arabInternet2001/documents/pdf/document15.pdf.

Greenberg, Karl (2001), "Automakers Rev Up Online Efforts, But Some Dealers Are Skeptical," *BrandWeek* (December 10) 10.

Greenspan, Robyn (2002), "In Any Language, Hispanics Enjoy Surfing." Internet: www.cyberatlas.internet.com.

Gregory, Jim (2002), "The Name Game," *Fortune.* Internet: www.fortune.com/sections.

Grönroos, Christian (1990), "Relationship Approach to Marketing in Service Contexts: The Marketing and Organizational Behavior Interface," *Journal of Business Research*, 20 (January), 3–11.

Gruener, Jamie (2001), "How to Measure Storage ROI," *Network Connections*, 8–10.

Gruner, Kjell, and Christian Homberg (2000), "Does Customer Interaction Enhance New Product Success?" *Journal of Business Research* (July), 1–14.

Guglielmo, Connie (1997), "No Sacred Trust: Personal Data Up for Grabs," *Inter@ctive Week* (December 8). Internet: www.zdnet.com/intweek/printhigh/120897/cov1208.html.

Guglielmo, Connie (1998), "Audio Gives the Web an Earful," *Inter@ctive Week* (February 9). Internet: www.zdnet.com/intweek/print/980209/283997.html.

Guglielmo, Connie (1998), "Stream Market Splits into Two Camps," *Inter@ctive Week* (February 4). Internet: www.zdnet.com/zdnn/content/inwk/0504/281720.html.

Hagel, John and Marc Singer (1999), *Net Worth: Shaping Markets When Customers Make the Rules* Boston: Harvard Business School Press.

Hallerman, David (2002), "Online Ad Pricing: Count Heads or Count Results." Available at: www.emarketer.com (Date of access April 25, 2002).

Hanson, Ann (2001), "Gimme Shelter," *BrandWeek* (December 10), 16.

Hertzberg, Robert (1996), "RealAudio's Convictions Lead It to Top of Charts," *Web Week* (January: Volume 2, Issue 1). Internet: www.internetworld.com.

Heyman, Karen, Paul Hoffman, Tom Negrino, Richard Raucci, Anne Ryder, Charles Seiter, Dave Taylor, and Karen Wickre (1996), *Yahoo! Unplugged.* Internet: www.idgbooks.com/yp/yahoounplugged/history/wbhist1.htm). (Also at www.idgbooks.com.)

Iansiti, Marco and Alan MacCormack (2001), "Developing Products on Internet Time," *Internet Marketing.* J. Sheth, A. Eshghi, and B. Krishnan, eds. Orlando, Florida: Harcourt Inc., 239–251.

"Internet Is Powerful Complement to Traditional Advertising Media" (2002), Available at: www.advantage.msn.com (Date of access: December 20, 2001).

"Internet Usage at Work Spikes 23% to More than 42 Million Office Workers," (2001), ITU (2001a), Internet Report. Internet: www.itu.int/ITU-D/ict/publications/inet/2000/flyer/flyer_next.html.

"IRI and DoubleClick Study Shows Online Advertising Drives Sales of Consumer Packaged Goods Brands," (2002), Press release available at www.doubleclick.com.

ITU (1999), Development of the Network.

ITU (2000a), The Internet in the Andes: Bolivia Case Study. Internet:
www.itu.int/ITU-D/ict/cs/bolivia/material/bolivia.pdf

ITU (2000b), Internet Indicators. Internet:www.itu.int/ITU-
D/itc/statistics/at_glance/basic00.pdf.

ITU (2001b), Internet on the Nile: Egypt Case Study. Internet:
www.itu.int/osg/spu/wtpf/wtpf2001/ casestudies/egypt.pdf.

ITU (2002), Kretek Internet: Indonesia Case Study. Internet:www.itu.int/ITU-
D/ict/cs/indonesia/index.html.

Jackson, Ted and John Baskey (2000), *How to Use Balanced Scorecards to
Implement E-Strategy*. Boston: Harvard Business School Publishing Report.

Jarvis, Steve (2001), "Follow the Money: Web Analytics Help Marketers Fix Sites,
Revise Strategies," *Marketing News* (October 8), 1, 10.

Jarvis, Steve (2002), "How to Set Up Shop to Take Advantage of the Next
Recovery," *Marketing News* (March 18) 4.

Jeanette, J-P and H. D. Hennessy (2002), *Global Marketing Strategies*, Boston:
Houghton Mifflin Company.

Kalakota, Ravi and Marcia Robinson (1999), E-*Business: Roadmap for Success*.
Reading, MA: Addison-Wesley.

Kaplan, Robert and David Norton (1993), "Putting the Balanced Scorecard to Work,"
Harvard Business Review (September–October), 134–147.

Kasanoff, Bruce and Toria Thompson (1999), Advanced Strategies for
Differentiating Customers and Partners: Software That Enables 1 to 1
Relationships. Stamford CT: Rogers and Peppers Group Report:
Accelerating 1 to 1. Internet: www.1to1.com.

"Key Business and Marketing Trends Survey Analysis," (2002), Patrick Marketing
Group Report (March). Internet: www.the-dma.org

Kim, Amy Jo (2000), "Secrets of Successful Web Communities," *Naima* (May).
Internet: www.naima.com/articles/webtechniques.html.

King, Julia and Thomas Hoffman (1999), "Pace of Change Fuels Web Plans; Sites
Must Shift Offering Every 60 Days to Thrive," *ComputerWorld* (July 5), 1.

Kirkpatrick, David (2002), "Beyond Buzzwords," *Fortune* (March 18), 160–168.

Kotler, Philip (2003), *Marketing Management*, 11th ed. Upper Saddle River, NJ:
Prentice Hall.

Kotler, Philip, and Gary Armstrong (2001), *Principles of Marketing*, 9th ed. Upper
Saddle River: Prentice Hall.

Laseter, Tim, David Torres, and Anne Chung (2001), "Oasis in the Dot-Com
Delivery Desert," *Strategy+Business* (issue 24), 28–33.

Li, Kenneth (2000), "Publish Online or Perish?" *The Industry Standard* (April 3), 60.

Long, Geoff (2000), "Bhutan Goes Online: A Modern Folktale," Reports from
Developing Worlds. Internet: www.icrc.ca/reports/read_article_englihs.cfm?
article_num=611.

Mannisto, Laura (1999), "Examining the Opportunities and Challenges for ISPs in Developing Countries." Internet: www.itu.int/ITU-D/ict/papers/1999/LM-ISPForum-Nov99.pdf

Mardesich, Jodi (2001), "Too Much of a Good Thing," *The Industry Standard.* Available at: thestandard.net (Date of access: May 15, 2001).

Marlatt, Andrew (1998), "Newsmaker—Rob Glaser: RealNetworks," *InternetWorld News* (April 27). Internet: www.internetworld.com.

Mazur, Laura (2001), "Life Stages Hold Key to Improving Customer Bonds," *Marketing* (August), 16.

Melymuka, Kathleen (2001), "The Balanced E-Scorecard," *ITWorld* (March 12). Internet: www.itworld.com.

"Meeting Generation Y" (1999), *NUA* (July 19). Internet: www.nua.ie/surveys/analysis/weekly_editoria/archives/issue1no84.html.

Miller, Thomas (2001), "Can We Trust the Data of Online Research?" *Marketing Research* (Summer), 26–32.

Minges, Michael (1999), "Counting the Net: Internet Access Indicators." (Internet: www.itu.int/ITU-D/ict/papers/1999/MM-Int99-Jn99.pdf

Minges, Michael (2000), "E-Commerce in Three Landlocked Nations." Internet: www.itu.int/ITU-D/ict/cs/material/ e-commerce%20in%203R.ppt.

Minges, Michael (2001a), "Mobile Internet." Internet: www.itu.int/arabInternet2001/ documents/pdf/document15.pdf.

Minges, Michael (2001b), "Measuring the Internet in South East Asia." Internet: www.itu.int/asean2001/documents/pdf/Document-25.pdf

Modahl, Mary (2000), *Now or Never*. New York: HarperBusiness.

Moon, Youngme (2000), "Interactive Technologies and Relationship Marketing Strategies," Harvard Business School Article 9-599-101 (January 19).

Moran, Susan (1996), "Amazon.com Forges New Sales Channel," *Web Week* (August 19: Vol. 2, Issue 12). Internet: www.internetworld.com/print/ww-back.html.

Murphy, David (2001), "Connecting With Online Teenagers," *Marketing* (September 27), 31–32.

Murphy, Kathleen (1996), "Plug-In Weeds Out Advertising," *Web Week* (May 20: Vol. 2, Issue 6). Internet: www.internetworld.com/print/1996/05/20/webweek.html.

Neal, William D. (2000), "Branding in the Third Millennium," *Marketing Management,* Vol. 9, Issue 2, p. 64.

Negroponte, Nicholas (1995), *Being Digital*. New York: Vintage Books.

Newbery, Michael (1998), "How to Upset a Web Cache" (October). Internet: www.vuw.ac.nz/~newbery/rant.html.

"New eGlobal Report" (2000), *Business Wire*. Internet:Lexis-Nexis Academic Universe (March 28, 2000). Internet: www.lexis-nexus.com/universe.

Newell, Frederick and Katherine Newell Lemon (2001), *Wireless Rules*. New York: McGraw Hill.

"New Study from McKinsey and Media Metrix Gives, Online Marketers an Advantage in Targeting Consumers" (2001), From Report: Internet Consumer Segments Identified for First Time (April 17).

"New York E-Commerce Association Presents Experts on Online Branding; Industry's Leading Internet Companies Discuss the Challenges of Creating Differentiation on the Web," *Business Wire* (March 22, 2000) p. 1.

Nickols, Fred (2000), *Strategies: Definitions and Meaning* (February 16, 2002). Internet: home.att.net/~nickols/strategy_definition.htm.

Nielsen//NetRatings press release. Internet: www.nielsen-netratings.com.

"No Surprise: Total Ad Spending Down 9.8% for 2001, Compared to Results in 2000" (2002), Internet: www.cmr.com/news/2002/030602.html (Date of access: April 24, 2002).

"On-Line Investing: 'Datek Online: A Haven for the Hyperactive'" (1998), *Forbes* as cited in *Datek* (May 4). Internet: www.datek.com/marketing/about/in_news/forbes0598.html.

"Online Shopping Promises Consumers More Than It Delivers" (2001), Press release available at www.bcg.com.

Orbitz (2001), Press release. Available at: 212.133.71.16/hsmai/news (Date of access: April 26, 2002).

Pastore, Michael (2001), "Banners Can Brand, Honestly They Can, Part II." Available at www.cyberatlas.internet.com (Date of access: December 20, 2001).

Pastore, Michael (2001), "Blue Collar Occupations Moving Online," (April). Internet: http//cyberatlas.internet.com

Pastore, Michael (2001), "SMS Continues to Take Messaging World by Storm," *CyberAtlas* (April 4). Internet: cyberatlas.Internet.com/markets/wireless/article/0,,10094_733811,00.html.

Pastore, Michael (2001), "Why the Offline are Offline," (June 14). Internet: cyberatlas.onternet.com.

Pastore, Michael (2002), "Incentives Still Key to Mobile Advertising." *Cyberatlas* (April 15). Internet: cyberatlas.internet.com.

Pastore, Michael (2002a), "Online Consumers Now the Average Consumer." Internet: cyberatlas.internet.com.

Pastore, Michael (2002b), "Chinese-Americans Have High PC, Internet Penetration Rates," (February). Internet: http//cyberatlas.internet.com.

Pastore, Michael (2002c), "Broadband Users Pull Ahead in Online Hours," (March). Internet: http//cyberatlas.internet.com.

Pellegrino, Robert, Doug Amyx, and Kimberly Pellegrino (2002 working paper), "A Methodology for Assessing Buyer Behavior: Price Sensitivity and Value Awareness in Internet Auctions."

Peppers and Rogers Group (2001), "1to1 Mobility: Customer-Based Strategies for a Wireless World." White paper.

Peppers, Don (2000), "Getting to Know You Without Knowing You," Peppers and Rodgers Newsletter (Spring). Internet: www.1to1.com.

Peppers, Don, and Martha Rogers (1996), *The One to One Future*. New York: Doubleday.

Peppers, Don, and Martha Rogers (1997), *Enterprise One to One*. New York: Doubleday

Pitt, Leyland, Pierre Berthon, Richard Watson, and Michael Ewing (2001), "Pricing Strategy and the Net," *Business Horizons* (March), p. 45.

Ponnaiya, Elzaurdia and Sanjay Ponnaiya (1999), "The Distribution of Survey Contact and Participation in the United States: Construction a Survey Based Estimate," *Journal of Marketing Research* (36), 286–294.

Pravica, Danica. (2000), "Who Do You Want to Know Today?" *Computing Canada*. Vol. 26, Issue 1, p. 15.

"Pretty Good Deal" (1996), *Suck* (November). Internet: www.suck.com/daily/96/11/18/daily.html.

PricewaterhouseCoopers, LLP (2002), IAB Internet Advertising Revenue Report: Third Quarter 2001 Results. New York: PricewaterhouseCoopers New Media Group. Available at: www.iab.net (Date of access April 10, 2002).

"Products of RelevantKnowledge" (1998), *RelevantKnowledge* (October). Internet: www.relevantknowledge.com/Products/index.html.

"Profile of Andrew Sather" (1998), *Highfive Profile* (Issue 9). Internet: www.highfive.com/profile/past/profile_07.97.html.

Radding, Alan (2001), "A Tale of Two Users," *Network Connections*, 20.

Randall, Neil (1997), "The New Cookie Monster," *PC Magazine* (April 22). Internet: www.zdnet.com/pcmag/issues/1608/pcmg0035.htm.

Ransdell, Eric (1999), "Network Effects," *Fast Company* (September), 210–216.

Rappa, Michael (2000), "Business Models on the Web," (April 29). Internet: ecommerce.ncsu.edu/business_models.html.

Rappa, Michael (2002), "Business Models on the Web" (February 17, 2002). Internet: digitalenterprise.org/models/models.html

Raskino, Mark and Emily Andren (2001), "Climbing the Slope to E-Business Recovery," Gartner Research Report (December 14).

Ray, Michael L. (1973), "Communication and the Hierarchy of Effects," in *New Models for Mass Communication Research*, P. Clarke, ed., Beverly Hills, CA: Sage Publications, 147–175.

Reid, Robert H. (1997), *Architects of the Web*. New York: John Wiley & Sons (also on Internet: www.architectsoftheweb.com/jw).

Reim, David (2000), "Brochures, Brands, and Relationships," *Medical Marketing and Media* (February).

"Relationships Rule," (2000), *Business 2.0* (May), 303–319.

Renner, Dale (2000), "Closer to the Customer: Customer Relationship Management and the Supply Chain," Andersen Consulting. Internet: renner.ascet.com.

Rose, Bill and Larry Rosin (2001), "Internet VII." *Arbitron/Edison Media Research Report.*

Rozanski, Horacio D., Gerry Bollman, and Martin Lipman (2001), " Seize the Occasion! The Seven-Segment System for Online Marketing," *Strategy+Business*, 3rd Quarter.

"Safeguarding the Web" (1998), *ZDNet Special Reports: Products* (February 5). Internet: www.zdnet.com.

Saunders, Christopher (2001), "E-Mail Marketing Revenue to Top $2 Billion in 2001," Internet: www.internetnews.com

Saunders, Christopher (2002), "CMR: Web Ad Spending Dropped 14.7%," *Internet News*. Available at www.internetnews.com (Date of access: April 10, 2002).

Sawhney, Mohanbir (1999), "Making New Markets," (May) *Business 2.0.* Internet: www.business2.com/articles/1999/05/text/newrules.html.

Sawhney, Mohanbir (2000), "How It Works," *Business 2.0* (February), 112.

Schlender, Brent (2002), "All You Need is Love, $50 Billion, and Killer Software Code-Named Longhorn," *Fortune* (July 8) 56–68.

"Search Engines Are an Indispensable Utility for Internet Users" (2002). Press release at www.pewinternet.org.

Seybold, Patricia (1998), *Customers.com.* New York: Random House.

Sheth, Jagdish N. (1995), "Relationship Marketing in Consumer Markets: Antecedents and Consequences," *Journal of the Academy of Marketing Science*, 23 (4), 255–271.

Shevack, Brett. (2000), "Beyond That First Burst of Awareness." *Brandweek*, Vol. 41, Issue 22, p. 41.

Silk, Jon (2001), "SMS Marketing Finds Its Voice," *Internet World Show Daily*, December 13, 7, 32.

Slott, Mira. (2000), "Store Strategies at Center Stage," *Home Textiles Today*. Vol. 21, Issue 43, 35–38.

Sonnenberg, Frank (1993), "If I Had Only One Client," *Sales and Marketing Management*, 56 (November), 4.

Spector, Robert (2000), *Amazon.com: Get Big Fast.* New York: HarperBusiness.

"State of the Practice: Intranets Are Busting Out All Over" (2000), *IDM* (April). Internet: idm.internet.com/idm/vol2/11.

Strauss, Judy and Donna Hill (working paper), "Consumer Complaints by E-Mail: An Exploratory Investigation of Corporate Responses and Customer Reactions."

Strauss, Judy and Raymond Frost, (1999), *Marketing on the Internet: Principles of Online Marketing.* Prentice Hall.

Strauss, Judy and Raymond Frost (2000), *E-Marketing*, 2nd ed. Upper Saddle River, NJ: Prentice Hall.

"Study Reveals Previously Unmeasured Characteristics of U.S. Online Hispanic Population," (2002), HispanicAd.com Press Release (May 12).

"Survey: Lycos Users Most Concerned About Credit Card Security" (1998), *InternetNews* (March 5). Internet: www.internetnews.com/bus-news/1998/03/0501-lycos.html.

"Sweden Remains the World's Dominant Information Economy. . ." (2001), IDC Press Release (February). Internet: www.idc.com.

Taylor Nelson Sofres (2001), Global eCommerce Report. Internet: www.tnsofres.com/ger2001/download/index.cfm.

"The E-Commerce Balancing Act" (2000), *SAS* (November/December). Internet: www.sas.com

The Global E-Commerce Report (2002), Taylor Nelson Sofres Interactive (www.tnsofres.com/ger2002/home.cfm)

"The New Stock Traders: They're Gusty, They're Savvy, and They Don't Need a Broker" (1998), *BusinessWeek* as cited on *Datek* (May 4). Internet: www.datek.com/marketing/about/in_news/bw050498.html.

"The Questions of Cookies" (1998), *AdKnowledge* (September). Internet: www.adknowledge.com/cgi-bin/show?Reference/ques_cookies.html.

"The Value of a Corporate E-Mail Address" (2001), eContacts Media Kit.

"The World's Online Populations" (2002), *CyberAtlas* (February 27). Internet: www.cyberatlas.com/bigpicture/geographics/article/0,,5911_151151,00.html.

U.S. State Department, *Hidden Killers* (1998), The Global Landmine Crisis. Internet: www.state.gov/www/global/arms/rpt_9809_demine_ch3h.html.

"Vast Improvements in Prompt Email Response" (2001), *1to1 Magazine* (November/December), 11.

Vincent, Lynn. (2000), "The Brand That Binds," *Bank Marketing*. Vol. 32, Issue 11, 24–29.

Vogelstein, Fred (2002), "Looking for a Dot-Com Winner? Search No Further," *Fortune* (May 27), 65–68.

Vonder Haar, Steven (1998), "Can Yahoo! Stay the Meteoric Course?" *Inter@ctive Week* (April 29). Internet: www.zdnet.com/zdnn/content/inwk/0516/310746.html.

Vonder Haar, Steven (1998), "Roll 'Em: Bringing Video to the Net," *Inter@ctive Week* (June 15). Internet: www.zdnet.com/intweek/print/980615/327251.html.

Vonder Haar, Steven (1998), "Web Firms to Track Individual Ads," *Inter@ctive Week* (January 12). Internet: www.zdnet.com/intweek/print/980112/270968.html.

Wang, Nelson (1997), "Startup Offers Service to Fix Undercounting of Page Views," *Web Week* (October 13). Internet: www.internetworld.com/print/1997/10/13/news/19971013-startup.html.

Watson, Richard (Ed.) and Pierre Berthon, Leyland Pitt, George Zinkhan. (2000), *Electronic Commerce*. Orlando, FL: The Dryden Press.

Watson, R. T., P. G. McKeown, and G. M. Zinkhan, "Electronic Commerce and Pricing," working paper as cited in Pitt, Berthon, Watson, and Ewing (2001), "Pricing Strategy and the Net," *Business Horizons* (March), 45.

"Web Still Growing by Two Million New U.S. Users Per Month," (2002), *MM&M* (March), 10–11.

Weisul, Kimberly (1998), "Online Brokerages Target Niches," *Inter@ctive Week* (May 4). Internet: www.zdnet.com/intweek/print/980504/314056.html.

Weisul, Kimberly (1998), "Online Trades Jump 25 Percent," *Inter@ctive Week* (June 1). Internet: www.zdnet.com/intweek/daily/980601n.html.

Wellner, Alison (2000), "The Internet's Next Niche," *American Demographics* (September), 18–19.

Wellner, Alison (2001), "A New Cure for Shoppus Interruptus," *American Demographics* (September).

Wells, Nigel, Jeff Wolfers, and Richard C. Riecken (2000), "Finance with a personalized touch," *Association for Computing Machinery. Communications of the ACM,* Volume 43, Issue 8, 31–34.

Whelan, David (2001), "A Tale of Two Consumers," *American Demographics* (September), 54–57.

Wilson, Ralph (2000), Review of Trout & Rivkin's "Differentiate or Die: Survival in Our Era of Killer Competition," *Web Marketing Today*, p. 1.

Wolfinbarger, Mary and Mary Gilly (2001), "Shopping Online for Freedom, Control and Fun," *California Management Review*, (43), 39.

Wood, Marian (2001), *Prentice Hall's Guide to E-Commerce and E-Business*. Upper Saddle River, NJ: Prentice Hall 2001.

World Bank (2000), World Development Report 2000/2001, Table 4, p. 280.

"Yahoo!'s Yang: Web Is Now a 'Lifestyle Medium'" (1998), *ZDNN* (March 12). Internet: www.zdnet.com.

"You Say PC, I Say TV" (2000), *CyberAtlas* (February 2). Internet: www.cyberatlas.com.

Chapter 5 Notes

1. American Marketing Association (1996), *Code of Ethics.* Chicago, IL: American Marketing Association.

2. S. Warren & L. Brandeis, "The Right to Privacy," 4 *Harvard Law Review* 193 (1890),

3. 381 U.S. 479 (1965).

4. 410 U.S. 113 (1973).

5. Restatement [Second] of Torts, § 652 (1977).

6. W. Adkinson, J. Eisenach & T. Lenard, "Privacy Online: A Report on the Information Practices and Policies of Commercial Web Sites," The Progress & Freedom Foundation, March, 2002, available at www.pff.org.

7. <u>Timothy R. McVeigh v. William Cohen, et al.</u>, 983 F. Supp. 215 (D.D.C., Jan. 26, 1998).

8. "Privacy Online: A Report to Congress," p.12, Federal Trade Commission, June 1998, available at www.ftc.gov/reports/privacy3/toc.htm.

9. Children's Online Privacy Protection Act of 1998, 15 U.S.C. 6501 et seq.

10. Federal Trade Commission Children's Online Privacy Protection Rule, Final Rule, 16 CFR Part 312, November 3, 1999, available at www.ftc.gov/os/1999/9910/64fr59888.htm.

11. Fair Credit Reporting Act, 15 USC 1681 (1992).

12. Electronic Communications Protection Act (ECPA) 18 USC §§2510-21, 2701-11 (1994).

13. The Direct Marketing Association guidelines are available at www.the-dma.org/library/guidelines/onlineguidelines.shtml.

14. Directive 95/46/EC of the European Parliament and of the Council of 24 October 1995 in the protection of individuals with regard to the processing of personal data and on the free movement of such data. Article 25.

15. Updated Safe Harbor Principles are available at: www.ecommerce.gov.

16. "Commission Staff Working Paper: The Application of Commission Decision 520/2000/EC of July 2000 to Directive 95/46 of the European Parliament and of the Council on the Adequate Protection of Personal Data Provided by the Safe Harbor Privacy Principles and Related Frequently Asked Questions Issued by the US Department of Commerce," Commission of the European Communities, Feb. 13, 2002, available at www.europa.eu.int/comm/internal_market/en/dataprot/news/02-196_en.pdf.

17. "Privacy Online: A Report to Congress," p.12, Federal Trade Commission, June 1998, available at www.ftc.gov/reports/privacy3/toc.htm.

18. 17 U.S.C. §§107 and 109 (1998).

19. 17 U.S.C. §506(a) (as amended 1997).

20. 17 U.S.C. §512 et seq. (1998).

21. 17 U.S.C. §1201et seq. (1998).

22. See, "Unintended Consequences: Three Years under the DMCA," Electronic Frontier Foundation, May 3, 2002, available at: www.eff.org.

23. WIPO Copyright Treaty, adopted by the Diplomatic Conference on Dec. 20, 1996, WIPO Doc. CRNR/DC/94 (Dec. 23, 1996) and WIPO Performances and Phonograms Treaty, adopted by the Diplomatic Conference on Dec. 20, 1996, WIPO Doc. CRNR/DC/95 (Dec. 23, 1996).

24. 15 U.S.C. §1051 et seq.

25. 15 U.S.C. §1125.

26. *Playboy Enterprises, Inc. v. Calvin Designer Label*, 985 F. Supp. 1220 (N.D. Cal. 1997).

27. *Playboy Enterprises, Inc. v. Welles*, 7 F. Supp. 2d 1098 (D. Cal. 1998).

28. *Estee Lauder Inc. v. The Fragrance Counter and Excite, Inc.* (S.D.N.Y. complaint filed Mar. 5, 1999).
29. *Ticketmaster Corp. v. Microsoft Corp.*, No. 97-3055 DDP (D. Cal. filed Apr. 28, 1997).
30. *Washington Post v. TotalNEWS, Inc.*, 97 Civ. 1190 (PKL) (S.D.N.Y., filed Feb. 28, 1997).
31. 35 U.S.C. §101 et seq.
32. *Amazon.com v. Barnesandnoble.com* (W.D. Wash., filed Oct. 21, 1999).
33. *M. A. Mortenson Co. v. Timberline Software*, 998 P.2d 305 (Wash. 2000).
34. *Groff v. America Online*, 1998 WL 307001 (R.I. Super. Ct., May 27, 1998).
35. 18 USC §1831 et seq.
36. *New England Circuit Sales v. Randall*, No. 96-10840-EFH (D.Mass., June 4, 1996).
37. *eBay, Inc. v. Bidder's Edge, Inc.*, 100 F.Supp. 2d 1058 (N.D. Cal. 2000).
38. Directive 96/9/EC of the European Parliament and of the Council of 11 March 1996 on the legal protection of databases.
39. 948 F.Supp. 436 (E.D. Pa., 1996).
40. *America Online v. Christian Brothers*, No. 98 Civ. 8959 (DAB) (HBP) (S.D. N.Y., Dec. 14, 1999).
41. *Washington v. Heckel*, 24 P.3d 404 (Wash. 2001), cert. denied, 122 S.Ct. 467 (2001).
42. *Intel Corp. v. Hamidi*, 94 Cal. App. 4th 325 (2001), review granted (April 23, 2002).
43. 267623 *Ontario Inc. v. Nexx Online*, No. C20546/99 (Ontario Super. Ct., June 14, 1999).
44. 47 U.S.C. §230(c)(1) [Communications Decency Act of 1996].
45. *Zeran v. America Online*, 129 F.3d 327 (4th Cir. Va. 1997), cert. denied, 524 U.S. 937 (1998).
46. *Godfrey v. Demon Internet Limited*, (UK) [1999] EWHC QB 244.
47. 117 S.Ct. 2329 (1997).
48. *Multnomah County Public Library et al., v. United States, et al.*, No. 01-CV-1303 (E.D. Pa., May 31, 2002).
49. *Zippo Manufacturing Company v. Zippo Dot Com, Inc.*, 952 F. Supp. 1119 (W.D.Pa. Jan. 16, 1997).
50. *Digital Control Inc. v. Boretronics, Inc.*, 161 F.Supp. 2d 1183 (W.D. Wash. 2001).
51. *ALS Scan, Inc. v. Robert Wilkins*, 142 F. Supp. 2d 793 (D.Md. 2001).
52. vmag.cilp.org.
53. www.arbiter.wipo.int/center/index.html.
54. "Combating Internet Fraud and Deception," Federal Trade Commission, May 2001, available at www.ftc.gov/bcp/internet/cases-netsum.pdf.

Chapter 16 References and Sources

Chile

Chilean Telecommunications Bureau (Annual Report 2001, www.subtel.cl)

ENTEL Chile Annual Report 2001 (www.entel.cl)

National Institute of Statistics, Santiago, Chile (www.ine.cl)

Telecommunications Suplement, El Mercurio Newspaper May 17, 2002
(www.emol.com)

Publications and Studies made by The Chamber of Commerce of Santiago
(www.camaracomercio.cl)

People's Republic of China

CCID Consulting. "Report of B2B E-Commerce in China,"
www.ccidconsulting.com/. 2001.

CNNIC (China Internet Network Information Center). "The 9th Survey of China
Internet Development." www.cnnic.cn/. 2002.

Yang, Weidong. "A Roadmap for China E-Commerce Development," ZDNet China.
www. zdnet.com.cn/. March 20, 2001.

Germany

Eimeren, Birgit van/ Gerhard, Heinz/ Frees, Beate (2001): „ARD/ ZDF-Online-
Studie 2001: Internetnutzung stark zweckgebunden," Media Perspektiven
8/2001, p. 382-397. Internet: www.ard-
werbung.de/showfile.phtml/2001_08_01.pdf?foid=2

NUA/ The Age (2002), "Australians not interested in mobile Internet," (June 12
2002). Internet: www.nua.com/surveys/index.cgi?f=VS&art_id=
905358050&rel=true

GfK (2000), "Internet Boom Set to Continue," (February 4, 2000). Internet:
194.175.173.244/gfk/english/index.html

GfK (2001), GfK Online-Monitor – 7.

Australia

The Australian Bureau of Statistics (a government organization) is the most
authoritative source of this information (www.abs.gov.au).

India

Chand, Fakir "Barriers holding up e-biz explosion in India," August 3, 2001 retrieved
from www.rediff.com/money/2001/aug/03fakir.htm on May 23, 2002.

Cheung, Eddie "Profiling Indian Internet users: Part 2," January 10, 2001retrieved
from www.emarketer.com/analysis/easia/20010110_india2.html.

DQ Week, "India ranked 32nd in Internet usage in the Global E-commerce survey,"
January 10, 2002 retrieved from www.dqweek.com/content/search/
showarticle.asp?artid=31297

Northern Ireland

www.nua.ie is a major source of regular updates for trends in this area.

A recent study (December 2001) by IDS *Internet Usage by Irish Businesses* www.irishbusiness.ie/publishing/internet-reports.htm contains a lot of data on Internet adoption in Northern Ireland

Internet Usage in Business, Key Note, July 2001, www.keynote.co.uk.

The Foresight Northern Ireland Report on ebusiness (2001) contains useful guidance on the ebusiness process for local organizations, with profiles of four industry sectors (Engineering, Life and Health, Textiles and Apparel, and Food and Drink) and some local case studies www.foresight-ni.org.uk/ebusiness/ebusinessreport.htm.

Invest Northern Ireland www.investni.com is due to develop quickly, following the integration of three significant providers of business support in the local community.

KableNet www.kablenet.com provides news and information on the growth of Internet services in local government throughout the United Kingdom

Oultwood www.oultwood.com/localgov/northernireland.htm describes the development of online services for rate payers and local businesses in each of the 26 local government areas in Northern Ireland.

UK Online for Business www.ukonlineforbusiness.gov.uk is a substantial and growing resource, with information for businesses of varying size in different sectors of the local economy .

Property News.com www.propertynews.com is a local site on which property buyers and sellers can explore the local market.

The Northern Ireland Aerospace Consortium www.niac.org.uk and SORCE www.sorce.net/org are two examples of local organizations that started to make significant use of the Internet as a promotional and trading medium.

Rural Northern Ireland www.ruralni.gov.uk provides current information and news about trends and developments that affect the local agricultural community. The value of such communication technology grew in significance during the 2001 outbreak of foot and mouth disease, which imposed massive restrictions on all movement on and off farms.

Poland

Augustyniak, Szymon (2002), "Do Unii przez Internet" (May 20). Internet: www.cxo.pl/news.asp?id=179.

Bonarowski, Michal (2002), "Podpisz się komputerem," *Polityka* (June 29).

Economic Academy in Krakow, School of Marketing (2000), "Badanie Polskich Uzytkownikow Sieci Internetu." Internet: badanie.ae.krakow.pl.

Iszkowski, Waclaw (2002), "Coraz wiecej watpliwosci. Relacja z Forum PIIT,"

Polska Izba Informatyki i Telekomunikacji (June 13). Internet: www.piit.org.pl/poj_news.xml.

(1) Kowalczyk, Mariusz (2001), "Zamiec w sieci," Wprost on-line. Internet: tygodnik.wprost.pl/index.php3?numer=1023&art.=129565&dzial=3.

(2) Kowalczyk, Mariusz (2002), "Cyberokazja: Tanio, taniej, Internet," Wprost on-line. Internet: tygodnik.wprost.pl/index.php3?numer=1023&art.=12174&dzial=3.

(3) Kowalczyk, Mariusz (2002), "Janko Internauta: Społeczenstwo informacyjne czy skansen?" *Magazyn Internetowy WWW*, (June).

Latek, Katarzyna (2002), "Encyclopedia.com," Wprost on-line. Internet: tygodnik.wprost.pl/index.php3?numer=1023&art.=12074&dzial=3.

Leszczyński, Grzegorz (2002), "Badanie e-sklepow," *E-Marketing* (April). Internet: www.e-marketing.pl/badania/pecom.php.

Levy, Steven and Stone, Brad (2002), "Rewolucja Wi-Fi," *Newsweek Polska* (June 23).

Mielnik, Jakub (2002), "Odwrot Strony," *Newsweek Polska* (January 2).

Nua Surveys (2002), "Europemedia: Polish Internet Spending to Soar" (June 28). Internet: www.nua.com/surveys/index.cgi?f=VS&art._id=905358110 &rel=true.

Piasek, Arkadiusz (2001), "10 lat Internetu w Polsce: wyniki ankiety," *PCWorld* (September 14). Internet: www.pcworld.pl/news/news.asp?id=5012.

Pisera, Rafal (2002), "Wakacje z komputera," *Newsweek Polska* (June 6).

Polska Agencja Rozwoju Przedsiebiorczosci (PARP), (2000) "Wykorzystanie Internetu w malych firmach," (October). Internet: www.parp.gov.pl/demoskop.php.

Samuelson, Robert (2002), "Stara gospodarka ratuje nową," *Newsweek Polska* (March 12).

Siluszek, Andrzej (2002), "Urzedowa mizeryja online," *Magazyn Internetowy WWW*, (June).

Wodecki, Andrzej (2002), "Studia w Internecie," *Polityka* (June 29).

Turkey

CRC Research and Consultancy, Inc. (www.crc-tr.com).

cyberatlas.Internet.com/big_picture/geographics/article/0,,5911_574601,00.html.

turk.Internet.com/haber/yaziyaz.php3?yaziid=3071

www.nua.com/surveys/index.cgi?f=VS&art_id=905355675&rel=true

www.nua.com/surveys/index.cgi?f=VS&art_id=905355952&rel=true

Kircova, Ibrahim, (2002a) Sanal Pazarlama Dunya'da ve Turkiye'deki Gelismeler, Sanal Pazarlama Paneli, Istanbul Ticaret Odası, 10 Mayıs.

Kircova, Ibrahim (2002b) Internette Pazarlama, Beta Basim Yayim Dagitim A.S., Istanbul.

Superonline (www.superonline.com.tr).

Index